CHART OF CCC CAMPS IN CONNECTICUT

Town Post Office / Location	Camp Name	#	Company	Began	Closed
Clinton / Killingworth	Roosevelt	S-60	171	5/23/33	3/31/37
Cobalt / Meshomasic SF	Jenkins	S-57	181	6/15/33	1/7/36
Danbury / New Fairfield / Squantz Pond SP	Hook	S-62	172	5/24/33	10/30/35
Danbury / Wooster Mt. SF	Fechner	S-69	2102	6/4/35	5/24/37
Eastford / Natchaug SF	Fernow	S-56	183	6/29/33	5/28/41
East Hampton / Salmon River SF	Stuart	S-70	1194	7/8/35	5/31/37
East Hartland / Tunxis SF	Robinson	S-53	180	6/13/33	7/28/41
Haddam / Cockaponset SF	Filley	S-64	1195	12/11/33	7/30/41
Kent / Macedonia & Kent Falls SP		SP-1	P-11057	6/ 10/35	6/10/37
Madison / Cockaponset SF	Hadley	P-65	2101	6/4/35	4/4/41
Niantic / Stones Ranch Military Reservation	Chapman	S-61	177	6/1/33	10/30/35
Portland / Meshomasic SF	Buck	S-61	1197	6/4/35	7/22/41
Stafford Springs / Shenipsit SF	Conner	P-68	1192	6/4/35	5/23/41
Thomaston / Black Rock SP	Roberts	S-59	175	5/30/33	9/28/37
Torrington / Burrville / Paugnut SF	Walcott	S-54	176	5/24/33	5/28/37
Torrington / West Goshen / Mohawk SF	Toumey	S-52	173	5/27/ 33	7/26/41
Union / Nipmuck SF	Graves	S-55	174	5/27/33	4/22/36
Voluntown / Pachaug SF	Lonergan	S-58	179	6/6/33	5/28/42
West Cornwall / Sharon / Housatonic Meadows SP	Cross	S-51	182	6/ 2/33	4/1/41
Windsor / Poquonock / Agricultural Experiment Station	Britton	P-66	1193	6/4/35	5/26/37
Winsted / Barkhamsted / Peoples & American Legion SF	White	S-63	106	5/24/34	1/6/42
New London / Supply Depot at Government Dock			190	4/35	1936?

Connecticut Civilian Conservation Corps Camps:

HISTORY, MEMORIES, AND LEGACY OF THE CCC

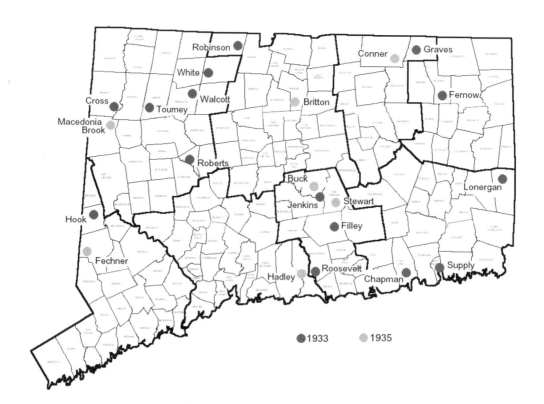

Robinson

White

Cross Walcott
Toumey
Macedonia
Brook

Roberts

Buck
Jenkins Stewart

Hook Filley

Fechner

Hadley Roosevelt
Chapman

Conner Graves

Fernow

Lonergan

Supply

● 1933   ● 1935

To Jason,

Connecticut Civilian Conservation Corps Camps:
HISTORY, MEMORIES, AND LEGACY OF THE CCC

Martin Podskoch

Martin Podskoch

Edited by David Hayden

Podskoch Press, LLC
East Hampton, Connecticut

Connecticut Civilian Conservation Corps Camps:

HISTORY, MEMORIES, AND LEGACY OF THE CCC

Published by
Podskoch Press, LLC
43 O'Neill Lane
East Hampton, CT

podskoch@comcast.net
www.cccstories.com
www.adirondackstories.com
www.firetowerstories.com
www.adirondack102club.com

HC ISBN 978-0-9794979-9-5
PB ISBN 978-0-9794979-8-8
Manufactured in the United States of America

654321

Cover Design by Amanda Beauchemin
Design & Layout by Amanda Beauchemin of Ford Folios
Maps by Paul Hartmann

TABLE OF CONTENTS

FOREWARD

The many works of the Civilian Conservation Corps in Connecticut State Parks and Forests are an ever-present and enduring legacy. The thousands of conifer tree plantations, scattered in most of our parks and forests, are still there and thriving. The many miles of graveled roads, some now paved, with their stone bridges and culverts, were so well constructed and engineered, that they are still in daily use. Perhaps, the most important but unrecognized inheritance are the many lakes, ponds, picnic pavilions and park and forest recreation areas which were constructed by the CCC boys and now have become some of Connecticut's premier State Parks and Forests.

I am sure many of you will recognize and have probably visited Squantz Pond, Macedonia Brook, Housatonic Meadows, Kent Falls, Mohawk Ski Area or Forest, Burr Pond, Black Rock, Peoples Forest, Stratton Brook, Chatfield Hollow, Mashamoquet Brook, Green Falls Pond and others which were initially partly or mostly developed as recreational areas by the CCC's.

When Marty Podskoch was doing his research for "Civilian Conservation Corps Camps in Connecticut", he was talking to our Town Historian about setting up local talks and finding the locations of CCC camps. The Historian told Marty that he should contact me as I had worked for the State Parks and Forests for forty years and could be of help. Marty phoned and we talked for hours and have since traveled to many sites of former CCC camps throughout the state. In most cases, we found only solitary chimneys; old outlined pathways and roadways between the remains of concrete foundations of barracks and other buildings, wells, a few pipes and other unidentifiable debris. In a few isolated instances, garages or a building or two were in use. Mostly, in our travels, we kept running into elderly men who would say with pride, "How do you like that dam, road or building? I built that when I was a CCC boy and by gosh – we built it right and it's still as good as the day we finished it!" When we questioned them further on what they did in World War II and their future careers, we were astounded at how successful they were in their later lives. Many had taken advantage of the GI bill, had gone to college, and had gone into a profession.

In the seventy-five years since the Great Depression and The New Deal, we have had several slight economic downturns, inspiring a number of government programs patterned after the Civilian Conservation Corps. These programs were instituted during the 1970s and the 1980s.

From 1974-1988 I was in charge of the YCC or Youth Conservation Corps in the western half of Connecticut. For eight weeks each summer, youths, ages fifteen to eighteen worked at minimum wage on varied conservation projects. They cleared brush and built hiking trails, footbridges, boardwalks through swamps, picnic pavilions, fish rearing pools, planted trees and shrubs and also repaired some of the old CCC works. They also retrofitted many of our park and forest facilities for handicap access.

There were four mobile teams of ten persons randomly picked by computer resulting in a diverse, yet balanced, representation of the community: half girls, half boys, poor inner city, affluent suburban and very well-to-do.

Two adult counselors led the teams: one male and one female, usually schoolteachers with some do-it-yourself skills. We also had an eight-week summer residential camp program with several camps for forty kids each working on state parks, forests, fish and game areas and flood control areas. During the first week, the projects only required simple skills, giving the counselors and the team time to learn to work together. Then, as the projects became more complicated, requiring carpentry, masonry or other skills to build footbridges, fish rearing pools, picnic pavilions, canoe takeouts and many other projects, the kids were taught all the skills to successfully complete them. The girls, as well as the boys, became able carpenters and masons. The objective was to construct needed projects that would last fifty years and be of high quality, also the objective of the original Civilian Conservation Corps.

A few team members did not succeed and were fired but most accepted the responsibility and grew up into great kids who would be future citizens that you would gladly hire. Our reputation was such that sometimes principals or probation officers sent us their problem children and most times we could turn these referrals into potential great employees.

For instance, I had two girls from a big city mill town, one, whose ambition was to be a clerk at Dunkin' Donuts and the other wanted to be a cashier at First National. They showed interest in wildlife: therefore, I placed them for several weeks with our Wildlife Biologist and his two graduate assistants doing a special research project. They loved it and changed their life goals. They were such terrific kids that I helped them find summer jobs to help pay for college. At Hammonasset State Park, one was in charge of all the campgrounds and the other girl was in charge of all the ticket booths. They both now have Master Degrees and have good jobs: one is a supervising biologist in New England and the other is in charge of all animals used in cancer research at a major University. This is typical of the many success stories of the Youth Conservation Corps kids.

The Young Adult Conservation Corps, or YACC was a year-round program for high school dropouts ages sixteen to twenty-six. Team members were hired for forty hours a week at the minimum wage to work days in our State Parks and Forests and to attend high school equivalency classes several nights a week to get their GEDs. Some of the girls were single parents, who arranged for childcare while they worked or attended classes. Most of these girls received their GEDs, learned useful and employable skills, successfully raised their children and greatly raised their future prospects.

One of our major projects under this program was the construction of an Atlantic salmon holding facility. Five male team members were from the inner city. One was fired, another quit in a few weeks, and the last three worked successfully for two years. Prior to this, they had never worked more than a month or so at some dead-end job, but when they left, they had learned enough carpentry and other building skills to get well-paying jobs rehabbing buildings and apartments in the inner city. You can see how these programs were highly successful in developing great citizens and accomplishing the same needed quality work on our parks and forests, just like the original Civilian Conservation Corps. So the next time you visit one of our state or national parks or forests, look closely and you may see some of the dividends of the original CCC programs or those later Conservation programs that not only built useful and enduring projects, but made better future citizens and enriched young lives. What better investment can we make than in our youth and that of improving our recreational areas and natural resources?

Retired State Recreation Specialist Carl Stamm on a walkway in Rhododendron Sanctuary in the Pachaug SF in Voluntown built by YACC students. The CCC had built the original walkway in the 1930s. Podskoch

Marty Podskoch (left) and Carl Stamm with former State Governor Jodi Rell at the CCC Museum in Stafford Springs on Feb. 12, 2009.

This book is dedicated to the three million CCC men who worked in the United States and its territories on conservation projects such as planting trees, building state and national parks, fighting fires, building roads and bridges, helping farmers and ranchers prevent erosion, and aiding citizens during disasters.

PREFACE

My interest in the Civilian Conservation Corps (CCC) began while gathering information in the Adirondacks for my fire tower books during the summer of 2004. One day I visited Joanne Petty Manning of Saranac Lake whose father, Bill Petty, had been the District Forester at the DEC Office in Ray Brook and had a large collection of photos and information on fire towers. She brought out a large box of photos and in it was a packet of six or more photos that didn't relate to the Adirondack fire towers.

One showed a large group of young men posing for a picture. The men wore dungaree shirts, pants, jackets, and a variety of hats. Some were holding shovels. Other pictures showed a group of guys leveling a dirt road, young guys planting trees, boys eating at picnic tables with tents in the background, and a group photo of older men posing for a picture. Joanne told me that these were of the Civilian Conservation Corps and I decided to copy them just in case I needed them in the future.

My northern Adirondack fire tower book came out in the fall of 2005. This was my third book on the men and women who worked on the fire towers of the Catskill and Adirondack mountains. I wondered what I'd do for my next book. I remembered Joanne's photos of the CCC and then I knew what I wanted to work on. I had just finished writing about the men and women who worked in fire towers saving the forests from fires now I'd write about the young men and veterans who worked in the CCC who built up our forests and state and national parks.

I began searching for information on the CCC of New York by giving talks throughout the state and writing newspaper stories about the CCC camps. Gradually I was able to locate many former CCC enrollees and their families. After six years of work and over 100 interviews, my book Adirondack Civilian Conservation Corps Camps: History, Memories, and Legacy of the CCC was published in 2011.

In the mean time I had moved to Connecticut in 2005 and it dawned on me that I should also gather information on the CCC camps in Connecticut. I had to find the men who were still alive in my new state. It also required a lot less driving.

In the meantime I had moved to Connecticut in 2005 and it dawned on me that I should also gather information on the CCC camps in Connecticut. I had to find the men who were still alive in my new state, which required a lot less driving.

At the end of 2007 I began calling libraries, historical societies, and senior living communities to see if they would be interested in giving a presentation on the CCC camps in Connecticut. I also sent news releases and photos to newspapers describing my search for information concerning CCC camps and asking readers to contact me.

The response was tremendous. Many of the old boys or family members contacted me and shared their photos and stories. I either went to their homes or called them on the phone for interviews. By the end of 2008 I had given 56 presentations and I was on my way for a second book on the CCC.

There were times of frustration when I was told, "Oh, if you were only here a month or a year ago when Joe was alive. He had great stories." Then there were the times a son or daughter told me, "I only wish that my father told me about his days in the CCC. I don't even know what camp or state he was in."

My book is not a comprehensive history of the Civilian Conservation Corps but the history of the 21 Connecticut CCC camps and the stories of the young men who left their homes to earn $30 ($25 went home) a month to help their families survive during the Great Depression. The reader will see how these young men developed a sense of worth. Many had only an eighth grade education and were wandering the countryside and city streets in search of a job. Once in the CCC they felt important. They learned how to take orders, developed a love of nature, and learned a trade, all of which gave them a sense of self-worth. They knew they were helping their country and their family.

As you drive through the Connecticut countryside you pass by the lofty plantations of white pines that were planted by the CCC during the 1930s. You will also pass by and maybe camp at the many state parks that were established or developed by the young enrollees or the Spanish American War and WWI veterans.

Now sit back and enjoy an illustrated chronicle of the CCC boys who worked in the state parks and forests. You will also find the stories of Connecticut young men who were sent to Western states and found adventure there.

Marty Podskoch

podskoch@comcast.net
cccstories.com • adirondackstories.com • firetowerstories.com

Marty Podskoch and family at home on Lake Pocotopaug in East Hampton, Conn. (Front Row) "Vinney" & Jenna Podskoch, Kira and Lydia Roloff. (Back Row) Matt, Ryan, Lynn Podskoch, Kristy & Matt Roloff, and Marty. Phyllis Tribuzio

CHAPTER 1
CONNECTICUT CCC CAMPS – THEIR HISTORY

One of the most important events in the history of the United States was the election of Franklin D. Roosevelt (FDR) as President during the Great Depression. With over 13 million unemployed FDR promoted many relief programs that created jobs for the unemployed. The Emergency Conservation Work Act, better known as Civilian Conservation Corps, was the first such program passed by Congress in 1933 during Roosevelt's first "One Hundred Days" and is also considered his most successful program and certainly his most popular. During its nine years 3 million young men worked conserving our natural resources throughout our country and possessions.

Conservation was important in the Roosevelt family. FDR and his cousin Theodore "Teddy" Roosevelt had a deep love for conserving the land and forests in the United States. Both were governors of New York State (NYS) and presidents of the United States.

While President (1901-1909), Teddy helped preserve approximately 230,000,000 acres in the United States. In this new land the government established five new National Parks, 16 National Monuments, 51 Wildlife Refuges, and huge reserves and National Forests.[1]

Gifford Pinchot, a college trained forester, influenced both Teddy and Franklin. Pinchot urged the use of scientific management of the natural resources of the West and worked to prevent developers from destroying the land. Teddy appointed Pinchot to head the new US Forest Service.[2]

When FDR became President in 1933, Pinchot warned him about the depletion of our forests and impressed upon him the importance of purchasing large tracts of privately owned forest lands. When Congress passed the Weeks Act in 1911 it enabled the government to purchase private land. This made it possible for the creation of the national forests east of the Mississippi. Pinchot also urged FDR to purchase the 50 million acres of recently abandoned farmland east of the Mississippi and employ men who were on relief to reforest these lands.[3]

FDR grew up at his family's estate, Springwood, in Hyde Park, NY where he enjoyed roaming the forest and hills near the Hudson River. Later he went into politics and was elected to the state senate in 1910. Here he became the Chairman of the Committee on Forestry. FDR took over the family estate in 1910 and the following year he hired a forester who developed a management plan for Springwood. In 1912 he had a few thousand seedlings planted, the first of some 550,000 trees planted over the next forty years.[4]

In 1928 FDR became governor of New York and advocated for government intervention during the Depression. FDR developed relief programs for the unemployed. One program gave 10,000 men jobs working in the state forest and parks. They built park buildings and roads, planted trees, and did erosion control projects.[5]

During his years as governor FDR encouraged the state legislature to pass laws promoting conservation and development of the state forests. In 1931 FDR proclaimed Conservation Week. His press release stated his goals: "...to bring to the attention of the people the great public benefits that are dependent upon the wise use and perpetuation of our forests, the protection of the birds and animals that they shelter, and the safeguarding of our water from alienation and pollution."[6] FDR encouraged the state to purchase substandard farmland and then reforest the land. In 1931 the state legislature approved a $19 million bond issue to purchase submarginal farmland. The Conservation Department supervised this program and purchased farms that had at least 500 acres. In 1932 the state hired 10,000 temporary workers from the relief rolls to plant trees. The land was reforested and helped in preventing soil erosion and provided forests for future timber production.[7]

The Great Depression

The Great Depression was a traumatic period for millions in the United States. It began when the stock market crashed on October 27, 1929. Many economists thought it was merely a bump in the market but the slow economy dragged on. President Hoover believed that local governments and private charities should provide relief to the unemployed and homeless and not the federal government. Breadlines and Hoovervilles (homeless encampments) sprang up around the United States.[8]

During the Great Depression many people were forced to live in shanties. Library of Congress

There were nearly 2 million unemployed men and women who wandered the US on foot and freight trains, lived in caves and shantytowns in search for a job and security. In this group were a quarter million called "the teenage tramps of America" who were in the same search to find security.[9]

In 1932 George Rawick estimated that one in four of the youth between ages 15-24 were unemployed. Of this age group only 29% did part-time work.[10]

Joe Arnold of Branford described his life during the Depression, "My mother Marguerite had four children: Marguerite, Eugene, and John. I was the eldest. I was born on March 28, 1918. I had a good life and finished 9th grade when my father lost his roofing business due to the Depression. He tried several small businesses and eventually went to work for his brother out of town. My family lost our home and we moved to New Haven, Conn.

"Then my father left my mother with four children. I had to quit school and help my mother. I read about the CCC in an article in *Time Magazine*. In approximately March 1937 I went to the town hall and signed up. They sent me to Camp Cross in West Cornwall in the northwestern part of the state."

The US was not only facing a financial catastrophe but an environmental crisis as well. States were unable to control the frequent forest fires and the diseases and pests that decimated the forests. Poor farming practices, overgrazing of public lands, and overcutting of forests led to erosion of topsoil. Streams became uninhabitable leading to the decline of fish. Frequent flooding occurred.

During the 1932 election the Democratic Party nominated Franklin D. Roosevelt. His slogan in the campaign was a "New Deal" for America. He promised to work to reverse the economic collapse that Hoover failed to achieve. With over 20% of US workers unemployed, FDR pledged to help the "forgotten man at the bottom of the economic pyramid."

In his July 2, 1932, acceptance speech at the Democratic Convention in Chicago, Roosevelt made the following promise to create meaningful public relief:

Let us use common sense and business sense. Just as one example, we know that a very hopeful and immediate means of relief, both for the unemployed and for agriculture, will come from a wide plan of the converting of many millions of acres of marginal and unused land into timberland through reforestation. There are tens of millions of acres east of the Mississippi River alone in abandoned farms, in cut-over land, now growing up in worthless brush. Why, every European Nation has a definite land policy, and has had one for generations. We have none. Having none, we face a future of soil erosion and timber famine. It is clear that economic foresight and immediate employment march hand in hand in the call for the reforestation of these vast areas.

In so doing, employment can be given to a million men. That is the kind of public work that is self-sustaining, and therefore capable of being financed by the issuance of bonds which are made secure by the fact that the growth of tremendous crops will provide adequate security for the investment.

Yes, I have a very definite program for providing employment by that means. I have done it, and I am doing it today in the State of New York. I know that the Democratic Party can do it successfully in the Nation. That will put men to work, and that is an example of the action that we are going to have. [http://www. presidency.ucsb.edu]

Americans were looking for a change in leadership and in November they chose Franklin D. Roosevelt over Hoover by a landslide vote, 22,821,857 to 15,761,845. FDR was sworn into office on March 4, 1933. After FDR was sworn into office he decided to forego the traditional balls and celebrations and sat down with his cabinet and began working on solving the economic crisis.

President Franklin D. Roosevelt signing the Emergency Conservation Work bill. CCC Legacy Archives

Hundred Days & Emergency Conservation Work Act

On March 9 he declared a "Bank Holiday" that closed the banks for four days to help stabilize the financial system. Then FDR and Congress passed the Agricultural Adjustment Act, a farm relief law that paid farmers subsidies for not planting part of their land and reduce livestock. Is purpose was to reduce crop surplus and in turn raise their value.

On March 21, 1933 Roosevelt called the 73rd Congress into Emergency Session to hear and authorize his program. He proposed to recruit thousands of unemployed young men, enroll them in a peacetime army, and send them into battle against the destruction and erosion of our natural resources.

"I propose to create a civilian conservation corps to be used in simple work, not interfering with normal employment, and confining itself to forestry, the prevention of soil erosion, flood control and similar projects. I call your attention to the fact that this type of work is of definite, practical value, not only through the prevention of great present financial loss, but also as a means of creating future national wealth."[11]

Organized labor unions were concerned that the CCC would lower wages. They were also worried if the Army was involved in running the program it might lead to regimentation of labor. Others feared the CCC would take jobs from men working in the forests.[12]

On March 27 FDR introduced Senate Bill 5.598, the Emergency Conservation Work Act (ECW).

It went through both houses of Congress and on March 31, 1933 FDR signed the ECW Act, more commonly known as the Civilian Conservation Corps. This provided work for 250,000 unemployed young men ages 18-25. FDR brought together two wasted resources, the young men and the land.[13]

By the end of the "Hundred Days" FDR had pushed 15 major bills through Congress, such as the Federal Emergency Relief Administration (FERA), which provided funds for grants to states to establish relief programs, the Tennessee Valley Authority (TVA), which provided hydro-electric power, flood control, and soil conservation to seven southern states, and the National Industrial Recovery Act (NIRA), which stimulated industry and established labor standards.[14]

Organization of the ECW (CCC)

On April 5, 1933 FDR signed Executive Order 6101 authorizing the ECW (CCC) program and appointed Robert Fechner director. He was a vice-president of the American Federation of Labor. James J. McEntee became his assistant.

FDR established an Advisory Council composed of representatives from the Secretaries of War, Labor, Interior, and Agriculture. These agencies worked together with Fechner in performing miracles in organizing large number of enrollees and camps throughout the 48 states, Alaska, Hawaii, Puerto Rico, and the Virgin Islands.

The Army mobilized the nation's transportation system to move thousands of enrollees from induction centers to working camps. This was the largest peacetime

ECW (CCC) Director Robert Fechner (5th from left with dark coat) visited the Paul Smiths camp in 1933. Workers are busy building camp. NYS Archives

The Army organized and supervised the CCC camps. These officers supervised Camp White in Barkhamsted. John Eastlake

mobilization of men the United States had ever seen. Most of the young enrollees came from the East while the majority of the projects were out West. The Army used its regular and reserve officers, together with regulars of the Coast Guard, Marine Corps and Navy to temporarily command camps and individual companies.

The Departments of Agriculture and Interior planned and organized work projects.

The Department of Labor, with the help of state and local relief offices, selected and enrolled the young men. Each state had a quota for enrollees based on population. The qualifications for the junior enrollees were: single, male, 18-25 years of age, unemployed, on the relief roll, healthy, and not in school. They signed up for a six-month period. Later enrollees could re-sign three more times for an additional 18 months. They were paid a dollar a day. The enrollee received $5 for spending money and the government sent $25 directly to the parents each month. If the men found employment they could ask for an honorable discharge.[15]

Only 37 days elapsed from Roosevelt's inauguration on March 4, 1933. Henry Rich of Alexandria, VA was the first enrollee on April 7. Ten days later Camp Roosevelt, the first CCC camp in the US, was established near Luray, Virginia in the George Washington National Forest.[16]

FDR promised to have 250,000 men in camps by July 1. All the agencies and branches of the federal government cooperated in implementing the program. His goal was achieved in July and junior enrollees (ages 18-25) were housed in 1,463 CCC camps.

In the July 8, 1933 issue of the weekly CCC newspaper, "Happy Days," FDR welcomed the CCC enrollees:

"I want to congratulate you on the opportunity you have, and to extend to you my appreciation for the hearty cooperation which you have given this movement, so vital a step in the nation's fight for progress, and to wish you a pleasant, wholesome and constructive stay in the CCC.

"I welcome the opportunity to extend a greeting to the men who constitute the Civilian Conservation Corps. It is my belief that what is being accomplished will conserve our national resources, create future national wealth and prove of moral and spiritual value, not only to those of you who are taking part, but to the rest of the country as well.

"You young men who are enrolled in this work are to be congratulated. It is my honest conviction that what you are doing in the way of constructive service will bring you, personally and individually, returns the value of which it is difficult to estimate.

"Physically fit, as demonstrated by the examinations you took before entering the camps, the clean life and hard work, in which you are engaged, cannot fail to help your physical condition. You should emerge from this experience, strong and rugged and ready for entrance into the ranks of industry, better equipped than before."

Afro-Americans were also accepted into the CCC because the law creating it barred discrimination based on race, creed, or color. The unemployment rate of Negroes was twice that of whites. The CCC administration became frustrated when several southern states like Georgia, Arkansas, and Florida refused to enroll few or no Negroes in 1933. When the federal government threatened to withhold state quotas of CCC camps they gave in.[17] Discrimination, however, led to separate Negro camps with

Director Robert Fechner (center) and President Franklin D. Roosevelt are surrounded by CCC enrollees when they visited Shenandoah VA on August 12, 1933. Legacy Archives

white Army officers in command. Only when there weren't enough Negroes for a company were they integrated with whites. In Connecticut the camps were integrated but in nearby New York there were separate "black" or "colored" camps.

In April 1933 there were two modifications to the ECW. On April 14th the program included the enlistment of approximately 14,000 unemployed American Indians.[18] There were only a few such camps and they were on the Indian reservations. Most of these enrollees were married and lived at home. By 1942 over 80,000 Native Americans had worked to reclaim the land.

Another change in the program was the hiring of approximately 25,000 local experienced men (LEM). At first they were called "experienced woodsmen." For every camp with 200 enrollees the camp could hire 16 local experienced men.[19] These men were experienced in carpentry, logging, masonry, etc. They trained the young enrollees in skills that many would use later in life. They also taught the workers proper use of tools, safety skills, discipline, and cooperation. The LEM program benefited the local communities by giving jobs to the unemployed whose salaries pumped money into the local economy.[20]

A third modification of the program occurred when veterans were admitted into the CCC. Their average age was 40. Many were unemployed and filled with despair during the Depression. Many had physical and mental impairments from WWI. They first became a problem to the government during the spring and summer of 1932 when they came to Washington, DC and demanded a bonus that was promised them when they received Service Certificates in 1924. The government responded by saying they had to wait till 1945 to cash them in but the unemployed veterans wanted to be paid right away. When this "Bonus Army" refused to leave the city, President Hoover had General Douglas MacArthur and the Army drive the veterans, their families, and friends out of the city and burn the protestors' shelters.[21]

The Bonus Army came a second time to Washington DC in 1933. FDR's reaction to the Bonus Army's march was different. He didn't send the Army but instead sent his wife, Eleanor. She listened to their concerns and told her husband. On May 11, 1933 FDR issued an executive order authorizing the enrollment of approximately 25,000 veterans of WWI and the Spanish American War. There were no restrictions as to age or marital status and the men were

During the summer and fall of 1933 CCC enrollees lived in Army tents. This is the Voluntown Camp Lonergan. Work has begun on the barracks and headquarters buildings. CT CCC Museum

housed in separate camps while working on conservation projects suitable to their age. By the end of the program nearly 250,000 veterans had participated. Veterans received a dollar a day but ¾ of their monthly salary went to their dependents. If they didn't have dependents it went into an account that they received when they left the CCC.[22]

Early Years

The CCC was popular throughout the US. A poll of Republicans showed that 67% supported it, and 95% of Californians approved. Even the Chicago Tribune, an enemy of FDR, and the Soviet Union praised the program. A Chicago judge thought the CCC was largely responsible for a 55% reduction in crime.

By April 1934 the program had almost universal support. The $25 monthly allotment to the enrollees' parents improved the US economy. Families could now provide a better life for their children. During the fiscal year 1935-36 the federal government sent to families throughout the US approximately $123,000,000. At first enrollees were limited to working one 6-month enlistment to allow others a chance to sign up and take advantage of the opportunity to work. Communities near the CCC camps benefited economically, too, because the enrollees pumped into the communities approximately $5,000 a month with their purchases at local businesses.[23]

Word about the camp's positive effects spread throughout the nation. The young men were working hard, eating well, gaining weight and strength, and improving millions of acres of private, state, and federal lands. They built new roads, strung miles of telephone lines, fought

(L–R, Front Row) Foremen R.B. Hosier & D. F. Knox. (Back Row) Forestry Engineer W. F. Schreeder, Supt. H. V. Potter, State Forester A. F. Hawes, Supt. Co. 1195 R. F. Coughlin. 1940 Camp Madison Yearbook

Number of Camps (June 30, 1935)[27]

California	155	Colorado	31
Pennsylvania	113	South Dakota	31
Michigan	103	Indiana	29
Wisconsin	103	Nebraska	27
Illinois	88	New Jersey	26
Missouri	88	Louisiana	25
Idaho	82	Alabama	24
Oregon	75	Florida	23
Minnesota	74	New Hampshire	23
New York	69	Oklahoma	23
Washington	69	South Carolina	23
Virginia	63	Arizona	22
Massachusetts	58	Connecticut	21
Tennessee	57	Wyoming	20
Texas	55	Maine	19
Arkansas	50	North Dakota	19
Iowa	41	Utah	19
Ohio	40	New Mexico	17
Kansas	39	West Virginia	17
North Carolina	38	Maryland	15
Vermont	37	Nevada	14
Kentucky	34	Rhode Island	7
Mississippi	34	Delaware	3
Georgia	33	Dist. Columbia	2
Montana	32		

fires, cleared forest of dead trees, and planted millions of trees. Newspapers published their accomplishments and many who opposed the program were won over. FDR decided to extend the program for one more year.

By 1935 the CCC program was enjoying one of its best years. The enrollees were no longer living in cold, drafty tents and wearing poor fitting uniforms. Senators and congressmen realized the benefits to their constituencies and urged Director Fechner for more camps in their states. By the end of 1935 there were 2,600 camps, some in each of the 48 states. They performed over 100 types of work. Local men worked as superintendents, foremen, blacksmiths, tractor operators, and mechanics and most of the salaries were spent locally and so benefited the whole area.[24]

The number of enrollees doubled since its beginning in 1933. There were now 505,782 men and more than 100,000 men who were officers, supervisors, foresters, education advisors, and LEMs.

In 1935 the CCC continued to be popular. Congress voiced their approval and extended the program to increase the enrollment to 600,000. This included enlarging the supervising staff to 6,000 Army, Marine, and Navy Reserve officers. The CCC expanded the age requirements for enrollees from 18-25 to 17-28 in order to fill the larger quota. This made at least 40,000 youths aged 17 eligible.[25] There were many young men who lied about their age or applied using their older brother's name. Now they could apply legally.[26]

The government set a goal of enrolling 600,000 men for 1936 but a new FDR advisor, Harry Hopkins, impeded

the attainment of that goal.

In 1935 FDR had selected Harry Hopkins, former head of the Federal Emergency Relief Administration, to be the Director of Work Projects Administration (WPA). Hopkins created new rules for the selection of enrollees. These rules were based on relief rolls and ignored the quota systems previously used in the states. Director Fechner did not agree and protested. This caused confusion and delays in the enrolling process. By September 1935 only 500,000 men were enrolled. This number was never reached again during the duration of the CCC. Near the end of 1935 another problem faced Fechner in attaining 600,000 enrollees. FDR secretly told him that since an election year was coming he wanted to balance the budget by a drastic cut in the number of enrollees and camps. This plan eventually caused Roosevelt problems in 1936.[28]

Middle Years

In January 1936 when Roosevelt announced the elimination of 489 CCC camps nationwide.[29] This reduction resulted in a huge outpouring of disapproval that reverberated throughout the nation. The politicians on both sides of the aisle in Congress showed their disapproval. They knew the CCC program was successful in creating jobs and helping their constituents in the communities where the camps were established.

FDR refused to listen to the protests and announced a reduction in enrollment to 300,000 men and 1,400 camps.

Citizens responded with an outpouring of letters to FDR. Even Democratic members of Congress protested the reductions. Finally, FDR and his advisors cancelled their proposals and kept the same number of CCC enrollees and existing camps. The CCC program continued to produce successful work during 1936 despite these governmental hassles.

In 1936 the CCC was not only popular with the Republican presidential candidate, Alf Landon, but it had a 67% approval of the registered Republicans.[30]

Although the ECW was originally called the Civilian Conservation Corps it did not become official until June 28, 1937 with an act of Congress.

In 1937 FDR decided to cut cost by reducing government spending to the states. This resulted in states reducing the number of camps working on park, forestry, and fish and game projects.[31] The number of state camps in Connecticut was reduced to 10. In the fall these camps closed: Black Rock in Thomaston, Roosevelt in Killingworth, Britton in Windsor, Stuart in East Hampton, and Wooster Mt. in Danbury.

Later in 1937 Congress responded by extending the life of the CCC for three years and separated the CCC from the federal relief organization by establishing it as a regular government bureau.[32]

The enrollees received a present from President Roosevelt in 1938, new uniforms. Since its beginning in 1933 the enrollees used WWI Army surplus uniforms. On FDR's visit to Warm Springs, GA he was upset to see the CCC men wearing poor quality uniforms. He felt this shoddy clothing weakened the men's morale. FDR had the Department of Navy design a new forest green uniform that became widespread the following year.32

Despite the popularity of the CCC, Congress decided not to make it a permanent government agency. For the next two years Congress funded the program as an independently funded agency. Perhaps it was because Congress thought it was a temporary relief program to help with the Depression.

Later Years

In 1939 Fechner was faced with new challenges. The threat of war in Europe and possible German invasions of England and France. Threats of war spurred the economy to produce materials for our allies. Factories needed workers and the number of CCC enrollees began to decrease.

Roosevelt decided to reorganize several agencies. Congress created the Federal Security Agency (FSA) that consolidated several offices and boards under one director. It brought the CCC into this agency. Fechner was furious. He was no longer the director of an independent agency and now had to listen to the directives of the FSA Director. Fechner asked the President to change his plan but FDR refused. To show his indignation Fechner submitted his resignation but later withdrew it. Many think this conflict with Roosevelt led to Fechner's ill health and in December he had a massive heart attack and died on December 31.[33]

The CCC Legacy Foundation states: "Fechner was the CCC. His honest, day-by-day attention to all facets of the program sustained high levels of accomplishment and shaped an impressive public image of the CCC. He was a common man, neither impressed nor intimidated by his contemporaries in Washington. Fechner was considered deficient and lacking vision in some areas but his dedication was second to none. His lengthy and detailed progress

Three of these enrollees are wearing the new forest green uniforms that were issued in 1938. It was a big improvement over the old WW I uniforms. The other two enrollees are wearing their spiffy double breasted suits ready to impress the young ladies in nearby Voluntown. Gary Potter

reports to FDR were valuable information. He was a good and faithful servant who was spared from witnessing the end of the CCC program."[34]

During 1939 these camps were operating in Connecticut: Toumey, East Goshen; White, Winsted; Lonergan, Voluntown; Robinson, East Hartland; Cross, West Cornwall; Fernow, Eastford; Filley, Haddam; Buck, Portland; Hadley, Madison; and Connor, Stafford Springs.

In 1940 the CCC was now confronted with the loss of their leader and a President and Congress who were more concerned with the conflicts in Europe than the CCC. Congress appointed Fechner's assistant, John J. McEntee, as its director. McEntee was a very knowledgeable person but did not have the patience of Fechner. The new director had conflicts with Harold Ickes, the Secretary of the Interior, who disapproved of McEntee's nomination. McEntee struggled to keep the program going and received little praise for his efforts.[35] He worked until the program ended in 1942.

In 1940 when France fell to Germany public support for the CCC began to waver as the threat of war increased. Emphasis in Congress was now focused on the defense of our country and mobilizing for a future involvement in war. Demands for ending the CCC increased in Congress.

Despite the CCC difficulties, it continued to be a popular program. FDR tried again to reduce the CCC for economic reasons during the election year of 1940 but Congress refused and added $50 million to the 1940-41 appropriations. The number of enrollees continued to be approximately 300,000.[36]

In Connecticut there were 10 CCC campsites during the beginning of 1941 but with the increase of factory production the number of camps in the US was reduced to 900 camps and 135,000 enrollees. By the end of the year there were only two camps in the state: Lonergan in Voluntown and White in Winsted.[37]

Towards the end of summer in 1941 the CCC faced new challenges: the decrease in applicants, desertions, and resignations due to better jobs. There were now less than 200,000 enrollees and approximately 900 camps. The citizens and newspapers who had supported the CCC now questioned its continuation. Unemployment was down and the defense of our nation was of the utmost importance.[38]

On December 7, 1941 the Japanese bombing of Pearl Harbor had a traumatic effect on the nation and the life of the CCC. The US had to focus on defeating its enemy and any projects not directly related to the war effort were considered non-essential and many were dropped. Congress appointed a joint committee to study the various federal agencies. The CCC came under close scrutiny towards the end of 1941 and the committee recommended the abolishment of the CCC by July 1, 1942.[39]

During 1942 Camp Lonergan in Voluntown was the only operating camp in Connecticut.

On March 25, 1942, the ninth anniversary of the establishment of the CCC, FDR sent a letter to CCC Director James McEntee to congratulate him for his work:

"There is a real place for the CCC during this emergency and it will be called upon more and more to perform tasks which will strengthen our country, and aid in the successful operation of the war. Many of the young men now in the camps will enter the nation's armed forces. When that time comes, they will be better prepared to serve their country because of the discipline, the training and physical hardihood they gained in the Civilian Conservation Corps."[40]

The CCC plodded on for six months knowing that the end was near. Finally in June the House of Representatives voted 158 to 151 to curtail funding to the CCC. Then the Senate voted on a bill to continue the CCC that twice ended in tie votes. Vice President Harry Wallace voted to continue funding. Then the Senate-House Committee came up with a decision that authorized $8 million to liquidate the agency. Both the House and Senate confirmed the end of the CCC and it became history.

When the US entered WWII it became apparent that the CCC program would end. Provisions were made to end work projects. States made provisions to turn over the camp buildings and all operating equipment such as tools, tractors, trucks, etc. to the Army for the war effort.[41] During the war a few of the camps in the US were used as Prisoner of War (POW) camps but none in Connecticut were used for that purpose. Most of the CCC camp's buildings were taken down and used by the state while some were sold to individuals just to get rid of the buildings.

Accomplishments

The CCC, composed of both young men and veterans, played a significant part in saving and restoring our natural resources. Listed here are some of its major accomplishments throughout the US.

CCC Programs in US & Territories

- employed 3,463,766 men
- enrolled 2,876,638 Juniors, Veterans, and Native Americans
- enrolled an estimated 50,000 in territories of Alaska, Hawaii, Puerto Rico, and Virgin Islands
- planted between 2-3 billion trees
- built more than 3,000 fire towers
- constructed 46,854 bridges
- developed 52,000 acres of public campgrounds
- constructed 125,000 miles of roads
- built 13,100 miles of foot trails
- built 318,076 check dams for erosion control
- fought fires totaling more than 8 million man-days
- strung 89,000 miles of telephone wire
- protected 154 million sq. yd. of stream and lake banks
- stocked 972 million fish
- performed mosquito control work on 248,000 acres
- assisted farmer's land by controlling soil erosion and improving 40 million acres of farmland
- provided 814,000 acres of barren and denuded range land with vegetation
- restored 3,980 historic structures
- provided an economic boost to local businesses
- enrollee dependents received $662,895,000 nationwide
- physical health of the enrollees improved through vigorous work and good food
- the education program taught approximately 40,000 illiterate enrollees to read[42]

CCC Program in Connecticut

- employed 30,670 men (1933-1942)
- enrolled 28,447 Juniors and Veterans + 2,223 officers and supervisors
- 22,114 men in CCC camps
- most of the pine and spruce plantations on State Forest and Park lands were planted by CCC
- thinned 28,000 acres of young forest to improve the health and growth rate of the forest
- thinning provided: 82,000 cords of firewood, 29,419 fence posts and highway guard rails, and 1.4 million board feet of saw logs
- about 5 man-days per acre were spent on the management of forest stands that had not seen

treatment since they were first cut over, burned or damaged by storms

- 1,606,730 acres treated for gypsy moths; this took 416,000 man-days and 200,000 of those days doing gypsy moth control work
- Danbury camp in Wooster Forest cut and destroyed over 100,000 dead and diseased elm trees
- worked 50,685 man-days doing forest fire prevention and pre-suppression work
- removed dead and dying material along highways and burned 100' strips on both sides of the highways
- built 50 miles of fire lanes which provided access to remote areas and served as fire breaks
- built 1,200 water holes to aid firefighters
- built nine fire towers that helped with the early detection of forest fires
- planted shrubs and trees to bear fruit, seeds, and nuts for wildlife
- created over 1,100 acres of recreation facilities
- built 500 fireplaces and 1,100 picnic tables
- 1,100 picnic tables
- dug wells for drinking water
- developed system of ski trails
- constructed bathhouses in many state parks
- created 150 miles of truck trails and about 500 miles of old log roads were cleared
- built two nature museums
- helped towns recover from floods and hurricanes
- cleaned out 3,750 flooded buildings after 1936 flood
- helped clean up after 1938 hurricane
- improved streams by rip-rapping, planting the banks, and building V-dams[43]

Camp Roosevelt constructed a large dam, creating Schreeder Pond. Amidst the white pine trees that were planted by the CCC is the beautiful Oak Lodge that is now a nature museum. Podskoch

FDR's CCC program was his most successful New Deal Program. It had overwhelming support from the enrollees, political parties, families, towns, states, and nation. The CCC had a lasting effect on the lives of the enrollees by giving them a sense of worth because they had a job and were helping their families. Enrollees learned self-discipline, developed a lasting love of nature, learned how to get along with many types of people, and in many cases learned a trade they used when they left the CCC. The enrollees' experiences in the CCC benefited the US when it went to war with Japan and Germany because the Army trained them so that they had discipline and knew how to lead. Many who were leaders in the CCC became sergeants when they joined the army and navy.

The Post War Years

There were a few attempts to revive the CCC concept after WWII. The Student Conservation Program (SCP) proposed by Elizabeth Cushman in her 1955 senior thesis at Vassar College was implemented in 1957 in the Olympic and Grand Teton National Parks. Young people performed jobs such as trail work and collecting entrance fees. In 1964 the Student Conservation Association (SCA) began. Elizabeth Cushman Titus became the president of the organization. It involved high school, college, and graduate students in the 50 states. The volunteers restored habitat, built trails, destroyed invasive species, and did erosion control work. During the summer over 600 youths (15 and older) worked in crews of 6-8 under the supervision of an adult. Work was on federally controlled lands such as national parks, national monuments, national wildernesses, and those under the Bureau of Land Management. The Departments of Agriculture and Interior and some states operated the conservation projects. Volunteers had to provide their own transportation to the projects. They worked from 21-30 days on projects. At the end they had a 4-5 day recreation trip.[44]

In 1970 the Youth Conservation Corps (YCC) began. The program employed teens (15-18) for 8-10 weeks in the summer doing conservation projects on federally managed lands. This federally funded program involved the youth in projects involving repairing and restoring historic structures, removing exotic plants, marking boundaries, restoring campsites, constructing trails, and doing wildlife research. There were 46,000 enrollees in 1978 in the 50 states, Puerto Rico, Virgin Islands, and Guam. The program ended in 1981 due to federal budget cuts.[45]

In 1993 a Community Service Trust Act passed during the Clinton presidency created AmeriCorps. Each year 75,000 adults covering all ages and backgrounds have the opportunity to work with local and national nonprofit groups doing projects to protect the environment or help individuals. Some of the projects are: helping communities during disasters, fighting illiteracy, cleaning streams and parks, tutoring disadvantaged youths, building homes for the needy, and operating and managing after-school programs.[46]

This beautiful stone nature museum was constructed by Camp White enrollees in Peoples Forest near Winsted. Podskoch

Organization of the Civilian Conservation Corps
LINES OF AUTHORITY

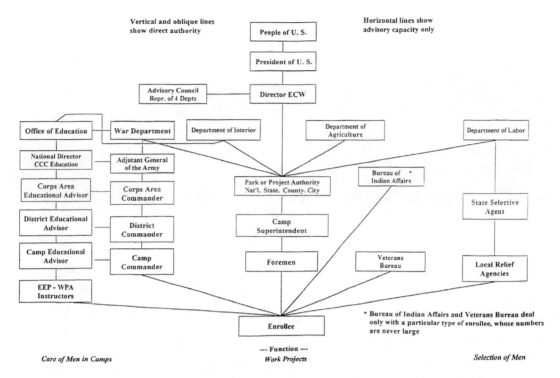

Organization of Civilian Conservation Corps, Lines of Authority. CCC Legacy Archives

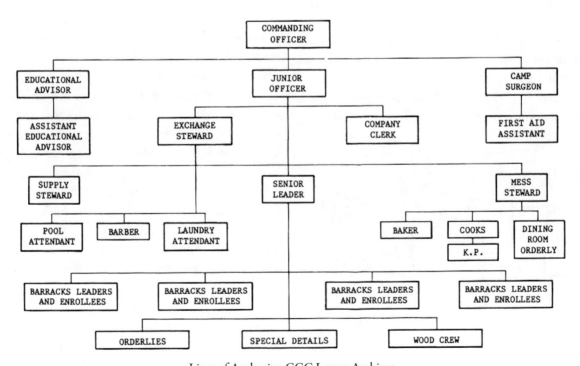

Lines of Authority. CCC Legacy Archives

CHAPTER 2
CAMP ORGANIZATION

A 1935 group photo of Clinton Camp Roosevelt, Company 171, S-60 located at Chatfield Hollow SP in Killingworth. George Diekewicz

Nine CCC Coprs Areas

CCC camps were organized into nine regional Army Corps Areas. Connecticut was in the 1st Corps Area along with the states of Maine, New Hampshire, Vermont, Massachusetts, and Rhode Island. An Army general commanded each corps area. The corps area was divided into districts. The general's job was to send messages from the corps area to each district camp, which had an executive officer, an adjutant (an officer who acts as military assistant), a medical officer, and a chaplain.[1]

In 1933 the 1st Corps Area was divided into six districts. Connecticut was in the Fifth District with headquarters at Fort Wright on Fishers Island, NY.

Each camp had a company number received when organized at an Army post. Example: Clinton was Company 171. The first number, 1, stood for the 1st Corps Area and the number 71 stood for the 20th company formed. Each camp also had a state letter and number. An S- was a camp in a State Forest, SP- State Park, P- Private Forest, AF- Army. Example: Clinton's camp was S-60. It worked in state forests. The number 60 stood for the 60th camp formed in First Corps Area.

Camp Organization

The Army supervised the men while in camp and provided them with food, clothing, equipment, shelter, and medical care. Each camp had a captain who was in charge of administration, discipline, and welfare of the men. He had one or two lieutenants for assistance. Some camps had an Army doctor/surgeon. If they didn't the Army contracted with a local doctor to do physicals and handle emergencies. In order to help with the supervision of the enrollees, the Army selected enrollees with leadership qualities. They helped supervise the barracks and work assignments. Leaders received $45 and assistant leaders $36 a month. Twenty-six leaders were assigned to each camp. Of these 26 men the Army had eight who worked in the camp and the other 18 were assigned to the superintendent.[2]

The camp was like a little town. At first during the summer of 1933 men lived in surplus army pyramid tents or wooden tent frames. Later the Army hired local carpenters to build wooden buildings that better protected the men. There were approximately 24 buildings in each camp. There was a kitchen/mess hall, recreation hall, barracks, officers'

Nine CCC Corps Area map. CCC Legacy Archives

quarters, school/classroom, infirmary, garages for Army and state trucks, vehicle repair shop, blacksmith shop, officers' headquarters, latrine/shower, water and sewage facilities, streets, and sidewalks. The camp had electricity and telephones. The buildings had large stoves that used coal or wood for fuel.[3]

Infirmary

Each camp had an infirmary with 4-8 beds. It had a stove and basic first aid materials and medicines. Each infirmary had one or two assigned enrollees who were there 24/7. They had general knowledge in first aid. They cleaned cuts and did bandaging and brought the ill food. If an injury was serious the enrollee called the Army surgeon or the contracted local doctor. If the patient needed to

go to a hospital an Army ambulance took him to New London, Conn. and then transferred him by ferry to the Army hospital at Fort Wright on Fishers Island, NY. There were accidents and even deaths of enrollees. About half of the deaths were attributed to vehicles. The enrollees drove the trucks and had frequent accidents due to poor road conditions or lack of experience on the part of the young drivers. Other causes of deaths were drowning, pneumonia, falls, fighting fires, and falling objects.[4]

Cover of the 1937 Fifth District First Corps Area 1937 Yearbook

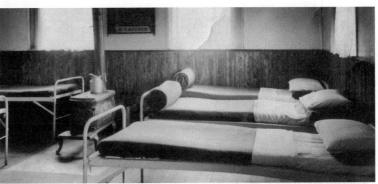

This is the Camp Cross infirmary in West Cornwall. An enrollee was responsible for taking care of patients and minor injuries. Some camps had an Army surgeon based at the camp while others camps hired local doctors when needed. Podskoch Collection

A 1939 view of Camp White from the Administration building roof with five barracks, a mess hall, a recreation hall, an infirmary (lower left), surrounding the flag pole and square where the men gathered in the morning and evening. The garages and maintenance buildings were down a hill to the left and a root cellar had been dug into the hill on the right of the buildings. Tony Gagliardi

When an enrollee was injured or sick he was taken to the camp infirmary for treatment. If the injury required hospital care, the patient was taken by camp ambulance to the Army hospital at Fort Wright on Fishers Island. This was the Camp Fernow ambulance with enrollees: Putney, Parsons, Guilford, and Disturco. Gary Potter

CHAPTER 3
ENROLLEE'S LIFE IN CAMP

Signing Up

At first unmarried, unemployed men between 18 and 25 years of age whose families were on the relief rolls were eligible to sign up. Candidates applied at the nearest public welfare office. In 1933 there were five applicants for each opening. There were four enrollment periods, January, April, July, and October. The number of spots depended on the town's quota and vacancies available. In 1935 the ages were changed to 17-23 to fill the enlarged quota. In 1933 the enrollees could only sign up for six months to allow others a chance to join. This rule changed so that the men could sign up four times for a total of two years. Once selected the enrollee then had to pass a physical exam and take the oath of enrollment.[1]

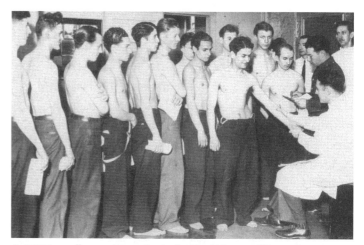

A CCC enrollee getting a physical exam. Library of Congress

Coming to Camp

In 1933 they were transported to an Army base for one or more weeks of conditioning. Groups of 200 men formed a company and were sent to establish a camp. After 1933 the men were assigned camps.

One can just imagine how many enrollees were homesick as they rode in canvas covered Army trucks or on railroads to their new camp. The young men left their homes in the large cities or small towns and traveled to the backwoods of Connecticut or way out west to Colorado or Montana. It was a real culture shock. Many had roamed aimlessly through city streets or rode the rails. Now their life was regimented and they had to follow orders and a schedule. Some men couldn't take this new life and left after just a day or two. The Army didn't chase after them but they received a dishonorable discharge.

Some men went to various camps in their state while others went across the US on trains to National Parks and Forests in California, Nevada, Idaho, Montana, Wyoming, etc. The men did not have a choice of camp location but went willingly to get a job and help their families. Then they had to adjust and live with about 200 other young men.

The new enlisted men went to the camp supply office for their clothing and equipment. The clerk gave them work clothes, boots, shoes, underwear, toilet kit, coats, rain gear, and uniforms.

This is the entrance to Camp Lonergan in Voluntown which greeted the enrollees in June 1937 as they approached their home for the next six months. Gary Potter

CCC enrollees at Camp Roosevelt in Killingworth lived in Army tents in 1933 while local carpenters built the barracks and other buildings. The gas pump was near the truck garage. George Diekewicz

Enrollees doing exercises before going to work in the forest or park. NYS Archives

Camp Fernow rec hall with pool tables, ping pong table, and chairs for relaxing. During the winter two wood stoves and a fireplace kept the room warm. Elizabeth Germaine

Daily Routine

Monday – Friday

6:00 am Reveille (either a bugle call or a whistle)

6:30 am Breakfast

7:00 am Police (clean) the barracks and camp

7:50 am General assembly, raise the flag, roll call, and work assigned

12 noon Lunch

4:00 pm Work ends and return to camp

5:00 pm Retreat ceremony involving the lowering of the flag, announcements, and dinner

6-10 pm Free time to play sports, listen to radio write letters, play cards or 'shoot the bull' with friends, or attend classes

10:00 pm Lights out[2]

The camp workweek consisted of 40 hours. The eight-hour day included an hour for lunch and driving to and from a work project. Many projects were 20-30 minutes from camp. A minimum of six hours of work a day was required. If it rained during the week, work had to be made up on Saturdays.[3]

The young men worked either in the camp under Army supervision or out on projects under the state's supervision. Eighty-four percent worked on projects, 12% were employed in camp, and 4% were sick or absent.[4]

Weekends

Saturday

The enrollees had free time unless they had to make up time due to poor weather or emergencies like fires or flood damage to towns or roads. Some men had a pass to go home. In the evening some went to a nearby town to go to the movies, a restaurant,or a bar, or maybe dancing or bowling.

Sunday

Sundays were also 'free time'. Many attended religious services held in camp. There were also trucks available to transport enrollees to local churches.

The young men kept their barracks in an orderly fashion because the Army officers had frequent inspections. This barracks was at Stafford Springs. CT CCC Museum

Camp Lonergan baseball team played other CCC camps and nearby town teams.
CT CCC Museum

These Camp Graves enrollees cooling off with a swim at a lake in
Union Historical Society

Camp Activities

Enrollees had opportunities for recreation in the evenings and on weekends. Most camps provided a building for a library or a space in the education building or recreation hall for reading books and newspapers. The rec hall sometimes had a pool and ping pong tables, and tables for card and board games. They also had a beautiful stone fireplace that provided warmth on cold days. Some enrollees brought their guitars and other musical instruments for playing music. Enrollees formed bands that performed for the camp.

In the rec hall was a PX or Canteen where enrollees could purchase, soda, candy, cigarettes, pipe tobacco, and toiletries. A leader or assistant leader supervised the store. Profits from the sales went to purchase items for the camp such as, a pool table, team uniforms, sports equipment, paint, lighting fixtures, etc.

There were opportunities for hunting, fishing, and trapping in the nearby forests, rivers, and lakes. In many of the camps baseball, basketball, and football teams were formed. Boxing and wrestling matches were also popular. Some camps built their own ring for matches. The camps had intramural competition with barracks or the team competed against nearby CCC camps or local town teams.

Field Days

"CCC Field Days" were held almost every year. Each district or sub district chose a town and enrollees from all of the camps came to test their skills in various sports. They participated in a parade and then competed in track & field events, boxing and wrestling matches, and baseball games.

Other Activities

Sometimes the camp had dances and invited locals to attend. Many romances developed with enrollees and girls they met in the nearby towns. Sometimes they married and settled in the country towns.

Plays and musical performances were held in the rec hall. Enrollees formed bands and performed for the camp. Federal Emergency Relief Act (FERA) sponsored traveling groups of actors who performed plays at the camps.

The Army provided religious service at least once a month in camp. If camp was close to a town, the Army provided trucks for transporting the enrollees to religious services on Sundays. There were also Catholic, Protestant, and Jewish Army Reserve chaplains who traveled to camps and held services. There were a few volunteer clergymen who held services in the camp without remuneration, except for board, transportation or lodging.[5]

Enrollees' Cars & Characters

Rules prohibited the ownership of automobiles at camp, but at many camps the officers looked the other way as long as the cars were kept elsewhere. Many enrollees hid their cars in the woods near camp. In those days one could purchase a jalopy for $20 to $60.

There were many unusual characters with nicknames like: "Loan Shark," "Gold Bricker," "Camp Bully," "Camp Comedian," "Shorty," "Slim," "Junior," "Muscles," "Chow Hound," "Stooge," "Apple Polisher," "Brown Noser," and "Stool Pigeon." The "Gold Bricker" was adverse to labor. The 'Loan Shark' was the camp entrepreneur. He would gladly buy a $1 canteen book for 50 or 75¢ and then resell it at face value, $1. He would also lend out money and discount it at 50 or 75 percent, but would seek his money on payday.

Thieves were punished not by Army officers but by the camp's "kangaroo court," which doled out punishment unbeknownst to the Army officers. The punishment was severe enough that the thief had second thoughts about stealing from his so-called friends again. Generally, penalties involved some kind of duty performed for members of the court, such as doing their laundry or pressing their shirts and pants-military style of course.

"Chow Hounds" had no table manners. They would first grab a platter of food and gulp it down and hopefully wait for the cook's call for seconds. Food was served either cafeteria or family style. In the latter, a "Chow Hound" was the first to grab the platters of meat, potatoes, and vegetables. Then load his plate and even his pockets with anything that was portable.

Connecticut Chief State Forester Austin Hawes stated

that there was waste and poor cooking at many of the camps because the cooks lacked experience. He felt the army should have hired trained cooks and it would have paid off in the long run.[6]

Education

There was no mention of education in the ECW Act but towards the end of 1933 Fechner appointed Clarence S. Marsh as Director of Education. An education advisor assisted each corps area commander. The Office of Education who administered the program in their area selected him.[7]

In 1934 the education program began operating in June. Criticism was leveled at the methodology used for teaching and even Fechner had doubts that it might impede the work program. His doubts never materialized. The enrollees' skills and education varied from men with little schooling to those who were university graduates. By 1937 the program taught more than 35,000 illiterate enrollees to read and over a thousand received a high school diploma and 39 men received a college diploma.[8]

Each camp had a Camp Education Advisor (CEA) who designed vocational and academic programs, taught classes, and brought in instructors and speakers. An enrollee worked as his assistant. The advisor held voluntary classes in the evenings. Classes covered a wide range of topics: mechanics, photography, forestry, engineering, surveying, high school diploma, carpentry, electrical, woodcarving, and other subjects. There were also correspondence classes from colleges. The education program's success depended on the competency and work of the CEA and cooperation of the camp commander.[9]

A wood sawing and chopping contest was held at Camp Fernow in Eastford that pitted enrollees from many Connecticut CCC camps. CT CCC Museum

On Sept. 31, 1935 these Camp Fernow enrollees are leaving camp. Some have their guitars and certificates they earned. Two Army officers and forestry foremen in the back row are sending them off with hopes of getting a job. The Army transported the boys by bus or train to their home town. Gary Potter

The mess hall at West Cornwall was a busy place at breakfast and supper where the enrollees could have as much as they wanted to eat. Many of them gained a lot of weight and muscle working in the forests and parks. Gary Potter

CHAPTER 4
CCC PROJECTS IN CONNECTICUT

SHORT HISTORY OF THE CCC

After Congress passed the Economic Reconstruction Act and it was signed by Roosevelt on March 31, 1933 the task began of securing unemployed young men in the country to do projects that would improve the country's natural resources especially the forests. Some of the projects were planting trees, preventing forest fires, floods and soil erosion, controlling plant pests and diseases, etc. in the national parks and national forests.[1]

With this authorization, President Roosevelt created the Civilian Conservation Corps and asked that 250,000 men be enrolled and stationed in camps run by the Army throughout the country by the end of the year. He appointed Robert Fechner as director who would be assisted by the departments of Agriculture, Interior, Labor and War. Each state received a quota based on its population. Connecticut's quota was 3,250 men. From this number 3,000 were young unmarried men between 18-25 years old and 250 were local experienced men (LEM). On June 7, 1933 Roosevelt signed an executive order adding 25,000 WW I veterans. Five hundred men was the quota for Connecticut.[2]

All the officers of the U.S. Forestry Service, U.S. Park Service and all state foresters were invited to a meeting in Washington on April 6 to receive instructions on running the program. Participants were surprised that there was no detailed information on how it was to be administered, the types of work permitted, or how it was to be financed. Chief

A group of Army and Connecticut Conservation Dept. Forestry personnel at Camp Fernow in Eastford. The Army supervised the enrollees in camp while the forestry dept. supervised the camp projects. Ted Schulz

Forester for Connecticut, Austin F. Hawes, wrote that the next day he asked the Chief of the U.S. Forest Service, Major Robert Stuart, if he knew any of the details of the program. Hawes wrote, "Apparently the President had not delegated authority to anyone to work out details of this great undertaking. It appeared later in his administration that this was one of Roosevelt's faults. It was evident that Major Stuart felt keenly that he had not been taken into the President's confidence, and I believe that this was a contributing factor in his untimely death later in the year."[3]

The participants heard that the enrollees would be conditioned at Army camps and then sent to work camps operated by foresters. Hawes and two other foresters were appointed to a committee to make recommendations.

Austin F. Hawes

Austin F. Hawes (1879-1962) served as Chief Forester for Connecticut from 1904 - 1909, then in Vermont until 1921. He eventually returned to his old position in Connecticut and held it until 1943. He wrote about his experiences supervising the development of Connecticut's forests. In 1957, he completed a 359-page manuscript entitled 'History of Forestry in Connecticut'. This chapter contains information from his manuscript that describes the development and accomplishments of the CCC.

'History of Forestry in Connecticut' has been digitized by the Connecticut Agricultural Experiment Station in New Haven and is available for download at www.ct.gov.[†]

fpr.vermont.gov

† Full url: http://www.ct.gov/caes/lib/caes/documents/publications/special_bulletins/hawes_%282014%29_ct_forest_history.pdf

They recommended that work camps be administered by the US Army and leave the foresters to concentrate on work projects. Roosevelt finally agreed on this partnership between the Army and the foresters.[4]

Col. William H. Wilson, the Army commander of Fort Wright on Fishers Island, supervised the Connecticut CCC camps. An Army captain or 1st lieutenant supervised the daily operation of each camp. A 2nd lieutenant assisted the commander.[5]

Camp Superintendent

Austin Hawes' first task was hiring superintendents and foremen for each camp whose responsibility was supervising the men in the fieldwork. Hawes stated there was an abundance of qualified men seeking employment due to the Depression. He conducted personal interviews and hired experienced engineers, foresters, and businessmen. Luckily, these men were hired before Washington Congressmen learned of the political patronage that could have been gained. Later, they sent Hawes lists of competent grade foremen to choose, but Governor Cross said politics should not be involved in the forestry work.[6]

The camp superintendent was in charge of the work projects. His salary was $200 a month. Eight to 10 foremen assisted him. Once the men left camp at 8 am to work on projects, they were under the superintendent and the Conservation Department (CD). The superintendent drew up projects or received projects formulated by heads of the CD. Projects included order of preference, maps, estimated man-days, and schedules for each project. Copies of the plans were sent for approval to the US Forest Service, the camp superintendent, and the CD Office in Hartford.

The Camp Hadley Superintendent and his staff in Madison (1940). Shepard

The superintendent assigned work to his foremen and organized the enrollees into small work crews.[7]

The superintendent had to send monthly detailed reports to Hartford showing work accomplished, man-days spent on the projects, and work that was contemplated. They also showed fuel and oil consumption, tools needing replacement, and the type of work done by heavy equipment and trucks.

The foremen were paid $70 a month. The camp also hired a blacksmith, a tractor operator, and mechanics. Several enrollees worked in the office doing clerical work. Most of this money went to local men thus boosting the economy of the local towns. All of the financing of the CCC came from the federal government and was distributed by the Army Finance Officer.

Camps

At the beginning Connecticut established 8 camps with 250 men in each. Then the state received authorization for four more camps with 200 men. This brought the total of enrollees to 2,800. To complete the state's quota (3,250) two more camps were added.[8]

When the first camps were established in the summer of 1933 the attitude of many of the enrollees was that they were on an outing. For a few months enrollees could not be discharged unless they refused to work or broke a camp rule. State Forester Austin Hawes said, "Most of the men loafed on the job and many were absent without leave. These faults were rectified and men discharged if they were absent twice without leave, or if they were habitual loafers. At first the towns sent some undesirable boys but as the purpose of the camps came to be better understood, a better grade of boys were sent."[9]

The government began giving inducements to enrollees who had leadership qualities. The position of Leader was established with a salary of $45 a month and of Assistant Leader at $36 a month. Each camp had approximately 200 men. They had 10 Leaders and 16 Assistant Leaders to help keep the young men in order and do their assignments.[10]

To handle all of the bookkeeping for the program, Austin Hawes hired Courtice Berry. He and his staff worked near Hawes' office in the State Office Building in Hartford. Hawes stated, "Berry was meticulous in handling the innumerable details of ordering tools and supplies, in the selection and supervision of blacksmiths who kept the tools in good shape and in regard to the bookkeeping."[11]

District foresters supervised the work projects and the superintendents in the camps in their districts. Hawes periodically inspected the projects and wrote recommendations to the superintendent. W. Foster Schreeder supervised surveying and type mapping projects while Hartford engineer, Henry R. Buck, supervised the road building.[12]

In 1935 the state established six new camps: Hadley, Britton, Buck, Conner, Fechner, and Stuart. These two camps were closed: Chapman and Hook. The state then had 16 forestry camps and one state park camp.[13]

In 1936 Connecticut Emergency Relief Commission reported 4,172 men in CCC camps. Part of their salary ($25) went home to their families and the annual amount was $1,251,600. All but ten towns in the state had enrollees. The large cities had most of the enrollees: Hartford, 1,583; New Britain, 1,548; New Haven, 1,294; Bridgeport, 1,216; Waterbury, 1,197.[14]

In 1937 the federal government lowered the age requirement from 18 to 17 and this increased the number of enrollees in the state. Some people said this lowered the quality of the work while others claimed it provided much needed education. Twenty-six percent of the men were now 17 or younger; 26% were 18. Not all of the Connecticut boys were in state camps. Twenty-nine percent worked in other states and of these 21% were in other New England states and 8% were in Oregon.[15]

Camp Names

The state named the camps after these men: Governor Cross, camp #51; James W. Toumey, professor at Yale School of Forestry, #52; Lucius F. Robinson, chairman of the State Park and Forest Commission, #53; Senator Frederic C. Walcott, #54; Henry S. Graves, Dean Yale School of Forestry, #55; Dr. B. E. Fernow, 1st technical forester in US, #56; Dr. E. H. Jenkins, former Director of Connecticut Agricultural Experiment Station who started forestry in Connecticut, #57; Senator Augustine Lonergan, #58; Harley Roberts formerly from Taft School of Watertown who worked for the establishing of Black Rock State Park and Mattatuck State Forest, #59; President Franklin D. Roosevelt, #60; Professor H. H. Chapman, President of the Commission on Forests and Wild Life, #61; James W. Hook, Chairman of Connecticut Unemployment Commission in 1933, #62; Alain C. White,

generously contributed to the establishment of state parks and forests in Litchfield, #63; Walter O. Filley, 4th state forester of Connecticut, #64; Arthur Hadley, former Yale president and supporter of forestry, #65; Dr. William Britton, State Entomologist, #66; Henry Buck, an engineer who was killed in an automobile accident while supervising camp road construction, #67; General Fox Conner, First Corps Area Commandant in Boston, #68; Robert Fechner, CCC Director, #69; and Robert Stuart, Chief US Forester in 1933.[16]

When a young man enrolled in the CCC he was sent to New London and transported by ferry to Ft. Wright on Fishers Island. Doctors gave him a thorough examination and inoculated him for paratyphoid and vaccinated them for small pox. After the medical checkup the men were sent to a particular camp.[17] After 1933 the men went to the New London Supply Depot for a physical and processing. Then

(L–R) 1 A Camp Walcott leader shows off his uniform with the Sgt. Insignia on his left arm. CT CCC Museum 2 CCC enrollees getting a physical exam that included shots by an Army doctor. www.newdealblog.com

A survey crew composed of Camp Toumey enrollees: Wilson, Mancuso, Quintas, and Yakso in the Mohawk State Forest. Mancuso Family

they went by bus or truck to their assigned camp.

The camp workweek consisted of 40 hours. The eight-hour day included an hour for lunch and driving to and from a work project. Many projects were 20-30 minutes from camp. A minimum of six hours of work a day was required. If it rained during the week, work had to be made up on Saturdays.[18]

The young men worked either in the camp under Army supervision or out on projects under the state's supervision. Eighty-four percent worked on projects, 12% were employed in camp, and 4% were sick or absent.[19]

At first most of the work was done using hand tools. Later projects such as road and dam construction required heavy-duty equipment and provisions were made for their purchase. In June 1936 the 16 camps had this amount of equipment: 24 half-ton trucks; 107 1½-ton dump trucks; 65 1½-ton rack trucks; one 15-ton tractor trailer; 12 tractor trail builders; 15 compressors; 24 jackhammers; 11 graders; 14 tractors; 3 diaphragm pumps; 2 cement mixers; 1 rock grinder; 1 rotary scraper; 7 snowplows; 5 welding outfits; 2 transits; and 4 motion picture projectors.[20]

"Side" or "spike" camps were established when projects were quite a distance from the main camp. CCC Director Fechner did not want the men to spend half of their workday traveling. The side camp had approximately 10-20 men who lived in tents and were supervised by a forester or foreman. These camps could not have more than 10% of the company's strength. They had a cook tent for preparing meals and enough supplies for a week or more.

Work Projects

Some of the most important projects of the CCC camps were: constructing roads and trails; improving

Enrollees used a Cletrac tractor to move logs in the winter. Stan Slusarczyk

forests; surveying forests and typemapping; controlling and preventing fires; improving streams for fish; developing recreational areas; constructing administrative buildings; insect and disease control; and working in nurseries.[21]

Truck Trails

The law creating the CCC did not mention building roads as an objective of the program. The US Forest Service created the term "truck trail." They specified that they could not be wide highways. The roads had to be well drained and surfaced with gravel. Clear-cutting of trees along the sides was not permitted. The roads were 10 feet wide with 2-foot shoulders. Roads were built to federal specifications. The subbase was 8-10 inches of broken rock that was covered with 4 inches of fine gravel or shale.[22] The roads were to be used by tourists to enjoy the forests and to help foresters in fighting fires. Foresters used selective cutting techniques which involved cutting only mature trees. The construction of roads made it easier to take out wood and caused less destruction to the forest. The CCC men also built trails to make it easier for tourists to explore the parks and forests.[23]

On July 1, 1938 the state completed 150 miles of truck trails, cleaned out 500 miles of old woods roads, and built and marked 80 miles of foot trails. About 35% of the CCC labor was used in road construction.[24]

The Connecticut Forest and Park Association (CFPA) dedicated Toumey Road on June 15, 1935. The road starts from Rt. 4 at the top of Bunker Hill and travels to the summit of Mohawk Mountain. At the dedication, Henry S. Graves spoke on the life and work of Yale professor, James W. Toumey, for whom the road was named.[25]

Mapping

In 1933 only 74% of the state's forest had been mapped and only 58% was typemapped. By July 1, 1938 the CCC boys, supervised by state foreman and foresters, increased the surveyed state forest to 97.9% of the 69,985 acres. The men marked the outside borders with metal discs. About 95% was typemapped which means marking the types of trees in the forest. The mapping of the state forests showed that 65% was mixed hardwoods, 8% hard and soft woods, 8% softwood plantations, and 7% abandoned farm land. The remaining 12% was hardwoods, cedar swamps, water, ridges of oak, and open land.[26]

Carpentry/Stonework

The CCC built or improved several administrative buildings. They improved the old farmhouse where Ranger Hubert Hubbell lived in the Mohawk Forest. They built a 60 x 24-foot shed for the sawmill that Curtis Veeder presented to the state. Workers also built a sawdust storage shed, and warehouse and shed for lumber. The sawmill began operating in November 1935. It produced a large amount of lumber used for construction projects.[27]

They also built a forest ranger house in Tunxis Forest and converted an old farmhouse into a home and office for the forest ranger in Peoples Forest. The men also built sheds for the storage of lumber and nursery stock.[28]

At the American Legion Forest, the CCC built an administrative building for the Western District containing offices and drafting rooms. They also repaired three old houses for the District Forester and for two forest employees.[29]

The Paugnut Forest had a stone house built for recreation.[30]

The Meshomasic Forest had a sawmill with a cement foundation constructed along with a brick charcoal kiln, a lumber shed, and a plant for creosoting fence posts.[31]

In the Eastern District this construction was completed in the Natchaug Forest: improved the ranger's house, built a planer shop, sawmill, machine shop, sawdust shed, and three

This beautiful stone office building at Burr Pond was built by Camp Walcott enrollees. CT CCC Museum

lumber storage sheds. The state purchased a used sawmill and steam boiler for $250 using Federal funds.[32]

At the Nipmuck State Forest, the CCC built a small caretaker's cabin.[33]

At the District Forester's home in the Nye-Holman Forest, the CCC did improvements and made an office and drafting rooms.[34]

In the Pachaug Forest workers built a shingle mill, a lumber storage shed, a brick charcoal kiln, and a sawmill with a cement foundation. They also improved the house of the forest ranger.[35]

In the Cockaponset Forest, the men built a brick charcoal kiln, a garage, and a lumber storage shed. They also did improvements on the ranger's home.[36]

The Nature Museum in the Peoples Forest was one of the outstanding buildings constructed by the CCC. They used fieldstones for the exterior and finished the interior with chestnut. The design was similar to the Bear Mountain Museum in NY. Russell Lund maintained and supervised it for several years. He also developed a nature trail.[37]

Insect and Disease Control

The CCC camps expended about 18% of their force in controlling insects and diseases in the forests on both public and private land. In the first five years they expended over 416,000 man-days. The CCC devoted about 70% of the work to fighting the gypsy moth that was spreading throughout the northern section of the state. The Federal Government established a barrier zone between New York and Western New England and included Fairfield and Litchfield counties. The CCC fought the insects from a few

Camp Cross enrollees from West Cornwall are spreading gravel on a truck road. Gary Potter

CCC boys "Bug Patrol" examining trees for gypsy moth egg masses in the winter. Carol Smith

areas east of the Connecticut River and then westward to the barrier zone. They used a variety of methods in fighting the insects: wrapping burlap around trees and crushing caterpillars from June to August; ground spraying during June and July; and scouting and painting creosote on egg masses from September to June.[38]

Dr. Burgess, head of insect control, insisted on scouting of lightly infested areas. As a result of this CCC boy spent a day covering only 5-10 acres a day. During the first three years boys scouted 1,036,000 acres but they only found one egg mass per 10 acres. Hawes stated that "the Gypsy Moth cannot be eliminated and that only heavy infestations are dangerous to our forests."[39] The CCC concentrated on the heavily infested areas on the west side of the Connecticut River: Burlington, Canton, Granby, Hartland, New Hartford, Simsbury and Eastford, Stafford, Union on the east side of the Connecticut River.[40]

Workers placed burlap bands around the tree where the caterpillars rested in the early summer heat. Men then crushed the caterpillars but it took 5-7 man-days for an acre and destroyed between 50-300 per acre.[41]

Blister rust is a fungus that damaged millions of white pine trees in late summer or fall. In order for the blister rust to spread it needed a host (ribes bushes such as currants and gooseberries) to complete the cycle. During the spring enrollees scouted state and private forests for ribes plants within 900' of white pine trees. They pulled the plants out and let them dry so they were no longer a threat. The CCC fought the gypsy moths by searching for and destroying the egg masses in the fall and winter. They painted the egg masses with creosote. In Connecticut CCC boys spent 66,000 man-days pulling out gooseberry and currant bushes that were near white pine trees.[42]

In 1933 Dutch elm disease was found in Connecticut and 57 trees were removed in the next year. In 1935 and 1936 men removed 76 trees in each of these years. Most of these trees were removed in lower Fairfield County. The state established Camp Fechner at Wooster Mountain in Danbury. They removed over 100,000 dead and dying trees that were mostly small. Four infected trees were found in the town of Old Lyme. CCC boys from Camp Chapman removed these trees.[43]

Fire Control

The CCC constructed two wooden fire towers: one each in the Cockaponset and the Meshomasic state forests. They also took the steel fire tower that was at Savin Rock and erected it in West Hartland in the Tunxis Forest. In Redding the local Protective Association donated land to the state where a steel tower was constructed. In 1937 the CCC built a steel fire tower on Mohawk Mountain replacing the old wooden tower built in 1922.[44]

Over 50 miles of firebreaks were built to prevent the spread of forest fires. The CCCs removed dead trees from a 100' wide strip and then removed all trees and brush from a 15' wide strip.[45]

Water holes were built to provide water to fight fires. Men dug about 1,000 waterholes in state forests and 200 on private land. The saucer shaped holes ranged from 6' to 12' wide and 6' deep in the center and held from 350 to 1,000 cubic feet of water. Their shape enabled animals to safely walk in or out.[46]

During the fire season each camp had a crew of ten men trained to fight fires along with their regular landscaping work. When the camp received a telephone call for help, a gong or whistle was sounded and the crew ran to trucks with firefighting equipment. Some crews were so fast that they left camp in less than a minute.[47]

Parks & Recreation

In Connecticut the State Park Department, under Superintendent Arthur Parker, was responsible for developing recreational facilities. Only Macedonia Brook Park was entirely under Parker's supervision. There were three other CCC camps located on state parks but they were under the Forestry Department because most of their

Each camp had a trained fire crew of 10 men. The Haddam fire crew is donning their Indian water tanks for a drill in 1936. CT CCC Museum

In 1935 Camp Stuart in East Hampton rebuilt the Comstock Covered bridge that crossed the Salmon River. CT CCC Museum

work covered forestry projects.[48]

Superintendent Parker supervised CCC workers on many projects. On Haystack Mountain in Norfolk, they built and graded a road to the observation tower. They also built a graded road at the Kent Falls Park. At Mohawk Pond they made an entrance road. A road was constructed through Devil's Hopyard State Park (SP). CCC enrollees demolished a cement fish shed at Rocky Neck State Park. Later the cement was used to construct the foundation for a pavilion. Road work was also done at Black Rock SP, Mount Tom SP, Hammonasset Beach SP, Squantz Pond SP, and Macedonia Brook SP. The CCC worked on the recreational pond at Buttonball SP but it wasn't completed.[49]

Limited recreational facilities were developed at fifty areas in the state forests. In the picnic areas the CCC built: 500 fireplaces and 1,100 tables. They dug 30 wells, drilled four wells, and enclosed eight springs for drinking water. Swimming facilities were created at Bragg Pond by building a dam in the Tunxis Forest. Enrollees built bath houses on the Farmington River in the Peoples Forest. They also worked to protect the river by building stone revetments (sloping structures placed on banks). In 1933 workers built Massacoe Pond in Simsbury Forest for swimming. In Cockaponset Forest a large dam was built on a brook creating a large swimming area and recreational area. CCC built bath houses on Great Hill Pond in Meshomasic State Forest (SF), Morey Pond in Nipmuck SF, and at Green Falls and Phillips ponds in Pachaug SF. A stone dam was built at Day Pond in Salmon River SF. Here they also rebuilt the Comstock Covered Bridge. In the Peoples SF four Adirondack lean-tos were built and one in the American Legion Forest.[50]

Ski Trails

Ski trails were constructed at the following state forests: Mohawk, Tunxis, Paugnut, and Salmon River. The latter site was hardly used due to insufficient snow.[51]

Bridge Construction

The CCC men at Camp Fernow constructed the 74-foot Fernow Bridge over the Natchaug River using stone and timber from the forest. On June 4, 1934 Governor Cross dedicated the bridge. The floods of 1936 damaged the bridge but the boys repaired and strengthened it.[52]

Dam Construction

Superintendent Titcomb spent $1,000 reconstructing the timber dam at Burr Pond. After Camp Walcott was established on May 28, 1933, Austin Hawes and Henry

Skiing was popular at Camp Roosevelt at Chatfield Hollow State Park. CT CCC Museum

This beautiful bridge with native stone abutments was built by Camp Fernow enrollees over the Natchaug River. CT CCC Museum

Buck went one night to look at the dam that was in danger of breaking. They met with the mayor of Torrington and Supt. Buttrick and had repairs made, but it continued to leak. Finally, they decided to build a new cement dam and placed foreman Noble in charge. It was a major project of the CCC camp.[53]

There were two other dams constructed. One was at Day Pond in the Salmon River Forest and one at Darling Pond in the Natchaug Forest.[54]

Stream Improvement

The CCC did many stream improvement projects on the Natchaug, Salmon and Black Ledge rivers. The latter stream had a complex system of barriers and check dams that significantly improved the fishing. The Board of Fisheries and Game Department supervised the work.[55]

Silviculture

Silviculture or forest stand improvement consumed about one-fifth of the CCC labor. Many of the state's forests were damaged by severe cutting practices, fires, and ice storms. Little had been done to improve the forests. The state used "salvage cutting" which meant the cutting of all the trees and replanting. This took about 30 man-days per acre.[56]

Another technique used by the CCC was the "weeding of young stands." They cut out the inferior trees with billhooks (cutting tool with a wooden handle and a curved hooked blade) and machetes so that the favored species would have space to grow. This method only required about 4 man-days of labor per acre.[57]

About 28,000 acres of state forests received some type of improved cutting by July 1, 1938. Most of this work was done by CCC enrollees. They cut 82,000 cords of wood, 50,000 poles, 1,400,000 bd. ft. of logs, and 177,000 fence posts. Almost half of the cordwood was burned at the camps for cooking and heating. The remainder of wood was sold for either charcoal or wood.[58]

The state built kilns at Meshomasic, Cockaponset, and Pachaug State Forests. Each kiln held approximately 50 cords of wood. The wood burned between 4-6 days with 10 days to cool. The result was about 40 bushels of charcoal for each cord. There was quite a high demand for the charcoal. Charcoal was used for picnics, fireplaces and drying tobacco. Approximately $100,000 came from the sale of charcoal.[59]

Tree Planting

Tree planting was another important work performed by the CCC. During the first five years about 3⅓ million trees were planted in Connecticut. Some of the chief trees planted were: white, red and Scotch pines; Douglas fir; European larch; and Norway and white spruce. The seedlings were supplied by these three state nurseries in Natchaug, Nye-Holman, and Peoples forests.[60]

Disasters

In the spring of 1936 heavy rains caused the Housatonic and Connecticut rivers to overflow their banks and flood many towns and cities in Connecticut. On March 22 Hawes offered Governor Cross the aid of Connecticut's CCC camps. Camp White Superintendent, Otto Schroeter, was placed in command and when the flood subsided 1,636

Two charcoal kilns were built in the Cockaponset State Forest by foremen and Camp Filley CCC boys in Haddam. DEEP State Parks Archives

A crew of CCC boys from Camp Britton in Windsor came to the aid of the people of Wilson whose town was flooded by the Connecticut River in 1936. Ed Kelly

enrollees began helping 24 towns and communities. They cleaned out flooded homes and buildings and sprayed them with chloride of lime. Enrollees buried animals such as cows, cats, and dogs. They cleaned 2,950 dwellings and buildings such as schools, barns, churches, etc. The young men worked 26,047 man-days. On April 29 Hartford's mayor, Thomas Spellacy, honored 1,200 CCC enrollees who had worked in Hartford with a dinner at the Foot Guard Armory. He also presented each enrollee with a wrist watch as thanks for the hard work.[61]

Forestry Research

In 1937 Dr. Raymond Kienholz, who was the superintendent of Camp Robinson, was appointed by Austin Hawes to be the Specialist of Silviculture. Kienholz established his headquarters in the Tunxis State Forest. He directed the enrollees at Camp Robinson in establishing many experimental tree plots.[62]

His work began at the latter point of the CCC program in the state. He was in charge of all the forestry research work. He and his assistants studied the diseases and defects in 1,250 plots in the state forests. Kienholz and his assistants recorded the effects of the 1938 hurricane on the state forests.[63]

Connecticut Payback

During the beginning stages of the CCC program, the state foresters received a telegram asking them to reimburse the Federal Government with half of the profits they received from the sale of wood products. Connecticut

agreed and by the end of the nine years CCC program, State Forester Austin Hawes said, "...the state reimbursed the (Federal) Government a greater amount than all the states combined. This was partly because we placed more emphasis on forest stand improvement than most states, and partly because of our excellent market for fuel wood."[64]

The forest products cut by the CCC from Dec. 1933 to July 1, 1938 totaled $179,394.50. When one deducts the hiring of horse teams of $2,888.65 the total was $104, 505.85. The US Treasury received $49,954.76.[65]

Camp Closings

When the CCC camps closed no funds were available for their maintenance. The following camps were demolished when the camps were closed: Roberts, Chapman, Graves, Hook, Fechner, and Stuart. Camp Jenkins in Cobalt was used as a central warehouse for the other working camps. Camp Britton in Windsor was on property owned by the Connecticut Agriculture Experimental Station and reverted back to them. Camps Roosevelt and Walcott retained some of the buildings because they were located on ponds.[66] Camp Lonergan in Voluntown was the last Connecticut CCC camp. It closed on May 25, 1942.

(L–R) 1 An Army officer (left) supervising the tent mess kitchen that fed the 250 enrollees during the summer of 1933 at Camp Roosevelt. DEEP 2 Al Baldini (front, left) from Hartford with friends in front of Army tent at Camp Roosevelt in June 1933. Pam Baldini 3 Lt. Gilbert cooling off in the hot July summer of 1933 by his tent at Camp Roosevelt where he and Capt. Michner supervised the CCC enrollees. Pam Baldini

After a hard day working on roads, trails and cutting wood, most of Camp Roosevelt enrollees wore their CCC uniform and lined up for chow with their mess kits in hand for supper. DEEP

CHAPTER 5
CLINTON / CHATFIELD HOLLOW STATE PARK / KILLINGWORTH

HISTORY

Camp Roosevelt (also called Camp Clinton because that was the nearest post office) S-60, Company 171 was located in the Killingworth block of the Cockaponset State Forest (CSF). It was the first CCC camp in Conn. and named to honor President Franklin D. Roosevelt who initiated the nationwide CCC program.

CSF covers over 16,000 acres of south central Conn. and parts of the forest are in 11 towns. The forest is named after Cockaponset, a Hammonassetts' chief who is buried in a section of Haddam called Ponset. The natives' village was on a fortified round hill in Chester. The Hammonassetts lived in the present-day towns of Madison, Killingworth, and Clinton.[1]

On May 23, 1933, 250 enrollees arrived at present-day Chatfield Hollow State Park (CHSP) and pitched their army tents in a large field near Chatfield Hollow Brook. By the fall wooden buildings had been constructed and the men lived in five barracks.

Indians frequently came to this area to fish and hunt. Indian artifacts have been found near Indian Council Caves where they found refuge and had council meetings under rock overhangs. The present-day park road follows parts of the old Indian trail that meandered along the brook amid white pines.[2]

During the 1600s English colonists settled in Chatfield Hollow and used the stream for power. Three Chatfield brothers came from England about 1639 and their descendants built a grist mill along the brook. There are metal fragments in the brook that suggest there had

been a smelting furnace to make tools from native ores. There are also some cellar foundations and an old watermill showing evidence of the early settlers.[3]

The June 19, 1933 issue of the Hartford Courant reported 20 men from Camp Roosevelt in Killingworth were in an accident when the truck they were riding overturned on the Killingworth North Madison Road. Sixteen of the men were injured, two of whom were in critical condition. Nine of the injured were taken to the Middlesex Hospital in Middletown and three were treated at the New Haven Hospital and later released. Four men in the accident had no injuries and they helped the injured.

The convoy of five trucks were on their way to a baseball game in Madison. The last truck was driven by enrollee Frank Romananowicz of New Haven. As it traveled down a hill in North Madison, Frank lost control and the truck rolled over with its wheels in the air. One enrollee thought that a big rock in the road caused the accident. When the truck toppled over, most of the men were thrown from the vehicle but Romananowicz and Fiorenzo were pinned in the truck cab.

Thomas Oneski of Norwich, one of the uninjured and a clerk at the camp, sent one of the uninjured to call the other trucks back. When the trucks returned there were now approximately 40 men who lifted the overturned truck off the two men. A passerby stopped and volunteered his car. An enrollee drove it with some of the injured to the Middlesex Hospital. The other injured were taken to the Middletown hospital. One of the truck drivers got lost and wound up at the New Haven Hospital.

In June of 1933, this fleet of Army and Conservation trucks transported enrollees and supplies to work projects. Pam Baldini

While carrying Camp Roosevelt boys to a baseball game in Madison, a truck like this flipped over, injuring most of the occupants. CCC Legacy

Indian caves where Hammonassetts gathered. DEEP

When the wooden buildings were completed in the fall 1933, the enrollees had a warmer place to live for the winter. Here is a May 1935 group photo of the enrollees with the Army officers and Conservation Dept. workers seated in the middle of the second row. George Diekewicz

A 1934 aerial view of Camp Roosevelt showing the long garage on left, barracks, mess hall, administrative building, rec hall, and infirmary on the right. The dam and pond are in the upper right corner, and park road on upper right. DEEP

(L–R) 1 The path led to the Camp Roosevelt headquarters where the Army officers and camp superintendent and foresters worked. The enrollees gathered at the flag pole in the morning for the raising of the flag and roll call. Then in the evening they gathered for the lowering of the flag and then off to supper. DEEP 2 The enrollees moved into wooden buildings. The one on the left was at the end of the camp and the lower long building on the right might have been the garage. DEEP

Dr. John Spignesi of Clinton, who was also the contract doctor for Camp Roosevelt, was located in Madison and he came and gave first aid to some of the injured.

In June 1933 Camp Roosevelt sent three crews to Hammonasset Beach where they built new entrance roads and improved lanes and graded older roads. Enrollees removed scrub growth of marsh alder and replanted them along the top of the sand berm between Meigs Point Road and the beach. They worked there until October 1935 when they were replaced by WPA crews who continued the roadwork project.[5]

In 1934 enrollees began their largest project, the construction of an earth, stone, and masonry dam on Chatfield Hollow Brook that created Schreeder Pond. The seven-acre pond has been a popular site for swimming and fishing for almost 80 years. The pond was named after William Foster "Gus" Schreeder, who was Conn. Regional Forester of the Southern District and a former CCC camp supervisor. In 1948 Schreeder became the State Forester of Conn.[6]

Camp Roosevelt men built many hiking trails in the park beginning in 1934. Crews of young men were supervised by foresters. One trail led to Indian caves and another took hikers to an old millpond. Former CCC enrollee (1933) Kornel Bailey wrote in his History of the Hiking Trails in Cockaponset Forest (in Connecticut Forest & Park Archives): "This Chatfield Hollow Trail was very well constructed, with many graded sections, stone steps and stone culverts that are in perfect condition today."

In 1936 enrollees built Oak Lodge on the west side of Schreeder Pond. Skilled masons and carpenters supervised the enrollees in the construction of the stone foundation, fireplace, chimney, and the post and beam building, while the camp blacksmith made wrought iron parts for the doors. In 1986 Oak Lodge was placed on the National Register of Historic Places. During the summer the lodge is open as a nature museum.[7]

There was one fatal injury on March 9, 1934 when Morris L. Cooper was working in a gravel pit and a large frozen chunk of top-soil fell on him that caused a hemorrhage in his lungs.[8]

Camp Roosevelt closed on March 31, 1937. Some of

Two CCC enrollees are working on a stone bridge abutment next to Chatfield Hollow Brook. DEEP

The millpond at the end of the paved Chatfield Hollow Road that the Camp Roosevelt enrollees restored by cleaning out the mud and rebuilding the dam. DEEP

An enrollee stands on a wooden tower that is almost complete except for the closed in observation cab. This was another project done by Camp Roosevelt. The tower was used by hikers and for spotting fires. Today only the cement footings remain. DEEP

CCC enrollees dug and built this well for visitors near the millpond at the far end of CHSP. They also built the wooden arched bridge over Chatfield Hollow Brook (right center). DEEP

Enrollees and foremen working on the early stages of the stone and concrete dam that held back Chatfield Hollow Brook. The photo was taken on the north side and the dam and roadway are on the right. DEEP

the camp buildings were retained because they were near the pond. The Bureau of Teacher Preparation at the New Haven State Teachers College rented the remaining camp buildings.[9] State records indicate that the college continued using the buildings in 1942.[10]

After WWII the pond, beach, and recreation area increased in popularity and in 1949 Chatfield Hollow became a state park.

LEGACY

Thanks to the hard work of the CCC enrollees of Camp Roosevelt during the 1930s, Chatfield Hollow State Park is a wonderful place for anyone to enjoy fishing, swimming, picnicking, and hiking. The seven-acre Schreeder Pond and forest areas offer plenty of sites to set up a picnic using the tables and fireplaces near the beach or wooded groves. Visitor enjoy the variety of hiking trails to Indian caves, exploring jagged rocky ledges, and walking by cooling streams winding throughout the park. A variety of nature programs and informative talks about the park are offered during the summer at the Oak Lodge.

Directions:

From Middletown take Rt. 9S for 8.3 mi. to Exit 9, toward Killingworth/Clinton. Turn right onto Rt. 81 for 7.9 mi. to a roundabout and take the 1st exit onto Rt. 80W. Travel 1.4 mi and the park entrance is on the right. Follow the park road to a dam and pond on the left. Drive over the dam and the camp was located on the left. The Nature Museum is on the right under white pine trees near the pond.

Walls and stone work on dam are almost complete and the small Chatfield Hollow Brook when dammed became Schreeder Pond. Conn. CCC Museum

The foreman or camp superintendent (wearing shirt) looking over a beam that will be used in the construction of Oak Lodge. The enrollees are busy adding exterior sheathing to the walls. The fireplace and chimney will go in the remaining space. DEEP

The interior of Oak Lodge that featured huge beams and large stone fireplace on the opposite side. DEEP

Children and adults are playing and swimming in Schreeder Pond. On the other side is Oak Lodge and on the left and right are Camp Roosevelt buildings. DEEP

Today the Oak Lodge is used as a nature museum and is open during the summer. Podskoch

For over 75 years visitors have enjoyed swimming, hiking, and picnicking at Chatfield Hollow State Park. People are shown enjoying a picnic celebrating the 80th anniversary of the CCC near the Oak Lodge. DEEP

41

MEMORIES

"A Short History of Our Camp"

The May 1935 issue of the Clinton CCC camp newspaper called The Roosevelt Rambler, had an article entitled "A Short History of Our Camp" that gave a very good description of what happened during the first two years of Camp Roosevelt.

Accompanied to the boat by a band escort, the boys left Ft. H. G. Wright, NY, enroute to the Cockaponset State Forest and established the first CCC camp in Connecticut. As was fitting, it was named after our President.

Arriving at the present location, it was found that the area had to be cleared of trees and brush. Hospital tents were set up as quarters for the men and the Army and Forestry personnel. The kitchen was established under a tent fly with an old Army range being utilized to do all the cooking. Under the supervision of a corporal several men assumed the duties of cooks, some successfully and some otherwise. Mother Earth served as a table for one and all.

At this time the Army personnel consisted of Captain Michner, Company Commander, Lt. O. H. Gilbert, mess and supply officer, Sergeant Wilson, First Sergeant, Sergeant Williams, Mess Sergeant, and Corporal Woodhouse as cook. Dr. Spignesi of Clinton was surgeon. He was later relieved by Dr. Murphy.

The Forestry Dept. consisted of Mr. McLaughlin, camp superintendent; T. B. Aldrich, road foreman; T. Farr, A. R. Yale, F. C. Butterfield, and C. J. Anderson, forest culture; D. B. Heatley, recreation projects; J. T. Bottomley, fire trails; F. J. Martin, MacCracken, and Potvin, gypsy moth; Noble,

camp engineer; Johnson, blasting and compressor foreman; Robinson, mechanic; and Martin, blacksmith.

The work projects got under way in the early part of June. Those consisted of the construction of Chatfield Hollow Road, the upper dam, the improvement of trout streams, thinning in the woods about camp, and planting and transplanting of trees. These projects were all undertaken without the aid of machinery; the men on the various crews performing their daily tasks using ordinary hand tools.

The floor of the washroom was started in the early part of June. This was the first sign of construction of the camp. Later the kitchen and recreation hall were erected. Construction was started by the 189th Company, who were preceded by the 190th Company. It got to be a great racket to report sick around eight o'clock in the morning, and try to get a day off. It was quite a shock to some of the boys when they finally caught up with them.

The pond was used to wash clothes, bodies, and mess gear. A radio was received and placed under the tent fly, thus establishing our recreation hall. Sometime later a storm not only wrecked the radio but also blew over all the tents and caused other damage.

With the advent of fair weather, a baseball team was organized and a few games were played with the Clinton and Madison teams. About the middle of June, while on the way to Madison, the boys met with an unexpected accident. One of the trucks overturned and several of the boys were badly bruised. Unfortunately, one of the boys was severely injured and as a result spent a year convalescing at the Walter Reed Hospital, in Washington, D.C.

Early in September floors were built for our tents.

Camp Roosevelt rebuilt the mill dam Chatfield Hollow Brook and created a pleasant place for picnics and relaxation. Podskoch

The mill pond and bridge to picnic tables that enrollees built. DEEP

These enrollees are airing their tents with the door flaps open to keep cool as crews of carpenters were busy across the camp road building permanent wood buildings. DEEP

This was the first sign of living under civilized conditions. During this same period the kitchen and mess hall were completed. One can hardly imagine the change which this made at that time. In a short time the digging of the well was completed and a tank and pipe lines were installed which made possible the use of showers and other facilities in the wash room. However, the majority of the men were not used to having a wash room here, and continued to use the pond.

The building of the barracks was started by the 189th Company. Barrack number one was constructed first and was ready for occupancy on Oct. 10, 1933. Barracks number two, three, four, and five were finished in order. At this same time the Army and Forestry quarters were also completed. The last piece of construction was the garages, which completed the work of the 190th Company.

Previous to the work of construction many changes were made in the camp personnel. Sgt. Wilson was relieved of his duties and was replaced by Sgt. Dwyer. Captain Michner turned over the command of the company to Lt. Gilbert and returned to duty at Fort Wright. Lts. Clark and LeVoie were assigned to duty as Mess Sergeants and Supply Officers. On Nov. 23, 1933, there was another change of command. Captain Manning assumed command of the company and Lt. Gilbert resumed his former duties. Lts. Clark and LeVoie were assigned to duty in other camps.

In the meantime, the camp was furnished with a tractor, grader, and a full quota of trucks. With this equipment the dam and (swimming) hole were completed while the

Chatfield Hollow Road was also reaching completion. Several changes were made in the forestry staff. Mr. Parr, Jackes, and McCracken were transferred to another camp. Mr. Evarts replaced Mr. Martin as the camp blacksmith. Later in October we welcomed Mr. Phelps, Lawler, and Miller who were put in charge of the work at Hammonasset Beach.

Our first winter was a hard one, but the men suffered no ill effects. Numerous cold snaps were encountered and were topped by the blizzards during Jan. and Feb. 1934. Owing to the depth of the snow it was necessary for the men to clear roads by hand in order to reach the highway.

Early in January Lt. Gilbert was relieved by Lt. Patzold while Lt. Lennon relieved Dr. Murphy as camp surgeon. Lt. Massello also reported to duty but returned to Fort Wright after a few weeks. Late in February Mr. Goebel reported to camp and assumed duties as Education Advisor. Shortly after, Dr. Chafetz replaced Lt. Lennon as camp surgeon. April brought us another change of command. Captain Manning was replaced by Lt. McCarthy, who was succeeded by Captain Keeney on May 16th. A short time later Lt. Benson reported to replace Lt. Patzold.

At this time the scenery about the camp started to change for the better. The mud hole in front of the (undecipherable) was eliminated by excavating the dirt and trucking it to another location. A road leading to camp was built and extended to the rear of the barracks. This road will eventually span the new dam and connect with the Chatfield Hollow Road. Volunteers were called out to help beautify the camp. Fences and walls were built, grass planted and a boxing ring and baseball field started. Volleyball contests

The completed dam and bridge that Camp Roosevelt enrollees built created Schreeder Pond. The CCC boys also built the log shelter on the hill. DEEP

and softball games proved to be the major recreational attractions. A baseball team was organized and a dozen more games played with other camps and surrounding town teams. A fairly successful season was enjoyed but the boys were handicapped owing to the lack of practice and their own playing field.

July brought us more changes in the Forestry Staff. Mr. Johnson and Robinson were transferred to Camp Jenkins, Mr. Wilkes reported as auto mechanic, while Mr. Chipman replaced Mr. Noble. Mr. Duprey replaced Mr. Potvin in gypsy moth work. Lt. Katzman reported for duty and assumed the duties of Mess Officer and Welfare Officer. Lt. Benson terminated his active duty in August as did Lt. Katzman. Lt. Marsden reported for duty at the same time while late in September Lt. Chapin reported.

October saw two more changes in the personnel of the camp. Mr. McLaughlin resigned as camp superintendent to accept a position at the University of Utah. He was succeeded by Mr. Humphrey who was in charge of the work at Camp Hook in Danbury. Captain Keeney was succeeded by Lt. Morgan who assumed command of the company on Oct. 27th.

The work and projects in all this time progressed very rapidly and fine showings were made by all the crews. The Chatfield Hollow Road was completed and the Spruce Lodge Road was immediately undertaken. This project was one of the most difficult encountered, rock ledges, and boulders predominated. However, despite the obstacles, the road was carried through and is now finished except for a few final touches. A survey has been made of the Etzler Road and construction has already been started.

The "Water Hole Gang," true to their name, set out to build the new dam which will impound a lake, directly in the rear of the camp. It is expected that this project will be completed by Oct. of this year. Upon completion, a road will surmount the dam and tie in with the Chatfield Hollow Road. The gypsy moth crews have been busy from the start of camp and have covered many miles and towns in their search of this pest. The wood chopping crews, bothered by gnats in the summer and frostbite in the winter, have accomplished much. Fire and scenic trails have been cleared out as has a goodly supply of fence posts, cordwood, and mill lumber during the past two years. The type-mapping and surveying crews have also accomplished much in the classification of trees, the establishment of boundaries, and paving the way for the general improvement of the forests.

At Hammonasset Beach many changes and added facilities have been made possible through the efforts of the boys who toiled there, winter and summer. Parkways and drives have been built, swamps drained, and public camping grounds doubled in area.

The past winter has been a mild one in comparison to the one previous, however, many a weary night was spent by the boys on "fire guard." This task of checking the wood stoves at night though dreary, was essential for the protection of the sleeping members in the advent of a fire. Many activities were enjoyed during the winter months, these consisted of basketball, minstrels, boxing, skating, skiing, and snowshoeing. Added attractions and entertainment were the weekly movies and vaudeville shows presented by ERA units from New York. In this manner, the winter soon passed quickly for the members of the company.

During this period several changes were made in the forestry staff. Mr. Weatley and Mr. Martin were transferred to other camps and replaced by Mr. Devino and Mr. Demasi. Mr. Sinott also joined the staff but was replaced by Mr. Falvey.

With the advent of warmer weather, the members of the company are now busily engaged in improving the appearance of the camp. Each night finds a goodly number of men working on the fields which are to be utilized for volleyball, softball, and quoits. A baseball team has been organized and once again the boys were looking forward to a very active summer.

On May 1st Lt. Lindahl was ordered to duty at Fort Wright and turned the command of the company over to Captain Hamilton. In their efforts to impress their new commander, the men are now working hard to make the camp one of the prize camps of the district.

To one who has watched the growth of camp it is an easy task to visualize all the changes and improvements in the appearance and general setup of the camp. However, the casual visitor has no conception of the effort required or the pride of the men in their company which transformed the camp from a clearing in the woods to its present aspect.

"Camp Roosevelt Truck Crashes Injuring 16"

The June 19, 1937 issue of the Hartford Courant reported 20 men from Camp Roosevelt in Killingworth were in an accident when the truck they were riding overturned on the Killingworth North Madison Road.

Sixteen of the men were injured two of which were in critical condition. Nine of the injured were taken to the Middlesex Hospital in Middletown and three were treated at the New Haven Hospital and later released. Four men in the accident had no injuries and they helped the injured.

The damaged truck was one of five that had left camp and were on their way to play a baseball game in Madison. The last truck was driven by enrollee Frank Romananowicz of New Haven. He was the last of the convoy as it traveled down a hill in North Madison. The enrollees were riding in an Army truck covered with a canvas. One enrollee thought the truck hit a rock on the road causing the accident. When the truck toppled over, most of the men were thrown from the vehicle but Romananowicz and Fiorenzo were pinned under the body of the truck. All the wheels of the truck were in the air and the truck.

Thomas Oneski of Norwich was one of the uninjured and a clerk at the camp sent one of the uninjured to call the other trucks back. When the trucks returned there were now approximately 40 men who lifted the overturned truck and the two men pinned men were removed. A passerby stopped and volunteered his car. An enrollee drove it and took some of the injured to the Middlesex Hospital while the other injured were transported to the Middletown hospital. This truck driver got lost and wound up at the New Haven Hospital.

Dr. John Spignosi of Clinton and the contract doctor for Camp Roosevelt was located in Madison and he came and gave first aid to some of the injured.

The driver was unconscious and had a skull fracture and internal injuries. Frank and Salvatore Fiorenzo of Stamford had compound fractures of both legs and back injury. The two were listed in critical condition.

Alfred W. Baldini

In the winter of 2015 Pamela Baldini called me and said her father-in-law, Alfred W. Baldini, was in the CCC and wanted to know how she could find more information about when and where he served. I told her how to get his discharge papers.

Pamela sent for Alfred's papers. On March 24, 2015 she emailed copies of his discharge papers and promised to send me additional information.

On June 16, 2015 Pam sent me a copy of her father-in-law's camp photos and this description of Alfred:

"Alfred Baldini was born in Bloomfield in 1913. His parents were Alfredo and Erminia (Parozzoli) Baldini. Both were born in Italy.

"After skipping two grades he graduated from Hartford Public High School in June 1930. His discharge said that he had worked for a year as a spot welder at Liberty Oil Burner Co. in Hartford and was paid $12 a week. He then was unemployed.

"Jobs were not plentiful and the CCC was an opportunity for him. He often talked about being in the first group and served six months. His records show he joined on April 29, 1933. He went to Fort Wright on Fishers Island for a 'reconditioning' program and his effort

(L–R) 1 Alfred Baldini was just 5' 6½" tall and weighed 136 pounds when he came to work at Camp Roosevelt on May 23, 1933. 2 Capt. Michner supervised Camp Roosevelt in the summer of 1933. 3 Al Baldini (right) and two enrollees off to work in an Army truck. 4 Alfred (front) and his road work crew using only shovels and picks. In later years CCC camps got more power equipment to make road building easier. Photos courtesy of Pamela Baldini

was 'satisfactory.'

"On May 23, 1933 the Army sent Alfred to Camp Roosevelt in the Cockaponset State Forest in Killingworth where he was a laborer doing reforestation work. While there each month his mother Erminia received a check of $25 at her home in Hartford for her son's work.

"After working six months he was honorably discharged on Sept. 11. Maj. F. E. Parker stated he had a 'satisfactory' performance. It also states he left to accept a job. Capt. Michner signed his final papers."

Pamela sent me a CD containing 24 beautiful photos of her father-in-law and activities going on at Camp Roosevelt. It was very rare for the young 1933 recruits to have a camera since the boys were very poor.

"Alfred often spoke about the road work details and when we traveled the shoreline, he would point out areas he worked in.

"When Al arrived at camp there were no trails and no buildings. Everyone lived in tents.

"My father-in-law said for recreation they went swimming at Lake Terramuggus.

"Al mentioned the pay was sent home to his mother and he got to keep $5. Al spoke about an important government official's tour of the camp and the preparation for the visit. I cannot remember who the official was or anything else about the visit.

"He married Rena Tolve and they had two sons: Richard and Alfred.

"Alfred died on Feb. 10, 1999 in East Windsor."

For recreation Alfred (top) and four friends went swimming at Lake Terramuggus. Pamela Baldini

(L–R) 1 Al Baldini (right) and two enrollees with a dog in June 1933 at Camp Roosevelt. 2 Alfred ready to chow down after working in the Cockaponset Forest. The Indian tanks and hoses in the background were used to fight fires. 3 Alfred (right) and friends in Lake Terramuggus. Photos courtesy of Pamela Baldini

Al Pisarski

Al Pisarski, an enrollee at Camp Roosevelt, wrote this letter to the Bristol Press describing his daily life.

Camp Roosevelt
Company 171st C.C.C.
Clinton, Conn.
May 31, 1933

Editor Bristol Press,

We are hereby giving you the facts of "Camp Roosevelt." I must say that there are two hundred men in this camp. We men get up at 6 am for reveille. At 6:30 we make up our bunks. Chow call is at 7 am, and we have until 7:50 when we fall out for assembly to go to work. There are different section gangs which are as follows: Pine Shoot, Camp Police, Improvements, Kitchen Police, Water Hole, Surveyors, and Road Gang. Each gang has a section foreman besides a State Forester who will supervise all the work. Eleven-fifty am is recall for chow which is served at 12 noon. At 1 pm we go back to work where we stay till 4:30. We eat at 5:30 and have the rest of the day to do as we please.

Our living quarters are canvas tents, each of which is occupied by 24 men. We have 11 of these tents which are policed every morning. The boys have built a small dam that has converted a small brook into a 7-foot deep swimming hole where a majority of the boys enjoy themselves after a hot day's work. We are now expecting athletic equipment that will be sent soon to the boys for their use. We expect to pick different teams from the sections and there will be plenty of competition when we get a baseball team started.

The nearest town from camp is Madison which is about 9 miles away and it's there that the boys go for entertainment such as dancing, shows, etc. It may be a long hike but the boys don't mind it when they think of what's in store for them when they get there. Our smallest member is from Bridgeport, who is 4 feet 8 inches tall. The tallest member is 6 feet 3 inches and they make a swell pair when they get together. On Sunday a bunch of the boys are transported to a church in Clinton by an army truck which takes them back also. The penalty for not keeping clean is a ducking in the brook, clothes and all.

Saturday noon always sees a bunch of boys on the road hitchhiking to their home town for the weekend. There are always at least one hundred and twenty-five men going home. We can go home every weekend and national holiday.

Visitors are allowed to come and visit the camp at any time. We already had quite a few. We are going to have a bugler in camp from now on who will give all calls. One of the boys brought a flag and we have to salute it when it goes up or down. Electricity hasn't been extended to camp yet, so we have to use candles and flashlights at night until a construction crew can come up and string wires out to here from town.

We have a couple of barbers here who cut the boys hair for I.O.U.'s until pay day when they collect everything at once. You can have four styles when you get a haircut: 1. The regular civilian cut. 2. The close crop or military trim. 3. The bald dome or horseshoe type. 4. The old rinktum or shaved head. The most of the boys get a military trim so they won't feel embarrassed when they go home.

Mosquitoes were the enrollees' chief worry at first. Different methods were used to keep them away. When we first got here they looked as big as airplanes and stung like bullets. But the boys are getting used to them now as time goes on. The latest song for the C.C.C. boys is as follows:

"All we do is sign the payroll.
All we do is sign the payroll.
All we do is sign the payroll.
And the check goes marching home."

Signed,
Al Pisarski

Enrollees posing by tent where they slept during the summer of 1933 at Camp Roosevelt in Killingworth. CT CCC Museum

George Diekewicz

George Diekewicz shared his Camp Roosevelt CCC stories and photos at the 75th Anniversary of the CCC at Chatfield Hollow State Park. Podskoch

The 75th Anniversary of the CCC was celebrated on Aug. 17, 2008 at Chatfield Hollow State Park (CHSP). There were many CCC alumni and their families and one of the men was George Diekewicz who was with his grandson Eric Britschock. George told me that he had lived and worked at Camp Roosevelt, which helped build CHSP. I asked George if I could visit and interview him. He agreed and I arranged to visit him in a few weeks.

In September I went to Alexandria Manor in Bloomfield and interviewed George in his room. Before I could ask him a question he eagerly began telling me stories about his jobs at Camp Roosevelt.

"The captain made me an assistant leader in my barracks. My job was to make sure the guys obeyed the rules. One of the rules was that every morning the men had to make their beds and keep their area organized. I had a cook who wouldn't make his bed. When the Army Lieutenant inspected my barracks, he gave me hell for the unmade bed.

"When the cook came back to the barracks I told him that when I got back from the shower if his bed wasn't made, he'd have to kiss the floor. I had to talk rough to the guys to get them to listen. When I got back his bed was made. I was relieved because he was a big guy and I didn't want to fight with him.

"My main job in camp was chopping wood. I cleaned the forest of dead trees and those that were falling over or leaning on other trees.

"We had the weekends free so most of the time I hitchhiked to my home in Norwich."

I asked George to tell me about his family and how he got into the CCC.

"I was born on Nov. 8, 1914 in Wilmington, DE. My father, Demitri, came to the US from Russia in 1908 and worked mostly on farms. My mother Mary came over to the US in 1910. I had two brothers, Adam and John, and two sisters, Vera and Mae.

"We moved a lot, first to New Jersey where my dad worked on farms along the coast. Then we moved to New York and finally to Sommers, Conn. He then had a farm in Hazardville. Dad got into the booze business. He had a still in our barn and guys came to buy it. Luckily he never got caught.

"Jobs were hard to find during the Depression. I heard people talking about the CCC so when I was 19 years old I joined in November of 1933. The Army sent me to New London and I took a ferry to Fort Wright on Fishers Island. I got a physical and some training. Then I went back on the ferry and was shipped to Camp Roosevelt in Killingworth. They were just building the pavilion when I arrived.

"We had competitions against other CCC camps. I was going to enter the axe chopping contest. One day while

(L–R) 1 Captain McClough was in charge of Camp Roosevelt and he is near the garage where the trucks were stored. 2 As leader, George Diekewicz made sure the boys in his barracks kept it neat; he was paid 45 dollars a month compared to the others who received 30 dollars a month. 3 Two boys cutting logs at the Chatfield Hollow State Park. Photos courtesy of George Diekewicz

practicing I cut my foot. It was deep and about three inches long. They took me to the infirmary and a guy bandaged up my foot. Luckily I was able to go to the championship in Higganum. My opponent got a nice clear soft log and I had a hard curly maple log so I came in second place."

Q: When did you leave the CCC and what did you do after?

A: "After about two and a half years I left the CCC because they wanted to send me to Oregon and I didn't want to go.

"I had quite a few jobs afterwards. I dug a trench for a boiler room in Versailles (near Baltic). I also got a job logging. I cut 90 eight-foot logs a day that were used for railroad ties. Then I worked for Inland Paper Board Co. Then I moved to Baltic Mills. I was a card grinder where we made cotton material. I then worked at Kendell in Windham as a machinery repairman. I retired in 1979.

"In 1938 I got married to Margaret Spinella in Waterford Works, NJ and we had two children, Janet and MaryAnn. My wife and I enjoyed traveling after I retired."

Q: What did you learn from being in the CCC?

A: "I liked being in the CCC because I was earning money. I learned carpentry skills that later helped me build my own house in Norwich."

On Sunday, Aug. 29, 2010 George Diekewicz passed away.

These three enrollees are eager for the wood chopping contest with another camp. George Diekewicz

Herb Boughton

After serving in the CCC at Camp Roosevelt, Herb Boughton served in the Army during WWII.
Ernie Boughton

While walking at Day Pond in Colchester during the winter of 2008, I met a group of ice fishermen. I asked if anyone had a parent or friend in the CCC. One man, Ernest Boughton from Colchester, said his father, Herb, was in the CCC. Ernest said his father lived in Wallingford and gave me his dad's phone number.

On Feb. 19, 2008 I called Herb and asked him to tell me about his CCC experiences.

"I quit school after 8th grade to help my family. My father Levi and mother Gertrude had seven children: Dwight, Bob, Marion, me, Gordon, Edna, and Richard.

"At first I worked at Mr. McClay's camp in Fair Haven. It had a swimming hole where all the kids gathered. Then I read about the CCC in the newspaper and signed up in the spring. I think it was around 1938. They sent me to Camp Roosevelt in Killingworth. When I got there I was homesick for a while but got over it. I was fortunate to have a good friend at camp, Ray Farren, who was also from New Haven.

"At camp I had a few jobs. I did landscaping and built trails in Chatfield Hollow State Park. I also cut trees in the nearby Cockaponset Forest.

"After work and supper I read books and newspapers in camp. Sometimes I walked to my sister Marion's home in Killingworth Circle on Route 79.

"On the weekends we had movies right in camp. The nearest town to camp was Madison but I never went there.

I was kind of a loner. I spent my monthly $5 in the PX for cigarettes and candy.

"We had other activities in camp to keep us busy. I liked to play horseshoes.

"Once a month I hitchhiked home to see my family and friends.

"After working in the CCC for a year I left and got a job in the Winchester Factory. I worked in the rolling mill until 1942.

"Also in 1942 I married Doris Rosa and we had eight children: Carol, Kathie, Ernest, Larry, Mark, Mary, Christine, and Paula.

"When I was 21 years old I was drafted into the Army. The Army sent me to Fort Eustice, Virginia and then to Fort Taunton, Mass. They shipped me to Iceland for three years where I guarded an airfield.

"After the war I worked as a dock builder for Blakeslee Arpaia until I retired.

"I enjoyed working at Chatfield Hollow. I also learned how to take care of myself. In later years it was nice to visit the park with my family and enjoy the pond and trails that we CCC boys built."

Herbert W. Boughton, 89, of Wallingford, died Friday, July 1, 2011.

Kornel Bailey

While searching for information on the internet about Camp Roosevelt I found an article entitled, "History of the Hiking Trails in Cockaponset Forest" by Kornel Bailey. It was posted on May 1, 2003 by Robert Butterworth, Connecticut Forest & Park Association (CFPA) Volunteer Trail Maintainer of the Northern Section of the Cockaponset Trail.

In the article Bailey stated: "Camp Roosevelt was the first CCC camp in the state and was one of the largest with 250 men. It was established May 23, 1933 in Chatfield Hollow, Killingworth Block of the [Cockaponset] forest. The area was later designated the 'Chatfield Hollow State Park.' It was surrounded by the state forest. The camp was closed before Oct. 1937. I was in this camp from the opening day until the first week in January 1934, and I believe the hiking trail was constructed after I left the camp."

This last sentence spurred my quest to contact Kornel or a member of his family. After contacting CFPA they said Kornel had passed away but his son was alive somewhere in northeastern Connecticut.

After a search through the internet I located his son Richard. He shared the information that was recorded for local public access TV in Haddam around 1980 when his father was 70 years old. Richard also sent me his father's discharge papers that he obtained from the National Personnel Records Center in St. Louis.

"Kornel was born in 1909. He grew up in New Haven and joined the Boy Scouts at age 11 where he learned a lot about the outdoors including tree identification which he was very good at. He also had outdoor experience including volunteer work clearing trails for Connecticut Forest & Park which had its offices in New Haven.

"After he was laid off from a job in 1933 he talked to Mr. Ross, who was the forester for CFPA about the CCC. Ross said that CFPA could recommend men who were used to working in the woods to the CCC. The CCC was looking for men who had worked in the woods since most of those joining were 'city boys' who knew nothing about the woods. He said he would recommend Kornel as a LEM (local experienced man).

"When he joined on May 18, 1933 he was sent to Fort HG Wright on Fishers Island for five days to be processed, get shots, be issued clothes, etc. The Army had him doing conditioning work until May 30th when he went with the other LEM's to Camp Roosevelt in Chatfield Hollow, which had just opened. They had to put up their own large circus-like tents that each slept 50 boys on cots. The tents would be used until the fall. A construction crew came in a while later to start building the barracks, mess hall, etc. He also said they started enlarging a small swimming hole to a large lake by constructing a large stone and concrete dam.

A group of enrollees taking a break from cutting and chopping trees with their foreman on the left. CT CCC Museum

Kornel Bailey brought his love of trees to Camp Roosevelt where he worked as a crew leader thinning the forest and searching for gypsy moths in the Cockaponset State Forest. Richard Bailey

Walter Baranowsky

Walter Baranowsky of Bridgeport worked at Camp Roosevelt at Chatfield Hollow SP. Patrick Baranowsky

"He was at Camp Roosevelt for about nine months. Because he had experience he was made an assistant leader but he lacked any education in forestry (he dropped out of high school after two years). He started by leading a crew that was thinning trees and cutting them up for cordwood. All the work was done with two-man crosscuts and axes. He only did that for about three weeks before men from Yale with education in forestry came in to lead the crews. He then was switched to lead a crew scouting for gypsy moths, a job that didn't need forestry education. He was discharged from the CCC on Feb. 12, 1934.

"After my father was discharged from Camp Roosevelt, my sister and I believe my father was hired by the US Forest Service and was stationed in Kentucky for two years. He got married in Dec. 1935.

"My father's love of the outdoors was a major part of his life. He was awarded the Silver Beaver Award in 1950, which is the highest award for leaders in the Boy Scouts. He was chairman of the Connecticut chapter of the Appalachian Mountain Club and was director of the AMC's August Camp for several years. He got his job as caretaker for the Middletown, Conn. reservoirs primarily because of his forestry experience which was needed for managing the watersheds. He was very active in CFPA trails work for almost 50 years. I think he was on the Board of Directors for a while."

Kornel Bailey passed away on May 30, 1996.

On Jan. 29, 2010 I interviewed Mimi Venezia Baranowsky by phone at her home in Milford, Conn. about her husband's life and experiences in the CCC.

"My husband Walter Baranowsky was born in 1916 in Bridgeport. His parents were George and Valerie and they had seven children: six boys and one girl. Walter was the youngest. During the Depression his father worked in a grocery store and a factory. [His parents were immigrants from Poland circa 1910.]

"One day when he was taking lunch to his father, he was hit by a bus and hospitalized. When he got to high school I think he had a year of trade school. Walter quit school because he had to help his family during the Depression.

"Since jobs were hard to find Walter joined the CCC in around 1935 or '36.

"Walter didn't mind leaving home because he was helping his mother with money she received each month. He had a wonderful disposition. His camp was in the woods and he loved the outdoors. When I first met him he wanted to take me to the camp."

Q: What did he do for jobs and what did he do after work and on weekends?

A: "I remember once he prepared breakfast but since he loved the outdoors he got switched to building trails.

"In the evenings they used to walk to town in Clinton to go to the bars and on the weekends he hitchhiked home occasionally. He loved to go roller skating and dancing."

Q: When and why did Walter leave the CCC?

A: "Walter thought the CCC was a great place but decided he had to look for another job. He was discharged in 1936 or 37 and got a job at Jenkins Valve Co in Bridgeport, Conn."

"That is when Walter and I met. We eloped in October 1940 because he was Polish and I was Italian. [Mimi's parents were Italian immigrants, circa 1900] Back then parents didn't want their children to marry a person who was not the same nationality. We kept it a secret till we told our parents and were married in church in February 1941. We had two children: Joann and Patrick."

Q: Did Walter participate in WWII?

A: "When Pearl Harbor happened he decided to join. I said he should wait. He was then drafted but failed the physical with hearing in only one ear.

"I worked at Remington Arms and he went to Avco building propellers. After the war he worked at Singers. Then he worked for Northeast Utilities. Walter went to night school and he became a machinist. He retired in 1983 and he died in 2006."

Q: What did he think of the CCC and how did it affect him?

A: "Walter liked the CCC because he got along with everybody and you listened to other people's opinions. He also loved being outside in nature. If it wasn't for the CCC, he probably wouldn't have been athletic and be the person he was."

I was fortunate to get these comments from Walter's grandson, Patrick W. Baranowsky.

"Walter was a quiet and extremely giving person with an incredible sense of duty. This is why he joined the CCC.

I noticed similarities during my life as he helped my parents financially when they were young, gave his car to me when I was in college, and worked double shifts for years to ensure a comfortable retirement for Mimi and himself.

"Being a quiet person, while building the Chatfield Hollow trail that includes the Indian cave, he found a rock outcropping that would enable him to survey the entire park. This was his place of solitude and he would spend a lot of personal time there.

"After he got married, he wanted to show this special location to Mimi, and perhaps the subsequent trail development and growth of vegetation changed his orientation enough that he could not recall its location. Decades later (in the early 1980s), he and Mimi took my brother and me there as they did every summer. My brother and I started climbing some rocks, jumped a very steep (perhaps over 20 feet deep and 3 feet wide) rock crevasse, and started yelling to Walter and Mimi to check out the amazing views we encountered. Mimi would not join us because she was afraid of heights and the crevasse scared her. Then Walter's face lit up as we had just found his special location.

"He was such a loyal and caring husband that he never would have found this with his wife. She would not have crossed the crevasse, and he would never leave her side when just the two of them were together. When she realized what we had found, she got the courage to join us and the four of us sat on that large rock for about a half hour while Walter told stories about how he could see the activity around camp and know when he needed to return for meals. Every year after that until I went to college and stopped my annual week-long visits to spend with them, we

This group of enrollees is working on the stone and cement dam that created Streeter pond in Chatfield Hollow SP. Walter is the boy kneeling by the board. Patrick Baranowsky

Camp Roosevelt boys in a gravel pit where they loaded truck with gravel for road construction. Walter is kneeling, the 2nd person from the left in the 2nd row. Patrick Baranowsky

would go back to that rock.

"Walter once told me that the cook was not friendly or cooperative. One time, he was on the trails past dinner time, and when he arrived at camp, the cook would not feed him. Walter was responsible for getting up early in the morning to heat the water for showers. The cook had to shower first so breakfast would be ready for the camp after their showers. That next morning, my grandfather did not turn on the hot water, and when the cook realized why, they formed a truce and Walter never went hungry again.

"The walk to the bars that you mention was many miles. When we would visit and travel on the road from Clinton to Chatfield Hollow, my grandfather would keep saying to my brother and me, 'We were still walking,' about every minute after we passed Clinton and until we arrived at Chatfield Hollow. He would catch a ride when he could find one, but many times, they spent most of the night walking back and forth, just to experience some civilization beyond the camp. He enjoyed telling us these CCC stories."

Edward Gentile

Ed Gentile by the entrance to the CCC Camp Roosevelt Headquarters building where he did typing and other office work. Ed Gentile

Edward Gentile of Kensington heard that I had given a talk about the CCC at the Voluntown Library in January, 2008 but didn't know how to contact me. He sent the following letter to me in care of the Voluntown Library.

April 28, 2008

Dear Mr. Podskoch,

I recently learned of your doing research and writing a book on the CCC camps.

I was in the Civilian Conservation Corp for a very short period of time, 7/17/35 to 9/8/35. I was assigned to Camp Roosevelt 171st Company in Killingworth. The area was referred to as the Cockaponset State Forest. I was assigned to what was referred to as the 'Road Gang.' We built dirt roadways through the forest. In addition, we started to excavate an area for a pond. This is now Chatfield Hollow State Park.

I recall the foreman telling the boys, "If you come upon any black snakes, throw them into the woods, and don't kill them." I was deathly afraid of snakes and if I came upon any black snakes, I would move away from the area.

The barracks held about 30-35 men. When I got to the camp, a super took me to a barracks I was going to be assigned to. He showed me a bunk and said, "This is the only one I have, you're going to have to bunk next to a N_____." I said, "You mean a colored guy?" He abruptly replied, "Yes." I met the colored guy later in the day and we became good friends.

His name was James Marcellini. I would kid him, my being of Italian descent, I would say to him, "I suppose you're going to try to tell me you're Italian!" We would laugh so much about it.

I was called into the office one day and the super said, "We see by your application info that you type." I said, "Yes." I was immediately put behind a desk in the office. I detested it. I decided to leave the CCC. I told a little white lie and said that I was going back to school. My discharge paper lists the reason for leaving: 'To further education.'

I did not go back to school. In fact, many years later I took the state high school exams and received my diploma that is dated December 20, 1999. I was 81 years of age.

Very truly yours,
Edward F. Gentile

A road constructed by the 'Road Gang' at Chatfield Hollow State Park during the 1930s. CT CCC Museum

When Ed Gentile arrived at Camp Roosevelt this is what he saw. The flag pole on the left is where the Army officers took roll each morning and the flag was raised. The gas pumps on the right were near the truck garage and the row of buildings housing the camp headquarters, barracks, and infirmary. Ed Gentile

A CCC enrollee using hand tools for road and trail construction. Pamela Baldini

On July 20, 2008 I talked with Ed by phone and asked him to tell me about his family.

"I was born on Feb. 27, 1918. My father Frank had a grocery store attached to our house. My mom ran the store while Dad worked in Stanley Tools factory. Dad worked in the section that made tool handles. He did well in the store and in about 1925 he built a new brick building with apartments upstairs on the second and third floor.

"My mother Julia had seven children: Albert, Elizabeth, Mary, me, George, Rita, and Francis.

"The Depression hit and Dad lost everything. There were so many on relief. We got an identification card that indicated how many people were in the family. You got a rationed amount of food based on the number of people in the family. People were so poor you would see ladies pulling wagons and they went inside and got a bag of coal.

"I dropped out of school in 10th grade because I couldn't get into the School for Dramatics because of discrimination. I went to work. I lied and said I was 16 and worked only on Saturdays in First National Grocery store from 8 am to 9 pm. I got paid a dollar a day. On the other days I did odd jobs, like shoveling snow.

"There was a city store and Dad got a job as a butcher. Upstairs in his building there was an office for the CCC.

"A friend of mine joined the CCC and he told me about it. I followed his advice and went to New Britain and signed up. I was 17 years old. I was happy to do something that was constructive like going to a job and knowing that my mother was going to get 25 dollars. It made me feel good.

"One of my first jobs was working with a crew that was excavating for a pond. They had a tractor pulling a scoop to make the pond.

"My next job was building trails through the woods. We used picks, shovels, and rakes.

"In the evening I liked to read while others played cards. Sometimes on the weekends a friend and I would hitchhike to Clinton Center. We wore our uniforms and people were willing to pick us up. We walked around town and bought ten-cent hamburgs and looked for girls.

"On some weekends I thumbed a ride home. We left right after work on Friday. I was looking for my mother's cooking.

"They had some team sports but I never joined one. I did, however, do some wrestling in a makeshift ring."

I then asked him what he did after he left the CCC.

"I did odd jobs working Saturdays for a year and a half or two. Then I got a job in Marlin-Rockwell in Plainville. I ran an internal grinder and made ball bearings. I stayed there for about a year and worked from 6 pm to 6 am.

"In 1940 I married Mary DeMarco and we had three children: Donna, Francis, and Steven.

"On my birthday of that same year, I went to work for Hamilton Propeller, a division of United Aircraft that is now United Technology. I was active in organizing Local #743 International Assoc. of Machinists, A. F. of L. I kept attending their meetings. Then I was elected shop chairman. Any grievances had to come through me. I did that for three years. Then I was elected chairman of the negotiating committee and executed the first union contract.

"My union participation continued. The International Associations of Machinists (I. A. of M) Office in

Washington, D.C. appointed me as a 'Special International Representative' in 1943. At 25 years of age I was the youngest representative of the I. A. of M in the United States. I participated in the negotiating of the first union contracts for Pratt & Whitney in East Hartford and Stanley Works and Stanley Tools in New Britain.

"During the time that I was the shop steward, I had a company executive who was crying because he couldn't get any help. I told him there were a lot of colored people in Hartford looking for a job. He said, 'No.'

"We left his office and sent a letter to the Secretary of the Navy telling him about the attitude of the executive towards negroes. We also sent a copy to our union headquarters in D.C.

"Then I got a call from Washington, D.C. They said President FDR was going to issue an order forbidding discrimination. For years I wondered if that order was ever issued.

"A year and a half ago at my granddaughter's wedding, I met a young woman who was a legislative assistant to our senator. I told her the story of what happened at my job to see if an executive order was ever issued by FDR. A few weeks later I got a letter from her showing the executive order issued by FDR. I think I was responsible for that order. It reminded me about that Negro who slept next to my bed in the barracks at Camp Roosevelt and was the object of discriminatory remarks and I stood up for him.

"For the short period that I was in the CCC I found a different world with kids from all over the country with different religions, nationalities, and races. Other guys were sent out all over the US. That was an education in itself.

"I was surprised one day when my grandson told me he went fishing. I asked him where and he said Chatfield Hollow State Park. I almost flipped and told him I played a part in building it."

On July 22, 2011 Edward Gentile passed away.

"Chapel in the Woods"

Peter Kindlmann wrote me an email about the "Chapel in the Woods" in Chatfield Hollow SP.

"My wife and I live in Guilford and make frequent visits to Chatfield Hollow State Park for exercise and recreation. I'm a retired engineer and she is a still semi-active potter. Each time I see the dam, the Oak Lodge nature museum or carefully built steps in some sections of the trails, I think

of the 1933-37 CCC work. I also wonder about details of life in the camp when I pass the remnants of the chapel on the variously called 'Nature Trail' or 'Witch's Hollow Trail.' Only the chimney and concrete foundation anchor points remain.

"The only reason I believe it to be the remnant of a chapel is that in 2008 I took a picture of a wooden trail map someone had made that was up in an official-looking display. I don't recall when that display disappeared, but it was many years ago now. Regrettably, any trail guide maps with comments about numbered stations has not been available for years, either. So I don't know who the 'custodian of local lore' on this point might be."

I was fortunate when Andy Annino, a DEEP worker at Chatfield Hollow, sent me this additional information on the Chapel:

"The Chapel in the Woods is located on the Yellow Nature Trail near the entrance to the park. It is mentioned in a booklet called 'Witches Hollow Nature Trail' that was available for hikers. Here is the description at site 13:

13 Watch Out for Goodie and Betty Wee

The inhabitants of Chatfield Hollow, the area once known as 'Witches Hollow', tell fanciful legends of two mischievous witches, 'Goodie Wee' and her daughter 'Betty Wee.' They were alleged pranksters having been accused of enchanting the cream from their neighbors house and pre-venting it from being made into butter.

The remains before you are of a chapel built by the Civilian Conservation Corps. The Corps also built the dam which created Schreeder Pond below you. They complained of pranks played on them while working on these projects. These pranks were attributed to the spirits of the two witches, Goodie and Betty Wee.

At Chatfield Hollow, it's 'take only pictures, leave only footprints!' Here are two witches to enforce the code!

"The Chimney and remnants were either a chapel or open air shelter definitely from the CCC boys. We were always told it was a chapel."

"Chapel in the Woods" chimney can be
found on the "Yellow Nature Trail" at
Chatfield Hollow SP. Peter Kindlmann

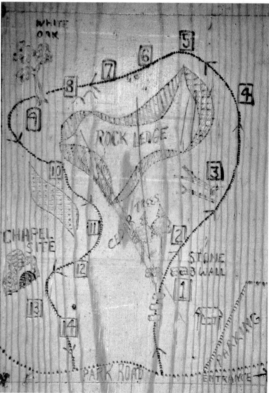

This wooden kiosk contained a wooden map (right) that showed the location of the Chapel
chimney. The box held maps for hikers. The kiosk has disappeared since this photo was taken.
Peter Kindlmann

CHAPTER 6
COBALT

HISTORY

Camp Jenkins, S-57, Company 181, was established on June 15, 1933 in Cobalt, Conn. approximately 5 miles east of Middletown. The 250 enrollees arrived at the site just off Gadpouch Road at the foot of Great Hill in the Meshomasic State Forest (MSF) and began laying out the camp and pitching their tents.[1]

MSF was the first state forest in Conn. and the second state forest in the US. The word meshomasic is a Native American word meaning place of many snakes as there were numerous timber rattlesnakes. MSF began in 1903 with 70 acres and has expanded today to over 9,000 acres. The state established it "to provide private landowners with good examples of good forest management practices."[2]

The state named the camp after Dr. Edward Hopkins Jenkins (1850-1931) who was the director of the Conn. Agricultural Experiment Station (CAES). In 1872 Jenkins graduated from Yale and continued his studies in chemistry at Yale to 1875. He then went to Moecken, Germany and studied till 1876. The next year he began working as a chemist in Middletown at the CAES, which then moved to its present location in New Haven. In 1879 he received a PhD from Yale. From 1881-1883 he worked at the Windsor Agricultural Station where extensive studies were conducted on corn and tobacco. In 1882 he became the vice director of CAES. In 1899 Jenkins hired Walter Mulford, who became the first State Forester in the US. In 1900 he became the director of the Conn. Experimental Station. In 1926 Jenkins wrote The History of Connecticut Agriculture. Dr. Jenkins worked for nearly 47 years with CAES.[3]

Charles H. Tracy was the camp superintendent of Camp Jenkins. Under his direction enrollees improved North Mulford Road and almost completed construction of Reeves Road in the MSF.[5] They also constructed a wooden tower in MSF to spot forest fires.[6] During the summer crews scouted for gypsy moth egg clusters, cleaned out underbrush where there was an infestation, removed any hollow trees, and banded the remaining trees with burlap to prevent the spread of caterpillars.[7] Scouting continued in the winter and enrollees destroyed egg clusters by painting them with creosote.

Camp Jenkins enrollees did recreation projects in MSF. They constructed a pier and bathhouse nearby on Great Hill Pond. They also developed a picnic area in a pine grove on Reeves Road.[8]

By June 30, 1934 Camp Jenkins had done a lot of forestry work in MSF. The young men cut 462 cords of wood for fuel, 350 posts, 108 poles, and logs totaling 28,878 bd. ft. Their silviculture work included: cleaning 602 acres of dead wood, thinning 293 acres, cleaning 78 acres for planting, and cutting 55 acres for reproduction.

Camp Jenkins entrance just off Gadpouch Rd. in Cobalt.

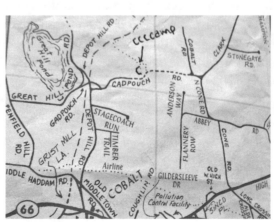

Camp Jenkins was right off Gadpouch Road in Cobalt. Pete Foster

A 1933 aerial photo showing Army tents spread around the camp where the boys lived while the permanent wood buildings were later built. DEEP

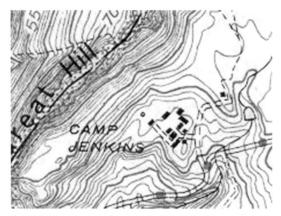

This 1940s topo map showing the location of approximately 10 buildings. The building farther to the right was a farmhouse.[4]

Camp Jenkins had seats built on the side of the hill for group photos like this but mostly for their boxing events and shows. CT CCC Museum

Camp Jenkins enrollees did a lot of silviculture work in the nearby Meshomasic State Forest. Some of the boys are posing for a photo by the sawmill shed. CT CCC Museum

Carlton Durgan by the Camp Jenkins fireplace from the infirmary is the only remaining structure. Podskoch

A group of boys posed for a group photo on the bleachers set in the hillside. CT CCC Museum

This totaled 1,028 acres of treated forest.[9]

On June 4, 1935 Lt. George D. Freeman led a cadre of enrollees from their Cobalt camp some two miles to the new CCC site for Camp Buck on Great Hill Road in Portland. The Army described it as a hillside swamp. The young men pitched their tents in a dry corner and got to work preparing the site.[10]

Another important contribution to the MSF by the CCC was the construction and maintenance of car roads and bridges, foot trails, and wood roads (for firefighting and logging only). By June 30, 1936 there were 12.5 miles of auto roads (gravel), 52.5 miles of wood roads, and 3.9 miles of foot trails.[11]

Camp Jenkins also worked in nearby Hurd State Park approximately 4 miles south in Middle Haddam near the Connecticut River. One of the projects they began was constructing a mile of the entrance road in the park. They sub-graded and side-graded the road but the enrollees were removed from the project in the fall of 1935.[12] From 1937-38 this road was completed by the WPA. The WPA then extended the road for another mile to the quarry shelter.[13]

One project that enrollees didn't have to go far to work on was at the nearby cobalt mine. Over two hundred years ago there were many attempts to mine the precious stone of cobalt at the SE base of Great Hill. There were three to four shafts in the sides of the ravine along Mine Brook and Gadpouch Rd. The July 2, 1937 issue of The East Hampton News reported: "For two years, members of a Civilian Conservation Corps company encamped only a few hundred feet from the mine shaft, and working in conjunction with the State Forest and Park Commission, cleaned up the forest debris and underbrush that had been accumulating for years, set up tables, benches, and cement fireplaces for picnic parties, and cleaned out the longest of the two horizontal shafts still easily to be found. With caution, picnickers today may walk on logs in the muddy floor of the mine to the very end of its 75-foot length." Today the picnic area has disappeared and the state enclosed the vertical shaft with a fence.

The Cobalt camp had an education advisor who coordinated education classes and recreation activities. Classes ranged from basic school subjects to hobbies and vocational subjects. The Bristol Press (undated) reported that Meyer Fishbein taught a ground aviation class and guided the enrollees in building model planes.

The camp newspaper, The Jenkins Journal, in the December 1934 issue stated there were three excellent teachers. The Education Advisor was Henry Ruskin said that classes were available in dramatics, composition, drawing, spelling and arithmetic. There were also nearly 150 books in the Education library for enrollees to sign out. Every Thursday evening there was group sing at 6:15.

The state closed Camp Jenkins on Jan. 1, 1936. Some of the buildings were saved and used as a CCC central warehouse for the 10 camps in the state.[14] When the remaining Conn. CCC camps closed in 1942 some buildings were removed while a few were retained by the state Conservation Department and used as a warehouse by the Forestry Department.[15]

LEGACY

The CCC built many miles of truck roads to remove logs for wood products and for fire protection in the Meshomasic State Forest. Enrollees also constructed trails that are used today by hikers and hunters.

Directions:

Go to the intersection of Rts. 66 and 151 in Cobalt. Drive north on Depot Hill Rd. for approximately 1 mile. Turn right on Gadpouch Rd. and drive for approximately one half mile. Look on the left for a dirt road that goes uphill. Park here, walk uphill, and turn left on the dirt road. As the road levels out, turn left, and you will see one of the few remaining CCC structures, a stone fireplace. The main buildings were on the right and forward. A good time to explore is in late fall or winter to avoid brambles and bushes.

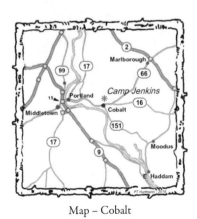

Map – Cobalt

MEMORIES

These are articles from Camp Jenkins' monthly newspaper, The Jenkins Journal.

The Educational Program had a choice of many evening classes that enrollees could take. Lt. George D. Freeman taught arithmetic, algebra, geometry, history, and Mr. Hazeltine taught journalism. Classes were held in the old Infirmary building.

Each month someone in each of the five barracks wrote what was happening. Often it described members in a humorous way. Barracks No. 2 reported:

Enthusiasm for football has reached the Barracks, and is a cause of many a headache received in a collision with the oval shaped weapon directed with the unmistakable skill and precision of Ossio's arm.

Woe are we! "Squako" has a bigger and louder instrument of torture which is put in use every evening. The barracks also received a contribution of a guitar from one of the singing rookies whose voice, when mingling with Mozzer's and Osella's, almost sounds like Caruso's.

Mandl, of the Portland Bridge Company, says that his interest in women has waned considerably since the coming of cold weather.

During the cold weather and early darkness, expeditions to Middletown with the use of thumbs are not enjoyed, and to improve this, the boys from No. 2 just charter an Army truck through a little extra patience in cleaning up.
- The Jenkins Journal, Oct. 1934

"My Job in the C.C.C."
by Confidential

The blast of the Sgt.'s whistle at 7:15 am is the cue for us to go to work. Without hesitation we start out for the trucks, into which we clamber with the swiftness of mountain goats to gain a comfortable and warm shelter of the cab. With the start of the truck, there is a silent painful battle for this prized position. The ride to our destination is far from pleasant. The cold wind pierces right through the heavy clothing, thereby giving a chill which combined with a frozen nose and frozen feet, leaves you in a frozen disposition.

Arriving at our work place, our assistant leader drives us right into the brush to cut dead chestnut trees. Our talented axmen takes his keen edged axe and in less time than it takes to tell, has one tree or more for us to saw. The

Camp Jenkins enrollees just arrived at a work site ready for the day's assignment from the foreman or forester. CT CCC Museum

assistant talented axman helps in the felling of these dead denizens of the forest. The sawing part of the job is left to "Tony", my pal, and myself and is accomplished with the speed and precision of expert woodsmen. These posts are twelve feet long and over four inches in diameter and then carried on our shoulders to a certain pile where they are trimmed and inspected.

The falling timber is a grave danger and accompanied by sharp axes, which are often misplaced, makes a safe job very dangerous. Under these circumstances the hours fly fast and posts accumulate rapidly.

After lunch the official tenor of the gang can be heard mingling his notes with the ringing of the axe. The spell of the wood enters the talented axman's head, and he goes to work with vigor that was not dreamed of in the morning. Thus, the day's work ends with the results of our toil all piled up ready to be hauled out by horses.

- The Jenkins Journal, Oct. 1934

"The Forgotten Crew"

The morning was cloudy and misty with rain, which drove the boys back to camp after an attempt at work. The ride back to camp was far from comfortable with the cold rain soaking through to the skin and the wind, which was colder than the rain, adding more to the discomfort that the boys had to endure. Arriving in camp the boys changed into dry clothing and warmed themselves. But we are ahead of our story.

Noon, the sky brightened, and with cheers the boys went out to work in anticipation of having a full weekend off. The cheering was short lived, for the sky became darker than ever and to our utmost disappointment, another

soaking was inevitable. The trucks were back for the boys, but since our truck did not arrive, four of us went back into the forest to get as much protection from the rain as possible. During the time we were in the forest our truck arrived, and the rest of the crew, thinking that we went in some other truck, did not call us. Woe unto us. The cold rain beating on our heads drove us out of the woods to see if the truck was there. Then came the realization that we were stranded and forgotten in the rain, ten miles from nowhere. The one thing left to do was to wait for another truck if any. But the truck was long in coming. The afternoon was cold, and it poured "kittens and puppies." We looked in vain for shelter. It did not take long before there was not a stitch of dry clothing on us. Rock ledges did not keep the wind away from us, and gradually freezing was not pleasant. A fire was needed to keep us warm, so we decided to try to start one. It is possible to start a fire in the rain, but did you ever try it? We did and it was only with long painstaking exertion that we succeeded.

In camp the boys were playing cards after supper. One of them remarked about the absence of "Wings," a fellow who was with us in the cold, cold rain. Word was passed slowly along until it finally reached the ears of Mr. Parr, our superintendent. A pick-up truck was sent to the rescue.

In the forest we were huddled around the fire shivering in the cold rain which was trickling down our necks. Was long after sundown, when it would have been nice to have been able to climb into a nice, warm comfortable bed. Despair grew in our hearts. Then glancing down the wooded mountain we saw light winding up the road. Immediately a loud cheer broke from us four "Children of the Storm."

Cover of the Jenkins Journal, Nov. 1934.

Camp Jenkins enrollees lined up to go into the mess hall. CT CCC Museum

The mess hall was lined with picnic tables and the boys took their mess kits to the serving area up front by the kitchen. The Mess Sgt., lower right, supervised the men. Two wood stoves provided heat when needed. CT CCC Museum

The ride back to camp was not very comfortable. It was pitch dark, the wind cold, and we were wet, tired, and sleepy. Someone made the remark that a flat tire would make it the end of a perfect day, when suddenly the day did end perfectly. We had a blowout! It was not exactly a trifling thing to change a tire in the darkness, but it was finally done, and we again started for camp with the dreadful fear of having a wheel fall off! More than one sigh of relief went up when we finally did arrive in camp.

- The Jenkins Journal, Nov. 1934.

"What a Job!"
by Confidential

Come Friday and the end of a hard week's work. Pleasant thoughts of a wonderful weekend at home were being entertained by me when I saw to my dismay that my name was on the "KP" list. My ardent desire to go home led me to do the next best thing. I went to the First Sgt.'s office in quest of a night fireman's job. My request was unhesitatingly granted.

Then the work began. The first three hours were spent cutting kindling wood for the next morning. This was an easy matter which required only patience.

Returning to the kitchen I found some food which had been left for me by the Mess Sgt. Before I could put this away, however, Sgt. Dave Lirese, the esteemed "Top Kick," came in. The Sgt. had ten to twelve men of all ages from six to sixty with him introducing them to me as brothers. A hungrier pack of brothers I have never seen. Before they left they had devoured every morsel of food within their reach and drank all of the coffee that I could make.

While feeding Lrese's "kinsmen" the kitchen fires slipped my mind. After their departure I was so engrossed in cleaning up the mess that they had made that I had forgotten to replenish them with fuel. When I did start to feed them, I discovered that my art of stocking coal fires was practically negligible. In fact, I had put the fire out altogether. It was now twelve o'clock and red hot stoves were needed by three. This was the last straw. I was beaten.

I sat there brooding over my misfortune when to my luck, in came "Wings" Matthews. A helpful young man like him is often heard of, but seldom seen. Here he was, however, seeing my plight, he immediately came to my rescue. His knowledge and experience in all the tricks of fire making did me a great deal of good, because in about a half an hour, the fire was blazing merrily. The wind was blowing fiercely outside, but our success with the kitchen stoves drove me to new conquests. In no time I had the fire under the "G. I. cans" blazing. Bringing in the wood and feeding the fire was no easy matter, especially with the cold piercing through my none too heavy clothing, but this was done cheerfully, and with the help of my friend "Wings," the work was done thoroughly. Thus the time was spent until three o'clock when it was time to awaken the cooks. With their arrival there were new and different tasks at hand.

The lack of sleep was beginning to tell, and grogginess began to overcome me. The rush hour drew near, and in my condition, it loomed as an enormous job. Fires, fires and more fires; many and different were the fires that I had to make, and with the cooks laughing at my misfortune, it was most irritating and tiresome. Finally, the fires were lit, and I sat down.

Thus ended the night. I got up, walked into my barracks, got under the blankets, and in a few moments fell into a sound, dreamless sleep.

By the way, I did not go home for the weekend.

I dedicate this article to my good friend in need, "Wings."

- The Jenkins Journal, Nov. 1934.

The Creosote Plant in the Meshomasic Forest

Creosote is distilled from tar and along with coke is the principal by-product of gas manufacture. It is used to preserve wood because it is poisonous to fungi, permanent, cheap, repels water, and won't corrode metal tanks.

The CCC built a creosote plant to treat wood posts from non-durable wood. It was an open tank that used a non-pressure method.

Workers placed well-seasoned, debarked logs into the tank. The logs are fitted with iron to prevent splitting. Between 75 and 100 posts are immersed in 3½ feet of creosote. The liquid is heated to 220 degrees for five hours and then cooled for 5 hours. The heat expands the wood and the air and water are driven out. The wood then cools, contracts forming a vacuum and absorbs the creosote. Each posts absorbs between a half to a full gallon per post. It can treat approximately 3,000 posts per month.

- The Jenkins Journal, Oct. 1934.

Barracks No. 4 News
by "Zip" Ziplow

We the honorable members of Barracks No. 4 are gratefully pleased with the change of lighting system in our abode. Before the change our barracks looked like a dismal spot in the dark. The improvement has made the place look more like a building of modern civilization than a medieval structure. The boys will not need to cripple their eyesight now when reading.

Our star tackle, Mickett, was greatly disappointed because of an injured leg but more grieved over the fact that his girl witnessed the game with one of her many beaus.

- The Jenkins Journal, Nov. 1934.

Barracks No. 2 News

Our humble abode is a gathering place for all the "ear benders" in camp including one of the greatest called

the great Buzachowski. During the evening it sometimes changes into a madhouse of flying bodies as the boys work out some famous plays used by the late Knute Rochne.

Our crooning halfback, Ossie, gives us a serenade now and then, when he is not absorbed in squawking in protest of the lack of firewood beside stove No. 1. His crooning is not bad at all, believe me.

Oh those guitars! Practically everyone tries choking a song out of them and rarely succeeds in anything but torture to the uninterested listeners.

When "Squake" Appruzoso's accordion is accompanied by those guitars, you've got to be rugged like Toth to stay in the barracks.

During the night there are so many different sounds that they mingle into music when heard by a musically minded personage like myself. This orchestra is regularly accompanied by a song from Campesi at certain intervals.

- The Jenkins Journal, Nov. 1934.

Football

The organization of the Camp Jenkins football team was delayed for about a month, and therefore the team was not in good shape when it played its first two games.

The first game played by the team was with Tufts A. C. of Middletown, a semi-pro team. In this game our team held its opponents scoreless in the first quarter, but a touchdown in the second quarter put the Tuft's team in the lead. Mickett, who played excellent football at his position as end, was taken out of the game due to a sprained ankle. The Middletown team won by a score of 14-0.

The second game was played with the Northwesterners of New Britain. This also resulted in a defeat for the Jenkins eleven. The Northwesterners, likewise a semi-professional team and one of the undefeated teams in New Britain, was organized several years ago. This team outweighed and outplayed our boys, winning by the score of 19-0.

- The Jenkins Journal, Nov. 1934.

Basketball

The basketball season is close at hand, and a call will be sent out soon for candidates to report for practice. Captain Thomas will cooperate in any way possible and will coach the team.

- The Jenkins Journal, Nov. 1934.

Angelo Alderuccio

Angelo Alderuccio of New Britain standing by the misplaced Camp Jenkins sign on Gadpouch Road in Cobalt. He worked there from 1934-35.

Kathy Goodspeed of East Haddam contacted me after reading about my search for CCC enrollees. She said her father, Angelo Alderuccio, had been in the Cobalt CCC Camp. I asked her if I could interview her father and if he would be interested in showing me where the camp was. I had visited a site on Gadpouch Road that had a sign stating the location of Camp Jenkins but it just didn't look like there was enough area for a camp site and there were no remnants of a camp.

Angelo agreed and on August 23, 2008 I met Angelo, Kathy, and her husband Russ at the Cobalt Post Office parking lot. We drove up Depot Street and then on to Gadpouch Road. We stopped and walked over to a state sign stating that this was the site of Camp Jenkins. Angelo looked around and he said, "This is not the site. It doesn't look anything like the place I spent a year."

On my previous visit to the area, I had walked farther up Gadpouch Road to where a road went to the left. I followed it and found another road that led to a clearing and an abandoned fireplace and chimney. So I told Angelo, Kathy, and Russ to follow me to the site I had visited. As we walked Angelo said, "This is more like my camp. This is the road we drove up to camp."

When he saw the fireplace he said, "This is where the infirmary was."

The state had misplaced the sign and I now knew for certain that I had the correct location of Camp Jenkins.

We tried to look for more signs of the abandoned camp but it was like a jungle overgrown with invasive plants, vines, and thorny brush. I could only walk if I had a machete. We'd have to wait for the winter to explore again.

I asked the group to come to my home so that I could interview Angelo.

Q: Angelo, tell me about your early life and family.

A: "I was born on July 17, 1914 in New Britain. My parents were Cesario and Beatrice. My dad was a barber in New Britain. He got sick and he had trouble with his vision. Dad then joined the WPA and did manual labor. My parents had nine children: Lucy, Sarah, Mary, me, Frank, Felice, Jimmy, Joe, and Johnny. It was hard for them to raise a large family during the Depression. My brother Frank was also in the CCC at Camp Buck. He only stayed for three months and joined the Navy.

"The older kids in the family had to help by getting jobs. I quit school in the 7th grade and I got a job as an errand boy at Atkins Printing Co. I worked there for two years. While working I went to night school and passed 8th grade. Then I got laid off and joined the CCC.

"I lived in New Britain near gas tanks. Here they made their own gas out of coke. My friends and I were called the 'Gas House Gang.' During the Depression we took the good coke out of the ashes that were thrown out. A woman bought the coke from us. We got 15 cents for a bushel. We picked up two bushels and got enough money to go to the movie theater. There was a guy outside selling hot dogs for a nickel and the show was a nickel. So three guys went into the movies on the profit we made."

Angelo Alderuccio standing on the road that led to Camp Jenkins where he was during 1934-35. Podskoch

(L–R) 1 "Captain Walter D. Thomas was in a cavalry division during WWI and he often rode around camp on his horse. He lived in a house on Great Hill Lake," said Angelo Alderuccio. 2 Angelo Alderuccio (2nd from left) taking a break with his friends in the woods. The older man in the back was the foreman or local experienced man (LEM). 3 Angelo (seated) joking with friends. Photos courtesy of Kathy Goodspeed

Q: How did you learn about the CCC and how was camp life?

A: "I think I learned about the CCC in the paper. I had a job selling papers and shining shoes. I got the papers for 2 cents and sold them for 3 cents. On April 28, 1934 I went someplace in New Britain and signed up. I was happy joining the CCCs because my mother was going to get some money. My mother saved the 25 dollars each month that she received from my work and bought her first washing machine.

"The army sent me and the other enrollees to the army base on Fishers Island. I was only there for one night and then they sent me and three other recruits by army car to Cobalt.

"Honestly, I liked the togetherness of living in camp. I lived in Barracks No. 1. We had 40 men in it along with the supply sergeant, Laskey, and the top sergeant, David Larese. They had separate partitioned rooms. The other barracks each had 50 guys. We worked, ate, played, and slept together. We were tired at the end of the day. We took a shower in a building that was separate from the latrine. It had an open area with 20 showers. It had a big concrete slab floor. I had two good friends who were from Middletown: Cannata and Casperino. There was a boy from New Britain who was our barracks leader. He had been in the army before and he woke us up every morning.

"Our camp was integrated. There were 4-5 Negroes in barracks No. 5. We got along well except for one fight and the white guy lost.

"I do remember two other fights. The guys went out in the woods and settled it. When one guy had enough, they shook hands and that was it.

"In our barracks there were three stoves. It got pretty cold in the winter but the stoves and three woolen blankets kept me warm. We gave one guy 50 cents a month to light the fire in the morning so it would be warm when we got up."

Q: What kind of jobs did you do?

A: "My first job was the cutting up of dead chestnut trees. The logs had to be 12 feet long and the smallest diameter had to be at least 4 inches. We took them to a spot in the woods and later a man came with a team of horses and pulled them out on a sled. They went to the tobacco farms for poles that held up the netting to shade tobacco.

"We used a two-man saw or axe for cutting trees. We also cut oak for guard rails. They were taken to the creosote plant that was nearby. I never went there.

"Our other jobs were cutting cord wood and building fire lanes. We cut brush and trees in a 50-foot swath so fire wouldn't cross over.

"There were a lot of snakes there. Ranger Joe Sennet knew where all the rattlesnake dens were. His nickname was 'Rattlesnake Joe.' I did see one rattlesnake while I was working and I'm sorry I killed it. I wanted the skin. It had 4 buttons on the rattle. One guy brought a copperhead into the barracks. He had it tied so it wouldn't bite anyone. The next week I saw a big black snake. Boy, did I run fast.

"On rainy days we burned brush in open places.

"We also built roads. Some places they had to blast through the rock. That is where we used our 16-pound sledge hammers to break the pieces up.

"One time there was a fire on Great Hill Mt. We carried Indian tanks and put out the hot spots.

"On rainy days we still worked. We burned big piles of

brush that we cut when clearing the woods.

"In the winter we did the same jobs. There were no bulldozers. We did all the work by hand."

Q: Did you ever get sick and have to go to the infirmary?

A: "There was a guy who was in the infirmary who knew some first aid. There wasn't a doctor. If you got really sick they took you to Fort Wright Army Hospital on Fishers Island. I never got sick. I did almost get injured once when my axe cut through my shoe but luckily it only got to my sock. The only time I went there was on a rainy day. I brought lunch for one of the sick guys."

Q: Did anything funny, scary, or sad happen while at camp?

A: "One of the funny things that happened in our barracks was when the guys were upset with one guy who was a loud sleeper. So one night when he was asleep four guys carried the guy in his bunk outside. He woke up in the morning totally surprised to see where he was.

"The latrine was two benches in the middle with 8-10 holes on each side. We sat back to back and side to side. Water was running constantly in the toilets.

"One time a guy rolled up a bunch of newspapers and lit it. He put it in the first hole and the water carried it past the guys that were sitting on the toilet. Their rear ends got singed but nothing serious.

"Another time someone took a big black snake and threw it into the shower room while the guys were showering. The guys got scared and ran out.

"In the morning Sergeant David Larese was outside the barracks and he opened the side windows. He then blew a whistle really loud and yelled, 'Hit the deck! It's daylight in the swamps!' and we got up.

"On Monday mornings we had to change our bed sheets. We put the top sheet on the bottom and took the bottom sheet to the supply shack to be washed. We then got a clean sheet for the top."

Q: What did you do in the evenings?

A: "We just milled around or hung around the barracks. A few times they showed us movies. They also had contests such as wood chopping. My friend Ziggy was the champ.

"On certain evenings of the week in the summer, we went to a place like an arena. It was on the bank of the hill and they had benches to sit on. They dug a groove in the bank and put boards there for us to sit on. Any guys who could perform, sing, dance, or play an instrument, would entertain. Other camps came with boxers and we had a boxing ring to have matches. Here we would also have a sing-along and everyone sang.

"The second best thing was the rec hall where they sold cigarettes, soda, and candy. I didn't go in there much but shot the breeze in my bunk. The guys just liked to sit around and talk. We had guys of all nationalities and religions but we all got along beautifully. We were all there for one thing, to get money for our parents.

"Almost every weekend I went home. We bummed rides from Cobalt to Middletown. Then we worked our way to St. Sebastian's Church and hitched rides to New Britain. We had no trouble at all getting rides because people saw us with a CCC uniform. I had a brother-in-law, Howard DeAngelo, who always took me back to camp.

Camp Jenkins had a boxing ring and matches were held with other CCC camp enrollees while spectators sat on benches that were built on the side of a hill. CT CCC Museum

Camp Jenkins had many activities to keep the enrollees busy such as boxing, football, and baseball. One of the boys is dressed up for a game with another CCC camp. Angelo is pictured 2nd on right. Kathy Goodspeed

"After my friend Ziggy left Camp Cobalt he came to visit two or three times.

"I stayed at camp on weekends if I had KP duty but it wasn't often because my friend Salvatore Scalora was a clerk in the forester's barracks. He did the assigning of KP and he only gave it to me once. For KP we had to wash big pots and pans. The lieutenant came in one time and checked the pots with his glove. He ran his fingers along each of the pots and pans. When he found a dirty one he threw them all back into the sink and we had to do them all over. We stayed there till 10 o'clock at night.

"We also had a mine near camp. There was a cedar fence around the mine shaft. One time my friends and I crawled in. It was low and we went in about 50 feet."

Q: How was the food?

A: "We ate in the mess hall. It was big and held 200 guys. The food was good. Our cook was an ex-marine. His pies were out of this world.

"At meal time we lined up with our mess kits. They put the dry food in the cover part and the bottom part was for watery food. I even went for seconds for the creamed beef on toast. They called it 'SOS.' The food was so good that I gained 12 pounds while I was there. When we finished eating we walked over where there were three garbage cans outside the mess hall. We dipped our mess kit in the first can, then in the second, and finally in the third. Boy, the water was hot! By the third can your kit was clean."

Q: What did you do for recreation? Did you join any teams?

A: "The camp had a football team but I never joined. They played other CCC camps. I was too tired at night to go out to play football.

"Once in a while they took us to Middletown to the movies. On Sundays we went early in the morning to church in East Hampton."

Q: Why did you leave the CCC?

A: "I didn't sign up for another year in the CCC because I thought I was going to get a job in New Britain because it had a lot of factories. My brother-in-law picked me up. When I went home, however, I couldn't get a job. I just hung around. That's when my father got sick and I went over and worked for the WPA. I got $6.50 in scrip for working two days a week. We had to go to a store that said, 'We accept scrip.'

"I worked for the WPA for about two years. Our work was using a pick and shovel.

"In the winter we dug up maple trees in the woods and laid them down. They were small maple and ash trees about 10-12 feet high. We covered the roots with dirt and in the spring we planted them all over the city.

"After that job I went to Corbin Cabinet Lock Co. and I was a trucker. I took materials to different departments.

"In 1940 I married Virginia Autunno. We had three children: Anthony, Roseanne, and Kathleen.

"I was never in WWII. They took my four brothers but not me. I was married and had a child so maybe that was why they didn't take me. I was also getting a deferment because I worked in a company doing defense work.

"Later in the 40s, I got a job in Union Manufacturing Co. We made chucks and die block sets. Then they went on strike. I went to New Britain Public Works in the 50s and worked in the sewer dept. I retired in 1981."

Q: Angelo, when you look back at your time in the CCCs what did you accomplish?

A: "In the CCC I learned to get along with everybody. It took me off the streets and I was able to help my family."

The next year Kathy Goodspeed sent me an email. "My father passed away peacefully on December 15th at the age of 95. He loved that CCC camp! It gave him something he took with him for the rest of his life. I am so grateful to you for giving that experience to me – for me to capture some of his past life was such a gift. Thank you!"

Edward Warner Bjork

In the summer of 2009, Lynn Bjork of Amston invited me to her home to share information about her father, Edward Warner Bjork, who was in the CCC at the Cobalt camp in 1933. She showed me a wooden box and said, "My father made this foot locker out of scrap wood to hold his valuables." She opened the lid and on the inside was carved:

E W B
Co 181 Cobalt Conn
June 1st 1933 to

"I don't have any children or family to leave this trunk to, but I know you are interested in the CCC," she said. "Would you like to have it and use it in your CCC presentations?"

Without any hesitation I said, "I'd be honored to show it to others and share your dad's story."

Lynn then handed me some typed pages. "My father

typed his life story so that I'd have a record of his life and family. These pages have to do with his time in the CCC. I think you'd enjoy reading it."

The following is an excerpt from Edward Warner Bjork's autobiography.

I was born on September 13, 1916 and had one brother and two sisters. We lived in East Hartford during the Depression. After two years in high school, I left school to go in the CCC in 1933. We were paid $30 a month. Twenty-five dollars was sent home to help pay rent. We were given $5 a month for expenses.

First the 181st Co. was put together on Fishers Island off New York, where we were formed and issued so-called uniforms all left over from WWI. No two of us looked

Lynn Bjork proudly holding her father's 1933 foot locker that he made and used while working at Camp Jenkins. Podskoch

Camp Jenkins boys loading cord wood on sleds and used a tractor to move the wood. Connecticut Agricultural Experiment Station

alike! Some were issued combined navy and army clothes, some just navy, and some just army clothes. The only thing we all had in common was hobnail shoes.

On June 1, 1933, after about two weeks of getting to know rules and regulations we were sent to Cobalt, Conn. Meshomasic State Forest, one of the first camps in Conn. We arrived at dusk and set up our tents on the only level ground around. That night the mosquitos were as large as humming birds. The next morning we found we were in the middle of a swamp! For about a week we cleared off a hill and moved our tents up there Then we started on the barracks which we built ourselves, under supervision of course. After that we started working in the forest. We built water holes in case of fire. We built trails, cut wood for people on welfare, learned to use TNT. We also cut telephone poles and cleaned out dead wood from the forest. Then we went to Groton and looked for gypsy moths, worked in sand pits shoveling into dump trucks by hand. There were six to eight men to a truck. There were no front end loaders!

We rode to Marlborough and drove around ten curves in the road. We cut wood there (no chain saws, just axes, and crosscut saws).

In the wintertime we rode in open trucks in zero degree weather, but I will have to say, we did have warm clothes by then. By wintertime we were issued all kinds of winter gear and no one ever froze.

When we were working in the forest our dinner was delivered by truck from camp, but as we had fires going we had to heat up the meals.

Now to get back to the barracks, there were three log burning stoves in each barracks. At night when any one got up to go to the washroom and latrine, the man would check the stove to make sure the fires did not go out! As for recreation, a ring was set up in a hollow and benches were built on the slope. We had boxing matches between other camps. "Red" Vertefeuille who later became a policeman in Willimantic, was considered champion of Conn. CCC camps. He later died of cancer of the throat while on the police force. I still have a scar on my chin to remember him.

After the first winter I got a job with First National Stores Warehouse, so I was discharged from the CCC. I was now bringing home $22 a week. I gave my folks $10 a week for room and board. With the remaining $12 I bought my clothes and a motorcycle, a 1927 Indian Scout. At that time, 1934, a lot of people were on the move all over the country looking for jobs. I was 18 years old.

Lynn said, "After Dad's days in the CCC, he joined the Navy. He lost a foot while in the Navy and was honorably discharged. He passed away in 2007. Dad told me that the CCC made him become more responsible."

Carlton Durgan

At a hiking conference at the Connecticut Forest and Park Association in Rockfall, I met Lynn Kochiss, an avid hiker, retired teacher, and resident of Gadpouch Rd. I told her I was searching for information on Camp Jenkins that had been near her home. She told me to contact her neighbor, Carlton Durgan, who had worked at the camp after it closed.

In Jan. 2009 I visited Carlton Durgan at his home on Gadpouch Rd. and asked if he would go with me and explore the Camp Jenkins site. He agreed.

As we drove up Gadpouch Rd., Carlton told me that he was born in East Hampton on June, 6, 1935. He said, "I lived close to Camp Jenkins but I don't remember the men working there because it closed when I was one year old."

"There was a cobalt mine over there on the right. The state put a metal fence around the mine shaft so no one would get hurt. In the old days the men shoveled and dug for cobalt on Gadpouch Rd. They dug about 10 feet deep.

"My boss couldn't watch everyone because his men were spread out at different sites.

"They had a hook hammer (like a knife) and chopped away at the stone to look for the cobalt.

"In the 1950s I got a job with the Conservation Department. My job was 'maintainer' in the forest. I did whatever the chief wanted me to do. I don't remember the boss' name. He lived with his wife and two children in one of the old CCC buildings in the front of the old camp. We showed up in the morning and he told us what to do. We did some clearing out of the mines and some trucking. I worked there for a short while, about two years. The boss was frustrated because there wasn't enough time for the workers to work.

"When I was working, there were only two buildings left from the camp. The philosophy was, if they weren't using a building, it had to be torn down. I think they took the last two buildings down in the 1970s."

"I remember the pond directly in front of the back building. The inside of the building was filled with a lot of wood items. It wasn't heated."

As we walked through the snow, to the left of the fireplace we found this old hand water pump. Podskoch

Then Carlton found the old concrete box at the base of what used to be a pond. It might have been used as an overflow device. Podskoch

Henry Mallett

On May 23, 2008 I spoke at the Mansfield Public Library on the CCC where I met Jane Zadnik of Manchester. She told me her father, Henry Mallett, worked for the Conservation Dept. during the Depression at Camp Jenkins in Cobalt. A few weeks later she sent me photos of her dad and told me about his life.

"I don't know much about my dad's work in the CCC. Actually he never really said much about his life in the CCC. He was stationed at camps Graves, Jenkins, and Buck. My father graduated from UConn in 1934 with a degree in Forestry and by Oct. 1934 he was at Camp Graves in Union.

"His parents Charles and Anna Mallett were from the Woodbury area. My grandfather was a tenant farmer so they moved around a lot. Dad was an only child. He was quite poor and worked his way through UConn. My father probably didn't go home very often because he didn't have any transportation.

"After leaving the CCC job, he worked in the print shop at The Hartford Insurance Co. where he met my mother, Helen Gardner. They were married on Nov. 30, 1939. He was in the Army from 1942-43. I'm an only child and was born in 1946.

"Both of my parents died in 1981."

Henry Mallett (left) worked as a forester for the Conn. Conservation Dept. at three CCC camps: Graves, Jenkins, and Buck. Jane Zadnik

A CCC Army truck trying to plow the road to Camp Jenkins. Jane Zadnik

CHAPTER 7
DANBURY / SQUANTZ POND

HISTORY

Camp Hook S-62, also called Camp Danbury because that was the nearest post office, was located at Squantz Pond State Park (SPSP) near Pootatuck State Forest (PSF) in the town of New Fairfield. The camp was named for James W. Hook, Chairman of the Conn. Unemployment Commission in 1933.[1]

Squantz Pond (c. 288 acres) is 8 mi. north of Danbury in the towns of New Fairfield and Sherman. It is a natural pond and Candlewood Lake formed in 1923, is nearby.[2] The pond is named after Chief Squantz of the Schaghticoke Indians who sold the land to settlers of Fairfield County in the early 1700s. On the hillside overlooking Squantz Pond is Council Rocks. There is a large balanced rock slab that looks like it might topple over. The slab is bordered by rocks on each side forming a natural amphitheater where Chief Squantz held councils.[3]

Pootatuck State Forest was named after another Native American tribe in the area, the Pootatuck (also Potatuck, Pohtatuck), which lived before the Colonial period in the western part of Connecticut. They lived in the Fairfield County area where Southbury, Woodbury, and Newtown are today. The Pootatuck did farming and fishing. Some of the crops they raised were beans, squash, corn, and tobacco. They also hunted in the rugged hillsides.[4]

PSF (circa 1200 acres) is located mostly in the town of New Fairfield and a small portion in Sherman. The park overlooks Squantz Pond and Candlewood Lake. Most of the forest was acquired in the 1920s for about $10 per acre.[5]

Camp Hook was established on May 24, 1933 when 212 men arrived from Camp Wright on Fishers Island where they had spent time for physicals and basic training. They set up their tents and began working on the camp site, including the construction of wooden barracks.

Camp Superintendent Harold D. Pearson organized and supervised the camp work projects. Some of the projects were: building roads and fire ponds, planting trees, salvaging dying chestnut trees for posts and poles, and thinning forests to produce firewood.[6]

At the beginning of the summer of 1933 two crews were busy with road construction and continued working till April 1934. In September 1934 there was only one crew working on the park drive.[7]

By the end of 1934 a road from the park and through the forest had been partially completed at both ends. Enrollees also constructed a mile-long foot trail along Candlewood Lake.[8]

The enrollees harvested valuable wood in the Pootatuck Forest. By June 30, 1934 they had removed 371 cords of wood for fuel and made 376 posts, 32 poles, and logs totaling 3,124 board feet.[9] Woods improvement projects lasted for six weeks in February and March of 1934. Enrollees thinned the forest and removed dead trees.[10]

By the summer of 1934 silviculture work continued in the Pootatuck Forest. They cleaned 150 acres of dead wood, thinned 107 acres, cleaned 15 acres for planting, and did reproduction cutting (cutting mature trees, for the

(L–R) 1 Camp Hook was established in May 1933 on the shore of Squantz Pond State Park in New Fairfield. 2 Camp Hook was established near the shore of Squantz Pond (upper right). Enrollees lived in tents and later permanent wooden buildings (lower left) were built on a hill overlooking the pond. 3 By the fall of 1933 enrollees had moved from the tent camp to the permanent camp. Photos courtesy of CT CCC Museum

An undated group photo of Camp Hook enrollees and leaders by the garage and barracks in the background. CT CCC Museum

(L–R) 1 A 1934 aerial view of the completed Camp Hook. The road coming from Squantz Pond is in the upper right. Today one chimney remais while level indentations in the earth indicate where the buildings stood. DEEP State Archives 3 At the end of each work day the boys at Camp Hook got dressed in their uniforms and stood at attention for the lowering of the flag. Then they went to the mess hall for dinner. CT CCC Museum

seedlings to grow) on 102 acres. The total area that was treated was 374 acres.[11]

Another trail was constructed to Council Rocks and the enrollees built a lean-to on the lakefront.[12]

On Dec. 7, 1934 Arthur V. Parker, Superintendent of Conn. State Parks recommended to the State Park and Forest Commission that Camp Hook "should be the first one [CCC camp] to be discontinued or transferred, as it is so placed to dominate the park."[13] Education was an important part of Camp Hook. The Education Advisor, H. Hyman, supervised the camp monthly newspaper called the "Squantz Reveille." In the May 1935 issue it listed these courses that were offered: Arts and Crafts with ERA instructor Mr. Popke, Current Events with Mr. Hyman, Entomology with forester Mr. Warren, Photography that included taking and developing photos, a radio class directed by ERA instructor Mr. Dushay, a Dramatics Class led by Mr. Passmore and classes in elementary subjects such as English, spelling, history, etc. taught by ERA instructors.

Mr. Passmore also directed the camp band. The band competed on May 9, 1935 against all the CCC camps in Connecticut. The competition was held at the Hartford Women's Club Auditorium. They came in first place and received a loving cup.

On June 19, 1935 the Squantz Players presented "The Valiant" at the New Fairfield Town Hall. The play was directed by Mr. Passmore and ERA instructor Ben Blumenthal.

Enrollees also participated in many sports. The baseball team was managed by Mr. Passmore and coached by Mr. Jim Sawyer. The camp constructed a volleyball court near the baseball field. Horseshoes were a popular game at camp. Mr. Crosby gave swimming lessons in the evening.

The Squantz Reveille reported in June 1935 that four enrollees went to Fort Adams near Newport, RI for a seven-day life-saving swimming course.

The baseball team in 1935 played these CCC camps: Robinson, Roberts, Walcott, Toumey, and Cross. They also played these local teams: Golden Hill, New Fairfield, and Falcons.

By the summer of 1935 Camp Hook had finished the park drive but had a little more side grading to complete. The improvements made the park more accessible and from 1935-36 the park attendance doubled.[14] Camp Hook had a significant effect on Squantz Pond State Park, which had been created in 1928. They improved the park road, constructed a parking area, and built trails for hiking. By the summer of 1936 more than 357,490 visitors had come

Country or "Hillbilly" bands were popular at Camp Hook. CT CCC Museum

There is a large boulder marking the entrance to Camp Hook. It is located above the Squantz State Park beach and parking lot. Podskoch

The June 1935 front page of the monthly Camp Hook newspaper. CT CCC Museum

This beautiful fire place and chimney is one of the few remaining structures left of Camp Hook. Podskoch

Map – Danbury Squantz Pond

to the park to spend more than 40,500 camp days. Today each year over 100,000 visitors enjoy the park.[15]

Camp Hook closed on Oct. 30, 1935. Workers dismantled most of the buildings but left four so that the salvaged material could possibly be used.[16]

LEGACY

Today the Pootatuck Forest is managed for sawtimber, firewood, and wildlife habitat, as well as recreational activities such as hiking, hunting, and birdwatching. Fishing, picnicking, and swimming are very popular at Squantz Pond State Park.

Directions:

From East on I-84: Take Exit 6 in Danbury. Take a right at the traffic light onto Route 37. Follow the signs on Route 37 until you arrive in New Fairfield Center. Take a right at the traffic light onto Route 39 traveling north for approximately 4½ miles to the park entrance. The entrance will be on the left at Sherwoods Rd. Camp Hook was on the hill above the state beach and parking area. There is a large boulder with a Camp Hook sign. Only one camp building and chimney remain.

MEMORIES

Poems by "Doc" Leiken

"A Plea"

My hand is sore
I cannot write
In my poor pen
There is no might
Yet writing news
Is not just play
To one whose thoughts
Are sure to stray
To love, to home
And girls, so pray,
Please come again
Some other day

"Nonsense"

If I were you
And you were me
The both of us
Would surely be
As much alike
As we could be
If I were you and you were me.

"More Nonsense"

When I shall die
And I am dead
I'll lay so quietly in bed
And angels hovering around my head
Will prove to you
That I am dead.

Michael Popovich

On May 9, 2012 I visited Michael Popovich at his home in West Hartford where at 98 years old he still lives alone and does all his own cooking and cleaning. Podskoch

On Oct. 23, 2008 I met Michael Popovich and his daughter Elaine at the Wallingford Library where I gave a talk on the CCC. He said he was in the first group of men at the CCC camp at Squantz Pond. He gave me his phone number and I promised to interview him by phone.

I was eager to talk to Michael and telephoned him four days later at his home in Elmwood (near Hartford). He told me he was born on Oct. 17, 1914 in Waterbury, Conn. His father George worked part time at Chase Brass Rolling Mills while his mother Mary raised her five children: me, Theresa, Mary, Anna, and George.

"Since I was the eldest in my family I had to help my parents and get a job. I quit school after ninth grade.

"My father signed me up in the middle of April 1933 in Oakville, a section of Waterbury. They took me and a group of boys by bus to New London. I was scared because I had never left home before. I didn't know anyone.

"They transported us by boat to Fishers Island for about a week and a half. The army outfitted us with clothes and a duffle bag to carry them in. We also did exercises. We slept in barracks. That was the first time I was by the ocean.

"My group got transferred to Danbury in a WWI Liberty truck that had solid rubber tires and a canopy top. The area was just woods when we got there. It was right across from Squantz State Park. We parked by an opening in a field, right by the water. They told us to set up our tents but we didn't know anything about putting them up. Then an army officer showed us how to do it. The tents were large and held eight guys. Our camp wasn't near the pond but away and on a hill.

"It was about noon when we finished. We had sandwiches for lunch. They dug a hole or privy in the woods that was quite far. There wasn't an outhouse with seats. It was just a hole. I think we got the drinking water right out of the pond. There was a lister bag that held water for us to drink. It was a large canvas bag supported by a tripod. The canvas bag would sweat and help cool the water.

"The first night we were really tired. The beds were folding Army cots. Camp was just a mess but in a week it was all straightened out. I heard a lot of woods' noises: the sounds of frogs croaking and birds chirping. We were lucky we never saw any bear. No one ever saw a deer.

"In our tent there was a guy who snored a lot. One night four guys carried him out of the tent on his cot and placed him by the pond. He slept there all night.

"Every morning they had a regular bugle to wake us up. Then we went to have breakfast. It was great. We had a lot of eggs and cereal. There was a big squad tent to get our food. We ate outside on picnic tables. If it was raining, we ate in our tents. We had our own mess kits and used that instead of dishes. After we ate there was a barrel of boiling hot water. We dipped the mess kits in and swished them around.

"Our first job was building a fire lane through the state forest. We had to make it 10' wide on each side of the main road. We cleared the bushes and trees. We burned the trees and brush. After the area was cleaned we began building a road through the forest. We used mostly shovels, picks, and sledge hammers to break rocks. We used wheelbarrows to move the dirt and stones and dumped them on the side. There were a lot of city boys who didn't know how to work and the foreman showed them how. I used the jackhammer for the rocks.

"There was a good atmosphere with all the guys. There were hardly any fights.

"After supper we played baseball or went swimming in Squantz Pond. The swimming area had already been built. It was really nice, clear, cold water. There was no parking lot. People just parked on the grass. It was a new small park. It didn't have anybody supervising it. There was no entrance fee like there is today.

"If it was raining we didn't have to work. We just stayed in our tents. Since our tents were on a hill we had to make ditches around the tent to divert the water from coming in.

"On the weekends we didn't have to work. Sometimes we hitchhiked to Danbury and just walked around. I never went to a movie. One time there was a county fair in Danbury and we spent some time there. There were a lot of farm girls I called 'farmerettes.'

"We also walked over to Candlewood Lake and watched the nice motor boats go by. We also fished in the lake and Squantz Pond. If we caught fish, we brought it back to the mess tent and the cooks fried them for us to eat.

"On Sunday an Army truck took us to Danbury to go to church. I went to the Catholic Church.

"Sometimes we walked 3 miles to the small family store in New Fairfield. I got to be pretty friendly with the family who owned it. I always bought an ice cream or drank a quart of milk.

"I worked there for six months and then my time was up.

"It was the autumn and my father made me quit because I had to help him at home with farm chores. We had a five-acre farm. I just listened to my dad. I was the oldest one and had to help my family. We had one cow, hogs, and about 40 chickens.

"Then I got a job in Waterbury Steel Ball Bearing Co. Then I worked for Chase Brass in Waterbury. I operated an 18' rotary furnace. It heated up copper and brass ingots. I only worked at nights and because of the job I was developing a small ulcer. I went to Samson Tech. during the day and worked at Chase at night to pay for my schooling.

"I quit working at Chase and got a license for repairing airplane engines in Hartford. Then I went to Pratt & Whitney and assembled engines.

In 2009 Michael Popovich visited his old Camp Hook at Squantz Pond with his family.

"In 1940 my friend John Chuchlow and I bought an airplane from Bridgeport Air Service. It was a B-1 Ryan, the sister of the Spirit of St. Louis. We took lessons at the Bristol Airport in 1941. I kept it at Mt. Tobe Airport near Waterbury. We just flew around there. Sometimes we took up to four passengers for rides and we charged them a dollar or two.

"When the war came we couldn't fly so we sold it. After that I only flew with friends.

"In 1941 I married Grace Fecteau of Waterbury and we had three daughters: Carol, Elaine, and Joyce.

"In 1964 I worked at the nuclear power plant in Middle Haddam. I was working with the fuel rods till the atomic power plant closed and I was transferred back to Pratt & Whiney. I worked there for 40 years.

"The CCC built character in the young men. I had to learn to get along with everyone. I also learned how to build a road and how to use dynamite. It was a good experience for me."

Ray H. Space

Ray H. Space was born on Oct. 20, 1917 in Patterson, NJ. His mother was Bertha Wallace Space.

During the Depression he joined the CCC and worked at the Squantz Pond camp.

Robert Miller, a reporter for the Danbury News-Times, wrote about Ray Space in an August 10, 2008 story:

In 1933, in the midst of the Great Depression, Ray Space, Sr. was at sea, like millions of other American teenagers.

There were no jobs to be had – the national unemployment rate was 25 percent. People were hungry and dispirited. The social safety net we're accustomed to today had yet to be woven.

And then he found a lifeline. He signed up with the newly created Civilian Conservation Corps, left his home in Bridgeport, and went into the woods.

At Camp Hook in New Fairfield, he found work cutting roads and killing gypsy moths at Pootatuck State Forest and Squantz Pond State Park. He found work that gave his life meaning.

"It's the best thing that ever happened to me," said Space, who now lives in Stratford. "I could have taken the wrong way, but I got a bed to sleep in and beautiful meals to eat."

When he left the CCC Ray worked as a truck driver for Vought-Sikorsky Aircraft. He then owned and operated school busses which then laid the foundation for his desire to own and operate school buses serving families in the Westport community. He did this for 20 years. Ray was praised for saving a little girl's life by performing the Heimlich maneuver while driving a school bus.

Ray married Anna Luciano of Westport and they had one son, Ray "Corky" Space.

On Friday April 15, 2011 Ray H. Space died at the age of 93.

Mickey Gallo

On March 8, 2009 Paul Gallo of Rocky Hill sent me this email about his dad, Mickey Gallo, who was at in the CCC camp at Squantz Pond in 1933.

"Nice article in today's Courant, Marty. My dad was at Camp Hook, Danbury. After he passed away at the age of 93, I took the sepia tone pictures that he took and developed at the camp and I made a scrapbook and added captions. I donated all of them in a 3-ring binder to the CCC Museum in Stafford Springs in the early 1990s.

"My dad is often not wearing a shirt. If I had a build like him, I would go shirtless, too. I placed a yellow circle around my dad in pictures that he's in. Please be mindful that I made up the narratives on each page in order to weave a story.

"The one true hand-me-down story of my dad was when he first arrived at camp. He easily took care of the Camp Hook boxing champ in the second round. He never continued to box there; only did it to prove to himself that he could do it.

"Here are some of my dad's photos from Camp Hook and captions I wrote." [Photos on next page]

This was a real hot summer day! You rarely heard a complaint, though. We were always ready to pitch-in and help each other when needed.

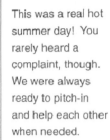

Dad (circled) and other Camp Hook workers on a hot day building roads.
Paul Gallo

Some of those summer days and nights were brutally hot!

We would get cleaned up for dinner and usually hang around until dark.

Dad (circled) with friends by their tents by Squantz Pond in the summer of 1933.
Paul Gallo

CHAPTER 8
DANBURY / WOOSTER MT.

Camp Fechner in Jan. 1936 with Wooster Mt. in the background. Arlene Rivard

HISTORY

Camp Fechner P-69 Co. 2102 was located on Rt. 7 at Wooster Mt. State Park in Danbury. It was located approximately two miles south of the present-day Danbury Mall and I-84.

Wooster Mountain was named after a Revolutionary War hero, General David Wooster (1711-1777) who fought in the French & Indian War and the American Revolutionary War. He died at the Battle of Ridgefield on the side of the Patriots.[1]

Camp Fechner was named to honor Robert Fechner who was the Director of the CCC program from 1933-39. Franklin D. Roosevelt appointed him the administrator of the Emergency Conservation Work Act in 1933. Fechner was a machinist and started the Machinist Union. As director he was an excellent organizer and administrator. He passed away at work in 1939.[2]

On June 4, 1935 a cadre of 23 men formed at Camp Hook, Co. 172 at Squantz Pond with the purpose of establishing a camp at Wooster Mountain State Park. First Lt. A. E. Killen led the group.

The May 1935 issue of the Camp Hook newspaper, Squantz Reveille, described the establishment of the camp. "Camp Hook will be at Sugar Hollow on the Danbury Norwalk Road (Rt. 7). Our camp will act as a parent company to the new one, that is, all the camp detail needed to start the camp running will be supplied by this company.

"These men will be transferred to Sugar Hollow: senior leader, O'Connor; clerk, Rarus; PX, steward, Bigos; store keeper, Shortell; mess steward, Murphy; first cooks, Karkut & Primrose; second cooks, Heffner, Musto & Jaroszynski; truck drivers, Conforti and Hucaluk; nurses, Lindsay & Fairfull; chief KP, Pullman; dining room orderly, Martino; officers' orderly, Maruszozak; incinerator fire, Karmelowicz; bath house orderly, Sobolnicki; and KPs, Keller, Matcheski, Nicoletti, and Vertefeuille."

Captain E. G. Schwartz took command of Camp Fechner on June 24, 1935. During July new recruits arrived and lived in tents. A. R. Olson became the camp Superintendent and began preparing work projects. Olson was assisted by the following men: Arthur B. Ceder, John U. Campane, Ransom W. Davis, Andrew Gujdon, Frank G. Pescatore, Clifford Ongley, William J. Nalewak, and James P. McDonough.[3]

The empty field was the site of Camp Fechner, which is now used as a shooting range. The shooting targets are located at the foot of Wooster Mtn. The old mess hall is used by the Danbury Shooting Sports Association. Podskoch

The chief project of the camp was to control Dutch elm disease (DED). The camp was established to help the Connecticut Agricultural Experiment Station.[4] DED is a wilt fungus that grows in the sapwood of elms. It was spread by the elm bark beetle. DED got its name because Dutch scientists first identified the disease in 1917 in Holland. The fungus spread throughout Europe killing many elm trees.

In 1930 the fungus appeared in the US in a shipment of logs in Ohio. It then spread eastward infecting most of New England. In 1933 it was first found in Connecticut and most of the 235 infected trees were found in the SW section of the state. New Haven, known as "Elm City," lost almost all of its elm trees.[5][6]

Seven scouting crews covered over 80,000 acres treating infested elm trees. Samples were often sent to a laboratory in Morristown, NJ for testing. Crews eradicated unhealthy elm trees by cutting them down and burning them.[7]

Another tree insect Camp Fechner fought was the European Pine shoot moth. From Nov. 1935 to June 1936 enrollees destroyed 378,653 infested tree tips that were on mostly Red Pine trees.[8]

Summary of Completed Projects
Sept. 1935 - June 1936

- Dutch Elm Disease Control: 56,222 trees removed and 15,788 acres scouted
- Forest Stand Improvement on Wooster State Park: 39 acres thinned and 138 cords of wood cut
- European Pine Shoot Moth Control: 773 acres of pine plantations worked; 445,645 infested tips destroyed
- Flood Emergency Work in CT Valley: 913 man-days
- Trailside Clearing for fire-fighting: 3.3 miles
- Water holes for fire-fighting: 14 water holes
- Road Construction: Camp entrance road and graveling at Pootatuck Forest 0.7 mi.[9]

The camp built a 60-foot steel fire tower approximately 8 mi. SE of their camp in the Town of Redding on Fire Tower Rd. (off Old Redding Rd.) in Top Stone Park. They also constructed an 18' wide, 2,000' long road to the tower for the observer and the public. Crews beautified the area around the tower by thinning trees and shrubs to allow flowering trees and shrubs to blossom. Brush was piled creating shelters for wildlife. Several times Camp Fechner was called out to fight fires on the Connecticut and New York border.[10][11]

The enrollees did stand improvement on five one-acre

The 60' fire tower built in Redding by Camp Fechner. easternuslookouts.weebly.com

Photos of activities at Camp Fechner from the First Corps Area, Fifth CCC District Yearbook, 1937.

parcels of private land to show the public how to properly manage their forests.

Camp Fechner didn't have to go far to find forests that needed improvement. Their camp was at the base of Wooster Mountain State Forest where enrollees thinned 120 acres.[12]

During the 1936 flooding of the Connecticut River, Camp Fechner's men were transferred to Camp Roosevelt in Killingworth on March 23. The enrollees helped clean up in the towns of Chester, Essex, Portland, East Haddam, and Haddam. They cleaned and disinfected 39 buildings and 163 houses. On April 10, 1936 Company 2002 returned to their camp at Wooster Mountain State Park.

The Education Program led by Mr. Hyman offered programs in basic and vocational subjects. In 1936 these classes were held: Leather Craft, Model House Building, First Aid, Swimming & Diving classes, and Model Airplanes.[13] The program was expanded in 1937. Here are the classes and their instructors: Safety, Capt. Schwartz; Woodcarving, Henry Anton; Forest Protection, Mr. Nalewak; History & Discussion, Capt. Schwartz; Forest Conservation, Superintendent A. R. Olson; Machine Operation & Mechanics, Mr. Davis; Leathercraft, Mr. Popke; Driving, Mr. Campane; Roads, Trails & Structures, Mr. Art Ceder; Tree Identification, Mr. Trafton; Forest Improvement, Mr. Ongley; and First Aid, Dr. Schoff.[14]

The Education Advisor also helped plan recreation, which included: swimming in Sugar Hollow Pond across Rt. 7 from the camp, volleyball, a baseball team that played local town and CCC camp teams, diving, basketball, horseshoe pitching, and a golf course between Barracks No.

1 & 2.[15] In 1937 boxing and softball were added to the camp activities. One boxing bout was held at the Young Men's Catholic Club Team in Danbury. Softball games were held on Saturday and Sunday evenings on a field near the camp and Rt. 7. Players were reminded to "be careful in chasing balls across the highway. Forget the ball and look before crossing the highway."[16] In 1937 Walter S. Grimala became

The March 1937 Fechner Forum cartoon

(L–R) 1 A cover of the March 1937 issue of the Fechner Forum, the monthly camp newspaper, supervised by the Education Advisor. 2 Camp Fechner mess hall is the only building left at Wooster Mountain State Park. It is now used by the Danbury Shooting Sports Association. Podskoch 3 In 1940 Camp Fechner was turned over to the Wooster Mountain State Park Cooperative Shooting Range. It is operated by the Danbury Shooting Sports Association. It is used as a skeet and trap shooting area. Only the CCC mess hall remains and is used by the shooting club. Podskoch

the new Education Advisor. He instituted these additional courses: Aviation, Letter Writing, Personal Improvement, Woodworking, and Journalism. He organized a summer program covering agriculture and animal raising. Courses included: Entomology, Poultry Raising, Hog Raising, Truck Gardening, and Landscape Gardening. Capt. Schwartz handled the poultry project. Mr. Grimala, who taught the course on swine, planned on having a pig pen built. Messrs. Ceder and Pescatore taught truck gardening. Messrs. Davis and Gujdon instructed a group in raising flowers. The WPA facilitated the offering of a course in Aviation.[17] Camp dances were also held. On July 27, 1936 a band from Bridgeport provided the music. The Feb. 1937 issue of Camp Fechner News reported a dance was planned in Danbury and urged the enrollees to be on their best behavior.

Camp Fechner closed May 24, 1937 and the WPA helped take down the buildings. They moved the lumber to other state parks.[18]

LEGACY

The Wooster Mountain State Park provides hiking, hunting, skeet, trap and target shooting.

Directions:

From Exit 3 of I-84 go approximately 2.6 miles south on Rt. 7, Sugar Hollow Rd. and the camp site is on the right.

Map – Danbury Wooster Mt.

MEMORIES

The following excerpts are poems and stories written by enrollees from the Camp Fechner News.

"Reincarnation"
by James Gassinger

It was not so long ago,
when I was down and out,
Always looking for that break,
that never would come about,

Running around from town to town,
always on the go,
What would finally become of me?
I really did not know.

My clothes were worn and tattered,
and the nights were often times cold,
And a cup of coffee, at least to me,
was worth its weight in gold.

I tried to earn my way;
to make an honest living,
But jobs to men in tattered clothes,
people are not giving.

Then one day,
I forgot where it happened to be,
I saw a poster,
exploiting the advantages of the CCC

I read it over, once or twice,
and stood there feeling numb,
For it suddenly dawned on me –
My one big chance had come!

I hurried to the recruiting office,
and filled an application,
And strode from there
all filled with exultation.

They gave me a uniform,
all pressed and looking neat.
A chance to earn my way;
to stand on my own two feet.

To some this may sound silly,
a sort of fantastic poem,
But gee, it's kind of tough,
to be left in this world alone.

Many times I've shuddered;
to think my fate would be
Without determination
and the help of the CCC.
- Camp Fechner News, Jan. 1937

"Meditation"

The blow of a bugle, the cry of "Let's go,"
I roll out of bed while dreams of go into oblivion,
I dress, oh so quickly, and out of the door I fly,
I see the grey dawn breaking up in the sky.
I look out all around me while dark shadows creep,
And into my brain fond recollections creep,
Of childhood days when life was gay,
When life was warm as the sun's beaming ray.
Of worries and cares I knew not then,
Back in those days, those days back when.
Then a shout, a whistle, or a pal's hearty "Hello."
And back into the past sweet reminiscences go,
And I return to reality, to face life alone,
Or at least, till the weekend when I get home.
- Camp Fechner News, Jan. 1937

"A New Lease on Life"
by Alexander Clinton

During our first two weeks in camp we were the butt of several practical jokes. Some of them were pretty raw but they were all in fun, after a while things settled down to where everything was plain sailing.

After two weeks of conditioning we were assigned to crews and sent to the woods. I was assigned to Dutch Elm Sanitation. Most of the work was in swamps and I saw more mud during my first day than I had ever seen before.

On my first day of work, as I was bending over picking up the remains of a giant elm, a voice behind me said, "You look hot buddy." I turned around and saw a husky fellow about twenty or so. He continued, "There is a well just over the hill. Why don't you walk over and get a drink?" I thought he was pulling my leg because he grinned unconsciously as I stammered my thanks.

After wiping my muddy hands upon some moss I made my way over the hill in search of the well. What a life! I tried to wipe a lump of mud from my eye and left a larger lump of mud in its place. This sort of discouraged me as I despaired of ever being able to make a go of it. I was so preoccupied with my thoughts that I wasn't watching where I was going. Consequently, my boots which were two sizes too large became caught in wild grapevines and I found myself sitting in the mud. This all tended to make a bad matter worse. I arose, straightened myself out a bit and after a little cussing that would have done credit to a sailor; I took a path which luckily led to the well.

After quenching my thirst, I felt a good deal better and began to see things in a better light. I made my way back along the trail which led over a hill. As I gained the summit I thrilled to the sight below where amid a group of elm trees I saw a team at work. The sound of saw teeth chewing the hard wood resounded throughout the entire valley. But the sound of the saw was not the only song which emanated from the clump of elms. The saw team was comprised of two coffee colored youths, well-built and husky, who were harmonizing on the spiritual "Go Down Moses."
- Camp Fechner News, March 1937

Melvin "Bob" Claude Lockwood

The CCC was Lockwood's first job at age 19 and he did an excellent job as supply clerk. Jan Howard

On April 23, 2008 I gave a talk on the CCC camps in Conn. at the Brookfield Historical Society. At the end of my talk Jan Howard told me her father was in the Danbury CCC camp at Wooster Mountain. She also showed me a group picture and pointed to a young man. "I believe my father is the man kneeling at the far right next to someone who is standing," she said. I really don't know much about his time in the CCC. But I got some information from his brother, Lewis, about his early life.

"Lewis told me that my grandfather had married a woman from the Caribbean island of St. Kitts. When my grandfather saw his wife holding their youngest child over a well, he had her placed in a mental institution in Middletown. She might have been suffering from postpartum depression but in those days doctors didn't know about it. My uncle said my grandfather then took my father and his four brothers and dropped them off at an orphanage in Hartford. My father was never adopted but his other brothers were all placed in foster homes. My father stayed in the orphanage. When he was 19 he went into the CCC and was sent to Danbury."

Jan asked me how she could get more information on her father in the CCC. I told her to contact the National Archives and Records Administration in St. Louis, Mo.

Nine months later, Jan sent me a copy of her father's records and a camp photo that she obtained from St. Louis.

Melvin "Bob" Claude Lockwood enrolled in the CCC on July 27, 1935 and was a member of Company 2102 at Camp Fechner in Danbury. Bob weighed 142 pounds and was 5' 10" in height. He was born on July 16, 1916 in Westford, Mass. The 19 year-old had graduated from high school. He stated that he never had a job and his mailing address was R. F. D. #1 Unionville, Conn. He said he'd be best qualified as a clerk because he had no experience working outdoors, but when the time came to leave the

A group of enrollees from Camp Fechner displaying a flag they earned in competition. Bob Lockwood is standing in the second row, third from right (his head centered in the window). Jan Howard

CCC he hoped to get a job in commercial art or forestry.

His first job at Camp Fechner was company clerk. He worked in the camp office and did jobs such as keeping files and doing secretarial work. He received two excellent ratings and one satisfactory rating for his work. On Oct. 1, 1937 Bob became the supply clerk. He did this work until Feb. 5, 1937.

During his CCC time he displayed leadership qualities. On Sept. 1, 1935 he was promoted to Assistant Leader. He received $6 more per month in addition to his monthly $30. Twenty-five dollars was sent home monthly to his father.

A year later Bob was promoted to supply clerk. In this job he had to keep exact records of supplies coming into the camp. He became a leader and received a monthly salary of $45.

On Feb. 5, 1937 Bob was discharged from Camp Fechner.

Jan told me, "My mother Marjorie Rydell was from Danbury. Somehow my parents met and fell in love while my father was in the CCC camp. They got married in 1937.

"In 1940 Dad lived in Danbury with my mother and me and was a bookkeeper at one of the hat companies. According to my half-sister, he also worked at one time for a newspaper, but in what capacity I don't know.

"When I got older I became interested in genealogy and I learned more about my father's life. According to one of her half-sisters, he was a good husband and a loving father. He had also attended two universities and had earned four degrees. He had also been involved with the Boy Scouts and a member of the PTA. At the time of his death in 1973 he

Bob Lockwood (center) clowning at the dinner bell with friends at Camp Fechner in Danbury. Jan Howard

was a probation officer of the Juvenile Court for Muskegon Co., Minn.

"I have never stopped and walked around the site of Camp Fechner on Rt. 7 in Danbury," said Jan, "though I have driven past its former location many times."

Peter J. Arsenault

Peter J. Arsenault wrote about his experiences at Camp Fechner in Danbury and it was posted on the internet.

"I joined the CCC because when I graduated from high school I could not find a job. I heard about the CCC and being from a family of 12 children it would benefit my family by my joining the CCC since they would not have to feed me and would get $25 a month.

"I was in Company 2102, Camp Fechner, in Danbury, Conn. in 1935 to 1936. The company worked in the forest cutting down trees and burning the wood because the trees were infected with Dutch elm disease.

"One of my jobs was the first aid man for Camp 2102. I became a medic because I had a high school education. The navy doctor gave me a first aid book to study.

"To make extra money I sold CCC banners and pillow tops with verses of mother and sweetheart to the CCC boys in my camp. I heard about this in a newspaper that came to the camp. It went to all the CCC camps.

"I was friendly with Raymond Dean. He introduced me to his sister, Margaret ('Peggy'), and when I left the CCC in 1939 I married her. We were married for 55 years when she passed away.

"During the war I worked for the U.S. Aluminum Co. in Bridgeport, Conn. I was a supervisor in the physical lab. We made airplane cylinder heads.

"In 1982 I organized National Association of CCC Alumni (NACCCA) Chapter 92 in Milford, Conn. I also became Northeast Regional Director for the CCC alumni. The CCC is something I will never forget."

Peter Arsenault died on Jan. 30, 2006 at the age of 90. He was the son of Avit and Mary Ann Gallant Arsenault and was born Oct. 20, 1915 in Prince Edward Island, Canada. He had three children: Peter, Jr., Thomas, and Marie. He had lived in Milford for 54 years.

William Affek

Arlene and her husband Bob Rivard met me at the Lebanon Historical Society on April 14, 2010. Arlene told me her father William Affek was in the Danbury CCC camp and she was interested in getting his discharge papers. I told her how to get them and she promised to share her information with me.

On Jan. 8, 2013 I visited Arlene and Bob at their home in Lebanon and I was surprised to also meet Arlene's mother, Emily Affek. As we sat at the kitchen table Arlene showed me the blank questionnaire I had sent her almost three years ago. She explained how she has been recovering slowly from the traumatic effects of Lyme disease the past 12 years and was unable to answer the questions. I then asked Arlene to tell me about her father's life and experiences in the CCC.

"My father, William Albert Affek, was born in Newark, NJ on June 10, 1916. His father Albert worked on their family farm and also worked at some of the local mills. Dad's mother was Suzanna and she had four sons: William, Walter, John, and Stanley.

"Dad graduated from the Putnam Trade School in May 1935 and was unemployed for two months. The offices of the Social Service Department and Department of Labor in town knew that Dad's family was poor and recommended my father to be eligible to join the CCC. My father was the eldest in his family and they were lucky that their son could get a job. I think my father was happy to get a job and be able to help his family.

"On July 6, 1935 Dad went to the Jewett City Town Hall and signed up for the CCC. On the application form he stated that he had worked a year doing carpentry and felt he was best qualified to do carpentry work at the camp. I do remember my father showing us a doctor's house in town where he replaced the roof. It was a huge house and that roof he worked on still looks great.

William Affek (left) worked at Camp Fechner where he worked cutting down diseased elm trees. Arlene Rivard

"On July 18, 1935 he went to the Replacement Center in New London and signed up for the CCC.

"Dad was sent to Danbury in the western part of the state. It was a trip of over 100 miles. I'm not sure if he went by himself or with a group of other boys. He was probably happy to go and help his parents but I'm sure he was a little nervous because he was a homebody kind of boy and I'm sure he missed his family.

"He told me he loved being in the CCC because when he got there he got new clothes and boots. He was poor and wasn't used to the nice clothes. His discharge papers said he worked as a laborer. He did tree work. I heard his camp's main job was cutting and destroying the diseased elm trees. Dad also told me he did sign carving and woodworking. He told me the CCC wanted him to go out west because they needed someone to carve signs but he refused because he wanted to be back home.

"My father said he had fun with all the guys. He used to make some extra money by giving haircuts. He was good at cutting hair. There were a few Negros in camp and there was some prejudice against them. Dad said he had to go in the back of the camp to cut the Negros' hair. Dad wasn't prejudiced like a lot of the guys were in those days."

Then Arlene asked her husband to get a group picture of Camp Fechner. "I got this photo at a large CCC Reunion at Rocky Neck State Park. I met Peter Arsenault who was also at Camp Fechner. He had an extra group photo and he gave me one. Dad is in the second row and to the left of one of the leaders with a large hat."

"One funny incident happened in camp. My father and a group of friends were walking in the nearby woods when they saw a black bear approaching them. They ran down the mountain to the camp as fast as they could.

"On the weekends Dad stayed at the camp. He didn't hitchhike often probably because it was too far but he did so a few times. He loved to play the harmonica and that was probably one of his hobbies.

"After 9 months in the CCC, Dad was discharged on March 31, 1936. His records show that he got 'satisfactory' rating for his first three months. During his last 6 months he received an 'excellent' rating. I'm not surprised by that because he was always a hard worker.

"When he came back home he found jobs in the local mills. He then worked in a cabinet shop in Norwich. Then he worked in the Plastic Wire and Cable Co. in Jewett City.

"During WWII Dad's three brothers were in the Army.

Dad, however, didn't have to go to war because he was the eldest and only survivor since both parents had died."

Arlene then reached over the table and handed me a picture of her father and his three brothers.

"I forgot to tell you that his brother John was also in the CCC at the nearby Voluntown camp. Also, my father always referred to the CCC as 'CCC camp.'

"In 1947 Dad married Emily Sudol and they had two children: my brother James and me.

"For the rest of his life he worked at E. B., Electric Boat Co. He was a carpenter in the model shop. There he and the other men made all the parts for the submarine out of wood for testing. One day he brought home a wooden faucet he had made. It was very small. He wanted to show us an example of what he made.

"During the early 1970s Dad got sick and had a stroke. He had to quit work and was on disability. Then in 1975 he passed away.

"Dad always said that the CCC was the best experience of his life. He talked about his CCC camp all of his life. He liked the money that he earned for his family. He had a lot of fun with the other guys. He always talked about the boots and warm coat that he got and the food was good. He loved everything about the CCC."

CHAPTER 9
EASTFORD FERNOW

HISTORY

Company 183 was organized on June 5, 1933 at Fort Wright on Fishers Island, NY about six miles off the coast of New London. Capt. Pharr commanded the company. Enrollees underwent training for approximately two weeks. On June 24, Lt. Kiemling took a cadre of one private and nine enrollees from the company and went to the Natchaug State Forest (SF) and established a camp site.[1]

On a sunny hot day on June 29, Company 183 left Fort H. G. Wright, at 8:45 am on the Gen. Greene ferry for New London. After they arrived they boarded buses, trucks, and three private cars at 9:45 am and the convoy headed for the Natchaug SF. The convoy reached Hampton Reservoir and began traveling on a narrow truck trail and the trucks became mired in mud. After much effort the convoy reached Kingsbury Rd. After five hours the convoy reached the camp site. The enrollees first task was pitching tents and downing a hearty meal of good old-fashioned canned beans.[2]

The next day the men were assigned to details to prepare the camp site. Construction officer Lt. Rublee, foreman Fred Monroe, and forty enrollees began constructing a latrine, icebox, and water hole. Other details gathered fire wood, moved supplies, constructed a road into camp, and other camp organization tasks.

The camp was named after Bernhard Fernow who is considered the father of American forestry. He was the third chief (1886-1898) of the United States Division of Forestry set the foundation for the US Forest Service in that was established in 1905 under Gifford Pinchot.[8]

The construction detail's next project was the construction of the lavatory, kitchen, and administration building. These were the only camp buildings constructed by enrollees. The rest would be done by civilians.[9]

At first enrollees traveled to camp from Rt. 44, then south on Chaplin Road (Rt. 198), then left on Pilfershire Road 1 mile to Kingsbury Road on the right. On this road they passed the Nathaniel Lyon Memorial on the right that contains a large stone fireplace and chimney. These remains were the birthplace and home of General Nathaniel Lyon who was the first Union general killed in the Civil War. In 1861 he died in the battle of Wilson's Creek where he is credited with saving Missouri for the Union. Just a little farther was the camp entrance. It was also possible to come to the camp from the south by traveling on Kingsbury Road.[10]

By 1934 the camp buildings were completed with the barracks, mess hall, and clinic forming a square with the flag pole in the middle. CT CCC Museum

Camp Fernow was named after Bernhard Fernow, the "father of professional forestry in the US."[7]

Lyon family fireplace and chimney near Camp Fernow. CT CCC Museum

(L–R) 1 In order to shorten the driving time to their camp site, Camp Fernow enrollees used native stones and timbers to construct this beautiful bridge over the Natchaug River. CT CCC Museum 2 The Austin F. Hawes cabin in the Natchaug State Forest. Conn. Agriculture Experimental Station 3 A view of the Camp Fernow buildings taken from the water tower and looking westward towards the Natchaug River. CT CCC Museum

CCC enrollees used native timbers sawed at the camp sawmill to build this post and beam lumber shed near the saw mill. The boys received hands on experience by a foreman skilled in carpentry. CT CCC Museum

Between 1933-34 enrollees built a lumber shed and a warehouse. They also installed a second-hand No. 1 Lane sawmill that had a 52" diameter tooth saw with a pipe and sawdust blower on a concrete pad. They used it to make lumber from the Natchaug Forest.[15] CT CCC Museum

The DEEP still uses the lumber storage shed built by the CCC in the 1930s. Podskoch

Capt. James S. Thompson oversaw a lot of projects that were completed to beautify Camp Fernow. The camp won many awards because of his efforts. CT CCC Museum

New Bridge

In July 1933 a decision was made to create a new entrance that would shorten the distance to the camp. Foreman Bob Coughlan and his crew of surveyors looked for the best location and by early August a site was selected for a bridge over the Natchaug River. On Sept. 1 the crew began digging to bedrock on the west bank for an abutment. Engineer Louis James came to supervise construction. A coffer dam was built with sand bags to keep out water while enrollees poured the foundation. Pumping was also done every morning to remove water as the boys worked.[11]

Then a stone mason, Augustus Casciani, arrived to supervise the stone work and his 25-man crew. The boys enjoyed working with him despite the hard work of gathering stones from the river bed. Finally, the two abutments and two center piers were completed above the water line. Another crew was busy in the forest cutting 27' long bridge stringers and taking them to the camp sawmill and slabbed on one side. Soon the stringers were stretched across the river and 3" thick planks were spiked to them. Then guard rails and bridge rails made from 6" thick chestnut poles were added. August and crew then built stone posts on top of the cement plates. In no time vehicles were passing over the bridge.[12]

Enrollees completed the 16' wide by 74' long bridge across the Natchaug River by the middle of March 1934. It was designed by Henry R. Buck. On June 4, the camp had a dedication. Some of the honored guests were: James McEntee and Ross Abare who represented CCC Director, Robert Fechner; Major General Knight who represented General Fox Connor; Connecticut Governor Wilbur H. Cross; and Austin F. Hawes, Conn. State Forester.[13]

The enrollees cut and split over 500 cords of fire wood in 1934. CT CCC Museum

Enrollees Rzepiejewski and Scavetta are probably thinking, "Do we have to work today?" CT CCC Museum

Projects

In 1933 Camp Fernow did stream improvement projects on 2½ miles of the Natchaug River. They built 53 deflectors (logs or rocks that extend from the bank into the stream to stabilize stream banks by moving the current away from the banks), two boulder dams, 24 artificial boulders (stone in concrete), and six shelters to improve the habitat for fish. The following spring of 1934 Camp Fernow did the same type of work on Roaring Brook in Willington and Union.[14]

Civilian labor was brought in about Oct. 1 and they constructed barracks, dispensary, and foresters' and officers' quarters. Work was completed by the end of the month and workers began constructing 20-stall garages.

Capt. James S. Thompson assumed command on Jan. 26, 1934. Lt. Kiemling began working on improvements and projects to beautify the camp. He first rebuilt a 40' high, 500 gal. capacity water tank. The camp was built on a field with walkways that were just hay and mud. Kiemling drew up plans to landscape the camp. Loads of gravel were hauled in for walks that were then lined with stones. Then loam was spread and grass planted for the quadrangle. Many trees and shrubs were planted to beautify the camp. Kiemling had the buildings painted with artistic decorations.[16]

During Capt. Thompson's tenure the camp did many other landscaping projects. Camp Fernow was the first one to do landscaping within a CCC camp. The CCC Corps Area Headquarters promoted this landscaping program to all the other New England camps.[17]

In March of 1934 the Education Department was established with LeRoy A. Dissinger as Advisor. He added other teachers for the program and developed many classes for the enrollees.[18]

Camp Fernow was involved in building roads in the Natchaug SF. They constructed and maintained Kingsbury and Fernow roads. The latter connected the camp with the new bridge built in 1934 over the Natchaug River.[19]

On April 1, 1934 Mr. Currier was relived of the position of Superintendent and replaced by Harold D. Pearson.[20]

The construction of a State Store House was completed on April 25, 1934. It now supplied the Forestry Departments of seven CCC camps.[21]

The State Park and Forest Commission reported that by June 30, 1934 enrollees cut 589 cords of wood for fuel, made 347 posts and 417 poles, and cut 59,311 board feet of logs.[22]

Bernhard Fernow would have been proud to see the excellent work the enrollees performed doing silviculture. By June 30, 1934 enrollees cleaned 275 acres of dead wood, thinned 339 acres, 50 acres of reproductive cutting, cleaned 79 acres for planting for a total of 743 acres treated.[23]

During the latter part of November 1934 the first ERA dramatic troupe of players performed the play "Tommy." The plays were performed on a portable stage with floodlights in the rec hall.[24]

From Dec. 1934 a crew of nine scouts under foreman Dolor LaBelle searched for egg masses in Eastford, Pomfret, and Ashford. The crew covered 917 acres and destroyed 64,900 egg masses by painting them with creosote. In the spring and summer the crew banded the trees with burlap.[25]

Foreman James Krayeske led the White Pine Weevil Control crew that worked in the white pine plantations in the Natchaug SF. The men inspected and removed 6,423

Activities at Camp Fernow.[27]

Camp Fernow boys building a log tower used for locating fires. CCC CT Museum

weevilled tips. They placed them in a canvas bag slung over their shoulder and later burned the tips.

On Jan. 8, 1935 the monthly meeting of camp commanders and superintendents was held at Camp Fernow at which approximately 50 members attended.[26]

Camp Activities

Various vaudeville troupes visited the CCC camps providing them with entertainment. On Jan. 19, 1935 Vaudeville Unit No. 1 put on an entertaining show. After their show a group of enrollees put on a show of their own for the visiting actors in the officers' quarters. They also sang "CCC Boys" composed and written by members of the troupe.[28]

In Feb. 1935 Education Advisor LeRoy A. Dissinger received three instructors to help in teaching. Classes included the basics of reading, writing, and arithmetic. There were also these: Glee Club, Drama, Wood Carving, and Auto Mechanics.[29]

During the fall and winter movies were shown on Monday evenings in the rec hall. Guest speakers were also invited to the camp on a variety of subjects. The rec hall had two pool and two ping pong tables for enjoyment.[30]

The camp basketball team won the Plainfield Community League championship on March 25, 1935. In

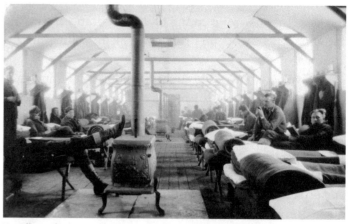

Enrollees relaxing in their barracks after a busy day of working in the Natchaug State Forest. Some are reading, smoking, sleeping writing letters, or playing cards. E. Germaine

the play-off series Camp Fernow defeated the Plainfield Clowns and St. Andrews teams.[31]

On April 1, 1935 J. Francis Dillon became the new Education Advisor replacing Mr. Dissinger who moved on to be the District Education Advisor.[32]

On May 8, 1935 Dr. James S. Corkery became the new camp surgeon.[33]

On the morning of June 4, Guy L. Colson, 1st Lt. led a cadre of 23 enrollees from Camp Fernow to East Douglas, Mass. to organize a new camp and Co. 1199.

Construction of an addition to the mess hall and a

Members of the Camp Fernow baseball team that played local town and CCC Camp teams. CT CCC Museum

Foreman Winch (wearing hat) posing with the Camp Fernow members in the sawing and wood chopping contest held at their camp. CT CCC Museum

In August 1935 the CCC District Wood Sawing and Chopping contest was held on Aug., 29, 1935 at Camp Fernow. The choppers had to cut through 9-10" thick logs in thee marked spots. Henry Langlois and Thomas Raimondo represented Camp Fernow. The saw teams also had to make three cuts. Representing Camp Fernow were Walter Kania and Edward Kornacki. Neither home team contestants won.[38]

new barracks began on June 5, 1935 and were completed on June 28. A second anniversary party of the camp was also held on that day.[34]

The camp had two alternating fire crews of ten men each under the supervision of foreman Richard B. Hosier. The crew that remained at camp was ready for any fire calls. Their truck was equipped with shovels, pumps, Indian tanks, etc. While at camp they did work such as landscaping and grading. During the spring of 1935 they responded to 12 fires in the towns of Columbia, Hampton, Danielson, and Wauregan. If the fire warranted more men, a crew of volunteers was quickly formed. The fire season lasted from late March till early June.[35]

Sports

Sports were an integral part of the camp. Captain Thompson contacted the Willimantic "Y" and received special rates for enrollees to participate in winter recreation. In the summer the camp had inter-barracks competition in baseball and volleyball in which almost all of the enrollees

participated. The camp also had baseball and basketball teams that competed against other camps and town teams. In 1935 the camp baseball team won the Plainfield Community League championship.[36]

In 1935 Mr. Ledger, a member of the education staff, started a class in boxing. Two matches were held with Camp Jenkins in Cobalt.[37] Matches were also held at Crystal Lake and Stafford Springs. There was no camp football team but the boys enjoyed playing touch football. During the winter enrollees enjoyed skiing, skating, and ice hockey. In the summer they boys went either to the "Y" in Willimantic or Halls Pond 1¼ mile from camp. Some of the enrollees got into weight lifting and wrestled in the rec hall.

Also in August a crew was constructing a 2½ mile trail along the east side of the Natchaug River. The trail would join Trail #2 and travel along Beaver Dam Brook to Kingsbury Rd.[39]

Then on Sept. 7, twenty CCC camps competed for the State Swimming Championship at Colt Park in Hartford.[40]

At the end of September 1935 a "Timber Estimating"

Camp Fernow personnel in 1936 with camp mascot, "May Pay Day" in the front left and Army officers, state foremen, and foresters in the center of the first two rows. The cooks in white are seated on the ground. Gary Potter

Enrollees found this orphan fawn and named her "May Pay Day." She was loved by all the boys and was the camp's mascot. Here, Dr. Gross is feeding her milk. CT CCC Museum

The new Natchaug River Bridge withstood the 1936 Flood without damage. CT CCC Museum

In July 1936 construction began on a tennis court. It was located behind Barracks No. 1.[54] CT CCC Museum

project was completed by foresters Milton Arnold, Richard H. Florian and a small crew of enrollees. The project began in 1933 and the men covered approximately 6,000 acres in the Natchaug SF and 15,000 acres in the Purchase Areas. The result of the study helped in making a permanent plan of managing the forests and constructing roads, fire lines, and thinning the forest.[41]

The blister rust crew ended its season on Sept. 20. Foreman Howard N. Wells supervised the work over a six-month period. They destroyed 12,878 currant and gooseberry bushes covering 43 acres of state land and 4,164 acres of private land.[42]

In November 1935 a library was constructed in the Administrative Building and it opened up into the rec hall and was opposite the P. X. It had a traveling library of books and magazines for the enrollees.[43]

Two crews resumed thinning the hardwood stand of approximately 20 acres in the Beaver Dam Brook Block during November. It was between the Natchaug River and Kingsbury Rd. The men were supervised by foremen Richard Hosier and Howard Wells. Trees of inferior quality were removed.[44]

In Jan. 1936 Capt. James Thompson was transferred to East Hartland and 1st Lt. J. J. McCarthy assumed command of the camp. The following month Captain Albert McCullough became the new commander. At the end of March, McCullough was transferred and McCarthy again assumed command. Under his leadership he received praise for supervising his enrollees during the massive cleanup work during the 1936 Flood. His men moved into towns such as South Windsor, East Hartford, Hartford, Warehouse Point, and other areas devastated by the flooding Connecticut River.[45]

Robert Sargent, a member of Camp Fernow, was commended by the Flood Authorities for his work during the 1936 Flood. When the pumps installed by the WPA were not working properly, Sargent was placed in charge. He succeeded in getting them to work properly and helped in the flood cleanup.[46]

Hartford Mayor Thomas J. Spellacy had a special testimonial dinner for all of the CCC enrollees who worked to clean up his city. He also presented them each with a wristwatch.[47]

Trail Roads

By Feb. 1936 Trail #1 (Kingsbury Rd.) going north and south in the Natchaug SF was completed. Trail #2 (Fernow Rd.) going east and west was in construction. These roads were important in improving the condition of the forest where they used proper silviculture methods. Workers could remove diseased and less desirable trees and used them for saw logs and fuel wood. The old fields were then planted with valuable conifer trees. Roads were also important in case of fires.[48]

By June 1936 NSF had 5.9 miles of auto roads, 1 vehicle bridge, 25.2 miles of wood roads, and 1.8 miles of foot trails.[49]

In June 1936 the Education Dept. moved into Barracks No. 5. It was divided into three rooms for instruction and an office for the advisor. New floors were installed in the barracks and rec hall. The ice box and root cellar was enlarged and remodeled. Plans were made to get a deep water well for the camp because of insufficient water in the summer.[50]

On June 18 the camp celebrated its third anniversary with a social dance at Al-piee Tabar in Willimantic. Helen Price of new London furnished singing, dancing, and tumbling. On that same day the camp mascot, "May Pay Day" was shot by a farmer for eating his garden. The camp enrollees mourned her death. At about the same time two young deer were brought to the dispensary to be nursed. They were named "Ike" and "Mike."[51]

During the middle of July 1936, Lt. McCarthy was transferred to Company 1191 in Kent. Captain Earl H. Marsden became the new commander. Two months later Captain Marsten was transferred to Company 190 in New London and Lt. McCarthy returned to command the Eastford camp.[52]

After McCarthy returned, Camp Fernow received the "Honor Pennant" for its district for the third time in four months.[53]

The education department was successful in sending enrollees to the Willimantic State Training School and many completed their courses. This was the first time that a Conn. CCC camp completed vocational classes.[55]

During the fall and winter enrollees were able to go to the Willimantic "Y" on Wednesday evening for inter-barracks basketball, swimming, track, boxing, wrestling, and life-saving class.[56]

Camp Fernow received the "Honor Pennant" of the Fifth CCC District after the January 1937 inspection. This was the third time in four months that Camp Fernow received this award.[57]

1937 Classes

During the winter enrollees took vocational classes at the Willimantic Trade School. At the end of classes 38 certificates were awarded to enrollees.[58]

The Education Dept. added these new classes at camp Fernow during the 1937 summer: Mess Management, Agriculture & Animal Husbandry, Leader Training, Personal Interviews, English, Spelling, Arithmetic, Photography, Hog Raising, Agriculture, Citizenship, and Woodworking.[59]

Camp Fernow was fortunate to have its own doctor. In 1937 it was Carmine Thomas Angelone. The next year it was Dr. Harry W. Broadbridge. In Oct. 1939 Broadbridge was transferred to the Salisbury, NY camp.

The cover of the June 1936 Fernow Forum depicting the camp buildings.

The new classrooms in Barracks No. 5 in 1936 at Camp Fernow. CT CCC Museum

This is the staff of Camp Fernow composed of Army officers, Conservation Department foresters, and foremen. Many of them taught evening classes at the camp. CT CCC Museum

1938 Hurricane

The bridge built by the CCC over the Natchaug River was buffeted with high water both in the spring flood of 1936 and again in the summer of 1938 but it withstood the onslaught unscathed. But the terrible hurricane on Sept. 21, 1938 was too much for the bridge. A flood broke the Phoenixville Dam on the Natchaug River and the surge of water destroyed the center stone foundations and the wooden timbers.[60]

The education advisor worked with a group of enrollees to publish a weekly newspaper called the "In Fernow." It contained camp news, editorials, "News Reviews" (national and world), "Windbag," humorous camp stories of enrollees, and, of course, pictures of girls. In 1939 Peter C. Quinn was the education advisor.

The Jan. 1939 issue of the In Fernow reported enrollees building a small memorial structure near Gen. Nathaniel Lyon's fire place chimney. It was dedicated to Knowlton Lyon who was related to Gen. Nathaniel Lyon of the Civil War.

Construction of a gym was reported in the Feb. 1939 issue of the In Fernow. It would have basketball hoops, wrestling and boxing ring, parallel bars, rowing machine, and a hand ball court.

Many enrollees asked why there wasn't a football team and the administration stated that there were regulations in the First Corps Area that prohibited it. The reason was that because there were many injuries some of which were very serious.[61]

1939 Classes

During the spring 1939 these classes were held: Aviation, Journalism, Carpentry, Crafts, Archeology, Forest Conservation, American History, Tree Identification, and Commercial Arithmetic.[62]

Miss Evangeline Church taught English, spelling, history, and also arithmetic to ten enrollees interested in getting a grammar school equivalency certificate. During the summer they were tested and graded at the University of Connecticut.[63]

Evangeline Church

During 1938 Miss Evangeline Church, who was hired by the WPA as a teacher, gathered a group of Fernow enrollees who were interested in archery and taught them how to make bows and arrows. By mid-summer she took the enrollees outside for target shooting. Her classes were cut short with the extra work that the enrollees had to do because of the 1938 Hurricane. The following spring classes continued and more students joined. Then camp administration fixed up an abandoned barn and it was decorated and named "The Wigwam" or "Indian Lodge." Here the young men began making the American flat bows. Previously they had been making English long or semi-long bows. Her group continued practicing outside and giving demonstrations at towns and other CCC camps. This led to the formation of another archery class at Camp Conner in Stafford Springs. During the summer enrollees made 31 bows that they hung on the walls of "The Wigwam." In 1939 Camp Fernow had a competition with Camps Filley and Conner.[64]

In October 1939 Camp Fernow enrollees signed up again for these classes: carpentry, drafting, trade mathematics, and electricity. The classes were held on Monday and Tuesday evenings. Fifteen enrollees completed typing and shorthand classes at Putnam Community Center. They celebrated with a dance at the Putnam High School.[65]

The tennis court was completely renovated in the summer of 1939. To help defray the costs a small fee was charged for the users. Tournaments were held throughout the summer.[66]

Various agriculture projects began during the summer of 1939. A plot of land was plowed for a vegetable garden. Flowers and bushes were planted in the camp quadrangle. Pheasants were also raised by the company.[67]

Bridge Work

During the spring and summer enrollees began work on the damaged Natchaug Bridge. The old center piers and abutments were blasted and removed. In July 1939 these supplies arrived at the Hampton Station for the bridge: 735 bags of cement and three 70' I-beams.[68] In August these bridge supplies arrived: 7,538 lbs. of 1'-36' long reinforced steel. Workers began work on forms for the final back wall of the abutment and then cement would be poured.[69] In late August the three I-beams arrived. An 18-wheel trailer from Camp buck delivered them.[70] Enrollees placed the three 71' long steel I-beams over the river. It took 2,222 man-days to rebuild the bridge.[71]

On Sat. Aug. 26, 1939 the Gold Star, VFW of Willimantic presented their second annual show at Camp Fernow. The Post Drum Corps presented a concert in the rec hall and this was followed by four boxing bouts. The event was sponsored by Willimantic Postmaster James J. Lee and Post Commander Arthur Langlois.[72]

Several products made at Camp Fernow were on display in Aug. 1939 at Jordan's Hardware Store in Willimantic. The items were bows and arrows made by the Archery Class, many pieces of art made with Plaster of Paris by the Craft Class, camp newspapers, furniture made by the Carpentry Class, and Indian artifacts found by the Archeology Class.[73]

On Sept. 26, 1939 Capt. John E. O'Hair who had been at Fernow since Jan. 1938 ended his command.[74] On Sept.

12, Lt. A. L. Willis became the new camp commander. His last position was commanding the East Wallingford, VT camp.[75]

A Farewell Dance at the Willimantic Town Hall was held at the end of September for the 57 men leaving the camp. The Silver Rhythm orchestra supplied the music. This left approximately 100 men remaining at Fernow. Later replacement came from the Reception and Transportation Center in Hartford.[76]

At the end of 1939 enrollees received a new forest green uniform. Enrollees would now wear the uniforms – except when working – but especially when they went to town.[77]

The Oct. 14, 1939 In Fernow issue reported that during the fall and winter, Camp Fernow's enrollees were able to take classes at two locations besides those offered in camp. The first was at the Putnam Community Center in the Putnam High School. The other was at the Willimantic Trade School. The Putnam Center also provided four W. P. A. teachers who came to Camp Fernow each week.

The Putnam Community Center added four new classes at camp: Social Dancing, American History, Archeology, and Indian Lore.[78]

Arthur Basto
(1896 - 1980)

Arthur Basto taught Camp Fernow enrollees about Indian archeology and explored the Natchaug Forest for Indian artifacts. He furnished various tribes in the area with historical data that was unknown to them.

In recognition for his valuable service to studying and preserving the Indian history, in July 1939 Basto was made an Indian Chief by the New England Federation of Indians at a ceremony in Westerly, RI.[79]

Arthur Basto's boyhood interest in arrowheads and other artifacts surfaced during cultivation activities on his family's farm and resulted in his lifelong passion for archaeological research and preservation. Self-educated in the field of archaeology, Arthur Basto was a locally recognized authority on natives of Northeast Connecticut, and he was a popular speaker whose audiences included professional archaeologists as well as the general public.

In 1936, he began methodical excavation and recordkeeping at a site on his family farm which was located along Little River. That site proved to be the location of a

The archery team practicing at Camp Fernow. CT CCC Museum

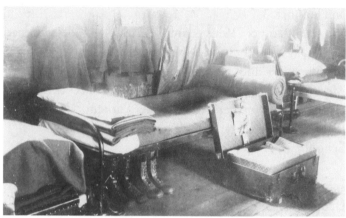

The enrollees had weekly inspections. You can see how orderly each bed was and even their trunk was inspected. Doesn't it look like our kids' and grand children's bedrooms are today? CT CCC Museum

former native village. Arthur Basto supervised and taught the Yale archaeology students who assisted with excavation, recording of data and cataloging of artifacts from the site. Results were published in the Bulletin of the Archaeological Society of Connecticut in 1938 and 1939. Arthur Basto donated his entire collection of artifacts (about 4,000 items) to the Peabody Museum at Yale University.

The Arthur Basto Archaeological Society holds membership meetings four (4) times a year at the Sprague Town Hall, located at the corner of Rts. 207 and 97.[80]

Archery Team

In Oct. 1939 four members of the archery class, led by their instructor, Evangeline Church, traveled to the University of Connecticut to participate in a "Play Day." The enrollees participated in many events involving the university students. The feature event was the "Columbia Round" that consisted of 80 archers lined up and shooting at 20 targets. Those watching were surprised at the CCC archers who used handmade bows and arrows compared to the others who used commercially made equipment.[81]

Also in Oct. 1939 a camp orchestra was formed. It consisted of five enrollees playing a piano, guitar, violin, and two harmonicas. The men hoped to expand to more members and play at dances.[82]

In 1939 Lt. A. L. Wills tried to secure reduced movie tickets at the Capitol Theater in Willimantic. Theater manager Pickett said that it wasn't possible but offered the Lt. five free tickets per week. Lt. Willis decided to use the tickets as a way of getting the enrollees to keep their

barracks spic and span. He announced the awarding of the free tickets each week to the barracks that was the cleanest. Each morning the barracks were inspected and on Friday the two winning barracks were announced. The winning barracks then had their leaders choose the men that showed initiative and ingenuity in improving their barracks. The first place barracks received three tickets and the second place barracks got two.[83]

In the fall of 1939 Camp Fernow conducted an orientation program for 87 new recruits. After the new recruits arrived they had dinner in the mess hall. Lt. Wills welcomed the men. The next morning at breakfast the new recruits learned about the different phases of camp life from

The Eastford camp cut down trees to show the boundary lines of the Natchaug State Forest. CCC CT Museum

the commander, education advisor, welfare officer, senior leader, mess steward, canteen steward, and company clerk.[84]

Vocational Classes

Enrollees had the opportunity to take vocational classes at the State Trade School in Willimantic Classes began on Oct. 6 and were held on Mondays and Tuesdays throughout the winter. The classes offered were: drafting, carpentry, electricity, and trade mathematics.[85]

After serving their six-month term at Camp Fernow, 47 members resigned for another term and they left by truck on Nov. 1, 1993 and went to start a new camp in Florida, Missouri. They were going to construct the Mark Twain Memorial Park and were under the command of Subaltern Clausen.[86]

The Natchaug Bridge was opened to traffic at the beginning of Nov. 1939 but would officially be opened and dedicated at a later date.[87]

Best Camp Award

In an effort to win the Corps Area Honor Pennant for the Best Camp, a weekly contest was held to see what two barracks were the best after an inspection. To encourage hard work a weekly prize of three free Willimantic Movie Theater tickets were given out to each winning barracks. Competition became so intense that the prizes were extended to the top three barracks.[88] The camp enrollees also painted many of the inside of the buildings in pleasing colors. The barracks windows were also fitted with curtains.[89]

The Camp Fernow sawmill began operating in November 1939. Foreman C. P. Barrington supervised the 13-man crew. Another crew of Barrington was busy cutting logs doing boundary work. The logs were cut into boards.[90]

In December, 1939 Lt. A. L. Willis was replaced as commander and Subaltern F. J. Leonard took over the camp. This was the first non-military leader for Camp Fernow. This was the new way that the CCC camps were being run

Camp Fernow had 18 trucks that were owned by either the Army or the CT Conservation Dept. The camp used them to transport men and materials. CCC CT Museum

Most of the time the young enrollees did a great job of driving but there were times when there were accidents. Here a pick-up truck rolled over in a ditch. CT CCC Museum

A Camp Fernow enrollee working on the damaged pickup truck. CT CCC Museum

In February 1935 these men from Camp Fernow are trying to extricate this tractor that has slid off the road. CT CCC Museum

These 17 Camp Fernow boys are ready to cut trees in the Natchaug SF with a forester (front row, left) and the foreman seated in the truck. CT CCC Museum

All the camp trucks were housed in garages. Here truck driver Ed Kornasky by his truck that he drove enrollees to work, sports events or to the movies in Willimantic. CT CCC Museum

by citizens and the Army officers were being recalled to service for the possibility of war.[91]

The trucks in each camp were work horses performing many duties such as transporting men and materials. In 1939 Camp Fernow there were 3 Chevrolet pick-ups, 8 Chevrolet rack trucks, and 7 REO dump trucks. Camp mechanic Charles B. Jacoby reported the trucks of the State Forest Service traveled approximately a quarter of a million miles over an 18-month period. The actual mileage was 208,351 miles and these trucks used 29,326 gallons of gas and 3,548 quarts of oil.[92]

The Dec. 16, 1939 issue of the In Fernow reported that foreman A. O. Alleard's crew of 20 men had a 40% increase production over a work period of 100 man-days. Using brush hooks, axes, and machetes they covered 300 acres from October to mid December. The work was in four blocks at Beaverdam, Chaplin, Westford, and Eastford.

Camp Fernow boys had a great meal on Christmas day that included these items on the menu: roasted turkey with walnut dressing, cream of tomato soup, celery, mashed potatoes, giblet gravy, turnips, buttered peas, parker house rolls, butter, cranberry sauce, mixed nuts, chocolates, mince pie, ice cream, bag of fruit, and for all that stayed – cigarettes![93]

The camp basketball team used the Willimantic Armory for their weekly practice and home games. Some of their opponents were the Taftville Eagles, Camp Filley, and Camp Connor.[94]

In Feb. 1940 the CCC dentist, Dr. E. J. Carroll, and his assistant paid a visit to camp Fernow for their six-month check-up of enrollees. The doctor did extractions, fillings, and gave oral hygiene instructions to the young men.[95]

Throughout the year Federal CCC inspectors visited the CCC camps and evaluated the programs. On Feb. 8, 1940 Corps Area Education Advisor, Fred E. Lukens visited Camp Fernow's Education Advisor, Mr. Quinn, and his instructor Strock who was in charge of the Equivalency testing. Later in the month truck inspector Stephen Russell made his monthly visit and did his inspections of camp vehicles and office records. If there were any major repairs they were sent to the Boston CCC garage.[96]

Religious programs were held frequently especially Catholic programs because most of the enrollees were of that faith. In March a Catholic mission was held by District Chaplin Rev. William J. Dean and Rev. Edward O'Keefe S. J.[97]

In the spring 1940 WPA instructor Miss Evangeline Church continued teaching these classes: Handicrafts, Grammar School Equivalency, and Archery in the Indian Lodge. Her archery team had lost only one match in the past. Competition matches were held in Goodyear, Putnam, and Fernow.[98]

By 1940 Camp Fernow had completed Fayette Wright Road in the NSF.[99] By the end of 1940, there were 9.4 miles of roads in NSF.[100]

During the summer of 1940, Company Commander F. J. Leonard gave the approval for Army trucks to transport enrollees for swimming at Halls Pond. The "Buddy System" was used where experienced swimmers swam with novice swimmers.[101]

On May 28, 1941 Camp Fernow closed. H. V. Potter was the camp superintendent at the closing. The Army retained custody of the camp.

LEGACY

Camp Fernow enrollees left their mark on the Natchaug SF. They thinned the forest to permit trees to flourish. They built the Natchaug Trail that allows both young and old to enjoy the beauty of nature. The CCC also built picnic areas. The Natchaug River is noted for its good trout fishing. The roads built by the CCC are still used today for tourists, hikers, bikers, and horseback riders.

Directions:

From the intersection of Rts. 44 and 196 in Eastford, go south on Rt. 196 for approximately one-half mile. Then turn left on Pilfershire Rd. and travel 1 mile to Kingsbury Rd. on the right. You will pass the Nathaniel Lyon Memorial on the right that contains a large stone fireplace and chimney. Drive a short distance and you will pass an old ranger house. A little further there is barn on the right and the camp was in the open space in back of the garage. Going south on the road the sawmill and storage shed are on the left.

Enrollees Rowkowski (left) and Panfilis having some fun at Camp Fernow. CT CCC Museum

This fisherman is enjoying fishing near the CCC constructed bridge that crosses the Natchaug River and leads to the Camp Fernow site. Podskoch

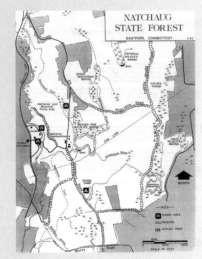

Map – Natchaug State Forest

Natchaug State Forest

Camp Fernow S-56 was on land in Nathaniel Lyon State Park in the town of Eastford in northeastern Connecticut. The camp was bordered on three sides by the Natchaug SF.[3]

The forest got its name from the Indian word 'natchaug' which means 'land between the rivers'. It refers to the junction of the Bigelow and Still Rivers which form the Natchaug River at Phoenixville. The forest is located in what was a portion of the hunting grounds of the Wabbaquasset Indians.[4]

It was originally called Eastford Forest when the state acquired 586 acres in 1917. At present, the Natchaug SF yields over 13,000 acres.[5]

MEMORIES

This CCC camp song was written by enrollees Donald S. Peters and Francis Maher and dedicated to Captain James Thompson. It was sung by Camp Fernow Glee Club on WTIC at Avery Memorial Hall on Feb. 15, 1935.

"May Pay Day", Camp Fernow's mascot. In July of 1935 she was about two months old. CT CCC Museum

"To Our Mascot"

Who's the one that's loved by all?
Tis' May Pay Day, shy and small
With eyes of forest brown
She made a hit in Fernow town.
So here's to May that dear young deer
Who's brought to Fernow woodland cheer.
- Fernow Forum, July 1935

The Camp Fernow flagpole in the center of the courtyard.
CT CCC Museum

"Camp Fernow Just for You"

Our fair flag is waving
Over the field;
Our men are fighting
With the spirit
That will not yield.
Three cheers for Fernow
We're all for you
Once again we will triumph
Camp Fernow just for you.

When the day is over
And our work is thru,
We'll get together
And we'll sing
Of our love for you.
Three cheers for Fernow
We're all for you
Once again we'll triumph
Camp Fernow just for you.

Winter has come to Camp Fernow. CT CCC Museum

"Winter Again"
by Russell Poll

Once again we don our Winter coats,
For Summer is on the wane;
With every sun we note the change,
'Twill soon be Winter again.
Our clothes, no doubt, may be too small,
Or they may be too big;
But when we feel the chill of Fall,
About our clothes we won't holler at all.
Now take my advice and don't cry in vain,
Cause Winter's paying us a visit again.
- Fernow Forum, Oct. 1935

In July 1935 enrollees were thrilled to discard their mess kits for meals in the mess hall. No longer did they have to stand in line to be served. They were now served at tables, family style. Fernow Forum July, 1935.

"Chow"
by Pat Maher

On Monday we had bread and gravy,
On Tuesday 'twas gravy and bread;
On Wednesday and Thursday gravy and toast,
Which is nothing but gravy and bread.
On Friday I went to the "Louie,"
And said, "Please give us something instead."
So Saturday morning just for a change
We had gravy without any bread.
- Fernow Forum, Oct. 1935

The Mess Hall at Camp Fernow. CT CCC Museum

"Camp Fernow"
by Harry Huildford

Camp Fernow, the home of the CCC,
Upon a knoll surrounded by trees.
We do all kinds of work,
Our duties we never shirk.

For two hours of duty isn't much fun,
Some people would rather face the barrel of a gun.
We all dress up for evening mess,
Ties, slacks, shoes, all spick and span I must confess.

Now that the day's duties are over,
Some go to town but most of us remain under cover.
- Fernow Forum, Oct. 1935

CCC Camps in Connecticut were integrated and for the most part the boys got along well. CT CCC Museum

"Our Forest"
by Charles Allen

A safe retreat from summer's heat
Fresh green on winter's snow
Our forests stand in stalwart bands
To greet the folks who know.

To weary souls they're restful goals
On nerves distraught with care
They spread a balm of soothing calm
No doctor can prepare.

Quite free to all who heed the call
Supreme in scenic lure,
Their verdant arms out flung with charms
Inviting, safe, secure.
- Fernow Forum, Feb. 1936

Camp Fernow was surrounded by the beautiful Natchaug State Forest. CT CCC Museum

"True CCC"
by Charles W. Lemanski

Who wants mansions? Who wants wealth?
I'm not greedy - I want health!
This wide forest is for me;
That's my life! A CCC.
- Fernow Forum, June 1936

Captain Thompson and the mess hall staff that included cooks, KP (kitchen patrol), and servers. CT CCC Museum

"To Our KPs"
by A. S. Jackson

One moment, please! Did you wash the pots
And pans you used when you cooked our lunch?
Clean and in order for supper time?
Doesn't that sound like a pretty good hunch?
One moment, please! Did you burn the scraps
And cover the grub away from the flies?
The view of a campsite spick and span
Is pleasant, indeed; to a sportsman's eyes.
- Fernow Forum, June 1936

"Vets"
by Ray Tavernier

Six months, a year, a little more,
The "Vets" are leaving, their term is over
They had no work, no job in view,
So they joined the C's like me and you.
But time and tide wait for no man,
And the time to leave is now at hand.

Then from the city and towns,
The "Rookies" come from all around,
Fat and thin, short and tall,

Watch them come, "Rookies" all.
They'll take your place when you are thru,
And do the work you used to do.

This camp to them is a strange land,
So be a sport and lend a hand.
For tho' it's strange and sort of new,
They'll someday be a "Vet" like you.
- In Fernow, Jan. 1939

"Disappointment"
by Salty Peters

When you want to play some pool,
Waiting is the general rule.
You wait around for an hour or two
To find, at least, the game is thru.
You quickly rush up to the table
And grab the stick if you are able,
Only to hear to your dismay,
That it isn't, as yet, your turn to play.
- In Fernow, Jan. 1940

Playing pool was very popular in the camp mess hall.
CT CCC Museum

"Goodbye"
by Ray Tavernier

As the cold north wind is blowing
And the winter months are nigh,
When from this camp you're leaving
To your friends you'll say goodbye.
The time is short, and words are few
As the time has come to say "adieu."
Not goodbye as some will say
For I know we'll meet again some day.
Friends you'll meet and then you'll part

But you'll always be within my heart.
But write a letter now and then
To let me know that we're still friends.
- In Fernow, March 1940

Friends enjoying some down-time together in their barracks at
Camp Fernow. CT CCC Museum

The July 1935 cover of the Fernow Forum

Camp Fernow's Capt. Thompson is saying goodbye to the well-dressed enrollees whose six-month
term is over. They are waiting for a truck to take them home. CCC CT Museum

Harold Mattern, Part II

Harold Mattern is cheerfully sharpening his saw, which is held firmly by the handmade jig. Lee Mattern Salina

Harold Mattern worked at many CCC camps in Connecticut and eventually worked for the Conservation Dept. This is a continuation of Harold Mattern's movement from Camp Graves (Chap. 21) in Union to Camp Fernow.

"In April 1936 I was 21 years old and I left the Union camp because it was closing. They asked me what camp I'd like to go to. Since Camp Fernow in Eastford was about 14 miles from my home and the closest camp, I asked for Eastford.

"Some of the buildings, still exist today like the garage, lumber shed, and the sawmill. It was a steam driven sawmill. Charles Barrington was the sawyer. He was a big guy who liked to chew tobacco. He wore a big cowboy hat.

"One day there was a bad accident in the mill. One log rolled over and flipped. It hit a plank and broke the chin of a foreman named Myron Hadfield.

"My first job was cutting cordwood. I was a leader and I cut logs, too. In camp we had a buzz saw that was driven by a tractor with a belt. It cut the logs into cordwood.

"For my second job I worked to eliminate white pine blister rust. I spread the guys out in a line. We walked through the woods and when we found black currant or gooseberry bushes, we pulled them up and hung them up to dry. The berries were the host for the blister rust. We made sure there were no gooseberries within 900' of the pine trees.

"We had about 20 guys. One guy on each end of the line carried pieces of paper. When the line walked to the end, the end guy left a piece of paper. When we turned around there were pieces of paper that marked where we had covered. We searched for the berries in the spring and summer. It was kind of a monotonous job to do.

"My third job was trying to stop the white pine weevil. It was an insect that laid its eggs on the shoots of the white pine trees. When it hatched out, the white grub ate down and killed the lead shoot and made the tree grow crooked. We used a clipper to cut below the weevil. We placed the cutting in a canvas bag. At the end of the day we burned them up. We did this during June because we wanted to get them at the worm stage.

"Also during the months of March to the middle of May it was the fire season. When there was a fire we were called out.

"Then the tool clerk left for a job with the state highway department. My old superintendent from Camp Graves came to Fernow and he gave me the job of tool clerk.

The sawmill located in Camp Fernow was steam driven. CT CCC Museum

Three Camp Fernow boys taking a break by their stacked cordwood. CT CCC Museum

This is the type of truck that brought the enrollees to Willimantic.
CCC CT Museum

"On the weekends most of the time I came home. I either hitchhiked or one of the foremen went to see his girlfriend at UConn so he gave me a ride. On Sunday night I walked to Storrs and got another ride with another foreman, Clifford Mason. He was in charge of fighting the gypsy moths. He was a graduate of UConn Forestry School.

"The other times I got home by hitchhiking to Willimantic and then got another ride to Storrs.

"When I stayed on the weekends at camp, the Army had trucks that took us to Willimantic on Friday and Saturday nights. We went to the movies that were 10 cents or to dances.

"That is how I met my wife, Virginia James, in Willimantic. It was about 1940. She worked in Woolworths store and later on for Southern New England Telephone Co. I learned that she had been in high school with my brother Kenneth. She also knew a few other people I knew.

"For sports I went to the Y in Willimantic on Wednesdays. We played basketball. It wasn't organized teams just pick-up games. Some guys played on the camp baseball team. They played against other CCC camps.

"Guys did the washing of their laundry but I took my laundry home and my mom washed my clothes.

"I spent my money mostly on movies and food. We got paid at the end of each month.

"I stayed at Fernow for a little over two years. I left in July 1938. I moved to Camp Robinson in East Hartland.

"Later I came back to Camp Fernow and stayed there till May 1941.

"Then I joined the Army and went to Camp Edwards on Cape Cod for training. In December they sent me to Quincy, Mass. to protect the Fall River Shipyard. I stayed

there till Feb. 8, 1942 and they shipped me overseas to Australia. At first they shipped us on a troop train for five days across the US and then by boat to Australia.

"In Australia we set up search lights in Brisbane (eastern coast) and protected the coast. We also shipped stuff on a narrow gauge train to Townsville (northeast coast).

"In 1943 I came home and got married. I got a job as foreman for the state and worked as a skilled tradesman and I did forestry work."

On June 8, 2012 Harold Mattern passed away at his home in Storrs, Conn.

Maynard L. Brown

Maynard L. Brown worked at Camp Fernow and later served in the Army during WWII. Edna Brown

On Sat., May 31, 2008 I met Edna St. Onge Brown at the Putnam Library. She told me that her husband, Maynard L. Brown, was in the CCC camp in Eastford. I later interviewed Edna and her son Maynard.

Edna said, "Maynard joined the CCC to help support his mother. His father left his mother before he was born. Maynard also had a twin sister, Minnie.

"His mother remarried and lived with relatives and did some housework.

"Maynard had to quit school in 7th grade and worked for the town. When you worked for so many hours, you got a slip to get food. The town gave cheese and some other commodities.

"He joined the CCC about 1936 and I was about 16 years old. Maynard came down to my uncle's house in

Putnam to see his half-sister, who was married to my uncle.

"I only remember him telling me that he climbed trees with ropes and spurs."

Maynard [Jr.] added, "My dad showed me how he used to climb trees in the CCC using spikes. I was about 12 years old and I asked him if I could try them but he said, 'Not till you're 21.'

"Dad used to do tree cutting jobs around our town and I used to be his helper sending him things on a rope. He even worked at Gertrude Chandler Warner's home who wrote the famous Boxcar Children books."

Edna continued, "My husband had buddies who lived here in Putnam. They hitchhiked home together.

"He used to walk me around my hometown.

"Then my family moved from Putnam to Attawaugan near Danielson.

"He got out of the CCC and worked on a road crew in Putnam.

"One month before my 19th birthday we decided to elope and get married in South Bridge, Mass. We were all ready to go when my best friend who was going to be my maid of honor said she couldn't go because she was pregnant and very sick. So my father and mother said they'd go and stand up for us. Maynard had a car with a rumble seat and my parents sat back there. They were good sports and even endured some rain on the trip. We were married on July 20, 1940.

"Maynard got a job for Medbury & Trowbridge working on roads.

"In 1944 he got drafted into the Army. He was discharged in May 1946.

"We had two children, Maynard and Paula.

"After the war my husband worked for UConn till he retired.

"My husband died in 1981."

Theodore "Ted" Schulz

Theodore "Ted" Schulz came to my CCC talk at the Voluntown Library on Jan. 29, 2008.

The next day I called him at his home in Preston, Conn. and asked about his life and his time in the CCC.

"I'm 86 years old. I was born in Norwich on July 14, 1922. My father, Theodore, was from Germany. He was a businessman who ran a fish market and later a restaurant. He also put on clambakes. Dad then owned Happyland

Ted Schulz worked at the Eastford CCC Camp. Ted Schulz, Jr.

Dance Hall/Casino. It had a big dance hall with an 8' veranda around three sides, and a dance floor large enough to hold four squares for square dancing. It was located in the Happyland section of Preston on the banks of the Poquetanuck Cove by the drawbridge. Parts of the Happyland casino building were from a building the trolley would stop at that was in the Hallville section of Preston where the senior housing is today.

"My mother, Erna Richter, was also born in Germany. My mother raised a step-daughter, Lucy, from Dad's previous marriage and my mom had two sons, me and Roland.

"My mother got ill and went back to Germany in 1926 with my brother. I lived with my grandparents and sister.

"Then Dad died in 1938 after the terrible hurricane destroyed his business. My grandparents then passed away and I was all by myself to find a job.

"In the fall of 1939 I read about the CCC in the newspaper. I went to the Norwich City Hall and signed up on Oct. 3, 1939. We went to Hartford by bus and then we were trucked to Camp Fernow.

"I was in a new place and I was very unsettled. I had lost my dad and grandparents and I didn't know how I felt.

"Camp was strange at first. It was new. It was integrated, too. I bunked between two Afro-Americans. We got along OK. I was used to it because I had blacks in my high school class.

"At Fernow I made some friends. One of my friends from Preston, George Moran, joined the CCC after me and came to my camp. This made camp a lot more enjoyable.

"First I worked on marking state forest land. We

cleared a 10' swath on the state property border line. We made a firebreak by dragging the brush back about 50' from the border line so that if a fire broke out it wouldn't come on state land.

"My second job was mostly cutting up fallen timber from the '38 hurricane in the Natchaug State Forest.

"Another job is that we got trained in firefighting. Some weekends you had to stay at the camp if there was a danger of fire. I did fight some fires. Some were pretty tough. One time while I was a leader, one of my guys got tied up in a barbed wire fence and it got hectic because the flames were coming close but I finally got him free.

"One time we went to Camp Lonergan in Voluntown to gather white cedars that were growing wild in a swamp. We took them to the Chaplin Nursery and transplanted them.

"Other guys had jobs such as clearing a field where seedlings were growing.

"We also cut up cordwood from the hurricane. We worked in 2-man teams. We sawed up the trees and then used mauls and wedges to split the wood. Each 2-man team had to produce a cord a day and if you were done in the morning you just goofed around. Sometimes you worked all day because wood was scarce. Then local workers hired by the government used teams of horses and sleds to take the wood out.

"Another job I had was boiler fireman at the sawmill and machine shop. I had to keep the boiler stoked by throwing wood in. I then threw a switch to transfer power to either the shop or mill. It was tough if they were sawing and you had to keep the steam up to 100-pound range or the saw would bog down in a log. Charles Barrington, our foreman, was the sawyer.

"Then I got the rank of assistant leader and it gave me $6 more a month and 2 stripes."

I asked Ted if he or anyone else ever got hurt at the camp.

"One fellow was cutting up slab wood with a buzz saw and as he pushed the table forward his 'chopper mittens' (gloves with a cloth inside and leather outside) got caught and he lost his thumb and two fingers. What a blood-curdling yell he gave out. He was taken to the dispensary but I never found out how he made out.

"There weren't any flush toilets, just the old fashioned outhouse with about 12 holes. In the wintertime, they had a garbage can outside the barracks for you to use at night.

"In the evenings we went to the recreation hall and canteen. Another place to go to was the education building where they had photography classes.

"There was also a shop with carpentry tools. I had a deer antler and a skull. I cut out a board and attached the deer to the board and took pieces of paper and glue to form over the skull part.

"I also took school classes because I quit school when I was in my junior year of high school when my father was ill. When Dad died I worked on a farm picking strawberries and melons. I also worked at a poultry farm in Ledyard.

"There was also another building where a lady taught archery and where there were other things that you could make.

"While I was in Camp Fernow I took night classes in machine shop at the Willimantic Vocational School. I learned how to read blueprints, use a micrometer, lathe, drill presses, and a shaper.

Ted Schulz's father owned the Happyland Dance Hall / Casino in Preston. Ted Schulz Jr.

Theodore "Ted" Schulz wearing his uniform at Camp Fernow. Ted Schulz Jr.

Camp Fernow boys with the 2-man saw they used to cut cordwood in the Natchaug State Forest. DEEP

Boys waiting to begin sawing in the 2-man competition at the Eastford Camp. CT CCC Museum

The sawmill where Ted worked as the boiler fireman. DEEP State Parks Archives

Ted Schultz joined the Army during WWII. Ted Schultz Jr.

"On the weekends I walked to the main road and hitchhiked to Willimantic and then down to Norwich. It was easy to catch a bus back to Willimantic and then hitchhike to camp. When I stayed at camp on the weekends I went out to movies in Willimantic with my friends.

"For recreation they had an open camp chopping and sawing contest. I liked the sawing contest using the 2-man crosscut saw. I entered with a friend and we did win.

"The food at camp was good. They trained guys for cooking at Fort Wright. Also, some got on-the-job training.

"On May 28, 1941 I was transferred from Camp Fernow to Camp Filley in Haddam. They made me an assistant to the education advisor. I helped the teacher out because I had a ranking of assistant leader at Camp Fernow. The work wasn't heavy manual stuff like the guys did on the outside but you had to do whatever he told you to do.

"In the evenings I went to a trade school in Middletown. I took classes in machine shop work to fulfill a 200-hour class that I had started in Willimantic. I finally got my certificate after I quit the CCC and took classes in

"In the evening I took classes at camp and I got an award for proficiency in history from the DAR of Willimantic. I went every night to class and I got a certificate. After WWII I took classes for a GED and I used my certificates that I earned in the CCC to get my degree." Ted Schulz Jr.

Norwich.

"After I spent two months in Camp Filley they moved me to Voluntown on July 30, 1941 because Camp Filley was closing. I worked there mostly clearing brush along the forest roads. I was an assistant leader of forestry.

"On Oct. 2, 1941 I was discharged after spending two years in the CCC. If I had been a leader I could have stayed longer. Leaders could stay longer than the two-year limit.

"After the CCC I worked constructing the south yard of the present day Electric Boat Co.

"In 1942 I joined the Army in August, and did training in Camp Hulen, near Palacios, Tex. Then we went to England and Europe. I served with the 273rd Ordnance Maintenance Co. and received a Purple Heart.

"My brother Roland fought in the German Army. Roland became a POW in a Russian camp where he did hard physical work. The Russians sent him home.

"My mother who left the US when she was ill, wrote quite frequently to me from Germany.

"After the death of my mother in 1984 my brother Roland and I were reunited in 1985 and I went through Checkpoint Charlie to meet my brother and his family in what was then East Germany.

"After the war in 1945 I worked in two garages.

"I got married in 1952 to Teresa Teague. We had four children: Tracy, Theodore, Timothy, and Terri.

"Then I worked for Christie Plating Co. for 20 years. I then worked at Capehart Industries, and the SEAT Bus Co."

Ted, when you look back at your time in the CCC what did you learn? I asked.

"I learned how to work and be a good citizen. The CCC offered me a chance to take vocational classes. There

I learned the skills of working in a shop. I learned how to run a lathe. The CCC benefited me when I got a job in an automotive garage where I worked overhauling starters and generators. I liked being in the CCC."

Theodore "Ted" O. Schultz passed away on Dec. 30, 2009 at his home in Preston.

William "Bill" L. Krois

Bill and Agnes Carroll Krois on their wedding day.
Arlene Morrissey

On May 21, 2009 I interviewed 94 year-old William "Bill" L. Krois from his home in North Andover, Mass. by telephone. He told me about his CCC days at Camp Fernow.

"I was in the CCC beginning in April 1934 till the spring of 1936.

"I joined because I had to help my family. My father Max was a farmer in Southern Germany before coming to the US. He came to the US during the Depression. He did whatever he could to help his family survive.

"Dad was married twice. With his first wife he had four children: Mary, Catherine, Frances, and Tecla.

"Then he married my mom, Theresa. They had five children: Max, Joseph, me, George, and Jane.

"Dad died when I was 9 years old. My mom had to struggle to survive. The older kids had to help by getting jobs. I was lucky that I didn't have to quit school and in 1933 I graduated from high school.

"My neighbor Joe told me that he was joining the CCC so I said, 'Let's go.' I had an adventurous spirit and didn't mind going away.

"I signed up in Greenwich, Conn. I went to New Haven by train and then up to Fort Devens, Mass. where I got clothes. Then I was transported by bus to Camp Fernow in Eastford.

"At first I worked on roads and then I worked with a survey crew. I wasn't that enthusiastic about working in camp but I was so happy to help my mother to support the family.

"Then I worked as the assistant to the education advisor, Fran Dillon. I typed letters and helped with programs during the day. Fran was a very nice guy who graduated from college but couldn't get a job.

"The food at camp wasn't like home cooking but we survived. They served pork, roast beef, hot dogs, and cabbage. In the evenings I did a lot of reading. Lights were shut out at 9 pm.

"For sports they were going to build a tennis court but it never got done. I played on a football team and played games in Willimantic.

"On weekends I mostly stayed at camp. I didn't have too much money to go places. A few times I hitchhiked home or went to Willimantic. One time I hitchhiked to Greenwich and a guy tried to proposition me. I told him, 'See my nose? I'm a boxer and a football player and I wouldn't want you to mess with me.' He didn't bother me when I said that.

"I left the CCC because I was able to get a job. My cousin worked for Life Savers and she helped me get a job. I worked as a mail boy in Port Chester. I worked there for a year and a half. I had an idea to get into sales. I asked the vice president and he got me a job in Lynn, Mass. I got a room for $3 a week and got paid $85 a month. I stayed for seven months.

"I played football and got an injured tooth that became abscessed. I went to the boss and said I couldn't work because of the pain.

"Later a sales manager called me and sent me to New Haven. I worked there till I was drafted on April 1, 1941.

"In 1944 I got married to Agnes Carroll. We had three daughters: Carroll, Nancy, and Elizabeth.

"I was in the Army till July 11, 1945. Then I went back to Life Savers but they said I didn't have to come back. Luckily my wife's relative worked for Borden's Co. and they got me an appointment. I became a salesman and stayed there for 35 years.

"The CCC was very educational for me. I learned how to associate with other ways of living and to deal with them. I also developed my interest in reading."

William "Bill" Krois was born on March 10, 1915 and passed away on Friday, May 21, 2010.

Walter Kania

Walter worked as a laborer in the Camp Fernow sawmill and then worked in the boiler room. Walter Kania

Ninety-five year-old Walter Kania told me about his experiences in Camp Fernow in Eastford, Conn. and Meeker, Col. Podskoch

In 2009 Walter Sekula, a former CCC alumni and advocate for the CCC in Conn. and the US, told me his friend, Walter Kania, had a large collection of pictures from his days in Camp Fernow. Finally, in April 2010, Sekula and I drove to a nursing home in Danielson where Kania was a resident. He told me about his life and CCC experiences.

"I'm 95 years old and I was in the CCC for 3½ years. I was born in Southington on Sept. 5, 1915. My father Frank was a tool polisher during the Depression at Pexto Manufacturing. I had five sisters and a brother.

"I graduated from high school. There weren't many jobs available but I was working 10-12 hours a day on a farm. As winter was approaching I needed another job. Then I heard about the CCC. I went to the town hall and asked if I could join. They said no because my parents owned a home. But I was lucky and they let me sign up on Oct. 4, 1934. They sent me to Eastford and Camp Fernow.

"My job was working in the sawmill. We took large green logs and cut them into lumber. It was hard work. The boards were heavy. Then I got moved to the boiler steam room that powered the sawmill.

"When the Flood of 1936 hit, the flood washed out the bridge our camp recently built over the Natchaug River. I asked to go and do flood work at the towns along the Connecticut River but I had to stay and help keep the camp running.

"In 60 days they made me an assistant leader and I got paid $36 a month. After a while they raised me to leader and got paid $45.

"One job I wouldn't sign up for was truck driver because I saw a really bad accident and I swore I'd never drive.

"Our camp had a few Negros. The Army told us there would be no prejudice. I worked with a few of them. They were darn good workers. They were right off the city streets but learned fast how to use a shovel and pick.

"I never went to the infirmary. If you got hurt, you just kept going and let it heal.

"On weekends I played center field on the camp baseball team. Sometimes I hitchhiked home because Southington wasn't too far.

"Since I was a leader I was allowed to stay more than the 2-year limit. After three years at Camp Fernow they asked for volunteers to go out West. I signed up and wound up in Meeker, Col. That is where I met Walter Sekula.

"I worked in the kitchen. We started at 5 or 6 am and then had an hour break till the next meal. I worked three days and then I had a day off. We named the mess sergeant 'Bean Man' because he was Mexican and thought we should have some type of beans with every meal. He drove the enrollees crazy. It got so bad they refused to work till they had more meat and no beans.

"Walter Sekula was one of the three notorious chow hounds. He was the first in the mess hall and last to leave.

"After 6 months I decided I had enough. I was

discharged on Dec. 20, 1938. Walter Sekula and I always traveled together. So when we were discharged we hitched rides on box cars and went to Mexico. We loved the life of a hobo. Then after a few months we came home.

"I had jobs in various shops and my last job was in Jacob's Rubber Shop in Danielson and in Dayville, Conn. We made molded rubber inserts mainly for the automotive industry.

"On Sept. 7, 1940 I married Alice E. Renaud. We had two sons: Charles and Robert.

"I wasn't in WWII because I had a stomach ulcer and part of it and my intestine were removed in the 50s.

"My experience in the CCC was good for me. I learned how to be a good worker and take care of the forest. I also learned how to fight fires."

Then Walter Sekula reminded Kania to show me his CCC photo album. He remembered all the guys' names as if it was yesterday and said I could borrow the album to copy the pictures. I thanked him for sharing his stories and great pictures

Walter Kania passed away in Brooklyn, Conn. on May 8, 2011.

William Nieminen

On Sat. May 31, 2008 I met Barbara Urban at the Putnam Public Library. She told me her father, William Nieminen, worked at Camp Fernow. She didn't have much information on his work there but after securing his CCC discharge papers this is what she learned.

"My father was born on April 28, 1906 in Greenland, Michigan. His family moved to Chaplin, Conn. He graduated from grammar school, attended two years of high school, and attended 1½ years at Ford Trade School. Afterward he worked in the Connecticut forest as a woodsman.

"At the age of 27 he joined the CCC on May 31, 1933 at Fort Wright on Fishers Island, NY. He spent a month at Fort Wright in a reconditioning camp. On June 29 he was transported to the Town of Hampton and Camp Fernow where he worked in the woods. His mother, Aina Rajakka, received the much-needed check of $25 a month that he earned at camp.

"After a year working at Camp Fernow he was honorably discharged on April 16, 1934 because he had found employment.

"My mother shared letters she got from Pat Maher, who was a good friend of my dad at Camp Fernow. Pat was transferred to Camp Triangle in Blachly, Oregon and he wrote the letters from out West."

John J. Collins Jr.

John Collins at his home in Watertown on Sept. 25, 2010.
Podskoch

It was a cold winter day on Jan. 24, 2006 when I traveled to Thomaston to speak at their town library. I was accompanied by my CCC buddy, Walter Sekula from Norwich. He loved to travel with me and share his CCC stories with my audiences. We stopped for a bowl of hot soup at the local diner. The large plate glass diner's windows were frosted over because of the humidity inside and the frigid weather outside.

During the winter Walter (left) went ice skating on a nearby pond with his friend Kornacky. Walter Kania

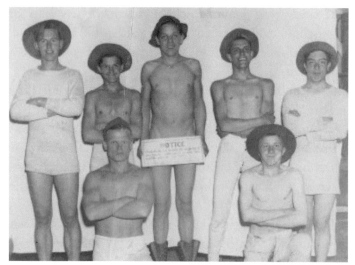

John Collins (Back Row, L) and barracks friends having fun. John Collins

John Collins (Back Row, R) and friends watching a baseball game at Camp Fernow. John Collins

We then went to the Thomaston Library and I was amazed at the number of people who came to share their remembrances of their fathers in the CCC and the history and location of the Thomaston CCC camp.

Then a man in the back slowly stood and said he had been in Camp Fernow. He shared some of his stories but I knew he had a lot more to tell.

Unfortunately, I didn't have his name but I was able to get it from a librarian who knew him. His name was John Collins from Watertown.

On Jan. 27, 2008 I telephoned him and he shared his life story.

"I was born on Oct. 17, 1920 in New Britain. My father John worked for Chase Metal Works in Waterville and we had it tough. I remember wearing cardboard in my shoes.

"I was one of the original dropouts from school. My family moved from Thomaston to Waterville when I was in 9th grade. I got discouraged and dropped out. I tried to get work and I heard about the CCC. My parents signed me up at the age of 17. They told me I had a chance to go to Colorado but I wound up in Eastford in 1938 or 1939.

"The army took me by bus from Waterville to New Haven. There were other guys going with me, too. I didn't know any of them. They took us to the armory in New Haven. They separated us and I went to Eastford. Guys were passing out when they got the needles.

"They took us by bus. They assigned us to a barracks. I was a little homesick but I loved it there. I was a country boy and loved the woods. It was a good life and I was thankful

to be healthy and earning money. The CCC kept me off the street.

"I had a lot of friends. Our barracks leader was Whitey Vasaloff. He was Mr. Clean, a physical culture guy. He lived in Waterbury and often my dad picked me up and brought him home, too.

"One of our jobs was to get rid of dead wood. I loved to hear the twang when I chopped into a dead tree. We cut it up to length and another detail came and hauled it into camp.

"We also planted trees. Sometimes we planted 3,000 trees a day. We used a short handled grub ax. I made a hole and shoved the seedling in and tamped the soil with the grub ax.

"Every morning I was in charge of the flag. At Reveille and Retreat I put up the flag and took it down. It was kept in the headquarters.

"We did a lot of firefighting. When we came back sometimes, there were fire trucks with Indian tanks and fire hoses and pumps. Anyone who volunteered to fight a fire was compensated with an hour off for every hour he worked fighting a fire.

"We went in with axes. I hooked up the hose and had to walk the whole hose to make sure it was OK and free of leaks. Also I had to help keep it from burning. If there weren't any tanker trucks we got water from streams and ponds.

"I do remember the food trucks. They sent good food and they always had apple sauce. We had lemonade in thermos cans (10-15 gallons).

"There were times we had some fun. One day a tree had fallen in an old family cemetery nearby. A kid from Hartford and I were sent by truck to clean up the tree. We were doing good, and I said, 'Holy smokes did you hear that?' He responded, 'No I didn't.' I started moaning and he jumped right off the tree trunk and ran out of the cemetery. I couldn't get him to come back.

"I got involved in camp life. Everything had to be in place in our footlocker. We had inspection every Friday. If you didn't pass you were 'gigged' for the weekend. You couldn't leave camp and had weekend details, such as policing the area.

"One day the cooks promised filet mignon but it turned out to be baloney, but most of the meals were very good. The breakfast with pancakes was my favorite. We also had scrambled eggs.

"During the evenings you could sign up for sports and classes. I played baseball and track. We went to towns like Putnam but something happened and we were run out. We also played other CCC camps. I played center field.

"I signed up for an archery class. We had a woman teacher. We paid $10 for lemonwood to make a bow. She said it was the best. She also taught us how to make arrows. We shot outside. She took us to a small stream and had us dig and look for arrowheads and Indian relics. I found an arrowhead and I still have it.

"Every weekend I hitchhiked home but sometimes Dad picked me up. I was pretty lucky getting rides. I used Rt. 44 and another week I used Rt. 66. I'll never forget this one hot day and I had no rides. Finally, somebody picked me up and took me to the east end of Middletown. He said, 'You look pretty thirsty.' He stopped and went to the back and opened his trunk. There was a trunkload of Pepsi Cola and ice. He gave me one and I was so happy. It quenched my thirst.

"Another time I was going back through East Hartford and when I got to Manchester a well-dressed elderly man stopped and asked me where I was going. I told him I was going to the CCC camp in Eastford. He said, 'Hop in. Can you go for a meal?' I said 'Yes.' He said, 'Well, I have a cottage with some food.'

"At his cabin he cooked me a roast beef dinner. After that he said, 'How about some ice cream?' I said, 'Sure.' So he gave me some and drove me all the way to the CCC camp. In those days people were generous and gave people rides, not like today.

"Then my mother got sick and I asked the captain if I could get stationed at a camp closer to home. So they transferred me to Camp White in Riverton near Winsted. I think it was late August. This was another great camp.

"They first put me to work in the saw room. They taught me how to sharpen saws and axes. I worked with an older CCC guy.

"I wanted to get out into the forest and work and asked for a transfer. They assigned me to work with this guy who hauled wood. We picked up wood with a truck and it was used for fuel.

"After six months I signed up again. In the meantime, I had an uncle who was a foreman in Chase Metal Works and he got me a job. Once you were able to get a job you could ask for a discharge and I was granted one.

"Then in 1942 I was drafted into the Army. The CCC was a great help for me when I was drafted. I was assigned to a barracks and I had experience making beds. The company commander came in and came to my bed. He tossed a coin upon my bed and it bounced up. The commander said to the other guys, 'The next time I come in and toss up a dime, it better bounce up like Collin's did.' Boy, the guys were mad at me.

"In 1945 I went back to Chase Metal Works as a crane operator.

"The next year I married Dorothy Van Buren. We had a boy named Terry and girl Diane.

"I worked at Chase Metal Works for 27½ years. The plant was closing so I quit and worked for the Conn. Highway Dept. for five years. Then I got a job for Army Corps of Engineers on flood control dams on the Naugatuck River. My job was to make sure the gates were operating

John J. Collins of Watertown worked at Camp Fernow in Eastford and Camp White in Winsted. During WWII, he was a medic with Company F, 309th Infantry Regiment, in the 78th Division. Collins received the Bronze Star for valor and two Purple Hearts. John Collins

properly and to keep brush off the rocks of the dam. I also worked on the Northfield Brook Dam and maintained it. I also did plumbing, carpentry, and painting. I retired in 1985.

"When I look at my time in the CCC I can definitely say it was a good life. It got boys like me off the street. It taught us how to live a good life."

John J. Collins Jr., affectionately known as "Father John," died Monday, Aug. 6, 2012.

Zigmund Shuster

Zigmund Shuster served in WWII with Company B, 709th Battalion from Jan. 14, 1943 to April 17, 1946. He was a Corporal with the Military Police and deployed to France on V-Day.
Katherine Hunt

Katherine Hunt of Bridgeport contacted me and said that her father, Zigmund Shuster, had served at two CCC camps: one near Grand Junction, Colorado and the other at Camp Fernow in Eastford. I asked her to interview her father and she called him. This is what Zigmund said about his life and time in the CCC.

"My father, John, had all kinds of jobs. He sold Raleigh Products. He took me once in a while to work. I went with him to Seymour and met Sikorski. I saw the helicopter he invented. Dad knew Russian and spoke to him.

"My mother had four children, Walter, Bruno, me, and Anna. We lived on New St. in Shelton. My mom got a lung disease and was sent to Colorado with a chance to get better. She, however, died. I was just five years old. We were placed in an orphanage for about a year in New Britain. Dad remarried. My step-mother had two children. All of us

kids slept in the attic. She was real good to me.

"When I was in 7th grade I had appendicitis. I missed two weeks of school in June. Luckily, I survived. The school said I had to do the last half over and stay to make it up after school but my dad pulled me out of school. I got a job working in the bowling alley in Ansonia. I got five cents a game setting up pins. I had to work to help my family.

"There were a whole bunch of guys from Shelton who joined the CCC. So I signed up at the Shelton City Hall.

"It was an adventure. I didn't hate it. It was a good life.

"At first I went to a camp in Colorado outside Grand Junction. Army trucks picked us up at the railroad station. It was very cold. The driver said the camp was just around the corner. The wind was blowing hard and it was blowing snow under the canvas. Fifty miles later we got to camp.

"In camp there were four buildings where the guys slept. They had three stoves inside each barrack. One guy had to keep the stoves going day and night.

"The bathroom was a galvanized 50-gallon barrel outside the door to take a leak at night.

"When we first got there we went for a ride and visited Indians in a tepee. They charged $3 to look around. They also sold axes that they made out of stones and metals.

"My first job I built a road. We used to go up a mountain and smash rocks. They were about 5' high and 12' wide. Then we'd roll the pieces down the mountain. I later saw a pile of smaller rocks by a miner's claim. These rocks were a lot easier to move. We rolled these stones down the mountain. They were loaded onto trucks and taken to build a road.

"Another job I did was cutting trees. When we cut trees some guys had axes and some had saws. They cut the wood in 4' lengths and sold the wood.

"Our days were regimented. We had to get up at a certain time, work all day, and come back to camp after work. The When the bugler called we lined up according to height. One guy was 6' 11". Then the bugler blew the horn, the 2nd Lt. turned toward the flag and we all saluted the flag. Then he said, 'Dismissed.' He left and we went to our barracks to get ready for supper. We had to put on our old WWI uniform for dinner.

"One time I turned around and I lost my eyesight. Then I heard a humming sound and passed out. I fell down just as they were lowering the flag. Somebody lifted me up and told me to go to the doctor, who, gave me salt tablets. After that they passed salt tablets every morning.

"In the evening there were classes if we wanted to take them and sports.

"Some guys went half a mile to visit some women and the guys came down with VD. Once a month we had to take off our clothes and wear raincoats while the doctor examined us. He gave penicillin shots if we needed them. One guy had syphilis and he went crazy with the news. He had to go to the infirmary for treatment and he calmed down.

"The food we got in the mess hall was good and there was plenty of it. After supper was our free time. One time after supper a guy showed me how to throw a knife. I enjoyed doing that. They had a baseball team that played other teams. When it was warm we swam in the river.

"I remember going to see my brother, Bruno, who was in another camp in Colorado near a river. My brother was a cook and he cooked for me.

"After six months I went back to Connecticut and was sent to Camp Fernow. They taught us how to sharpen axes and how to use a saw. We worked mostly in the woods. I worked there for six months and came home.

"I worked in a basket shop for about a week and a half but I just couldn't get how to do it.

"Then I was drafted into WWII. I went to Paris about three days after it was liberated. I was a military policeman.

"After the war ended we were transferred to Germany. It was a terrible mess from the bombing. Women were picking up bricks and taking them in wheelbarrows.

"When I was discharged I came home. I took up plumbing under the GI Bill. I worked for Ralph Mann & Sons.

"When I was 25 years old I eloped with my girlfriend Katherine. We had two children: Zigmund and Katherine.

"The CCC was good for me because I got to travel and

I learned how to work hard."

At a CCC Reunion at Rocky Neck in 1986 where 2,200 CCC members and guests attended a picnic, Zigmund Shuster, a leader at Camp Fernow, described in a Sept. 8, 1986 newspaper article in the Chronicle what happened during the 1938 Hurricane: "We were in the barracks and, I tell you, most of us were scared. I made the men huddle close to the front door so if the roof caved in we'd be able to get out. A big piece of equipment was blown sky-high and landed on the barracks roof. Some guys panicked and tried to get out the door. Some of us formed a barrier to prevent this. Pieces of that equipment fell around the front. If we'd let anybody out, chances are they'd have been killed. As it was, the camp took a beating and we had a big cleanup right there in camp.

"I loved being close to Willimantic where I saw the movie 'Rose Marie' (Nelson Eddy and Jeannette MacDonald) at that theater on Main St. (The Capitol). We'd try to catch the movie bus that was going back to camp. Yep, I made liberty in Willimantic, the Thread Capital of the World.

"I knew of parents who were offering a dowry for their two daughters whom they wanted to see married off. They hoped a young man in the CCC would marry them.

"We were in the nicest camp of them all, there in the Natchaug Forest. It was located in Eastford but we got our mail in Hampton.

"The CCC was good for me because I got to travel and I learned how to work hard."

Zigmund Schuster died on March 9, 2013.

Walter McVety

On Oct 4, 2014 I interviewed Walter McVety by phone and he told me about himself and his family:

"I was born on Nov. 25, 1918. My father never stood out in any way, just a regular joe, He was raised in St. Francis orphan asylum. He was let out at the age of 14 and became a teamster in New Haven.

"My mother, Christine Middlebrook, had three children by her first husband named Race. Their names were: Pliny, Stella, and William Race They were well grown up by the time we came along on her second marriage to Henry McVety. They had three children: Joseph, me, and Jeanette who was the youngest.

"After one year in high school I dropped out at the age

These Camp Fernow boys are posing outside Barracks No. 1 in 1939.
Gary Potter

Walter McVety worked at Camp Fernow.
www.legacy.com

of 16 to get work to help my family. We didn't have enough to eat in the Depression. Potatoes were five cents for a peck. I'd ask the butcher for some bones for our dog and my mom boiled them and made stew. I'd go to the vegetable stands and get the boxes for firewood. Sometimes I found some cabbage leaves and a half rotten tomato and mom used it for stew. I went to a department store and did the running for the driver and he'd give me 50 cents at the end of the day. We were registered with the Social Dept. and my mom got so much for each kid. We got a ticket for the grocery store and traded it for food. It was difficult and took its toll on my mother."

Q: How did you learn about the CCC?

A: "The CCC was the thing of the times. Maybe my mother heard about it. I lied about my age. I signed up in the spring of 1936 at the Orange Street Armory in New Haven. Then a bus took us to Camp Fernow.

"My older brother, Joe, was in Camp Hadley in Madison. Our friend, David Dunn, was in Camp Roosevelt. My brother stayed in for a couple hitches and then signed up for the Army."

How did you feel about leaving home?

"I was sad to leave home. I came home every chance I had. At 4 pm on Friday when the week was done I'd hitchhike home. I went on Rt. 6 to Middletown and then home.

"We slept in a barracks and had a 'ditty box', a safe box, for your clothes. Sometimes we used two boxes to play cards on in our free time in the barracks."

Q: Do you remember any of the guys in camp?

A: "I remember one big black guy. He was a nuisance when he got drunk. One time he came through the barracks screaming and tore all the pipes down. We rushed to fix them up. We were up till 2 am using a flashlight to put up the pipes. I also remember an officer named Sgt. Monroe."

Q: What were some of your jobs?

A: "At that time there was a scourge in the forest called gypsy moths. They had guys who climbed up the trees and had special climbing shoes. When they found the egg masses they painted them with creosote. I serviced the climber using a rope.

"If there was a forest fire and I worked on that, I got three days off. I fought a fire once and carried an Indian tank. I was just a skinny guy, about 98 pounds, but I did carry my weight. I think the fire was over by Norwich.

"I remember working on casting a cement flat area to be used for garbage cans. I had a wheelbarrow full of cement but I spilled the whole load full of cement in the wrong form and Sgt. Monroe got mad as hell.

"I can't say I enjoyed the full time I was there even though I liked the food. We had some fun playing tricks on each other."

Q: What did you do in camp in the evenings?

A: "In the evenings I read or listened to the radio. I wasn't good at sports. I was born blind in one eye, had rickets, and my chest was deformed. On weekends they had dances in Willimantic but I never went to Willimantic.

"I can remember walking up to the camp and guys said you have to watch out for the bobcats that come out of the mountains. I was a scared of walking around."

Q: Why did you leave the CCC?

A: "I left because I didn't like it. I went home and I got a job as a dishwasher at the Oasis Restaurant in Orange on the Milford Turnpike. The restaurant closed in winter so I got a job with the WPA. I had a pick and shovel job. I worked with a mason putting gutters in the street. They made them out of red brick. Then I went to Spring Side Home. It was at the foot of a hill. At Potter Field we leveled out the land for more graves.

"I was drafted into the Army during WWII. I went to Ft. Devens and was discharged because of my eye.

"Then I went to National Folding Box Co. I did piece work. I bundled boxes and tied them up.

"I got married on June 27, 1943 to Ruth Andrews. We had three children: Kathy, Walter Jr., and Robert. Two of my children died. You just have to pound the pavement and keep going.

"I had a chance to go into maintenance work but my boss wouldn't release me. I left anyway and I got a job as a mechanic at Connecticut Bus Co. I needed a Public Service license, even though I wasn't driving passengers. They gave me a test with a patch over my good eye, and I looked under the patch and cheated. I got the job.

"After 14 years I got a job with Armstrong Rubber Co. and worked as a mechanic for 17 years. They closed and I got a job repairing washing machines called 'Kleen-O-Matic'. I worked there for 26 years. I retired at 89. Even after retiring I went over on Saturday and Sunday and repaired machines."

Q: What effect did the CCC have on you?

A: "The CCC gave me a chance to make money to help my family."

On Sept. 16, 2014 Walter McVety passed away.

Louis Tomasiello

Louis Tomasiello of Waterbury joined the CCC and did forestry projects in the Natchaug State Forest in Eastford. Later he became the Supervisor of Waterbury Parks Dept. Podskoch

When I interviewed Colorado CCC alumni Joe Iadarola of Watertown, he said his son's father-in-law, Louis Tomasiello, had also been in the CCC, too. I then called Louis and arranged for an interview at his home in Waterbury.

On Oct. 13, 2008 I visited Louis Tomasiello at his home on Travse Street. The house and yard were well maintained and groomed. I later learned that his grounds reflected his CCC experience and his last job working for

A CCC fire-fighting team ready to put out a forest fire with Indian Tanks on their backs. Gary Potter

the City of Waterbury.

As Louis and I sat in his living room he told me that he was born in San Lupo near Naples, Italy on March 11, 1923. His parents Adiego "Diego" and Anne Santopietro moved to the US while Louis was still an infant.

His father got a job as a tool setter at Chase Brass & Copper Mfg. Co. in Waterbury, but the plant was working only three days a week so they were poor. Louis was the oldest of six children, followed by Diego, Annette, Joe, Vicky, and Ann.

He said, "Since I was the eldest I had to help my family. I quit school after 8th grade. I worked as a pin boy at a bowling alley. There weren't machines to set the pins. Boys were paid for each game.

"My friend joined the CCC and went to Colorado and that is how I found out about the CCC. I was 16 years old and joined in the spring of 1939. I was the only one from Waterbury and signed up at the town hall.

"They took me to Eastford. When I got there they were just fixing the river banks and the bridge that had been washed away.

"Then I was a rack truck driver and I drove without a license. I drove the boys to work and worked right along with them. Sometimes they brought us lunches and if we were close to camp I'd drive them back to camp. The food was great. I didn't have to do KP duty when I was a truck driver. They took my name off the list.

"The trucks were kept in a garage. The garage had one mechanic and one or two guys working with him.

"All the truck drivers had to park their trucks in such a way that they could be removed quickly in case the garage was on fire. I had to back my truck into the garage and release the brake. I attached a rope with a hook to the bumper so if there was a fire we could pull the trucks outside by hand.

"After we started working on roads I began driving a bulldozer. The forester taught me how to run it. I also drove the truck.

115

"In the spring we planted trees. I had a bag of seedlings and a grub hoe. They were mostly spruce and white pine trees.

"Sometimes we manned the steel fire tower near Pomfret. There were two guys up there. They had a map table and if you had a fire you'd call another tower and use triangulation to locate the fire.

"In the evenings they had classes for us. Some classes were held in the carpenter workshop that had a table and band saw. That's where I learned carpentry so I was able to build my own house 52 years ago.

"I also went two nights a week to a trade school in Willimantic and learned how to use a lathe, miller, and a shaver.

"On some evenings we played baseball with friends. There wasn't a place to play basketball.

"Sometimes on the weekends I'd hitchhike home. I had to wait till Saturday so I wouldn't be hitchhiking on the road Friday night. I took Rt. 66 to Middletown. If I stayed at camp, the Army took the guys to Willimantic to the movies or dances.

"After about a year and a half at Camp Fernow, I figured it was time to come home and get a job. I left in 1941 and took a job as a tree surgeon clearing lines for Conn. Light Power and Telephone Company.

"Then I was drafted in the Army in 1942. I went to England, Scotland, and Wales. Ten days after the invasion I went over to Normandy. I was in communications and laid wire from the command post to the artillery. My commander was General Patton.

"When I came home from WWII, I married Marie Filippilli on Nov. 28, 1946, Thanksgiving Day. We had three daughters: Phyllis, Linda, and Nancy.

"At first I did trimming trees. Then I began working for the Waterbury Park Dept. where I ran the greenhouse and nursery. After working there for 20 years I took a civil service test and I became superintendent of parks. We had about 30 parks and 15 were large parks. I loved that job. After 40 years of service for the Parks and Recreation Dept. for the City of Waterbury, I retired in 1985. I then did some carpentry.

"I went back to Camp Fernow when I came back from the war and the barracks were still there. The CCC gave me a deep love of the forest and trees. I then chose the job of caring for the trees of Waterbury. I just loved that job."

On May 1, 2010 Louis Tomasiello passed away.

Milton Arnold

Milton Arnold's high school graduation photo.
Joan Hageman

While I was a member of the Colchester Land Trust our secretary, Joan Hageman told me her that her father, Milton Arnold, was 96, and had worked in the CCC. I had

(L–R) 1 "They gave me different jobs. My first job was cutting cord wood in 4' lengths and leaving it to season. When it was needed they went out for it and used it for heating the barracks. We cut the wood with 2-man saws. The barracks were just north of the sawmill." CT CCC Museum 2 A bulldozer working behind Barracks No. 5. Gary Potter 3 Today, Camp Fernow's garage is used by the Conn. DEEP. Podskoch

just started working on an Adirondack CCC book and I figured that it would be a good idea to interview him in case I ever did a Connecticut CCC book. She arranged an interview with her dad on Nov. 28, 2006.

I drove past the Comstock Covered Bridge that went over the Salmon River up a dead-end road and found the large colonial home where Milton lived. I was invited in by Milton's son Jon and we sat in the large living room and began the interview.

Milton told me he was born on Oct. 18, 1910 on Edgerton Street in East Hampton. His father was a pattern maker for the N. N. Hill Co. where he designed patterns for toys. Milton had a brother, Norman, who was a professor of biology at Dartmouth.

I asked Milton how he came to work for the CCC.

"After graduating from UConn in forestry and biology, I needed a job. There was a big demand for men to work at the newly formed CCC camps in Connecticut. When I was in college I worked in the summer in Colorado inventorying land and forests. This experience helped me get a job as forester and foreman at Camp Fernow in Eastford. I had from 30-50 men working under me depending on what we were doing.

"I had to buy a Model T Ford to get there. There was only a dirt road to camp. There were two large Army Hospital tents in a large field. The tents held about 50 kids in each. They had canvas cots to sleep on. The boys had WWI Army mess kits. There were Army officers in charge and one Marine.

"The first night the officers and I were in a wall tent. A heavy rain blew the tent down and broke it in half. I guess we went into another small building for cover.

"The next day we had to build mess tables and put up more tents. They did a lot of work to build up the camp.

"They built a wood floor for the hospital tent. The tents had Sibley wood stoves. The stovepipe went up the center of the tent.

"There was a separate tent for cooking. The food was adequate, but the breakfasts were really good. The officers ate in an overhang tent, the foremen ate by themselves. The boys sat on the ground with their mess kits.

"There were 200 boys so they needed at least four big tents.

"The camp doctor had a small hospital tent.

"We did not have trucks for the first two weeks. We used an old barn to store our tools. There were crosscut saws, crowbars, shovels, and axes.

"I was assigned one crew of boys to chop wood.

"I think it was in July that we started our work projects. One of the first jobs of the foresters and foreman was to enhance the population of the trees in the forest by removing the poor trees.

"By the Fall a wooden main building for the officers was finished. Then the barracks were completed. They also built a large garage for the trucks.

"On Sept. 29, 1935 I married Joyce Brown who was my high school sweetheart. We met on the Air Line train that we took to high school in Middletown since East Hampton didn't have a high school.

"When we graduated I went to UConn and Joyce went to the University of Vermont. She got out in 1931 and worked in her family's fish and line mill on the Salmon River. That mill went out of business when a flood knocked out the dam that made the mill's power.

"The first winter was tough at Camp Fernow. We had a lot of snow. We cut dead and live trees for wood. At first we didn't have teams of horses to haul the wood out. Then they hired an Indian who had a team and he hauled the logs out.

"In the spring of 1934 we got more trucks, a tractor, and equipment to build roads. The tractor helped to haul wood out of the woods on a sled.

"My next job was to enhance the Natchaug River for trout fishing. I had to direct the flow of the river to make deep holes for the benefit of fish.

"Harold Mattern, who worked many years in the CCC and later for the Conservation Dept., came to our camp and took charge of the tools. If you needed a tool you asked him. He had a large sharpening tool in the sawmill.

"The job that kept me working the longest was mapping the trees in the Natchaug State Forest. I had a survey crew that located the boundaries and cut out a 20' wide strip around the state border and put up signs on the border.

"I surveyed the timber in the forest, the types of trees, and the amount of board feet. My crew and I walked through swamps and old fields. We mapped the land and forests in mile squares. We also made maps of all the roads and timber growth.

"After a few years at Fernow I was sent to Camp Filley in Haddam in about 1936 and worked in the Cockaponset State Forest. I did a lot of mapping there.

"We got a new shipment of enrollees who were mostly

This hole was dug for a telephone pole. CT CCC Museum

Milton Arnold is bracing a tree to two other trees. Joan Hageman

Milt Arnold taught his CCC boys how to survey. Here is a crew in the Mohawk SF. Elizabeth Germaine

from New York City. We had to show them how to cut and saw trees. Some of the forest had been burned or cut down and used for firewood. The boys burned the dead trees.

"Every spring we got seedlings from nurseries. One guy did the whole job of planting. He used a mattock to make the hole, then he placed the seedling in the hole and 'heeled' it in by kicking his boot heel back hard against the hole to straighten the seedling and set it tight. We planted white pine, spruce, white spruce, and larch. Scotch pines grew in dry spots.

"After a while I went to the Mohawk State Forest with another guy named Dick Florian. We inventoried all the timber. I wasn't there long and then went to the Housatonic State Forest.

"At this forest I left my home in East Hampton at 4 am on Wednesdays and worked for five days, including the weekends. When I got there I loaded the kids in a pickup truck. We climbed up Canaan Mt. It was snowy. Some places we had to lower kids over ledges to do measurements. I had a board where I wrote it all down. We ran lines of men 500 feet apart. We recorded streams, fences, and the types of trees in each quadrant area. To get the age of the trees we used a drill bit to get core samples.

"My next camp was at Shenipsit State Forest in Stafford Springs. I started taking down buildings in Camp Graves, which had been closed in Union, Conn. As I was removing

nails in a 3' long board, a piece of wood went through my arm. I went to the local hospital to get it removed.

"In 1938 I was in Camp Lonergan in Voluntown. Here I was a forestry foreman. I was in charge of thinning a cedar swamp. Other crews were working on roads while others were doing blister rust control work.

"Then the 1938 Hurricane struck. I was in the woods. It was very windy and sections of buildings were flying. Danny Devine was building a dam and a tree fell on him. We had a hard time getting him out of there. We went out with bucksaws and cleared the roads in eastern Connecticut. The whole camp was out working except the cooks.

"I stayed at this camp until I had to go for a physical for my eye. By that time I had three kids at home. I moved my family to Litchfield. There I worked for the State Fish and Game Dept. doing projects to provide better habitat for wildlife. We built farm ponds from 1-50 acres in size on state land. In 1972 I retired."

On Nov. 7, 2010 Milton Arnold died at age 100.

Charles Gould

Charles Gould, a resident of Jerome Ave. in Bristol and a CCC veteran of Camp Eastford, was interviewed by Gustav Sporn in a Sept. 6, 1986 issue in the Bristol Press. Gould attended a CCC Reunion at Rocky Neck in 1986 where 2,200 CCC members and guests attended a picnic. Gould put his experience in perspective when he said, "We got a dollar a day but we had $10 worth of fun."

He recounted an incident that happened one night when a group of recruits who came from reformatories in Cheshire and Meriden started badgering a 6' 4" Negro enrollee from Hartford. A fight ensued and three of the tormentors were, according to Gould, "Laid out."

That night the troublemakers were confined to their tent and guarded by enrollees with baseball bats. In the morning the men were shipped back to their reformatories.

Gould shared a tent with seven other boys, six of whom were from Bristol. He said, "From that day on, everyone at camp got along just as if they were brothers."

Gould was a truck driver in camp where enrollees built roads, bridges, cleared brooks, and planted trees. He was at Eastford from June to Sept. 1933. He concluded, "We had good shoes and plenty to eat. For many CCC boys it was the first time for both."

CHAPTER 10
EAST HAMPTON / SALMON RIVER STATE PARK

HISTORY

On June 4, 1935 Lt. Lorenz led a group of 23 CCC enrollees from Camp Walcott in Burrville to form Camp Stuart S-70 along the Salmon River in East Hampton. The young men pitched their tents in an open field that later became the baseball field. The men worked on the entrance to the camp and prepared the way for more enrollees and officials who came during June and July. The new group of men was classified as Company 1194.[1]

Dr. Ornstein, the medical doctor, arrived on June 6th. He was followed by 1st Lt. A. E. Baldwin, Lt. H. D. Holt, and Lt. H. J. Kropper, who became the commanding officer.[3]

More tents were pitched to accommodate the 160 enrollees. Over the next three months a mess hall/kitchen, five barracks, an infirmary, a garage, an education building, shower/toilet, and officers' quarters were constructed. The men moved to wooden barracks by the first of September.[4]

A well driller was hired to find water. When he hit water it gushed out with such force and volume it flooded the campsite. Today this artesian well continues to flow and many people get water at the park's two water pipes.[5]

On Oct. 14, 1935 1st Lt. Kropper resigned and 2nd Lt. John C. Vaughn from Camp Walcott in Burrville, assumed command. A smoker was held for Kropper and he was given a Gladstone traveling bag, a pipe, and a tobacco pouch from members of Co. 1194.[6]

The Education Director of Camp Stuart was Frank Romeo. He went to Springfield College and earned his masters degree in education. He had many teaching experiences ranging from camp counselor in Maine, Army instructor in WWII, and teacher in high schools. He began work in Aug. 1935.

For the fall he offered 25 different classes and activities such as Forestry, Woodworking, Radio, Electricity, Typing, Dramatics, Orchestra, Glee Club, Auto Mechanics, Truck Driving, Journalism, Writing, Drawing, Cooking, Leather Craft, Harmonica Band, Camp Orchestra, Auto Mechanics, Truck Driving, Electrical Club, etc.[7]

The Players Club was very active producing plays and presenting them at the camp and many public organizations. On Oct. 11th they presented a play at the American Legion Hall. They also did a program for the residents of Colchester at Day Hall that benefited the Bacon Academy junior and senior trip to Washington.[8]

In November, the Players Club practiced at the North Westchester Congregational Church Social Room. They then performed for an audience that included residents of North Westchester, Westchester, and company enrollees.[9]

The Players continued their programs during December at these venues: Congregational Church in Hebron, Nathan Hale High School in Moodus, and the Christmas Party at the company mess hall on Dec. 19th.[10]

On Nov. 14, 1935 Captain Charles H. Rohrbach assumed command of Camp Stuart. He had previously commanded Camp Chapman in Niantic. Born in 1895 in Bridgeport, he graduated from Yale, and attended M. I. T.

Robert Y. Stuart

The camp was named to honor Robert Y. Stuart (1883-1933) who was a graduate of Yale School of Forestry. He worked for the US Forest Service under Governor Gifford Pinchot in Pennsylvania, where he bought more State forest lands, established fire lookouts and a started a Forest nursery.

Stuart returned to the US Forest Service in 1927 where he promoted forest research and tree planting in the National Forests. Before President Roosevelt took office in 1933, Stuart had outlined a plan to complete the National Forest. He also had a long list of projects and plans for the CCC camps to complete. Stuart fell from his 7th floor office and died in 1933.[2]

www.foresthistory.org

Camp Stuart was established in the Salmon River Forest in East Hampton. Walt Olson & Chatham Historical Society

CCC boys working on the Camp Stuart road and pathways. Walt Olson & Chatham Historical Society

Camp Stuart road by one of the five barracks. The buildings were covered with tarpaper. The roof had ladders to help clean the three metal chimneys. Walt Olson & Chatham Historical Society

This is the site of the artesian well that was drilled behind Camp Stuart in 1935 to supply the CCC camp. Today it continues to supply visitors to the Salmon River State Forest with fresh water. Podskoch

Two of Camp Stuart's cooks and mess sergeant outside the mess hall. CT CCC Museum

and Cornell Aviation School. After participating in WWI he worked as comptroller at Remington Arms. In 1933 he worked at CCC camps at Squantz Pond and Chapman.[11]

Towards the end of 1935 Mr. Pelletier and his crew built a diversion dam on the Salmon River that became a great swimming pool in the summer. He also constructed a flight of steps down the bank of the river to aid fisherman.[12]

In December, an East Hampton resident donated a siren that was placed below the peak of the Headquarters' Building. If a fire was called in or found there was a button for someone to push to sound the alarm.[13]

Recreation activities were popular in the winter. The basketball team went by truck to practice in Colchester. In January the team played a game at Park Hall in Colchester and a dance followed. A hockey rink was built at camp and four lights were installed for night skating but the weather was too warm and ping-pong and basketball were popular.[14]

In Feb. 1936, the weather got colder for skating and it snowed quite heavily. Skiing was also popular with the many nearby hills to ski down.[15]

Camp Stuart's first major project was the restoration of the Comstock Covered Bridge in 1935. It was originally built about 1771 and had been rebuilt in 1863. The bridge

crossed over the Salmon River and was the main route (Rt. 16) of travel from Colchester to Middletown. It was not till 1932 that the state built the new concrete bridge downstream. In Nov. 1935 Raymond Shappoll assisted Mr. Noble in working on the Comstock Bridge.[16] The CCC enrollees replaced the old siding with boards from a nearby barn and installed doors to prevent vehicular traffic.[17]

The first snowstorm of the year hit Camp Stuart on Sunday, Jan. 19, 1936. There were many vacancies for breakfast and many AWOLs because of the storm. Many weren't able to make it back to camp from their weekend trip to their home on Monday morning for roll call because of the poor road conditions. Fortunately the Colchester Town snowplow cleared the roads in and about camp.[18]

During December enrollees renovated the Comstock Bridge School. Two enrollees installed electrical equipment and the Players Club provided the funding for the project. The Players Club, boxing team, and dancing classes used the main room. A small adjoining room was used as a woodworking shop. Capt. Charles H. Rohrbach loaned the shop the following equipment: lathe, jigsaw, buffer, sander, and crosscut saw. The hallway was set aside for the Radio and Electrical Club.[19]

In Jan. 1936 these courses were available from the Education Dept: Typing, Radio, Forestry, Mechanics, Dancing, Hygiene, Mathematics, Boxing, Basketball, Photography, Carpentry, Woodcraft, Gen. Science, English, Psychology, Grammar, Dramatics, Tree Surgery, and Forum (Current Events). Each week Camp surgeon Dr. Ornstein gave interesting health lectures covering topics such as: surgical shock, medical instruments, surgery, bandaging, fractures, Red Cross First Aid certification, etc.[20]

Besides keeping the enrollees physically fit and helping with illnesses, Dr. Ornstein made sure the Mess Hall was in A-1 condition. He made bimonthly examinations of the food handlers and daily examined the kitchen, latrine, washrooms, and barracks. Garbage was removed every day from camp and the grease trap was skimmed regularly. Water and milk were tested monthly by the Dept. of Health.[21]

The Jan. 1936 issue of the Camp Stuart Courier reported that the artesian well recently drilled was tested by the Health Dept., which gave their approval. The Leaders Club held monthly meetings at Sammy's Diner in Colchester. Camp supervisors spoke at the Jan. 1936 dinner. This was followed by a dinner and dance. The Colchester Girls Club came and served as dance partners.[22]

Camp Stuart enrollees attended local church services and had an Army Chaplin, Capt. William B. Johnson, stationed at the camp. Priests and ministers also visited the camp for religious talks. Father Hinchey of East Hampton was honored with a smoker on Feb. 4, 1936. Also during that month Rev. C. H. Fields of the East Hampton Congregational Church gave a slide lecture entitled, "Nature and God."[23]

The Players' Club presented a play and dance on Feb.

During the 1930s Camp Stuart enrollees helped restore the Comstock Bridge that for over 100 years was the principal means of crossing the Salmon River. It was restored again by the state in 2012. DEEP State Parks Archives

26th at the East Hampton American Legion. The East Hampton Orchestra provided music along with the Camp Stuart Harmonica Band. At night the camp had an M. P. who patrolled the camp to guard against prowlers. The patrol was given a powerful lamp purchased using camp funds.[24]

The Stuart Camp newspaper was renamed in May and was called the Stuart Gusher after the new artesian well. When the driller hit water it was a gusher that was so strong it flooded the campground.

During the month of March 1936 Camp Stuart was quarantined for a time due to scarlet fever.[25]

During the spring of 1936 enrollees turned to new forms of recreation. The horseshoe courts became popular along with baseball. The pool tables were still popular and trips to the movie theaters in Colchester and East Hampton were a big favorite. The theaters' owner, Mr. Alpert, was generous in reducing the tickets from 35 cents to 20 cents to the CCC boys.[26]

During the summer inter-barracks volleyball and softball leagues were formed. A boxing ring was built and Mr. Bride of East Hampton instructed the boys. In September lights were added to the ring.[27]

Football was the new sport that was inaugurated in the fall of 1936. The new coaches were Messrs. Bissell, Heatley, Pelletier, and McAvoy. The following schools donated football equipment to the team: Trinity College in Hartford, Taft School of Watertown, Choate Prep of Wallingford, Kingswood School of Hartford, and Roxbury Prep of Cheshire. On Oct. 16th, 25 enrollees traveled to Middletown to watch a Wesleyan football game. The following weekend 25 enrollees watched a Trinity College game.[28]

The Stuart football team lost its first two football games. On October 31 a much stronger and experienced Camp Lonergan team crushed them by the score of 39-0 at a field in Norwich. Camp Stuart guard, Joe Nowakowski suffered a broken elbow and was taken to the Fort Wright Hospital. The next game in East Hampton was against the New London Supply Depot team. Camp Stuart lost 0-7.[29]

After the football season enrollees began practicing basketball on a new court at camp. Practice also began in November for the Camp team that was coached by J. S. Bissell who was a star player at Trinity College.[30]

A WPA Vaudeville show from Bridgeport entertained enrollees on Monday, Oct. 5, 1936. They performed 12 acts

Camp Stuart enrollees did projects to improve the Salmon and Blackledge rivers. To the right of the river are logs built into the river bank to prevent erosion. DEEP State Parks Archives

Local historian Dean Markham seated on one of the logs placed by the CCC enrollees on the bank of the Salmon River. The steel rods holding the logs are still in place. Podskoch

CCC enrollees completed this beautiful stone and cement dam that created Day Pond. DEEP State Parks Archives

that were enjoyed by the boys.[31]

Education Advisor J. S. Bissell offered 37 classes and activities for the Camp Stuart boys. Besides the classes that were offered in the past these were the new offerings: Landscaping, Handicrafts, Concrete Construction, Photography, Vocational Guidance, CCC Administration, and Educational Films. Classes were held in these locations: Comstock School House, Mess Hall, Officers Mess Hall, Blacksmith Shop, Rec. Hall, Legion Hall (basketball), Garage, and Dark Room. Some classes and activities were also held on the weekend. The foremen, foresters, and Army officers, Capt. Rohrbach and Dr. Ornstein, taught classes.[32]

An added entertainment to the camp was added in Nov. 1936. The enrollees chose to have movies shown each Wednesday nights. The camp made a contract with Films Inc. and enrollees agreed to pay 40 cents each month.[33]

The November 1936 issue of the Stuart Gusher newspaper reported enrollees searched for a lost hunter in the woods near Marlborough on Nov. 18th but no mention if he was found.

Enrollees continued to be involved with local residents. In November eight enrollees participated in a minstrel show with the East Hampton 4-H Club. Miss Beckwith, principal of the East Hampton Grammar School, directed it. She also taught an English Class to enrollees at camp.[34]

The following is a record of attendance for the education classes in December 1936. English - 6, Machine Operation - 15, Forest Protection - 22, Journalism - 15, Road, Trails, and Structures - 16, Forest Improvement & Use - 9, General Conservation - 7, Tree Identification & Nature Study - 13, Mess School - 12, Office Relations - 5,

Photography - 16, Saw Filing - 5, Supply Management - 2, Surveying - 5, Typing - 22, Arts & Crafts - 14, First Aid - 20, Music - 1, Basketball - 16.[35]

The February 1937 issue of the Stuart Gusher reported these speaking guests at camp. Fred Stone, Athletic Director of Weaver High School in Hartford, gave a talk on his visit to the 1936 Olympics in Germany. He emphasized the value of clean living, sportsmanship, and the use of leisure time. Then F. W. Putnam, a representative of the Refrigeration and Air Conditioning Training Corp. in Youngstown, Ohio, talked about the value of good character, a good record, and the future of a career in refrigeration and air conditioning. Finally, P. L. Newton from Fox's Dept. Store photography department showed a 16 mm sound film on "Skiing" that showed the fundamentals and excitement of the sport.[36]

Another project that Camp Stuart performed was stream improvement work on the Salmon and Blackledge rivers. The latter flows into the Salmon River. The

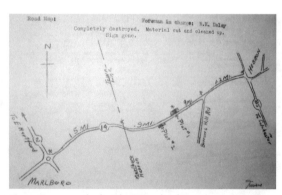

Camp Stuart worked with private land owners to show them how to clear the land and plant seedlings. These were called demonstration plots and foreman Daley supervised two in Hebron on present day Rt. 66. CFPA Library

Enrollees cutting wood with a buzz saw at Camp Stuart. Walt Olson & Chatham Historical Society

These enrollees are taking a break from trimming brush and moving rocks while building trails in the Salmon River State Forest. CT CCC Museum

These enrollees are cutting cord wood. During their first year Camp Stuart men cut 1,050 cords of wood. Walt Olson Chatham Historical Society

enrollees built V-dams, walls, and fish pools. They also planted trees along the rivers. The work helped create a fisherman's paradise.[37]

Foremen Ted Pelletier and Charles Sniffin worked till the end of 1936 on this project.[38] Forester Raymond K. Daley Jr. and crew did improved cutting and weeding in Oct. 1936 in the Day Pond block.[39]

The third major project of Camp Stuart was the construction of the stone dam that created Day Pond in the town of Westchester. Camp Superintendent Stanley Niven supervised the dredging and removing of all vegetation from the old pond that had been used to power a sawmill. Foreman D. B. Heatley supervised enrollees in building a 100' long dam of stone and reinforced concrete that was 18' high and anchored on bedrock. They also added fish ladders for fish to travel to the Salmon River for spawning. Some 30 men worked on the project that took 18 months to complete. The enrollees also built a picnic area.[40] The men also built the 3,350' road to the 160-acre Day Pond Park. Foreman John Bloom supervised the top grade of the road in Nov. 1936.[41]

The Day family originally owned the park and adjoining forest land during the colonial period. They built an overshot waterwheel dam that powered an up-and down saw for the sawmill. In 1879 Edward C. Brown bought Day Pond and there is a story told that Brown would place a log onto the carriage and start the mill. He then went home for breakfast and when he returned to the mill the log was sawed.

In 1935 the state purchased the pond and surrounding forest. In 1949 Day Pond became a state park.[42]

There were other projects in the Salmon River State Forest. Enrollees built truck trails and did silviculture, gypsy moth eradication, and fire hazard reduction work. The gypsy moth crew was composed mostly of men who left the closed Cobalt Camp.[43]

Near Camp Stuart enrollees built three ski trails: a novice, an intermediate, and an expert trail. The latter was considered by many as the toughest in the state. Experts from the Appalachian Ski Club laid out all of the trails.

Another important project was the planting of trees and doing silviculture work in the forest. By June 30, 1936 Camp Stuart had planted 23 acres of trees.[44]

During the months of March and April 1936 the Connecticut River flooded and caused extensive damage to the nearby towns and cities. Camp Stuart and other CCC camps were called on to help clean the damaged homes and businesses. Camp Stuart helped in restoration work in East Hartford and Glastonbury.[45] Camp Stuart Superintendent Stanley Niven was in charge of all the flood relief work in Hartford.[46]

As spring approached in March 1937 two fire crews of 10 men each were organized and worked close to camp in case of a fire call. One group led by Charles Sniffin did general clean up at Day Pond. The second crew led by Ted Pelletier worked at the gravel pit in camp.[48]

Also during March, three crews led by Ray Daley, Stanley Kogut, and David Heatley did improved cutting in the Meshomasic State Forest.[49]

At the end of winter Camp Stuart basketball team defeated Camp Roosevelt 41-20 and won the Eastern District CCC championship. They then traveled to the Waterbury YMCA Gym where they competed against Camp Kent. It was a close game but Kent defeated Stuart

These boys built up their muscles loading gravel on dump trucks. The gravel was used for building roads at Day Pond and trails in the Salmon River SF. CT CCC Museum

1194th Company at East Hampton, Conn

This photo collage shows Camp Stuart and the enrollees and their work projects.[47]

One of Camp Stuart's fire crews holding their fire-fighting equipment that included axes, shovels, Indian water tanks and council rakes. The latter are held by the 4th and 5th boys from the right. Council fire rakes are used for raking fire lines to mineral soil, digging, rolling burning logs, and cutting grass, small brush and small trees. They are rakes with sharp teeth. The crew's foreman is on the left. CT CCC Museum

Captain Charles H. Rohrbach took this photo of Camp Stuart enrollees doing flood relief work during the 1936 flood in one of the towns flooded by the Connecticut River. They cleaned homes and factories. Walt & Sue Olson

Enrollees also rebuilt a dam in nearby Westchester and created Day Pond SP that has a swimming and picnic area. There are also hiking trails and year-round fishing. DEEP

35-29.[50]

On May 31, 1937 Camp Stuart closed. The camp was demolished because there were insufficient funds to maintain the buildings.[51]

LEGACY

Camp Stuart's projects during the 1930s have made Salmon River State Forest a popular destination for picnickers, hikers, and fishermen. The forest contains nearly 6,000 acres for hikers to explore. In addition to its outdoor offerings, pumps allow visitors to take home fresh water. The artesian well that provided CCC enrollees water now supplies visitors with free fresh water.

Directions:

From Portland drive 6 miles east on Rt. 66. Then turn right onto Rt. 16 and travel approximately 5.8 mi. Here you will go over the Salmon River with the Comstock Covered Bridge on your left. Then turn right on Gulf Rd. As you go down into the Salmon River State Park turn left at a small parking area. Walk down this barricaded road and over a small walking bridge. There is an overgrown open field on the right where Camp Stuart was. The artesian well is on the left side of the hill. You will also find cement foundations and a water fountain.

This is the entrance to Camp Stuart. It is located just off Rt. 16 as you drive into the Salmon River State Forest. There is a small road to the left that leads to a bridge and a large field where the camp was located. Podskoch

Camp Stuart enrollees planted these white pines over 75 years ago. They offer shade and tranquility to the visitors of the Salmon River State Forest. Podskoch

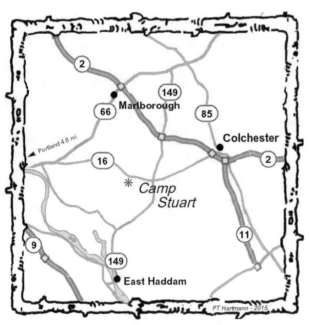

Map – Camp Stuart in East Hampton

MEMORIES

A Rookie Request
by J. Della Gelfa

"Dear Santa Claus," a Rookie wrote,
"I am an enrollee
And this you know, I'm always broke.
So please don't pass by me.

Now what I want is very neat.
It's called a parlor stove.
I need it bad, to warm my feet,
It's cold in the morning, by Jove.

The Recreation Hall is new
But please don't come in there,
Because the boys will wait for you
When you come through the air.

So come to barracks four
And fill my woolen socks.
My bunk is nearest the door,
But please, my shirt don't hock."
- Camp Stuart Courier, Dec. 1935

A Camp Stuart boy in front of the administration building in the Salmon River SF. CT CCC Museum

"And That's Why"
by Jerry Dela Gelfa

One morning a certain enrollee went to the C.O.'s office and asked for his immediate discharge. Upon being asked for his reasons for his hasty departure he simply recounted the following events of the previous day:

6:00 - Leader attempts to rouse him, but he just grunts and doesn't move.

6:02 - Somebody overturns bunk. Suspects Leader.

6:10 - Dresses up, minus one sock.

6:15 - Shivers around stove which is practically out because of his refusal to help bring in the wood.

6:30 - Goes to the washroom where someone takes his cap by mistake.

6:45 - Hears chow bell and in a mad rush scrapes his shins against an innocent box.

7:00 - Sits down to eat and discovers his fruit and cereal absent from the table.

7:15 - Makes his bunk and accidentally drops pillow on floor. In haste to clean pillow he forgets to sweep under his bunk.

7:30 - Leader makes him polish the stoves.

7:45 - Stands for inspection and receives a personal lecture for condition of his bunk.

8:00 - Goes to work and forgets his mittens.

10:45 - Drops plank on his foot and limps around the rest of the morning.

12:00 - Spills stew on floor of Mess Hall and Mess Steward orders him to report to kitchen for extra duty after supper.

12:45 - Leaves camp for work again and as he watches a passing truck, gets his feet tangled and stumbles into a brook.

1:00 - Arrives on the job where he is welcomed with a direct hit by a snowball.

4:00 - Trudges to camp, scans bulletin board where he finds his name on weekend KP list.

4:15 - Washes up and misplaces his comb. Also forgets to put on tie for evening meal.

4:45 - Gets a severe reprimand from Captain at retreat for being without tie. Someone in the rear gives him the "royal razzberry."

5:00 - Doesn't hear chow bell and dines on two slices of bread.

5:30 - Barracks leader makes him wash windows as

punishment for rising late.

6:00 - Starts washing Mess Hall floor.

8:00 - Finishes scrubbing of floor and tells Mess Steward what he thinks of that honorable person.

8:01 - Assigned to clean grease trap.

9:30 - Limps wearily back to barracks where he finds the fellows wrestling on his bunk. Shoos them off bunk and finds two springs missing.

9:45 - Tries to crawl into bed and finds he is short-sheeted.

10:00 - Lights go out and he realizes he has locked his keys in his box.

10:05 - The fellow in the next bunk starts snoring and continues to snore the rest of the night.

12:00 - Finally falls asleep from fatigue.

- Camp Stuart Courier, Dec. 1935

"Lights Out"
by J. Della Gelfa

When taps are blown and lights are out;
I lay awake and dream
Of this and that and all about
The things we daily scheme.

Oh, when the life seems pretty tough
I feel like quitting them
And say, "I'm licked and had enough."
And leave the camp and men.

But can I daily do my best
If I can never cease,
When day is done and others rest,
More work leaves me no peace.

When I return from hated toil,
I ask my weary mind
Must I always be forced to spoil
My restful hours of time?

But can I call myself a man
If I pack up and leave?
And tell my folks from work I ran
And pay ne'er more receive.

- Camp Stuart Courier, Dec. 1935

"This Couldn't Have Been Brown"

A young man from the city,
Saw what he thought was a kitty.
He gave it a pat, and soon after that,
He had to bury his clothes.
Indeed, it was an awful pity.
- Camp Stuart Courier, Feb. 1936

The cover of the Sept. 1936 issue of The Stuart Gusher shows an enrollee with choices of roads to travel in life. The Gusher had many articles that encouraged the boys to get an education, and maintain good health and a strong work ethic.

Charles Hall

I was fortunate to meet two people in my town of East Hampton whose grandfather worked at Camp Stuart. They just had a few stories to tell me because they were very young when he passed away. The first person was Frederick "Skip" Fitch of Tartia Road.

"Charles Hall was originally from Moodus where he was born in 1874. His father, Charles Hall Sr., was born before the Civil War in 1847 and died in 1941. I don't know a lot about my great-grandfather.

"In 1900 my grandfather moved to East Hampton. He was a carpenter. Then he worked at one of the bell factories in East Hampton. He made 10 cents an hour when the factory was open. He did whatever job he could to take care of his six children and his farm.

"During the Great Depression my grandfather got a job as a foreman at Camp Stuart near the Comstock Bridge in East Hampton. He taught the CCC boys carpentry. One of his jobs was the building of both gates at each end of the bridge.

"He probably rode 'Old Nell,' his horse, to work which was about 3 miles each way. His farm was on the corner of Rte. 66 by present-day Sam's Garage.

"I always listened to the old timers tell their stories. I wish I could have remembered more stories that my grandfather told me."

On Nov. 20, 2013 I met Jeanette Knotek whose

Charles Hall supervised the building of the gates on the Comstock Bridge that prevented cars and wagons from using the bridge. Podskoch

grandfather was Charles Hall, too. This is what she remembered about him.

"My grandparents, Eva and Charles Hall, had six children: Clara (my mother), Gilson, Charles, George, Anna, and Eva (Fitch).

"Grandfather Hall was a carpenter. I remember him sharpening saws. My grandparents lived between Moodus and East Hampton.

"There weren't many steady jobs during the Depression, so my grandfather did any kind of work he could find.

"Aunt Eva Hall Fitch told me the story that my grandfather went on a horse and wagon to the CCC camp and stayed there from Monday through Friday. He worked on the doors on both sides of the Comstock Bridge. He also supervised the CCC boys in rebuilding the bridge.

"When he left Camp Stuart he worked for Bevin Bells Co. in their foundry.

"In their later years my grandparents lived on N. Main St. in East Hampton. I wish that I knew more about his life."

Joseph Biegaj

During WWII Joseph Biegaj served in the Army. Bill Biegaj

Bill Biegaj of East Hampton met me on one of my monthly Chatham Historical Society walks in East Hampton and said his father had worked in the CCC. He sent me information about his dad's life, CCC discharge papers, and experiences in the CCC camp in East Hampton.

"My father Joseph Biegaj was born on Oct. 29, 1912.

(L – R) 1 When Joseph Biegaj and other enrollees came to Camp Stuart in July 1935 their meals were prepared in a mess kitchen under two tarp tents. There was a lister bag filled with drinking water hanging on a tripod on the left. The boys washed and rinsed their utensils in the galvanized garbage cans. One was filled with soapy water and the other with hot water for rinsing. A truck is unloading supplies near one of the tents. 2 After a busy day working in the Salmon River Forest, Camp Stuart enrollees walked to the nearby Salmon River for a swim. 3 One enrollee in his work clothes and an Army helmet is being tossed into the river. Photos courtesy of Bill Biegaj.

His parents were Joseph and Rose. He had eight siblings: Mary, Joseph, Stanley, Lucien, Helen, Jean, Loretta, and Frank. His sister Helen died as a teen during the scarlet fever epidemic in the 1920s.

"Dad only went to 7th grade and quit school to help his family since he was the second eldest in the family. He probably did odd jobs and his CCC enrollment form stated he had been unemployed since 1929.

"It was not until he was 22 that he heard about the CCC and signed up on July 5, 1935. He was sent to New London for a physical exam and for various shots. On Sept. 30th he was assigned to Camp Stuart in East Hampton. He was probably nervous leaving home but he really needed money to help his family. The camp was out in the woods near the Salmon River. My dad was a city boy who was born and raised in New Britain and had never slept in the woods before.

"My father said he did work using a jack-hammer, carpentry work, and he was proud that he helped build a dam on the Salmon River. After a hard day's work he said they were fed enough food and did not go hungry.

"On March 31, 1936 Dad signed up for another six months. He also got his younger brother Lucien to sign up and he got into Dad's camp. They enjoyed hanging around together. This also meant that their parents got a total of $50 each month for their sons' work.

"In his free time he enjoyed playing football and baseball. Sometimes on the weekends he and his friends walked all the way to Middletown to try and meet girls and find entertainment.

"After working for a full year Dad was honorably discharged on Sept. 30, 1936. His discharge papers said that his work was 'Excellent.'

"My dad benefited from working in the CCC by learning the skills of a carpenter. When he came home he got a job doing carpentry work in a large factory.

"In 1951 my parents got married and had two sons: Joe Jr. and me.

"Dad always told me that he wanted to see the dam he worked on in the Salmon River but he never went back to his old camp site. When my wife and I moved to East Hampton I wanted to take him to the Salmon River but he died shortly after our move.

"After my wife and I heard your talk on the CCC camps, we went to the Salmon River State Park and searched for the dam. As we explored we were fortunate to find some of the remains of the stones that my dad had toughed. He was so proud of his work in the CCC."

Karl Mandl

Karla Moore of Berlin met me at a CCC reunion at the Connecticut CCC Museum and told me about her father, Karl Mandl.

"My father, Karl Mandl, worked at Camp Stuart, the East Hampton CCC camp in the Salmon River State Forest. Karl was born in New Britain in March 1918 and his parents were Karl and Bertha. They had six children.

"Karl quit high school and took a year working in the CCC because his dad may have lost his job. He had to help his family because he was the eldest. On Oct. 18, 1935 Dad enlisted at the Replacement Center in New London. He was just 17 years old.

"One Sunday afternoon my family and I traveled with Dad to Day Pond in Westchester. Dad told us how he cleared the forest there. The CCC also built Day Pond dam. He also said he was the boss over men that were older than him.

"On the weekends Dad said he and a buddy hitchhiked and walked back to New Britain.

"After a year at Camp Stuart, Dad's discharge papers state that he was honorably discharged on Sept. 1, 1936. His performance at camp as a senior leader and laborer was 'excellent.' This was a month before his six-month tour was up so that he could return to school for his senior year. He graduated in 1937. Dad became an accounting clerk at Cudhy Packing Co. Then during WWII he enlisted in the Navy.

"After the war he married Cecilia Wright in 1945. They had five children: Karla, Karen, Kathleen, Kristine, and Karl.

"Dad then went to Bryant College and studied accounting. After graduating in 1949 he worked as an accountant for Webster Blanchard & Willard which later became Price Waterhouse. He was a finance director for the town of Berlin. Later, from 1977 to 1983, he was budget director for the city of Waterbury. He retired in June 1994 as director of finance for the town of Middlebury.

"When he looked back at his days in the CCC he told me that the most important thing was that he assisted his family when they needed help. He also said he developed a good sense of discipline."

On April 23, 1998 Karl Mandl died at his home at the age of 80.

Five CCC boys posing with one of the camp dogs by the entrance sign to their camp. CT CCC Museum

Karl Mandl (1st on Left) worked for almost a year at Camp Stuart as a laborer and a leader of his barracks. CT CCC Museum

CHAPTER 11
EAST HARTLAND

HISTORY

Camp Robinson, Company 180 S-53, was located in the Tunxis State Forest (TSF) in East Hartland, 11 miles northeast of Winsted.

On June 13, 1933 Company 180 arrived at an old abandoned farm on Rt. 20 (N. Hollow Rd.) about 1 mile north of the village of East Hartland. The enrollees cleared the land and set up their tents.[1]

Camp Robinson was selected as the best CCC camp in Connecticut during the first period of enlistment in 1933. The camp was administered by Capt. Holoway and Superintendent Kienholz.[3]

CCC work projects were concentrated on protecting and developing the Tunxis State Forest. The forest contained approximately 5,639 acres and had one of the highest altitudes in the state, 1,360'. Camp Robinson developed many ski trails and open downhill ski slopes. The area became very popular. At the end of Balance Rock Road, enrollees built a large parking area and a 17' x 25' log cabin for ski enthusiasts in 1937.[4]

The ski cabin was heated by a massive stone fireplace to the south of the ski slope. Today the slope is overgrown and unrecognizable. The cabin reflects the high standards of design and craftsmanship. "The building is nicely proportioned and detailed with pyramidal corners and exposed roof trussing. It is limited use as a trailside pavilion. The dirt road to the cabin is lined with some stone walls and cul-de-sacs, that were built by the CCC. No early ski facility survives in Mohawk State Forest, making the Tunxis Forest Ski Cabin one of the oldest, if not the oldest, structures associated with downhill skiing in the state."[5]

Enrollees constructed many miles of roads and foot trails. They built a half-mile double-width truck trail to Bragg Pond. Enrollees improved and surfaced the town road from East Hartland to Camp Robinson. Two other roads they constructed were Pell Rd. (East of Emmons Pond) and Morrison Hill Rd. (West Hartland).[6]

Camp Robinson sign in front of the farm house on Rt. 20 in East Hartland in 1933. CT CCC Museum

Camp Robinson was established on an abandoned farm. The enrollees lived in tents till permanent barracks were constructed. CT CCC Museum

An aerial view of Camp Robinson during the summer of 1933 when boys were living in tents. CT CCC Museum

Hartford County Bar Assn.

Lucius F. Robinson

The camp was named for Lucius F. Robinson (1863-1941), a noted Connecticut lawyer and environmentalist. He was a Yale graduate, President of the Bar Association, and director of several insurance companies in Hartford.

Robinson served on the Connecticut Forest and Park Commission from 1913-36, and as chairman from 1917-1937. During this time 12,000 acres of parks and 80,000 acres of state forest were added. He was also president of the Hartford City Parks. Governor Wilbur Cross asked for his expertise in the creation of the Merritt Parkway.[2]

CCC enrollees constructing a log ski cabin on Balance Rock Road in the Tunxis State Forest. Jeff Ward

Camp Robinsons' fleet of Army and Conservation Dept. trucks were used to transport men and materials. CT CCC Museum

These CCC boys are proudly posing by the log lean-to they built on a trail in the Tunxis SF. CT CCC Museum

These young CCC men are taking a lunch break while doing forestry and trail work in the Tunxis SF. CT CCC Museum

These photos show the construction phases of a bridge. The photo on the left shows enrollees using cribbing across a river. The photo on the right shows the completed trail bridge from a different angle. CT CCC Museum

CCC Camp Robinson with its wooden buildings, water tower and old farm house in the upper left. CT CCC Museum

Enrollees doing stone work on the Ranger cottage. Walter Spellman

Enrollees landscaping the grounds at the completed Ranger cottage. DEEP State Parks Archives

This crew of Camp Robison boys have their axes and other tools ready to clear trails and cut trees in the Tunxis SF. CT CCC Museum

They also constructed these foot trails: the 1-mile long No. 1 trail from Rt. 20 to Bragg Pond, the 1-mile Roaring Brook trail in the Hartland Hollow Block to Indian Council Rocks and falls on Roaring Brook.[7] Another trail they built was the Falls Brook trail. The two-mile loop that began at Rt. 20 in Hartland and passed many waterfalls, cascades, and pools.[8]

Insect control was another work project. Camp Robinson was near the New York border and Connecticut was trying to stop the spread of the Gypsy moths from the Hudson Valley. Enrollees scouted for gypsy moth egg masses and destroyed them by painting them with creosote.[9]

At Bragg's Pond in East Hartland Camp Robinson strengthened the dam and built several fireplaces and a bathhouse. Tourists enjoyed swimming in the pond, hiking the trails, and picnicking in the designated areas.[10] The 1938 flood, however, washed out the Bragg's Pond dam and the dam was not rebuilt "due to the Metropolitan Water Board Reservoir."[11] Stream improvement was another work of the enrollees. They improved two miles of the Farmington River. They built 33 artificial boulders, one boulder dam, and 26 deflectors.[12]

The 1934 Report of the Connecticut State Parks and Forest reported Camp Robinson was building a fire line on the border with Massachusetts. They removed dead trees in a 100-foot wide strip and grubbed a 15-foot wide center strip. The strip was mostly on state forest land.[13]

Camp Robinson helped move the steel tower from Savin Rock (West Haven) to West Hartland, where it was used to spot fires.[14]

From July 1, 1933 to June 30, 1934 CCC enrollees worked with the state and planted the following trees in the Tunxis State Forest: 23,400 red pine; 8,200 white spruce; 1,000 Colorado spruce; 1,000 white cedar; 300 Riga Scotch pine; 1,000 European larch; 16,600 Norway spruce; 1,000 Douglas fir; and 1,000 hemlock. The total was 53,500 trees.[15]

Forest Products Produced from Tunxis State Forest

Years	Cords	Posts	Poles	Board Feet	Source
July 1932 - June 30, 1934	402	180	216	14,279	Report of the CT State Parks and Forest, 1934, 101.
July 1934 - June 30, 1936	1,115	184	146	29,471	Report of the CT State Parks and Forest, 1936, 72.
July 1936 - June 30, 1938	792	...	110	10,856	Report of the CT State Parks and Forest, 1938, 48.
July 1938 - June 30, 1940	1,831	280	279	11,800	Report of the CT State Parks and Forest, 1940, 57.

The Oct. 1935 issue of the Robinson Register reported that work was progressing on the new Ranger cottage just across the road from the camp. The foundation was laid and men were working on the structure where Dr. Raymond Keinoltz, the forestry research technician, would be housed.

Colonel Schroeter, who worked previously at Camp Chapman, became the new camp superintendent in the fall of 1935. He replaced John Wulff.[16]

By June 30, 1936 there were 4.8 miles of car roads, 55 miles of wood roads, two vehicle bridges, and 9 miles of foot trails in the Tunxis State Forest.[17] During the spring of 1936 Camp Robinson assisted Hartford and surrounding communities during the catastrophic flood that damaged thousands of homes and businesses. Otto H. Schroeter, Superintendent of Camp Robinson, was chosen to supervise all of the CCC camps that were working during the flood.[18] In Oct. 1936 a public address system was installed at Camp Robinson for announcements, dance classes, and public speaking. It was funded by profits made at the canteen.[19]

A Sept. 1935 group photo of Camp Robinson. Gary Potter

After working the Tunxis SF the enrollees came back to camp and got ready for supper. In the evening they took courses in many topics such as forestry, mechanics, etc. CT CCC Museum

Camp Robison enrollees having fun in a tug-of-war. CT CCC Museum

These enrollees worked at the gravel pit and loaded trucks with grave used in road construction. CCC CT Museum

State Technician George A. Cromie supervised a landscape crew of 14 enrollees establishing a nursery in an abandoned field near camp. They removed most of the white birch and in the spring they planned to transplant thousands of hemlock, white pine, and mountain laurel from the Tunxis Forest.[20]

During the beginning of 1937 Mr. Loughlin's carpentry crew completed a log cabin on Ski Trail No. 1.[21]

The basketball team started their season without any practice session because they lacked a gym. The result was losing their first six games. They lost four games with the Southwick Boys' Club and two losses to the Poquonock Townies.[22]

Education advisor Richard A. Fear stated that new clubs were formed in January 1937: The Aero Club, the Arts and Crafts Club, and the Tunxis Press Club. Mr. Fear was proud that about 20 men were preparing to take a test in Hartford to get a high school diploma.[23]

The new enrollees were fingerprinted. Their prints were filed with the FBI in Washington.[24]

Monthly "Smokers" were very popular entertainment at camp. In January 1937 the first part of the entertainment program was a discussion of the US Constitution. Next came a clog dance by three enrollees, followed by singing,

During the winter the boys were kept busy after a snowstorm shoveling the camp roads and walkways. CT CCC Museum

three wrestling matches, and three boxing matches.[25]

During January and February 1937 the Tunxsonian reported various speakers came to camp. Thomas Merritt took a group camp photo and then gave a talk to the Photo Club about techniques to improve their picture-taking and developing skills. Next, Army Chaplin Lt. W. E. Garabedian gave a talk on flags used in America from Leif Ericson to the present. In March, a Connecticut State Police officer talked about highway safety and explained driving laws. Mr. Wellbourne from the Goodyear Tire and Rubber Co. gave an illustrated talk on the processing of rubber from trees to the finished tire.[26]

On March 4, the Glee Club came in second place

These CCC boys posing by the Camp Robinson sign. The camp closed after eight years of forestry work in the Tunxis State Forest. CT CCC Museum

Photos of Camp Robinson activities from the 1937 First Corps Area. Fifth CCC District Yearbook.

at the Hartford Woman's Club. Camp Ross came in first place.[27]

Seventy men from the Forestry Club and other Camp Robinson enrollees traveled on March 10 to Hartford and attended the Sportsmen Show at the State Armory.[28] On March 29, 1937 a "Farewell Smoker" was held to honor the 27 boys leaving at the end of their 6 months and the 11 men who reenlisted and volunteered to go to Oregon.

At the end of 1937 Col. Otto H. Schroeter, who was the camp superintendent since 1935, was assigned to Camp Cross at Housatonic Meadows. He was honored at a banquet at the Old Well in Simsbury.[29]

In December, Dr. Cheney from the Connecticut State College gave a talk on astronomy. The men enjoyed his talk on the solar system. The professor was also a magician and the boys enjoyed his interesting magic tricks.[30]

In February 1938 Capt. James S. Thompson congratulated the veteran enrollees for welcoming the new recruits and making them feel at home and not hazing the new recruits as had been done in the past. He stated there were no reports of homesickness or men who went AWOL.[31]

In April 1938 Camp Robinson celebrated the fifth anniversary of the CCC. The first dance of the spring season was held on Tuesday, April 5 and girls from the

surrounding towns were brought to the camp. The next day Senator Walcott, State Selecting Official B. H. Van Buren, and Marion Lee of the Emergency Relief Division visited the camp.[32]

After six months of work 15 members of the Tunxis Forestry Club completed five miles of the Blue Trail that begins at Pine Mt. and ends at the Massachusetts border. The Blue Trail begins at Bragg Pond Picnic Area.[33]

The spring sports season began in April with boys playing on the tennis, badminton, and volleyball courts. Boxing was held at an outdoor arena with bleachers. The camp baseball team began practicing on the camp baseball field where they won two successive State CCC Championships. There were also inter-barracks baseball and softball leagues. Swimming was held at Braggs Pond. Dick Fear coached the track team that competed against nearby CCC camps and high schools. Fishing in the local streams for trout was also very popular.[34]

Dr. Shapiro the camp surgeon instructed 31 men who earned their First Aid cards.[35]

During the summer of 1938, a 116' x 20' education building was built next to Barracks No. 5. It contained two classrooms, a library, a reading room, and education advisors' offices.[36]

The agriculture education program was expanded by

(L–R) Two views of the Ranger cottage today. There is an addition that was built for a youth program called the Wilderness School. Podskoch

The Camp Robinson site is now a state highway maintenance garage on Rt. 20.

25 garden plots for boys who signed up to raise vegetables. The poultry program was expanded with 150 new baby chicks. The old oil house was moved near the hen house and became a brooder house.[37]

On May 24, 1938 junior students at the NYS College of Forestry at Syracuse University came to Camp Robinson for a tour of the camp and its' forestry projects. A dinner followed and sporting events in softball, tennis, volleyball, and badminton were held.[38]

Dr. Raymond Kienholz, Director of Research in Connecticut CCC camps, established his headquarters in the Tunxis State Forest. He directed the enrollees at Camp Robinson in the establishment of many experimental tree plots.[39]

The 1940 State Park and Forest Commission Report stated that Camp Robinson constructed two more roads in the Tunxis State Forest: Pine Mt. Rd. and Hall Rd. The length of car roads in Tunxis State forest increased to 12.1 miles by mid-1940.[40]

The camp had a variety of recreation activities. They had a baseball diamond, a tennis court, two volleyball courts and a small pond (Emmons) for swimming. There was a recreation hall where the boys played pool, checkers, ping pong, and card games.[41] Camp Robinson had a baseball team that played in the Connecticut State CCC league. In fact, they won two successive state championships.[42] Another form of recreation was the Camp Robinson Glee Club. They won a silver cup in a state competition.[43]

Camp Robinson was one of the first CCC camps in New England to have a separate education building. The Army built it during the summer of 1934. It contained two classrooms and an office for the education advisor. The education program was moved to a barracks building during the summer of 1938. It was partitioned into a classroom, a reading room, a library, and a game room.[44]

After eight years of operation, Camp Robinson closed on July 18, 1941. K. Gometz was the last camp superintendent. The US Army retained custody of the camp.[45]

After Pearl Harbor, Camp Robinson's buildings were turned over to the Army which cut 16 small buildings into sections and moved them to Bradley Airport. They burned the rest of the large buildings: five barracks and garages. This caused an uproar from the public because of the waste of lumber. This practice of destroying buildings was not repeated at other closed CCC camps.[46]

On July 14, 1944 the camp was turned over to the State Forestry Dept.[47] Today, only the Stone Headquarters and Ski Cabin remain. A state highway maintenance garage and storage facility occupies the grounds of what was once Camp Robinson.

In 1933 Dr. Raymond Kienholz was the superintendent of Camp Robinson and in 1938 he became the Director of Research in Connecticut CCC camps. White Memorial Foundation

LEGACY

Visitors to the Tunxis State Forest continue to enjoy the benefits of Camp Robinson. The forest totals 9,152 acres that are on both sides of the Barkhamsted Reservoir in the towns of Hartland, Granby, and Barkhamsted. During the winter skiers enjoy the ski trails and during the rest of the year visitors enjoy the CCC hiking trails or mountain biking on the numerous woods roads.

Directions:

From I-91 take Exit 40 to Rt. 20 West towards Bradley Airport. Travel for 3.1 mi. Continue on Rt. 20 towards E. Granby and go for 13.8 mi. You will come to East Hartland at the intersection of Rts. 20 and 179. Continue on Rt. 20 on North Hollow Rd. for approximately 1 mi. You will pass the Wilderness School (240 North Hollow Road) on the left. The Ranger Cabin built by the CCC is used by the Wilderness School. Go 0.1 mi and on the right is the State Highway Maintenance garage and facility. This was the former site of Camp Robinson.

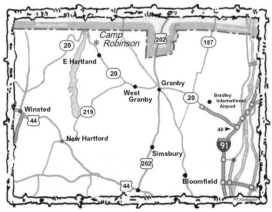

Map – Camp Robinson in East Hartland

MEMORIES

"The Enrollee Speaks"
by Julius Konworski

First impressions are most generally lasting ones. I dare say that I have never been favorably impressed by anything other than by my arrival at this Camp Robinson.

Shortly after leaving my home town, I began for the first time, to notice the beauties of nature. For the first time I seemed to feel an inexplicable desire to be free as the birds that I could see flitting from tree to tree. Some vague desire to suddenly strive to do something constructive seemed to invade my entire person, and for once in my brief life I seemed to sense a feeling of utter security and happiness.

Among the many things which impressed me on my way to camp was the ever increasing beauty and number of trees that just seemed suddenly surround us as we sped along the long road to Robinson. Upon arrival at camp, I was greatly impressed by the simple beauty and arrangement of the entire camp grounds and of the tidiness of the barracks and the friendliness of all the men, especially of the leader who immediately set about to make us comfortable.

The leader assigned to show us the camp area gave us quite a surprise when he pointed out the tennis, volleyball, and basketball courts. I had never realized that the CCC camp could be so well appointed.

I've been in camp for some time, but I doubt if I'll ever change my attitude towards the camp, its leaders, or surroundings.
- Spectator, Oct. 1939

A CCC camp dog sleeping on the road.
Kathleen Esche

"He's Past 13 But He Doesn't Look Old"
by Emil Verrilli

He's past 13 but he doesn't look old
For his eyes are bright and his back is bold,
He holds his head high and his tail he wags,
When I ask him for a walk through woodland crags,
He chases rabbits and other game,
And doesn't mind the wind or rain.
He barks at everyone and tries to act tough,
But those of us who know him, can see right thru his bluff,
I retire for the night and he guards my door;
He sleeps as my protector and he enjoys it too;

For his affection is the same whether I am happy or blue.
I tell my troubles and he never says a word,
Just listens sympathetic, as the every word were heard,
If dogs have a heaven, the same as mortals do,
I'm sure old "Bud" will get there, too.
- Spectator, Oct. 1938

A West Cornwall CCC truck flipped over on its side.
Sheila Ceder

"If He Had Known"
by Daniel Greer

If he had known a curve was ahead,
If he had known he wouldn't be dead.
If he had known that speed doesn't count,
He would have saved his bank account.
Now if he took that curve with ease,
He could have gone where ever he pleased.
But now it's too late, God Bless his soul,
He only raised the death toll.
- Spectator, Oct. 1938

"Please Be Careful!"
by Daniel Greer

When bumming home, please be careful,
And what I'm saying is sure an earful,
Please watch out for those speeding cars,
If you don't you will visit Mars.
Always keep left of the road,
And when bumming at night, wear light clothes.
Now take these hints I beg of you,
And after each weekend we'll be seeing you.
- Spectator, Nov. 1938

"Joe Dunn's Thanksgiving"
by Gerard Claing

As darkness shrouded our camp with its mantle of diamond studded velvet blackness, a few of us, just a bit too stuffed with Thanksgiving turkey, lingered about the fireplace listening to the old timers reminiscing of the days gone by.

"This sure was a great Thanksgiving Day," remarked one guy.

"Yes, sure was," answered another, "but yet as thankful as we are for everything I can recall someone who has a few reasons more than we to be thankful."

"Who is that?" inquired another.

"Remember Joe Dunn, the fellow who was S. L. (Senior Leader) up in Vermont?" A chorus of "Yes" and "Sure do" answered this query.

"Well," continued the speaker, "I met Joe the other day and things are sure breaking right for him and his wife."

"Remember how he met that little wife of his?"

"Who doesn't? Let me see, it happened something like this:

"Joe strapped on his knapsack and picked up his gun. He was going on a week's leave (from CCC) and was spending it on a hunting trip in the woods near his camp. Well-wishers crowded around their popular S. L., helping him with his accouterments. Some snapped his snowshoes to his pack while others offered suggestions. Finally, Joe trudged out of sight through the wood.

"Hours later he arrived at one of the CCC built shelters known as 'The Pine.' Hurriedly he made up his camp and cooked up a mess of beans. Supper over with, the dishes washed, he banked the fire for the night and turned in.

"Morning found Joe digging his way through a bank of cold glistening snow. Dark clouds covered the sun and a cold wind howled through the tree tops.

"By nightfall, the snow fell quite steadily and Joe pitched his camp in a thick hemlock grove. As he cooked a hunter stew upon a glowing fire, he remembered that the morrow was Thanksgiving Day. Mentally he listed a few of the things he had to be thankful for: his job in the CCC, the opportunities for improvement, and preparation for the better things to come.

"The sun rose up red and cheery on the following morning. Joe, having broken up camp very early found a set of fresh deer tracks near a recently frozen spring. For hours he followed the wily deer until suddenly he saw it, in the gathering dusk, not fifty yards away. Quickly he drew up his gun and taking deliberate aim killed the magnificent buck with one well-placed bullet. Carefully he skinned the animal and having severed a hind leg, cached the rest where he could find it later.

"Almost exhausted he climbed up the mountain side looking for a place to pitch his tent. He had scarcely reached the top when he spied a cabin a short distance away.

"Cautiously he approached the cabin door and knocked. A moment later it swung open and he stood face to face with a slender, dark-haired girl.

"'Howdy, Miss! Is your father home?'

"'I have no father,' replied the girl, and tears came to her eyes. She added, 'My mother is very sick.'

"'What is troubling her?'

"'She broke her leg in a fall.'

"'Did you get a doctor?'

"'A doctor! Oh no, I could never leave her alone.'

"'May I see your mother?'

"'Yes! Come this way.'

"Joe walked through the cabin to a nook that served as a bedroom and found an elderly women writhing in painful agony upon the bed. Quickly he bared her leg and thanking God for his knowledge of First Aid improvised a rough splint to keep the leg in a more comfortable position while he dashed off to a nearby village for the doctor. Upon bringing him back, Joe helped him set the broken limb.

"The following spring Joe got himself a good job and in June we were invited to his wedding. He married that little French (Canadian) girl whom he had met in the Vermont hills and who he still calls his 'Thanksgiving Sweetheart.'"

- Spectator, Nov. 1938

"Life Isn't What You Make It"
by Lewis Conant

Life is what you make it
Who quoted that famous line?
You have got to make it
If it isn't all just fine.

If you should slip upon a stairway
And break a bone or two
That certainly won't be your way

Of planning things to do.

We have to force a smile at times
When everything is gray.
With every task an uphill climb
We keep on hoping for our day.

The sun isn't always shinning
When we wish it would
For humans are always pining
For everything that's good.

No, life isn't what you make of it
As some would have you believe
But it's best to live and take it
For it does no good to grieve.
- Spectator, Nov. 1938

The education advisor supervised the enrollees in the production of the camp newspaper. Over the years it had these titles: "Robinson Mountaineer," "Tunxis Press," "Tunxonian," "Spectator," and "Robinson Register."

Many of the enrollees hunted during their free time and were quite successful in the Tunxis State Forest while others had unusual prey. Here are the results of the 1939 hunting season, according to the January Spectator:

Aresco	1 baby duck
Boulanger	1 crow, 5 rabbits, 1 sparrow, 1 chipmunk
Carnell	16 rabbits, 11 squirrels, 1 woodchuck, 1 porcupine, 6 houseflies
?????	1 cat
Nelson	3 squirrels, 6 rabbits
Cyr	1 partridge, 1 hawk
Kirychuck	1 rabbit (massacred with buckshot)
Mufatti	2 partridge, 18 rabbits, 8 squirrels, 2 suspicious-looking tree stumps
Dombroskas	1 field mouse (tch tch)
Nipert	1 weasel (no offense Robins), 3 rabbits, 2 squirrels
Yeltema	1 complete failure
Kowalchuk	15 squirrels, 1 chipmunk
Frisketti	8 squirrels
Beausoleil	11 mice, 4 rats
Verrilli	1 rat, 36 EPDs
Vincinni	5 rabbits
Conant	2 rats, 2 mice

"The 'Rise' of Whitey Conant"
by EX-member CC1-139966

Night guard's whistle
Get up, Whitey
Some Day this'll
Make me mighty
Mad, and I'll go
Up to the C.C.C.
Say, 'I'm thru',
So Captain gimme
My discharge an'

I'll be leavin'
For Civilian Life
I'm grievin'
Cripes, there's no heat
Guess I'll have to
Wash and go to eat.
So much to do,
Captain Hayes is
Coming today
And he raises
Hell with my day.
Think that I will
Get leave some how
Before they kill me
With the chow.
I'm getting old
Three months to go
This joint is cold,
Hope it don't snow.
I have been here
In the CCC
More than a year
That's enough for me
There's the chow bell,
Now I have to
Get up – Oh hell!
Where's that damn shoe
- Spectator, Jan. 1939

"It Happened One Night"
Anonymous

I have an ambition. You have an ambition. Yes sir, we all have some aim in life. Well, Dembroskas, that keen-minded, six-foot brute, had an ambition, too, and a very high minded one at that. He wanted to be a big game hunter. He never had a chance to realize his aim, however, until he joined the C's and here he was given his chance. He had heard stories of ferocious bobcats, a man-eating snipe, six-foot jackrabbits, and a blood-thirsty fox that roam the virgin forest of East Hartland. He fairly burned with the desire to go out and bring back one of these dangerous animals and so one dark night, he set out, single-handed and armed with naught save a harmless 10-gauge double-barrel shot-gun.

"I'm gonna get a bobcat," he remarked before leaving, "and when I spot one, it won't stand a chance. I'm dead-eye Dick, and I'll blast it into eternity!" There was a gleam of supreme courage in his eye as he swaggered out of the door.

It was a dark starless night, rather warm and calm, almost too calm. As he walked along, playing his light here and there, a feeling of nameless dread permeated his big frame. Why, he couldn't understand. The darkness had never affected him before yet this night seemed to cloak him oppressively, driving his courage away and leaving him with a panicky sort of fear, a feeling that he had never experienced.

Suddenly two gleaming eyes staring out of the darkness brought him back to reality. All fear left him as a great desire to slay this beast surged within his breast. Only one thought dominated his mind. This time those eyes gleamed so brightly in the strong light it was a bobcat and here was his great chance.

"Gee those eyes are kinda close together for a bobcat's. Maybe he's cross-eyed. They're awful small, too. It must be tough for what else would be roaming in the woods at this time of the night." Thus ran his train of thought.

All this thought was a matter of seconds and the next instant a loud report shattered the night setting the echoes reverberating.

"Oh boy! I got 'em. Only one shot too. Will those guys in the barracks sit up and take notice when I walk in with this baby."

With this, he walked over to where the quarry lay in a pool of blood, knelt down, and picked up the remains of a poor little field mouse.

- Spectator, Jan. 1939

A Camp Robinson boy dressed up and possibly going home or to town.
CT CCC Museum

"Dedicated to Lewis Conant"

Ho hum – work to be done
Why did I ever join the C's?
All grind – no fun;
Too many officers to please.
What's that? An inspector coming tomorrow?
(And they shot Lincoln.)
Come pay day – how I'll drown my sorrows.
Every guy, officer and gal I'll shun –
No, wait a minute, a gal –
That's what I need;
A wife, not just a pal.
(Oh, for a home cooked feed!)
Gee, and I'm getting old –
Yeah, I'd like to settle down.
But where's there a girl in this part of the world?
You're right, buddy, they can't be found.
East Hartland, my, my, what a town!
A glorified gas station, that's all it is!
By woods, woods, and woods it's bound.
Ah! – What excitement, what enjoyment it gives!
Yeah! – Where? – Ho hum.
- Spectator, Dec. 1938

"Life of the KPs"
by Kenneth Calkins

This article is written to give some of you fellows an idea of what kind of life the kitchen police tolerate.

The night guard wakes us up at 5:30 am. We get up, make our bunks, wash-up, then report to the kitchen. When we arrive there each of us has a different job to perform. One KP puts bread and sugar bowls on the tables and gets the bread for the lunches. The head KP cuts his butter and sees that the fruit is passed out. Another gets the dishes that he cook needs to put the food on. The meal by this time is ready to serve. After everything is ready the chow bell is rung.

After breakfast is served the tables are cleared and washed. About 8 or 8:15 am we are ready to start washing dishes and pans. When this job is finished two or three of us peel the spuds for supper. Sometimes there are other ingredients to get ready so we prepare these. Then we sweep and wash the kitchen floor and try to keep it clean.

The outside man has his own special job to do. He has to

sweep the floor, clean the incinerator, the small grease trap, and police up around the mess hall. He also has to keep the fire going in the field kitchen, keep the wheelbarrows full of coal and see that the G. B. cans are always full of water. On Wednesday morning he has to wash the mess hall floor.

We have to go through this same routine three times every day, five and sometimes six days a week. So now you fellows can see what kind of a life the KPs have. When quitting time comes, we are ready for bed and a good night's rest.

- Spectator, Dec. 1938

"After the Storm"
by Dr. Raymond Kienholz

The somber woods are clothed in ice,
Dipped in a silver bath.
Each twig is held in a crystal vice,
The sleet storm's aftermath.

Slanting rays of the morning sun,
Transform each humble tree.
And when the storm and sleet are done,
Not any twig is free.
The pliant birch, a graceful plume,
Bends o'er the rutted road;
She waits release from her icy tomb,
And the Storm King's load.

The rigid oak holds his head upright,
Disdainful of every foe.
His spreading crown defies the might
The North winds snow.

The ferns and grasses bear a crop
Of the clear frost's veil;
Like the shimmering background drop
Of some acted fairy tale.

All the twigs and withered grass,
A frigid armor bear;
And magnified as through a glass,
Are wondrous, lovely, fair.

The murky fog cuts off the sight
Of melting, icy mounds,

Marred is the silence of the night,
By sudden, crashing sounds.

The silver hoard is changed by rain –
The alchemist at play;
And morning finds the world again,
As any other day.
- Spectator, Mar. 1939

Frank Matulewicz

Frank Matulewicz in front of his home in Bethlehem, Conn. In 1935 Frank worked at Camp Robinson in East Hartland. Podskoch

On April 16, 2008 I traveled to the beautiful country town of Bethlehem, Conn. to interview Frank J. Matulewicz. I was surprised to learn that many immigrants from Lithuania, the country of my mother's parents, settled here and were farmers.

Frank told me, "I was born on May 3, 1917 in Torrington. I had a younger brother William. My father Bolus worked at American Brass where he lost his arm in a roller press. He got $300 compensation but he kept on working. He died when I was just two years old. My mother, Mary Yurashus, married again to William Marculinas.

"My stepfather bought a house but he had a hard time paying the mortgage. After my third year of high school I quit school to help my family. In 1935 I went to the welfare department for help and they got me into the CCC.

"We went first to New London and got physical exams and shots. I saw a parade of CCC boys marching with picks

142

and shovels. It looked funny. I wondered what I'd be doing.

"Then they took us in a truck to Camp Robinson 180 in East Hartland. There was one guy with me from Torrington but he was sent to the Burrville Camp.

"It was tough being away from home because I had had my own room and now I lived with 40 guys in a barracks. I asked, 'Where's the bathroom?' And they said, 'Up there. Follow that path.' It was a pit latrine. It was nothing like home.

"My work was fixing roads and I used a jackhammer. I also planted trees along Barkhamsted Dam. Other people were just cleaning out the valley of trees and cemeteries where the new dam would be.

"I was also on a fire crew. The fires weren't too big. They were mostly brush fires. I used Indian tanks, shovels, and rakes.

"We took the old chestnut trees out of the forest because they were dead. They used them for telephone poles. We used a grappler hook and it took about six guys to carry them out. It was hard work but I didn't mind it.

"I never got seriously hurt to go to the infirmary. There was a Dr. Shapiro who was there all the time in camp. One time we got all sunburn. We had taken our bunks outside and fallen asleep and got a bad sunburn. We went to the infirmary and the doctor put something on our backs and chest. I later had a melanoma when I was older. It might have come from that bad sunburn.

"The food was good. We had a Chinese cook who did a great job. One day we caught a lot of bullfrogs and he

cooked the legs for us.

"After supper we played cards, shot dice, and read a lot. They had a canteen but we liked to walk to the store about a mile away in East Hartland.

"We always had an initiation for the new guys who came to camp. The new guys had to stay under a tree in the dark and wait for something to come out but nothing ever came out. It was fun to watch them.

"In our spare time after work or on weekends we took walks to East Hartland where there was a little store. We bought tobacco, etc. One guy wanted to go down every night to buy yeast cakes for his pimples. Sometimes we threw a football or baseball around but I didn't play on an organized team. There were times when I had KP duty on the weekend.

"Once in a while we went home on the weekend. We usually hitchhiked. On my way back to camp one driver left me off at the wrong place and I had to walk quite a bit to get back to camp.

"After being in camp for 18 months I left. I got a job with the Torrington Co. They made bicycles, needles, and bearings. I worked there for about five years.

"In 1940 I married Helen Krauchlis. We didn't have any children.

"I was drafted into the Marines in November 1942. I went to Paris Island but developed an ulcer and was discharged in January 1943.

"I bought a liquor store in Torrington and ran it for about 20 years. Then I went to Cape Cod and retired in 1987.

"I kept in touch with two guys from the CCC: Tom Videtto in Torrington and George Lazuskas.

"While in the CCC I learned about how nice nature was and how to help it along. The forest was really cleaned up by us. We cut all dead trees and thinned the woods. The dead wood was used for cord wood. We put wood in cords, 4' x 4' x 8', and left it on the road. Farmers, etc., came along and took it. We learned discipline from Capt. Smith."

Frank J. Matulewicz died on June 8, 2009.

Adolphe Kosnoff

On June 30, 2008 I interviewed Adam Kosnoff at his home in Wallingford. He told me about his brother, Adolphe Kosnoff, who worked at Camp Robinson:

"My brother, Adolphe, who we called 'Sid,' was

Frank Matulewicz (right) and a friend pose in front of Camp Robinson sign near Rt. 20 in East Hartland. Frank Matulewicz

A view of Camp Robinson from a tree or camp water tower. Roberta Kosnoff Sciacca

This is Adolphe "Sid's" barracks. The Army made the men keep it clean and orderly. Roberta Kosnoff Sciacca

The Camp Robinson Mess Hall. Roberta Kosnoff Sciacca

born in September 1918. Our father Anthony died in 1928 when I was only 5 or 6 years old. He had worked in Winchester Arms Factory in New Haven. Our mother, Mary Ungiecheaur, had to raise her five children by herself for a time till she remarried. My brothers and sisters were: Helen, Adolphe, and twins John and Anthony, who died at 16. I was the youngest.

"Adolphe was the eldest boy and he had to help my mother a lot. He quit school after 8th grade. He worked on farms in Hamden where he picked beans, strawberries, etc. He joined the CCC at 17. I think it was 1935.

"They sent him to Camp Robinson in East Hartland. He enjoyed being there. Adolphe loved to chop wood. He also worked on eliminating blister rust. He pulled up currant bushes.

"One time my mother, stepfather 'Dan,' and us kids went to visit him. We thought it took an awful lot of time

Camp Robinson enrollees went swimming in nearby Braggs Pond that had a dock and diving board.
Roberta Kosnoff Sciacca

to get there. When we got there, he wasn't there. My mother was hysterical. We got home and she was worried. The next time we saw him. He said he went to Bridgeport with his friend, Walter. We had gone to pick him up and bring him home but we just looked around, saw his barracks, but not him.

"Another time when he was splitting wood the axe slipped and went through his boot. He had to go to the infirmary.

"Then a sad thing happened when his camp was searching for someone who was lost. They found the missing person hanging in the woods.

"On the weekends he did some skiing and went swimming at Braggs Pond. It was between East Hartland and the camp. I was there once but now it is a swamp. Sometimes he and his friends went by truck to Winsted to the movies or to hang around. He didn't come home very often because it was pretty far away.

"Adolphe stayed there for about a year. I think he had enough of this work and jobs became more plentiful. Adolphe got a job at Sargent Lock & Tool Co. and worked as a molder of brass.

"In April 1942 he joined the Army and went to England, Africa, and Italy. He was overseas for 3 years.

"Adolphe married Ruth Koelle from New Haven. They had five children: Roberta, Mark, Kevin, Karen, and Ann.

"I went with my brother about 1965 to the camp and we only saw the headquarters' building. Just the concrete posts of the barracks remained.

"Adolphe liked being in the CCC because we were brought up in the woods and he liked the outside work. He said it was the best thing ever made.

"My brother passed away in 2004."

I then interviewed Adolphe's son, Mark. "My dad

said he was working for a dollar a day. He was just 16 years old. He hitchhiked back and forth from camp to Hamden. There were times when my step-grandfather, Danforth, drove up on a weekend to visit or bring my dad home.

"My uncle Adam and I would drive up the back roads to go back and my uncle remembered what he did as a kid when he visited my dad.

"Adam left my dad's album at the Stone Museum to share with them. But a few weeks later we went up there and they said they misplaced it. Luckily I had them copied.

"Dad loved to cut wood and burn wood in his stove. He taught my brother and I how to cut wood with an axe. It definitely came from his days in the CCC."

Arthur Longley

Art Longley from Hamden worked at Camp Robinson in East Hartland. www.legacy.com

At a CCC Reunion in Chatfield Hollow State Park in 2008, I met Art Longley but wasn't able to interview him that day. Luckily Art wrote me an email on Jan. 29, 2009:

Request:
Looking for old buddies that were in Camp Robinson, 180th Co. CCC, East Hartland, CT, 1939 to 1941. My brother was in Camp Robinson before me. Curley was his nickname.
- Art Longley

I responded to his inquiry stating I didn't know about his brother but I would like to find out about his life and experiences in the CCC.

"Here is some basic info about my life. I was born on Feb. 19, 1922 in New Haven. My parents were Arthur and Marie (Lendroth). I was the youngest of five. Ellen was the oldest, followed by Edwin, Robert, and Doris.

"After my third year in high school, I quit and searched unsuccessfully for a job.

"I joined the CCC on April 15, 1939 and became a member of Company 180 in East Hartland. I didn't feel bad about going away from home because my brother had been at Camp Robinson for two years and I had visited him many times. I went swimming at Braggs Pond and had picnics. Braggs Pond got washed out during the 1938 flood. One day my brother Edwin ('Curley') and another guy were digging a test hole for a new dam and it caved in on them. They were very lucky to get out alive.

"On the day that I arrived, I was in line at the supply room waiting to get fitted for shoes and clothes when someone read the roster and asked, 'Who's Longley?' I replied, 'Here.' Three guys came over and one said, 'It must have been the milkman.' I was only 110 pounds. My brother who had just left this camp weighed 165 pounds and was as hard as a rock.

"Camp was tough at first. Then I got to know some of the guys. Since I went to the same camp that my brother was in for two years, his friends helped me along. That really helped.

"Some of my friends in camp were: Lou Kulpa, Chris Marrinelli, Joe Shermanski, and Curley Provanzo from New Britain. Later in life I met up with Lou Kulpa a couple of times and Curley drilled an artesian well at my business.

"My main job at this camp was doing gypsy moth control and this is all I did there. We searched for gypsy

These boys look pretty happy at Camp Robinson in East Hartland. Roberta Kosnoff Sciacca

moth egg masses and painted them with creosote.

"In the winter there wasn't much to do in the evening. We mostly listened to the radio. In the summer we went swimming, played horseshoes, took walks, played ball, wrote letters, played ping pong, and hung out at the canteen.

"On the weekends I took it easy. I'd go to town, go home, or be on fire watch.

"The food wasn't that bad. Some guys complained all the time. The food did get a little bad towards the end of the month. We all survived.

"After 18 months in the CCC I left because I got a job at Pond Lily Co.

"During WWII, I served in the Army. When I got out, I got a job as a mechanic. I then moved up to supervising the garage for Cott Beverage Corp. After working there for 12 years, I opened up a garage, Circle A Automotive and Truck Repair, in Hamden. My son owns it now.

"I was married twice and I had four children: June, Dawn, Arthur, and Sharon.

"The CCC life was good for me. I learned many things that were helpful throughout life. The camp had classes at night. I took a mechanics class. It helped me get three stripes in the Army. I've gone back to my old CCC camp site many times with my brother, wife, daughter, and friends. I have a lot of good memories of my time at Camp Robinson."

Arthur Longley passed away on Dec. 22, 2010 at the age of 88.

Eugene J. Bellucci

On Sept. 18, 2010 Eugene Bellucci attended a CCC Reunion in Stafford Springs and shared his stories. Podskoch

Eugene Bellucci (back row far right) with his good friends at Camp Robinson in the summer of 1933. They lived in the tent (behind them) that had a wooden platform. Eugene Bellucci

"I was born on Dec. 4, 1914. My father, Michael, worked for New Haven Gas Co. He was hit by a car as he crossed the road and died at about the age of 50. My mother, Armida, was left alone with four children: Aida, Frank, me, and Edward. Mom got a job at a nursing home. She never got married again. When she got older she moved to Savin Rock Area. It was a resort, a big place with rides. My mother lived to be 96.

"I graduated from West Haven High School. Then I worked for a peddler. I helped him buy produce at the market. We drove around town in a truck. He'd holler, 'Vegetables!' I'd deliver the produce to the homes.

"In 1933 I signed up for the CCC in New Haven. They took me and other guys by truck to New London. We went by boat to Fishers Island for training. We read and learned about forestry. At first I was a little lonesome. We stayed for about ten days and lived in tents. Then we went back to New London and then truck to East Hartland. It was different living way up in the mountains compared to New Haven.

"I didn't mind leaving home. I met some nice guys at Camp Robinson. We first lived in tents. I have a few pictures and one has my six friends in a tent. The buildings were put up pretty quickly. Some of the boys helped the foremen build.

"My first job I was with a crew clearing the forest. Then the officers found out about my clerical ability. I was made the camp clerk. I took a correspondence course in accounting. They made me an assistant leader and I got paid an extra 6 dollars a month. Our military and civilian offices were in separate rooms.

"On the weekends I hitchhiked home. Since I worked in the office I got to know the officers well. They helped me by giving me a ride to Wallingford because many of them lived in that area. From there I took a trolley or bus home.

"In East Hartland I met a girl at a church dance. I'd let her know when I was going to town by calling her from the company office where I worked. We'd go out to dinner. One time she drove me to Winsted and we went to a movie.

"On June 30, 1934 I was honorably discharged. I got a job as a soda jerk in New Haven near the Shubert Theater where I met a lot of famous people.

"While in camp I got a degree in accounting from a correspondence course. This was a big help in getting office jobs. My first office job was with Connecticut Refining Co. We sold gas under the name Benzoline. I was the office manager till my boss died. His wife hired someone else and we had a disagreement and I left. Then I worked C. W. Blakeslee Construction Co. I worked at their concrete plant. After 8 or 9 years as manager I worked for an automotive company, Nizen Motor Parts. I then went into business by myself doing accounting.

"During WWII, I was with Benzoline. My boss put me in charge of the rationing board. When I got drafted I was excused from the draft because of that job.

"In 1938 I married Elsie Ferrucci and we had two children, Elaine and Eugene Jr. Elsie died in 1976.

"A few years after leaving the camp I went back to my old camp with my children. I had had a great time there and it was a good learning experience."

Eugene J. Bellucci, 98, of 125 Putnam Ave., Hamden, died May 30, 2013 at Hamden Health Care after a brief illness.

John Piotrowski

On Jan. 26 2008 I gave a presentation on the CCC camps in Connecticut at the Thomaston Library. In the audience was John Piotrowski and his wife Ethel. John told the audience about his experiences at Camp Robinson in East Hartland.

"I came from a large family of seven children. It was hard for my father to raise his family during the Depression. Both of my parents came from Poland and they had it hard because they had to learn the language of their new country. My dad, John, worked as a laborer at the Eagle Lock Co. in

At the Thomaston Library in March 2008 John Piotrowski shared his CCC experiences. Podskoch

Terryville. There were times when dad didn't work all the time. My mom, Romualda, did her best to feed and clothe her children: Theodore, Edna, me, Raymond, Regina, Lucile, and Edwin.

"In 1916 I was born in Terryville, the third oldest. We older kids had to get jobs to help their family.

"I think my mother heard about the CCC. She may have contacted the 1st selectman. My mom and I went down to the town hall on July 1, 1934 and signed up. I just had my 18th birthday.

"Then we went to the Bristol Armory and got on an old grey Army bus that went to New London. We took a ferry to Fishers Island where we were processed and given a physical and shots. We were issued Army clothes that were cavalry uniforms from WWI. Then we were asked where we wanted to go: Flagstaff Arizona or a camp in Connecticut. I chose Connecticut because I heard it was too cold in Flagstaff.

"The Army sent me by bus to Camp Robinson in East Hartland.

"Leaving home didn't bother me. It was in the woods and I loved it there.

"I had a few jobs. We started work at 8 am. We were driven out to a site in a truck and picked up at 3:30.

"For my first job I was assigned to a stone mason. He lived in Hartford where his dad was in the masonry business. We built the fireplaces in front of the lean-tos in the Peoples State Forest.

"We also built a road to Barkhamsted that included building walls along culverts. In fact I left our names in a

John and Ethel Piotrowski holding the CCC ring that John gave to Ethel while they were dating. Ethel gave me the ring to share when I give CCC talks. Podskoch

A close-up view of Piotrowski's CCC ring that has a surveyor's transit, and two trees. Podskoch

Prince Albert can in the wall. It was about 2' down and the opening was visible but I never went back to see if it was still there.

"Then I was transferred to a type mapping crew. This was a survey of the land and types of trees in the area. I worked with a man, who I think his name was Robert McCovy. He was a Yale Forestry School graduate. There were also two CCC boys in my group. I was the compass man. We went in a straight line and mapped the area between two roads. We worked in thousand-yard increments. We had a scout who ran both ways of the line and yelled out what he saw, for example, 'swamp', or 'confer' or 'stone wall,' etc. The third guy, the leader, drew maps and took notes. I had a compass to go in a straight line unless I got to a pond and had to go around. The worse parts were the laurel bushes, big boulders, or ledges.

"While we were working we saw herds of deer.

"For lunch we were handed a bag with sandwiches and tea in a Thermos. Some guys wanted coffee so they brought a pot.

"I also worked part time with a surveyor. I was a pole man.

"After work we went to the mess hall for supper. The food was great except for Sunday night when they had 'bleep on a shingle.'

"A pig farmer came every day to pick up the garbage to feed his pigs. Then he'd butcher a pig and gave it to the camp.

"In the evening I mostly read in the library. In the rec hall there was a pool table. A friend of mine from Bridgeport beat me with a run of 50 balls.

"There were ski trails and a ski hill that the CCC boys built. The camp had skis. Once I went skiing and tried going downhill but crashed.

"Boxing was also popular. I had friend, John Morisey of Deep River, who trained outside. He won in the 150-pouind class in Hartford and other amateur fights.

"I played basketball in Winsted. We went by truck in the night to play. I didn't make the team.

"Every weekend I went home. We hitchhiked on Rt. 8. We wore our uniforms and people picked us up all the time. I liked to visit my girlfriend.

"After that I worked for about three months in the infirmary. The only injuries were from axe cuts on feet and toes and wood slivers.

"In the infirmary we had two rooms: an office and a room with two beds. If there were any serious injuries they were sent to Fishers Island. We had one case of appendicitis. There was a doctor who went from camp to camp. In fact, he never came to our camp.

"The dentist came about once a month to pull teeth. I had one tooth that was pulled by him.

"When they decided to send a cadre of 25 men to Vermont I was one of the group. We were going to open a camp near Ludlow (Okemo). Our camp was located at the ski resort.

"In the Vermont camp I also worked in the infirmary. There was a carpentry crew building the barracks. I think it was a hired crew. The CCC boys lived in tents.

"In July or August of 1935 I was transferred to Fort Ethan Allen artillery range in Essex Junction. I was in the infirmary with a doctor from Tufts Medical College.

"There were no serious injuries but I did get frostbitten from walking in the slush and cold.

"We also had tents with wooden floors and we ate with mess kits.

"After a year and a half in the CCC, I saw snow on Mt. Mansfield and I didn't want to spend the winter up there.

"I left and got a job in New Departure Roller Coasters in Bristol. I worked on parts and machinery. I got an apprenticeship and transferred and got a job doing tool and die work. I was there for five years. Then I worked in a shop making parts. I also worked for a power company where I drilled and tapped holes in pipes that were in the ground. They had to dig holes for me so I could do the work.

"In September 1939 Ethel and I got married. We had five children: Frances, Edwin (d. 1985), Patricia, Ann, and Raymond.

"During the war I was deferred because I did work related to the war effort and because I had two children.

"After the war I worked at Associated Spring Co. for 30 years and retired in 1978.

"In the CCC I grew up a little bit. I went from a skinny boy to a man. I learned discipline and how to take and give orders."

Then Ethel brought out a small box. In it was a silver ring with an emblem showing a surveyor's transit, a tree, and a pine tree. She said to me, "My husband John saved up his five dollars and bought it at the camp store. He gave it to me as a token of his love for me. None of my children want it. Would you like to have it?"

I said, "I'd love to have it and show it to my audiences when I talk about the CCC."

John M. Piotrowski passed away on Jan. 17, 2011 in Morriston, Fl. at the age of 94. His wife Ethel died on March 7, 2013.

Michael Bacha

Michael Bacha of Shelton joined the CCC in 1938 and worked at Camp Robinson. Michael Bacha Jr.

CCC historian Kathleen Duxbury of New Jersey told me she met Michael J. Bacha of Slanesville, West Virginia at a CCC Gathering in Branson, Missouri. He told Kathleen that his father, also named Michael, had been in the CCC in Connecticut. They lived together in Slanesville so I arranged for a telephone interview with Michael Sr. on Jan. 20, 2011.

"I was born in Shelton, Conn. in 1921. My father, Joseph, an immigrant from Austria worked as a machinist at the mill. My mother was named Mary; my three sisters were: Anna, Mary, and Helen.

After the 10th grade I left high school to help my family where I worked at the mill with my father. "A recruiter came to our town of Shelton and talked to us at a ballgame about joining the CCC. In 1938 I signed up in Shelton. They took about eight guys from our town by bus to East Hartland.

"After working a while in the woods, they asked if I wanted to be a leader. I led a group of 10-15 guys and we cut cordwood.

"I don't remember too much fooling around or joking. We were very serious. I was the team leader. We were cutting

Camp Robinson boys taking a lunch break in Peoples SF. Roberta Kosnoff Sciacca

(L–R) 1 Michael Bacha's experiences in the CCC helped him when he was in the Navy in WWII. Michael Bacha Jr. 2 Bacha and other Camp Robinson enrollees cut and stacked cordwood they got from the Tunxis State Forest. Roberta Kosnoff Sciacca

Ralph "Bud" Meredith

Ralph "Bud" Meredith in front of the Conn. CCC Museum in Stafford Springs where he attended a reunion of CCC alumni. Podskoch

trees that weren't straight. It was called 'liberation cutting.' There were other groups that worked on projects such as building roads.

"While working in the woods I got cut in the leg by a bush hook. We had a doctor who stitched me up right below the knee.

"It wasn't bad leaving home because I went home almost every weekend. A lot of guys had cars and we hitched rides with them. We all pitched in for gas.

"At night we had classes. I took some high school classes.

"After supper we played basketball at a court they built outside. There were no teams. We were way in the woods.

"After a year in the CCC I got a job with Manning, Maxwell, and Moore. We made gauges for machinery in Bridgeport. My job was as a gauge calibrator. I worked six months and then worked at Sponge Rubber Co. Then I quit work and took classes at night and finished high school. I learned how to silver solder. I also learned on my own how to fix watches and clocks. I still tinker with them today.

"In 1942 I joined the Navy. I went aboard the USS Denver, a light cruiser."

"I got married to Catherine Arent in 1945 in California. We have two children, Catherine and Michael.

"After 30 years in the Navy I retired as Lieutenant.

"Then I took two years of college classes in Norfolk, Va. where I studied hotel management and received a degree.

Michael Bacha passed away on Aug. 28, 2013. On March 25, 2014 his wife, Catherine, died. They had been married for 68 years.

Charlene Farley of Fairfield contacted me in the summer of 2008 and told me her father, Ralph Meredith, had been in the CCC. I asked her if she would be interested in bringing her father to the CCC Reunion at the CCC Museum in Stafford Springs in October. She said that she would try to attend.

On Oct. 11, Charlene and her father came to the CCC reunion all the way from Fairfield, an hour and a half trip. Here is what he told the audience about his life and his CCC experience:

"I was born on June 18, 1917. My father William worked at Yale Locks Co. My mother was Florence and I had a sister, Jean.

"I only went two years to high school. I quit because my dad was having a hard time keeping our house. He only made $18 a week.

"I worked with show horses that were in Madison Square Garden. I also had a job working in a pharmacy in Old Greenwich. I also worked as a glass blower. There were quite a few guys in Greenwich that were in the same financial situation as my parents. I had a buddy, Walter Starkens, who is now in Arizona. He was in the CCC before me and told me to get in.

"In 1935 I went to the first selectman in Greenwich. I told him I needed to help my father. The selectman helped me get into the CCC.

Camp Robinson's rec hall was used for dances, speakers, variety shows, and a place for enrollees to relax, play pool or cards. It also had a store that sold soda, candy, cigarettes, etc. Roberta Kosnoff Sciacca

"On June 22, 1935 I enrolled in the CCC. I had just turned 18. I first went to New London and then the Army sent me to Camp Robinson in East Hartland. I was assigned to one of the six barracks.

"We did a lot of forest work on diseases that attacked the trees. We cut off the infected branches.

"I enjoyed the camp food. In those days you were hungry after a hard day in the woods. I didn't complain.

"After supper I went to the rec hall and had a coke for 5 cents and bought cupcakes. In the evening we also played baseball and cards.

"We used to play tricks on guys, too. In the evening we'd nail their shoes to the floor and when they got up in the morning they had a hard time getting them on.

"On the weekends I used to go home. One Friday night a friend from Bridgeport brought me and two other guys to his town. Then I hitchhiked home.

"I liked it there and wanted to stay but my aunt, who had money, advised my dad to have me get another job. My father talked to the commanding officer about getting a better paying job for me. My captain said I could get a discharge if I got a job.

"When my sister got me a job as a welder at Electrolux, I was honorably discharged on Sept. 13, 1935 after serving almost three months in the CCC.

"During WWII, I joined the Army but failed the physical because of hearing problems. I went to a doctor who blew out my ears to get rid of a wax buildup. Then I had my physical redone and I passed. I went to the Panama Canal for three years. I was a cook for the General.

"After the war I got a job working for the town of Greenwich.

"In 1950 I got married to Lucy Mae Easma Ramsey who was from Maine. We met at a dance. She had two daughters, Sheila and Geneva, from a previous marriage. Then Lucy and I had two daughters, Beth and Charlene.

"About 15 years ago I went with a friend to see my old CCC camp. It had changed a lot. All of the buildings were gone.

"The one thing I learned from the CCC was discipline so that when I went into WWII, I was used to taking orders. I also learned the importance of getting along with people and making the best out of life."

Ralph "Bud" Meredith passed away on Jan. 4, 2011 at 93 years of age.

Roger Aubrey

Roger Aubrey at a CCC Reunion in Burrville is telling other alumni and friends about his time at Camp Robinson. Podskoch

On October 19, 2009 Roger Aubrey came to a CCC reunion at Burr Pond in Burrville, Conn. I was surprised because he drove over 200 miles from Sugarloaf, Penn. (near Hazelton) to attend the reunion.

"I was in the CCC from July 2, 1940 to June 30, 1941. I graduated from Willimansett High School near Holyoke, Mass. It was hard to find a job so I joined to help my family.

"My parents, Elijah and Regina, had nine children to feed and clothe. Doris and George were the eldest. I was next followed by Jeanne, Donald, Lucille, Robert, Ruth,

These boys are eager to buy soda, candy and cigarettes at the camp canteen in the rec hall. National Archives

and Gertrude.

"Dad was unemployed for several years. He did any job he could. At that time it was the worst part of the Depression. Someone told my dad about the CCC. Mom and Dad talked to George and me about joining. We followed their wishes and signed up. They took us to Camp Robinson in East Hartland.

"There wasn't any problem in being away from home because we had to help our parents. There were no ands, ifs, or buts. It was also easier since my brother and I were in the same barracks.

"For me it was a good life. I had a job doing something for my family. I looked upon it as a challenge. I didn't mind being away because we were only about 35 miles from home.

"My first job was working for the education advisor, Richard A. Fear. I was his secretary. I might have gotten the job because in high school I took commercial courses such as typing, bookkeeping, and shorthand.

"I took care of the library, taught typing, and ran the 8 mm movie projector. The movies came in the mail. I did this for about three months. Then I was promoted to junior leader.

"From Aug. 21 to November I was the canteen steward. Lt. Kimball chose me for this job. I worked during the day ordering supplies. Candy and ice cream were the best sellers. Hood Ice Cream came from Springfield, Mass. I got candy and gum from a vendor who stopped by. I also sold bottled soda, shaving cream, aftershave lotion, lip ice, and deodorant.

"I also was the mail clerk. The mail came to me and I arranged it alphabetically. I also sold stamps, letter materials, and pencils.

"Every month I made out a report to Lt. Kimball. The head man in camp was Capt. Jules L. Paradeans who had fought in WWI with the Belgian field artillery.

"I opened the store to the boys at night from 7-9 pm. It paid me an extra $10 a month. I was getting a total of $46 a month. $22 went home to my parents.

"Part of my job was cleaning the rec hall. I did this in my free time. The senior leader supervised and controlled the activities of the boys in the rec hall. The rec hall consisted of camp headquarters, canteen, and main rec room.

"From Nov. 16, 1940 to March 15, 1941 I was the secretary for the state offices and the general clerk for the LEMs. The LEMs were always asking me to do something.

"Then from March 16 to June 30, 1941, I was called a technical service clerk. I did miscellaneous jobs such as the payroll for all administrators of the camp.

"I kept getting inside jobs. I missed doing outside work like the other guys were doing. When I was young I loved being in the woods and I always wanted to be a forest ranger.

"My brother George was in for only a few months with me. He worked on building Hurricane Ridge Rd.

"After supper I'd go in the rec hall. It was next to the last building on the north side of camp. I played ping pong there or tennis on a court outside with a fence around it. I was a left-hander and had the advantage. I was the camp champ in both. There weren't any tournaments. The senior leader was the champ and I beat him. They had tennis rackets and balls at the rec hall. We had to sign them out.

"On Thursday nights they took us on trips to Hartford or Springfield. Most guys liked Hartford. Sometimes we

Some enrollees like Roger Aubrey (above) who knew typing or stenography worked in the Administration Office and did record keeping, ordering, etc. CT CCC Museum

stopped at a roadside stand that had a 'Ginny Grinder.' It had meats, tomatoes, lettuce, and soda for about 35 cents. Most memorable to me was going down hills and country roads. The trucks had side benches for about 20 guys. We folded the benches up for about 30 miles. We enjoyed standing and singing. We just sang songs till we got to Granby. Our voices echoed through the valley. Then when we got to Granby we sat down.

"On the weekends I tried to go home. If I stayed at camp I played pickup football. There were no formal teams.

"I never got hurt working but I saw a couple guys who banged up their legs with an axe. We had a rotating Army doctor, Phillip Schultze, who took care of the sick.

"I decided to leave the CCC when my year was up. Dad's former company, B. F. Perkins, started getting orders again. My brother was working at the Springfield Armory making rifles.

"When I got home my first job was working from 6 pm to 6 am in a cotton factory in Holyoke. My next job was at a plant making beer filters. Then on Feb. 18, 1942 to April 25, 1943, I got a federal job at Bradley Field.

"On Sept. 6, 1943 I married Jeannette Lavallee. We had four children: Priscilla, Jim, who died in a plane crash, Margaret, and Joanne.

"I was drafted into the Army on April 12, 1943 and went to Fort Devens, Mass. on April 19th. Then I went for basic training in Miami. I passed a test and went to teletype school in Tampa, Fla.

"My next job was doing Air Force supply work in Oklahoma. In 1944 I did photo reconnaissance in England and did support work for Patton's Army. Before the D-Day Invasion my squadron took pictures of all the bridges between the Channel and Paris, France.

"After the war I worked at Westover Field in Chicopee, Mass. in the supply department. In 1954 I went to Dover Air Force Base in Dover, Del. where I worked for 30 years. I retired in 1984.

"I have gone back to Camp Robinson about 10 times. One of our WWII friends lives in Granby. I was always at a desk and I missed doing outside work. I really wanted to be a forest ranger.

"In the CCC I learned to have confidence in my abilities to please whomever I was working for. I had the belief that whomever you worked for you had to work hard for them."

Roger lives in Lewes, Delaware.

Gaetano "Guy" Aiello

Guy Aiello worked for over a year at the CCC camp in East Hartland where he mostly did masonry work. He is with his wife Isabel and daughter Angela. Angela Andreoli

In 2013, I met Angela Andreoli of East Windsor at a CCC Reunion at the Conn. CCC Museum. She told me that her both her father, Guy Aiello, and father-in-law, Walter McVety, had been in the CCC.

"My father enjoyed driving our family to the park and was very proud of his masonry work in the CCC."

The next year Angela sent me this information and photos of her father, Gaetano "Guy" Aiello.

"My father was born on Sept. 27, 1914 in Faroleto Antico, located in the SW part of Italy. His parents, Augustino and Angela, had six children: Mary, Frank, Gaetano, Peter, Thomas, and Rosina. My father only graduated from 8th grade.

"Guy was 16 years old when his family moved to the US and lived in Hartford. My father said the move was very traumatic for him.

"He attended the Arsenal Trade School in Hartford for 9th grade. Then he worked at Romal Saglio's farm in Andover, Conn. and was paid $4 a week. On June 17, 1930 he became a citizen of the United States.

"When my father was 19 years old he joined the CCC and was sent to Co. 180 in East Hartland. During the first four months he did reforestation work in the Tunxis SF. Then from April till November 1934 he did masonry work. His discharge papers state that he did excellent work. Then on Dec. 1, 1934 my father was sent to Fort Wright Army

(L–R) 1 The Oak Lodge stone chimney at Chatfield Hollow SP. Angela Andreoli 2 One of the masonry projects that enrollees did at Camp Robinson was the ranger cabin. Podskoch 3 The Hurricane of 1938 caused tremendous damage to Connecticut's forests. Harold Mattern traveled to many of the forests measuring the downed trees and calculating the amount of lost timber. DEEP

Hospital but it doesn't state his illness. He was discharged on the 31st of Dec.

"Dad earned $30 each month: $25 was sent to his uncle, Frank Fazio, in Hartford and he had $5 spending money.

"After the CCC Dad worked in the construction and plastic industry. Then he worked in a ball bearing plant for 15 years.

"My father married Isabel LaBianca and they had four children: Angela, Ann, Lawrence, and Thomas.

"I asked him how the CCC helped him. He said, 'I learned to read and write in English.' All through his life he was very proud to have been part of the CCC."

On Nov. 16, 1982 Guy Aiello passed away.

Harold Mattern, Part III

Harold Mattern worked at many CCC camps in Connecticut and eventually worked for the Conservation Dept. This is a continuation of Harold Mattern's movement from Camp Graves (Chap. 21) in Union to Camp Fernow in Eastford (Chap. 9), and then to Camp Robinson.

Harold Mattern said, "I came to East Hartland to work with Dr. Kienholz, a botanist and foreman at the camp. He was doing research on the growth of trees. I knew my tree species and I was the person he was looking for.

"While in Camp Fernow I bought a 1936 Chevy. My father had saved money that I sent home and he gave me the money to buy the car. I paid $100 at Bowser Motors in Willimantic. I rented a garage to hide it because you couldn't bring a car to camp. The garage was about four miles from camp. Dr. Kienholz knew I had a car, in fact he found me the garage to rent.

"When I went home I charged guys 25 cents apiece to give them a ride.

"While working with Dr. Kienkolz I learned a lot about flowers and ferns. He was doing studies on the forest floor. We went to farms in different areas and identified the plants. He drove a federal govt. pickup truck. Sometimes he had another person go with him but it was mostly me that worked with him. I enjoyed working with him very much. He took a lot of pictures and I carried his equipment. He did all the technical work.

"The doctor was married and lived in East Hartland with his wife and two children.

"I had this job till Sept. 21, 1938 when the hurricane hit Connecticut. We then worked on measuring the logs and calculating the volume of wood in the downed trees.

"We first went down to Camp Buck in Portland where there was a big blowdown. We were able to drive in because crews had cleared the road of trees. I had a couple of guys with me. We cut and measured the logs and got the diameter of the trees and their volume. This work kept me busy for a long time.

"Later I came back to Camp Fernow and stayed there till May 1941.

"Then I joined the Army and went to Camp Edwards on Cape Cod for training. In December they sent me to Quincy, Mass. to protect the Fall River Shipyard. I stayed there till Feb. 8, 1942 and they shipped me overseas. At first they shipped us on a troop train for five days across the US and then by boat to Australia.

"In Australia we set up search lights in Brisbane (eastern coast) and protected the coast. We also shipped stuff on a narrow gauge train to Townsville (northeast coast).

"In 1943 I came home and got married. I got a job as foreman for the state and worked as a skilled tradesman doing forestry work."

Harold Mattern died on June 8, 2012.

CHAPTER 12
HADDAM

HISTORY

Company 1201 established Camp S-64 on Dec. 11, 1933 in the Cockaponset State Forest (CSF) in Haddam, Conn. It was the 13th and last camp established in the state. It was unique in that the enrollees didn't sleep in tents when they arrived because the wooden buildings were ready.[1]

Company 1201 established Camp S-64 on Dec. 11, 1933 in the Cockaponset State Forest (CSF) in Haddam, Conn. It was the 13th and last camp established in the state in 1933. It was unique in that the enrollees didn't sleep in tents when they arrived because the wooden buildings were all ready.[3]

The Feb. 28, 1934 issue of The Bristol Press describes the effect of a blizzard on Camp Filley's New York City recruits:

"C.C. Lads Have New Experience"

When tales of experience during the recent blizzard are recounted, none probably will find more interested listeners than those of some 200 Civilian Conservation Corps boys stationed at Camp Philly in the Cockaponset State Forest here. The boys were recruited mostly from the streets of New York. Before coming to camp many had not ventured into a forest; few had ever faced the dilemma of being snowbound with avenues for food supplies cut off by eight and 10-foot snow drifts.

On Dec. 11, 1933 enrollees, dressed in WWI Army clothes, arrived at their new home, Camp Filley in Haddam, where they would spend their next six months working in the Cockaponset State Forest. DEEP State Parks Archives

At the entrance to camp there was a large boulder inscribed with "US-CCC, Camp Filley, 1201-CO."

www.geni.com

Walter O. Filley

The camp was named to honor Walter O. Filley, who played an important part in the development of forestry in Connecticut. He was born on July 27, 1877 in New Haven. After graduating from New Haven High School, he spent 10 years in the photography business. He graduated from Yale University in 1910, was an assistant instructor at the Yale School of Forestry, and then became an assistant at the US Dept. of Agriculture Conn. Experimental Station. He was the fourth State Forester and Treasurer of the State Parks and Forest Commission.[4]

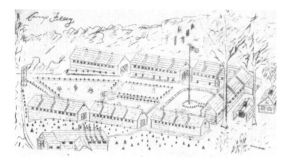

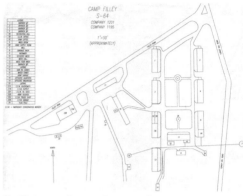

A drawing of Camp Filley by enrollee Kenneth Baron. The Officers' Quarters (bottom left), four barracks (two on each side above Officer's Quarters), Recreation Hall (to the right of the lower barracks), Wash Room (to the right of the upper barracks), Mess Hall (long building facing flag), Mess Gear Wash (behind Mess Hall in front of Infirmary), and Infirmary (farther behind Mess Hall).[2]

(Left) An aerial view of Camp Filley in the Cockaponset State Forest in Haddam in 1933. CT CCC Museum (Above) Camp Filley layout of buildings and roads. DEEP State Parks Archives

Visions of some reduced rations through failure of army trucks to cut a way through the drifts came to the boys. The camps 5-ton tractor was marooned four or five miles away on a road job on which the boys were working the day before the storm broke.

If there were any signs of stress among the lads, it required only the far-reaching experience of their camp superintendent, Richard Coughlin to counteract their fears. Using snowshoes, Superintendent Coughlin set out in the storm to drive back the marooned tractor. Before nightfall he had started the tractor on its rough voyage over the drifts, none of which was too tough to stand up against a bucking. Once back to camp a snowplow was attached and breaking out to the state highway accomplished so trucks could reach the supply depot and bring in rations.

The company was on hand to cheer Coughlin when he returned. The ovation he received was worthy of a "conquering hero" returning with a battle prize.

CSF covers over 16,000 acres of south-central Connecticut in 11 towns. The forest is named after Cockaponset, a Hammonasset chief who is buried in a section of Haddam called Ponset. The natives' village was on a fortified round hill in Chester. The Hammonassetts lived in the present-day towns of Madison, Killingworth, and Clinton.[5]

The land in the CSF was acquired by purchasing agent Elliott Bronson and then turned over to Conservation Dept. District Forester W. Foster Schreeder and Camp Superintendent Robert F. Coughlin who searched the deeds and titles. They then began work on surveying the boundaries of the CSF during 1927-28. From 1931-32 more land was purchased through the efforts of State Forester Austin F. Hawes.[6]

Once Camp Filley was settled one of its first projects was cutting out the ten-foot wide boundary lines of the Cockaponset State Forest. The enrollees set two-inch diameter iron pipes at the boundary corners. They then placed boundary disc markers with brass caps at intervals of 75-100 feet.[7] By Sept. 1934 approximately 19 of the 21 miles of boundaries were completed by the boys. Foreman Conlin supervised the boundary crew that had many boys from upstate NY who had some experience working with an axe and saw in the Adirondacks.[8]

Camp worked on the following projects in the CSF: picnic areas, fire trails and roads, surveying, forest improvement, fire ponds, a fire tower, charcoal, and gypsy

Camp Filley enrollees helped masons from Middleton in the building of this charcoal kiln in the Cockaponset State Forest. DEEP State Park Archives

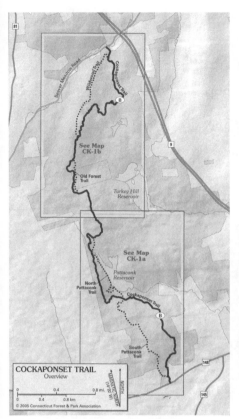

Cockaponset Trails built by the CCC.[13]

Enrollees built a lumber shed in 1934.[16] In 1940, enrollees poured a cement foundation and built a sawmill shed on it (shown on right).[17]

Men wrapped trees with burlap to help in killing the caterpillars. Connecticut Agricultural Experiment Station

Enrollees used these coupons to buy items at the camp Canteen. Gary Potter

moth control.[9]

One of the first roads built by enrollees was Filley Rd. which is just off Turkey Hill Rd. The half-mile road went from Turkey Hill Rd., past the camp, and then to Ranger Rd. where the forest ranger's home and garage were.[10] In 1936 enrollees worked on the construction of Buck and Beaver Meadow roads in Haddam.[11] By 1940 enrollees had constructed Cedar Swamp Road in Chester and Jerico Road in Haddam.[12]

In 1934 Camp began construction of the Cockaponset Trail. It began at Beaver Meadow Rd. near Exit 8 of Rt. 9 and twists and turns through CSF for over 7 miles going past the Pattaconk Reservoir to Rt. 148. Camp enrollees did most of the northern section. Hikers marvel at the intricate stone stairways and rock walls the enrollees built more than 80 years ago.[14]

Camp worked to arrest the spread of gypsy moths. Crews searched for egg masses and painted them with creosote to kill them. The trees that weren't infected were banded with burlap on their trunks during the summer to trap the caterpillars.[15]

In 1934 the Army and Navy Club began awarding a prize for the best camp in the state. On June 30, 1934 Camp received the Best Camp prize for the third quarter. The camp was led by Captain Roland W. Sellew, 2nd Lt. John C. Vaughn, 1st Lt. Richard K. Brown (Surgeon), and Superintendent Robert F. Coughlin.[18]

Superintendent Coughlin was assisted by the following foremen: Arthur H. Christie, recreational center; Milton Arnold, type mapping; Adrian Barry, water holes; William Collin, boundaries; Daniel Devine, construction; Walter Hall, cuttings; Albion Jack, gypsy moths; George Jayne, fire lines; Henry Potter, roads; William Ridley, machine operator; Stephen Russell, mechanic, and Harry Thomas, blacksmith.[19]

The Army selected some of the 200 enrollees to help with supervision in the barracks, canteen, mess hall, etc. In 1934 Camp Filley had a Senior Leader, Frank Catapano, who was in charge of the Leaders who were paid $45 a month and Assistant Leaders who were paid $36 a month. The Leaders in 1934 were: Henry Avery, Edward Clark, Robert Cornwall, Kenneth Deering, Stephen Fedunk, Jack Glasser, Herman Hegyi, Nick LaMonica, and Leon Ruderwicz. The Sub-Leaders were: Albert Bleckaer, Joseph

An Aug. 1935 group photo of Camp Filley. CT CCC Museum

A road constructed by Camp Filley in the Cockaponset Forest. DEEP State Parks Archives

The Beaver Meadow picnic area near the Odber Mill site. Enrollees constructed five fireplaces and approximately 16 tables. CT CCC Museum

Crucilla, Thomas Delahanty, John Finney, Jack Godberg, Basil Hudywa, Richard Kenney, William Kochler, Arthur Larson, Joseph Lhothan, Annello Lopez, Bernard Marvel, Anthony Masselli, Francis Mulligan, Alfred Peckrul, and Rudolph Ruderwicz.[20]

The Aug. 1, 1934 issue of the camp newspaper, The Filley Flash, reported that the Middletown Exchange Club visited Camp Filley. The club was honored with a banquet at which W. O., the man for whom the camp was named, State Forester A. F. Hawes, and Conn. Transient Camps head, Mr. Currier all spoke. Boxing matches were held after the banquet.

At the end of the summer of 1934 enrollees celebrated with an old fashioned clam bake. The Sept. 1934 issue of The Filley Flash stated they thought there was enough food but the "lobsters disappeared all too fast. The end of the clambake found but little of the large heap of food unconsumed." After the supper Father Guerriero, Mayor Bielefield, W. O. Filley, and A. F. Hawes gave speeches. Then the camp orchestra provided music.[21]

On July 31, 1935 Co. 1195 was organized at Camp

Chapman in Niantic, Conn. 1st Lt. George D. Freeman supervised the company of 120 men in conditioning exercises and camp fundamentals. On Aug. 9, 1935 Co. 1195 moved to Camp Filley and replaced Co. 1201. Captain Leavitt continued supervising Camp Filley along with Superintendent Robert F. Coughlin, Education Advisor Mr. Compana, camp doctor, Dr. O'Neill, and the forestry personnel.[22]

Projects

In the August 1936 issue of The Filley Flash Superintendent Coughlin reported on the past and future work of Camp:

The camp constructed about 8 miles of truck trails, 12' wide with 9' of gravel. Most of the work was done by hand but later aided by a Caterpillar tractor having trail builder attachments and a Cletrac 35 tractor.

Enrollees continued scouting and eradicating gypsy moths on about 40,000 acres of state and private land in the towns of Haddam, Chester, Middletown, and Middlefield.

The camp supervisors planned on thinning 1,000 or

(L–R) 1 Visitors inspecting the bridgework on Filley Rd. near Pattaconk Recreation Area. DEEP State Parks Archives 2 The CCC built many waterholes in the Cockaponset SF. They built where there were springs and lined them with stones. They provided water to fire fighters in the forest. DEEP State Parks Archives 3 A wood chopping contest in Eastford. CT CCC Museum

more acres of forest and removing dead and undesirable trees in order to promote the growth of desirable and productive trees.

They planned on building three recreation and picnic areas to accommodate 20 cars, five latrines, five fireplaces, and picnic tables. Enrollees completed the Beaver Meadow and Pattaconk recreation area. Work was to begin at the Turkey Hill reservoir where they planned to build a series of trails.

The next project was to weed the plantations where trees had been planted over the past years. They also planned on surveying 160 miles of roads in the Cockaponset forest.

With regard to fire prevention the camp planned on building 50 water holes at strategic locations in the forests and roads to provide accessible water to fight fires. They also began cutting fire lines through the forest and boundary lines to make it easier to access areas in the forest.[23]

The camp provided transportation to churches on Sundays. Also on Sundays at noon Army Chaplain Capt. W. B. Johnson held a non-sectarian service.[24]

Sports

Sports were an important part of camp life. In the spring Camp Filley had a baseball team that played other CCC camps and local town teams. The 1935 team had a 0.66 winning percentage. The enrollees also enjoyed playing intramural volleyball and softball and swimming at neighboring Higganum Reservoir, Turkey Hill Reservoir, and Cedar Lake in Chester.

Other athletic events were held for the enrollees. During the summer of 1934 Camp Filley enrollee Milton Kodz from Jordanville near Utica, NY came in second place in the Connecticut CCC Wood Chopping Contest. On Sept. 20, 1934 Kodz and these men: Grant Adams, Henry Avery, Lyle Glendenning, Al Kent, Ed Koweleski,

Art Locke, and Chet Tatko entered the New England CCC Wood Chopping Contest at the Eastern States Exposition in Springfield, Mass. Kodz came home with the championship.[25]

Education Advisor Spear and Capt. Sellew tried to organize a football team in 1934 but were unable to obtain equipment. Although the enrollees didn't have a football team they were able to attend Yale football games and the entrance fee was $1.10 per game.[26]

During the winter of 1933-34, the Filley basketball team was able to play their home games at the Middleton State Armory and practice at the Middletown skating rink. Their opponents were Middletown Trade School, Wilson AC, Moodus Town team, Portland AC, and Camp Chapman. The next winter Camp Filley's basketball team played in the Industrial League at the YMCA in Middletown and other CCC and high school teams.[27]

On Oct. 10, 1934 The CFPA met at camp and presented the camp with the Association's Best Camp Award in Connecticut for the third period.[28]

Also in October Countess Alexandra Tolstoy, a nearby neighbor of Camp Filley and an exile from Russia, talked to the enrollees in the camp recreation hall about the Russian Revolution. Her father, Leo Tolstoy, a Russian novelist, short story writer, essayist, playwright, and philosopher, wrote War and Peace and Anna Korenina. The Countess told the enrollees that her father didn't oppose the Russian Revolution but the bloodshed that resulted from it. She left Russia because the new government radically differed from her father's principles. The Countess said she couldn't get a passport to Western Europe because those in power wanted her to be the curator of schools and museums dedicated to her father. She left Russia and lived two years in Japan before coming to the US. She felt the American farmer had the ideal life and came to Connecticut. She had no money and she and two other women worked up to 14 hours a day on a farm where they had 1,500 chickens and two cows. She also wrote every day and read material on politics and literature.[30]

Alexandra Lvovna Tolstaya (1884-1979) with her father Leo Tolstoy.[29]

Schedule of Evening Classes in 1934

Monday
6-7 pm First Aid - Algebra
7-8 pm First Aid - English Radio
8-9 pm First Aid - History - Debating

Tuesday
6-7 pm First Aid - Movies
7-8 pm First Aid - Movies
8-9 pm First Aid - Movies

Wednesday
6-7 pm First Aid - English - Auto Mech. - French
7-8 pm First Aid - Music - Surveying
8-9 pm First Aid - Civics - Music

Thursday
6-7 pm First Aid - Arithmetic
7-8 pm First Aid - Current Events - Gen. Forestry
8-9 pm First Aid - First Aid - Spelling

Friday
6-7 pm Radio
7-8 pm History
8-9 pm Civics

Henry B. N. Spear, Education Advisor[31]

Silviculture

During the 1935-36 winter crews worked in the Cockaponset State Forest. Crews tinned 269 acres and removed 586 cords of wood and most was sold while 181 cords were used as fuel in camp. Workers also produced 623 hardwood highway posts and 9,575 board feet of saw logs. During the month of February, 90 acres were thinned.[32]

1936 Flood

On the evening of Thurs., March 19, 1936 Camp received a call for help from the town of Middletown because the Connecticut River was flooding the town. Captain Leavitt sent two shifts of 70 enrollees each to help the residents. Capt. Levit, Lt. Vaughn, and Superintendent Coughlin supervised the men who worked day and night rescuing families from their homes, saving their furniture, patrolling the bridges, protecting the businesses from looting, and directing traffic. Camp used its ambulance and trucks to help the Middletown residents. Some enrollees volunteered to work up to 36 straight hours during the early surge of flooding.[33]

When the flood receded, enrollees continued to work during March and April in Middletown and surrounding towns of Haddam, Deep River, Cromwell, Hartford, and Chester. This work was important to prevent the spread of diseases. Camp enrollees earned praise for their relief work.[34]

Recreation Projects

Camp Filley foreman R. B. Hosier supervised his crew of 20 men in building and maintaining picnic areas in the Turkey Hill Block. The Beaver Meadow picnic area had four fireplaces and 16 picnic tables on the banks of Beaver Meadow Brook. There were also tables, fireplaces, and

CCC enrollees preparing to leave camp to aid with flood relief. Gary Potter

Bob Butterworth by an incinerator built by Camp Filley enrollees at the picnic area on Turkey Hill Rd. CT CCC Museum

The camp library was a place enrollees could visit that was quiet for reading books, magazines and newspapers. It was also used for writing friends and family. Kathleen Esche

Camp Filley built this wooden observation tower on Turkey Hill Rd. DEEP State Parks Archive

bathhouses at the Pataconk Picnic area on Filley Rd. at the Pataconk Reservoir. The third recreation picnic area was under construction at the Turkey Hill picnic area on Filley Rd. on Turkey Hill Reservoir. Enrollees acted as guards and caretakers who kept the areas clean and helped visitors.[35]

Education

In 1936 Barracks No. 5 was converted into a schoolhouse and writing and reading room. The building had new lighting fixtures and comfortable furniture that created a friendly quiet atmosphere for reading and writing letters home. The library's number of books increased by 200 from a donation from the Russell Library in Middletown.[36]

During 1937 the Education Dept. began to emphasize vocational classes to prepare the enrollees for jobs. Classes included typing, aviation, woodworking, mechanics, etc. Traditional classes were featured: spelling, arithmetic, English, current events, and geography. Some of the new classes were boxing, orchestra, dramatics, ballroom dancing, and swimming at the Middletown YMCA. The education building received a collection of books from a traveling library and also from the Curtis Memorial Library in Meriden.[37]

The April 1938 issue of The Filley Flash listed the following recreational activities: inter-barracks softball, horseshoes, inter-barracks volley ball, chess tournaments, card tournaments, weight lifting, track, flower gardens, bead work, metal and leather work, wood work, fencing, ping pong tournaments, wrestling tournaments, swimming, letter painting, mural painting, dancing, boxing, raising hogs, and baseball.

During July and August of 1938 Company 1195 built the Turkey Hill Observation Tower along the Cockaponset

Trail that was also built by the CCC. It took 71 days to construct the 23' high tower using timbers from the nearby forest. Two sets of stairs and a landing led a 10 x 10' wide platform where hikers got a spectacular view of the surrounding area. Since the area had been destroyed by an earlier forest fire, hikers had an unobstructed view of the trail head on Beaver Meadow Road to the northeast, Turkey Hill Reservoir to the south-southeast, and maybe a view of Camp Filley to the east. The cost of the tower was $282.43. Years later the tower was removed possibly due to deterioration of the timbers. The only remnants of the tower are four concrete footings.[38]

In 1939 two popular classes offered at Camp Filley were typing and Tree Surgery. Mr. Connors came twice a week from Middletown to teach typing classes that had the largest enrollment. Mr. Anderson taught Tree Surgery, Elementary Forestry and Nature study, all were practical courses that included tree identification and rope climbing. Graduates had an opportunity to seek employment as a tree surgeon.[39]

In October 1938 Camp Filley men cut up trees at the Congregational Church in Haddam downed by the 1938 hurricane. Thankful Arnold House Museum, Haddam

Two Camp Filley enrollees looking at announcements on the bulletin board by the Headquarters Building. CT CCC Museum

There were some new sports in 1939 besides the traditional, basketball, baseball, and softball. A 12-man archery team was organized. The boys made their own bows and arrows. They also constructed four target stands. The targets were constructed of twisted straw rope that they sewed together in a circle and covered with oilcloth. Capt. Schwartz painted the colored circles. Both Capt. Schwartz and Education Advisor Miner made their bows out of lemonwood.[40]

The boys built a 50-yard rifle range in the back of camp with seven targets with abutments. The men stood on a platform and use the surveying transit and Capt. Schwartz's high-powered telescope to see the hits. The Camp Filley rifle team lost twice to the local Higganum team. Horseshoe pitching was very popular on their three courts. Mike Vecchitto was the camp champion with 101 wins and only five losses. He was the past champion of Meriden in 1937.[41]

In June 1939 foreman Lawlor's crew cleared a site at the intersection of Filley Rd. and Old County Rd. for the construction of a portable saw mill to deal with the wood salvaged by Camp Filley after the devastating 1938 Hurricane. The work was part of the Fire Hazard Reduction Program.[42]

Enrollees had the ability to participate in religious services while in camp. In June 1939 Rev. Harry L. Huss, S. J. made weekly visits to Camp Filley on Tuesdays to give nine enrollees instruction before receiving the sacrament of confirmation. Huss stayed over night and in the morning had Mass for camp enrollees in the school building. Then

he visited four other camps. After weeks of instruction the nine Camp Filley enrollees traveled to Co. 2103 in Westfield, Mass and received confirmation with other CCC boys in the same district.[43]

After over five years of heavy use, Camp Filley's buildings were repaired in the summer of 1939. Seven Middletown carpenters replaced joists and beams under the buildings; installed new flooring in the infirmary; enlarged the sterilizing room in the kitchen; replaced all doors and screens, installed new sinks and doors between the shower and washroom; and constructed a new root cellar and oil storage shed.[44]

On Feb. 13 & 15, 1940 Camp Filley had a Sportsmen's and Conservation Show. Exhibits of sportsmen's equipment, foresters' work, and animal and tree exhibits were displayed in the school building and recreation hall. Sportsmen, taxidermists, and conservation groups had special exhibits and sporting goods. There were 48 specimens of birds, animals, and fish displayed by taxidermists and Connecticut State Fish and Game Commission. Eighteen enrollees acted as guides for the visitors. The boys constructed a hunter's cabin using slab wood in the recreation hall. The cabin surrounded a working fireplace. The cabin walls had hunting rifles, traps, deer heads, and hides with hunting and fishing brochures on the table. The March 15 issue of The Filley Flash stated the show was a tremendous success and there was hope of another in 1941.

After over seven years of work in the CSF, Camp closed on July 30, 1941. At first the Army retained custody of the camp.[45] On July 1, 1943 Camp was turned over to the Conn. State Forestry Department. The state then sold five buildings for $1,000 for salvage and kept the remaining 18 buildings.[46]

Former Department of Energy and Environmental Protection (DEEP) Museum Director Nicole Chalfant Shaw said in 2010: "All of the buildings were eventually removed and the land was left to return to a natural state. What remains is one of the best-preserved footprints of a CCC camp in the state. The trees and underbrush have grown up, but it is easy to see the indentations where the ground was leveled for each building. Still visible are all building foundations, connecting roads and paths, the camp dedication monument, and three cobblestone chimney stacks. Depressions clearly mark the location of the barracks, recreation hall, wash/supply room, mess hall, infirmary, and smaller ancillary structures.[47]

(L–R) 1 A fireplace and chimney are all that remain of the Camp Filley Rec Hall. 2 The camp stone is still at the Camp Filley site where it was placed in the early 1930's. The inscription is: "US-CCC, Camp Filley, 1201-CO." 3 Bob Butterworth, a CFPA trail maintainer in the Cockaponset State Forest, is standing on a hiking trail stone step built by Camp Filley during the 1930s. Most of the trails and stone stairs are still in use today. All photos courtesy Podskoch

"The 9.7-acre Camp has been designated a state archaeological preserve and placed on the State Register of Historic Places, becoming the first CCC site to be so protected and honored. Camp joins 25 existing state historic sites, of which only 8 are on DEEP property."[48]

LEGACY

The trees that the CCC planted over 80 years ago are actively managed for wood products and provide a diversity of plant life for wildlife habitat. Recreational opportunities abound including: hiking, cross-country skiing, fishing, snowmobiling, swimming, boating, and hunting. The CCC built most of the Cockaponset Trail and their hard work and craftsmanship can still be seen in the stone retaining walls and staircases. Some of the popular hiking trails are the Turkey Hill Loop near the Turkey Hill Reservoir and a 20-mile trail system around Pattaconk Reservoir Recreation Area near Chester. Some trails are only footpaths, while others are open to mountain bikes or horses. Many enjoy swimming, paddling, and fishing on Pattaconk Lake.

Camp Filley enhanced the Cockaponset Forest by building up the woodlands that had deteriorated over the years due to poor logging practices and forest fires. They planted trees, fought tree insects, and did silviculture work. Enrollees constructed the northern section of the Cockaponset Trail that is an integral part of the Blue-Blazed Trail System that is managed by the CFPA. The CCC also constructed Filley Rd. that opened the forest to tourists, hikers, and sportsmen. They constructed truck trails that enabled fire fighters to get to the forest fires more quickly

and loggers the ability to remove forest products.

Directions:

Take Rt. 9 to Exit 8 in Haddam and drive NE on Beaver Meadow Rd. At the 5-way intersection at Arnolds, turn a hard right and go south on Turkey Hill Rd. Follow to the first right and turn onto Filley Rd. Park behind the large red barn on your right. The abandoned Camp Filley is behind the barn.

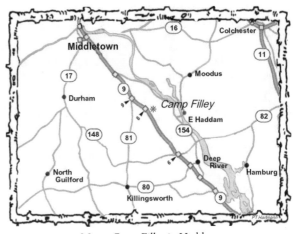

Map – Camp Filley in Haddam

MEMORIES

This poem was written by George Doll, a former leader at Camp Filley. The poem was published in 'Happy Days', a weekly CCC national newspaper.

"On My Way Home"
by George Doll

The robust life of the CCC
Will no longer be in store for me,
For in a few days – please don't talk,
I'll be on my way to New York.

One year of bliss and serenity,
And construction and entomology;
Alas the end! I must rescue my walk
For I'll be on the way to New York.

Camp Filley, for which I will pine;
The haven of my rousing good time.
But with regulations forming a staunch bulwark,
I'll soon be on the way to New York.

The things I have planned are of no avail
For I must cast off and set sail;
The road at last has reached a fork,
I must take the one to New York.

In spite of the fact I must pack,
I may change my name and come back;
Then when I think of leaving, I balk
But I'll soon be on my way to New York.

A place I've struck. I've been told
But Bickford's cellar will keep out the cold;
At any rate, the time, I'll watch like a hawk
For shortly I'll be on my way to New York.

E're I shove off I'll be of good cheer,
Aided, perhaps, by a few glasses of beer;
No more beans with very little pork,
For I'll be on my way home to New York City.

As I have slowly attained the height
So I must quickly turn out the light,
For someone in Washington has pulled the cork
And I must be on my way to New York.

Farewell to you Officers, Foresters and men
When I depart I may not return again;
Without a job, soon one must I stalk
For I'll be on my way to New York.
- The Filley Flash, July 1934

Boys dressed up and ready to go home. CT CCC Museum

"Adios"
by C. Terek

We leave you tonight for our home towns,
Our duties we hope are fulfilled;
Although the parting is hurting – leaving against our will,
So we hope in the fall
To pay you a call
And renew old acquaintances again.
- The Filley Flash July 1934

"The CCC in Forestry"
by August Jonza

When dawn doth come to view,
A frozen silence beams;
A group of men in slumbering dew
Are finishing their dreams.

At first the sound of whistles creep
To ears of those concerned;
Pretending to be sound asleep,
They wait the final word.

Then at last the whistles roar,
To wake the sleeping mind;
Still none respond, but wait for more,
Then the leaders grind.

O'er their bodies blankets fly,
The men get in a rage,
And how they cuss, "Oh, my! Oh, my!
One wouldn't believe their age.

Finally, they're all on foot,
And start to think of food,
'Cause when they're up, an empty gut
Gives them an awful mood.

Mon'ot'on'ous, as they would say,
To wait for morning feed,
There sure would be some Hell to pay,
If there was not enough to eat.

After breakfast some would stall,
And some rest on their beds,
In would come leaders big and small;
And make them fix their beds.

Inspection was the only phase
That they did ne're ignore,
For in that phase were many ways,
That would make the sergeant sore.

Inspection was soon over,
And men began to lurk,
For they had to rove,
In different kinds of work.

Amen, the details, there was one,
So ruthless and discrete;
Cause all day long they had to run,
And walk upon their feet.

The only consolation
The men would always say,
"Is the good ole army rations,
Beans served every day."

The afternoons were lonesome,
Thus, the men would laze;
To foremen it was boresome,
Today, tomorrow, always.

This is where this poem ends,

I hope I've made it clear to see;
The life of many hefty men,
"The CCC in Forestry."
- The Filley Flash, May 1934

"Cruel Winter"
by John Pitts

Ah! Cruel winter soon you'll fade
For the preparations of spring are being made.
You who vanquished the beauty of flowers,
With whistling wind, and icy showers.
You who changed the leaves from green to brown
And who destroyed the entrancing lakes,
Changing its rippling waters to barren ice cakes.
You who caused the birds to take wing,
Then coldness unbearable you started to bring.

Ah! Brr! soon for your biting wind
There'll be cool breezes of spring again,
For your lifeless snow enveloping hills,
There'll be violets, buttercup, and daffodils.
For your cold hard snow clouds of grey,
There'll be the warm billowing skies of April and May.
- The Filley Flash, July 1939

Winter at a CCC camp. Mark Kosnoff

"KPs Lament"
by Anthoy Masselli

(To be sung to the tune of "Twenty-One Years")

If you are a KP
You must wake up in time,
To serve bread and butter

To a mile-long chow line.
You wake up so early
You think it's still night,
And start in working
Before it's daylight.

Wash dishes at breakfast,
And dishes at noon,
More dishes at supper –
You'll go crazy soon.
Oh, don't be a KP
If you want to stay young,
For the work of a KP
It never gets done.
- The Filley Flash, Jan. 1937

The other things to do.
The C.C.C. I'm telling you
Is no place to get blue.

Now folks at home so dear and true,
A word we'd like to say,
The Captain and camp life here,
We'll take most any day.
- The Filley Flash, Feb. 1938

While working in the woods camp Filley boys take a break by a warm campfire. CT CCC Museum

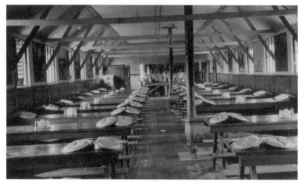

The Camp Filley Mess Hall with tables set with cups and dishes, salt & pepper shakers, and sugar bowls. The cooks, servers and KP workers are ready to serve a meal. Kathleen Esche

"So Sayeth the Rookies"
by F. P. Button

When we rookies first came to camp,
Our life we thought was free,
But soon to our surprise we found
Good times was not the key.

Our life is ours to some extent,
Some ways we must reform
But for the Government and camp,
Our work must be in form.

So here in camp we work and slave,
Our duties to keep up,
From hunting bugs in the woods
To cleaning mess kit and cup.

Not mentioning shoes to shine and all

The camp newspaper, The Filley Flash, was an important part of camp life for the enrollees because it included camp projects, coming events, jokes, cartoons, poetry, art, sports, education and health news, and guidance articles. It came out monthly and was produced by the enrollees under the supervision of the Education Advisor. Thankful Arnold House Museum

Bill Livingston

Bill Livingston chopping a tree in the Cockaponset State Forest.
Bill Livingston

Edward J. Bartek

Edward J. Bartek lived an extraordinary life part of which was working at Camp Filley in Haddam. Tom Bartek

The following story was found at the James F. Justin Civilian Conservation Corps Museum web site: justinmuseum.com.

"I was a member of Co. 1195th CCC camp in Haddam, Conn. The year was 1938. We were paid $30.00 per month and $22.00 was sent to our home. They took out $.50 cents for our laundry, $5.00 for a PX book and gave us $2.50 in cash. It was the best thing FDR ever did. It took us kids off the streets and did a lot to make men out of boys. The food was very good. We worked outside in the woods, cutting down dead trees, fighting fires, building roads, etc.

"On Friday nights we had boxing. The matches were three rounds and the winner got one full carton of cigs.

"Also, every Friday we had either the Army, Navy, Coast Guard, Air Corps, or US Marine Corps gave us a pitch to join up. I picked the US Marines. When I first went into the Marines my pay was $21.00 a month. We were paid more in the CCC and the food was a hell of a lot better.

"In the Marines I saw four years of service with two years overseas with the 1st Marine Division and saw action from Guadalcanal on up. Some of the men that I was with in the Marines were also in the CCC.

"After the war I went to the University of Massachusetts under the PL 16 for Disabled Veterans. After that I spent my life as a golf course superintendent. On January 8th, 2004, I was 83 years old."

Edward J. Bartek was one of the many children during the Great Depression who was raised in an orphanage and foster homes. At the age of 16 he left high school, lied about his age, and joined the CCC in 1938. He worked at Camp Filley in Haddam as a surveyor and dynamiter clearing roads in the Cockaponset State Forest.

On March 14, 2010 an article by Anne M. Hamilton appeared in the Hartford Courant entitled, "Edward J. Bartek Rose from Horrific Childhood to Pillar of Wisdom." In it she describes how Bartek triumphed over a childhood straight out of a Dickens novel to become a successful teacher and the creator of a philosophical worldview he called Trinityism.

Bartek was born in Hartford, on Nov. 25, 1921. His parents were Michael and Anna (Zabiecka) Bartosiewicz. Bartek had one brother, Charles.

"I had an unfortunate childhood because I grew up in an orphanage," said Bartek to another Hartford Courant reporter in 2006.

Edward spent eight years at the Hartford County Home at Warehouse Point, and St. Francis Orphan Asylum in New Haven [orphanages]; and in three foster homes. He graduated from St. Peter's Elementary School in New Haven and attended West Haven and Hartford high schools.

Anne M. Hamilton wrote: "The conditions overall were terrible. Bartek was separated from his sibling. At times, he was given poor or insufficient food. In one home, he was isolated in the attic and no one spoke to him for months. He was not allowed to visit the bathroom when he wanted, and he could take a bath only once a month.

"The mistreatment affected him socially.

"'He didn't fit in, and he had no one to show him the ways of acting in public,' said his son, Alex Bartek.

"Although he had few friends, he was bright and was pushed two years ahead in school.

"Bartek dropped out of Hartford Public High School at age 16 (1938). He lied about his age and enlisted in the Civilian Conservation Corps, working as a surveyor and dynamiter helping to clear land for a state park in Haddam."

"'He felt isolated,' said Alex. 'He went inward. All he had was imagination and thinking.'

"Bartek joined the Navy in World War II and served on ships in both the Atlantic and Pacific. When his ship crossed the equator, Bartek refused to go along with the traditional hazing that sailors inflict on one another and was subsequently shunned by the crew for the rest of his tour of duty.

"'He had no clue how to interact with people,' said Alex. 'Nobody talked to him, but he didn't even know what was happening.'

"He changed his name to Bartek after the war because his family name was perpetually mispronounced. (In the Navy, his mates didn't even try and called him Jones.) After the war, Bartek returned to Hartford and worked at Hamilton Standard Propeller, at the state of Connecticut's unemployment compensation office, and at Travelers Insurance Co.

"He was married in 1949 to Eugenia Redekas, who died in 1987. They had two sons: Alex and Thomas.

"With the help of the G.I. Bill, Bartek attended Hillyer College, now the University of Hartford, and earned a bachelor's degree in the mid-1950s and later a master's degree. He began teaching English at A.I. Prince Vocational Technical School in Hartford and became head of the department. He retired about 1976 after more than 20 years of teaching.

"His lifelong obsession with writing resulted in more than 35 books, all self-published. He wrote voluminously on many topics but mostly about a complex philosophical system he devised called Trinityism.

"'His life's passion was thinking about ordering the universe,' said Alex. His philosophy involved thinking about the physical world in groups of threes: water, steam,

and ice, for example, or neutral, plus, and minus, or hot, warm, and cold. On another level, the divisions included soul, mind, and body, or the physical, spiritual, and sensual worlds.

"'He came up with laws of a broader nature to explain everything in our existence,' said Alex. 'It gave him an insight into people's problems.'

"Over the years, my father tried to popularize his theories. He wrote several hundred letters to the editors of local newspapers. He spoke on the radio and used his theories to counsel people with psychological and marriage problems. He taught ethics and philosophy at Tunxis, Manchester, and Middlesex community colleges. He wrote two volumes of his autobiography, a book on dreams, and one on fables."

Patton Duncan, a physics professor at Capitol Community College and an admirer of Bartek's thinking said, 'He tried to unify spiritual, scientific, and rational thinking in one whole. He didn't have one idea; he created a system like Plato, Kant or Aquinas. His work attempts to create a synthesis of philosophy, science, and spirituality.'

"He concentrated for many years on poetry – he wrote 10 volumes – and was a founder and former vice president of the Connecticut Poetry Society and a founder and president for 15 years of the society's local chapter, the Wit and Wisdom Writers Club. He organized several poetry festivals at Manchester Community College and readings at local nursing homes. In 2005, he was honored by being named to the Manchester Arts Commission Hall of Fame.

"'His poetry was very, very easy to understand,' said Linda Richardson, a member of the club. 'He used poetry to get his philosophy across.'

A Camp Filley survey crew in the Cockaponset SF.
DEEP State Parks Archives

His years of isolation made Bartek awkward socially. He couldn't make small talk and was humble and unassuming, but he had several close friends with whom he shared poetry and philosophy. He was quiet, but 'strongly opinionated about everything.'

Ellsworth "Al" Clarence Hartman

Ellsworth "Al" Hartman (top left) and his bull gang and four friends doing road work. The foreman has a pipe. Linda Johnson

Al Hartman (top) and his friends at Camp Filley in 1934. Linda Johnson

On March 1, 2012 Linda Johnson sent me this information about her father, Ellsworth "Al" Clarence Hartman who worked at the Haddam CCC camp. Hartman was born on Sept. 24, 1915 in Buffalo, NY. His father Charles had steady employment as a railroad engineer but during the Depression he probably was out of work. His mother, Louise Kreuger, had 13 children and Linda's father was in the middle.

"My father only went to tenth grade and may have had to quit school to work and help his family. He heard about the CCC and joined. Dad went to Camp Filley in Haddam where he ran a bulldozer. He also talked about cutting trees.

"On the weekends Dad played the harmonica and entertained the guys. He was a real ham. Dad loved his beer and he probably went drinking at a bar.

"He earned $30 a month and $25 was sent home to his parents. When he found out his brothers were helping themselves to the money he earned, he said, 'Why should I work?' So he didn't sign up again.

"Dad told me the thing he learned the most from working in the CCC was how to get along with people other than his family.

"After he left the CCC he worked at Republic Steel in Lackawanna, NY.

"He married Margaret Markwart in 1940 and they had two children, Norman and me.

"Then Dad worked at a knife factory. His last job was as a bus driver for Niagara Frontier Transit Authority in Buffalo.

"When I was 12 years old my parents took me to Dad's camp in Haddam. We saw mostly woods and he pointed out roads he built. He also told me Leo Tolstoy's daughter, Alexandra, lived near the camp. She had two white German shepherd dogs and he remembered her calling for them in Russian."

In 2002 Al Hartman passed away.

Nicholas & Wasil Alshuk

On Dec. 29, 2008 I received this email from Kathleen Esche from Presque Isle, Wis.

"I was just reading the newsletter from the Kent Historical Society and your recent CCC talk. I'm originally from Connecticut (now living in Wis.) and have been doing genealogy on my family for many years now. It turns out that some of my family, the Alshuks in Seymour, Conn., were at a CCC camp. My great-uncle Nicholas had some pictures in his photo album (sadly he died on a ship while in WWII). I'm not exactly sure if he was there in Haddam or if his brother Wasil was there.

"There were three brothers in all. Wasil was born in 1914, Nicholas in 1921, and Tom in 1923. All three fought in WWII.

"Attached are the CCC pictures. I don't have the album

(Clockwise from Left) 1 CCC boys resting in the woods while building trails in the Cockaponset SF. 2 Resting after working in the woods. 3 Two CCC ax men. 4 Camp Filley barracks – ready for inspection! All photos courtesy of Kathleen Esche

anymore and it's been a few years but I recall thinking that some of the items might have been postcards. I did notice that one picture says 'Nick' on the bottom so that was one of my great-uncles (he's the one that died during WWII)."

I called Kathleen's Uncle Tom who said he wasn't in the CCC but Wasil and Nick were.

These four photos (above) are the unidentified CCC Haddam Camp photos from Kathleen's deceased Uncle Nick's photo album.

Peter S. Valenti

Peter Valenti by the state garage he helped build while working at Camp Filley in Haddam. Podskoch

In September of 2010 I visited Peter Valenti at his home on Bear Rock Rd. in Durham, Conn. He introduced me to his wife, Phyllis, and I was surprised when she told me she was the sister of Nick Naples who was a good friend of my father-in-law, Burt Way. She told me that the house where she and Peter lived was her family home that her father had built.

We sat at the dining room table and Peter began telling me about his life and time in the CCC.

"I was born May 9, 1920 in Darien, Conn. My father, Pasquale, came from Calibria, Italy and he was a gardener in Darien. My mother, Caterina, had seven children: Anna, Bruno, Mary, me, Frank, Anthony, and Patsy.

"After I graduated from high school I was on my own searching for a job. My brother Bruno was already in the CCC at Camp Buck in Portland. I signed up in February 1938 because I wanted to go someplace where you got three square meals a day.

"First they sent me and a group of guys to Fort Devens, Mass. for about a month of training. Then they shipped us to different camps. They sent me by truck to Camp Filley in Haddam.

"My first job was with a woodcutting crew. Then I worked building roads and cleaning up the park by Lake Cockaponset in the Cockaponset State Forest.

"Then I became a truck driver. I drove the camp ambulance, a Chevy truck from WWI. Normally I drove by myself but sometimes I took someone with me.

"The only exciting trip I had was going to Winsted after a truck taking the boys to Winsted for a night out on Friday turned over because the driver was hot rodding. Twenty-five guys were in the back. We got a call to come up and help. By the time I got there they were all taken care of.

"I had a military driver's license but I didn't have a state driver's license. One day I drove an Army truck on my own to get a state license in Middletown. When I got there the inspector asked, 'What do you have to take the test in?'

"I showed him the Army truck and he said, 'You mean to tell me you drove it up here without a license?'

"I said, 'Yes. I have an Army license.'

"The inspector replied, 'I'm going to have to arrest you.'

"I said, 'Go ahead.'

"I called Captain Schwartz. He said, 'Let me talk to that gentleman.'

"He then said to the inspector, 'I'd like to see you arrest that boy.'

"Then the inspector sat down and filled out the license and I never had to drive and take the test.

"I worked two years at Camp Filley and the last year and a half I drove the ambulance. I took patients to New London and went on the ferry to Fishers Island, NY. Then I drove about 10 minutes to the Army Hospital at Fort Wright.

"The most unusual experience I had was during the hurricane of 1938. I was in the camp when the hurricane hit. The winds were terrible. We heard the loud bangs from the trees breaking.

"After it was over we had to clear the fallen trees. There was one guy who was cutting a leaner tree, one stuck on another tree, but it wouldn't fall down. As he was cutting to free the tree, it sprung up and flipped him over backwards and knocked his front teeth out. I had to drive him in the ambulance to Fort Wright.

"In the infirmary Johnny Marmish from Massachusetts took care of the guys who had accidents. There was one guy who was hit by a shovel in the gravel pit. He also took care of anybody who was sick. Our doctor, Dr. Mazzacane, came once or twice a week and he was an Army man.

"I helped build the state garage with LEM Davis Lawler. He was an excellent carpenter. I think I sawed every rafter that is in it. This garage was used by the Army trucks.

"The guys liked to joke around. We had a barber who came to camp once a week from Middletown. He had a Model T. One day some guys jacked up the drive wheel on the back of his car. When he got ready to leave he tried to go but couldn't. He got PO'd. He told the captain and we all got restricted to camp for two weeks because no one would admit it.

"We burned wood in three stoves in each barracks and when the fires burned out we froze. Every other window was left half open year round because of the fear of carbon monoxide poisoning.

"During the weekdays we listened to a radio or went swimming in nearby Cockaponset Lake. In the fall we picked hickory nuts.

"I was the catcher on the baseball team. We played Deep River and Middletown. Our games were played on the Higganum town field. During the winter we didn't have a basketball team.

"On the weekends we went to Middletown. On Friday

Peter Valenti drove trucks (above) and an ambulance at Camp Filley. Roberta Kosnoff Sciacca

The state garage that Camp Filley enrollees built to store their trucks. It is still used by the DEEP. DEEP State Parks Archives

nights we went to the movies and bought food at the bakery.

"I decided not to sign up again for the CCC when my time was up in February because I had met my future wife, Ruth Van Cleef of Haddam. I used to go every day to pick up the mail at the post office. That was when I met Ruth in town while she was with her friends. They were all graduates of high school. We became friends and I used to go walking with her. Very seldom did we go to the movies in Middletown but when we did, her dad took us in his truck.

"We got married on February 11th, 1940. This was even before I got out of the CCC. After our wedding I was discharged from Camp Filley. My wife and I had three sons: Peter, Edgar, and Robert.

"I didn't have a job so we moved to Darien. We rented an apartment and I worked with a man who owned a business called Service Unlimited. We did everything like painting, mowing lawns, etc.

"In 1943 I joined the Marines and was stationed in the Pacific. I was a mechanic and stationed on five islands. We moved around quite a bit.

"When I got back to the US, I went to work with The New Haven and Shore Line Railway. I was a mechanic. Then I went to Pratt and Whitney and worked for 28 years. I worked in plant services in Middletown. I did all types of work in maintenance. Then I became a foreman during my last 20 years.

"The CCC was a good influence on me because it gave me a job and I learned how to be a hard worker."

William "Bill" Vance

Bill Vance shared his life story while a resident of the Jerome Home in New Britain. Podskoch

After meeting Bill Vance on Sept. 20, 2009 at a CCC Reunion in the Salmon River State Park in East Hampton, I interviewed him at his nursing home in New Britain.

Q: Tell me about you and your family.

A: "My family lived in Waterbury. My father's name was James and he worked as an electrician and lineman. My mother, Josephine, was busy with eight children: James, Dorothy, Loretta, myself, Gertrude, Patsy, Joanie, and Margie. I was born on Aug. 15, 1919. When I was in my third year of high school I quit. I really don't know why I quit but I did. I started looking for a job but there just weren't any."

Q: Why did you join the CCC?

A: "My family lived in a six family block home. The guy on the top floor had boys and one, Joe Donnelly, was in the CCC. He spent a lot of time in Colorado. Joe told me about his trip and it sounded good to me. So in the spring of 1939 I signed up. They sent me and other boys by bus to Hartford and then by train to Middletown. We then got a ride in an Army truck to Camp Filley in Haddam."

Q: What jobs did you have?

A: (Laughing) "For my first two months I dug ditches but I hurt my finger in the truck. We had Ford trucks. When we arrived at the job we had to take out the steel bench seat that we sat on. As I was taking it out with a guy at the other end, he let go of the seat out of the truck and it landed on the ring finger of my left hand. I spent a couple months recovering. I had a small job of raking the campgrounds.

"About every couple of days the doctor came to the infirmary and looked at my finger. It was very swollen. The orderly changed the bandage until it got better. That was in early in July.

"When my finger was better I was told to report to the company clerk who was going to leave and go to a camp in Colorado. I took a test and was very fast at the typing part because I had taken typing in high school. I got the job and worked for two months in the office and I became the company clerk. I was doing all the work in the office. It was an OK job and it was clean work as opposed to my first job of digging ditches.

"Then the 1938 Hurricane hit and I was sent out cutting trees. There was a lot of cleanup work. You just can't imagine how much work there was. It was very hard with trees holding up trees. We were very busy cleaning roads for traffic to get through."

Q: What did you do in your free time?

A: "In the evenings we just hung around camp. Sometimes on the weekends I'd hitchhike home. It was about a 35-mile trip. I'd wear my uniform and people would stop and give me a ride. I didn't do any sports but there was boxing. The guys set up a ring and had matches on the weekend. There were a lot of good boxers from New Britain.

Q: How long did you stay in the CCC?

A: "After six months I decided to go home. I figured I could get a job. I found work as a glass cutter on Jefferson St. Then I got lucky and got an apprenticeship at the Farrell Foundry in Waterbury making machines.

"In 1944 I was drafted into the Army. I was shipped to the Philippines and worked in the ordnance department where our job was to repair guns.

"After the war I went back to work in my old job in Waterbury. I stayed there till I retired.

"I got married to Margaret 'Peggy' Carey on July 6, 1946. We met at a dance. We had six children: Bill, Jim, Steve, Bob, Ray, and Sheila."

Q: Was the CCC good for you?

A: "Yes! By being in the CCC I learned how to work, to get a job, and to be able to stay in my home town."

On Jan. 4, 2010 William "Bill" Vance passed away.

Bill Vance attended a CCC Reunion at the Salmon River State Park. He is pictured with three other CCC alumni who shared stories of their time in the CCC. Alumni (L–R): Hugo DeSarro, Angelo Alderuccio, Bill Vance, and John Bauer. Podskoch

CHAPTER 13
KENT / MACEDONIA BROOK STATE PARK

HISTORY

In 1935 the National Park Service in Washington, DC offered Connecticut a CCC camp at Macedonia Brook State Park near Kent in the northwestern part of the state. At first a fifty-acre parcel opposite the old Dean place at Macedonia Brook on Fuller Mountain Road was considered for the camp site. The Connecticut Park and Forest Commission (CP&FC) unanimously accepted the offer.[1]

In May the state received word that the Army rejected the Dean site because the valley in Macedonia Brook was too fragile for a large concentration of men.[2]

A new site in North Kent was selected and rented. The parcel was just south of Kent Falls State Park on the Schagticoke Trail (Rt. 7) and adjacent to the New York, New Haven & Hartford Railroad tracks (NY, NH & H).

Macedonia Brook CCC Camp 11057 began on Mon., June 10, 1935 when Lt. F. G. Comerford led a cadre of 23 men from Co. 173 at Mohawk State Park. They left at 4:30 am and reached the new campsite at 6 am. By 9:30 am the tents were all set up.[3]

Supplies for building the camp arrived quickly. The Army hired carpenters and on June 19th the men began building the camp. In a month the barracks were ready for occupancy.[4]

On Fri., July 12, a train carrying 167 enrollees commanded by Lt. B. B. Trusoski arrived on the NY, NH & H Railroad and stopped at the entrance to the new camp. It took only 12 minutes for the men to unload their supplies. This was a unique situation to have a camp located near railroad tracks. The young men moved into the newly constructed barracks. Then a staff of LEM (local experienced men) arrived and the camp population rose to 202 men.[5]

The New Milford Times reported in the July 18, 1935 issue that the CCC camp in North Kent opened on Wednesday of that week. Informal exercises were held at 2 pm. The following local religious and political leaders spoke: Rev. Henry Bartlett, Kent Congregational church; Father Dowd, Sharon Roman Catholic church; Howard C. Giddings, First Selectman of Kent; F. H. Peet, the master of the state Grange; Paul Peter Mitnick, education advisor; and Lt. Commerford, camp commander.

Bill Bachrach of the Kent Historical Society discovered in his research that the scheduling of the construction

One of the few photos of the Kent camp along the Housatonic River in North Kent across from Kent Falls. The buildings from the bottom left clockwise were: Barracks #1 (near the R.R.); Library, Education, PX, and Rec. Hall; Barracks #3; Shower & Laundry, and Mess Hall (to the left of the flag pole); infirmary; Barracks # 4 and #5 bldgs. (near river); Officers' Headquarters (to the right of flag pole); Transportation (lower right near tracks). There was a small Guard House by the tracks. Peg Carlson

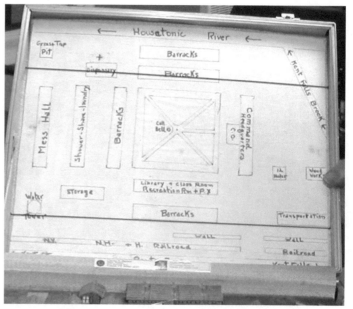

This is a small diorama model and map of the Macedonia Brook camp made by former CCC member Charles Bigelow. Podskoch

This photo collage shows Camp Macedonia Brook and the enrollees and their work projects.[8]

and supervision of the camp ran into bureaucratic and political infighting. The first issue was that the local US Congressman, J. Joseph Smith, sent a letter to Director James J. McEntee, the acting Emergency Conservation Work (ECW), questioning the employment of several New York carpenters in the construction of the camp buildings.

Bill wrote: "We have a series of telegrams and letters going back and forth and an investigator, who was sent to Kent from Massachusetts by ECW. We learn the power of Oscar F. Ross, Business Agent of Local 1005 (New Milford, CT) of the United Brotherhood of Carpenters and Joiners who was concerned that out-of-state carpenters were being hired for the construction. Then Mr. Ross accepted union dues from the Pawling and Dover, New York union locals and listed the out-of-state carpenter's residences as New Milford, CT. By October when the investigation was complete, the construction of Camp Macedonia Brook

had long been finished. There were some 55 carpenters, laborers, other tradesmen, and supervisory personnel (18 from Kent) who earned up to several months of needed employment."

The second controversial issue was determining who would be the civilian superintendent of the camp. CP&FC usually selected the camp superintendent and they chose Henry K. Herbinson. The Macedonia camp, however, was under the National Park Service in Washington and in late spring of 1935 new regulations specified that lead personnel would be "selected from Congressional lists." For half of July and most of August the camp was without a superintendent. The young men were without tools and had to remain in camp. On Aug. 14, 1935 the CP&FC stood by Mr. Herbinson and by August 29 the ECW in Washington agreed to Herbinson's appointment.

Superintendent H. K. Herbinson arrived on Thursday,

Aug. 29, 1935 and began supervising the construction of a three-mile road along the eastern base of Cobble Mountain in Macedonia Brook State Park. This would divert traffic from the old road along Macedonia Brook that was steep, crooked, and narrow. The Superintendent's Report of April 1, 1936 stated that the old road was "hazardous most of the time and impassable in spring." The old road had four bridges that had to be maintained while the new road had none. The young enrollees also built hiking and saddle trails, did mapping, and fought fires.[6]

Macedonia Brook State Park, located approximately 2 miles north of the village of Kent, began in 1918 when the White Memorial Foundation of Litchfield donated a 1,552-acre tract to the state. Originally the land was the home of the Scatacook Indians. In 1738 settlers moved into the area and lived at peace with the Indians who also helped the Patriots as scouts during the Revolutionary War. The land was used for farming and commercial purposes. Gristmills, cider mills, and sawmills were established in the area. Remnants of an iron forge are still visible in the southern end of the state park. The iron industry required a large amount of charcoal that eventually led to the depletion of the area forests. Efforts were made to conserve the wood but coal from Pennsylvania mines proved to be too expensive, which led to the closing of the Macedonia furnace in 1865.[7]

The enrollees had entertainment during the winter of 1935-36. Minstrel shows were very popular. On Feb. 20th a group of enrollees performed songs and dances in the Mess Hall. Four days later they performed at Camp Cross and then on the 26th they performed for the public at the Warren Grange. "Smokers" were held frequently in the Mess Hall. Here again the boys presented songs and dance routines.[9]

In the camp quadrangle was a large bell and flagpole where the enrollees gathered each morning and evening for the raising and lowering of the flag.[15]

The young men participated in sports such as skiing and basketball. The camp basketball team practiced at the Kent Town Hall because the high school didn't have a gym.[10]

In March the company commander, 1st Lt. Comerford treated his men to trips to the movie theaters in Waterbury and Watertown. There were also dances in the Mess Hall.[11]

During the extremely cold winter of 1935-36 the Housatonic River, which flowed past the CCC camp, flooded on March 12, 1936. The river was at a 75-year high and washed away three covered bridges that included the nearby 150-year-old Cornwall Bridge. A 2-mile stretch of NY, NH & H R tracks was flooded including the CCC camp. The CCC enrollees helped clear the area of ice and debris.[12]

The Macedonian camp was also flooded. The Macedonian, the camp newspaper, reported: "The Housatonic River flood kept our officers out of bed for three nights and caused little concern. Leaving the camp grounds a sea of mud and water – but soon dried back into a presentable appearance."[13]

Later that month the Connecticut River overflowed. The Macedonia camp sent 140 men along with six foremen to help in the cleanup. The men were housed with Co. 175 in Thomaston, near Waterbury. The enrollees also traveled to Hartford and did cleanup work in warehouses and homes.[14]

When spring arrived in 1936 Lt. Comerford set out a program of beautifying the camp grounds. Grass was planted throughout the camp, shrubbery and flowers were planted, symmetrical walkways, and rustic fences were added. A 450-pound bell was installed behind the flag pole.[16]

During the spring of 1936 the CCC boys improved several miles of the Appalachian Blue Trail that ran through Macedonia Brook State Park. Part of the Appalachian Trail runs along the Housatonic River across from the CCC camp near Kent Falls.[17]

Macedonia Brook Camp 11057 also participated in fire drills with the Kent Volunteer Fire Department and helped them fight fires. This helped strengthen their relationship with the local citizens.

The camp also participated in other local town functions. They cooperated in planning a President's Birthday party, town sports such as basketball and baseball, and participated in church services and functions. A group of four enrollees joined a local church choir.[18]

The June 1936 Macedonian reported the Kent Fire Dept. had a baseball game with the CCC officers and foremen and the CCC team won 7-5.

The camp mess took pride in being awarded one of the three best camps in the state. Part of this is attributed to the fact the cooks had worked together for 17 months.[19]

The CP&FC made monthly visits to the Macedonia Brook Park to survey the progress of the CCC work. One such visit was on Nov. 6, 1935. They walked along the new 1.5 mile roadbed and then went for lunch at the Kent Inn with Superintendent Herbinson and Commander Comerford.

The ECW Agency also made frequent inspections of the camp. One report contained a nutritious camp menu. Some of the items were: roast turkey, sage dressing, mashed turnip, brown gravy, hot Parker House rolls, and mince pie. The camp's safety features were reported to be fully in place. Sanitation was given a rating of "good."

The ECW report stated, "All waste [water] pass through one or both of two grease traps from which it is carried thru tile [pipelines] to a covered sump pit 18' square by 18' deep from which loose laid tile carries the overflow to smaller pits and rock-filled drains. Garbage [is] taken away daily by [a] local farmer..."

The New Milford Times reported on July 13, 1936 that H. S. Turrill MD of Kent submitted a report stating the beach at North Kent was not being contaminated by the CCC camp where there is "the best sewage disposal plant that is to be obtained."

During the summer enrollees were kept active playing inter-barracks baseball while the camp team played other CCC camps and local teams. In July a track and field event was held to celebrate the 1st anniversary of the camp. The camp surgeon, Dr. J. J. Pallotta, donated a trophy to the outstanding track & field man and 12 bronze medals for the winners of the other events. Enrollees were also invited to watch baseball events and boat races at the Kent School.[20]

During the summer many speakers gave talks in the camp. Mr. Brookman of West Hartford advised the boys on individual social and economic problems. Mr. La France from the Dept. of Interior showed a movie on recreation and education, and Len Howard a famous Litchfield stained glass artist gave instruction on his craft.[21]

The state ran into a roadblock in completing the

CCC enrollees built this huge stone wall and road that paralleled the stream in the Macedonia Brook SP. Podskoch

Macedonia Brook road project. The October 1936 CP&FC minutes reported "an unsuccessful attempt to negotiate a lease and option from Frank Buchinger for a 52-acre parcel on the southerly border of the park, to permit the construction of an additional half mile of road." This parcel was needed to connect the two parts of the state park.

Historian Bill Bachrach said CP&FC minutes stated: "By mid-1937 the road the CCC had built was not yet open for use 'because work still had to be done on the side grading and parapet walls had to be built on the highest retaining walls.' The walls are high indeed, as much as 14 feet, and it remains to be discovered if the 'boys' helped with that work or left it to more experienced Depression-era stone workers."

In February 1937 here is the staff that ran the camp. The Army personnel consisted of: Commanding Officer, 1st lt. F. G. Comerford; Adjunct, Lt. B. B. Truskoski; Camp Surgeon, Dr. J. J. Pallotta; and Education Advisor, Mr. R. R. White. The U. S. Park Service personnel was: Superintendent, H. K. Herbinson; Foremen, E. J. Sullivan, F. E. Brookes, C. E. Baum, W. W. Davison and E. W. Roche; Mechanic, A. E. Seiffert; and Blacksmith, F. P. Schirm. [22]

During the winter 1937 the survey crew supervised by Eugene Sullivan completed a lineal survey of the top of Cobble Mt. (1,450') in Macedonia Brook SP where the Appalachian Trail passes over. Hikers have a panoramic view of the Catskill and Berkshire mts.[23]

The basketball and baseball teams played these teams: Camp Cross, Camp Roberts, Camp Toumey, and Camp Fechner. In 1937 Camp Macedonia basketball team was undefeated and played for the state championship.[24]

In March 1937 Co. 1191 Macedonia Brook was awarded as the "Outstanding Company" in the 5th District and would represent Connecticut in competition for the First Corps Area (New England) prize.[25]

The Macedonian boys worked closely with the Kent Fire Dept. during the 1937 spring fire season. Forty boys were called out to fight a 4-acre blaze that threatened Macedonia Brook State Park. That same week they helped the Kent firemen contain a 100-acre fire at Bulls Bridge.[26]

The Macedonia Brook Camp closed on June 10, 1937. The CP&FC report of the General Superintendent dated June 30, 1937 stated: "Due to nation-wide curtailment of National Park C.C.C. work, Connecticut lost its one camp [Macedonia Brook] in the state [working] on a purely park program.

"There was another reason for closing the camp. The state did not own and had no funds to buy a small tract of land needed to finish the south end of the park road on which the camp was working. However, they did finish about three miles of road in good shape and it is in use as a substitute for the town road. The relocation carries most of the traffic to the west of the brook and out of the bottom of the valley, thereby saving a very characteristic feature of this park from being overrun and its value as a recreation area destroyed by the unnecessary car travel."

Bachrach stated: "We have no report or photographs of an opening ceremony for the road. This is odd because government agencies usually love to show off the successful expenditures of the public's dollars. We did find the recommendation that 'the new road be closed at night for control purposes.' Later CP&FC showed $5,000 projected for the 1939-40 State Park's budget for 'one hundred acres of woodland, needed for completion of the Macedonia Brook road.'

"It is uncertain how many years the new road stayed open. The old road along Macedonia Brook was improved and it is this road that carries vehicular traffic today."

In February 2006 Gary Nasiatka, Park Unit Supervisor for the Kent area, submitted a $50,000 grant to rebuild sections of the wall and road. He stated: "It's a shame to see the deteriorating wall. About 40,000 hikers, bicyclists, equestrians, and cross-country skiers use the road yearly." ("Loving Care Sought for Walls in Park," Patrick Sullivan, Hartford Courant, 2-23-06).

Bachrach added: "In September of 2009, a state grant enhanced by economic stimulus money provided $75,000

for restoration of the road's tallest stonework."

The Kent Historical Society (KHS) located the site of the Macedonia Brook camp site. Then they contacted Nick Bellantoni, the CT State Archaeologist, who immediately expressed an interest in coming out to see the site. On Tuesday, December 2, 2008, Bellantoni arrived with a cadre of state experts. They were joined by Dr. David Poirier, CT Council on Culture and Tourism, staff archaeologist; Stacey Vairo, National/State Register Coordinator, and Karin Peterson, Director of Museums, as well as Nicole Chalfant, DEP Museum Assistant and Jim Baeschle, Park Ranger for Macedonia and Kent Falls. Bill Bachrach and Marge McAvoy from the KHS and Shaun McAvoy from the Kent Conservation Commission rounded out the search party. They all set off across the railroad tracks and into the woods. After struggling through thick underbrush, they came upon various relics that were clearly part of the camp, although the actual use of some of them is still unclear.

Bill Bachrach stated: "What is certain is that we all want to do something to commemorate the piece of Depression-era history before it is too late. As a nonprofit 501(c)3 the Kent Historical Society will write a non-matching grant to the state for $20,000 to have the site surveyed, mapped, and otherwise documented. With that information in hand, further decisions can be made about what to do next. It is hoped that the site will be listed on the State Registry of Historic Places, and that further funding will be secured."[27]

The Macedonia Brook CCC camp built the beautiful trail along Kent Falls. Podskoch

LEGACY

The CCC camp built the scenic ¼ mile trail along Kent Falls and the park and picnic area at the base of the falls. Thousands of people visit the park and enjoy hiking up the scenic falls trail. Then many relax and enjoy a picnic at the many tables.

The Macedonia Brook CCC camp that was located across the road from Kent Falls SP did extensive work on Macedonia Brook SP building roads, hiking trails, and 51 campsites that are enjoyed by thousands of people each year.

Directions:

From Danbury follow Rt. 7 to the village of Kent. Then continue 4.5 miles on Rt. 7 to Kent Falls on the right. The CCC camp is across Rt. 7 and the railroad tracks in dense brush along the Housatonic River.

From Hartford travel west on I-84 to Exit 39. Then go west along Rt. 4 to the intersection with Rt. 118 in Harwinton. Drive west on Rt. 118 to the intersection with Rt. 202 in Litchfield. Turn left onto Rt. 202 and go west for about 7 miles to the intersection with Rt. 341. Turn right onto Rt. 341 and travel to the intersection with Rt. 7 in Kent. Turn right (north) onto Rt. 7 and the park will be located approximately 4.5 miles ahead along Rt. 7.

Visitors to the Macedonia Brook State Park near Kent enjoy the beautiful stone pavilion for picnics and reunions. DEEP

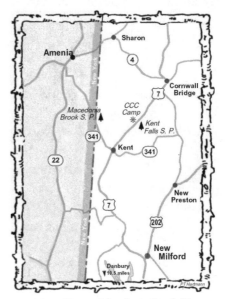

Map – Kent & Macedonia Brook SP

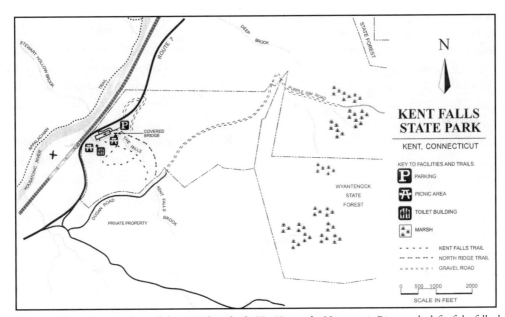

Map of Kent Falls SP showing the trail the CCC boys built. The X near the Housatonic River to the left of the falls shows the location of the Macedonia CCC camp in North Kent. DEEP

179

MEMORIES

"To Camp Macedonia"
by Joe Finnegan

My family needed money,
When I was going to school.
My clothes looked kind of funny,
But I learned the Golden Rule.

I hardly got two squares a day,
My clothes made me look like a tramp;
And finally in a thoughtful way,
I joined the C.C.C. camp.

With schooling I thought I was through,
But I was wrong I soon found out.
I took things from a different view,
And began to change my ways about.

I took the knocks that came along
For I knew they had to come,
And it didn't take me very long
When I began to have some fun.

We didn't receive a very big pay,
But I did my best for a dollar a day.
I was never very far from home
And my mind it soon began to roam.

I dreamt of such a wonderful treat
The folks and my girl so sweet,
'Twas on a Friday afternoon
When my week day chores were through.

When I had decided I'd go home
Because I felt so blue.
The next few hours were spent in talk
As to just how far it was to walk.

The fellow whom I talked o said
Before I got home I would be dead.
He also told me not to skip
But just to take a little trip.

He told me, much against my pride,
That I would have to bum a ride.

I started on my weary way
Expecting to be back Monday.

The stars were just beginning to show
And the traffic it was very slow.
Just two hours later a car pulled up
And I jumped in like a timid pup.

All the way home was the ride I got,
And I was thankful an awful lot.
I saw them all have fun galore
I started back to camp once more.

Now when you're coming down the street,
In your car so new and neat,
If a C.C.C. is going your way
Shortest of rides will make him gay.

So pick him up;
You'll not be harmed,
And you'll be thanked –
Or I'll be darned.
- Macedonian, Feb. 1937

(Editor's Note: Joe resigned from his camp on Feb. 2, 1937. He turned in this contribution the day he left.)

"A CCC Boy's Lament"
by William Potter

When I was born my mother said
Such a handsome boy should get ahead
My father foretold a professional career
While sister said, "An actor he'll be. He's such a dear."
Oh boy, if mother could only see me now.

The important incidents of my childhood days
Seem lost as through the past I gaze
But now I know that mother was a sage
For I walked and talked before one year of age
But fellows, if she could only see me now.

To school I went at the age of five
That school I quickly did revolutionize
The teachers in learning soon surpassed
And graduated three years before my class
But I say, just look at me now.

From thence into the world of business I ventured
In search of experience, knowledge or adventure
When Wall Street decided to bestow
Several positions as presidents I decide to blow
But my God, if they could only see me now.

My sister's words rang continuously in my ears
"An actor he'll be. He's such a dear."
So Hollywood was the next to know
That the sunshine from my smile was quite a glow
Oh honey-gal, if you could only see me now.

The Depression came and fortunes went
And left me alone without a cent
I decided that the world was all wrong
And said I would prove it before very long
Did I? Look at me now.

In order to carry out my prophecy
I decided to enlist in the CCC
This I did without further ado
And now I'm the guy that eats next to you
Yeah, look at me now.

If I'm all right look at me now
And that dirge you're singing is a lovely song
And to think I did this willy-nilly
My God! Look me up
I'll go quietly.
- Macedonian, March 1937

The cover of the March 1937 Macedonian.

Charles "Charley" Bigelow

Charley opened up his attaché case and showed me the model
he made of his CCC camp in Kent. Podskoch

There was one CCC camp in Kent that neither I nor the Kent Historical Society knew its exact location. After a year of research, we located the camp across the road from Kent Falls on Rt. 7.

In January 2012 I received an email from Joan Sharpe, the President of CCC Legacy in Virginia. She sent me the name of a man, Charles Bigelow, who was a member of the Kent camp, and she enclosed a picture of a 16" x 15" x 2" case with a model of his camp.

I called Charles at Blair Manor near Enfield and arranged to visit him on January 19, 2012. As I walked into the reception room a motorized wheelchair driven by a smiling man with a huge frame came toward me.

"Are you the guy interested in talking to me about the CCC?"

I said I was and went with him to the dining room where we could talk. Charles introduced Judy Johnson, the rehabilitation supervisor. We sat down and enjoyed a cup of coffee. Charley told his life story and how he joined the CCC.

"I was born on Aug. 31, 1919 in Willimantic. During the Depression my parents, Charles and Edna (Brown) split up. My father had no job and couldn't raise us. My mother could only raise one child, my sister Doris. My younger brother Francis and I became wards of the state. We lived in a foster home and worked for our foster parents. When I got to be 17, I learned about girls and the foster parents said I had to leave.

"That was when I learned about the CCC from a state agency in Willimantic. I signed up for six months. They took me to the railroad station and I traveled all by myself to Kent. An Army truck picked me up and took me about three miles north up Rt. 7 to Kent Falls. The camp was on the left side of the road and right along railroad tracks. We drove over the tracks and through the camp entrance. The buildings were located next to the Housatonic River. I was amazed that so many people lived there. I thought it was the end of the world and the beginning of a new life for me.

"In camp we were under the control of the Army. We rode on trucks and on the job we were under the Forestry Dept. Our work was done in Macedonia State Park. This was two miles north of Kent near the New York State line.

"Every morning and evening we gathered outside by the flag and stood at attention.

"The camp offered me the opportunity to get an education. I never completed high school. I only had two years of studying carpentry at a vocational school.

"My first job at camp was working with the education adviser, Mr. John Goebel. He offered me the job as his helper, but I didn't last long because I didn't have much education to help correct papers, etc. I took classes in history and math but I stopped going because they didn't offer a high school equivalency class.

"Then I got a job working in the PX where I sold merchandise such as candy, soda, cigarettes, tobacco, etc.

I handled money and took inventories. The PX was open evenings from 7-9 pm and on the weekends from 3-5 pm.

"While I was doing that job in the PX, I worked also during the week building rock walls at the Macedonia State Park. A truck took us in the morning to Kent and then about two miles north on Rt. 341 (Macedonia Brook Rd.) to the park. They put me with T. J. Rawza, a foreman who was from Hartford. We had a small bulldozer, air compressor, and dump trucks. I helped load the trucks with rocks we gathered in the woods. To this day I still have back problems that I attribute to that hard work.

"On the job we had to use a lot of dynamite. One guy, Joe Gories, from New Britain, was in charge. He got paid a little extra for his work. Just before they lit the charge I had to go to a safe area. Then they'd yell: 'Fire in the hole!'

"In camp and on the job my buddy was Ralph "Chewy" Hoag. He was 5'2" and I was 6'2". He was from Stafford Springs, Conn.

"We had this one guy who would always be bumming cigarettes from us but never paid us back. We decided to get even with him. One day we caught a snake. Just before he was going to get in the truck we put the snake on the seat. When he sat down, WOW – You should have seen him bolt out of that truck!

"Another time we rolled a cigarette and put a worm inside. We gave him the cigarette and when he lit it the worm started to cook and sizzle. After that he never borrowed cigarettes from us again."

On April 29, 2012 the Kent Historical Society invited Charley, his friend Erica and me to Kent to honor him for his CCC work. They took us to the wall that Charley helped build in Macedonia Brook SP. As we passed a section of the wall he said, "There's one of the rocks that I helped move and place in the wall." We stopped and pushed Charley in his wheelchair near the wall. He was so proud of his work. Podskoch

This is Charley Bigelow's only photo of his Macedonia Brook camp in North Kent. He said there was a guard shack by the railroad tracks at the camp entrance and he lived in Barracks No. 1 also near the tracks. Charles Bigelow

Then an elderly woman came into the room and Charley introduced her.

"This is my good friend, Erika Crossman. I was her husband's best man at their wedding. When he died we began going together. I never got married myself."

"If it rained we didn't go to Macedonia Brook. They kept us in camp and had us work there. One of the projects was building a rock wall along the tracks. There weren't many trains that went by. The tracks were owned by the New York, New Haven and Hartford Railroad."

Erika said, "Charley and I went up to the camp in 1988 and the rock wall was still there. We also stopped into the Kent Library and told them that Charley was there in the 1930s but they didn't have any information on the camp.

"The librarian said the local people didn't look favorably at the boys coming to town. They were probably worried about their daughters getting in trouble with the young men."

Then Charley opened a briefcase. Inside was a model of the Kent camp.

Charley said, "Erika helped me make this model. I made the buildings out of wood and she helped paint and draw the outline of the camp.

"As you drove over the railroad tracks coming into camp the transportation building was on the right and across from it was the outhouse. We had three trucks that were a combination dump truck and personnel carrier. The outhouse was a 12-holer. To the right of the outhouse was a wood workshop. Kent Falls Brook flowed to the right of these buildings.

"The center of the camp was like a town square with paths leading to the flagpole. This was where we gathered each morning for roll call and the raising of the flag. There was also a bell they rang for meals.

"There were four barracks. I was in Barracks No. 1, which was along the tracks. There were two barracks next to the Housatonic River and the fourth barracks was on the left side of the square. It was in front of the shower and laundry building. Behind the shower building was the mess hall. To the right of this building and next to the river was the grease pit. It collected the grease from the mess kitchen. Some guys who got into trouble had to go down into the pit and clean it. It was a terrible job. After working there the guys took off their clothes and hung them on a stick in the river and the force of the water almost cleaned them.

"The large building in front of my barracks had a library, classroom, recreation room, and PX.

"The largest building on the right side of the square was the Command Headquarters. The Army captain and assistant leaders lived and worked there.

"On the left side of camp near the tracks was a large water tower that supplied the camp.

"In the evenings we went to the recreation hall and played pool and cards or read books. Then we went back to our barracks and at 10 pm the lights were shut off for sleep. Our barracks had coal stoves for when it got cold. One guy had the fireman's job. He spent the night filling the stoves and making sure the buildings were safe.

"On the weekends we spent time across Rt. 7 where we played and relaxed on the grass by Kent Falls State Park. On Sundays the camp's baseball team played other camps. Sometimes I went to watch the games. They took us on trucks. While sitting in the truck it was the first time I heard the song, 'Take me out to the Ball Game.'

"There was a baseball team but I didn't make the team. The older guys were in charge and I didn't get picked.

"Some of the guys liked to fish in the river. My friend, Ralph Hoag, loved to fish. When he caught some fish he took them to the cook who cleaned and cooked them.

"There wasn't much to do in town so a lot of times I hitchhiked home. It took me several rides to get home. I stayed in Willimantic with my dad who was working for L. T. Wood in Manchester delivering ice.

"One Friday night some of us went on a pass for the weekend. There were about 20 of us. We got a ride on an open transport truck and we were taken to Torrington. That was some open air ride!

"We had to be back to camp by Monday morning for roll call. One time I was one day late because I couldn't get a ride. I was AWOL and they fined me $2.

"There were no dances and few restaurants in Kent Falls so we stayed in camp.

"The food was good. We ate in shifts. My favorite dish was pork chops.

"A funny thing happened one day in the mess hall. They didn't get all the soap out of the dishes and everyone got sick with diarrhea. All night the guys were running on the path to the outhouse.

"Fire drills were held in our camp because we had tarpaper covered buildings. The buildings were heated by using coal in the stoves. There were buckets of sand near the stoves in case of fire.

"I fought a forest fire in the nearby town of Salisbury. I was tall and they gave me a tank that I carried on my back. I thought this was fun to spray water. When it was empty I refilled it from a tank truck supplied by the local fire department. Each night we went back to our camp.

"If you got hurt or sick you went to the dispensary, which was near the river. There were 2-3 beds inside. The guys who were in charge were very knowledgeable and good with first aid. If there was a serious problem they brought in a doctor.

"After my six months were up, I decided not to sign up again. The camp was closing and I didn't want to go to another camp. Lt. Comerford and Fred Brooks of the Forestry Dept. wrote letters of recommendation for me. These were a great help when I went home to look for a job. My father was able to get me a job at L. T. Wood Co. in Manchester. I was 18 years old. I got my driver's license and could drive trucks. They gave me the job of working the third shift from 11 pm to 7 am. They trusted me working alone in a multi-million dollar plant.

"In 1941 I was drafted into the Army. I served overseas in England, Africa, and Italy.

"After the war I came back to my old job at L. T. Wood Co. in Manchester. I worked there till 1970. Then I worked at Pratt & Whitney as an inspector for ten years.

"In 1988 Erika and I went back to my old camp. The whole camp was absolutely gone. There was nothing left. It was funny that a piece of history was wiped out. I only had memories."

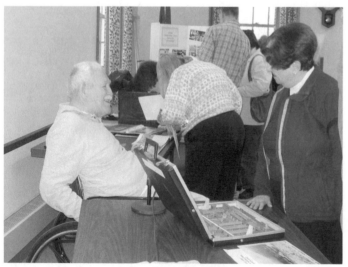

On April 29, 2012 Charley visited Kent Historical Society and was honored with a luncheon and an award for his work in the CCC. He told visitors about his life and experiences in the CCC camp in Kent. He also donated his diorama of his camp to the Kent Historical Society. Podskoch

Saverio Louis Scavotto

Saverio Scavotto from Enfield worked at the Macedonia Brook CCC camp in Kent. Bill Scavotto

Mildred Myers Scavotto from Rutland, Vt. sent me this information about her husband who worked at the Macedonia CCC camp in Kent.

"My husband, Saverio Louis 'Louie' Scavotto, was born on Dec. 7, 1917 in Enfield, Conn. His father, Louis, was a mason during the Depression and worked for the Town of Enfield in the WPA. His mother, Concetta 'Mary', had nine children: Saverio, Francis, Anthony, Nick, Ernie, Felix, Genevieve, Johnny, and Joe.

"My husband went a short while to high school but quit to help his family. There were quite a few fellows in his neighborhood who heard about the CCC and they all joined together. He went in to help take care of the kids in his family.

"Louie was sent to the camp in Kent, Conn. He always talked about the CCC and the projects he did. He loved it. He went in because his father was on WPA and there were nine kids to feed.

"My husband said he liked being in the CCC. All the fellows had a good time. They worked hard together. Every morning they went to work in a truck. They did all kinds of work from landscaping to road building. After work they went to the mess hall and my father said the food was great.

"Louie and his friends were great card players. So in the evenings that's what they did. He loved playing cards. He also liked playing ping pong in the rec hall.

"I think Louie spent a year in the CCC and then he

got a job working for United Aircraft in East Hartford. It is part of Pratt and Whitney. They made propellers. Then the workers went on strike so he became a painter. Next he went into business for himself and founded the Cambridge Decorating Co.

"On April 7, 1941 my husband and I were married. We had two children: Philip, and William, 'Billy'. We were married for 61 years.

"He retired from his business when he was 65 years of age.

"When my husband looked back at his time in the CCC, he always pointed out things the CCC boys did as we travelled.

"On April 19, 2004 my husband died in Westerly, RI."

Tony Gagliardi

Tony Gagliardi sharing Macedonia Brook camp CCC stories in his kitchen in Hamden. Podskoch

In the summer of 2008, Ron Gagliardi of Cheshire, saw an article about my CCC quest and called me to say that his father, Anthony, had been in the CCC. I arranged to visit Anthony at his home in Hamden.

His wife, Teresa, greeted me and took me to the living room where Tony was seated. He had a large smile and began sharing his CCC experiences.

"I was 17 years old and had just finished my third year of high school. I learned about the CCC because a bunch of guys in my neighborhood were in it. My mother told me to sign up for the CCC because we were poor and needed money. I was the second oldest in my family and I went

Tony Gagliardi was just 17 years old when he joined the CCC. Ron Gagliardi

down to the armory in New Haven and signed up.

"They sent me to Camp Wright on Fisher's Island near New London. This was for processing which included a physical. Then they shipped me by truck to Kent.

"The camp was near the Housatonic River and across the road was Kent Falls State Park. While living in the camp it felt like I was in the Army because officers ran the camp. The food was very good.

"There was an Army Chaplin in camp. One day he heard me swear. He yelled, 'I don't want to hear that word again!' From that day on I never swore again.

"I worked at the Kent Falls State Park. We serviced the area by cleaning the trails around the falls and picnic area. I enjoyed working with the other guys and made friends.

"A few times I went to Macedonia State Park for recreation and I saw the men laying stone for the walls along a long road.

"After work I played softball in camp. We also had a team that went from camp to camp.

"On weekends I went to town. I met a nice girl. Her family invited me over for supper and they treated me good. But then she was getting too serious and I wrote her a letter that ended our friendship.

"There were a few funny things that happened in camp. One was when the night watchman was walking around camp and he thought he saw a cat walking. So he walked up to it and said, 'Here kitty, kitty.' Well, it wasn't a cat but a skunk and he got sprayed really bad.

"From July to September 1936 I worked at the Macedonia camp. When September came I told my mother that I wanted to come back home and go back to school. She really wanted me to stay because she was getting my

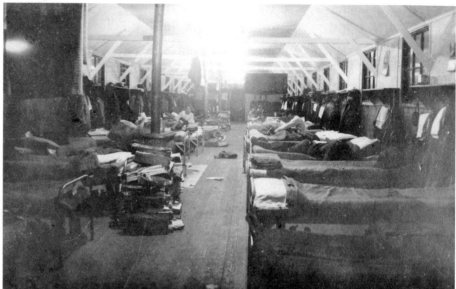

(L–R) 1 A Camp White enrollee breaking up stones with a jack hammer as Tony did. Paul Adykoski 2 Tony's barracks at Camp White where enrollees are relaxing after a busy day working. There is a stack of wood by the stove. Ron Gagliardi

pay of $25 a month. Luckily she agreed to my plea to get an education."

I asked Tony to tell me about his family.

"My father was Vincent. He worked as a mason when there was work. When he didn't have a job he worked for the WPA. My mother was Maria. She had nine children: Christine, myself, Marge, Florence, Vincent, Bernard, Phillip, Michael, and Ralph."

"I got a job as a pin boy in a bowling alley to help my family. I also bought my high school ring and 1937 yearbook.

"When I finished school in June, jobs were hard to find so I signed up again at the armory in New Haven for the CCC. I knew my work was helping my family. This time they sent me to Camp White in Barkhamsted.

"This camp was very good. First I worked at a quarry drilling holes in stones with a jack hammer. Then they used dynamite to blast them. They used the stones for making trails.

"Then they gave me a job in the office typing because I had an education. There was one other guy working with me. When the camp needed office supplies I went to Hartford. I got a ride in a small Army truck.

"I also had other jobs. One was working on a 'bug' crew. We searched for gypsy moths. I also worked on building roads.

"In the evenings I played ping pong or cards at the rec hall.

"On the weekends, if I had a chance, I went home. I left after work on Friday evening and usually hitchhiked. On my way back to camp my friends and I went to Hartford and usually got a ride on a truck that was going back to camp. Sometimes I'd get a ride with someone in camp who had a car. I'd get a ride to Waterbury and then hitchhike to New Haven.

"Some weekends when I stayed in camp I went to Winsted. I also went there for church on Sundays. They had a dance at our camp. I had a good time dancing. The next day the Colonel came up to me and said, 'You were quite a gay blade out there dancing.'

"I decided to leave camp because I knew what was ahead for me. I had to help support my family. I just had $5 a month for spending and I used it mostly to buy candy. I got a job in New Haven working at the Lehigh Coal Company. I carried bags of coal on my back. My pay was 50 cents an hour and totaled $5 for the week.

"After this job I realized I needed an education to better myself. I went to Boardman Trade School in New Haven. I learned how to read blueprints and how to use grinding tools. This helped me get a job at Geometric Tool

Company where I was a ground cutter for taps.

"On Oct. 9, 1943 I married Teresa Bonfiglio in New Haven. We had two boys: Ronald and James.

"In 1943 I joined the Navy. I stood watches on board and I was in charge of recreation. They sent me to school in Maryland and I studied recreation. When I went back on board I had a nice job of handing out volleyballs and basketballs. Then I lost that job. I later served on the battleship U.S.S. Indiana in the Pacific theater.

"After the war I tried to get my old job back at Geometric but couldn't get it. I decided to get a job as a carpenter making booths for bars for the New York Fixture Store. Then I worked making cement blocks for Plasticrete. My final job was as a mail carrier in New Haven. I retired in 1980 after 28 years of service.

"I felt the CCC was good for me, plus I was able to help my family with my monthly pay."

After the interview Tony and I shared a wonderful coffee cake Teresa had baked for my visit.

On Tues., Jan. 25, 2011 Tony Gagliardi passed away.

Tony (left) and friend dressed up for a dance at Camp White during the winter 1940. Ron Gagliardi

Tony Gagliardi with former Connecticut Governor Jodi Rell at a CCC Reunion at Chatfield Hollow SP. Podskoch

CHAPTER 14
MADISON

HISTORY

On June 4, 1935 2nd Lt. W. E. Chapin Jr., led a cadre of 23 men from Camp Roosevelt in Killingworth, Conn. to form the new Camp Hadley in Madison. The group left camp in two trucks containing camp equipment and rations for five days. Dr. Meyer Abrahams of NYC was the camp doctor.[1]

The truck caravan arrived in a beautiful pine grove on Copse Road in Madison. As the men arrived it began raining but this did not deter the men from their work. They pitched tents, set up the cooking stoves, and made a comfortable temporary camp by nightfall.

A June 1935 Hartford Courant article described that day: "Despite inclement weather and a campsite that was densely wooded and heavily underbrushed considerable progress was made and the entire camp was well established by night. The enrollees are busily engaged in clearing the underbrush around the campsite where they will live in tents until the buildings are constructed."

During the next few weeks the cadre cleared the area and planned where the buildings would be constructed.[3]

On June 24, 1935 Capt. M. G. Cohen assumed command of P-65 Co. 2101 that was housed in tents at Camp Roosevelt where they continued to live till the buildings at Camp Hadley were completed. O. R. Colangelo arrived on July 1 and became the education advisor. Instructors Welch and Ernest Dechant arrived and began assisting Colangelo. During this time, materials for a permanent wooden camp began arriving and construction began.[4]

At this time Co. 2101 with approximately 200 enrollees arrived at Camp Roosevelt in Killingworth and stayed at a tent camp established by Lt. Donald D. Hunt. On July 19, Capt. Harold D. Hersum of Maine assumed command of Co. 2101. They stayed there while buildings were completed in Camp Hadley in Madison.[5] Workers drilled a well at the Hadley camp and struck water at 200 feet.

Co. 2101 enrollees worked to complete Camp Hadley. Under the direction of Supt. Eliot of Guilford they cleared a large area near the camp for the construction of garages. They used dynamite to remove rocks and stumps. When the infirmary was completed Dr. Meyer Abrams moved his equipment in. The cooks moved their camp kitchen inside the mess hall and enrollees laid water and sewer lines. Headquarters and superintendent's offices were completed

The camp was named after Arthur Twining Hadley who was a Yale professor of political science (1879-1899) and later, at the age of 43, president of Yale (1899-1921).[2]

Camp Hadley Headquarters & Administration building was constructed in 1935. CT CCC Museum

Camp Hadley group photo circa 1935-36 with Capt. Capt. Harold D. Hersum in center first row with bulldog. CT CCC Museum

and furniture was moved in. Soon work was almost completed on the education building. The American flag was flying in front of the headquarters and cots were moved into the barracks.[6]

Although still living in tents at Camp Roosevelt, enrollees had activities in the evening. A Dramatics Department was formed in the summer of 1935. They had a minstrel show called "The Major Moe's Amateur Hour" which practiced two one-act plays and formed a glee club.[7]

After Co. 2101 spent two months camped out in Camp Roosevelt, Capt. McCulloch of Camp Roosevelt sent this letter to the Hadley enrollees:

On Thursday of this week you members of Camp Hadley quartered at Camp Roosevelt will move into your permanent encampment.

Your stay here has been a unique page in Camp Roosevelt's history. Undoubtedly every one of you will remember all through your fleeting years the two months spent in tents at the Civilian Conservation Corps camp in Killingworth. Every effort has been made to make your stay here an enjoyable one.

With few exceptions, your conduct has been commendable. Inter-camp entertainments and sports, which have been emphasized the past few months between Camp Hadley and Camp Roosevelt, in a great measure, prompted good will between the two camps.

The tent encampment period in the CCC was once termed the 'pioneering' period by an analytical editor. You men are now passing from your 'pioneering' period to a more permanent one of regular living quarters and work projects.

'Rookie' days are over, 'pioneers.' Best of luck and future happiness.[8]

Most CCC camps had a dog or sometimes a deer for a mascot but during the summer of 1935 Camp Hadley had a 13 year-old boy, Pete Gallagher, as their official mascot. He wore a CCC uniform and was called "Corporal." Pete said he was going to study to be a CCC captain. For now he had to return to school the next week. The camp newspaper didn't give any other information on where he lived or if he had any relatives in camp.[9]

Three days before they moved into their new camp, Camp Hadley's newspaper, The Pinch Hitter, reported in its Sept. 3, 1935 issue that Camp Hadley enrollees came to the aid of approximately 60 young girls at the nearby Atkinson School, a boarding school, when their water supply was interrupted. Camp director, Miss Francis Atkinson, called nearby Camp Hadley for help because the water pump wasn't functioning.

Sergeant Steve Moskell led a group of enrollees who didn't mind going to help the school and the dozen female councilors. The young men first tried digging up the water pipes but were unsuccessful. They then began a bucket brigade and furnished the girls with a temporary supply of water. They then went back to camp and left the work to professionals.

By early Sept. 1935 the barracks were completed at Camp Hadley and on Sept. 5, Co. 2101 with its 203 enrollees left Camp Roosevelt and went to their completed camp. They were accompanied by Lt. Hunt, Forestry Superintendent E. L. Eliot, and mechanic A. A. Parsons. The camp was now led by Capt. Harold D. Hersum. Dr. Meyer Abrams was the camp doctor.[10]

Enrollees were busy working on projects during Sept. 1935. Sixty enrollees rebuilt ¾ of a mile of the "Old Jack Day" road (present-day Warpus or Copse Rd.) that came from the main turnpike and extended past the entrance to Camp Hadley to the site of the new truck garages. They widened the road from 9' to 20' and graded it with gravel. The men cut trees and used dynamite to remove rocks and stumps. A neighboring farmer, Henry Menzel, donated a stone wall that the enrollees broke up and used for a base for the road. Madison First Selectman, Howard Kelsey, supplied the town tractor grader for the camp to grade the side and road.[11]

Camp Superintendent E. L. Eliot directed the clearing of a plot of land of trees, brush, and rocks for the new garages that would house the Army and state trucks.[12]

Another project was building a 12' wide road that would encircle the camp and eliminate the old road in the center of camp. The former company street would become a gravel path.[13]

By the middle of September 1935 a water tank was installed over the new water well. A pump now began supplying water to the officers' washroom. Work continued installing water lines in the camp. Now the camp didn't have to haul water from the town of Madison.[14]

Enrollees pitched in to make the camp presentable by clearing rocks and brush. They also took the various building materials that were scattered about and organized the wood, tar paper, and kegs of nails.

Also in September the camp was honored by a visit of the commander of the First CCC District, Brigadier General Fox Conner, who spent several hours inspecting the new camp.[15]

In October Camp Hadley was invited to a Halloween party and dance at Camp Roosevelt where they had spent two months waiting for their new camp.

The camp library received these contributions: 25 books from the Madison Library, 150 books from the

The 1935-1936 Camp Hadley basketball team with Joseph Fabiano (Top Row, L). Donna Sypniewski

Hartford Library, and many private donations.

During 1935 sports were very popular at Camp Hadley. A boxing team began practicing under the coaching of enrollee Joey Klempa who was the state light heavyweight title holder. Hadley also had a swim team that competed against other camps. They also practiced for a district inter-camp meet at Hartford on September 7 at Colt Park.

During the winter 1935-1936 the Hadley basketball team had a great season winning 15 out of 18 games. They defeated the following teams: Hand High School in Madison, Madison's G. O. P. (Grand Old Party), and CCC camps Roosevelt, Stewart, Buck, and Filley.[16]

A heavy rain began on Thur. March 12, 1936 and continued for nine days in Connecticut and all of New England. The Connecticut and Farmington rivers overflowed their banks and many towns were flooded and damaged. Several forestry foremen from Madison traveled to the affected areas in the Connecticut Valley and offered their help. On Saturday Middletown Police Chief Anderson called Camp Hadley for help to relieve Camp Filley men who had worked for 18 hours. Superintendent Eliot brought a crew of 50 men who patrolled the waterfront and Main St. On Sunday at 8 am another crew directed by D. F. Knox was stationed along the Connecticut River and at traffic barriers to restrict sightseers from the flooded areas. The enrollees were also assisted by men from Camp Roosevelt.[17]

In the spring 1936 enrollees built a volleyball court in the rear of the recreation hall and it provided for inter-barracks competition.[18]

The beautification of the camp continued under forester John Bottomley. He directed the two fire crews

Two enrollees on the water tower constructed in 1935 near the covered well. Donna Sypniewski

Work Projects of Camp Hadley from 1940 Camp Hadley Yearbook. Shepard

in securing trees, flowers, and bushes that they planted throughout the camp.[19]

On April 21, 1936 Frank Romer became the new Education Advisor. The education program contained many courses: Reading, arithmetic, letter writing, grammar, leatherwork, gypsy moth control, photography, road construction, first aid, dramatics, auto mechanics, conservation, swimming, music, mess management, leader training, forest protection, forest life, etc. The 1937 CCC Yearbook reported that 100% of the camp attended classes.

During April 1936 a house was constructed to store dynamite and caps. It was located on the road past the garages.[20]

The camp was continuously upgrading its facilities. In July 1936 Stanley Karas, in charge of maintenance, built benches around the mess hall to enlarge seating and he had the walls stained. The tables were covered with a glossy surface to resist wear and tear.[21]

During July the camp was treated to a dance and

vaudeville show. The Bridgeport Vaudeville Unit #2 performed a two-hour show. On July 20 the enrollees went to their monthly dance at the Madison Town Hall where they were entertained by the Hartford WPA orchestra. Young ladies from Middletown, Meriden, and New Haven attended the dance.[22]

Camp Hadley had good rapport with the town of Madison. The camp Entertainment Club gave a 1½ hour show at the Baptist Cottage.[23]

Camp Hadley enrollees worked principally in the Cockaponset Forest. They constructed truck trails, foot trails, planted trees, did forest improvement work, built fire lines, did gypsy moth eradication work, moved and planted trees and shrubs, constructed public picnic areas, and surveyed land.[24]

During the summer 1936 Camps Hadley and Roosevelt worked together building a part of Buck Rd. in Chatfield Hollow SP. The road used to be called Estel Rd.[25]

On Fri. Aug. 14, 1936 Camp Hadley was closed

Some of the many education and recreation activities at Camp Hadley. 1940 Camp Hadley Yearbook. Shepard

temporarily and quarantined when an infirmary attendant, Harold Johnson, became ill and was taken to Fort Wright Hospital because they thought he had a case of infantile paralysis. After a few days of observation doctors determined that it was another ailment and on August 17th the quarantine was lifted. Enrollees spent their down time painting the interiors of three barracks.[26]

Enrollees competed in a wood sawing and chopping contest at Camp Roosevelt in August 1936. Hadley took first place in sawing and second place in wood chopping.[27]

Also in August the camp acquired a 14-ton RD 7 trail builder bulldozer that did the work of 40 men. It leveled side banks of roads and moved rocks and graded roads. The camp also received a smaller Cletrac tractor for smaller jobs.[28]

Hadley enrollees neared the completion of Schubert Rd. in Chatfield Hollow SP. After this road was completed, the men began work on Winthrop Rd. (Rt. 80) Killingworth.[29]

The gypsy moth crew spent the winter and spring scouting for the egg masses and caterpillars. In the following spring they began placing bands of burlap on infected trees. During the day the caterpillars hid under the burlap where it was cooler. Then the enrollees killed the caterpillars under

This photo collage shows Camp Hadley enrollee's camp activities. Shepard

Joseph Fabiano of Waterbury discovered and helped extinguish a fire in camp. Donna Sypniewski

the burlap. At the end of the summer enrollees collected the burlap wraps from trees and packed them away for the next year. Then the crew resumed their scouting for egg masses.[30]

In October 1936 Barracks No. 3 was turned into a schoolhouse that contained a reading room, two classrooms, a journalism room, and an education office.[31]

Education classes began again in October 1936 and this was just in time for the new recruits. These courses and hobbies were offered: reading, math, English, letter writing, speaking, journalism, current events, radio repair, typing, leather craft, pest control, photography, truck driving, auto mechanics, road construction, special dancing, singing, stenography, orchestra, leader's training, dramatics, dynamics, ping pong, blueprint reading, fencing, movies, aviation, diesel engines, and woodworking. The enrollees were also able to take evening classes in Madison. They took shorthand and typing.[32]

When classes began 100% of the enrollees participated and there was 97% rate of attendance for classes.[33] This shows very few absentees.

The camp had a very good safety record except for an incident that occurred in the evening of February 1936. At 2 am night-watchman Joseph Fabiano of Waterbury while on his inspection of the recreation hall discovered a fire and he quickly extinguished it. He was aided by senior leader, Stephen Moskell of Meriden, who carried out Stephen Martin of Bridgeport who had collapsed from smoke.[34]

Safety practices were encouraged by instructors, foremen, and Army officers. In December 1936 Captain Hersum complimented the enrollees for completing three months without an accident.[35]

During the 1936-37 winter, the Hadley basketball team practiced on Wednesday afternoons with the Hand H.S. team in Madison. Camp Hadley played in the Community House League in Branford and the CCC League.

In April 1937 a photographer visited Camp Hadley and took activity, camp scenes, and group photos that were used in the Fifth CCC District Annual Yearbook.[36]

The spring education program in 1937 added courses in agriculture and animal husbandry. Enrollees learned how to raise pigs at their camp.[37]

In May 1937 the Gypsy moth crew led by foreman M. W. Kamienski did scouting and burlapping of infected trees in Gilford, Middlefield, Durham, and Branford.[38]

During the same month the library shelves were brimming with books. There were over 5,000 and most had

been donated by nearby town libraries, schools, or private individuals.[39]

In the spring of 1937 the federal government reduced the number of camps in Connecticut from 16 to 12. This resulted in the closing of camps and shifting approximately 400 men to a camp of their choice. About 40 men were transferred to camp Hadley.[40]

During the spring of 1938 enrollees who were studying for their grammar and high school diploma tests began preparing for the state exams that would be administered in June. Meanwhile, some enrollees attending the Madison evening school classes had a wide variety of topics to study: music, art, shorthand, dancing, bookkeeping, French, and dramatics.[41]

For the enrollees who remained at the camp on Friday evenings, the C. C. Club organized bingo parties. This helped the boys keep busy when many of their friends went home on the weekend.[42]

In March 1938 work began on building a schoolhouse to contain four classrooms, an advisor's office, a reading room, and a library.[43] Mr. Hosier and Mr. Shappelle and their fire crews were busy building the schoolhouse but they also did landscape work in camp.[44] They dug drains, built walkways, constructed walls and cedar fences, and planted flower beds.[45] A.M. Pierson Co., a wholesale nursery in Cromwell, donated shrubs and evergreens to the camp. Enrollee Arthur C. Brown of Hartford directed the work.[46]

The Clinton Players theater group provided free tickets to the enrollees at Camp Hadley. They attended many of the plays during the summer.[47]

Enrollees were also offered religion classes at

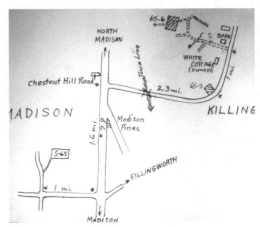

This map shows two one-acre parcels where Camp Hadley enrollees showed the owners of private property how to clear their land and then plant trees. These were in a demonstration forest to encourage owners to plant trees. This map was found in the CFPA library.

churches in Madison. Sixty boys attended Fr. Kane's Catholic Church and ten attended Rev. Mast's Protestant services held in camp.[48]

In the May 1938 issue of the Whisperin's newspaper foreman Potter and his work crew were reported as trying to finish a road project in Chester. Foreman Knox and his workers were just beginning to plant 25,000 spruce and pine trees. Besides sprucing up the camp with his fire crew, Mr. Shappelle and his crew were also cleaning up the picnic area at Chatfield Hollow SP.

On June 15, 1938 Capt. Roland W. Sellew left Camp Hadley and became the Superintendent of the Madison Military Academy. 1st Lt. Harold E. Miner became the new camp commander.[49]

A new activity was added to Camp Hadley in June 1938. Work began on building a chicken house for enrollees to learn how to raise chickens. This was the second year that agriculture classes were held at many of the CCC camps.[50]

On Sept. 21, 1938 the infamous hurricane hit New England and destroyed many homes and trees. Camp Hadley had some damage due to the 100-mph winds. Enrollees responded to the pleas for help by local towns and went out and helped their neighbors.[51]

During the new fall enrollment period in 1938, 72 men came to Hadley while 16 Hadley enrollees signed up and went out West.[52]

In November 1938 The Buzz Saw reported a new camp commander, Lt. Phillip Haas. Henry Potter continued as camp Superintendent.

As the year 1939 rolled in, the Leaders Club sponsored a dance on January 13th. The dance was held at the German Hall in Madison.[53]

Retired Connecticut State Recreation Specialist, Carl Stamm, is by the Camp Hadley stone incinerator. Podskoch

On Thanksgiving Day 1939 Camp Hadley had its annual football game on the Madison High School football field. About 500 spectators enjoyed the game. Barracks No. 4 won the inter-barracks game.[54]

In February 1940 Lt. W. Cleaves, Camp Commander, sent a memorandum to all enrollees in the Corps Area that prohibited hitchhiking. The reason he stated for the new regulation was that there were many accidents and one death due to hitchhiking. After enrollees were issued new spruce green uniforms it became harder for motorists to see the boys walking along the road at night. Appropriate disciplinary action would be issued for all those who violated the rule.[55]

On April 4, 1941 Camp Hadley closed while H. V. Potter was Superintendent. The US Army retained custody of Camp Hadley but the state had the responsibility to maintain it.[56]

In "The History of the Madison Grange #120" found in the Charlotte L. Evarts Memorial Archives in Madison, it said that the Grange secured a few of the Camp Hadley buildings for free. "Our Grange signed up for the Cockaponset buildings in Haddam and Madison-Killingworth. So for the weekends during the following months, members took down the buildings board by board and frame and carted them to town and stored the lumber in the Congregational Church horse sheds which stood at the location of the present parking lot of the Town Hall-Community Center."

With money they raised at fairs the Grange used the CCC timber and built their Grange Hall near the Village Green.

The Madison Grange was built using wood from a few of the abandoned Camp Hadley buildings. Podskoch

Here are some of the cement and stone structures at the old Camp Hadley site. On the left is a cement floor with pipes coming up, a stone fire place chimney, and a stone incinerator. Podskoch

Woodsy Club members and volunteers who helped clean up Camp Hadley. (Front row L-R) Jason Engelhardt, Ryan Handelman, Sam Wilson, Danny Weinreb. (Back row L-R) Bridget Gautrau, Alicia Imbergamo, Portia Blanchard, Taylor Day, Cecilia Bueno. Jason Engelhardt

Mike Caruso and Ed Kronberg, two former CCC boys at Camp Hadley, were there for the trail dedication and walked some of the trail and shared stories about their camp days over 75 years before. Both men now reside in Killingworth. Podskoch

LEGACY

Camp Hadley enrollees planted thousands of trees in the Cockaponset State Forest. The roads that they built are still used today by the many hikers, sportsmen, and families who visit the Chatfield Hollow SP. The roads are also used in timber harvesting and in fire prevention.

Sam Wilson, a Daniel Hand High School sophomore, took a hike near his home in the fall of 2013 on a Madison Land Conservation Trust (MLCT) trail. He found crumbling remains of stone chimneys, and cement foundations. He decided that he should do something about the overgrown and crumbling remains. An old sign at the trailhead referred to these remnants as the site of Camp Hadley. He didn't realize it, but this was the beginning of an enormous project that would involve many Madison residents of all ages. This lead to the discovery of the Civilian Conservation Corps (CCC) program that had been established during the Depression.

When Sam told his father about his idea to clean up the Camp Hadley site, his father contacted Joe Oslander, a MLCT board member and volunteer, and told him of Sam's idea. Joe put Sam in touch with Jason Engelhardt, a math teacher and advisor of the "Woodsy Club," in Sam's school. The club is composed of students with an interest in the outdoors and who get together to learn about their local forest environment and native cultures. The club liked Sam's idea and decided to work together with Sam and the MLCT to clean up and research the history of Camp Hadley.

After getting permission from the DEEP to work on the land, the Woodsy Club members and volunteers cleaned the trash and dense overgrowth that had accumulated since the closing of the camp in the 1940s.

Then they began making a large interpretive sign with a map, photos, and a brief history of the camp. This project required a lot of historical research, writing, and graphic design. The group raised $1,000 to cover the costs.

The students and adult volunteers placed markers at each of the building sites and points of interest in the camp.

On April 25, 2015 the MLCT celebrated the project's completion and over 100 people came to tour the Hadley camp trail.

Directions:

From I-95 take Exit 61 onto Rt. 79 north (Durham Rd). After approximately 1 mi., take a left at the 4-way light on Green Hill Rd. Travel west on Green Hill Rd. for 0.75 mi. to Copse Rd. Copse Rd. quickly changes to Warpas Rd. Trailhead is about 200' on the right. There is a small parking area on right at the trailhead.

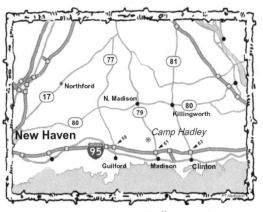

Map – Camp Hadley

195

MEMORIES

"If I Were a Leader"
Anonymous

If I were a leader I'd learn to know
That my position was a chance to grow,
I'd try to understand men who work,
To direct their efforts that none should shirk.

If I were a leader I'd always lead
I would never drive to attain more speed
Workers are human and humans must love
And they'll do more work when there is no shove.

If I were a leader I'd play the game,
Be as ready to praise, as I was to blame
Be sincere and just and never a snob,
But above all else I'd be on the job.

If I were a leader this truth I'd learn
That I was the key to the whole concern
And that harmony of the whole depends
On my leadership of my working friends.
- The Buzz Saw, Dec. 1936

The July 1936 cover of Camp Madison's newspaper, *The Buzz Saw.*

"Who?"
Anonymous

Little fishie in the brook,
CCC catch him on the hook.
Solitary vigil did he keep
For more than just a single week
In a hidden sunny glade,
For no one to know the place they made.

When the time and fish were ripe,
And all convinced the thing was dead,
A braver lad who did not gripe
Buried it in Bartnik's bed.
- The Buzz Saw, Aug. 1936

"The Stars Glittered"
by August Teri Savage

The stars glittered brightly in the sky,
That night I held her dainty hand.
She was all that beauty could imply,
Having all "these," "its," and "ands."

I used to be a misogynist
Until I met this gorgeous dame.
It was joy the way she loved and kissed;
Yet as I paused to learn her name

I was roughly pushed and jarred,
My teeth rattled and I nearly swore
To be interrupted by the night guard
Who told me not to snore.
- Whisperin's, Feb. 1939

"Mother Goose in the Forest"
Anonymous

Tom, Tom the camper's son
Dropped a match and off he run,
The fire with ease
Turned up the trees,
And Tom's in jail a fighting fleas.
- Whisperin's, March 1939

"Campfires"
by Stanley F. Bartlett

There's a spell about a campfire
That e'er holds me to the trail –
Although I never find success
I never seem to fail.
- Whisperin's, March 1939

CCC are burning brush that they have removed from a field.
Later in the spring they will plant seedlings. NYS Archives

"Brush Hauling"
by Anthony Kasinskas

It may be big or it may be small
We brush haulers have to take it all
We haul it about 50 feet in
Because we don't want to get turned in.

We brush haulers are always happy
So happy, that some of us got wacky
One boss says, "Drag it in and spread it out,"
Then another boss says to drag it out.

In any kind of weather, rain, sleet, or snow,
We brush haulers are always on the go
Because this life we're leading
Is better than being home and grieving.
- Whisperin's, March 1939

"Morning in Camp"
by Willard Shaw

Roll out of bed and open your eyes,
The whistle has blown and it's time to arise,
Into the washroom march the men,
To wash the face and hands again.

Then back to the barracks we all go,
Our faces flushed with a ruddy glow,
In we dash thru the barracks door,
To make our beds and sweep the floor.

The chow bell rings, the leaders shout
Come and get it or go without!
- Whisperin's, Jan. 1940

"Lover's Lament"
Anonymous

Scene: A darkened porch
Tips: Midnight present.
Action: If you love me, say so
If you don't love me, say so
If you love me and are afraid to say so,
Then let's go. I'm getting cold.

A Camp Hadley barracks ready for inspection.
DEEP State Parks Archives

Dominick Scarella

In June 2013 I received an email from Nancy Varthalamis of Commack on Long Island. She said that her father, Dominick Scarella, had memorabilia from three CCC camps: Camden, Maine; Madison, and Voluntown, Conn. She said had driving permits from Camden and Madison, two logs, and newsletters from the Lonergan camp in Voluntown, Conn.

Nancy wrote: "Before he passed away in 2001 he was beginning to reconnect with former CCC pals through the mail. He did not serve in WWII because of a bad leg. The friends he made in the CCC became his best fraternal memories.

"My father always talked about his time spent in the CCC. He had nothing but praise for it and how it helped him. He has photo albums, newspapers, and some other memorabilia from his time spent there."

I sent Nancy a questionnaire and here are her comments.

"My father was born on Aug. 4, 1920. His parents were Guiseppe and Constance Scarella. Dad had an older brother Patrick and an older sister Josephine. He should have graduated high school in 1939 but left in his junior year. It was not till after WWII that he completed his GED in 1947.

"I'm not sure how he found out about the CCC but I do know that Dad was happy to go off and work because of the Depression and difficult living arrangements at home. His older brother got married and brought his wife into their home. His parents always fought.

"Dad always spoke so highly of the camaraderie, the hard outdoor work and the extracurricular hobbies that they could partake in. He also learned dark room technique and took many photographs for the camp newspapers and himself.

"Dad's best friend was a man named Joe Hartford from upstate Connecticut. Dad made many friends. He has an autograph book filled with signatures and addresses for all of them to keep in touch after the CCC was being closed.

"Dad drove trucks into the woods where the boys were working. He said he learned how to drive carefully to take care of the lives of the men he was carrying.

"He also became a mess cook and those skills also stuck with him for the rest of his life. He cooked a lot under the head mess cook's supervision. He said most of the men were glad to have three square meals a day. On Saturday or Sunday morning Dad would make us stacks of pancakes, which would always lead into a story about feeding the men in the camp.

"I don't recall him ever talking about his being hurt at camp although he was sick as a young child with osteomyelitis which was a bone infection in his leg. That was why he never could get into any branch of the service once the war broke out.

"He did tell me about being very homesick once on Thanksgiving when he couldn't make it home and he had to eat in a diner. I called home from college a little homesick once and that's the story he told me over the phone. He

A tree view of Camp Hadley in Madison looking towards Warpas Rd. in the distance. Five barracks are on the right of the Company Rd. On the left were the mess hall, rec hall, flag pole in the square, and the administration building.

(L–R) 1 Nancy Varthalamis found her father's memorabilia of three CCC camps in his CCC trunk. 2 Dominick's driver's licenses for the Madison, Conn. and Camden, Maine CCC camps. Nancy Scarella Varthalamis

wanted me to stick it out and not quit.

"Dad actually took up flying lessons and we even have his log with all the various times and skills he practiced, but then the war broke out. I know he spent a lot of time with photography also, in his spare time. I think the men dated a lot and went into town because he had lots of pictures of groups of people having fun together."

Q: What do you think your dad accomplished in the CCC?

A: "I can't speak for my dad, except to recall he had only the fondest memories and was proud of the work he did in the parks and recreation areas he helped create, along with roads, camping areas, etc.

"Since it was a military-type organization, it had all the benefits of discipline, order, and well-roundness without the violence of war. He benefited from that as most men would."

Q: What did he do after you left the CCCs?

A: "Dad worked in a defense factory back home in Stamford, Conn. during the war. He married my mom in 1947 after he met her working in Pitney Bowes. Dad worked there for over 40 years. He built many of the postage meters that PB is famous for. He was particularly proud of the ones he made for the US presidents who retired. They got their own postage meters."

Q: How many children are in your family?

A: "My brother Robert (Bob) was born in 1949 and I was born in 1953. We lived in Stamford with our maternal grandparents and then when Dad was close to 40 we moved into our own new house in Norwalk where they lived until 1982. Dad had a workshop in the basement and underneath it was his old CCC footlocker. Inside it were pictures of

Betty Grable and other stars from the 40s. He had that until they moved to Florida in 1982. I don't know what happened to it. My father enjoyed a beautiful retirement in Florida with my mom up until his death in 2001."

Q: Did your dad ever go back to any of his camps?

A: "No, I don't believe he ever did, but I know he would have loved to. He was very sentimental and reminisced quite a bit about those times in his life. He was just beginning to receive some CCC newsletters in the mail when he died. In his eulogy at his funeral my brother and I mentioned how much the CCC's meant to him."

Boys waiting for transportation to take them home after serving their six months at Camp Hadley. Nancy Scarella Varthalamis.

(L–R) 1 Dominick Scarella (front) with Senior Leader Scalese (left) and Pop, the cook, in 1940. 2 While working in the kitchen Dominick had to ring the dinner bell. 3 Dominick (right) wore stripes signifying a leader in camp. With him are Pop, the cook, and friends by the mess kitchen. 4 On some weekends the boys had to take the cots out of their barracks for a good cleaning before inspection. Dominick is on his cot. All photos are courtesy Nancy Scarella Varthalamis

Mike Caruso

Mary Solera, a volunteer at the Killingworth Library, told me that a man came to the library after hearing that I was going to speak on the Connecticut CCC camps. He regretted that he couldn't come to my talk. Mary apologized for not getting his name and address and I thought that I'd never find out who he was. I have a passion for finding the few remaining CCC boys and chronicling their experiences in the CCC.

Then while gathering information from Carol Annino about her family's experiences, she told me that she, too, was a volunteer at the Killingworth library and would try to find the unknown CCC boy. A day later, Carol emailed me the name of a woman who was able to locate him and she told me his name, Mike Caruso.

Here is what he told me about his life and experiences in the CCC:

"The Depression was really tough on my family. My father, James, and mother, Mary, had it rough raising eight children in New Haven. My two sisters Rafelina and Adeline were the eldest. The twins John & Joe were next followed by James, who died when he was just a year and a half. Then my mother had George and another set of twins, Marie and me. We were born on Jan. 14, 1924.

"Then our whole family was thrown deeper into poverty when my father died from gangrene at the age of 33. He had been a foreman for the New York, New Haven &

A Cletrac tractor rolling a newly constructed road in the Cockaponset SF. DEEP State Parks Archives

Hartford Railroad line where his crew worked on the rails and ties. Then my father got an advancement and was placed in the tower and operated the signals.

"One day his old crew called him down from the tower and asked him to show how good he was at driving a spike into a tie. When he swung at the spike the head of the hammer bounced off the spike and the spike flew up and hit the side of a car. Then the spike ricocheted off the car and hit Dad in his hand. His hand got infected and it swelled up. At that time they didn't have medicine for gangrene. He died and my family was placed on welfare.

"The older children had to work to help my mother. I went to elementary school but after three months in high school I quit to help my family. I had a few jobs but not much money. At night I hung around the school with guys till 12 or 1 in the morning. Then I got a job at a produce market. I carried fruit in and out of the store.

"My brother John was in the CCC for two years and was the assistant to the superintendent at Camp Hadley in Madison, Conn. My brother Joe was supposed to go in the CCC, too, but he had a job so I used his name to join. I signed up in the fall of 1939 at the age of 15.

"With eight kids in our house I was happy to go away and be in the CCC. It was something new. Since my brother was there it made it easy to be away from home. We were both in the same barracks, too.

"My first job was as a truck driver. My brother learned how to do dynamite. One time he put 500 sticks into the big side of a hill and he told me to push the plunger. We'd yell to the other workers, 'Fire in the hole!' and they would relay the message to the rest of the men so no one would get hurt. The dynamite went off and I thought the whole

On Aug. 8, 2013 Mike Caruso revisited Camp Hadley where he worked during the Great Depression. He found the old stone and cement burn barrel along with some chimneys and foundations. Podskoch

mountain came down.

"Although we were in the Madison camp we were working at Chatfield Hollow in Killingworth where we were building a road. We also made box culverts for the new road. We used clay pipes under the road.

"Another job we did was that we made picnic tables and kept busy keeping the park clean. There were no toilets so if you had to go you took a shovel with you to cover it.

"We all got along well in camp. I just had one problem when someone stole something from my foot locker. He later confessed and was sent back on a bus to New York City.

"There wasn't much to do in the evening at camp. We could hitchhike to Madison after 6 pm but most of the guys stayed in camp. We played cards, went to the PX, or talked in the barracks.

"Once a week on Saturday they drove us to Madison to see a movie. At 11 pm we had to walk back to the truck to get a ride home. If you didn't make it, you had to walk back to camp.

"Some guys went home on the weekends but I only went home a couple of times.

"The food was good. Sometimes we had KP duty or latrine duty.

"After my six months were up in the spring of 1940, I decided to go home. I figured I could make more working outside the CCC camp. I got a job with my uncle fixing

On Aug. 6, 2013 the author took his granddaughters and Mike Caruso to explore Mike's old CCC Camp Hadley. Mike, Kira, and Lydia Roloff are seated on a large rock near the site of the camp garage. There is an iron wedge still imbedded in the rock after failing to split the rock. Podskoch

cars. He paid me a dollar a week. I also lived with him for the week. When he paid me on Saturday at 9, he sometimes asked to borrow the dollar that he had just paid me.

"My next job was working for a man named Hymie at his vegetable store in New Haven. I got paid $5 a week and I gave my pay to my mother.

"After Hymie's job I was drafted into the Army in January 1943. I took basic training in St. Petersburg, Fla. Then I was sent to Staten Island and went to mechanic's school. I did well in class and became a foreman of a motor pool. I went from a private to sergeant. Next I went to Bradley Field in Connecticut. There were just little planes there. There was a dirt runway and they were just beginning to modernize it. I stayed in an old CCC barracks. I was the first soldier to come there. We practiced flying in a glider. We rode in the glider along with two jeeps, a tractor, and 25 men sitting on both sides of the glider. They used a C-47 to lift us up from the ground by pulling with a nylon rope. There were two ropes, a short and a long one. The ropes had a hook that latched on and the C-47 pulled two gliders at once. We did this training at Westover, Mass. I was in a company of engineers.

"They took us up in the air and then the C-47 released us and we landed. We were practicing for invasions.

"In 1944 I went overseas to New Guinea and was in the invasions of the Philippines on Mindanao and Okinawa.

"After the war I came home in 1946. I got four bronze stars, two letters of citation, and a ribbon from the Philippine president.

"In October 1946 I married my girlfriend, Margaret Testa. We had three girls: Barbara, Sharon, and Kathleen.

"First I got a job working at the NY, NH, & Hartford RR. Next I went back to work at Carbonella Brothers Produce Market. I got paid $60 a month. Then I worked for the Gerrity Lumber Co. in Hamden for about 40 years. I enjoy working so I went to work at Morgan High School in Clinton. After working there for 11½ years, I retired at the age of 88 years.

"Before I joined the CCC, I used to hang around town with guys. The CCC was good because I didn't waste time and I stayed out of trouble. It was nice working outside and it was healthy. I hope they have CCC camps today because there are so many unemployed kids. The CCC taught me how to work and I was earning money for my mother."

Joseph Fabian Bergeron

Joseph Fabian Bergeron was the fire chief and fire marshal of Moosup. Ruth Bergeron

On Feb. 13, 2009 I spoke at the Plainfield Historical Society. Ruth Bergeron was in the audience and told me that her father, Joseph Fabian Bergeron, was in the Hadley CCC camp in Madison. I asked her to send me information about her father.

A few months later she sent me answers to my questionnaire, her father's discharge papers, and postcards he sent to Ruth's mother and family while he was in Camp Hadley. This is what I learned from Ruth about her father's life and his time in the CCC.

Joseph Fabian Bergeron was born in 1916 in Plainfield, Conn. His father, Fortuna, worked in a textile factory and had a small farm to help feed his family. His mother Georgiana Allard also worked in a textile mill, did seamstress work, and raised four sons and a daughter.

Ruth wrote: "My father graduated from 8th grade and went out and worked to help his family.

"On July 17, 1935, when he was 19 years old, he joined the CCC and was sent to Camp Hadley in Madison. Dad was a laborer, truck driver, and cook."

On Sept. 6, 1935 Fabian sent a postcard to his future mother-in-law, Edith Kennedy, with a picture entitled 'A Dam at Duck Holes'. It read:

I am in the new camp now. Got here yesterday morning at 10 o'clock. It's a very nice place over here. Took in a show last night in Madison. We have a lot of work to do before we get this camp straightened

out. It has been raining for the last three days out here. I'll write more about this place later.

Your Friend,
Fabian

On Sept. 6, 1935, Fabian sent a postcard with a picture of Old Linevan Falls Bridge to Emily Kennedy, his future sister-in-law:

Well, I suppose you are getting ready to fix your flower garden for next winter. There must not be many blooms left now. We are now in our new camp. The new barracks we live in are pretty nifty. We are now sleeping on good, soft beds, a little better than in the tents. This is all I can say for now. So take care.

Joseph Fabian Bergeron by a huge rock near his camp in Madison. Ruth Bergeron

On Sept. 14, 1935, he sent a postcard with a picture of the Madison Beach Yacht Club to Edith Kennedy.

Dear Mrs. Edith Kennedy,

Received your letter yesterday. Was very glad to hear that they are going to build a new road from your place to Moosup. Today is Sat. Worked all day. I have my job now working building roads. I have a few blisters on my hands from using the shovel. Been doing this work since Wed. We are building a new road into camp now.

Yours sincerely,
Fabian

Ruth wrote: "Sometimes on the weekend Dad hitchhiked home but mostly stayed at camp."

On Oct. 3, 1935 he sent a postcard with a picture of the Madison Golf Course and Caddy House to Mildred Kennedy, his girlfriend and future wife:

Went to a Grange meeting last night. I am planning to go home next weekend, but I am not sure because I will probably have to drive a truck and there are only a few drivers in the camp. We are going for free entertainment in Madison.

I had a small accident last week in the woods. Not with the truck. I got hurt by a stone on the side of a ledge we were working on. I was laid up a couple of days. I am back at work.

Fabian

On a postcard that depicts two fishermen on land trying to reel-in an enormous (fake) fish, dated Dec. 1, 1935, Fabian wrote this note to Mildred Kennedy:

Dear Mil,

Just a line to let you know that I will be home this weekend as I have a three-day leave. So I will be seeing you.

Your Friend,
Fabian

Ruth wrote: "One time Dad got very sick and went to the camp infirmary," wrote Ruth. "He had pains in his abdomen. On Feb. 24, 1936 the Army sent him by

Joseph Bergeron was taken to the Fort H. G. Wright Hospital on Fishers Island when he had appendicitis at Camp Hadley in 1936. Ruth Bergeron

ambulance to New London and from there he was taken to Fort Wright Army Hospital on Fishers Island. Dad had appendicitis and was operated on."

On a Feb. 28, 1936 postcard to Emily Kennedy, Fabian wrote:

Dear Friend,

Well, how is everything going? They took me out of bed and put me to work today. I worked about one and a half hours today. I can't do much. I am very weak. I have to walk a little for exercise. They got me under observation right now. I feel worse since I came here. I'll have to close till later.

A Friend,
Fabian

A week later, March 9, 1936, he sent another postcard to Emily Kennedy. He wrote:

It's raining here today. I feel better than I did. But I would feel a lot better yet. I'll be going home soon. If I get out of this hospital, I will probably be going home and maybe to stay but I doubt it will happen.

A Friend,
Fabian

Ruth wrote: "After spending five weeks at the hospital, Dad left on Mar. 31, 1936. Since his enrollment was over, he was honorably discharged and returned home.

"He got a job working at a local market and learned how to cut meat.

"On March 31, 1937 Dad married Mildred Ester Kennedy. I have two brothers, Edward and Paul.

"From 1943-45 Dad worked at Pratt & Whitney and he wasn't drafted into WWII because of a deferment.

"After the war Dad became an automobile mechanic. He also did some photography work. He was also very active in our local volunteer fire department where he served as fire chief and town fire marshal.

"The CCC was a good influence on my dad. He learned to be a good cook and how to work in the forest. His experience working and driving trucks had an influence on him becoming a mechanic, too.

"My father passed away on July 29, 2005."

Joseph Sadlowski

Joseph Sadlowski posing for a photo in the Cockaponset Forest where he worked for two years at the Camp Hadley CCC camp. Carol Ellithorpe

In June 2013 Carol Ellithorpe of Fountain Hills, Ariz. asked me to help her find information about her father's work in the CCC. She said, "I only have four pictures of his time in the CCC camp. Dad passed away over 20 years ago, and Mom doesn't remember much about Dad's early life except to say he was working at the CCC camp and they met while they were both fishing. Why is it we never think to find out this type of information before it's gone forever?"

This was one of the many stories that I have heard over the past years of children wishing that their fathers had told them more about their life and time in the CCC. I told her to send for her father's discharge papers which would give her some valuable information.

A few months later Carol sent me news from her father's discharge papers.

"My dad, Joseph W. Sadlowski, was born on Dec. 16, 1918 in Ansonia, Conn. His father, Joseph, worked as a laborer and his mother, Katherine, was a homemaker. Both his parents came from Poland. Dad went to schools in Ansonia and graduated from high school. To help his family he worked at a local bowling alley.

"He joined the CCC on Oct. 11, 1937 and was sent to Camp Hadley in Madison on Oct. 15. During his two years at Hadley, he had three jobs. For the first six months he did fire hazard reduction work. Then he worked building roads for 4½ months. His last job was chopping wood for 14

months. Dad received superior ratings for all of his work.

"On Jan. 27, 1939 Dad went to the infirmary for treatment of a sprained leg and remained there for three days.

"My father became an assistant leader on March 20, 1939.

"From July 1 thru September 15, 1939 he took these classes in camp: 'Tree Identification,' 'Photography,' and 'Leader Training.'

"I have some of Dad's CCC pictures. One is of a 1940's era flatbed truck decorated for use in a parade. There is a man standing in front of the sign on the side of the flat bed that reads: Conn Forestry Dept. CCC Camp Hadley, Madison.

"After almost two years, Dad was discharged on Sept. 30, 1939 because his 2-year time limit was up. His company commander was Phillip Hans.

"When Dad came home he was unemployed for 3 months. He applied for a job in the CCC and on Jan. 24, 1940 Dad signed up again for the CCC and was sent back to Camp Hadley where he received the job of 'Project Assistant.' He worked there for almost one year doing forest improvement projects. His camp commander was Constant L. Simonini. On April 3, 1940 Dad was made a leader at the camp. He worked under Camp Superintendent Harry V. Potter.

"Dad continued taking classes at camp. During the months of June thru August Dad took 20 hrs. of 'First Aid,' 30 hrs. of 'Leader Training,' 60 hrs. of 'Forest Improvement,' and 25 hrs. of 'Tractor Operation.'

"During his free time his records state that he 'read extensively: newspapers, books, and magazines.'

Joseph W. Sadlowski (left) working with a friend in the Cockaponset SF. Carol Ellithorpe

"On Dec. 5, 1940 Dad was honorably discharged from the CCC.

"Then Dad joined the Army on March 26, 1941. Dad never talked much about either his enrollment in the CCC's or his Army work in Townsville, Australia. He had something to do with communications.

"After his discharge from the Army on Aug. 5, 1945, he went back home to Ansonia, where his father got him a job at a factory. But Dad really didn't want to work in a factory and his father was really mad at him for not taking the job. Instead Dad started working for the State of Connecticut in the Forestry Department as a forest ranger. I'm sure his CCC experiences of working in the forest helped him get this job.

"It was while he was a forest ranger that he lived in the CCC buildings of Camp Hadley that were still standing. So I guess that was 1945-46, which is when my dad met my Mom.

"She grew up Green Hill Road, which is quite near Camp Hadley. The house is still there and owned by my cousin. My mom and dad married in 1948 and had three children.

"When my dad worked for the Connecticut Forestry Department, he was involved in building a fire tower somewhere in the Cockaponset Forest. I think it was in Killingworth. I don't remember a lot of details of my dad's work as I was only a kid then. I do remember climbing up to the top of the fire tower and being so amazed by the view! I do have a picture of Dad and one of his co-workers up at the top of the tower.

"Dad was in charge of several forests including Cockaponset. In 1968 he was 'transferred' to a forest in East Lyme, Conn.

"After 30 years working for the Forestry Dept. he retired. His work in the CCC and time working in the state forests is where he was most happy. He loved working in the woods. Dad passed away on Sept. 13, 1991."

"My Father, Joseph Sadlowski, and the CCC" by Carol Sadlowski Ellithorpe

I am surrounded by people, yet I am alone.

In all directions I see evidence of Civilian Conservation Corps (CCC) Camp Hadley, and I am trying to imagine what my father was thinking when he got to this, then-remote spot in the Connecticut wilderness. On October 15, 1937, when he arrived at Camp Hadley, Joseph Sadlowski was an unemployed young man of only 19 years of age from a rather large family who had lived his whole life in the city of Ansonia, Connecticut. His father worked in the Ansonia Copper and Brass Factory and he fully expected his son to join him at that place of employment or one like it after the Depression when there might be additional jobs available.

My father never talked to any of us about his time in the CCC so I am wondering what he felt, and for the first time, thanks to the imagination of a high school student and a myriad of volunteers, I can now see where the various buildings were in the Camp that shaped my father's future so profoundly. While this is a story of the resurrection of what remains of Camp Hadley, it is also a story of my father and the man he became.

Camp Hadley enrollee Joseph Sadlowski is sitting on the left side of the float the camp made that promoted their conservation work. Carol Ellithorpe

An interpretive historical marker along the trail erected by the Daniel Hand High School students and Madison Land Conservation Trust. Podskoch

I started researching my father's enrollment in the CCC in the fall of 2013 and thanks to one of only three photos my family has from that time, found that he spent his CCC enrollment at Camp Hadley, #2101, in Madison, Connecticut. Unbeknownst to me, at almost the same time, a young man by the name of Sam Wilson, then a sophomore at Daniel Hand High School, also got curious about the crumbling stone structures he saw while hiking a Madison Land Conservation Trust (MLCT) trail called the Camp Hadley Trail.

It is now March, 2015 and I am planning a trip, from my home in Arizona, to visit my mom and sister in Charlestown, Rhode Island in late April of this year when I received an email announcing a "Restoration Celebration" of CCC Camp Hadley. Wow, how opportune, I couldn't believe my luck, it was scheduled for April 25, 2015, right in the middle of my two-week visit! One of the things I had originally wanted to do on my visit was hike round the site of Camp Hadley. I had discovered that the land around the old camp was part of Cockaponset State Forest and the Madison Land Conservation Trust had established a hiking trail around the remains of the camp.

So, on that Saturday, my mom, sister and I drove to the Daniel Hand High School in Madison (which happens to be almost across the street from the farm that originally belonged to my Mom's parents) to attend the

On Apr. 25, 2015 over 100 people came to the Daniel Hand High School in Madison to the Camp Hadley Trail dedication program. Two former Camp Hadley enrollees, Ed Kronberg (left) and Mike Caruso, told the audience about their time at the camp. Podskoch

celebration. And, what a celebration it was! First was the indoor presentation, which included a welcome by Michael J. Maloney, President of the Madison Land Conservation Trust, CCC songs sung by Tom Callinan, Connecticut State Troubadour, opening remarks by Joe Oslander, also of the Madison Land Conservation Trust, and a short history of Camp Hadley by Marty Podskoch, CCC Historian.

Then two men who attended Camp Hadley, one of whom was Mike Caruso, now 91, shared their experiences and memories of their time there. But the part of the program that really intrigued me was finding out, from Jason Engelhardt, a mathematics teacher at the high school, that this entire process of locating and clearing the remains of Camp Hadley was set in motion two years ago by Sam Wilson.

Following the indoor part of the program, we then boarded a school bus (those seats certainly seemed smaller than they used to!) and drove to Camp Hadley to see the results of two years' worth of work by a dozen or so high school students, volunteers from the Madison Land Conservation Trust and local residents who became interested in the project that was in their "backyard". If it hadn't been for those wonderful people, there would have been very little visible for me to contemplate my father's time here. Instead there were remains of numerous buildings, most labeled, and with the hike being narrated by Joe Oslander of the MLCT, I was able to see where other less obvious features of the camp, such as the main road, were located.

Coming home, I wanted to share this amazing project with the membership of the CCC Legacy. So, with that in mind, I further researched this preservation project of the site of CCC Camp Hadley.

As already stated, the project was set in motion by Sam Wilson. Sam said, "I had no idea that conservation camps existed, let alone Camp Hadley right down the street from my house in Madison. I've always been intrigued by our nation's history, so I was very interested in restoring the camp and learning about how people lived during such a difficult time period. Now, anyone can visit and see how the camp was run decades ago."

Sam and his friends (including, but not limited to: Bridget Gautrau, Alicia Imbergamo, Portia Blanchard, Taylor Day, Cecilia Bueno, Ryan Handelman, Jack Dobson, and Dan Weinreb) wanted to clean up the camp site, so his Dad contacted Joe Oslander, a Madison Conservation Land

Trust board member, who, in turn, put Sam in contact with Jason Engelhardt, a Daniel Hand High School mathematics teacher, MLCT member, and the advisor for the schools Woodsy Club. The Woodsy Club is a club whose high school participants that have an interest in the outdoors get together to learn about outdoor skills, the local forest environment and native cultures.

The first thing they did was to put together a "to do" list of what they hoped to accomplish, what hurdles had to be surmounted, and how to get it all done.

The main items on the list included, but were not limited to: 1) Get permission from the Connecticut Department of Energy and Environmental Protection to undertake this project on state park land. 2) Create and install a large interpretive sign with a map, photos and a brief history of the camp along with smaller signs labeling the various building sites. 3) Last, but not least, clean up the dense overgrowth of vegetation and trash that had accumulated over more than half a century.

Joe Oslander handled the government end of things with its requisite paperwork. Sophomore Liam McCarthy and junior Catherine Peng took care of creating the signage. Liam, with his interest in history, did the research and writing and Catherine used her computer skills to design the sign. Portia Blanchard, a sophomore, applied for a grant from the Pardee Youth Fund (a trust fund administered by the First Congregational Church of Madison) to pay for the sign. They were pleased to provide the $1,000 needed for fabrication.

The physical work began during April vacation, 2014, when about a dozen students went to the Camp Hadley site on three mornings (along with several adult MLCT volunteers) to start clearing all that underbrush. Using shovels, leaf blowers, saws, and anything else that could be used to cut through the growth and to remove it from the remaining concrete slabs and foundations of the former buildings, they persevered and made a huge difference that gave everyone more incentive to keep going on this monumental task.

The clearing work continued throughout 2014 with many local residents, like Eric Alletzhauser and his two daughters, Emily, 11, and Lucy, 8, also making a dent in the work that lay ahead. Emily said, "I think it's really cool that we can kind of be connected to the past here. There are so many things that we really don't know what they were. I like trying to look at them and find all the different things that it could be."

The MLCT installed the interpretive signs and the trail was really starting to take shape, even more incentive to keep going!

It is estimated that all the volunteers have put in a total of 200 hours of labor through the spring of 2015. The MLCT would love to install more signs providing more of the historical information of Camp Hadley. If you are interested in supporting this effort, please contact Mike Maloney at mike@maloneyllc.com

What impressed me most about this whole project was the involvement of the students. Not only did they originate the project, use their physical and mental skills, but they really "got into it".

Jason Engelhardt, Mike Caruso, and Marty Podskoch at the entrance to the Camp Hadley Trail. Podskoch

Student and adult volunteers cleared cement foundations, stone structures etc. of dirt, leaves and other debris and posted identification signs. Podskoch

Some of their thoughts as quoted in 'The Lay of the Land', a Madison Land Conservation Trust publication:

"It's important to make sure history doesn't get forgotten. It's surprising that this camp, made during the Great Depression in our town of Madison, is practically unknown to everyone here. We dug up a bunch of artifacts, like a light bulb and some old cans. We started playing anthropologist by Googling the items to learn more about the time period."

- Bridget Gautrau, Junior

"On the first day, the sites were covered in leaves and branches, and weren't very identifiable. By the end of the first day alone, we had nearly cleared several sites and by the end of the week everything was cleared, including a newly restored trail."

- Alida Imbergamo, Junior

"This camp held a community, giving many hope and a reason to live. Knowing that we put forth our effort on the same ground as the original members of Camp Hadley really made us feel like we could make an impact."

- Portia Blanchard, Sophomore

Remember that young man that started this story? Well, my dad never did work in a factory. One of the last things his sister passed on to me before she passed away (at age 91), was that when my father returned from the war in 1945 he told his father that he would never work in the factory. He wanted to work in the woods. Well, despite his father's annoyance, he managed to get a job with the State of Connecticut, Forestry Department, and spent the rest of his life in the Connecticut woods he loved so much.

When he was hired by the State of Connecticut, he was housed in one of the buildings that remained from Camp Hadley. He met my mother while fishing in a stream in the rear of the farm that her family owned, just a stone's throw from Camp Hadley. He spent his whole career, 30 years, working for the Forestry Department in the Cockaponset State Forest. His time with the CCC developed his love for the outdoors that expands past his life into, now, three generations.

Did the CCC make a difference in my father's life? Oh, most certainly! As it did mine, my siblings, my daughter and her children. We all love the outdoors, thanks to the CCC and how it influenced my father's entire life thereafter.

Raymond Gianini

While working at Camp Hadley Raymond Gianini went to an Army cooking school and learned how to cook for the 200 enrollees in his camp. Mary Lombardi Gianini

After Deborah Gianini Fraser of Branford learned that I was giving a talk on the CCC at the Killingworth Library she contacted me in April 2013 and said her father, Raymond Gianini, had been at the Madison CCC camp. Deborah said that her father had passed away but her mother, Mary, had a lot of memories of her husband in the CCC and that I should call her.

On April 15th I called Mary Lombardi Gianini. She was very happy that I called and shared these memories of her husband.

"My husband Ray was born on March 5, 1922 in West Haven. His parents, Art and Jeanette, had parents who were from Italy. His dad made monuments for cemeteries. Ray was the eldest of four children. He had a sister Clara, a brother Art, and a younger brother that I didn't know well because he lived in California.

"Ray quit school after 8th grade and worked with his aunt and uncle. His uncle was a fisherman, in Stony Creek.

"I met Ray in 1939 when he came to our home in New Haven to date my older sister. She told me to go down and tell Raymond that she didn't want to go out with him. I went down and told him what my sister said and he replied, 'That's okay because I like you better.' That was the beginning of our romance and, eventually, our marriage.

"Soon after that he joined the CCC and went to the Madison Camp in Hadley. He was happy to leave home because he had a very bad home life.

"When he first joined the CCC he was a truck driver. On Dec. 19, 1939 he became a cook. He really loved that job. I have the certificate he earned by attending an Army cooking school. He had to get up at 4 am to start work and he stayed there till dinner was over and the kitchen was spotless.

"In the evenings he played cards and sometimes went to the center of Madison and walked around. Every other weekend he was off work and he came to visit me.

"There was one time when he got really sick. Ray came to visit me one weekend. He said he didn't feel well and went back to camp.

"When he got back to camp he was very sick. He doubled over and they sent him by ambulance to Fishers Island where there was an Army hospital. His discharge papers say he was at Fishers Island from July 18, 1939 for over 4 months. He came back to camp on Dec. 2, 1939.

"Then he became a second cook. He completed 144 hours of cooking instruction and on June 27, 1940 he received a certificate for 'Cooking.' He did this job till Oct. 19, 1940 when he was discharged.

"He left the CCC because he got a job at Winchester Rifle Arms in New Haven.

"We got married on Sept. 6, 1941 in St. Anthony's church in New Haven. He had been baptized, received holy communion, and confirmation in St. Margaret's Church in Madison. He did this as an adult because his mother did not take him to church. We had three children: Ray, Deborah Fraser, and Richard.

"Raymond was drafted into the Army on Dec. 21, 1942. First he went to Fort Devens in Massachusetts. Then he went to Kansas and Michigan. He was a cook in the Army just like he was in the CCC. I went to visit him in Michigan when I was 4½ months pregnant. He eventually was sent overseas to the Philippines where he spent most of his time. He came home at the end of the war with a terrible case of malaria which doctors believe may have contributed to his terrible heart condition.

"After Ray was discharged from the Army, he went back to work at Winchester Rifle Arms Co. but wasn't happy with his work. He left and worked at Armstrong Rubber Co. in West Haven. Ray worked there till he retired in 1984. He had a very bad heart and had 25 heart attacks.

On Jan. 3, 1987 he died at the age of 64.

"My husband loved the CCC! He had little schooling but he was well-read. He spent his spare time reading many books."

The next week I met Ray's daughter, Deborah Fraser, at my CCC talk in Killingworth. She said, "In my dad's free time he loved the ocean and enjoyed boating and fishing with my younger brother Rick. My dad was a member of the Coast Guard Auxiliary and loved being a part of that organization as well as being out on the water with other boating friends and our family.

"The cooking skills that he learned in the CCC continued not only into his Army life, but after his discharge. He made many a Thanksgiving dinner for our family at home and the best French toast in the world for Sunday breakfast."

John S. Balavender

John S. Balavender at a CCC reunion at Salmon River SP in East Hampton. Podskoch

On Sept. 20, 2009 John S. Balavender and four other CCC alumni came to a CCC reunion at the Salmon River SP in East Hampton. John shared his stories about growing up in New Britain and working at two CCC camps: Madison, Conn. and Meeker, CO. I planned on interviewing John at a later date, but I regret that he passed away approximately one month after the reunion on Oct. 21, 2009.

It was five years later that I was able to contact John's son Brien and his daughter Donna Larson and we arranged to meet at Donna's home on Feb. 13, 2016 where I was also able to meet John's wife, Helen. The three of us sat at the kitchen table and each shared their memories of John.

Helen started out saying, "John enjoyed being in the CCC very much. When his brother Eddie asked him to be in his wedding he said, 'No way! I'm going back to my CCC camp.'"

Q: Tell me about John's early life.

A: Helen said, "He was born in on May 3, 1918 in New Britain. His father was John and his mother was Mary. There had eight children: Katherine, Eddie, John, Verna, Helen, Henry, Raymond, and Steve. John went to parochial school and then Nathan Hale Jr. High School in New Britain. Life was tough during the Depression and since John was one of the older boys he quit after 9th grade to help his family. He did odd jobs and then heard about the CCC. He joined and in order to get in he had to pass a physical exam. He was sent to Camp Hadley in Madison."

Q: Do any of you remember what he did at camp?

A: Brien said, "He cut trees for firewood, built bridges, and grubbed out trees for roads."

"He said he also planted trees," added Donna.

"John often said when he came home on weekends that if he didn't have a ride back on Sunday, he'd walk from New Britain to Hadley," said Helen. "There were times when it was late at night and he'd hear dogs barking as he walked along the lonely roads."

"That's about a 30-mile walk," added Brien.

"My father had a lot of good friends at camp. One of them was Balukus. He's the one in this picture holding up my dad at Camp Hadley," said Brien. "The water tower is in the back. Another good friend was Dudley Brand from New London."

Q: After John's six months were up, why did he go to Colorado?

A: Brien said, "When they announced in camp to see if anyone would like to go out West to Colorado, I think his friends said, 'Let's all go together,' and Dad said, 'Let's go.' And they all signed up."

Q: Did he say what he did in Colorado?

A: "I'm not sure, but maybe the same things he did at Hadley," said Brien. "Here is a photo album of my father's CCC days. In it shows him cutting logs and men working ditches that they had dug. They are stacking logs on the sides of the banks probably to hold them back to prevent erosion. They did a lot to help the ranchers."

Donna remembered, "John said they'd get three or more day passes and they'd hop a train and take a trip to see more of the West."

"I remember Dad singing," said Brien, "'San Francisco the city by the bay. Seven-day pass and make an ass out of you and me.' I know he was never in San Francisco in the Army so maybe he hopped a train to California and that is how he got that song."

Helen said her husband often told her and others, "When I look back at my life, the CCC was a 'Hidden Army.' We were trained by the Army and when we entered WWII we were ready, especially the boys that had been in

(L–R) 1 When John Balavender joined the CCC he was just 17 years old. 2 John Balavender (left) and partner cutting a tree using a two-man saw. 3 John Balavender held up by his good friend Balukus at Camp Hadley. All photos courtesy Helen Balavender

the CCC."

Q: What did John do after the CCC?

A: Brien said, "When he left the CCC he worked at Fafnir Bearing Co. in New Britain."

"On June 6, 1941 he was drafted into the Army. We weren't at war and he was only supposed to be in for a year. He was 23 years old," said Helen. "Then when we were attacked at Pearl Harbor he had to stay in for five years."

Q: Where was your dad during the war and what did he do?

A: "Dad was in the U.S. Army's 176th Field Artillery Battalion, 9th Division. He served in seven major campaigns: Tunisia, Sicily, Normandy, Northern France, Rhineland, Ardennes, Central Europe, and Africa under the command of General William C. Westmorland. Dad drove a truck in a supply train that brought munitions to the front line. He tried to be a pilot but failed the test. Then they told him he could be a tail gunner but a friend of his told him that was a very dangerous job so he stayed driving trucks."

Q: What did he do after the war?

A: Donna replied, "He had a couple jobs but didn't want to go back to his old job at Fafnir Bearing Co. He worked as a carpenter building houses for a while. Then he began working with his brother, Steve, doing excavating work for foundations.

Brien added, "Then the two started B & J Trucking. They did a lot of hauling lime from Massachusetts to sewer treatment plants in Connecticut. When they got a bulldozer they got into excavating for underground utilities. Later on his sons Brien and Joseph took over B & J Constructions. Then Brien took the company over and his brother Joseph started a demolition company called SalCon.

Q: Helen, when did you meet John and when did you get married?

A: "In 1945, when John came home from the war, a friend introduced us. There was a time when we didn't see each other again but we got married on April 29, 1950. We had three children: Brien, Joseph, and Donna.

"I also had a brother in the CCC. My maiden name was Chymbor. It would be interesting to find out what camp he was in."

Camp Meeker enrollees and foreman placing logs as riprap in ditch to prevent erosion and possibly base for a bridge. Helen Balavender

(L–R) 1 Camp Meeker in central Colorado where John Balavender and 200 other Connecticut boys worked doing projects to help the ranchers. Helen Balavender 2 Brien and Helen Balavender and Donna Larson with Hadley Camp photo where John Balavender served. Podskoch

CHAPTER 15
NIANTIC

HISTORY

The Niantic CCC Camp Chapman S-61 Company 177 was established on June 1, 1933 at the Military Reservation at Stone's Ranch in East Lyme. This camp was composed of Veterans who had fought in the Spanish American War or WW I and were unemployed. It was named in honor of H. H. Chapman (1874-1963), who taught at the Yale School of Forestry, was chairman of Connecticut Forest and Parks Association, and President of the Commission on Forest and Wildlife.

Stone's Ranch was named after the former owner, Fred A. Stone, a famous circus performer and musical comedy star who set up his farm as a typical western ranch. In 1929 when Stone stopped using the ranch, he leased his 1,870 acre ranch to the Army to use for tactical training. In May 1931 the Connecticut State Legislature purchased Stone's Ranch from Fred Stone for $50,000.[1]

Ford Hilton grew up on Stone's Ranch where his father, Fordyce G. Hilton, Sr., was the State caretaker from 1938 to approximately 1960. Ford wrote, "A Brief History of Stone (sic) Ranch, East Lyme, Connecticut," and dedicated it to his father. Hilton stated there were two or three barracks, "across from the Ranch house. They were typical CCC wood single story with tar paper exterior and vertical 1 x 3 x 8 furring strips every 16."

One can tell that the kitchen in the ranch house was used for feeding the CCC camp because it had two large iron commercial looking wood/coal kitchen ranges in the kitchen area of the old Ranch House, as meals for the workers (enrollees) were prepared there, and served in the 'Fred Stone' addition (camp mess hall) which would have measured probably 30 feet by 40 feet or so.

"A huge stone fireplace/chimney formed most of the north wall of the addition and remnants of it still can be found there. This was not the main house chimney, but one of the log additions on the north end of the house. Lore had it this addition was built by Fred Stone and was where he and others rehearsed before going to Broadway in NYC.

Camp Chapman Co. 177 was established on Stone's Ranch in Niantic near Rt. 1. The mess tent is in the lower right with barrels of hot water for washing mess kits and utensils. DEEP State Parks Archives

Enrollees set up their Army tents in the large field on Stone's Ranch. A 36-gallon canvas Lister water bag kept the drinking water cool during the summer of 1933. CT CCC Museum

The mess kitchen tent with the cooks and to the right is the mess sergeant. CT CCC Museum

During the fall of 1933 CCC enrollees moved into the wooden barracks. CT CCC Museum

This piece from the June 1934 issue of the Camp Chapman News described the camp's first year.

History of Camp Chapman

"May 25th saw 200 young men huddled together at the army Dock in New London, each anxiously waiting for the boat that was to bring us to the final stages of our original destination. In the late afternoon we marched off the boat. At last we remember the famous 'Wait till you get the needle?' Many of us wanted to turn back but no one did.

"We first became acquainted with the Army when some sergeant blew a whistle and then shouted 'Forward March!' On we went to the supply house. There we were given the first supply of equipment. Just like getting a cat in the bag, we took the barrack bag. We didn't have time to check up on what we got. We were told to move on to the camp street until we came to 177 Co. It seemed as though the majority of men tried to group themselves together. The tents looked so cold and clammy to most of us. It is a safe bet to say that half of them never slept in a tent before. The supper gong soon sounded and the whole company street was filled with hungry men. It was a just hunger though.

"After supper most of us went to see the big guns. Gosh, we were certainly impressed by their size. After a thorough inspection of the island we called it a day and went to sleep.

One of the big guns at Fort Wright on Fishers Island, NY.

"Bright and early next morning a shrill whistle broke our sleep. It was rather tough getting up so early. A new day had dawned. Other adventures awaited us. After breakfast we were lined up and marched to the old Armory where we were given the well-known needle. In the same building we took the oath to live up to the rules of the C.C.C. and right then and there our pay began. It was good to know that we were working again.

"After we were there a few days, Capt. Sherman, our commanding officer, was replaced by Capt. Campbell. Remember the talk he gave us? He was a fine man.

"At last June 1st came. Up early in the morning and loaded down with baggage and equipment we were off on another adventure – To Star Ranch – our new home for the next year. For the rest of the day the place was a beehive of activity. It was under the direction of Lt. Seward the fellows put up the tents with skill and precision of a circus roustabout. Our first meal in the open air tasted a little different, didn't it? But it was good. Do you remember how Lt. Lennon made us pick up every little crumb that we dropped? Incidentally he is the only officer left of our original company. This whole month was devoted to the camp area cleaning.

"Along with July came Lt. Hawes. He gave us our first organized recreation, laid out the baseball diamond, the volleyball court, and started the ball rolling along. Who was in camp on July 2nd? Those of you who were there will never forget it. A terrific windstorm nearly blew the camp away. The cool heads of some of the fellows saved it from complete ruin.

At first the enrollees lived in tents. To the right is the latrine. DEEP State Parks Archives

"We ask ourselves where the months of July and August went to. The answer is that we were having such a nice time that we did not notice it go by.

"In September we were struck with deep regret when we learned that Lt. Hawes was being transferred to another company. How we hated to see him go. It was also in this month that the work in the forest began and that we enjoyed our first meal in the new mess hall. We were all dressed for the occasion with our best G. I. clothes. The barracks were well under construction and in a short time we were living in them.

"October brought the coming of Lt. Pohl, Lt. Comerford, and our present mess officer, Lt. Scott. Lt. Pohl was responsible for a great many improvements in the camp. With the leaving of Capt. Campbell, Lt. Pohl became commanding officer and the reign of happiness began. He worked wonders with the men. He was the man who gave us our first dance.

"November and the cold weather drove everyone to the recreation hall and we had a series of shows and plays.

"December brought us Capt. Rohrbach and a farewell party to Lt. Pohl. It was more like a funeral than a party. We hated to see him go. He hated to leave us.

"January brought the cold weather, the deep snow skiing, skating, the hockey team. They all contributed to our entertainment.

"February is remembered as the month of the big fire (the foremen's barracks), while March kept everybody busy with discharges and reenrollments.

"April and May has meant a great deal to the Veterans. The fast approaching June is forever in our minds and little else matters except the fact that we will be leaving shortly. And so ends this eventful history of the C.C.C. Veterans of the 177th Co. To be picked by the 'youth' of this company."[3]

I recall a massive coal furnace in the cellar with hot pipes extending to the upper floor registers.

"Behind the Ranch house in the valley at the southeast end of the field were two large bath and wash house buildings."

Hilton also stated that a friend of his father, George Wilke of the Blackhall section of Old Lyme, drilled two wells that fed the CCC camp water tank. One 500' deep well was at the top of Pump House Hill. It provided water for the old Ranch House, the CCC bath house and other camp buildings.[2]

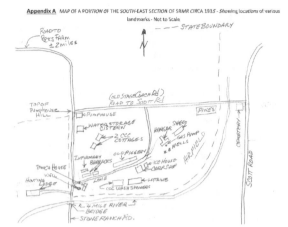

Map of Camp Chapman drawn by Ford Hilton.

Projects

The camp's first superintendent, Harold D. Pearson, was succeeded by Otto H. Schroeter. Enrollees did a lot of work at Stone's Ranch. They helped battle Dutch Elm disease and they planted the stand of pine trees in the area known today as "the Pines."

Another area where Camp Chapman worked was the Rocky Neck State Park located along Long Island Sound on Rt. 156 in East Lyme. Veterans began working there in June 1933 constructing a campground for the park. The state planned on 17 circular sites containing 12 campsites with a toilet and parking in the center of each. The CCC constructed four circular sites that were ready for campers during the 1934 season. For these four sites the enrollees dug five 48" wide wells approximately 12' deep. They lined the wells with concrete pipes, covered them securely, and

installed a hand pump.[4]

The CCC Veterans also put up a building for the camp watchman that was also used as the camp headquarters.[5]

Another project was the construction of a new park entrance called West Dr. so that the park would have an entrance and an exit road.[6]

Veterans also worked in the Nehantic State Forest (NSF) located in parts of Salem, Lyme, and East Lyme. The state acquired the first piece of land for the forest in 1925 and added to it over the years. It was the first state forest in New London County. Camp Chapman constructed a 2-mile road that traveled in a north/south direction in the NSF.[7]

The NSF, over 4,400 acres, is named after the Nehantic Indians who ranged from Wecapaug Brook, in what is now

Ford Hilton sitting on the steps to one of Camp Chapman's barracks with his mother (left) and his grandmother. Ford Hilton

These young Camp Chapman boys are taking a break from planting trees in the Niantic State Forest. CT CCC Museum

Enrollees carrying boards for work project. CT CCC Museum

The Veterans at Camp Chapman worked on building the road
and some rock walls at Devil's Hopyard in 1933. www.ct.gov

Rhode Island, to the Connecticut River. After the settlers arrived the Pequot Indians invaded Nehantic territory and took over half of the Nehantic's land.[8]

In September 1933 Veterans began roughing out a road in Devil's Hopyard SP. Plans had been drawn up by the Forest Commission four years earlier and Camp Chapman men cleared out 1,000 feet for a road. There was a lot of rock to be blasted and the stone was used to build walls.[9]

Chapman Veterans also worked at Fort Shantok SP (near Mohegan Sun in Montville). During the summer they built a truck road and fire trail there. They also worked to stop the seepage of water through the bottom of Tantaquidgeon Pond. They put a 200' long and 6' deep clay core at the foot of the dam. From the end of November till December they cleaned up the woods. This ended their work there as winter approached.

The camp infirmary didn't have running water and enrollee Whelan had to carry gallon containers of fresh water for his patients. Finally, in March 1934 water was hooked up to the infirmary.[10]

During the winter the basketball team had a successful season They competed in the Eastern Connecticut League and going into the last game of the season their record was 6-1. For their last game they traveled to Colchester and played at the Tip Top Hall.[11] Camp Chapman won the game 51-30.[12]

On Feb. 25, 1934 Mr. Pearson announced that his men cleared brush and trees from a 10' wide boundary space around the Stone's Military Reservation. They also resurveyed the area and set posts 150' apart marking the 17-mile boundary line.[13] Mr. Chipman supervised the men who were clearing the 32-mile boundary around the forest expecting to complete the work by April 1934.

In March the tool room was completed and Mr. Chipman was the first to draw tools from it for his crew.

Also in March the camp got a new superintendent, Otto H. Schroeter who replaced Harold D. Pearson.[14]

Camp Chapman received calls to help local residents when they had a fire. One instance was in March 1934. A reporter in the camp newspaper wrote this story: "Once again the members of the 177th Co. proved themselves to be heroes and worthy of mention. A fire broke out in the vicinity of the town of Hamburg on Sunday, April 22. Our company was immediately notified and in a jiffy the whole fire crew gathered together and set off. The boys did a great job in preventing it from spreading into a serious one. The boys who did a great job were as follows: Brazis, Donaruma, Gabor, Hennes, Jager, Katona, Marcinkas, Rotty, Francouer, and Valencourt."[15]

Also in April workers finished work on the officers' and foremen's quarters. The building had a beautiful fireplace and a patio outside.[16]

The camp PX (Canteen) sold many items to the Veterans. The profits of these sales went for the following purchases in April: $50 for rec hall furniture, $8 to tune the piano, $112 for baseball uniforms, and $15 for the Thursday night dance.[17]

In June 1934 new quarters were built for the cooks and their assistants. The infirmary was improved so that it was like a real hospital. Enrollees were also busy painting the new facilities.[18]

Camp Chapman had many sports such as baseball and the team played
local and nearby CCC camps. CT CCC Museum

After a year of service at Camp Chapman, many of the Veterans left camp and were replaced by younger men. The camp newspaper reported that Veterans were an experienced group and were looked up to and respected not only in camp but in the nearby towns. The younger replacements lacked experience and had "a tendency to fool quite a bit, especially in nearby towns with the result that too many complaints have been received concerning a number of foolish pranks."[19]

In 1934 Camp Chapman enrollees did road work at the Rocky Neck SP. They built the section of the road on the eastern edge of the marsh that is now used for bicycles and pedestrians. They also worked with park staff in building the administration building and creating camp toilets and campsites.[20]

At the conclusion of summer in 1934 the baseball team had a successful season under Coach Watterson.[21]

During the fall of 1934 Education Advisor, Mr. Watterson, encouraged Veterans to take education classes so that when they left camp they would have a better chance at getting a job. They were reminded that they could only stay in the CCC for one year. Many participated in classes in the Adult Education and Training Center in New London. They were able to choose from the following classes: Literature, Geometry, Spelling, English, Chemistry, Physics, Spanish, Diesel Engines, Arithmetic, Algebra, Geometry, Typewriting, Trigonometry, Electricity, Radio Repair, Auto Mechanics, Economics, Bookkeeping, History, Civics, and Shorthand.[22]

One of the adult classes on Tuesday nights from 8-9 pm was an orchestra class. There were approximately 10 enrollees playing musical instruments.[23]

Camp Chapman started out as an all-Veteran camp in 1933 and from the camp newspaper there seems to have been a transition to Veteran and Junior members in the fall of 1934. The Camp Chapman newspaper in the November issue offered this tongue-in-cheek advice to the rookies:

"Always offer a veteran first choice of all pies, cakes, etc. that may be brought to camp from home.

"Always offer clean shirts and pressed suits to a veteran in case he has a date and is not suitably clothed.

"Offer to make a veteran's bunk and sweep up for him when it is his turn.

"Always offer your cigarettes to a veteran whether he has them or not.

"Always offer to get a veteran's share of wood for the barracks."

In November 1934 Camp Chapman was preparing to have CCC-produced plays performed for their camp. The plays were produced in New England CCC camps and done with the cooperation of the NY Division of Public Welfare Dept. The camp secured the use of the Niantic School for these plays and admission was free.[24] During 1935 Camp Chapman was led by Capt. Charles Rohrbach assisted by 1st Lt. William P. Conlan, 1st Lt. Finton J. Phelan, 1st Lt. James E. Emmons, and Chaplain Capt. William B. Johnson.[25]

The Forestry Dept. was led by Superintendent Otto H. Schroeter who was assisted by engineer Zimmerman. These Local Experienced men (LEMs) supervised the work crews: Smith, Hale, Mack, and Koistinen road construction; Tober, pine shoot moth control; Shaw, landscaping; Knox, improvement cutting; Johnson, blister rust control; Wollman, blacksmith, and Fitzsimmons, mechanic.[26]

In January 1935 the Camp Chapman Clarion reported a few entertaining activities. Enrollees presented a minstrel show at the camp in December and there was hope to have another show in the future. One enrollee, James Bianco,

The cover of the Sept. 1935 Camp Chapman Clarion newspaper.

traveled to Hartford and was praised for his musical performance on radio station WTIC. Then on Jan. 24, 1935 the FERA players from Boston presented a vaudeville show for the enrollees.[27]

In January 1935 the education advisor offered these classes in Camp Chapman: piano, guitar, saxophone, trumpet, harmonica, orchestra, glee club, discussion group, science, biology, and woodworking. These hobbies were offered: shipbuilding, cedar chests, belts, iron work, fancy ladies silk handbags, silk handkerchiefs, and carved cones.

During the winter the enrollees could sign out a variety of books from the camp library. The library also had a variety of games: ping pong, checkers, chess, dominoes, and puzzles.[28]

General Fox Connor, the Corps Area Commander, encouraged the CCC camps to plant small gardens. Those interested in planting a 4' x 10' garden were able to get seeds for lettuce, tomatoes, Swiss chard, beets, carrots, beans, radishes, and turnips for only 10 cents.[29]

In the spring 1935 the Education Advisor, Joseph F. Watterson, proposed to start a vegetable garden to give enrollees experience in raising food for the mess hall.[30]

On May 9, 1935 the Women's Club of Hartford sponsored a statewide CCC entertainment in their auditorium. Eight Camp Chapman enrollees participated in the event singing songs and playing harmonicas.[31]

Enrollees were busy working during the spring on various projects. Seven-man crews led by Asst. Leader Karosos and enrollee Miller were pulling out Ribes bushes (currant and gooseberry) in the towns of Old Lyme, Lyme, East Lyme and also near the Norwich Reservoir. Their work protected the white pine plantations from getting blister rust. In June crews covered approximately 1,450 acres. While working near East Haddam workers were lucky to see the three-mile miniature railroad at the Gillette Castle.[32]

At Devils Hopyard SP a large crew was extending a 24' wide roadway. Foremen Mack and Koistenen supervised the workers who also made deep cuts and built high retaining walls. Most of the sub-grading of the road was completed and the gravel finish needed to be done. FERA workers constructed the stone arch for the bridge and installed a temporary round timber bridge near the scenic falls.[33] When Camp Chapman was closed work at Devil's Hopyard was continued by the CWA and FERA programs.[34]

Another crew at Rocky Neck SP planted 6,500 4-year old red pine trees over eight acres in the park. Another crew

led by foreman Smith completed a mile of the new road entrance to the park. A smaller crew maintained the road, laid turf-curbing, and spread gravel on the road.[35]

During the summer of 1935 baseball was very popular in camp. An inter-barracks softball league was held. Four barracks and an administrative team battled each week. The Chapman baseball team played in the Eastern CCC League.

The July 1935 issue of the Camp Chapman Clarion reported the maintenance crew constructed two 3-room cottages on the hill west of the camp near the cistern and south of the pump house. These were for Supt. Schroeter and Capt. Rohrbach and their wives. An electric power line was extended to the pump house and then a more constant water supply was provided to the entire camp. The dynamite crew of Potts, Inc. was preparing the old Colonial Stage and Hawkins roads for sub-grading. Another crew was breaking rock on the Peck Road.[36]

Mr. Tober's crew completed the maintenance of the Nehantic truck trail. Another road crew was widening Peck Road and extending the finish grade.[37]

The CCC also built a picnic area at Hog Pond. It is now called Uncas Pond after Chief Uncas, a sachem of the Mohegan Indians.

Dutch Elm disease was concentrated mostly in the Danbury area. But a few trees in Old Lyme were found to have the disease. Camp Chapman spent 1,677 man-days eradicating the infected elm trees. They cut the trees down and then burned them.[38]

The May 10, 1935 issue of the Camp Chapman Clarion summarized the accomplishments of the Niantic camp since 1933.

"From peeling potatoes in the kitchen to reading weather instruments on the hill, the men of this camp are doing forest work. The carpenters at Rocky Neck, the stone wall crews at Devil's Hop Yard, the road crews at Stone's Ranch are all working on forestry projects.

"Boundary lines and old wood roads have been surveyed and fire lined to permit easy access and to act as fire breaks in case of a forest fire. Often the men on those crews have walked one or two miles from the truck to get to their woods job. Other crews, the wood choppers have clear-cut areas in preparation for planting, for artillery ranges, and military maneuvers (at Stone's Ranch Military Reservation). These crews have thinned many acres along the new truck trail and deep into the woods, cutting over

1,000 cords of firewood, more than 3,000 fence posts, 15,000' of saw logs, and about 4,000 chestnut tobacco poles.

"Planting crews have set out about 35,000 young pine, spruce, and cedar trees as well as 1,000 game food shrubs. Water holes for firefighting pumps have been built at strategic points in the Nehantic Forest to aid in fire control. A picnic area has been arranged for public use on the State Forest. A crew is now cutting hardwood fence posts that will be later creosoted and placed along the state highways. A research crew has been making a detailed study of tree diseases through the Nehantic Forest which will be correlated with similar studies in other camps. These men must know or learn not only the tree species but also the disease species, soils, forest types, and some surveying. The cutting crews learned how to care for and use axes, bush hooks, saws, and scythes. They also learned how to fell trees, grade cord wood, posts, and logs, and how to identify species of trees.

"Chronological growth studies at Peck Farm (part of Stone's Ranch) and Nehantic Forest are being made by a foreman to collect data on the time of flowering, leafing, twig growth, fruiting, bark slipping, and foliage coloring of about 20 nature trees, shrubs, and barbed plants. The Agricultural Experimental Station has recently installed two thermometers in camp showing the minimum and maximum temperatures. This information is noted daily.[39]

Education classes continued in the summer of '35. Education Advisor Watterson was assisted by FERA teachers. They offered classes in commercial law, shorthand, history of inventions, nature study, psychology, advertising, and letter writing.[40]

The town of East Lyme was preparing for their Tercentenary Pageant and Mrs. Stephen Bond and Mrs. H. E. Hudson, directors of the pageant, asked Camp Chapman for volunteers to dress up as Nehantic and Pequot Indians, Lyme Haymakers, wrestlers, and musicians. The pageant was to be held on Aug. 16, 1935 on land adjoining Bridge Brook. Handicraft instructor Goddard guided the boys in making bows & arrows, hatchets, and pikes. Approximately 50 boys volunteered to be in the performance and FERA instructors, Miss Jackson and Mr. Leverne, helped in directing the rehearsals.[41]

On Thurs., Aug. 15, 1935 a wood chopping and sawing contest was held at Camp Chapman. The winners represented the camp in a district contest at the 4-H Fair in North Stonington. Also on August 15th the monthly dance was held at Camp Chapman. Camp trucks went out to neighboring towns to pick up guests and young ladies. One truck picked up guests at the Mohican Hotel at 8 pm and members of the camp administration escorted them to camp. A local New London orchestra provided music.[42]

In September 1935 a farewell dance was held for enrollees leaving Camp Chapman. The dance was held in the rec hall that was attached to the Ranch House.[43]

There were three important people who visited camp in September. Major Gen. Fox Conner came and made a thorough inspection of the camp. Dr. Thomas Hoffman, Core Area dentist, gave each enrollee an oral examination and treatment to those in need. The last guest was Dr.

Rocky Neck SP Beach in East Lyme, Conn. DEEP

Uncas Pond in the Nehantic SF is a popular swimming area. It was originally called Hog Pond and was later named after Chief Uncas. The CCC built a picnic area there and it is still used today. www.ct.gov

William S. Board, Asst. to the Pres. of Rollins College in Florida. He emphasized the importance of education in getting a job and for the enrollees to take advantage of the educational opportunities that were available at camp.[44]

In September, forester Shaw and his crew completed their waterhole work in the Nehantic SF. This afforded better protection of the forest by providing a ready source of water when needed.[45]

Trail work continued on the Stone's Ranch Military Reservation. Enrollees were rebuilding the old Harkins Rd. parts of which were the old British Military Rd.[46]

In September the District Forestry Wood Chopping and Sawing Contest was held at Camp Fernow. The Chapman team of Cacavalo & Kolodnicki came in 2nd place in log sawing and in the chopping contest Batick also came in 2nd.[47]

On Oct. 30, 1935 Camp Chapman closed. Since the government lacked funds to maintain the camp, the buildings were demolished.[48]

LEGACY

One of the most visited state parks on Connecticut's shore is Rocky Neck. Camp Chapman helped build some of the campsites, planted trees, built the entrance to the park, buildings and other park improvements that are still used and enjoyed by thousands of people each year.

Camp Chapman had a significant effect on the approximately 3,400-acre Nehantic SF. Enrollees built truck trails and waterholes and planted thousands of trees for future generations to enjoy. They also improved and developed places for fishing, swimming, picnicking, hiking, and hunting.

Camp Chapmen enrollees lived and worked on the 2,200-acre Stone's Ranch just two years after the State purchased it. The Army has benefited from the early work of the CCC who cleared the land, built roads, and marked its boundaries. When Camp Chapman closed in 1935 Stone's Ranch Military Reservation was used by the Army for infantry and tank training preparing our soldiers for action in WWII. It is still used today for infantry and tank training.

Directions:

Traveling east on I-95 take Exit 75. At the end of the ramp turn left, and go north on CT 161. Travel .45 mi. to the intersection of CT 161 and US 1 (the Boston Post Rd.) Then go west for approximately 3 mi. You will pass Scott Rd. and turn right on Stone Ranch Rd. Go to the end of the road and you will see a closed gate on the right. This was the entrance to Camp Chapman. Buildings were on both sides of the road but all are gone today. The Army uses Stone's Ranch for military practice. The area is closed to the public.

Map – Camp Chapman in Niantic

MEMORIES

These enrollees are happy that it's the end of a work day at 3:00 pm. They are sitting on the truck ready to go back to camp for supper. CT CCC Museum

Order of the Day
by Constantine Glowacki

6:15 am
As the bugler blows, hop out of bed
and jump into your clothes

6:30 am
Make your bunk and
clean around the trunk.

7:00 am
As you answer the call for chow,
get your breakfast and milk from the cow.

7:45 am
Fall in, one and all
in response to roll call.

8.00 am
As you hop upon your truck
and go to earn your daily buck.

12 noon
When you all gather in a bunch,
then you eat your noon day lunch.

1:00 pm
As the axes begin swinging,

the sledges assume a ringing.

3:30 pm
When the day's work is done,
you're tired but full of fun.

4:45 pm
Before you all go to eat,
you shall fall in for retreat.

5:00 pm
As you hear the call for supper,
go get your meat, bread, and butter.

10:00 pm
You hit the old hay
at the end of a perfect day.

- Camp Chapman News, Mar. 29, 1934

The mess kitchen tent at the end of the day. DEEP State Parks Archives

I contacted some locals of Niantic and East Lyme. Norman Peck Sr. of the East Lyme Historical Society said: "My cousin Murray Hill was in the CCC. He had two brothers, Francis and Bruce in Florida)

✽ ✼

On June 4, 2008 I visited Robert "Woody" Scott at his farm house on Scott Rd. in East Lyme.

"I was born in 1916. My family owned this farm since 1902. We raised strawberries and apples.

"So I was between 12-14 years old when the CCC camp at Stone's Ranch was operating. The camp was at the end of Stone's Ranch Road. The barracks were on both sides of the road. Before you went up the hill there was a "The ranch was originally owned by Morton Plant. He gave some of the land to Yale students.

"There was a big colonial house right by the turn-around. They held some functions there. I think they brought girls in for dances.

"The enrollees went right by my house on their way to work in the Nehantic State Forest. They built a lot of roads. One of them was Cemetery Rd. and a road to Norwich Pond.

"The guys used to go out with the local girls. They were a pretty good bunch of guys.

"The CCC was a good thing. It got the guys off the streets. They built roads in the Nehantic Forest, Devils Hopyard SP, and Rocky Neck SP."

Robert Woodrow "Woody" Scott, of East Lyme, died on Dec. 26, 2009.

Robert "Woody" Scott remembered the nearby Niantic CCC camp when he was 12-14 years old.
www.legacy.com

After interviewing Woody Scott I visited Margery Rix Ferencz at her home at the corner of Old Post Road (Rte. 1) and Stone Ranch Road.

"I was born in this yellow house in 1926. My name is Mildred Huntley Rix. My grandfather Huntley owned this land.

"My mother had an outside stand on Route 1 where we sold cigarettes, soda, and candy. The CCC boys came there and bought from us.

"My kid sister Helen loved those big hats they wore. One day a CCC boy put his hat on her head and she got head lice.

"My mother also boarded men who worked at the CCC camp. She gave them a real good home-cooked meal.

"When men came to our house my mother served

them dinner. I used to wait on their table. Sometimes there were four or five guys. She even fed the hobos when they came looking for food.

"Ken Palmer worked at the CCC camp and he became good friends of my parents. Later he worked at Bay Reuthers Boat Yard in East Lyme.

"A man named Brinkman was also in the camp and he stayed in this area when the camp closed.

"Bill Parks was another man who stayed here. He later married a local girl and had children.

"George Potts, a policeman in New London, might be related to another of the CCC boys who settled here and married a local girl.

"The CCC camp was located at the end of Stone's Ranch Road and the camp was on the right. As you entered the camp on the right was the ranch house and next to it was where they had dances. Across from the ranch house were the barracks buildings. The caretaker of the CCC camp lived in the ranch house. My father took me and the whole family to the dances in his Ford. The dances were in their mess hall. That's where I learned how to square dance. I was nine years old.

"When the camp closed we used to walk down Stone's Ranch Rd. and walk through the old camp. The buildings were abandoned and dilapidated. We'd walk straight through the camp to get to Scott Road."

❦ ❧

In 2008 I called Woody Scott's cousin, Allen Scott, a retired minister from East Lyme.

"I was born in 1923 so I was 10 years old when the CCC camp began. I remember the trucks going by our farm on their way to work. They built the roads through the forest. I also remember the truck that brought lunches to the workers at noon.

"Once we had a grass fire on our farm. My father and I were trying to put it out. Then a few trucks of CCC boys came. They were fast and put it out in about ten minutes.

"We had farm fields next to the CCC camp. I could smell the food cooking at the camp.

"I also remember them walking and singing as they passed by our fruit and vegetable stand.

"One boy told me he was getting out because he thought they were training the guys for war. But most of the boys liked living there.

"For years the camp buildings were there but then they disappeared."

❦ ❧

At the 50th Connecticut CCC Reunion held at the Rocky Neck State Park, Lloyd Chappel, a retired maintenance supervisor, told a Chronicle reporter how he worked in the CCC at the very beach where the reunion was held. In the Sept. 8, 1986 issue Chappel said:

"They had a ramp from the beach running up this hill (on which the stone pavilion is located) which they used to haul stuff. They worked on that concrete building there. They used horses for the hauling."

A goldbricker sleeping as his crew gets ready to go back to camp for supper. Howard White

"Order of the Goldbrick"
by Constantine Blowacki

If you wish to become a member of the Goldbricks,
Do one of these tricks:
Choose to stay all day
Then you'll lose part of your pay.
Refuse to earn your daily fee.
Then they won't refuse KP
Have a little dirt under your bunk
Then you'll spend the weekend cleaning your junk.
Fail to arise with the morning sun
Then you will receive a detail just for fun.
Pretend you are very sick

While you really goldbrick.
Make a little mistake to fail
To report for a smaller camp detail.
If your name appears on the list twice
Then you're skating on thin ice.
So beware!
If you really care.
- Camp Chapman News, Mar. 21, 1934

❦ ❧

"Fire Burns Down Barn"

"Who said nothing ever happens around here? On Monday noon everything was running as usual in the recreation room. The radio was going full blast. Whelan and Dunn were at the ping pong table and men were scattered here and there reading. All of a sudden we got an earful of Fitz's whistle. No one could understand the reason why he was calling the company out. It was only 12:45. Fitz, however, enlightened them soon enough. A barn was in the process of being devoured by flames at Peck's farm (part of Stone's Ranch).

"In a second the panic was on. A bunch of men jumped on the trucks. Some ran for the fire extinguisher and others got the implements to be used. In a jiffy we were on our way to the big fire.

"When we got there we found the remains of the old barn burned to the ground. There was nothing we could do.
- Camp Chapman News, Mar. 29, 1934

❦ ❧

"The Life of Capt. Charles H. Rohrbach"

"Capt. Charles H. Rohrbach was born in Bridgeport, Conn. He attended Central High School in Bridgeport and upon his graduation could proudly look back at his athletic contribution to his Alma Mater. Not being satisfied with managing and playing successful football in the position of end, he worked himself to the highest honor that a football player can dream of, that being appointed captain of his team. He then completed his studies at Yale.

"When war broke out he was an auditor with the

Remington Arms Co. Responding promptly to his country's call, he enlisted in the Air Services as a private first class and after three months training at M. I. T., Cornell University, and Ellington Field Texas, was commissioned 2nd Lt. with the pilot's rating of the Reserve Military Aviator.

"In 1918 he rose to prominence as an aviator flying at Roosevelt Field, NY; Mitchell Field, Long Island; and at some of the other most important fields in the US. He was also a pursuit pilot of the First Provincial Wing and functioned as a test pilot for a while but was not sent overseas.

"After the War he lived in Washington, DC for six years working as an income tax auditor for the government. Since that time he was employed in various accounting capacities with the Remington Arms Co. in several cities where they had offices and plants.

"In the Air Reserve Corps, he has successfully held commissions as 2nd Lt., 1st Lt., and Captain after doing active duty in such known air fields as Langley Field, Virginia; Bolling Field, DC; Phillip's Field, Aberdeen Proving ground, Maryland; Mitchell Field, Long Island; Cape Cod Airport and Boston Airport, Massachusetts.

"In CCC service he was stationed at Squantz Pond before being assigned to the command of this station in Niantic. His untiring efforts to make this camp one of the best in the district have won him the respect and support which is due him from his superiors as well as the esteem and love of his men."

- Camp Chapman News, Apr. 5, 1934

(Note: Captain Charles H. Rohrbach also worked at Squantz Pond in 1933 and at Camp Stuart in East Hampton in 1935. He had a home in Haddam Neck where he lived till he died in the 1960s.)

✄ ✄

Fire season usually began in the spring when the snow was gone and there were dry leaves and grass. In April 1934 this story appeared in the April 5, 1934 issue of the Camp Chapman News.

"About 10:45 on Friday morning the well-known tweet, tweet of Fitz's whistle was heard. Everybody rushed to the windows to learn the reason for this unexpected call.

"Upon falling out in the company street the fire crews were called out for action. Eight men responded to the call and rushed to the blacksmith shop for the necessary equipment and were then under way.

"After an unsuccessful attempt to get across the swamp, they returned in record time to get a truck.

"Upon arriving at the scene it was discovered to be a small blaze devouring some dried leaves and a small man was calmly watching them burn on his land. Boy, if you never saw any long faces before, you should have been there. But they all took the joke like a CCC does and it was agreed by all that it was good practice for the fire crews."

- Camp Chapman News, Apr. 5, 1934

✄ ✄

"Sincere Wishes"

When approximately half of the Veterans were leaving Chapman in June 1934 after working for a year at Stone's Ranch, Capt. Rohrbach complimented them: "You have learned how to live among men, play with them, eat with them, and fight with them, and you are going out with much more confidence in yourself than you have ever known before. The thirty dollars a month you have drawn in pay is not a fitting measure of what you have gained by being a CCC. You will go out now and take a job you would not have the guts to even try for a year ago and you will get that job and you will hold it.

"And so, tempering that feeling of personal loss which I shall have when you leave camp, you Old Timers, will be the assurance that the country, and you and I have gained a great deal by our association here at Star Ranch Camp. I still am going to miss you (and it is probably too much to expect) I hope you miss me, too.

"So long fellows! Good Luck! And as the doctor would say, 'Don't Forget to Wear Your Rubbers!'"

- Camp Chapman News, June 1934

✄ ✄

"A Farewell Message to you Veterans" by a Rookie

"The time is already here when it will be our sad duty to bid a 'Bon Voyage' to all the good old timers, a task which is not very easy.

"We feel like the youngster saying a melancholy goodbye to his older brother as he goes away. For now we will be on our own, fighting our own battles and settling our own disputes without the advice and guiding hand of a man who knows what to do and understands what it is all about.

"No more can we mingle our feet among the old timers on the proverbial brass rail, telling each other our troubles and pleasures. No more will prevail the intimate acquaintance with the well-known dog. No more will we hear and see the antics of our pals Dagle and Towgin. What will become of Haggerty when he becomes separated from Dunn?

"The uppermost thoughts of you Veterans seems to be, 'Oh boy won't it be great to stay in bed till 9 or 10 in the morning?' But the 9 and 10 at night is a time to think about, no more PX to run to, no pool table where the games are free, no pals to go with to town. ALL GONE. The days of the CCC are over.

"In my closing charge let me beg of you to go out into this world of ours with your chins up and show people that the boys of the CCC are men, and are to be considered as such. You have done your job well and now you are ready to meet the storms of life."

- Camp Chapman News, June 1934

❧ ⚘

"A Farewell to Axes"
by (Superintendent) Major O. H. Schroeter

"Just a few days to answer the 'morning call.' Empty bunks and mess benches will give mute testimony of those that left. The first hundred thousand of the Forest Army.

"Drafted from Connecticut cities and towns to you young men, has been delegated the task to clear up, rip up, burn up, and generally clean up hundreds of acres of wood and swamp land. Pick and shovel is hard work but it takes patience and energy to clean a path through underbrush and tangled briar patches. You have met this challenge with more energy and less complaints than people realize.

"You built roads, bunk and tool houses, did fire prevention work, boundary line clearing, and landscaping, fought forest fires and insect pests. You kept house, did the cooking, and kept yourselves clean and healthy, a credit to

the best pioneering traditions of our nation.

"To you who leave, best wishes, carry on and remember the three C's: COURAGE, CLEANLINESS, COURTESY!"

- Camp Chapman News, June 1934

Boys having fun at Camp Chapman. CT CCC Museum

These funny stories appeared in the Camp Chapman News 'The Raspberry Section' of Apr. 5, 1934:

"Big news! Bad accident! Zimba's precious bugle fell in the mess kit water. Don't feel so bad about it Charley. Maybe the notes will be cleaner."

"Get a load of this. The boys in Barracks No. 3 couldn't seem to fall asleep Sunday night. No one seemed to know the reason why. But the secret was solved the next morning. Palooka's very musical snore was missing to lull them into the arms of Morpheus."

❧ ⚘

"Barracks No. 3 has a new mascot for good luck. Lefty Uliase has recently captured a squirrel which resides in a redesigned dynamite box."

- Camp Chapman News, Mar. 29, 1934

❧ ⚘

"Thanks"
by John Downes

I give my thanks to Uncle Sam,

Because of him, I'm where I am.
Many thanks I give to the CCC.
It's been so good to my family.
I work again – so very glad.
To roam the streets is very bad.
It's life again to many boys.
It once was sorrow; now it's joy.
It gives them courage and hope again.
They have a chance like other men.
For others' sake, I'd like to see,
It last until eternity.
- Camp Chapman News, Sept. 1934

Ford Hilton at the entrance to Stone's Ranch Military Reservation. Over 80 years ago was the entrance to the Camp Chapman.

On Dec. 31, 2013 I met Ford Hilton, whose father was the caretaker during and after the time of the CCC camp, at the Rustic Inn in East Lyme and he took me to the end of Stone Ranch Rd. We stopped at the gate on the right that led to the Stone's Ranch Military reservation.

"I recall walking through the two barracks buildings on the left side of the road by the entrance to the camp with my dad. Another building behind that was probably the infirmary. It was circa 1939 or 1940. I also remember a large fireplace and chimney that were still standing. On the right side of the road near the camp entrance was the ranch house that had a large fireplace. Next on the right were the wash/shower room and latrine buildings. Farther up the road on the right was a three-bay building blacksmith/machine shop. The last building was an ice house. At the top of the

hill was a flat area that was the old air field. Stone had a T-shaped hangar for his plane with a gas pump in front. Next to the hangar was a shed.

"Up the hill behind the barracks on the left was the pump house, water cistern, and two cottages that were used by the Army captain and the other by the Superintendent."

Ford remembers seeing a stone chimney one of the few remaining structures of Camp Chapman in approximately 1940. Ford Hilton

Conrad J. Francoeur

Conrad J. Francoeur worked as a truck driver at Camp Chapman in Niantic. Elaine Edwards

When I spoke at the Bristol Historical Society in June 2010, I met Elaine Edwards of Cheshire, Conn. She told me her father, Conrad J. Francoeur, was in the CCC. A week later she sent me the following information about her father, who was in the Niantic camp.

"My father, Conrad J. Francoeur, was born on Feb. 6, 1913 in Valleyfield, Canada. When he was six years old his family moved to Bristol, Conn. His parents were Louis Francoeur and Clara Picard Francoeur. They had 14 children but only seven survived: Oscar, Ida, Alice, Valencia, Conrad, Paul, and Rita. My father only went to 8th grade and then went out to work and help his family.

"I'm not sure how he learned about the CCC but when he was 20 years old he joined on May 25, 1933. His discharge papers state that before he entered he was a truck driver. He joined at the beginning of the CCC program. Dad was sent to Fort Wright on Fishers Island where he and the other recruits were in a conditioning program.

"On June 2, he left Fort Wright and was taken by the Army to Camp Chapman at Stone's Ranch in Niantic. His letter of recommendation says he was the driver of the superintendent's car in addition to being a truck driver as listed on his discharge certificate

"After working at camp for a year he was discharged on June 30, 1934. He got a job at New Departure Co., in Bristol where he worked till 1979.

"He married Catherine Gaughan and they had four daughters: Elaine F. Edwards of Cheshire, Jacqueline F. Guyette of Waterbury (deceased), Sandra F. Mazurek, formerly Adams of Michigan, and Sharon M. Francoeur of New Jersey. My father passed away on June 24, 1993."

Patrick J. Ricci

After the CCC Ricci worked at Pratt & Whitney.
Carol Lambert

During my monthly Explore East Hampton Walks, Carol Lambert told me her father Patrick Ricci worked at

Patrick Ricci (left) with friend by barracks at Camp Chapman in Niantic. Carol Lambert

Besides doing carpentry work Ricci also worked cutting trees in the Nehantic SF. Carol Lamber

the Niantic CCC camp. She later sent me a copy of his discharge papers and information on his life.

"My father was born on Sept. 1, 1914 in Hartford. His parents Angelo and Esperanza (Viola) Ricci were Italian immigrants. My dad had two brothers John and Anthony and one sister Jean. When he got older he worked as a carpenter.

"When he was 19, Dad joined the CCC on Oct. 4th, 1933. He was sent to Fort Wright on Fishers Island at a 'reconditioning camp.' On Oct. 10 he was sent to Niantic Camp Chapman where he worked as a carpenter and laborer in the Nehantic SF.

"After working for one year at Niantic he left on Sept. 30, 1934. His records state his performance was 'excellent.'

"When he left camp, Dad received this letter:

My dear Mr. Ricci,

It gives the undersigned great pleasure to award to you herewith, in behalf of the state Forestry Dept. a Certificate of Merit" for exceptionally good work performed while enrolled in the 177th Co. Connecticut Civilian Conservation Corps.

Signed,
Capt. Charles H. Rohrbach and Camp Superintendent, Harold D. Pearson

"In 1939 he married Julia Kosar. They had two children: James and me. Dad worked at Pratt & Whitney Aircraft. He passed away on April 21, 2009."

CHAPTER 16
PORTLAND

Camp Buck group photo in Portland, Conn. DEEP State Parks Archives

HISTORY

Camp Buck, S-61, was established on June 4, 1935 in the Meshomasic State Forest (MSF) in Portland, Conn. when a cadre of 23 men led by Lt. George C. Freeman III left their Cobalt camp on Gadpouch Rd. at 8:30 am and drove approximately 2 miles to the new camp site on Great Hill Road. The Army described it as a hillside swamp.[1]

In the camp newspaper, The Buck Eye, enrollee Michael Kosko described what happened to him and his cohorts as they established Camp Buck:

"We arrived at the new site at 9 am with two new Army trucks loaded with supplies from New London. Upon arrival the first thing to do was to find a spot to put up tents. First up was the hospital tent. Next was the office and the infirmary. After the supply tent was erected, the sleeping quarters for the boys were pitched, and a pup tent for the commanding officer. Finally, the cook tent was ready for the preparation of chow.

"We ate on picnic benches. Then we took a truck to a nearby brook and filled G. I. cans with water. This water was treated with chlorine so that it could be safely used for cooking and drinking.

"During the first week in June, it rained day in and day out. The place looked like a mud hole. The boys filled in the ruts so the trucks could get to the main road two hundred feet from the camp site.

"Day by day the boys worked clearing away tree stumps that were inside the tents when they were pitched.

"On June 7, 1935, we received the first load of lumber which was a sign that the new camp would be constructed. Lumber continued to be hauled in until the camp resembled a lumber yard.

"On the 12th of June, construction officers came and surveyed the site, marking off the position on which each building was to be erected.

"On June 15, two carpenters and a foreman started to put up caffle (scaffold) boards for the buildings.

"The following week, sixty-four carpenters and laborers started construction.

On June 24, Lt. Freeman received two new officers to take charge of the camp. Capt. Hersum was to be commanding officer and Lt. Williams, the mess officer.

"On July first Lt. Freeman was transferred to another

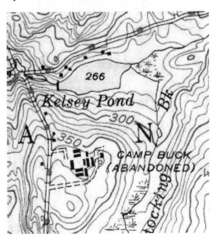

This 1945 Middle Haddam Quadrangle map section shows the Camp Buck buildings that were constructed in a swampy area near Kelsey Pond. Great Hill Road is to the left of the camp.[3]

company. The boys contributed a gift which was presented to him as a token of respect for their first commanding officer.

"On July 16 we received two more officers who were to replace Capt. Hersum and Lt. Williams. They were Lt. Ponnall as commanding officer and Lt. Iantosca as mess officer.

"July 16 we received 28 new men who were on detached service at the 181st Co. Cobalt camp with Captain Park K. Rockwell as their commanding officer of Co. 1197 that would reside at Camp Buck. The next day 56 more came. On the 18th twenty-eight more arrived and on the 19th 55 more arrived making a total of 167.

"On July 20 the original cadre moved into one of the barracks."[2]

At the end of three months most of the swampy area had been drained and the permanent camp buildings completed. The full contingent of Company 1197 arrived at Camp Buck on Sept. 13, 1935. Captain Park K. Rockwell, US Marine Corps. Reserve, and Superintendent Lawrence C. Blair worked together making the area livable and the site lost its "swampy appearance."[4] The next year the CCC boys planted shrubs, constructed walkways, and built a good road and entrance.

MSF was the first state forest in Connecticut and the second state forest in the US. The word meshomasic is a Native American word meaning place of many snakes. It has a native population of Timber Rattlesnakes. It began in 1903 with 70 acres and has expanded today to over 9,000 acres. The state established it "to provide private landowners

with good examples of good forest management practices."[5]

The camp was named after Henry R. Buck who graduated from Yale in 1902 with a degree in civil engineering. He established Henry Robinson Buck Inc., which was involved in surveying, engineering, and consulting. Buck worked for the state resurveying its boundries. Buck was very interested in Conn. forests and parks and became the Vice President of the Connecticut Forest and Park Association, VP of the Appalachian Mountain Club, and President of the Conn. Park Commission. He also worked with many CCC projects. State Forester, Austin Hawes, appointed Buck to design and build roads and forest trails in many Conn. State forests. On Aug. 11, 1934 Buck was travelling between his projects when his life came to a tragic end. He died in a head-on-collision travelling on Rt. 44 on Avon Mt. The following year the state honored Buck by naming one of the trails he designed in the American Legion Forest, Henry Buck Trail. They also named the Portland CCC camp after him.[6]

Most of the camp's projects were in the MSF in Portland. Some of their work included: improving forest stand, controlling gypsy moths, and building roads.[7]

The construction of a creosote plant near the Portland CCC camp was completed in 1934 by the nearby Cobalt camp in 1934. When the Portland CCC camp was established in 1935, Camp Buck enrollees operated the creosote plant. In the past, chestnut posts were used for fences and guard rails but when the trees died off the Agriculture Experiment Station found that creosoting other types of tree posts in an open tank lasted as long as the chestnut posts.[8] William C. Shepard was in charge of the creosote plant and sawmill. The creosote plant was then leased to the Webster & Webster Company.[9]

Projects at Camp Buck, 1935

- Cut and thinned stands of pine and larch
- Constructed forest roads, trails, and bridges
- Constructed picnic areas
- Slanted the sides of water holes
- Did road work in Kensington (section of Berlin, CT)
- Surveyed diseases of trees
- Preserved timber at the creosote plant
- Layed out and graded
- Landscaped[10]

The creosote plant pictured in 1938 was used by the Camp Buck enrollees to preserve wood used for guard rails and fence posts. The saw mill is on the right. DEEP State Parks Archives

Camp Buck Administration, Nov. 1939

- Commanding Officer - Captain P. K. Rockwell
- Adjutant - 2nd Lt. Angelo Iantosca
- Camp Physician - Dr. A. B. Goodman
- Education Advisor - Allan Lindstrom

Instructors

- John Pizzi, Hartford
- Michael Buczek, Meriden
- William Fink, New Britain
- Lafayette J. Robertson, Hartford

Forestry Dept.

- Superintendent - Lawrence C. Blair, Glastonbury
- Asst. Superintendent - Herbert S. Johnson, Higganum
- Senior Foreman - Paul C. Zimmerman, Lyme
- Junior Foremen -
  Henry Mallet, Woodbury
  Alfred Hunyadi, Bridgeport
  G. F. Chattfield, New Haven
  Clifford Robinson, Portland
  Frank Synott, Portland
  Daniel B. Wilson, Portland
- Junior Foresters -
  William P. McDonnough, New Haven
  Bradford Bidwell, New Haven
- Ranger - Joseph Synott
- Auto Mechanic - Earl E. Kenyon, New London
- Blacksmith - Charles Clark [11]

On Oct. 22, 1935 a 12-man fire crew supervised by Mr. Robinson traveled to West Peak in Meriden to fight a difficult fire. They were also joined by a crew from Camp Filley. The K. P. crew brought the men coffee and

Portland camp administrator group photo with commanding officer Captain Park K. Rockwell (center) surrounded by unidentified Army officers, superintendent, and foresters. Gary Potter

The Buck-Eye was the camp monthly newspaper. It had a variety of news including sports, humor, health advice, work projects, events, dances, education class info, and good old gossip.

sandwiches. Enrollees worked with three water pumps to extinguish the burning leaves and tree stumps. They worked till 8:20 pm and returned to camp at about midnight.[12]

The following evening a dramatics group from Camp Stuart presented plays and music for Camp Buck in the new Rec. Hall. The following week Amateur Night was held. The Dramatics and Entertainment Club organized the program and were assisted by Mr. Lyman from the Middletown High School. Officials of the local Hemlock Grange were guests of the camp.[13]

Camp Buck offered a variety of classes for enrollees. There were four instructors: John Pizzi, Michael Buczek, William Fink, and Lafayette Ebbertson. Some of the classes offered were: spelling, arithmetic, geography, history, grammar, radio, electricity, algebra, science, journalism, public speaking, dramatics, English literature, bookkeeping, typing, business English, and office practice. There were also hobby classes in woodworking, whittling, paper-shellac work, lettering, leather work, and metal craft.[14]

Enrollees were also able to attend classes at Wesleyan College in Middletown in the fall of 1935. Classes in English, Psychology, and Science were held on Tuesday and Thursday evenings from 7-8:15. This was the second tome the college offered free classes to Camp Buck.[15].

The first issue of Camp Buck's newspaper, The Buck Eye, came out in Nov. 1935 and listed the administration and Capt. P. K. Rockwell was the camp commander, and Lawrence C. Blair was the camp superintendent. There

1197th Company at Portland, Conn

A collage of the many activities and buildings at Camp Buck that includes the infirmary, mess hall, education and craft classes, boxing, baseball, and pool.[22]

were a total 206 enrollees that included 36 men who came from Camp Chapman in Niantic when it disbanded. Paul Zimmerman, the former Niantic assistant superintendent, also came and was in charge of camp Buck's layout, grading, and landscaping.[16]

Beginning in the Fall of 1935 enrollees had a variety of sports to keep them busy during the winter: basketball, wrestling, and boxing at the Y in Middletown.[17]

The camp newspaper reported in its December 1935 issue that the radio class led by instructor Michael Duczek visited radio stations WTIC and WDRC in Hartford. They were given a guided tour of the control rooms and studios. They also saw the instruments that were used for sound effects.

The camp fire brigade responded to two fires during

the early winter of 1936. The first fire was at the nearby home of Ranger Synnott's home. The young men quickly extinguished the fire and saved his home. The other fire was in the officers' mess hall. The fire crew used fire extinguishers to save the building.[18]

During the spring of 1936, a terrible flood devastated the Connecticut River Valley. Camp Buck's enrollees were one of the first groups to do rescue work. They did extensive cleanup work in Hartford and surrounding communities.[19] Camp Buck responded to pleas of help from people and businesses in Portland and Glastonbury. Here is one of the many compliments published in the March 1936 issue of The Buck Eye.

Joseph Katz a merchant in Glastonbury stated: "As one of the flood sufferers and as a merchant who was almost helpless due to the immense amount of scattered merchandise and lack of facilities for moving same, the help given by these boys was invaluable. Just as an illustration: in my house as flood raged and my cellar became full of water, I called in six of the (CCC) boys. In less than a half an hour they had moved more than four rooms of furniture up a flight of winding stairs without scratching or injuring a piece of furniture.

"In my stores they came to my aid three times moving stock and fixtures to higher levels and saving me thousands of dollars.

"Their conduct was excellent. They were most willing. They have done anything asked of them in a prompt manner and with a smile. Time after time they went into the cold swirling water over their boots and worked in muck and slush without a murmur. They have been on scout duty, patrol and rescue work. They are now engaged in rehabilitation."

Camp Buck continued helping other surrounding towns and joined forces with enrollees from Camp Lonergan of Voluntown. They pumped water from cellars, did repair work, and disinfected homes.

In recognition for their fine work during the flood, the manager of the Allyn Theater in Hartford gave free admission to 50 enrollees every Monday evening from Apr. to May 1936.[20]

During the summer and fall of 1936 the camp received many awards. It won the fifth district honor flag for five out of six months in the state and in the fall it was chosen to represent Conn. for the competition for outstanding company in the First Corp Area (all of New England).[21]

The Army provided recreational activities for the young men. One activity was the New England CCC forestry competition. In 1936 Peter Szlosek of New Britain won the Conn. CCC wood chopping contest. Then in September at the Eastern States Exposition in Springfield, MA Szlosek beat all his competitors.[23] In 1937 he then traveled to the sportsman show in Philadelphia.[24]

Road projects were very important for Camp Buck. The 1935 Connecticut State Park and Forest Commission Report (CSPFCR) stated that Camp Buck constructed Mulford Rd. in the MSF. Then in the 1936 CSPFCR reported that the CCC finished building Reeve Rd. These roads were used by visitors for recreation and by the state to fight fires and remove forest products. In the 1940 CSPFCR reported that work was done on the Mulford and Mott Hill roads.

As the young men worked in the MSF they were often surprised to find a timber rattlesnake resting under a log, sunning on a rock, or crossing a road. During the 1930s the attitude of the public was to destroy these poisonous snakes. Some town, county, and state governments offered bounties for killing them. Retired forest ranger for the MSF, Joseph Synott, bragged to the CCC boys that he was the rattlesnake champion. He claimed that at one time he had two barrels filled with rattle snakes in his cellar.[25]

The Oct. 1936 camp newspaper reported these work accomplishments: Completion of the Del Reeves Rd. under the leadership of John Novetany and a successful bug season by the Gypsy Moth Crew. One of the last year's projects was scouting for the gypsy moths in the Town of Berlin.

During the fall of 1936 there were two new classes. The taxidermy class, led by Raymond Merin the gypsy

The Oct. 1936 camp newspaper reported the completion of the Del Reeves Rd. under the leadership of John Novetany. DEEP State Parks Archives

The Camp Buck rec hall where boys could relax, read, play pool or cards. At the rear was the canteen where boys could buy soda, candy, cigarettes, etc. DEEP State Parks Archives

moth foreman, taught the boys how to mount birds and other animals. The Dramatic Club was led by Capt. R. K. Rockwell. The boys practiced doing short plays in the recreation hall where a stage was made and scenery and lights were used.[26]

The Education Director offered these winter classes: Arithmetic, English, Spelling, Electricity, Cooking, Carpentry, Metal Work, Road Construction, Forestry, Typewriting, First Aid, Sign Making, Leather Craft, Dramatics, Auto mechanics, Photography, Taxidermy, Beadwork, Leadership, and Boxing.[27]

The camp library received 300 books to its collection from these libraries: The Russell Library in Middletown, The Glastonbury Library, South Glastonbury Library, and the Westerly, Public Library in RI.[28]

Plans were made during the 1936-37 winter to clear another block of land in the MSF in the spring. Crews would clean the area of undesirable trees and then burn the brush. Then seedlings would be planted.[29]

On Jan. 14th, 1937 a bus from the district CCC Depot in New London arrived at camp with 26 new recruits from various towns in Conn. The first two weeks they were given a two-week training and conditioning course before they went to work in the field. Training included classes to acquaint them with camp procedures and they also did light work in camp.[30]

There were two guest speakers in January. On the 18th retired Portland minister, Rev. Albert Hughes, gave a talk on "Birthstones." He was very fond of hiking the local mountains and the feldspar quarries where he gathered many rare stones and minerals. This spurred the boys interest in searching for stones. Hughes' talk centered on the 12 birthstones for each month and their significance. Three days later, Dr. Henry Talbot from the State Board of Health gave an illustrated talk on "Personal Health and Hygiene."[31]

During the winter the boys were busy doing boxing and basketball. Nine boys were preparing for the Golden Gloves matches that would be held in January in New York. At first the basketball team didn't have a gym to practice in. Then Mr. Ahern, the principal of the Middletown High School, came to the rescue and offered his gym on Monday nights to the Camp Buck, Camp Stuart, and the Portland town teams. The team played in the YMCA League.[32]

The camp basketball team was busy defeating local CCC camps. On Jan. 7 Camp Buck defeated Camp Stuart

40-39 at St. Mary's Gym in Middletown. On Jan. 21 the team traveled to Madison and defeated Camp Hadley 35-33 at the Madison Town Hall.[33]

In February 1937 Captain Walter D. Thomas, Cavalry Reserves, became the new commanding officer of Camp Buck. He was assisted by 1st Lt. A. K. Buckanan and 1st Lt. C. G. Paolillo.[34] Two months later B. B. Truskoski became the Commanding Officer. The Buck Eye reported in its Oct. 1937 issue that Capt. P. K Rockwell resumed as commander of Camp Buck at the end of 1937 after being away for a brief period.

Camp Buck had an Aggie Club that gave the enrollees a chance to learn about raising farm animals and growing a vegetable garden. Ten enrollees invested $3 in buying a baby pig with the hope of selling it in the fall for $10. Another group of boys invested in baby chicks who then were able to sell eggs.[35] In April 1937 the garden club were lucky to have Mr. Farrell plough the garden with his red oxen. He then brought several loads of manure. Boys then signed up for a garden plot or have a two-man plot.[36]

The Handicraft Club was the only club led by a woman. Mrs. McDaniel taught metal tapping, wood burning, and art. The Dancing class was also popular. It was led by Mr. Connor who also taught typing.[37]

In April 1937 there was another change in camp administrators. B. B. Truskoski became the new C. O and he was assisted by A. W. Baldwin, Adjt. M. W. Price was the Education Advisor. L. C. Blair was the camp superintendent and R. Melius was his assistant.[38]

During 1937 the state built its first brick charcoal kiln

The charcoal kiln was built near Camp Buck in 1937. The enrollees cleared the MSF of dead and poor quality trees and made charcoal that was sold to the public and earned the state money. DEEP State Parks Archives

in the MSF. It burned forest waste from the 1938 hurricane. Camp Buck and other CCC camps were called in to clear trees in towns and in the forests after the hurricane. This wood was then made into charcoal and sold for a profit for the state.[39]

In February 1938 work began on the construction of the new school building that would be located behind Barracks No. 1 & 2. The land was surveyed and batter boards were placed marking the building's location. Posts were set in the ground for the foundation. Foreman Oscar Anderson supervised. Another construction project was the conversion of the large tractor trailer garage into an experimental laboratory. Experiments to preserve wood were done with other liquids besides the traditional creosote. Foreman Simon was the advisor for the State Forest Service and the State Experimental Station.[40]

An unusual inter-camp tournament was held between Camp Buck and Camp Filley on March 24, 1938. It consisted of indoor games such as chess, ping-pong, checkers, cribbage, pool, spelling and pinochle. The final result was a victory by Camp Filley with the score 22-18.[41]

Sad news came to Camp Buck on Jan. 12, 1939 when one of its enrollees, William Ray of East Hampton, died in the Middlesex Hospital. Six fellow enrollees were pallbearers for his funeral.[42]

Enrollees participated in sports during the 1939 summer. They had a choice of inter-barracks volleyball and softball, baseball, tennis, horseshoe pitching, and swimming at Great Pond. The Camp Buck baseball team played local CCC camps and played in the Middletown. Twilight League. At the end of the season the team's record was 12-5.[43]

The Army also provided an education advisor who organized classes for the enrollees. The June 3, 1939 issue of the national CCC newspaper Happy Days entitled "School Attendance Reaches New High" it stated that 160 Camp Buck enrollees attended morning classes for six months during May. The evening classes also stated the attendance was high.

The morning classes covered the following topics: woodworking, blacksmithing, machine operation & repair, dendrology, forest protection, machine operation & repair, and construction of roads, trails, and structures.

During mid-June all the classes were held in the morning because of the warmer weather and the evenings were devoted to recreation.

The morning and evening classes continued the following year with great success. There were 85 enrollees enrolled in academic subjects, 100 boys in informal classes (crafts & hobbies), 125 enrollees received daily instructions while working.[44]

In the fall of 1939 Camp Buck held one hour classes every Monday and Thursday. The boys liked this idea because it kept them inside for part of the morning and saved them from working in the early cold mornings.[45]

An inter-barracks softball league was held in the summer of 1939. At this time there were only four barracks that each had a team. There was also a team of camp officers and foemen that competed. Sadly, the O & F team lost all eight of their games.[46]

In September 1939 The Buck Eye began publishing a weekly newspaper with approximately four pages.[47]

In Oct. 1939 Foreman Leon H. Stone challenged his logging crew to provide 200,000 board feet to the saw mill that was located on the site of the creosote plant in camp. In Sept. the crew knocked out 50,000 board feet of logs, 175 highway posts, and 25 cords of wood. The crew was working on a 25-acre plot that had been damaged by the 1938 hurricane. After the logs were cut the hauling crew moved about 1,000 board feet daily.[48]

Enrollment in the CCC in CT dropped and there were no new recruits for Camp Buck in October and the allotment period was extended. The possible explanations for the decline were the beginning of war in Europe and the demand for war materials produced in factories caused a creation of more job openings in the brass and copper industries, airplane factories, and gun companies. Instead of 200 men Camp Buck had only 130. To help the situation

The sawmill used by Camp Buck is still used today by the DEEP. Podskoch

men from Massachusetts were sent to Conn.[49]

The enrollment center in Hartford, supervised by Camp Buck's Adjutant Mr. Lucinski, was moved to Camp Buck where new recruits were given physicals by Dr. Controno. Paperwork was handled in the camp administration office.[50]

The CCC made a change in administration positions. Reserve Army officers were no longer employed as leaders. At Camp Buck Lt. Lucinski became a citizen and still was able to continue working in the camp.[51]

During the fall Mr. Consolini's masonry crew was building approximately one culvert a day on road construction work. They were using 15" wide culverts. Another project was the building of a bridge at the creosote plant. This work was performed by Mr. Arnold and Mr. Simon's fire crews.[52]

In November of 1939 Camp Buck's fire crews were called out. The first came at night on the 18th in Glastonberry. The next afternoon a mop-up crew arrived to finish the job. Then on Sunday the 28th the fire crew was called up again for a small fire that was quickly extinguished and the boys enjoyed sandwiches for lunch.[53]

After four and a half years as leader of Camp Buck, Captain Rockwell left active duty and returned to private life on Dec 10, 1939. He and his family moved to St. Petersburg, Florida to join the medical staff of Safety Harbor Hospital.[54]

On December 11th 1st Lt. Paul W. Corrigan of Concord, New Hampshire became the new commanding officer.[55]

The following 1940 work projects for camp Buck were listed in the camp newspaper: winter-cutting and logging and transporting logs to camp saw mill; spring firefighting; maintenance of trails and roads; and tree planting. The camp planned on planting 100,000 trees on approximately 100 acres in the MSF. In the past 400-500 trees per man day were planted So with a crew of 25 men it was estimated it would take enrollees approximately 3-4 weeks to complete. Most of the land was on Resettlement Lands, land acquired by the Federal Gov. and turned over to the State Forest Service.[56]

On Feb. 8, 1940 Camp Buck held a dance in the Grange Hall from 8-11:15 pm. The camp provided transportation for girls that they picked up at the Green in Middletown at 7:30 pm and at the Post Office in Portland at 7:50 pm. Lt. Corrigan furnished the music using his record player and amplifier. Although there weren't many girls the enrollees had a ball even dancing with each other.[57][58]

There were frequent inspections of Camp Buck. On Jan. 20-21, 1940 District Education Advisor Mr. Scully inspected the library, crafts shops, and school rooms. He checked to see if the school had adequate amounts of text books and school supplies. He also observed classes while in session. He noted there were 15 in Elem. English & Math; 25 in Grammar School Equivalency; 18 in Leader Training; 3 in Photography; 8 in Press Club; and 12 in the Entertainment Group.[59] Three weeks later Scully returned and continued his survey of the enrollees reading levels.

The next inspection was by Capt. Pattee, the Construction Inspector. He found poor lighting in the library and classrooms and recommended the installation of 10 more lights and one outlet in all of the rooms.[60]

The following month Major General Woodruff, Commanding General of the First Corp Area, came to Camp Buck for an inspection. The newspaper said he was well pleased with the camp[61]

As the summer swimming season approached, Mr. Leonard, the camp Education Advisor and qualified American Red Cross Life Saving instructor, began classes in in swimming safety. He had also taught Senior Life Savers to two boys in each CCC camp in Connecticut and Rhode Island.[62]

The Education Dept. was fortunate to have three Wesleyan College students volunteer to teach enrollees high school classes. They came on Monday and Wednesday evenings. Dick Augenblick taught English, Bob Cohen taught two classes of Physics, and Sanford Cutler taught Algebra and Geometry.[63]

During the winter Bingo Parties were very popular in the Rec. Hall. At a Feb. 13th party 110 enrollees came and had a great time. Some of the prizes were candy, pipes, cigarettes, and tobacco.[64]

Another popular entertainment were Hollywood movies that were shown twice each month and the enrollees contributed 10 cents to help pay for the movies. The March 20th movie was "Beau Geste" that starred Gary Cooper, Brian Donlevy and Robert Preston.[65]

The enrollees had other monthly fees to pay. They paid 15 cents for the KPs. that worked in the kitchen. Most boys liked not having to do KP duty. The company barber charged 35 cents for each haircut. New enrollees paid $4.25 for trunks to keep their clothes and valuables. If the boys had photos developed in the photography room, they paid for the paper and chemicals. If a boy built something using wood in the Craft Shop, they paid for the wood.[66]

The Apr. 12th issue of The Buck Eye reported that on a Tuesday evening 50 enrollees were called to help in the search of a two-year old Amston Lake girl, Helen Montgomery, who had wandered from her home on the lake. At approximately 3 pm the parents noticed she was missing and called their neighbors, local fire departments, the state police, and Camp Buck enrollees in the search. It was not until 9 pm that state trooper Robert Ray and Albert Rivers found her sitting by a tree with her collie dog.

One of the many visitors to camp Buck were the supervisors of the Woodfield Children's Village (today called Family Services Woodfield) of Bridgeport. It was an orphanage for both boys and girls from the age of 18 months to 20 years old. The visitors came to see if it was possible for some of their older boys to join the CCC and what opportunities they would have in the CCC.[67]

In May 1940 the camp newspaper reported two crews were called to a forest fire in Rocky Hill. The first crew to arrive was led by Mr. Arnold. Then the pump crew led by Mr. Larrow arrived. They used 2,300' of hose and the pump and hose helped prevent the fire from spreading. Approximately 100 acres burned and this was the largest fire of the season. One enrollee was overcome by smoke and given first aid. The boys fought the fire for four and a half hours before it was under control. Two weary crews were happy to be back at camp and able to rest.[68]

A few days later three fire crews from camp were called out to a fire between Glastonbury and Manchester. The crews quickly brought the 17 acre fire under control.

In May 1940 Dr. Musick, the Army dentist, arrived in camp and examined the enrollees teeth. He did extractions and filled the teeth of the willing enrollees. There were some who dreaded a visit to the dentist. Most enrollees, however, were happy that they received free treatment.[69]

Mr. Merritt, the authorized CCC photographer, visited the Portland camp in May 1940 and took a group photo and other camp photos such as the rec. hall, library, mess hall, and camp officers. He then talked to the enrollees about his photography. Later a large sheet of 10 photos was available for purchase for 85 cents.[70]

The May 11th Buck Eye described the improvements that were being done on Camp Buck. All the buildings were given new porches and buildings needing roof repairs were scheduled to be worked on. The Press Room was made into a dark room and running water was installed. New lawns were put in where needed and old shrubs in the quadrangle were replaced along with flowers. The camp garden behind Barracks No. 3 & 4 was prepared for spring planting and the volley ball and tennis court were being repaired.[71] By June 16, the boys in the Garden Club planted the entire garden plot.

On Tues., May 26, 1940 a new work project in fighting tree insects began at West Peak in Meriden. Two crews from Camp Buck began spraying a poisonous lead solution on approximately 735 acres of forests. The crews used a special

Visitor to Camp Buck were greeted with this sign made of flowers on Great Hill Rd. DEEP State Parks Archives

Camp Buck enrollees used pumps, bulldozers, and dynamite in building Reeves and South Mulford roads through the MS. These roads enabled the state to remove logs to make various wood products and to fight fires. Conn. Experimental Station Archives

high pressure spraying truck with approximately one mile of hose. They used a mixture of fish oil and lead and the former helped to make it stick to trees. The mixture was to kill the gypsy moths and other tree insects. Two crews of 16 men each worked on a staggered schedule. One crew began spraying from 7 am until 1 pm. Then crew #2 took over and worked till 7 pm.[72]

In June the boys began swimming at the state beach on nearby Great Hill Lake. For safety the camp had a life boat, a roped off area for non-swimmers, and the "buddy system' was used that required all swimmers to never swim alone. The beginning of summer also brought the High School Equivalency classes to an end and 12 enrollees took the state tests. Each boy paid $2 to take the exam.[73] Mr. McCurdy, the Director of Physical Education and coach of the tennis, soccer, and swimming teams at Wesleyan College gave a lecture at Camp Buck on swimming safety.[74]

One night in August 1940 the entire camp was treated to a "Hot Dog Roast" at Great Hill Lake. Besides hot dogs the boys were served watermelon and iced coffee. After the picnic the boys had an outdoor movie, "The St. Louis Blues." The boys enjoyed the movie on blankets and chairs they brought. All had a great time.[75]

On August 8th Mr. Harr Smith, the Educational Supervisor of United Aircraft Factory in East Hartford, told the enrollees about the apprentice training program that he supervised. He said his company is looking for high school graduates who have had four years of math plus chemistry and physics. This was a good motivational speaker to spur the enrollees to continue their education in order to get a job.[76]

In June 1940 Mr. Fritz Gomez began planning the 19,000' South Mulford Road in the MSF. Then in the late summer John A. Simon began supervising enrollees who used a bulldozer and dynamite to carve through the rugged terrain. One crew worked in the gravel pit to supply the gravel for the road.[77] Meanwhile, enrollees were still working on the Reeves Road that was supervised by Mr. Joseph Consolini of Avon.

Another project in Sept. 1940 was the removal of the old Camp Buck water tower by the Corps Area maintenance crew who then constructed a new tower.[78]

In September The Buck Eye embarked on a challenging project, the publishing of a weekly newspaper. It had previously been doing two issues a month.[79]

On Thursday afternoon on Oct. 17th, 1940 two employment officers from the Underwood Fisher Co. in Hartford and Mr. Garvey from the State Employment Service interviewed 10 enrollees for immediate employment. The ten boys had been selected by the education advisor because of their past performance at camp. This was one of many ways the education advisor provided opportunities for the young men to get a job.[80]

After being the subaltern at Camp Buck since Nov. 1, 1937, Lt. William Lucinski was transferred to Stafford Springs on Oct. 25, 1940. The newspaper stated that Lucinski was admired by the enrollees and was greatly missed. He was replaced by Lt. Harold Nelson.[81]

The enrollees ended the month of October with a Halloween Party. The cooks served fried steaks smothered in onions, mashed potatoes, pie, ice cream, and cider. Then the boys passed out masks and they had a great time.[82]

An official photographer arrived at camp on Nov. 16, 1940 and took 94 photos of officers, foresters, enrollees, and classes. All the photos were in a yearbook that was sold for $1.89.[83]

The Buck Eye newspaper had frequent advice columns featuring topics as how to prepare for an interview, how to greet and walk with a girl, writing letters, safety while swimming, and prevention of athlete's feet,

During 1940 the Meshomasic kiln burned wood six times. Each time the kiln held approximately 227 cords and produced 45½ bushels of charcoal per cord.[84]

That same year the CCC helped construct a sawmill shed on a cement foundation near the saw mill and another building that stored lumber.[85]

Camp Buck did work to improve the state forest. They planted 775.8 acres of trees and did silviculture treatment to 2,433.8 acres in the MSF. From July 1, 1938 - June 30, 1940 the CCC planted 5,000 white pine; 4,400 Norway Spruce; 10,300 European Larch, and 1,000 Jack Pine totaling 20,700.[86] By June of 1940 there were 5,598.98 acres in MSF.

On July 22, 1941 Camp Buck was closed and E. H Walker was the last camp superintendent. The Army retained custody of the camp.[87] There are still a few of the Camp Buck buildings used at the DEEP Depot.

LEGACY

Today hunters, mountain bikers, and hikers enjoy MSF because the CCC built eight miles of dirt roads. The trees

Marty Podskoch and Carl Stamm gave the Portland Historical Society a tour of Camp Buck in March 2010. They are in the camp quadrangle by the flag pole. Just a few CCC buildings remain along with the sawmill and storage shed. Podskoch

the CCC boys planted are providing many wood products for the state.

Directions:

From Cobalt: At the intersection of Rts. 151 and 66 go north on Depot Hill Rd. for approximately 0.1 mi. Turn left on Old Middletown Rd. & travel for approximately .5 mi. Then turn right onto Penfield Hill Rd. and travel 2.0 mi. Turn right onto Stephen Tom Rd. and go .5 mi. to Great Hill Rd. Turn left and go approximately 0.2 mi to entrance on right of DEEP Portland Depot, 163 Great Hill Road, Portland. There are approximately two buildings remaining from Camp Buck.

From Middletown: Take Rts. 66 & 17A over the Connecticut River on the Arrigoni Bridge. At the intersection of Main St. and Marlborough Rd. (Rt. 66) go straight on Main St. and follow Rt. 17 A for approximately 2 mi. At the intersection of Rt. 17 go straight on Sage Hollow Rd. for .3 mi. Turn right on Rose Hill Rd. and go .2 mi. Turn left on Cox Hill Rd. and go 1.2 mi. to Great Hill Rd. Turn right and entrance to DEEP office will be 0.3 mi. on the left.

Map – Camp Buck in Portland

MEMORIES

"The First Day of a Rookie"
by J. Maloney

"Have you your papers with you?" was the first question they asked me as I fell in line behind a group of eager eyed new enrollees. I drew out some papers on which I signed my life away, some days previously. After being examined as to fitness for work for Uncle Sam. We were then led to the railroad station where upon boarding we were handed a ticket to be used for transfer to New Haven.

Upon arriving in the city of elms we were joined by more recruits with whom we traveled to New London. After being given various instructions, we were then transferred to different camps in the district. After taking the wrong road and arriving in camp later than scheduled and were scrutinized by the old timers. We finally had supper and were placed in various barracks. Some of the self-styled salesmen among the old timers made a handsome profit at selling boxes to us. So after being subjected to this strange abuse we crawled into our bunks and fell fast asleep. So ended a gruesome first day of a rookie.
- The Buckeye, April 1936

"A Day in the CCC"
by Kamm & Oliver

When you hear the bugle blow
To start the new born day
It's just a little message
To start you on your way.

Then you hear your leader shout,
Get up! Do your chores
Make those bunks
And sweep up those floors.

So you make your bunk
Then hurriedly dress;
Dash to the washroom,
To prepare for mess.

At revelry formation
The Captain quotes: "Stand by!"
We watch with greatest pride
"Old Glory" as she waves on high.

Then with quickening strides,
We hurry to morning mess,
And dig into our chow
With the greatest of zest.

After mess to the barracks,
For special detail
So in final inspection
We shall not fail.

Ready for work,
We dash to the truck
Speed out in the woods
To earn our daily buck.

Out ring the axes,
Down come the trees;
We topple the high timber
With the greatest of ease.

Then working steadily
Almost until noon,
By the pain in our stomachs
We know we'll chow soon.

Around a crackling fire
We eat our trusty meal
Then after resting our bodies
Much better we do feel.

Back into the woodland
We hastily flee;
Continuing our labor
Till half past three.

Now we are back in camp,
All dressed so neat
Standing at attention,
For evening retreat.

Then after evening mess,
In the library or school halls;
We diverse our entertainment
Till the final bugle call.
- The Buckeye, Dec. 1938

"Sunset"
by McGahan

At the close of day when the work is done,
I sit and gaze at the setting sun.
Such beautiful colors of golden hue,
With golden center enhancing the blue.

Who can describe its beauty? Behold!
Co colorful in its blue and gold!
Such a setting sun no artist can touch
Or transcribe its beauty with a brush.
God painted it there for us to behold
This painting of blue and gold.
- The Buckeye, Dec. 1935

This Camp Buck rookie is all dressed up with his new uniform. DEEP State Parks Archives

"Camp Buck as Seen by the Rookie (satire)"
by T. E. D.

When asked to give my views on Camp Buck, I was flattered but at the same time rather reluctant, as all I could say would undoubtedly be known already by the veterans. I finally consented when I was given the assurance that my name would not be divulged.

The Army truck picked us up in Middletown on the day I arrived and even at that early date, I was astounded by the friendliness of the boys of the camp. A leader who had been sitting with the driver, (later he turned out to be a senior leader) asked if anyone would rather sit in front with the driver, as it made little difference to him. Not wishing to hurt his feelings I accepted.

In camp the boys got our clothing for us, after first taking our measurements. Now clothing was issued to all of us rookies and with it came one extra piece of each so that if we lost anything, we would still have all we had signed for.

What we rookies did learn was the making of the beds in the morning, what really happened is that we were told to sit outside, while the assistant leaders made our beds and cleaned up. (this was done so that we would have a perfect barracks). Because the boys disliked carrying the night (urine) can, the leaders of each barrack gladly disposed of them for us.

Friday nights is the real fun (time.) Moffett, who as you know is the canteen clerk, passed out the free decks of cigarettes in appreciation of the patronage of the boys... the leaders put on an entertainment which is helped along by a talented Forestry Department. After that is over we go to a Mess Hall where a meal is served cafeteria style. Of course we always have ice cream and cakes but the best of it all is that we can order anything we like and the cooks make it up as we wait. Personally I like the tenderloin steaks they serve with French fries.

Over the weekend, as most of the rookies were broke, we planned to stay in camp. When the leaders found this out they said they would help us out. All the boys that cared to go to town were given a written introduction to some leader's girlfriend, and two bucks to take her out. We wanted to thank the boys for this favor but we were told that this was the usual custom here. (Later we found this to be true.) Do you wonder why we like this camp?

Working in this camp was beyond my expectations. The second day I went to work I was rather tired and when I had worked for about a half an hour shoveling sand, the forester in charge came over and asked: "Are you tired?" I said, "Yes." I was then told that I could go back to camp with the truck, get several hours sleep and come back when the truck returned with chow for the crew at 12. On the truck were 10 other men back for a rest. They sure treat us right here. But most of all I forgot was to tell you that we are each given sunburn lotion to assure our getting a nice even tan, quickly and easily.

Showers here are just like the "Y." Free soap, free razors and hot water any time you want it. They have recently installed tiled floors and a heater in the shower room as one of the boys objected to getting his feet cold. If you do want to go to the "Y" that is easily accomplished. Everyone on becoming a member of this camp is given a free membership and all they have to do if they want to go, is to see "Loey" and he will run them down in his car ... anytime.

"It's a grrrrrAND place!"

- The Buckeye, Sept. 1936, 3-4

"Medical Hints"
by Dr. A. A. LeVetere, Camp Surgeon

1. Be sensible – wear your winter clothing during the cold season.

2. Do not sleep without proper clothing at night.

3. Bathe frequently and keep the body clean and free from all odors, thus preventing disease.

4. Eat properly and sufficiently but don't gorge yourselves.

5. Visit the infirmary when sick, but do not feign illness or imagine.

6. Drink 5 to 8 glasses of water daily and make a habit to visit the latrine daily.

7. Do not take a laxative when you have abdominal pains. Consult the camp physician.

8. Get at least 8 hours of sleep daily. Give your body a break.

9. Keep your mind clean, healthy and pure. Visit the library and read good literature.

10. Classes are for your benefit. Make the most of them.

11. Keep the sex organs clean thus preventing disease irritation which may lead to a disastrous end.

12. Brawn without Brain is useless: Brawn with Brain is a winning combination. Which are you?

- The Buckeye, Nov. 1936, 7

"Check Yourself" (Manners with Girls)

When you meet a girl on the sidewalk and stop to talk, always remove your hat. Don't just tip it or touch it; take it off and leave it off until the conversation is over or until you have left her. Failure to remove your hat either shows your laziness or ignorance of proper manners.

If you stop a girl and want to talk to her, ask her if you may walk with her. Don't worry, you'll have plenty of time to talk to her and do so without bothering her.

When walking with a girl always walk on the outside. Never walk in public holding a girl's hand. It shows poor taste. If she needs assistance, she will let you know. If someone spoke to the girl when you are walking, tip your hat and acknowledge the greeting.

If you take a girl to a theater and there is no usher on hand, you lead the way. When leaving the theater lead the way out of the row, step aside and let her lead the way up the aisle. When entering a door open it and let her go ahead of you.

- The Buckeye, April 1938

The following are poems written by Portland CCC Camp Buck enrollees and published in February 1940 in "Woodnotes: A Collection of Poetry Written by Enrollees in CCC Camps of Massachusetts and Connecticut."

Poems by Norman Brien

Norman Brien was experienced in these fields: trees, insect pest control, timber stand improvement, and planting. He has shown ability as a leader in handling enrollees. He spent much of his spare time reading.

This young man at the Portland CCC camp on the fender of a Connecticut Conservation truck used in transporting men to work on road building, logging or bug control in the MSF. DEEP State Parks Archives

"Rabbit Love"

There is a fellow on our bug crew,
Whose name is Bernadine
And he is the greenest fellow I ever knew
One day while working in the line
He stepped up to mark a tree
And reaching it he suddenly changed his mind
For there sleeping on the ground,

Was a little striped creature –
As common an animal as there is around.
Said Bernadine, "It must be a rabbit,
I shall sneak a little closer,
Then I shall grab it."
Paumi the pusher was watching all the while.
He thought it was most amusing
And it certainly made him smile.
Now Paumi spoke up, "You'd better let that thing go,
It may look like a rabbit to you
But that's a skunk, you know."
During all this talking the skunk awoke and went,
We all considered it most fortunate
That he didn't leave his scent.

"Mountain Ledge"

I saw a mountain ledge today.
Its beauty thrilled me so,
The sun reflected from its side,
Made colors all aglow.
Rich shades of black and yellow
And the shades of a man well-browned –
Made me love that soaring peak,
That rose so high from the ground.
I saw pinnacles that towered
Into the blue of the sky,
They reminded me of sentries,
Looking down from posts so high.
I wondered as I stood there,
If other people passing by,

Camp Buck enrollees taking a break in the MSF during the fall.
DEEP State Parks Archives

Had stopped to admire the beauty
Of this craggy ledge so high.
I wondered how many people
Were blind to sights like these,
Caring not even if they existed,
Because them they didn't please.
I silently thanked my God,
For power to realize,
The beauties that are around us
And are unfolded before our eyes.

"When Summer Time is Over"

When summer time is over
And fall is on the air,
It's then I am the happiest
And forget all trouble and care.
When I see those rolling hills
And tall trees painted by God,
I am filled with the keenest pleasure
As o'er them I gaily trod.
I love to watch the squirrels
As they gather their winter supply,
Of meaty nuts and acorns
To eat when the snow is high.
And when I hear the cock partridge
Drumming on a fallen tree,
My heart is filled with rapture
And nature is close to me.

"Frowning Moon"

Last night I was walking
Under beautiful stars so bright;
A full moon was rising,
To fill the world with light.
Ever since I was a child
I believed the moon would smile,
When the world was peaceful and happy.
And free from trouble and trial.
Last night the moon was frowning –
He was watching the troubled world –
And slowly, so very slowly,
A picture then unfurled.
I saw a shell-torn country,
Right away I knew it was Spain;

I saw their people unhappy,
Suffering from hunger and pain.
I saw great armies parading,
And battleships go steaming by;
All just patiently waiting
Their war machines to try.
Many people are walking the streets;
They are our unemployed,
Deprived of a job and living –
Of hope and faith devoid.
Do you blame the moon from scowling?
After watching scenes like these
Do you wonder why he looks unhappy,
And why he seems so displeased?
When again the world is happy,
And we practice brotherly love;
I know the moon will be brighter,
And will be smiling from above.

"I Remember"

I am dreaming of yesterdays,
When I was a happy child.
My life was free of troubles,
And it seems I always smiled.
I remember my little dog "Spots."
He was a faithful friend;
And many a happy hour
Together we did spend.
I remember playing with brother
Through the long summer days;
The happiness that thrilled me
Will remain with me always.
I remember the winter snow –
The snowman was a thrill.
I remember days of coasting
Way over at Payne's Hill.
I remember my first day of school;
Everything seemed strange.
I was thrust into a new world,
And I was puzzled by the change.
I remember our summer vacation,
After our schooling was through;
Those days they passed so fast
It seemed as if they flew.
I remember summer days
Spent down at the swimming hole;

Days of peace and happiness,
With my fishing pole.
Those days have passed forever,
Never again to return,
Now that they are yesterdays,
For them my heart does yearn.
Then I grow old and lonely,
And life has passed me by;
I shall have those happy memories
Until the day I die.

Poems by Roger Kamm

Roger Kamm completed two years of high school in East Hartford. Athletically inclined. Has done clerical work for the Technical Service and took part in fire hazard reduction operations. Actively interested in Camp Buck newspaper activities.

"First Ordeal"

After the final roll call
Then they're given the oath,
Now they're members one and all,
Ready to take their post.
Soon marching in double flank
Their footsteps fall like rain,
One hundred wait in rank
To board the special train.
Arriving at the station
D two fifty-five,
Oh! What a jubilation,
When the train arrives.
The past is now forgotten
They only look ahead
To a new life they're starting,
A new future to be bred.
When the cars are filled
With rookies all so raw,
Their hearts are so thrilled,
Though they don't know the score.
The rookies are speeding
To their temporary haven
For the trail is now leading,
To good old Fort Devins,
At Devins they're outfitted
So they look their best

242

When they are admitted
To a camp out West.

These young CCC Buckeye boys are proud of their uniforms as they stand by the camp flagpole. DEEP State Parks Archives

"The Rookie"

A rookie isn't supposed to think,
He's not supposed to have a brain.
He's not supposed to know enough
To come out of the rain.
He's supposed to be the dumbest, too,
A man without a mind –
A fellow much more ignorant
You couldn't hope to find.
But you'll notice when he goes wrong
And the boys begin to holler
He'll say, "Have pity, I'm only a rookie
Trying to earn a dollar.
So being a rookie he gets away
With things the veterans can't
And when the trouble starts to brew
He'll always start this chant:
"I'm only a rookie
Who doesn't know the ropes."
And the boss will excuse him,
Rookies are dopes.

"T'was the Night Before Payday"

Prologue
T'was the Night Before Payday, and all through the camp
Not a Buckeye was smoking – not even the champ.
(cigarette chiseler)
Act One
At 6 am that – whistle blows;

They jump out of bed and into their clothes
"It's payday," they shout
As they scurry about,
And haunt the Rec Hall
Awaiting paycall.
Act Two
After the work of the long day is done
They all dress for town – and yow! How they run!
Intermission
Later that night they came straggling back
All out of fun, and some out of jack.
Epilogue
Oh Buckeyes give ear; this story is true
If you don't believe us, there's others who do.
The Buck Eye, Dec. 2, 1939

Hubert Sweet

After Hubert Sweet worked in the Portland CCC camp he fought in WWII. He was in the 45th Field Artillery and the 8th Infantry Division fighting in France, Germany, and Luxembourg. Hubert Sweet

Hubert Sweet of East Hartford came to the September 2012 CCC Reunion at the Connecticut CCC Museum in Stafford Springs and talked about his days in the Portland CCC camp.

"My father William worked for Cheney Brothers Silk Company in Manchester but during the Depression he was laid off. The company owned 400 tenant buildings and we lived in one of them. Dad worked on these buildings where he painted and mixed paints. I was the oldest and had to help my family when he lost his job. My mother, Leona Blair, had four other children: Francis, Valerie, Bill, and

Diane.

"I spent four years in a trade school, Cheney Tech, where I worked half-day in the trade school and the other half in regular school. I graduated in 1939. For my first job I worked wiring houses for a contractor. I did this till 1942 and then joined the CCC.

"The CCC was well-publicized in the paper and my parents encouraged me to sign up. It was in the summer of 1942 that I joined. I think my parents drove me to Camp Buck in Portland.

"For my first job they put me on a road gang and I didn't like it. Then I got a job breaking up stones with a sledge hammer. I got really good at it. You learned where to look for a seam and when you hit it, the rock split nicely. One time I stopped to eat lunch and I saw a large rattlesnake on the road. One guy held it with a forked stick and then let it go. There were quite a few snakes in that area.

"My next job they assigned me to was at the Cobalt Supply Depot. It was a few miles from camp. There were buildings left from an old CCC camp where they stored supplies. Another guy and I had a Chevy pickup that we drove to the depot. In the buildings there were supplies such shovels, sledge hammers, and picks that were used for road work. I helped put together orders for other CCC camps. When I wasn't busy I had a special grinder with two wheels. One wheel was round and the other had a V point. I used it to sharpen the bits for the jackhammers.

"Sometimes on the weekends I'd walk 5 miles to Middletown or just walk around in the nearby woods. I also had cousins who lived on nearby Great Hill Lake and I walked to their house.

"One scary thing that has stuck in my mind was one day when we were going over the Arrigoni Bridge that goes over the Connecticut River to Middletown. There was one Indian from our camp who was drunk and he climbed up on one of the rails. We were really afraid that he'd jump so we were lucky to grab him and pull him down. He then walked back to camp with us.

"After a few months I left the CCC because I got a job in Pratt and Whitney. They were hiring guys for the war. I went in as a machine operator. Later, I was promoted to be the lead man and was in charge of 15 guys. We made parts for the pistons in airplane engines.

"In 1943 the Army drafted me and placed me in the field artillery division. Then they shipped me off to Ireland in December 1943. I was in the D-Day invasion of France. On July 4th, 1944, I landed on Omaha Beach. We moved in 10 miles and set up our artillery. I was in four major European campaigns: Normandy, Roer River, Brest, and Crozon. I earned the Bronze Star, Silver Star, and Presidential citation. In 1945 I was discharged.

"In 1948 I got married to Sophie Golen and we had one daughter, Patricia.

"After the war I went back to Pratt and Whitney where I worked till 1983.

"When I look back at my time in the CCCs I learned how to do new things. I learned how to get along with people and how to have discipline."

Donald Butler Kelsey

Donald Butler Kelsey enjoying retirement. Rick Kelsey

Donald Butler Kelsey was born in August of 1921 and grew up on Great Hill Road on a farm next to Portland's CCC camp, Camp Buck. He enjoyed watching the camp grow and attending their weekly movies. Later, as a member and officer of the Portland Historical Society (PHS), he wrote about his experiences at Camp Buck in an article, "Memories of Donald Butler Kelsey, Camp Buck 1197 Co. of CCC." Donald passed away on October 26, 2002 before he could present his story at a meeting of the PHS.

"Memories of Donald Butler Kelsey, Camp Buck 1197 Co. of CCC"

In 1935 as the Depression worsened there was a need for more CCC camps. Four more were built in Middlesex County. One in Haddam, one in East Hampton (near

Salmon River), Cobalt on Gadpouch Road, and the one I am most familiar with, Camp Buck in Portland.

Camp Buck was located on Great Hill Road next door to where I lived. It is now a supply depot for the state D. E. P. and is in the rear of the present Co. No. 3 Firehouse. The state purchased the land from the family by the name of Sellew about 1930.

One Saturday in May I heard some noise over there and went to investigate. I was surprised to see it up. The men were busy putting away supplies and building tables and benches. In the mess tent the cook was setting up an army field kitchen with a work table, ice box dug into the ground, and a large stove which sat on the ground with an oven and stove pipe that went up about 8 ft.

The original contingent was comprised of 28 men, a sergeant and an Army lieutenant commander. The sergeant (believe his name was Tonsky) had served in the Army and controlled the men. I didn't know how I'd be received at camp, but I soon found out I was welcome as long as I stayed out of the way. One special friend of mine was Fred Moffitt from Seymour. Freddie was 18 years old, and had just graduated from high school. He worked in the supply room. When the officer found out that Freddie could type, he was made company clerk. He held that position for about three.

During the next month things started happening quickly. Lumber arrived, power was brought up, and the town widened the road and tarred it to the entrance of the camp.

A crew arrived to start the barracks and other buildings. The crew was made up of 25-30 local carpenters and about 25 laborers. The laborer job was to carry lumber, dig ditches for the water system and dig holes and set posts in the

ground for the buildings. My brother Cliff, who was out of work, got a job as laborer.

A private contractor was in charge of the construction. He pushed the crew as hard as he could because the sooner he finished the more money he made. The lumber used was 2 x 6" joists, 2 x 4" studs, 2 x 6" rafters, and 1 x 6" matched boards for floors, sides, and roof. Most wood was southern pine. All cutting and nailing was done by hand. Tarpaper was used on the roof and sides and homesote on the inside walls. All the buildings were completed in eight to ten weeks.

While construction was going on, a well driller came in to supply the camp with water, 15 to 20 gallons of water a minute was needed. They drilled for three weeks to a depth of 420 ft. when he was told to stop. There was plenty of water for an ordinary family but not enough to supply the camp. The driller then decided to keep drilling for two more days on his own. The first day a change in the type of rock was noticed. On the second day he struck a good supply. The final depth was 450 ft.

In August the men moved from the tents into the barracks and other men (new recruits) arrived.

A fleet of trucks came in. They were all new Chevrolets, eight dump trucks, and 10 rack bodies. Shortly after, an International trailer truck arrived for hauling equipment. The men built garages for them in the rear of the camp. The Army supplied one covered truck for picking up the mail and supplies every day.

In the late summer of 1935, a large parade was held in Middletown. The parade was to commemorate the 300th Anniversary of the Founding of the State of Connecticut.

Camp Buck constructed a float to participate. Frank Synott built a small log cabin (about 8' x 10') with a door,

Donald Kelsey (middle) in firemen's parade in Portland. Rick Kelsey

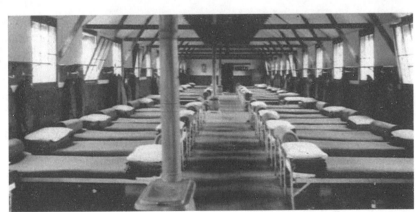

Camp Buck enrollees Moved from their tents to warmer more comfortable wooden barracks buildings. CT CCC Museum

chimney, and two windows. The cabin was then put on the back of the flatbed trailer, along with small trees, rocks, and other decorations.

Mr. L. C. Blair, who was the camp superintendent, asked my father if it would be all right if I rode on the float. I thought that would be fun and also Mr. Blair said his daughter might ride with me.

The day of the parade arrived. I found an old straw hat and a ragged shirt. A rattlesnake skin was tacked to the cabin wall near the door and I stood an old gun next to my bench.

Mr. Blair arrived about the time the float was to leave and said his daughter wasn't coming. I guess she didn't want to ride on a float with any boy. By the way, Mr. Blair was Paul Bengston's grandfather. His mother, Madeline (Buzz) Bengston lives on Cox Road.

I spent a lot of time at the camp, especially with my friend, Fred Moffitt. The guys saw us together so much they thought he was my brother. I used to help him in the PX which was open for business every weeknight. We sold soda (5 cents), ice cream (10 cents), candy (5 cents), cigarettes, and other things such as shaving cream and tooth paste.

The men kept busy beautifying the campgrounds, building garages for the trucks, and working in the forest. In the six years they were here they constructed approximately 15 miles of new roads and bridges which are still in use today.

One thing I remember well was the weekly movie shows. They showed some of the latest pictures, usually on Tuesday nights.

In the spring of 1936 all of New England suffered the greatest flood recorded. Whereas it didn't cause great

Camp Buck had Army canvas trucks to transport enrollees and materials. Theresa Strakna

damage to small streams in Connecticut, the Connecticut River reached its greatest height ever. All the homes were flooded, many up to the second floor. As the water receded a massive cleanup was necessary. The men from Camp Buck were called out to work in Portland, Glastonbury, and East Hartford. The work took nearly a month.

September of 1938 brought us the great New England hurricane. On September 20th I was in high school in what is now the middle school. When we went to school that morning it was raining lightly, but by about 9:30 it started to pour. By about 11:15 everything around the school was flooded and we were told school was closing at noon. I remember looking out the window toward what is now the post office and not being able to see across the street because of the rain. Both the cafeteria and gym were flooded to the doors.

The bus kids waited by the north door of the school for the school bus, about 12:30. I stepped outside and saw that the rain had let up. That's when I saw the Army truck from Camp Buck coming up Main Street. I waved my arms and motioned to them for a ride. The driver and officer with him saw me and stopped while I ran out and climbed in the back. We arrived at camp by way of Old Middle Haddam Road and Penfield Hill. Later that afternoon we had a phone call (phones were working) from Violet Clark, my classmate and neighbor from South Road, to see if my brother, Cliff, could pick her up. She was with the bus kids who had reached as far as what is now Kuskey's house on Cox Road. Cliff and I went around about way to get there and picked her up. Going back the road was flooding quickly by the meadows and the water was nearly up to the floorboards on Cliff's old '33 Ford. Violet couldn't get home because the bridge on South Road was out. Cliff finally rowed her across Kelsey's Pond in a boat. He had to be careful not to be washed over the dam as water was going over the whole dam about two feet deep.

The next morning, September 21st, we thought the rainstorm was over. There was no wind and it was warm. My mother needed a few things from the store and my Uncle Will needed a bag of grain for his cows so Cliff and I decided to go down right after dinner. In the meantime, Violet called from Synott's (her folks didn't have a phone) saying her folks also needed a few things. After dinner Cliff went down and rowed across the pond and picked up Violet and downtown we headed. We left Violet off at her Uncle George Clark's house on Depot Hill Road in

Cobalt. His house was just up the road from the Cobalt Market so Violet went to buy the groceries while we went to Portland. The time then was about 1 pm and the east wind had increased but it was not raining.

In Portland we picked up the cow feed at Cohen's Store which was then located on the corner of Freestone and Main Street. On the way back to Cobalt it got windy and rain started falling. A few trees had blown down along with some limbs.

At George's house we got Violet and headed home. As we turned the corner onto Penfield Hill Road a large tree came down and blocked the road. Back to Uncle George's we went and by this time rain was coming down in sheets and the wind was blowing a gale. The time was about 2pm.

George and his wife had four children and we all sat around the kitchen as the old house shook. No one realized this was a hurricane but we all knew it was a violent storm. At about 4 pm the wind and rain stopped and we all went out to survey the damage. All the large maples along the street were uprooted and there was no way we could drive the car home. We left the car there and Cliff and I walked home. We had to climb over and under trees all the way.

The next morning, September 22, dawned bright and sunny.

The crews from Camp Buck started to clear the roads both to Cobalt and Portland and by noon had most cleared. There wasn't any school for about two weeks. Well, so much for the "38 Hurricane."

The years after the hurricane the men of the camp cut wood and burned brush in the winter. In the summer they continued building roads. They built North Mulford & Dell Reeves Roads into Glastonbury and started on what is called Woodchoppers Road into East Hampton.

I did not spend much time up at camp during these years. There was work for me to do home on the farm. However, I did attend most of the weekly movie pictures.

By the middle of 1940 the nation's economy was improving and the men were leaving for jobs. Some of them left for CCC camps in Colorado and other western states. My friend, Fred Moffitt, left for a job in his hometown of Seymour.

Employment picked up so much in 1941 that Camp Buck was closed.

The camp was used during WWII for housing farm workers.

Robert T. Fitzgerald

On July 30, 2014 Bob "Fitz" Fitzgerald passed away at his home in Waterbury. Podskoch

I met Bob "Fitz" Fitzgerald and three other CCC boys on Aug. 21, 2010 at a CCC Reunion at the James L. Goodwin State Forest in Hampton, Conn.

Bob said people call him "Fitz." He shared his stories about working at Camp Buck in Portland and at Mesa, Colorado. I meant to call Bob and do an interview but for some unknown reason we never connected until I called his home in September 2014 and his wife Jean answered. She told me that Bob had passed away that July. I asked her if she or any other member of the family had any information on Bob's CCC experiences or stories, but she replied, "No."

I deeply regret that I wasn't able to interview Bob but I did find this information in the Aug. 3, 2010 issue of the Waterbury RepublicanAmerican.

(Front L–R) Frank Renzoni, Bob Fitzgerald, Pat Spino, Marty O'Brien (Back L–R) Marty Podskoch, Ted Renzoni, Henry Zapatka, Phil O'Brien, and Carl Stamm. Podskoch

Bob was born on Aug. 8, 1920 the son of William and Isabella (Kennis-Pasukinis) Fitzgerald. During the Depression he worked at CCC camps in Connecticut and Colorado. During WWII Fitz was an Army sergeant. After the war he graduated from Post Junior College and was on the dean's list.

Bob married Jean (Turnbull) and they had three daughters: Kathleen, Jean, and Roberta. For most of his life he was a carpenter. Fitz loved golfing and was an avid UConn Huskies fan. He enjoyed gardening and flea marketing. He had a talent working in leather and in marquetry, which is the art of applying pieces of veneer to form designs or pictures.

Nicholas & Costanzo Altieri

In July 2012 Joanna Price of Watertown sent me this information about her father and uncle in the CCC.

"My sister and I attended your talk in Kent, Conn, last Fall (2011). I had asked you about the country's largest collection of CCC memorabilia, and you told me it was in Edinburg, Va. I was really surprised, since I have friends who live there.

"Anyway, my father, Nicholas Altieri (b. 1-21-18), and his brother, Costanzo, were in the CCC. My father told me he was in Portland, Conn., and you told us that was Camp Buck. My father was from Waterbury.

"In the book you had there at the talk, we found a picture of "C. Altieri." My sister figured out that was Costanzo.

"Thank you so much for keeping the memory of the CCC camps alive.

"I thought you might like to hear a little more about my father. He was 10-12 when he came to this country from Italy. Because they didn't speak English, my father and all his brothers got put into first grade when they got here. I had always wondered why my father only completed one year of high school (he showed me that report card many years later – he was very proud of it). When I counted out the years, he would have been probably 19, or maybe as old as 21, when he completed his first year of high school. That's when he went into the CCC camp, to help his family. He was the oldest boy. I don't think he had a choice about staying in school. His father was probably an unskilled laborer at Scovill, I believe, and he was unemployed because of the Depression. There was something like eight or eleven

kids in the family (Dominic, Valentino, Nicholas, Altieri, Costanzo, Anthony, and a sister, Ruth).

"My father had been an apprentice barber by that time. While he was in the CCC camp, he gave the other guys haircuts for 25 cents, which was his own spending money."

I was unable to contact Joanne to get more details about her father's life but found that Nicholas passed away in Waterbury on Dec. 26, 2004.

CHAPTER 17
STAFFORD SPRINGS / SHENIPSIT STATE FOREST

HISTORY

Camp Conner, S-68 Co. 1192, was established in the town of Stafford Spring in June 1935. It was located on Rt. 190 five miles west from the village of Stafford Springs and three miles east of Somers.[1]

A story of the camps early history was written in the June 1936 issue of the camp newspaper, Shenipsit Lookout.

"On June 4, 1935 at 8 o'clock on a chilly morning Camp Conner was established. On that day a cadre of 23 men from Camp Graves under Lt. Bernard P. Moran arrived on trucks at the top of Somers Mountain. They unloaded several tons of supplies and equipment, took off their shirts, and started to work in building Camp Conner.

"It was a wild scene that faced them. They looked at an area covered with stumps and stones, partly hidden beneath ferns, which they had to turn into a CCC camp. They said to themselves, 'Boys, we've got a job on our hands.' They rolled up their sleeves, and went to work.

"The first thing that was done, as might be expected, was setting up a kitchen tent, so that the boys at noon would have something to eat. Then other tents were pitched for living quarters for the 23 men. Crews were sent over from Camp Graves, where the rest of the company was attached preparatory to the building of the camp and to help in preparing the ground."[2]

The camp was named in honor of Major General Fox Conner [1874-1951] who in 1933 was in charge of mobilizing and establishing the CCC camps in the US. Conner was then placed in charge of the CCC First Corps headquartered in Boston. He had prior experience in mobilizing men for war in 1917 when he was in charge of Operations during WWI. From 1921-25 he ran the Panama Canal. He left administering the CCC in 1938 when he retired. Generals Pershing, Marshall, Patton, and Eisenhower credit Conner with giving them and others the experience and training that enabled them to win WWII.[4]

This aerial view of Camp Conner in 1939 shows the headquarters bldg. at the upper center and Barracks No. 4 & 3 on the left and Barracks No. 2 and No. 1 on the right. In front of the headquarters was the rec hall, supply bldg., and mess hall with attached kitchen. The education bldg. was below Barracks No. 4 & 3. The infirmary was below Barracks No. 1. A large mound of coal was near the water tower. The shower/washroom was in the lower right area with a large wood pile to the left. There was a boxing ring on the lower left of the camp and below it was the Army garage. DEEP State Parks Archives

Major General Fox Conner (1874-1951) served as operations officer for the American Expeditionary Force during World War I. After the war he served in the Panama Canal, Hawaii. On Oct. 7, 1930 he became the CCC Commander of the First Corps Area which comprised the New England states. He is best remembered as the mentor of many of the Army officers during WWII, esp. Gen. Dwight Eisenhower.[3] mshistorynow.mdah.state.ms.us

The washroom was the second building constructed. It had a stove for warmth in winter and hot water boiler for showers and washing clothes. CT CCC Museum

On June 24, 1935 Capt. Arthur J. Wirth assumed command of Camp Conner. He supervised the construction of wooden buildings while the remaining enrollees of Co. 1192 were quartered at Camp Graves in Union.[5]

On June 28, 1935 FERA teacher, Franklin Learned, became the first education advisor. After a short time another FERA teacher, Roderick Rousseau, succeeded him. Classes were held at Camp Graves where the men lived in tents.[6]

The June 6, 1936 Shenipsit Lookout described the camp activity. "Work of construction pushed ahead rapidly. The first building to be set up was the mess hall, followed by the washroom. Work was then started on the other three

barracks and they were completed soon afterward.

"Camp Conner was a wondrously busy place in those days. At one time 75 carpenters were at work constructing buildings. The spirit and speed with which work was performed is indicated by the fact that on Sept. 5th, 1935 the camp was completed and the company pulled up its tent stakes at Camp Graves, and moved into Camp Conner." [7]

Once the camp was completed forestry work commenced on the first day of October 1935. Camp Superintendent Raymond Daly had his men work on gypsy moth control. Enrollees treated 77,310 acres of land for the control of gypsy moths.[8] Daly was assisted by Claire Gaudette, Charles Jacoby, Anthony Duart, Raymond Marin, P. J. Sullivan, Edward Sperandio, and Everett J. McConnell.[9]

On Dec. 9, 1935 Jerome O. Mahler replaced Daly as superintendent. Camp Conner did forestry work in the Shenipsit State Forest (SSF). The name Shenipsit comes from the Native American for "at the great pool," that refers to Shenipsit Lake. In 1927 SSF began with the purchase of land at the summit of Soapstone Mountain in Somers to erect a fire tower to keep a lookout over the forests of the eastern woodlands. Over the years, additional acreage was purchased to form over 7,000 acres in Somers, Stafford, and Ellington.[10] Camp Conner also did road construction and forest fire protection work in the Nye Holman and Nipmuck forests which had been formerly under Camp

(L–R) 1 The water tower was located at the rear of the camp near the elevated washroom behind. Edwin Strakna 2 This enrollee is part of the survey crew that marked out the road construction work with stakes on Soapstone Mountain. Conn. Agriculture Experimental Station 3 Enrollees drove a grader to level the gravel when they were building roads. Conn. Agriculture Experimental Station

1192nd Company at Stafford Springs, Conn

This collage of Camp Conner activities ranged from road work, night classes, sports and relaxation at the camp canteen.[19]

Graves' jurisdiction.[11]

On Jan. 15, 1936 1st Lt. Ernest W. Dehm replaced Capt. Wirth in command of Camp Conner.[12]

Over the severe winter of 1935-36 approximately 6 miles of road were washed out in the Shenipsit SF and were repaired by enrollees. They also did repair work on Stickney Hill and Morey Pond roads near Camp Graves.[13] Enrollees repaired the road to the fire tower on Soapstone Mt. During the spring they reforested 30 acres of unproductive land.[14]

During the terrible spring flood of March 1936, work crews from Camp Conner arrived along the Connecticut River before it crested. They did flood relief work in towns along the swollen river. Almost every man in the camp was involved in providing food and shelter to the flood victims. They had two camps: one was at East Windsor at Warehouse Point and the other at Hartford.[15]

Besides working in the forest a difficult job confronted the enrollees right in their camp. The grounds were littered with stumps and rocks and there was poor drainage. Enrollees brought in hundreds of tons of gravel for roads and paths. Tremendous amounts of earth were excavated and stumps and rocks were dynamited.[16]

Enrollees planted many evergreen trees along the entrance road to camp. A lawn was planted in the central square by the flag pole and they planted native flowering shrubs such as mountain laurel, dogwood, and blueberry bushes along the walkways.[17]

On April 9, 1936 Education Adviser Stanley Parker transferred from Camp Graves to Conner because Graves was closing. After almost seven months had passed, Herbert T. Baurer became the next education advisor.[18]

The education advisor provided a variety of activities

251

during the summer. Sports recreation was provided for all members of the camp. The following classes were also offered: Auto Mechanics, Life-saving, Photography, First Aid, Journalism, Civil Service, Typing, and Surveying. Tutoring was available for anyone interested. Discussion groups were held and speakers were also brought in. Enrollees were encouraged to take advantage of classes and provided with ways to search for jobs when they left the CCC.[20]

In the fall of 1936 the Camp Superintendent Jerome O. Maher discussed the work of Camp Conner in the October issue of the Shenipsit Lookout. He described the silviculture work and maintenance projects. He said enrollees developed picnic areas and recreational facilities in the nearby state forests. Workers did blister rust treatment of 22,000 acres of forests, and they scouted 78,000 acres for gypsy moths. They constructed 2.5 miles of truck trails, planted 37 acres of trees, constructed 18 water holes, did forest stand improvement work on 143 acres, developed 5.5 acres of picnic areas, constructed 19 fireplaces and 144 rods of fence. They did fire reduction work along a mile of road. Selective cutting of trees was done on 106 acres.

During the spring flood they did emergency flood relief work that totaled 1,500 man-days. They did 26 man-days fighting forest fires. Enrollees did boundary work on 8 miles of state land. Finally, they constructed a 2.3 mile

The education advisor supervised the Journalism Club that produced a monthly newspaper, The Shenipsit Lookout, containing these topics: commander's report, work projects, sports, guidance and advice columns, jokes, poems, gossip, visiting speakers, and Army inspections. Later the club produced a weekly newspaper. CT CCC Museum

telephone line from the camp to the fire tower on Soapstone Mt.[21]

During the late 1920s when Ida Pease sold her land on Soapstone Mt. to the state, she reserved the gold rights in the soil. Then when CCC enrollees were building the road on Soapstone Mt. they unearthed some gold. At first there were visions of a Connecticut gold rush. But on closer exploration no gold had been found.[22]

The 1934-36 Report of the Connecticut State Parks and Forest Commission stated the Shenipsit SF had 5.4 miles of auto roads and 13.8 miles of wood roads. Some of these roads were constructed by the CCC.

The Education Dept. advisor enlisted camp officials to teach many of the evening classes in October 1936. Blacksmithing was taught by Edward A. Ludwig the camp blacksmith, Leader Training was led by Captain Wirth, Tree Identification was taught by Junior Forester G. Bradford Bidwell, and Radio was led by William and Michael Witinok.[23] These additional classes were offered on Monday and Thursday evenings at the Manchester Trade School: Photography, Aviation, English, Arithmetic, Typing, Carpentry, Electricity, and Drafting.

On Nov. 24, 1936 the fifth monthly dance was held in the Stafford Springs Town Hall at 7:30 pm. The Ambassadors Orchestra provided the music and the WPA

This Camp Conner enrollee is using a jack hammer to break up stone or drilling to set a dynamite charge while building a road in the Shenipsit State Forest. His partner is by the truck that has the compressor to power the drilling. CT CCC Museum

The camp mess hall was always clean and orderly. Eight boys sat at each picnic table and the hall was heated by two wood stoves. The enrollees were served family style and they could eat as much as they wanted. CT CCC Museum

CAMP SUPERINTENDENT AND STAFF

ALBION W. JACK
Camp Superintendent

S-68-Conn.

WILFORD P. YOUNG
Foreman

J. C. GREENE
Foreman

E. M. HAWKES
Foreman

CHARLES JACOBY
Mechanic

C. GAUDETTE
Foreman

AUGUST P. BATAYTE
Foreman

Superintendent Albion Jack and is staff of foremen & mechanic who were in charge of the camp projects. Page was from camp yearbook. CT CCC Museum

also provided additional entertainment. The camp placed posters throughout the town to encourage young women to attend.[24]

On Nov. 2, 1936 Herbert T. Baurer of Waterbury and a graduate of Yale was appointed the new Education Advisor. One of his jobs was organizing activities. He was able to secure the gym in the town of South Willington for practice.[25]

Capt. Wirth provided "Movie Night" for his enrollees every Wednesday. He made arrangements with Films, Inc. to provide the movies.[26]

In January 1937 Jerome O. Maher left the position as Superintendent and was replaced by E. H. Humphrey of New Haven. He had begun service with the Forestry Dept. at the inception of the CCC in 1933 when he worked at Camp Hook in Danbury. Then he moved on to Camp Roosevelt in Clinton where he last served.[27]

In 1937 Camp Conner was run by the following Army staff: Capt. Arthur J. Wirth, 1st Lt. Ernest W. Dehm, Camp Doctor 1st Lt. Lloyd M. Wilcox, and Education Advisor Herbert T. Baurer.[28]

The technical staff included: Superintendent E. H. Humphrey, C. Bradford Bidwell, Clare D. Gaudette, Charles B. Jacoby, Wilfred P. Young, G. Kenneth Burwood, Edward A. Ludwig, and Paul C. Zimmerman.[29]

During the summer 1937 Camp Conner's baseball team played in the Stafford Springs Twilight League. They also played other independent and CCC camp teams. Some of the teams were: Crystal Lake, Somersville, Park Street, Enfield Prison, Maple Grove, and CCC Camps Robinson and Brimfield in Massachusetts.[30]

In August 1937 The Shenipsit Lookout reported that Camp Graves in Union, a sister camp to Conner, was to be taken down and the lumber would be taken to Voluntown's Camp Lonergan to be used for forms in building a new dam.

One of the new projects at Camp Conner was raising vegetables in the camp. Mr. Scott supervised the project. The enrollees planted corn, potatoes, carrots, squash, cucumbers, and parsnips. In the fall the crops were harvested and used by the camp mess kitchen. The project turned out fairly well except for the potato crop. [31]

The education classes began in the fall 1937 and Education Advisor Baurer announced these classes: basic classes of Spelling, Reading, Writing, and Arithmetic. The CCC camps were now emphasizing vocational training as a way of getting a job when the enrollees left camp. These classes were offered: Auto Mechanics, Electricity, Photography, Woodworking, Blueprint Reading, and Micrometer Caliper Reading. There were also classes for enrollees' leisure time: Oil Painting, Leather-craft, Music, and Radio Play Production. Baurer provided inter-barracks basketball games instead of having a camp team because he felt more men would have a chance to participate.[32]

In Sept. 1937 Barracks No. 3 was transformed into a deluxe classroom, assembly room, and reading rooms. Each room had sliding plywood partitions that allowed for quick changes. The reading room had comfortable chairs, pictures, and a table. The classroom had a chalkboard, desks, and chairs.[33]

In the spring 1939 Camp Conner continued to have good rapport with the Town of Stafford Springs. On March 23 a combination dance and minstrel show was held in the Town Hall. There was no admission.[34]

The May 1939 issue of the Shenipsit Lookout reported a new Education Advisor, Saul H. Dulberg and a new camp Superintendent, A. W. Jack.

Athletic activities kept the enrollees busy during the summer of 1939. Camp Conner had a traveling baseball team. There was also inter-barracks competition in softball, volleyball, and horseshoe pitching.[35]

The month of June 1939 was very productive in the field. A total of 1,299 man-days were used in fire hazard reduction work totaling 56.1 acres. Enrollees replaced culverts on Stickney Hill Rd. in Union, Soapstone Mt. in Somers, and Plantation Rd. in West Willington. Work consisted of building headwalls, blasting, clearing waterways, and grading. Mr. Hawkes supervised the crew in loading gravel. On one day this crew set the highest amount of trucks loaded in a single day, 63 loads. Mr. Knight's crew supervised a crew building a house for the Forest Ranger. His crew worked on excavating the cellar and on drainage work.[36]

During July the young men continued work on the Forest Ranger house, constructing forest fire breaks, excavating wells, transporting materials, constructing waterholes, fighting fires, maintenance, and nursery work.[37]

Major camp improvements were reported in July 1939. Almost all of the buildings were painted including the rafters in the barracks. A new wall was constructed in the washroom and new flooring installed in the rec hall. The roofs and smoke stacks were painted, too.[38]

At the end of the baseball season Camp Conner was undefeated. They then traveled 70 miles to play Camp Cross in West Cornwall, the Western CCC League champion. Camp Conner came out the victor. It was the first time they won an award for the best CCC camp in Connecticut.[39]

The Education Advisor reported this information about Camp Conner's enrollees. Twenty-six men had finished 11 years of schooling. Eight men graduated from Grammar School (8th grade), and morning classes were not being held in all of Connecticut CCC camps. In some camps classes were held on two or three days.[40]

There was a new club at Camp Conner in October 1939. An Archery Club began under the direction of Miss Evangeline Church. Some of the men traveled to Camp Fernow during the summer to learn how to make bows and arrows. Club members were outside after work almost every day practicing their archery skills. In the evening the members worked on their equipment in the schoolhouse.[41]

Mr. Sanger's shop class spent its time making toys for the sick and needy of the area. They made 175 toys in assorted colors of little rabbits and ducks on wheels.[42]

Sports kept the enrollees busy during the 1939-40 winter. The camp basketball team began using the Stafford Springs high school gym. The local police dept. began practicing on Wednesday evening with the Camp Conner team. Camp Conner competed against the following teams: Ellington, S. Windsor, Rockville, and Wapping (S. Windsor). They also competed against these CCC teams in Massachusetts: Brimfield, Chester, Holyoke, and Spencer.

(L–R) 1 These boys earned their time in the sun between barracks. The boys did their own laundry in the wash room and hung it on the clothes lines beyond them. CT CCC Museum 2 Camp Conner boys built water holes near springs and wet areas by digging a large hole approximately 5" deep and lining it with stones. This water hole was right in Camp Conner. Dan Niquist 3 An undated Camp Conner basketball team that played other CCC camps and nearby Connecticut and Massachusetts teams. Profit from sales in the canteen helped pay for sports equipment and uniforms. DEEP State Parks Archives

(L–R) 1 This observation tower replaced the old fire tower on Soapstone Mt. DEEP 2 The new Camp Conner water tower in 1940 with the headquarters building in the distance and the cook shack on the right. Edwin Strakna

Inter-barracks games were scheduled as preliminary games before the camp team played. On Friday evenings inter-barracks competition was held at the town bowling alley. Each barracks had two teams.[43] [44]

During Feb. 1940 a minor epidemic of bronchial colds hit Camp Conner. Fifty-one enrollees reported to the infirmary for treatment. An isolation ward was set up in Barracks No. 3. Dr. T. Goldstein supervised the care of the sick. He urged the enrollees to refrain from passing their cigarette butts because that could have led to the spreading of the illness.[45]

CCC dentist Dr. M. Musik made his quarterly visit to Camp Conner and examined all the enrollees. Then he did filling and extracting.[46]

Also during February Richard W. Howes of the Vocational Division of Conn. conducted a two-hour weekly teacher training workshop on Friday afternoon for all the foremen. He instructed them on the proper procedures of teaching vocational classes. Howes was in charge of all the curriculum materials used throughout the state's vocational schools.[47]

In 1940 the enrollees completed the construction of Avery Rd. and the Ranger's house. Camp Conner's men increased the amount of auto roads to a total 7 miles.[48]

After almost five years in operation Camp Conner closed on May 23, 1941. A. W. Jack was the last camp superintendent. The Army retained custody of the camp.[49]

After the attack on Pearl Harbor, Camp Conner was turned over to the Federal Security Administration to be used for agricultural workers. In 1943 farm families were transported from New York and housed at the old Camp Conner. The families came from "submarginal" low production farms. Later it was turned back to the State Forest Service.[50]

LEGACY

Camp Conner enrollees created an abundance of recreational opportunities at the 7,000 acre Shenipsit State Forest (SSF). They constructed the road up Soapstone Mt. (1,075') that led to the fire tower. The tower was removed in 1976 and replaced with a new observation tower where hikers can get amazing views of the Connecticut River Valley and the Springfield skyline. CCC enrollees also built picnic areas with fireplaces, tables, and wells for drinking water. Thousands of hikers, mountain bikers, and equestrians use trails constructed by the CCC.

The CCC planted thousands of trees, fought destructive forest insects, and did silviculture work in SSF that made it productive and the forest continues to be timbered today.

Directions:

From I-91 take exit 47 E and travel east on Rt. 190 for approximately 10 miles. You will travel through Hazardville, Somersville, and Somers. When you pass the Johnson Memorial Hospital on your left, the Connecticut CCC Museum and the site of Camp Conner will be on your right. The museum is in the old Camp Conner Administration Building.

From Stafford Springs on Rt. 32, travel west on Rt. 190 for 4.8 mi. The Connecticut CCC Museum is on your left and the site of Camp Conner.

Map – Stafford Springs

MEMORIES

The new Camp Conner water tower in 1940 with the headquarters building in the distance and the cook shack on the right. Edwin Strakna

"Hazing Ceremonies"

On Oct. 19, 1936 a group of Connecticut enrollees that were stationed at a camp in Claremont, NH were assigned to Camp Conner.

The next week 14 rookies came to Camp Conner and went through a hazing ceremonies. The night guard, "Sgt." Woods had the men do various duties their first night in camp. One enrollee had to watch the water tower by the light of an "obscured' moon, another man had to guard the latrine, two men guarded the door to the headquarters, and two more guarded the barracks against intruders.

The men did such a great job that the one assigned to the latrine bared Senior Leader Robinson from going to the latrine. Another person who worked in the office had difficulty getting in because of the rookie guard. It was a night they will never forget.

- Shenipsit Lookout, Oct. 1936

❦ ❧

"The Three C's"
by Alfred Schofield

If you get tired of bothering your mother,
If you don't get along very well with your brother,
If you have some trouble or other with your father,
Why not leave it behind without bother?
Join the Three C's.

If you can't get yourself a position,
If for a chance you always keep wishin',
If you want to make yourself into a man,
Why not follow this simple little plan,
Join the Three C's.

If you think you are fit for advancement,
There's no other job with more entrance,
Chopping and road building are part of the game,
With instructive classes to teach you the same,
Join the Three C's.

If you desire a chance to learn,
If for an education you constantly yearn,
Why not come to our classrooms for teaching,
Where practice makes perfect without any preaching.
Join the Three C's

Maybe you do only get a dollar a day,
Maybe you'll say it's not very much pay,
But consider your chances for recommendation,
By preparing yourself for some higher station,
Join the Three C's.
- Shenipsit Lookout, Jan. 1937

Boys by camp sign. CT CCC Museum

Theodore "Ted" Stearns

Ted Stearns with a leather purse on his lap that he made
while working at Camp Conner in Stafford Springs.
Podskoch

On May 26, 2008 I visited Ted Stearns at his home on Windham Rd. in Willimantic. Ted introduced me to his son John who lived with Ted. We sat down at his kitchen table and he handed me a leather purse, key case, and wallet.

"I made these for my mother when I was at Camp Conner. We had a couple that came up from N. Windham. The man was a leathercraft salesman. I used black cattle hide to make them. Some of it is like polka dots and here are her initials that I inscribed. I took this class every week. We paid him for the materials."

He then told me about his life before he was in the CCC.

"I was born on Aug. 5, 1922. My father, Robert E., ran a dairy farm and delivered milk going house to house in Willimantic. He milked about 50 cows. Dad owned Mountain Dairy. My dad died in 1937 of leukemia and my brother, Willard, took over the farm. I was just 15 years old.

"My mother was Alice James. She had six children: Cynthia who died as a child, Willard, Ellsworth, Robert, Steadman, and I was the baby of the family.

"I was 16 when I graduated from 8th grade. I was too much of a goof-off in school. I may have worked for my older brother in June 1938 till I started trade school in September 1938. I took electrical classes. I stayed for about a year.

"I knew a guy from Mansfield who was in the CCC and he told me about it. So I went to sign up. I think I did

it for the forestry experience. I went to Hartford and signed up on Oct. 2, 1939. They assigned me to Stafford Springs Camp Conner Co.1192.

"I was kind of nervous. I was never away from home and never stayed somewhere overnight. My mother drove me up to camp.

"When I got there, it was way in the country but I got used to it. The food was pretty good. It had a laundry & showers in one building.

"I was on a crew that worked in state forest areas. For example, we went to a 50-acre tract and cut a walkway inside the boundary. It was 25' wide.

"Another time three of us in a crew were building a driveway into a property owned by the state by Rt. 84 in Willington. It was called Rt. 15 then. The contractor was working on their road and we were working on state property. We were drilling holes into rock to blast it. We used jack hammers. I had the easy job, keeping track of the number of holes we drilled.

"We started with a 2" wide drill, then to 1¾", and finally to 1½". As we drilled the hole, we wore off the bottom and the sides of the bit. Every time we drilled, we had to add another length to the drill bits. The new bit screwed onto the other bit. They were in 2', 4', and 6' lengths. The three of us just did the drilling.

"On another job we went up to the laurel sanctuary on Rt. 190 in Union and did some clearing or patching of the road.

"There were some funny things that happened at camp. During my first week I was goofing off in the shower. A couple guys came in with a white towel. It was stenciled with somebody's number. So part of my indoctrination was to scrub off the numbers which were in indelible ink. They left and said they would be back and wanted it done or

The three leather goods Ted made (clockwise from top): hand
sewn and engraved purse, wallet, and key case. Podskoch

257

else. Maybe I beat it up and almost ruined the towel from rubbing it so much but when they came back and saw what I did they said, 'OK, I guess you tried.' and I passed.

"Sometimes on the weekends I hitched a ride home. It was about 30-miles away. Sometimes it was hard getting a ride. One time we walked down the mountain into Stafford Springs and we tried to get a ride. We were tempted to have one of us lie down and act like he was injured but we never did it.

"In our free time or on weekends we played cards or ping pong.

"After working at Conner for almost a year I decided to leave and was discharged on Aug., 13, 1940. I left because I thought I could do better. I was about 18. I got a job on a neighbor's farm as a hired hand.

"In 1941 I went to the Springfield Armory in Springfield Massachusetts and got a job. I worked in the motor pool and drove trucks. While working in Springfield, I lived with my brother Robert and his wife Doris. Then I lived with a fellow employee.

"I enlisted in the Army in Springfield on Nov. 25, 1942. In February 1943 I was called up to Ft. Devens for training. Then we got on a train for Texas. After 54 hours we got off in Texarkana, Tex. I stayed for about a year.

"The Army then sent me to NYC and placed me on a ship to England where I worked on tanks and did guard duty.

"Then I got on a ship to France. My job there was a mechanic working on jeeps and tanks. We all had certain classifications.

"On Dec. 29, 1945 I was discharged from the Army at Ft. Devens. I went back home where I did some farming. I worked at a poultry farm in Windham. I lived with the family and there was chicken in every meal! This ruined my stomach for chicken for the rest of my life.

"In 1948 I worked as a line helper for Conn. Light & Power. I worked my way up and became a lineman

"In 1950 I married Ruth Curtis from Terryville. We had a son, John in 1962. My wife died in 1976.

"When I froze my fingers in 1957, they moved me into the garage and I became the garage chief.

"After 35 years I retired in 1983. I remarried Vivian Kelly and went back to work for ten years at Tenett Tree Service, working on some old bucket trucks and some newer trucks. In my late sixties I would go on the road with trimming crews during storms.

"When I look back at my time in the CCC I learned discipline and how to behave myself. I also learned a little about jack hammering.

"When I went back to my old CCC camp a few years ago, boy, it had changed to beat hell. All buildings are gone except for headquarters. There's just an open field."

Ted Stearns passed away on Sept. 29, 2013.

Bob Hirth

Bob Hirth died on December 24, 2009 in Bristol, Conn.
funkfuneralhome.com

"I was born on Nov. 12, 1921 in Bristol, Conn. My father, Richard Hirth, was a tool and die maker at New Departure Co. in Bristol where they made ball bearings and coaster brakes for bikes. My mother, Josephine (Murphy) of Rockville, had three children: Winifred, Arthur, and me. I was the youngest.

"In June 1939 I graduated from high school at 17. During the summer I worked for a couple bucks a day at a farm.

"A friend told me about the CCC so in September I joined the CCC with a couple friends from Bristol. When I joined the CCC I had hopes of going to Colorado. I liked cowboys and Indians. It didn't bother me being away from home because I'd be working with a group of guys.

"They sent me to Camp Conner in Stafford Springs. An Army Reserve Colonel was our leader.

"When I got there, there were long rectangular buildings with about 2-3 stoves. It looked like a long barn. One guy was the night watchman. He kept the fires going.

(L–R) 1 The outside view of the four barracks and the headquarters bldg. on left at Camp Conner. CT CCC Museum 2 Bob Hirth liked to hitchhike home from Stafford Springs about every three weeks. He wore his uniform and drivers liked to give CCC boys rides. Bob Hirth 3 Bob was a mechanic in Ecuador. Hirth

Everyone had long underwear on depending on how close you were to the wood stove.

"I had two good friends in camp, Tom Moore and Tom Cronkite who were from Bristol.

"You had to be 18 years old to fight a fire. So I was just a water carrier. I carried Indian tanks to the guys who were fighting the fire.

"In the spring they gave us pine and maple seedlings to plant in the burned out areas.

"I built roads on Soap Stone Mountain. I cut trees with a two-man saw. A real old fashioned bulldozer pulled out the stumps. The driver was Bob Holcomb from New Britain. There was a fire tower with a ranger who was up in the tower. I could see him from where I was working. We were working pretty close to the tower.

"In camp they had a small library that some guys worked in. They had a couple barracks where the guys lived. If you had to take a shower it was in the center of the camp. There was no hot water. There was also an infirmary. I was lucky because I didn't get sick.

"The guys were always playing jokes. They always short-sheeted guys.

"In the evenings there was one guy who had a radio and we listened to Glenn Miller music. One guy had a guitar who played songs and everyone thought it was wonderful.

"On the weekends they had a truck that took guys to Skidico. It was a town near Stafford Springs.

"I'd hitchhike home about every third weekend. We left on Saturday mornings. We wore our uniforms so people picked us up. Sometimes it might take 4 or 5 hours to get home.

"When hitchhiking truck drivers took you into Hartford and it didn't take long to get a ride home to

Bristol. People in cars and trucks were happy to pick you up. People trusted you in those days.

"One Sunday night a friend and I never made it back in time and we came back late on Monday morning. We missed the morning roll call. Captain Wirth made us shovel coal from one pile to another and then move it back again. I think we shoveled for 4-5 hours. Then they fed us.

"The food was basically good. They gave us good wholesome food. There was enough to fill you up.

"At camp they had different activities. They did have boxing for the rough and tumble guys. They had a platform with ropes around it. I never got in it. There were a lot of tough city kids who did this. They had baskets for basketball. On weekends they showed movies at camp. We went to them when we didn't go home.

"Forest rangers were in charge of us when working on projects. They were older men and were about 35 years old. They supervised us planting and cutting trees. One foreman was in charge of roadwork. In the winter we did plowing and shoveling of snow. They kept us busy but we had good warm clothes.

"By the time May 1940 came, I was 18 years old. I knew I could get a job working on farms and earn a couple bucks a day.

"In the winter of 1940 I got a job in Whalen's Drug Store. That was when I fell in love with aviation. I went to aviation school for 18 months in Hartford. I became an aircraft engine mechanic. Then I took a test and became certified.

"I got a job at the Westover Field Airport. It was an Army Airbase in Massachusetts. I worked there for six months.

"The draft board was after me so I went to the Naval

Air Force and signed on Aug. 19, 1942 as an aircraft mechanic second-class. I was sent to Argentina and then to Newfoundland near Placentia Bay.

"In the spring 1944, two guys in my group were shipped to the U.S. Franklin, an aircraft carrier. Later, it was badly damaged and those two guys that I knew were killed.

"I was shipped to Sanford, Maine. It was nice there in the summer and I went to old Orchard Beach.

"Then in October I went to Clinton, Okla. and worked on experimental airplanes. I stayed there till end of the war.

"I came home after the war and got a job with Pratt & Whitney. I stayed there till November 1945 when I met a guy from South America. He said Panagra Co. from Lima Peru had a job opening. I went there in November and got the job as a foreman in Lima, working for the Limatombo Airport. I flew into Bolivia, Chile, and Ecuador doing repair jobs.

"I came back in 1949 and went back to Pratt & Whitney where I was a mechanic. Then I became an instructor on jet engines to all the airlines. I also taught the men in the military air force.

"I was married in 1951 to Dorothy (Kappell) Dahlgren, a widow with a daughter. We had: Jay (deceased), Donald of Westbrook, Ellen Cox of Bristol, and Nancy Chandler of Huntsville, AL. We were married for 36 years. Then she died of cancer.

"In 1982 I retired when I was 62.

"I was a bachelor for nine years. At the age of 74 I married Pauline (Goulet) Holden who had five children: Gary, Peter, Craig, Lori and Mary Beth.

"When I look back at my experience in the CCC I think I realized I needed more education. That's when I studied to be a mechanic and it became my work profession."

Joe Prucha

On June 9, 2007 I met Joe Prucha at the annual CCC Reunion at the Connecticut CCC Museum in Stafford Springs. He told me about his experiences at Camp Conner.

"I worked on the bug crew here. One of my jobs was climbing up trees and painting the gypsy moth egg masses with creosote. I had a can with a brush and creosote attached to my belt. It was a messy job but it was a job and I was thankful for that."

Joe then told me about his early life.

"I was born July 3, 1920 in this town. My father

Joe Prucha of Union visiting the CCC Museum in Stafford Springs. He worked there at Camp Conner from 1937-39. The museum is housed in the camp administrative building. Nancy Eve Cohen

William worked at the Nye-Holman State Forest by Willington. He worked in the tree nursery. He didn't get paid much. Then he lost his job. We sold a little milk, but it wasn't enough to carry us through. My mother, Anna, had seven children: William, Arthur, Emil, Joe, John, Helen, and Anna. I was in the middle.

"I graduated from grammar school. Then I quit because my family needed money. I worked six days a week for seven dollars at Pariezk Button Co. in Willington. I walked about 2 miles to get to work.

"In 1933 my brother William joined the CCC and worked for 18 months at Camp Graves in Union. My brothers Arthur and Emil both worked at Camp Fernow. They started in 1934. They both were there at the same time. Arthur ran a compressor in a quarry and Emil worked in the sawmill. They had stayed there for about 3 years, so I knew about the CCC.

"My brother Emil said he caught a black snake and put it under the sheets of a guy in his barracks. When the guy came in and climbed in bed he saw the snake and ran right through the screen door.

"When I was 17 I joined the CCC. It was around September 1937 that I went to the town office in Toland and signed up. They took me straight to Camp Conners and I got a physical.

"It was kind of strange when I first got to camp. I'd walk around and didn't know anybody. Then I got to know the guys who were sleeping nearby. It was a slow process. By the end of two years I knew most of them.

(Clockwise from Top Left) 1 Joe was on the bug crew at Camp Conner. He climbed trees and painted the egg masses with creosote. Conn. Agriculture Experimental Station 2 A Cletrac tractor was used for pulling logs and leveling roads on Soapstone Mt. DEEP State Parks Archives 3 Joe and the other Camp Conner enrollees enjoyed the rec hall where they played pool, cards or ping pong. CT CCC Museum

"There were two guys that were my real good friends, Raymond Mozzocki from Deep River and Sam Harrison, who used to sleep next to me.

"My first job was working on the road on Soapstone Mt. I used a pick and shovel. There was no heavy equipment. I did, however, see a cleat-track tractor pulling a log sled through the woods.

"Then I cut wood in the forest to thin the trees. The foreman marked the trees with a hatchet with a big C. Those were the ones we cut.

"Finally I was on a crew building springs and wells for the state park. We dug wells by hand till we hit water. Sometimes we had to blast the rock. When we hit water we lined the hole with stone. Then we put a concrete cap on top and added a hand pump. We dug the well in Morey Pond in Union.

"During the 1938 hurricane we did a lot of cleaning up of storm damage. Another job was we cleaned out areas for camping and picnics and built fireplaces. We did a lot of work near Somers, Union, and Stafford Springs. We also cleaned up the town roads.

"I never got injured from working but I did go to the infirmary when I got scarlet fever. I had a high fever of 107 and had strep throat. They gave me a handful of pills and I stayed there for a week.

"In my free time I played pool, ping pong, read, or studied in the Education room. It was not a part of rec. hall but was across from Barracks 3 & 4. I started in the auto mechanics class but there weren't enough guys for the class.

"I was a pitcher on the baseball team. We had uniforms and played other camps and sometimes farm prisoners. Osborn Prison in Somers was close by. We practiced in Somersville. We also had a basketball team.

"On the weekends I went home almost every time using my thumb. One time I walked all the way back to camp from home (11 miles) on a Sunday night and it was as foggy as hell. I remember I was walking past Stafford and a kid gave me a ride on his bike. I peddled and he rode on the crossbar.

"After working there for two years, I had to leave because you couldn't work for more than two years. I was discharged in September 1939.

"It was hard to find a job because I didn't have a car. I worked with my dad at the state nursery for about six months. I didn't like working in the hot sun but I had to.

"They were building Rt. 15. I got a job as a laborer for Savin Construction Co. in 1940. I worked there for about six months. I was laid off for the winter in 1941.

"In spring I went back to the road construction for M. A. Gambino. Then in the fall I was laid off in November.

"I was drafted in the Army in January 1943. I started in Fort Devens and went down to Sea Girt, NJ. After basic training we marched to Fort Monmouth, NJ. I was sent to Tampa for the signal corps studying radar. I went to the South Pacific on New Guinea and Biak Is. I was there for the invasion of Mauritius Is.

"In January 1936 I was discharged. "I enjoyed working here. It was great but there was still no work on the outside.

"Since I couldn't get a job I worked on my farm for a while. Then I got a job working on the construction of Rt. 15 to Hartford in 1947.

"In 1948 I worked for the State Dept. of Transportation. I was a tree climber trimming and spraying trees. In winter I rode in a snowplow truck. I did sanding from the truck. I threw the sand off the by hand.

"In June 1951 I married Jane Noff. We had six children: Marie, Michael, Larry, Joey, Lisa, and Rachel.

"I retired in 1986.

"My experience working in the CCC taught me how to get along with people. That was the best experience I ever had. I was only a poor boy living on a small farm. I was able to meet all types of guys from all over the state."

On May 1, 2012 Joe Prucha from Union, Conn. passed away.

Ralph Sturges

Ralph Sturges attended a CCC reunion at the CT CCC Museum in Stafford Springs and shared his stories of working at Camp Conner and Camp Lonergan in Voluntown. Later he became a chief of the Mohegan tribe and helped establish Mohegan Sun. Podskoch

At the annual CCC Reunion at the Connecticut CCC Museum in Stafford Springs on June 9, 2007, I was fortunate to meet and interview Ralph Sturges. He was dressed with a suit and tie a little different from the other CCC alumni that had gathered that day. But he proudly wore a baseball cap with the word Chief on it. I wondered what that meant. I later learned that he had Indian blood and was made a Mohegan Chief when he was chairman of the tribal council from 1989 to 1996, and in 1991 was elected Lifetime Chief.

When it came his turn to talk to the gathering, he said that he grew up a poor boy in New London and the CCC was a great blessing for him and his family because he was able to get a job and help his family.

Later that afternoon I was able to ask him about his life and time in the CCC.

"Before I joined the CCC I was 17 or 18. I heard about the CCC and went to the town hall in 1936 and I said: 'OK' to the recruiter. He said that I was going to Stafford Springs.

"I grew up in the city of New London where I was born on Dec. 25, 1918. I had a large family: four sisters and three brothers.

"I remember coming up here in Camp Conner. It was not like where I grew up. There were no homes. We walked around the woods and fields and heard the birds and the bees.

"When we began working there was no fooling around. The Army was in charge of the camp. When we went out to work, the foresters and foremen showed us how to saw and chop wood. At lunch time they brought us food to eat. We always had great food. We had some of the best cooks.

"The camp also provided us with good medical care. They had an education staff to teach us if we wanted to attend. Any time the education director was in the rec hall we could ask for help. They taught us how to be a young man.

"My job at camp was chasing bugs. We wrapped burlap around trees to stop the gypsy moths. I also fought fires. I never did a job without first being trained. You always knew your tools. When you were finished you were trained to clean them and put them away.

"On weekends you could sleep in, read newspapers or books.

"You see that road (Rt. 190) out in front of the Museum? A car would go by about every hour and a half. That's how quiet it was.

"There were also sports on the weekends. We had a football team and baseball team. There was also boxing and we went down to the nearby Crystal Lake for matches.

"Sometimes we'd walk down to Stafford Springs and sit in the park. Another thing they did was take us to Monson, Mass. for entertainment. We got there by going up Rt. 32 from Stafford Springs.

"After 6-8 months I left the CCC. When I had trouble

finding a job I joined again in 1937. They sent me to Camp Lonergan in Voluntown. It was during the terrible hurricane. First we went to Stonington to help clear downed trees. We were also looking for dead bodies. We moved trees off the highways and properties. We were told that one guy got hurt and we had to go and rescue him. After that we went to Westerly, Rhode Island. One time we worked all night to get a road open. It was hard because there were no electric street lights.

"We worked for weeks clearing the trees. The one good thing is that our camp cooked us great meals and they brought them to us in large containers.

"After the storm work I worked on a bug crew. The best part of this job was the forester. He knew all the tree bugs and explained to us why we were looking for them.

"He also showed us what plants we were pulling up. They were gooseberries that were the host for the blister rust that was killing the white pine trees. Some farmers got upset when we'd come on their land and pull up the gooseberry bushes but most didn't mind.

"People asked us, 'What are you doing with burlap around the trunk of the tree?' We'd reply, 'We are dressing up the trees.'

"Our barracks had two stoves and we used wood to keep us warm.

"Everyone did their own laundry. There was a sink and a washboard in the shower room. All our clothes had numbers in them to prevent stealing and they were checked when you were discharged.

"The Army had inspections every Friday and they checked the numbers in your clothes.

"Our camp had an infirmary if you got sick. One day I was chopping kindling and I missed the wood. I hit my palm with the axe. It was a bad cut. Our camp had an attendant who was always on duty. He did the best he could to take care of it. I had to stay for quite a while till I got better. A doctor from Old Lyme came and took care of my hand.

"If you needed a dentist you went to New London and went by boat to Fishers Island to the Army base.

"After the CCC I was in WWII. I served in the Army and was in the intelligence division in New Guinea and the Philippines.

"When I was discharged I signed up for the GI Bill and earned a college education. I worked in the Philadelphia area as a criminologist.

I returned to Connecticut and became the Chief of the Mohegan Indian Tribe. I was influential in guiding the construction and managing the building of the Mohegan Sun Resort.

"I remember Army basic training before I went to fight in the Pacific. The things I learned here in the CCC brought me back alive from the Pacific. I was able to survive all of the difficulties because of the things I learned while at Camp Conner.

"Most of the guys in the CCC came from the cities. This was the best thing that could happen to me and other guys who had not experienced the variety of people. There were bullies you had to confront. We had boxing. There was always someone to take you on. When you left the CCC, you were a man.

"When I look back at my days in the CCC I remember leaving camp along with the other enrollees and we all went home happy. I never met someone who didn't learn something. We all learned to be gentlemen."

Ralph invited me to visit him at his office at Mohegan Sun and he wanted to show me the marble sculptures that he had made. He also gave me his business card.

I was very busy that summer. In the fall I received the sad news. Ralph Sturges had passed away on Oct. 1, 2007. His wife, Ida, of 58 years, passed away that same year in May. They had one son Paul.

This is an excerpt from Ralph Surges' obituary in The Day of New London on Oct. 4, 2007:

Descended from the Baker line of The Mohegan Tribe, Chief Sturges petitioned the federal government for tribal recognition, eventually allowing for the establishment of Mohegan Sun. Owned and operated exclusively by The Mohegan Tribe, Mohegan Sun now stands on tribal land

(L–R) 1 This is the type of work Ralph Sturges did in the CCC to stop the spread of gypsy moths. The men in the photo are wrapping burlap around trees to shelter the caterpillars and then kill them. Conn. Agricultural Experiment Station 2 Chief Ralph Sturges of the Mohegan Tribe.

and is one of the largest and most successful casinos in the world.

In 1991, Chief Sturges was elected as Lifetime Chief by The Mohegan Tribe. In the Mohegan language, his chief's name "G'tinemong" translates as "He Who Helps Thee." With an unswerving regard for the welfare of his fellow tribal members, Chief Sturges worked throughout the latter half of the 20th century for federal recognition of The Mohegan Tribe and served as Tribal Chairman from 1989 to 1996. Sticking to his code of "Perseverance, Honor & Integrity," Chief Sturges pressed on in his efforts despite some initial setbacks, and was there in 1994 when the call came through granting federal recognition to the tribe. After working with both government officials and the financiers of Wall Street, Chief Sturges saw the rise of Mohegan Sun as its doors opened 1996. He also participated in the building's expansion in 2002. Mohegan Sun continues to grow, and is in the midst of another expansion entitled Project Horizon which is expected to be completed by 2010. Chief Sturges was present at the groundbreaking of Project Horizon in the summer of 2007.

Many honors and accolades were bestowed on Chief Sturges. In 2005, The Eastern Connecticut Chamber of Commerce honored him as Citizen of the Year, while the Big Brothers and Big Sisters of Southeastern Connecticut named him Man of the Year. In 2006, he was given an honorary doctorate by Eastern Connecticut State University. www.legacy.com

Sam Harrison

Sam Harrison came to a CCC Reunion at Camp Conner in 2007. He shared stories about first working at Camp Jenkins in Cobalt and later at Camp Conner. Podskoch

During a CCC reunion in 2006 at the Connecticut CCC Museum I was fortunate to meet Sam Harrison. He told me that he had worked at the Camp Conner infirmary and he had a lot of interesting stories.

On April 14, 2007 I interviewed Sam by phone at his home in Rockville.

"I was born in 1916 in Rockville, Conn. My father, John, was a weaver but he died when I was 6 years old. My mother Julia Geiser had five other children: Hazel, Evelyn, Bernice, Annie, and Russell.

"I worked in the summer selling papers and working on farms. I worked 6½ days a week but I only brought home seven dollars. I had a job working for a farmer named Rudy Moser who also had a dairy farm in Ellington. I carried 100-pound bags of grain for the cows. I helped milk the cows and bottle the milk. He also raised vegetables and tobacco. I walked ½ mile from home to town and met the farmer who picked me up with his truck. I helped him deliver milk and unloaded the truck.

"I quit school in 7th grade and continued working for Moser. His son Ben runs the farm now. He had a big orchard and a large apple cellar where he stored them. I sorted apples and delivered them to stores. Many of the stores had dirt floors that were cool and good for storing vegetables. I also carried 62-lb. sacks of potatoes to customer's and emptied them into barrels in their cellars.

"I worked a couple years after I quit school and I realized I was working too hard.

"Then I read about the CCC in the newspaper and I knew a businessman whose secretary also signed up the boys for the CCC. I signed up in the fall of 1935. I went with a group of guys to Hartford. They took us to New London and then by boat to Fort Wright. We stayed for about a week and got our shots. Then I went to Camp Jenkins in Cobalt near Portland, Conn.

"I didn't feel too bad about leaving home because it was something to do. I had four brothers-in-law who couldn't get a steady job. Some joined the WPA and were paid one dollar a day and I was paid the same plus I had room and board.

"My first job was cutting trees for cordwood. A lot was sent to Hartford. We cut the logs into 4' lengths. In Hartford they had buck saws and cut them into fire wood. They either gave the wood to the poor people or sold it.

"Our captain wore britches with leggings. He was in the cavalry during WWI. There were about six state

 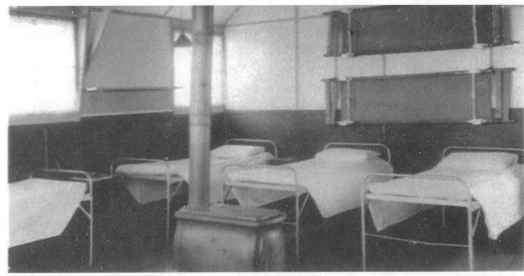

(L–R) 1 An Army officer supervising Sam at Camp Jenkins in Cobalt. He is wearing jodhpurs that were worn by men in the cavalry. The officer often rode around camp on horseback because he was in WWI. CT CCC Museum 2 This is a typical infirmary with 4-6 cots, a wood stove, stretchers, and first aid materials. Sam worked and slept at the Camp Conner infirmary for six months and did basic first aid, cared for sick, and brought them meals. It was a 24-7 job and he had every other weekend off. CT CCC Museum

foresters who supervised our work.

"For recreation we had a rec hall with a ping pong table. Once in a while we had a movie in the mess hall.

"I only was on KP duty once. After I got a job helping the captain. They had a bulletin board and I saw my name with an order to report to the captain. When I went to see him he said I would have a special job and that was taking care of his dog. I had to walk and feed him when the captain went home. That sure beat KP duty. I stayed in the headquarters with the dog on Saturdays.

"I stayed for six months in Cobalt and went home. I worked in mills in Rockville and mowed lawns.

"I think it was in the fall of 1936 that I signed up again for the CCC. I worked there for six months in Camp Conner. They asked me to work in the infirmary. I got $36 a month and that was $11 more than the other guys. They didn't give me any training just a white coat. There were six beds and one stove. I had to keep the stove going. There was a covered woodpile outside. I was right next to the latrine, a 16-holer. You could feel the wind coming up the hole and you didn't spend much time there. I had one guy that had pneumonia. I stayed there night and day. I only had every other weekend off. I had a book that I kept a record of the patients. I made up cough medicine and I took the patient's temperature.

"There were about 10-12 blacks in our camp. One day one came in complaining about a sliver in his finger. It was yellow and pretty ugly looking. He was short and weighed

around 210 pounds. We had a doctor that was assigned to 2-3 camps. The day the boy came in, I told him to come back the next day when the doctor would be here. He said it was swollen and throbbing so bad he couldn't wait. I said I'd give it a try. I had a little stove going with hot water going all the time to disinfect the needles, etc. He stood up against the wall and when I stuck the needle into his finger the pus flowed out slowly and he turned white and started falling. I grabbed him but couldn't hold him because he was so heavy. He dropped to the floor. I dragged him by his feet and pulled him from the wall where he had been standing. I couldn't revive him.

"I ran up to the headquarters and told the captain: 'This guy needs and ambulance!'

"They put him in an ambulance and I drove with him to New London. He was in pretty bad shape. We carried him on a boat that took us to the hospital in Fort Wright on Fishers Island. While on the boat I saw a guy who was from my hometown. It was a very cold ride.

"When we got to the hospital the doctors found out that he had blood poisoning. He never came back to camp. I never found out what finally happened to him.

"Most of the enrollees injuries were from chopping and sawing accidents. If it was a minor injury I bandaged them. If they needed stitches the doctor took care of them or they went to the hospital on Fishers Island.

"Our doctor's name was Goldsmith. He didn't wear a uniform like the Army officers. He supervised two other nearby CCC camps and a camp in Massachusetts. Every day he went home at 5 o'clock.

"I wasn't so crazy about the job but stuck with it because I got paid more than the other guys. I got the meals for the sick patients and had to keep the stoves going.

"There was a separate room for my bed and a room for an office that also had a stove.

"They had a recreation room but I couldn't go there because I had to stay at the infirmary. I only had some magazines to read from the rec. hall.

"I had a good friend in camp, Joe Prucha. We continued to be friends and later we worked together at the CCC Museum.

"On weekends I went home on a Saturday night only about twice a month. I was about 10 miles from home so I hitchhiked. A few times my brother-in-law picked me up.

"One time I got a ride during the winter from a guy driving a pickup truck. I had to sit in the back and it was very cold. My legs got so cold that when it was time to get out I fell down on the road because my legs were frozen.

"If you didn't get a ride you had to walk and boy if it was the winter you were cold.

"Both camps had good food and you had as much as you wanted. In the Jenkins Camp at lunch a big truck had 20-gallon tanks with soup in it. We used our mess kit to eat. We ate our lunch right outside and sat on a log. One morning it was 27 below and we had a hard time getting off the log because we were frozen to it. We dressed warm but riding in the canvas- covered trucks was cold.

"At Camp Conner we had baseball and basketball teams. We played local town teams and CCC camps.

"After working there for six months I left camp in 1937. My brother-in-law had a wood working shop so I worked with him for a while. Then I worked for the Rockville Hospital until I was drafted around September 1942.

"I went to Fort Devens and about 15 of us went to Ohio and then to the California desert. I got sick and was taken to a hospital and was operated on. After that I didn't go overseas. I did maintenance work.

"After WWII I worked for the Rockville Hospital doing maintenance work. At first the hospital was in a three-story house and the operating room was on the second floor. There was one large room for men on first floor and a large room on the 2nd floor for women. I had to get two guys, Herbie Krauser and his brother, to help me and the orderly to carry the patient up to the operating room. Usually Thursday was the operating day for kids. I'd leave my maintenance work and put on a white coat to take the orderly's spot. I also drove the ambulance. The orderly told me he was in the 1929 crash and told me stories that he was a millionaire but lost it all and almost went crazy.

"In 1952 I got married to Dorothy Worth. We had four children: Jerry, Susan, Bobby, and Freddy.

"The CCC was good for me because my experience in the infirmary helped me a little bit in working in a hospital. It probably helped me in getting a job at the Rockville Hospital. I also learned how to sharpen axes."

On Aug., 15, 2011 Sam passed away.

Gen. George Wozenski

Bristol native, George Wozenski, had an illustrious career in many battles in WWII. Bristol Historical Society

When I visited the Bristol Historical Society Museum members proudly showed me a portrait of Gen. George Wozenski hanging on the wall. They said he was a WWII

This is the Rockville Hospital where Sam worked before and after WWII. His experience working at Camp Conner was a good reference in getting the hospital job. echn.gykdev.com

hero and he had worked at the Stafford Springs CCC camp. At that time he was a captain in the Army Reserves.

Gary Potter, an avid historian in Bristol, shared an article he found about Gen. Wozenski in the Sept. 6, 1986 issue of the Bristol Press written by Gustav Spohn entitled "CCC Reunion Brings Back Yesterday." In the article it stated Gen. Wozenski saidv "I could show you colonels who shot up right through the ranks because of their previous experience in the CCC." He served for 3½ years in CCC camps in Boston; Rochester, Vermont; and Stafford Springs.

At the Stafford Springs Camp Wozenski was the commander. He was assistant commander in the other two camps. The general said that running the camps was very taxing because he was stretched in many directions. "You had to wear all the hats – mess officer, supply officer, finance officer and others."

He said that discipline was almost impossible to impose. "There was practically nothing you could do for disciplinary measures because everyone had a political friend. Nevertheless, the CCC was a good healthy life."

Captain Wozenski was relieved of his duty at Camp Conner and on July 9, 1937 he was commissioned into the regular Army at Fort Devens, Mass.

During WWII Wozenski received these decorations and citations: Distinguished Service Cross, Oak Leaf Cluster GO 82 Nov 44, Silver Star Medal Aug 43, Bronze Star Medal July 45, American Defense Medal, American Service Medal, Distinguished Unit Badge GO 33 FUSA 44, World War II Victory Medal, European African Middle Eastern Service Medal with Bronze Arrowhead, and the French Croix de Guerre, Belgian Fourragere, French Fourragere.

Here are two awards:

"The President of the United States takes pleasure in presenting the Distinguished Service Cross to Edward F. Wozenski, Captain (Infantry), U.S. Army, for extraordinary heroism in connection with military operations against an armed enemy while serving as Commanding Officer, Company G, 2d Battalion, 16th Infantry Regiment, 1st Infantry Division, in action against enemy forces on 11 July 1943 in the Gela-Niscemi sector, Sicily. Captain Wozenski, with about fifty men and officers, was holding a vital hill when the enemy counterattacked with about ten tanks and

approx. a battalion of infantry. The tanks surrounded the hill firing at point blank range when Captain Wozenski seized a rocket gun and, while constantly exposed to tank, artillery, machine gun and small arms fire, moved from point to point firing on the tanks and encouraging and directing his men to do likewise. He personally knocked out two tanks, one of them by firing into its rear after it had passed over his foxhole. Captain Wozenski's superbly heroic, calm determined conduct inspired his men to resist in an apparently hopeless situation and was a prime factor in the defeat of the enemy's counterattack. His gallant leadership, personal bravery and zealous devotion to duty exemplify the highest traditions of the military forces of the United States and reflect great credit upon himself, the 1st Infantry Division, and the United States Army.

"The President of the United States takes pleasure in presenting a Bronze Oak Leaf Cluster in lieu of a Second Award of the Distinguished Service Cross to Edward F. Wozenski, Captain (Infantry), U.S. Army, for extraordinary heroism in connection with military operations against an armed enemy while serving as Commanding Officer, Company G, 2d Battalion, 16th Infantry Regiment, 1st Infantry Division, in action against enemy forces on 6 June 1944, in France. On D-Day, Captain Wozenski's company suffered numerous casualties in reaching the fire-swept invasion beach. Boldly, he moved along the beach, at the risk of his life, to reorganize his battered troops. The reorganization completed, he courageously led his men through heavy machine gun and small arms fire across the beach and toward an enemy dominated ridge. Demoralizing fire from a powerful installation on the ridge threatened to stop the attack. Ordering his men to deploy to the flanks of the enemy position, Captain Wozenski, with great valor, advanced alone to within 100 yards of the emplacement. With cool and calm efficiency, he engaged the fortification single handedly with rifle fire to divert attention of the enemy from the flanking movement. Upon observing this valiant soldier, the enemy directed the fire of its machine guns on him but Captain Wozenski, with complete disregard for his own safety, continued the harassing fire until his men reached their positions safely. His inspired troops

charged the strongpoint vigorously and completely destroyed it, inflicting numerous casualties upon the enemy. Captain Wozenski's courageous leadership, fearless courage and zealous devotion to duty exemplify the highest traditions of the military forces of the United States and reflect great credit upon himself, the 1st Infantry Division, and the United States Army."
- http://www.homeofheroes.com

On July 14, 1947 he was appointed to the Connecticut Army National Guard as Brigadier General. He retired as Brigadier General.

Gen. Wozenski died in 1987.

Edwin R. Strakna

Edwin is clearing brush with a machete in the Shenipsit State Forest. Strakna Family

After finding photos of Edwin Strakna at the CCC Museum in Stafford Springs and also on the internet, I wanted to know more about the person in the photos. I searched the internet and located a few people in Maryland and emailed Theresa Strakna. I asked her if she was related to Edwin.

The next day I was happy to get an email from her. She said she was Edwin's daughter and offered to send me information about her dad who had passed away on July 28, 2014. Her sister, Cecilia Strakna, passed on a lot of information about Edwin's time in the CCC. The following is a description by Theresa and Cecelia about their father.

Edwin worked at Camp Conner in Stafford Springs

in 1940. This date is from a photo because the family was unable to obtain his discharge papers.

Edwin was born on Aug. 24, 1922. His parents, Albert Peter Strakna and Anna Barkiewicz were immigrants from Poland. Both his father and mother worked in a textile mill until his father injured his finger and the mill fired him. This was before the mills were unionized. Edwin was involved in the unionization of the textile mills in town. Later, his father did odd jobs including tending bar. His mother raised chickens, pigs, and vegetables, and sometimes bartered with neighbors for groceries and other items. They had four children Albert Jr., Edwin, Rita, and Robert.

Strakna went to St. Mary's Parochial School in Jewett City and was taught by French Canadian nuns. The nuns in his grade school taught the Polish kids to speak French and the French-Canadian kids to speak Polish. He had great experiences in Catholic school, learning French and Latin, and he excelled in music. He went to Griswold High School and graduated at the age of 16.

Edwin was about 18 when he joined the CCC. The program was designed to address the problem of jobless young men aged between 18 and 25 years old. He reported to his children that his CCC camp was the first truly "integrated" organization he ever was involved with. He said that most of the boys at Stafford Springs were either Polish-American, Portuguese-American, or African-American.

Interestingly, some of the Portuguese boys were dark-skinned, perhaps they were Cape Verdean, and when the Black boys first met them, they would ask, "You colored? You white?" The Portuguese boys always answered that they were white. The combining of these cultures made for some interesting stories. The African-American members of the camp thought that Edwin's hair, which was wavy and stuck up looked silly, so they gave him some pomade to flatten out his curls. Edwin was surprised to learn that some of the boys had to learn to wash their underwear more often, and they didn't shower often, saying that women preferred a 'manly smell.'

While he was in the CCC, Edwin learned to make corned beef hash, which became one of his signature dishes later. His photos show that he was working in the infirmary and clearing brush with a machete.

The weather at the CCC camp was colder than the weather on the coast of Connecticut, where he lived, and that when he took the train home to Jewett City, his friends would always make fun of him for being bundled up in warm clothing.

Edwin was very proud of the things that were built while he was in the CCC. He spoke of two specific projects; Beach Pond and Hopeville Pond. At Beach Pond, which straddles the border between Rhode Island and Connecticut, the CCC cleared excess vegetation and constructed bath houses and bathing facilities for the swimming area. Other projects involved clearing lots and building shelters for the public. The United States Government purchased the land for Hopeville Pond in the 1930s for recreational use. The CCC assisted with the construction of fire control ponds, forest roads, and adapting the Avery House for park use. When Edwin's family visited his parents in Jewett City, Edwin would take his family to these parks to show what he and his CCC camp worked on.

Edwin sent all of the money he earned at the CCC home to his mother to help the family. He was always very proud of his time in the CCC especially because he earned money for his family.

He joined the Navy in 1942 to fight in WWII. Dad was a 'sonar man' on the USS Terry DD-513. He participated in these campaigns: Battle of the Atlantic, 1943; Solomon Islands campaign, 1943-44; Mariana Islands campaign, 1944; and Battle of Iwo Jima, 1945.

After the war he went to the University of Connecticut under the GI Bill, earning a bachelor's degree. He then moved to Chicago and received a master's degree in Slavic Languages from the University of Chicago. In 1952 he married Christine Gellert, a Polish refugee in Chicago. Then they moved to Washington, DC where he worked for the Federal government as a translator. They had eight children: Gregory, Cecilia, Joseph, Theresa, Frances, Adam, Christopher, and Timothy.

Edwin began working at the CIA as translator in 1954. He worked during the Cold War and had the highest government clearance level. He retired early, but continued working as a translator doing contract work. During the 1980s, he worked with US Department of Justice Office of Special Investigations, interviewing Holocaust victims about Nazi war criminals living in the United States. Edwin really enjoyed being in the CCC. He and his wife went back to Connecticut to visit his old CCC camp. They often attended CCC reunions in Maryland.

Edwin Strakna passed away on July 28, 2014 at the age of 91, after a brief illness. He left eight children and 12 grandchildren. He lived a very full and interesting life and his family feels very lucky that he loved to talk about it.

Edwin worked in the Camp Conner Infirmary. Strakna Family

This photo shows Edwin (right) with four other recruits: "Nappy" (Fall River), Alex Reameau, George Hancock, and unknown. They were being processed at Fort Devens, Mass. in 1940. From here he was sent to Camp Conner in Stafford Springs. Strakna

"In the evening Dad played the guitar and sang – he was an accomplished musician." Strakna

CHAPTER 18
THOMASTON / BLACK ROCK STATE PARK

HISTORY

Camp Roberts was formed by Company 175 in Thomaston S-59, on May 30,

1933 at Black Rock State Park, 2 mi. SW of the city of Thomaston.

Black Rock derived its name from the mineral graphite that early settlers found in the Naugatuck Valley. Around 1657 settlers received the right to mine the black rock from the native Indians. Artifacts belonging to the Mohegan, Paugussett, and Tunxis tribes have been found at Black Rock State Park.[1]

In 1926 Connecticut received land for Black Rock State Park through the efforts of Black Rock Forest Incorporated, a citizen's conservation group that wanted to preserve woodlands.

Camp Roberts was located approximately 800' NW of present-day Black Rock Lake Dam in a field on the right side of Old Route 109. Black Rock Lake was across Rt. 109 on the left side. It was approximately 2 mi. to the camp's major work at Black Rock State Park.

Here is a description of establishing the camp in the 1937 First Corps Area, Fifth CCC District Yearbook.

"One afternoon in the month of May, 1933, a convoy of buses trailed slowly along the ravine penetrating Black Rock State Park and arrived at a clearing part of the forest. A large company of Connecticut boys clothed in Khaki, alighted and dropping their bags gazed on a scene which must have had a feeling of loneliness and despair. A large rocky ground, covered with stumps of trees, recalled to the imaginative mind long dormant, school memories of frontier days and our conquest of the West.

"After a hasty meal cooked over campfires, busy hands began the task of unloading tents and equipment. With the passing weeks vigorous exercise in the open air soon changed the physical appearance of the enrollees. Pale complexions turned to a healthy glow and hardened bodies, bronzed by the sun, offered a challenge to the winter to come." [3]

Captain Jules Paridaens supervised Company 175 in camp while Superintendent Homer C. Mead planned and supervised the outside projects.

During the fall local carpenters built permanent wooden buildings for the men for the coming winter. The buildings were positioned to create a quadrangle with a flagpole in the center of the green. Ornamental trees, shrubbery, and flower beds lined the borders. Enrollees gathered here in the morning for flag raising, roll call, and daily assignments. In the evening the men paid homage to the flag as it was lowered.

Camp Roberts' enrollees were involved in the

Thomaston CCC camp was named in honor of Harley F. Roberts (center wearing sweater & knickers), former headmaster at the Taft School in Watertown. This gathering was for a staff meeting in the Mattatuck State Forest (MSF) that Roberts helped establish when the Roberts' Black Rock Association donated the first land parcel to the state in 1925. This was the beginning of the MSF. DEEP State Parks Archives

Harley F. Roberts

The CCC camp was named for conservationist Harley F. Roberts (1861-1930) who was a teacher, assistant headmaster, and part owner of the Taft School, a preparatory school, in nearby Watertown. Roberts saw that most of the forests in the Naugatuck Valley had been destroyed and he lead the way by donating some land and securing gifts of land and money for Mattatuck State Forest. Black Rock State Park is part of that forest. He also helped organize and establish the Blue Trail System.

In 1912 the Taft School in Watertown became incorporated. Horace Taft (left) owned 5/6 and Harley F. Roberts owned 1/6 of the school.[2]

following work projects in the Naugatuck and Mattatuck State Forests: pest control, road building, fire control, and tree planting. The enrollees planted over 100,000 seedlings.

Enrollees constructed Spruce Brook Road that connects the Naugatuck town road with the Mattatuck Road. They also built picnic areas and swimming pools for public recreation.[5]

In August 1934 Camp Roberts produced its first newspaper, The Black Rocker. In the paper Capt. J. L. Paridaens stated that he was very proud of the staff for their work. Since the camp did not have a mimeograph machine like most CCC camps, the paper was professionally printed with the help of Mrs. F. H. Mattoon of the Thomaston Express. It had approximately four pages with three columns each. The staff charged 50 cents for a year's subscription and the newspaper sold ads to help defray the printing cost. Education Advisor, Donald B. Eddy, supervised the newspaper staff.[6]

The 1934 State Park and Forest Commission Report stated that in the Mattatuck State Forest 720 acres were cleared of dead wood, 695 acres were thinned, and 38 acres were cleaned for planting with the help of Camp Roberts.

The Bristol Press reported on July 29, 1933 that Camp Roberts was constructing trails through the Shade Swamp Sanctuary in Farmington. The enrollees also worked on eradicating gypsy moths. Crews scouted for egg clusters that contained several hundred eggs and killed them by coating them with creosote.[7]

Building roads sometimes required the use of dynamite to break up rocks. The Camp Roberts camp newspaper, The Black Rocker reported in the August 1934 issue that their camp had an outstanding dynamite crew. "With the assistance of Iantorna, Gatty, and Mills, Ace Dynamite men, Camp Roberts set an all-time record of 116 inches in 6½ hours. This was an average of over 18 inches per hour.

"The drills grew so hot from the incessant pounding that it was necessary to exchange them every few minutes in spite of the heavy gloves worn. Four drills were used up during the working period.

"This dynamite crew considers itself the best in the country. Camp Roberts invites competition."

The latter crew under foreman Hotchkiss was working near Watertown on what was called the "High Rock" project in the Mattatuck SF.

In December 1934 these enrollees were awarded certificates of merit for outstanding work by camp Superintendent Homer C. Neal: Louis Banatoski, Tylerville, surveying; John Breault, Bristol, road work; Theodore Cianchetti, Bristol, park work; George Gallagher, Bristol, moth and road work; Henry Nypert, Terryville, gypsy moth scouting; Edward Roche, Forestville, road

An aerial view of Thomaston CCC camp showing five barracks, a mess hall, officers' quarters and wash and shower room at the top. A flag pole stands in the quadrangle while the garages are on the lower right. Gary Potter

A 1935 group photo of Camp Roberts. Gary Potter

(L–R) 1 A camp cook ringing (part of a railroad wheel) to alert the enrollees that dinner was ready.[4] 2 This group is all dressed up to either go to town, see a movie and meet girls or ready to hitchhike home for the weekend. DEEP State Parks Archives

work; and Anthony Skinger, New Britain, gypsy moth and post exchange clerk. "Certificates of Merit Awarded CCC Workers." [8]

The U. S. Government sent vaudeville shows to CCC camps to entertain enrollees. In the winter 1934-35 theatrical groups visited Camp Roberts and performed four plays: "The Fall Guy," "One of a Family," "Friendly Enemies," and "The Whole Town's Talking." There were also two vaudeville groups that performed songs, dances, and jokes. [9]

Another source of camp entertainment was the Camp Orchestra composed of enrollees. They not only entertained their camp but performed at many outside functions: Camp Walcott, American Legion dances, Sons and Daughters of the Civil War Veterans in Bristol, and at radio station WTIC in Hartford. [10]

During the winter of 1934-35 the camp basketball team practiced on Tuesday evenings at the Taft School gym in Watertown and played at the Brooklyn Y quite regularly on Wednesday evenings. [11]

There was also competition outside in the snow having snowshoe races. Inside the rec. hall boys played checkers, bridge, set-back, and pinochle. Competition was fierce at the ping pong table. There was also a bowling tournament with work crew teams competing. [12]

Educational programs were held during the winter of 1934-35. Nature movies were shown during the winter on Tuesday and Wednesday evenings. [13]

In November 1935 these speakers gave lectures at Camp Roberts: William Greene, Director of Safety, at the Conn. Motor Vehicle Dept.; William Schofield, athletic coach at Crosby High School in Waterbury; M. Green from the local high school faculty; and attorney Keavney of Waterbury. [14]

The February 1936 issue of The Black Rocker reported that E. R. Hawkes from Camp White became the new camp superintendent. The other camp officials were: Lt. Pride, Commanding Officer; Lt. George R. Cunningham; Dr. Robert M. Oliver, physician; and Samuel J. Thornton, Education Advisor.

A few of the camp enrollees attended vocational training classes at the Waterbury Trade School. They made many wooden projects. [15]

After work and on weekends enrollees gathered around a radio in the barracks or rec hall to listen to music and sports. Their favorite shows in the order of their popularity were: Major Bowes Amateur Hour, Jack Benny, Rudy Vallee, Showboat, Fred Allen, Paul Whiteman-Bing Crosby, Burns-Allen with Ripley, Hollywood Hotel, Wallace Berry (Al Jolson), and One Man's Family. [16]

The March 1936 Black Rocker reported that the Education Dept. provided many interesting speakers. Sports editor of the Waterbury Democrat, John Cluny, spoke on these topics: creating good will at the Olympics and "Going to Press." Executive Secretary Conn. Prison Association, William D. Barnes, talked about rehabilitation and reform. Mr. Reilly of the Conn. Experimental Station told about blister rust and its prevention. The Personnel and Employment Manager of Scoville Mfg. Co. gave information on how to apply for a job, which was very helpful for these young men who desperately needed permanent work.

During the spring of 1936 Camp Roberts' enrollees

were busy getting ready for the sports season. The camp was one of the few Connecticut camps that had a soccer team. Herman Mainville, an enrollee and former player on the Plainfield A. C. Soccer team that was State Champions in 1935, was the camp coach. There was also softball intermural competition while the camp baseball team, coached by Dr. Frank Spindler, began practicing for competition with local CCC camps and town teams.[17] The young men were also busy playing volleyball and handball on the recreation field in camp.

At the District Woodchopping Contest at the Peoples SF on Aug. 17, 1936, Charlie Rood of Camp Roberts came in first place. On Sept. 7th Charlie went to the State CCC Championship at Stones Ranch in Niantic where he again came in first. His prize was baseball equipment and $10. He was then eligible to compete at the Eastern Sates Exposition in September where he came in second.[18]

When State Education Advisor, C. W. Gleason, visited Camp Roberts on Aug. 22, 1936, he praised Mr. Eddy on his education program that included these classes: Current Events, Auto Mechanics, Geology, Journalism, First Aid, Handicrafts, Dancing, and Orchestra.[19]

Camp Roberts also maintained the Naugatuck State Forest. It contained two large ponds, three gravel banks, and the three-mile Whittemore Rd. The road was named after the Harris Whittemore family of Middlebury and Naugatuck. The forest attracted thousands of picnickers, hikers, and campers. During the summer of 1936 enrollees also worked on constructing the Spruce Brook Rd. The mile-long road connects Whittemore Rd. with the Naugatuck town road that went up Hunter's Mt.[20]

In September 1936 foreman Herbinso's crew had a unique project. They were tearing down and removing the Diamond Match Co. mill in the towns of Oxford and Southford. The plant was approximately 1200 x 300' in size. The dam and the flume gate were to be untouched. Since the mill was located 30' below the highway, the crew had to build a bridge over a 30' wide gorge. The crew used roof trusses from the mill's boiler-house for the steel work. Wood from the engine room floor and boiler house roof were also used. The bridge abutments were built using 12 x 10' pine boards. When completed the bridge supported the loaded trucks. The crew began removing the brick walls and cleaned the bricks that were to be used in park construction. After a year of work it was hoped to make the area into a park.[21]

The Black Rocker newspaper reported in November 1936 the completion of the Naugatuck Dam in the Naugatuck SF. Mr. Bayette supervised the construction with the leadership of enrollees Charles Rood and his "Eight Horsemen." The dam measured 65' long, 2½' wide, and 11' high. It created a swimming pool. Foreman Bayette's crew under the direction of enrollee Gleason installed cobblestone gutters in the Naugatuck SF.

By the summer of 1936 four truck trails had been completed by the CCC enrollees. In the Naugatuck State Forest the Whittemore and Shepardson roads were built as well as a total of 4.1 miles of auto roads, 4 vehicle bridges, 43 forest roads, and 3 miles of hiking trails.[22]

In the Mattatuck State Forest the CCC constructed Gravestone Farm and Bacon Farm roads and also a total of 4.2 auto roads and 37 miles of wood roads used to remove timber and help in fighting fires. There were also 3 miles of trails for hiking.[23]

After the flooding in the spring of 1936, 130 enrollees were billeted at Camp Roberts and did relief work in the surrounding communities of Thomaston.[24]

The April 1936 issue of the camp newspaper gave the following camp administration information: Lt. Robert S. Pride, the commanding officer, was assisted by Lt. George B. Cunningham. E. R. Hawkes, the camp superintendent, was assisted by these foresters: C. H. Rogers, F. M. Nichols, A. Beardsley, V. Leonard, A. Rogers, W. H. Phelps, C. Hotchkiss, K. Bayette, and W. Mahoney. Frank Spindler was the camp physician and Samuel J. Thornton was the Education Advisor.

Samuel J. Thornton arranged for these lectures in April 1936. Gustave Bachmann, chairman of the State Temperance Union from Hartford, spoke on the subject, "Being Sorry Too Late." Reverend Sinclair, pastor of the Holy Souls Church in Waterbury and former missionary to China, talked about the ancient Chinese Empire. Lawrence Duryee, an engineer with the Connecticut Power and Light Co. in Waterbury, encouraged the enrollees to develop their talents in areas of interest. The final speaker, Arthur E. Blewett, an expert in nature studies, gave a talk, "The Amateur Naturalist." He encouraged the men to enjoy nature while working in the CCC and this joy should last a lifetime.

William Dorwin from the City of Waterbury's Park Department worked closely with the camp providing musical entertainment. The first concert was by the Stringed

Ensemble, an eleven-piece orchestra, which performed classical and popular music. The second concert was performed by the WPA Concert Band. Cosmo Vendetti led the musicians through a two-hour program of marches and popular ballads.

In the July 1936 issue of Black Rocker, Camp Roberts invited the public to view the road projects under the supervision of Foreman Hotchkiss. The first was Clark Rd. located one mile above Black Rock SP in the Mattatuck SF. Visitors could see the road lined with berry bushes, laurel, dogwood, and other flowering plants. Another road located above Black Rock SP is Jericho Rd. The largest project was near Beacon Falls where visitors could enjoy a picnic at the tables on Whittemore Rd. and swim in the two large waterholes that were also used in fighting fires.

Work crews led by foreman Hotchkiss worked on removing the brush and rotten timber on Bacon Farm Rd. In Beacon Falls foreman Bayette worked on the Spruce Brook Rd. [25]

In Oct. 1936 the camp enrollment was 128 men. Enrollees were kept busy playing inter-barracks touch football while some played basketball on the outside court. The latter were busy honing their skills for the upcoming winter basketball season. [26]

On Oct. 29, 1936 Camp Roberts' monthly dance celebrated Halloween in the camp's mess hall. Once again Hap Harrigan's Band furnished the music. Young ladies from the surrounding towns of Waterbury, Bristol, Thomaston, Naugatuck, Watertown, and Seymour helped make the dance a success. The boys decorated the hall with yellow, red, and orange trimmings. [27]

Foreman Leonard's woodchopping crew sent 200 cords of wood into camp during the month of November while Mr. Hotchkiss' road crew was busy clearing along Spruce Brook Rd. in December 1936. [28]

In December 1936 The Black Rocker reported that Chaplain Roy Honeywell obtained a movie projector for the camp. Thereafter the enrollees were able to enjoy a movie each week. At Christmas, Superintendent Hawkes provided a decorated Christmas tree and Reverend Jackson of the Thomaston Methodist Church led the enrollees in a group singing carols.

The camp newspaper cited the champions in the following fields: Debating-Bertier, Pool-LeRoy Mahew, Checkers & dancing-McNulty, Singing-Williams, Boxing-Fox and Davis, Basketball-Ciskowski, Ping Pong-Hillhouse,

Chess-Lamphier, Pinochle-Lashenka, Setback/pitch-Barry, Artist-Carpintino, Yodeler-DelBuano, and Entertainer-Davis.

During the winter Dr. Spindler, the camp physician, resigned to continue his education in New York City. The new physician, Dr. Oliver, not only helped the sick and injured but also gave courses in hygiene and general biology. In the spring he also coached the camp baseball team. The team played other CCC camps from Walcott, White, Cross, Robinson, Danbury, Hook, and Toumey and town teams from Waterbury, Thomaston, and Terryville.

On Jan. 21, 1937 Camp Roberts held their monthly dance in the camp rec hall and decorated the hall in red and gold. Young ladies from Waterbury, New Britain, and Beacon Falls attended and the "Hap" Harrigan Band provided the music. The dance was considered a great success. [29]

The February 1937 issue of The Black Rocker reported that the camp planned on doing forest stand improvement projects. Mr. Lenard supervised the work in Watertown and Mr. Cole was working in the Naugatuck SF in Beacon Falls. On Jan. 20, 1937 enrollees completed the 1.2 mi. of Spruce Brook Rd. in Plymouth. This project included a stringer bridge and a concrete slab culvert.

Thomaston Camp Roberts photos from the First Corps Area, Fifth CCC District Yearbook, 1937 showing some of the activities in camp.

The camp's education department offered vocational training in cooking and auto mechanics. Many enrollees took classes in mechanical drawing, printing, electricity, carpentry, and tinsmithing at Leavenworth Vocational Training School in Waterbury. The education director also organized these interesting classes: woodturning, drawing, wood-etching, photography, leather-craft, clay modeling, and life masks (a wax or plaster cast made of a person's face).

On Feb. 9, 1937 Dr. Ray Kienholz gave a talk on "Tree Identification." [30]

Joseph Jenkelunas, a FERA (Federal Emergency Relief Administration) instructor, taught the enrollees forward rolls, handsprings, hand-walking, and headstands. An undated The Bristol Press humorously reported: "If unsuspecting picnickers at Black Rock State Park next summer see scores of CCC boys swinging through the trees from limb to limb, Tarzan fashion, they can trace responsibility for these strange antics to the tumbling classes."

During the spring 1937 enrollees participated in these outside sports at these facilities: boxing ring and punching bag, volleyball court, horseshoe pits, and tennis court. [31]

With the arrival of new enrollees in the spring of 1937 a new round of education classes were available for the young men: agriculture projects, forestry, truck driving, leather crafts, rock collecting, auto mechanics as well as the basic skill classes of spelling, writing, and math. [32]

The springtime was a very busy season for the Camp Roberts fire crew. They were called out 25 times as reported in the April 1937 issue of The Black Rocker.

The camp provided entertainment for its members. There were weekly trips to town to go to the movies. The young men also formed a camp orchestra. They performed in the camp and at local towns. A dramatic troupe staged successful plays. Some of the talented enrollees were heard on WTIC radio station and performed at the YMCA in Hartford. [34]

The camp had monthly dances in the recreation hall and many boxing matches called "Smokers." Athletics was an important part of the camp activities. There were baseball and basketball teams that competed against other camps and town teams. The December 1936 Black Rocker reported that the camp had purchased a new basketball and shoes for the camp team. They hoped to also purchase new uniforms. On Tuesday evenings the boys practiced basketball at the Taft School in Watertown. They did ice skating and hockey across the road on Black Rock Lake.

In May 1937 weekly dance classes for the enrollees were held in the town of Thomaston. Local young ladies volunteered to be the instructors. [35]

During the spring 1937 Robert Fechner, Director of the Emergency Conservation Work, visited Camp Roberts and praised the camp for its appearance and work projects. He came for the dedication of the Stone House Museum built at the Peoples State Forest. [36]

Camp enrollees also participated in swimming, wrestling, tumbling, tennis, track, skiing, snow shoeing, and lifesaving. They also had pool tournaments in the recreation hall. [37]

Camp Roberts closed on Sept. 28, 1937. Most of the camp buildings were dismantled. The materials were used at Black Rock and other state parks. One building used by the Wigwam Gun Club remained in the 1960s but was later demolished.

Camp Roberts firefighting crew's equipment consisted of Indian tanks, brooms, axes, and consul rakes. During the spring the trained ten-man crew worked in or near camp and was ready to go as soon as the camp got a call for help. [33]

Route 109 is shown to the right of the Thomaston Dam that created Black Rock Lake by the U. S. Army Corps of Engineers.[38]

This is part of Black Rock State Park where CCC Camp Roberts built the pond, swimming area, and picnic area.

A trail in Black Rock SP leads hikers to historic black rock for a panoramic view of the park and surrounding area. Podskoch

In 1970 The U. S. Corps of Engineers completed the construction of a dam in the Naugatuck River Basin creating Black Rock Lake. Camp Roberts was located behind the Thomaston flood control dam and between the lake and below Rt. 109.

The Roberts Memorial, a natural monolith with a tablet to Harley F. Roberts of Taft School, is located near Black Rock Pond.

LEGACY

Today Black Rock State Park has 439 acres offering visitors swimming, fishing, picnicking, hiking, and camping with 96 sites.

Directions:

From Waterbury take Rt. 8 north and get off at Exit 38. Go east toward Rt. 6 west and Rt.109. At the intersection of Rts. 6 and 109 turn right and continue on Rt. 109 (Branch Brook Rd.). On the left you will pass the Thomaston HS and a large dam forming Black Rock Lake. After the high school you will go approximately 1.7 mi. and watch for a turn to the left onto Old Branch Rd. In the winter the road is closed but you can park in the parking lot and walk .7 mi. down towards the dam and the former CCC camp on the left. In the summer the road is open. Drive towards the dam and after .7 mi. look on the left for a narrow field that leads to the Camp Roberts site. Conservation Lake is on the left. All of the buildings are gone.

On Sept. 25, 2010 former Eastford CCC boy and employee at the Thomaston Dam and resident of Waterbury, John Collins, took Ted Renzoni and Marty Podskoch to the site of Camp Roberts. Here John and Ted are at the beginning of the entrance road to the camp just off the Old Branch Road and near Black Rock Lake. Podskoch

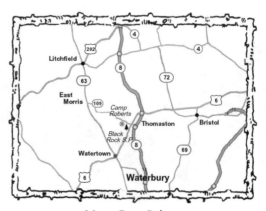

Map – Camp Roberts

MEMORIES

The August 1936 cover of the Black Rocker camp newspaper. These poems and stories are from the Black Rocker newspapers.

"Rookies Welcomed by Old Timers" by "Camp Trotter"

The rookies were welcomed wholeheartedly by the old timers on April 20, the day of their entrance into the camp. Long before they came the old timers planned a very entertaining surprise.

First on the program was getting all of them together, and marching them towards he flagpole. Then of course the new boys consented to play Indians and danced around the flagpole yelling something fierce. That was the best tribe of Indians the camp boys ever saw.

After they finished the dancing they were marched to the rec hall and there they sang all kinds of songs. Pretty good for the first time as most of the boys came from farms and never heard anything more musical than a bell on a cow.

After the musical program, the boys rendered solos.

After all this entertaining, the boys were all warm and so they decided to cool off a bit by taking a nice cold shower. As luck would have it five or six of them tried to back out of the shower saying they had theirs six months ago. But their pleading and begging fell on deaf ears.

Some of the boys got so excited after the bath that they went home, but later returned.

- Black Rocker, April 1936

"Mess Hall Manners" by Milton Morley

Every evening at 5 o'clock, the 175th Co. CCC get information for retreat. The flag is lowered and the men stand at attention. Then the command "Left Face" is given. Immediately one hundred and thirty men pivot as one and march with precision into the mess hall.

Upon entering they quietly take their places at the tables and wait for the signal to sit down and start eating. The order is given, the men sit down at their places and start passing the dishes to one another. There is no unnecessary noise and no loud talking. Each man takes his fair share and passes the dish on. When all have been served, they eat and talk quietly and joke among themselves. If there hasn't been enough food on the table to go around, the waiter is signaled and he gets another helping.

Upon finishing each man removes his knife, spoon, fork, cup, cereal dish, and plate and leaves it at a designated place. He then leaves the mess hall.

All but a few men at Camp Roberts do this. Those few know who they are. This is meant for you. Don't spoil our fine record.

- Black Rocker, Dec. 1936

These Camp Roberts' boys are taking a rest after working in the Mattatuck State Forest. DEEP State Parks Archives

"Beef Stew"
by Lou Grady

You get some beef and some carrots;
Some onions and a little celery too.
Cook them with spuds and string beans,
And you'll have some lovely beef stew.
On Monday they may feed us pork chops,
Spinach and a little gravy, too.
But the mess Steward will not be contented,
Until they feed us some beef stew.
This Dish may not sound delicious,
But it's eaten by kings and tramps.
It's served in hotels and lunch rooms,
But not like in the C.C.C. Camps.
We had a Mess Steward named _____
About meals he knew just what to do.
When the Mess had to save a little money
He would always serve us beef stew.
- Black Rocker, Feb. 1937

"Work"
by Lou Grady

I don't like to work in the summer
Because there's so much heat.
I guess I guess I'll have to though
To keep shoes on my feet.

I don't like to work in the winter
Because it is so cold;
But money jingling in my pockets
Makes me feel quite bold.

When flowers bloom I hate to work.
You know – in the spring
Because the birds up in the trees
Annoy me when they sing.

Some folks like to work in the summer,
Others in the fall. But me – somehow I don't seem
To like work at all.
- Black Rocker, Feb. 1937

Francis "Frank" J. Ciak

At a presentation at the Thomaston Library in 2008 I was showing pictures of CCC activities when a lady in the audience, Joan Savage, said, "That is my father in the picture of the photography club." We all turned to her as she continued, "When we were driving in the country he would say, 'See those trees. I planted them,' and 'See that road. I helped build it.' We didn't really understand what he meant at the time, but now I do."

After my presentation I encouraged Joan to ask the National Personnel Record Center in St. Louis for her father's CCC discharge papers. It would include when he signed, the camps he worked at, his jobs, and when he left the camp. A year later Joan called me to tell me about her dad's life and his time at the Thomaston camp.

"Dad joined the CCC on Jan. 9, 1935 in New London. He spent a week at Fort Wright on Fishers Island. On January 16 he was taken to Thomaston and became a member of Company 175. His records state he worked as alaborer doing reforestation work and that he received a satisfactory rating.

"My father said he joined the CCC because there wasn't any work. He quit Suffield High School in 10th grade to help his family. There were six other children in his family: Mildred, Sophie, John, Catherine, Stanley, and Tony. His dad was Joseph and his mom was Theresa.

"He told me that camp was difficult at times but he enjoyed it. He loved adventure and wasn't afraid to get his hands dirty. He worked hard. He was used to hard work because he started picking and planting tobacco when he was 7 years old.

"While at the camp Dad met Raymond Chagnon of

Frank Ciak was in the photography club (Back Row, Right) photo at Camp Roberts in Thomaston

Bristol, Conn. and they became good friends. They played basketball at camp. He and Dad were friends till dad died.

"In the evenings Dad and his friends walked to the center of town and went to the library. That is where he met my mother, Anna Shypinka. They went to movies and band concerts.

"On weekends he occasionally arranged for a ride or hitchhiked home to Sheffield. He liked to spend time with his brothers and sisters.

"Dad said the food at camp was boring. They ate lots of baloney and chipped beef on toast.

"For recreation Dad played baseball and basketball. In the summer he swam a lot at the lake in Black Rock State Park.

"While at camp dad signed up for some education classes. He completed a Red Cross first aid class. He also has a card stating he completed these classes: 'Conservation and Land Use,' 'Forest Protection,' 'Roads, Trails, and Structures,' and 'Tree Identification and Forest Life.'

"After serving a year Dad rejoined on January 31, 1936. He did road construction work and received an excellent rating. On Feb. 1, 1936 Dad was appointed assistant leader and received $36 a month pay.

"On April 29, 1937 Dad was honorably discharged. Dad was interested in getting married. Mom and Dad got married a little over a year later on July 16, 1938. They had two children: Francis and me.

"After leaving the CCC, Dad got a job at Plume & Atwood casting factory in Thomaston. He worked his tail off making steel. I saw him cry many times when he came home from work with blisters on his feet and hands. His job was pulling pots in the casting shop. When he came home he was bone tired.

"Next he worked for Solvents Recovery Service in Thomaston. He was the plant manager. When the 1955 flood destroyed his factory, it moved to Southington. Dad worked there till he was 50 years old when he retired because of ill health.

"Dad took me to where his camp was and to Black Rock State Park where he did a lot of work. He used to carry me across the Naugatuck River on his back because I was so small and he enjoyed pointing out his work.

"Dad passed away in February 1975.

"His work and experiences in the CCC helped him learn a lot about Mother Nature. He was always interested in the environment."

Joseph David DeGeorge

Valerie Amsel sent me this information about her father, Joseph David DeGeorge of Seymour, Conn., on March 6, 2014.

"My father was born on April 30, 1913 in La Crosse, Wis. His father was Joseph David DeGeorge Sr. and his mother was Frieda Harte. They had six boys: Fred, Perry, Clarence, Joseph, Elisha, and Woodrow.

"My father only went to 9th grade in high school possibly to help his family by looking for a job.

"When my dad was 20 years old he joined the CCC on May 30, 1933 and was assigned to Camp Roberts in Thomaston. His discharge papers state he planted trees, did survey and boundary work, gypsy moth removal, and helped construct many miles of truck trails. Dad was in the first group to work at Camp Roberts after Pres. Roosevelt started the CCC in 1933. He told me that in his free time he played tennis and sang in a barbershop singing group.

"He was there a little over a year and was discharged on June 30, 1934. Then he worked for Seymour Manufacturing as a store supervisor.

"On July 3, 1937 my dad married Josephine Louise Hurlburt. I was an only child.

"Dad was not eligible for WWII since he was born with Spina Bifida (incomplete closing of the backbone) although that never stopped him from very physical activity after having two surgeries.

"My father learned a good work ethic in the CCC which he passed on to all. He and his brothers talked little of their lives. He did, however, give a speech at one of his brother's funerals (which surprised all of us) about when his brother was hit by a car, and how happy they all were when he was able to come home from the hospital. His brother's children never knew about this."

Joseph David DeGeorge joined the CCC in 1933 and worked at Camp Roberts. He died on May 27, 2005 in Derby, Conn. Valerie Amsel

CHAPTER 19
TORRINGTON / BURR POND STATE PARK

Camp Walcott enrollees lived in Army tents while men constructed wooden barracks. CT CCC Museum

CCC boys taking a break from working on projects such as fighting fires, bug control, and road & trail building in the Paugnut SF. CT CCC Museum

HISTORY

Camp Walcott S-54 was established by Co. 176 on May 24, 1933 off Burr Pond Rd. approximately ½ mile west from Burrville Center on Rt. 8. The camp was located in a stand of hardwoods near Burr Pond in the Paugnut State Forest and was midway between Torrington and Winsted in the NW section of Connecticut.[1]

Enrollees lived in tents while wooden buildings were constructed. The young men moved into permanent buildings on Nov. 1, 1933. Most of the enrollees came from large towns and cities in Connecticut while 44 young men came from Massachusetts.[2]

Camp Walcott worked in the Paugnut State Forest and surrounding areas on the following projects: forest stand improvement, gypsy moth control, blister rust eradication, fire protection, and dam and road construction.

Paugnut State Forest (PSF) contains 1,702 acres and is located in four areas in north central Torrington. It abuts Burr Pond and Sunny Brook state parks. The main section of Paugnut totals more than 1,200 acres and was the site of Camp Walcott in Burr Pond SP. The forest honors the name of the local chief of the Newfield Indian tribe. When the chief saw his power, land, and prestige taken away by the Whites he sang a death song and plunged over the Robertsville Falls.[4]

Burr Pond dam dates back to Colonial days. The first dam washed out in 1840 and damaged the village of Burrville. The dam was repaired.

In 1851 Milo Burr rebuilt a log and earthen dam across the confluence of several mountain streams forming a pond that used water for power. The pond was named after Burr. A tannery and three sawmills constructed downstream consumed the pines and oaks from the surrounding area to

bioguide.congress.gov

Frederick Collin Walcott

The state named the Burr Camp to honor Senator Frederick Collin Walcott of Norfolk (1869-1949). He was a state senator from 1925 to1929, and a US Senator from 1929 to 1935. Walcott also served as the Connecticut Commissioner of Public Welfare from 1920 to 1946.[3]

meet the demand for lumber.[5]

In 1869 that dam was again damaged and repaired but over the years the dam was allowed to deteriorate because it wasn't needed for industry. In 1925 the state purchased the area and repaired the dam in 1926, 1929 and 1931. When Camp Walcott was established nearby the boys made repairs during the summer of 1933.[6]

When the state purchased the area the State Fish and Game Commission took over the jurisdiction of the pond and dam. They built a boathouse for the game wardens and stocked the pond.

In the spring of 1933 Burr Pond developed a large leak and most of the water escaped. A crew of enrollees cleared the underbrush on the sides of the pond while another group worked on repairing the dam. Another crew cleared a beach area and brought in sand for swimming. Enrollees also constructed a bathhouse.[7]

There were a few early projects at Camp Walcott. The first was the construction of the entrance road into Camp Walcott. They also built a three-mile trail around Burr Pond. Then they built approximately 2-mile Guerat Road through the center of the PSF. They also scouted the forests for gypsy moths.[8]

Another large project was the construction of a beautiful stone administration building. The enrollees were supervised by a stone mason.[9]

By June 1934 Camp Walcott had cut 127 cords of wood that were sold and 572 cords of wood for the camp, 160 posts, 271 poles, and 3,904 bd. feet of logs. Enrollees did silviculture work. They removed 77 acres of dead wood, thinned 341 acres, did 4 acres of reproductive cutting,

cleaned 18 acres for planting, and treated a total of 440 acres.[10]

On August 13, Capt. McCullough succeeded Capt. Benton as commander of Camp Walcott. During his year of service, he brought many improvements to the camp. He changed Barracks No. 5 into a recreation hall, laid foundations for buildings, planted grass and shrubbery around the camp, made gardens in the front and sides of barracks, completed the sheathing of the mess hall and kitchen, placed a life boat and life guard at the beach, made parking spaces for all the cars, erected signs and bulletin boards around camp, screened all windows, and installed a disposal plant for the kitchen.[11]

On March 26, 1935 Mr. Melius organized three eleven-man fire crews. Each crew had a foreman, 4 pump carriers, 4 water carriers, and 2 shovel and rake men. The crews were on call 24/7 and most of the Spring fires were in the Torrington vicinity. The boys' accumulated overtime was paid in days off after the fire season.[12]

In May 1935 enrollees were working at Haystak State Park on Rt. 272 in Norfolk. A crew was landscaping the entrance with pine and hemlock trees and laurel and juniper shrubs to prevent erosion and to add natural beauty. Another crew led by Maurice Visini was building a long steep wall along the road where there was steep cut into the mountain. The wall led to a parking area. A trail was planned that would lead to an old stone tower that gave the visitor a view of thee states.[13]

Also in May the camp baseball team began playing other CCC teams such as: Cross, Toumey, and White. There were other popular sporting activities such as pool

During the winter work crews from Camp Wolcott were busy searching for gypsy moth egg masses or doing silva culture in the Paugnut SF. CT CCC Museum

An enrollee sits on the entrance to the beautiful stone building that enrollees and skilled masons built. It was used as an administration building. The building was almost complete except for the stone stairway. Today the DEEP uses it for storage. CT CCC Museum

176th Company at Torrington, Conn.

A collage of some of the many activities at Camp Walcott.[14]

and ping pong in the rec hall.[15] The camp Forestry Dept. provided a nice wooden raft at the beach on Burr Pond for swimmers.

On June 2, 1935 one of Camp Walcott's enrollees, George L. Hickey, drowned in Burr Pond.[16] This tragic accident occurred just a few days before the camp administration started a program of swimming classes for all the camp enrollees. A certified swimming instructor, Cy Brunelle, first taught a group of 15 enrollees and after the swimming classes appointed them as assistant swimming instructors. Since camp Walcott was adjacent to Burr Pond the administration was concerned that no one would go swimming without proper supervision of an assistant instructor and only at certain times of the day. The enrollees were also taught the "Buddy System" so that there was always

someone present to give aid. The advanced swimmers had the opportunity to attain a Red Cross certificate. When swimming was permitted there was always an instructor on a boat to supervise the swimmers and they had to stay in a roped off area. [17]

Each Wednesday a vaudeville night was held with group singing and amateur performances to entertain the camp.[18]

Another form of entertainment was the Short Wave Radio Club. The members built their own radios and began talking to various parts of the world.[19]

On July 24, 1935 Camp Walcott held a Field Day that included foot races, wood chopping, and a tree identification contest. Then at the beach, Camp Walcott had a swimming contest with a team from Camp Hook in Danbury. After the competition a picnic was held at which 1,500 sandwiches,

Torrington / Burr Pond State Park

A group photo of Camp Walcott taken in September, 1935. Henry LeMay

75 gallons of punch, 5 crates of watermelons and 10 gallons of ice cream were quickly consumed.[20]

In the summer of 1935 Capt. James P. Walsh of Hamden became the new commander replacing Capt. McCullough. After two months Capt. Walsh left Walcott to lead a cadre of men to Oregon.

In October approximately 75% of the enrollees registered to take evening classes at Walcott College in Torrington. Some of the boys took three or more different classes. George Weiser and William Giglio of the Education Dept. at camp did a great job of planning and organizing the variety of classes and sites.

Every evening at 6:45 pm an Army truck took 20 men for high school classes at Torrington High School where they took Bookkeeping, Typing and Business classes. Their good attendance might have been attributed to the females in class.[21]

Enrollees also attended classes right in their camp. These classes were offered: Bookkeeping, Typing, English, Arithmetic, Accounting, Spelling, Current Events, and Journalism.[22]

In Oct. 1935 Capt. Hamilton left Camp Walcott after only two months in command. Although his tenure was

Camp Walcott men built this massive stone and earthen dam in 1936. They built a wooden bridge over the spillway for hikers walking on the trail around the pond. CT CCC Museum

brief the enrollees admired him for his work. He secured new football uniforms for the team and ran the best dances. He was replaced by Lt. Dittrich.[23]

The camp football team scrimmaged with two local high school teams. They lost 31-0 to Naugatuck and beat Torrington 6-0.[24]

In the fall of 1935 Camp Walcott held a Halloween Dance on Oct. 30,1935 at the Rialto Hall in Torrington. The dance began at 9 pm and a 10-piece orchestra and a vocalist provided the music. A waltz contest was held and the winning couple got a carton of cigarettes. For a half an hour the male wallflowers had the opportunity to get lessons from the ladies who taught them the popular dances: the "shag," "carioca," "polka," and "piccolino."[25]

On Nov. 8, 1935 Capt. Walsh returned from Oregon and assumed command again of Camp Walcott.[26]

In February 1936 Camp Walcott kept the young men busy during the winter evenings. There were classes in Handicrafts, Commercial Art, Photography, Carpentry, Model Airplanes, and Leather Crafts and there was a Dramatic Club.[27]

When the great flood occurred in March 1936 the enrollees rushed to save the Burr Pond Dam near their camp. They succeeded in preventing the south wing of the dam from giving way by using sandbags.[28]

Camp Walcott received praise for their work in doing relief work for the people of Hartford and New Hartford during the flood.[29]

A decision to make a stronger Burr Pond Dam was made and in June 1936 enrollees began excavation work for a modern dam. They excavated 1,256 tons of earth and 776 tons of rock. The new dam had 878 tons of concrete and 3,910 lbs. of reinforced steel. They also used 713 tons of masonry, 1800 tons of earth for fill, 202 tons of rock fill, and 403 tons of rip rap. Most of the work was done by

(L–R) 1 The survey crew was led by this forester who marked out roads and trails that were later built by Camp Walcott enrollees. A surveyor's transit is behind the forester. CT CCC Museum 2 Both LEM/foremen and enrollees drove Cletrac tractors in the Paugnut SF to build roads and move logs out of the woods. CT CCC Museum 3 Connecticut District camp administrators met at the Camp Walcott Administrative Building c.1936. Barkhamsted Historical Society

hand except for the moving of the large rocks that were moved by a homemade derrick. Although the work was done by novice enrollees, no accidents occurred during the construction. [30]

Camp Walcott had a positive effect on the development of the Paugnut State Forest. By July 1, 1936 there were 4.1 miles of automobile roads, 1 vehicle bridge, 7 miles of trail roads, 8 miles of foot trails. [31]

The camp football team had a slow start in Sept. 1936. In their first game with Camp White they lost 19-0. They hoped to improve by getting more practice and scrimmage games. The team acquired four more uniforms with a "W" on the jerseys. [32]

In September 1936 Capt. J. P. Walan was the Army C. O. assisted by Lt. Nelson Smith. Dr. J. V. DiRago was the camp doctor. W. O. Bruehl led the Education Dept. The following were the staff of the Forestry Dept: Superintendent R. E. Dexter, P. J. Demasi, Griffin, W. Rowe, and Ballarard (gypsy moth), Noble (engineer), L. R. Griswold (blister rust/silviculture), Wilcox and M. E. Visini (dam construction), G. Bardini (blacksmith), and A. Thompson (mechanic). [33]

In 1936 Camp Walcott was reclassified from S-54 to P-54. The camp went from a state forest to a park working camp. [34]

Also in 1936 Camp Walcott won awards for the best Mess Kitchen in District 5. All the cooks received their training right in the Walcott mess kitchen. [35]

In the April 1937 issue of the Walcott Warrior camp newspaper the Education Advisor, W. O. Bruehl, praised the 45 enrollees for their high attendance in Conservation Education courses. State Forester Hawes was

instrumental in providing information, films, and field trips for the instructors for these classes. Interest in the Aviation class attracted 33 enrollees. The carpentry shop was also busy with the young men making many projects. There was an Agriculture Program that was planned for the spring. A local farm donated a half-acre that was to be plowed for the enrollees to plant vegetables. Capt. Walsh conducted a Salesmanship course that helped prepare the men for a job in the business world. The course was very popular and attracted 77 enrollees. [36]

Camp Walcott was one of the first CCC camps to have a separate building used for educational purposes. It was called "School" and contained a printing room, darkroom for photography, a shop, and a radio shack. The education building was used as a reading room and a place to study. It was also used as a lecture hall where six conservation and 11

The cover of the Sept. 1936 Walcott Windbag

284

(L–R) 1 This level area near the old stone headquarters building is where all of Camp Walcott buildings were located. Today it is just a storage area. Podskoch 2 This pavilion on Burr Pond provides shelter to picnickers year round. Podskoch 3 Each year thousands of people enjoy the sandy beach and swimming in Burr Pond. Podskoch

other useful and popular classes were held. [37]

On May 28, 1937 the state closed Camp Walcott. Parts of the camp were retained because there was a pond nearby and they might have some future use. The camp was occupied temporarily by the US Geodetic Survey crew. [38]

In 1941 Camp Walcott was rented as a summer camp for boys and girls. The 1942 Report of the Connecticut State Parks and Forest Commission also stated that parts of Camp Walcott were retained by the state.

In 1943 the Conn. General Assembly appropriated $10,000 to develop Burr Pond for recreation. An approximately 2,000-foot road was built from the town road to the beach and a parking area for 50 cars was constructed. Then 200 cu. yds. of sand were brought in for a beach. [39]

Burr Pond was designated as a state park in 1949.

LEGACY

Camp Walcott had a tremendous effect in the development of Burr Pond into a favorite destination for

hiking, fishing, boating, swimming, and picnics. Their hard work produced a sturdy dam that has endured for 80 years. It has provided a beautiful body of water for swimming and fishing. The CCC trail around the pond is great for hiking. Visitors enjoy the park facilities year-round and it is a great place to get the whole family back to nature.

Directions:

From Waterbury take Rt. 8 north and travel 24.6 mi. to Exit 46. At end of the ramp, take a left onto Pinewoods Road. At the first stop sign go left onto Winsted Road. Follow Winsted Rd. for approximately 1 mile and take a right at the blinking yellow light (turn is marked with a park sign). Drive .5 mile up hill on Burr Pond Rd. Burr Pond SP is on the left. Drive on park road to large parking area on the left. Go to the left section of the parking lot and you will see a beautiful stone building. This was built by the CCC boys and the long narrow space in front of the stone building is where the barracks and other camp buildings were located. The address to the park for your GPS is 385 Burr Mountain Rd, Torrington, CT.

During the 1930s CCC enrollees built the trail around Burr Pond and visitors have been enjoying the picturesque walk for the past 80 years. The following are available at the park: bathrooms, a boat launch, food concessions, picnic shelter, and picnic tables.

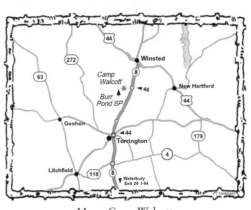

Map – Camp Walcott

MEMORIES

This group of six skinhead Walcott enrollees may have been the result of an initiation for the rookies coming to camp.
CT CCC Museum

"Impressions of a Rookie" by Charles McDonald

The day had arrived. The day that was to mark my entrance into the adventure and excitement of the C.C.C. camps. I could hardly wait for the hour when I was on board the train for New Haven, the first stepping stone leading to the seemingly very near camps of Connecticut. I had often heard and read that the C.C.C. fellow was referred to as being "the cream of the youth in these glorious United States." Soon I was going to find out for myself whether it was just mere talk.

I arrived at New Haven fully an hour ahead of time so that I would stand no chance of missing my golden opportunity. I entered the recruiting office, handed in my application, and then I was told to stand in a room until I had been given my physical examination. Following the examination, we were given a ticket, it was supposed to be good for a meal. I've often wondered what the meal was supposed to be good for?

Having partaken of the meal we were rushed aboard the train for New London. By this time, I was wondering whether I had joined the Navy to see the world or whether I had really joined the C.C.C. It was at New London that the rushing really started. We were checked in at the dock and then loaded aboard the ferry for Fort Wright. Upon arriving at the fort, we were marched to the barracks, where much to my disappointment we were ordered to remain in the barracks for the night. Later in the evening we were given another examination during which we received a 'jab' in the arm, which at that time seemed very slight to me, and so to bed.

The following morning when I awakened I found my arm stiff and sore from the jab of the preceding night. The hard-boiled sergeant didn't seem to mind it at all (After all he hadn't received the 'jab') and rushed us to the ferry which set out for New London.

We were rechecked at New London and paid off with the magnificent sum of eight cents that being our salary for one day's work. Then we were measured for our clothes, which I thought (after all, I was a rookie) would be perfect fitting. I certainly took a fit. Clothes of all sizes and shapes were thrown at us. The sergeant paid no attention to all of our sundry complaints, but ordered us to put them on and 'make it snappy.' We donned our non-descript uniforms and appeared in the yard looking like the misfit China Army. The sergeant then rushed us aboard another train. Then we were put on a bus at New Haven which dispatched us to Torrington and Camp Walcott.

Sure! I'm having plenty of excitement and the adventure is unbearable. After the newness wore off, I began to like the life, and now I was taking classes and lauding the C.C.C.
- Walcott Windbag, May 1935

"On Second Thought" by Ladislow Trucinski

The CCC life is not an easy one, men!
Sometimes things go wrong and we think
It's tough,
But it's worth all of the time we put in it;
And it's not a place for those who bluff.

Sinewy, broad shouldered men are they,
Real honest to goodness he-men.
Who are well-mannered gentlemen, too,
Now fighting for Uncle Sam again.

These men are the ordinary run of the mill.
Some are dumb, some are smart;
They enjoy singing, dancing, the movies and
Are not averse to affairs of the heart.

When you see them walking down the street,

They seem carefree, footloose, and free,
Their troubles are discarded for the moment;
Only their smiling faces do the people see.

But theirs is a job of great magnitude;
The destiny and future of America is theirs.
With a half a million men on the conservation battle
front,
Already fine fruit for their labor bears.

So give a cheer for these boys in khaki.
Theirs is not to ask but to do a job well,
And when the time comes for them to leave,
Their services will be easier to sell.
So give a thought to the boys in the CCC
Who someday the rulers of our land will be.
- Walcott Windbag, Nov. 1935

CCC enrollees being inspected by the company
captain. CT CCC Museum

On June 2, 1935 one of Camp Walcott's enrollees, George L. Hickey, drowned in Burr Pond. This poem was written by Frank W. Marinelli.

In Memory of George L. Hickey

Your gentle face and patient smile,
With deep sadness we recall,
You had a kind word for everyone,
And you are missed by all.

Mute is your voice, and still
The heart that loved us true,
Ah! Bitter and harsh the trail,
To part from one so good as you.

We miss you. Our hearts are sore.
As time goes by we'll miss you more.
Your cheery smile, your smiling face-
No one will ever fill your place.
- Walcott Windbag, June 1935

William Henry LeMay

In 1989 William LeMay celebrated his 50th wedding anniversary with his wife Elaine. He worked at two CCC camps, Burr Pond and East Hartland. Joyce Pelletier

On May 18, 2012 Joyce Pelletier of Colchester, Vermont contacted me by email and said that her father, William Henry LeMay, was in the CCC. She sent me the following information about her dad.

"My father, William Henry LeMay, was in two camps, Burr Pond and East Hartland. I only know a little about his life prior to my birth. The following is what I know.

"He was born in Warren, Rhode Island in 1914. His parents were Wilfred Napoleon LeMay and Roseanna Plante LeMay. Their first child, Wilfred was born in 1901. The next three children Emilia (1902), Napoleon (1903), and Lodia (1908) died at birth. Then came Emile Jean (1909-98), and William Henry (1914-98). The next two Irene and Alcide died at birth. Omer was the last child to live (1920 -2005). Many more children were born and died at birth or miscarriages to the total of seventeen in all. Records of the remaining children have never been found.

"My father only went to 6th grade. His family moved around a great deal. They lived in Rhode Island, Massachusetts, and Connecticut. William worked at many

William Henry LeMay (middle) in a Camp
Walcott photo in 1935. Joyce Pelletier

different trades before he joined the CCC. He had his own
shoeshine business, sold newspapers at the age of nine, and
worked in a meat plant.

"Desperate for work in 1935 Dad heard about the
CCC. I believe he read about it in the newspapers. He
joined in September 1935. He went to Burrville and worked
in Co. 176 at Burr Pond, where he stayed for some time.

"When he was discharged, he went back to Hartford.
Later he rejoined the CCC ranks in East Hartland. I believe
this was 1938.

"He married Elaine Caye on Sept. 9, 1939 in Windsor,
Conn. They had two children, David and me.

"After they married, they lived in Hartford until 1942.
When David was in poor health they moved out of the city
to Tariffville, which was part of Simsbury.

"From approximately 1940 until 1979 he worked for
three companies. He mainly worked at Pratt & Whitney
Aircraft as a tool and die maker. Later he did machine repair
work at Fuller Brush Co. When Fuller Brush moved to the
Midwest, he went to work at Grote and Weigel in Windsor,
Conn.

"When I asked Dad why he wasn't in the military
during WWII, it was because he worked at Pratt & Whitney
and that gave him a deferment.

"Dad developed lung cancer in the mid-1970s. It was
probably because he started smoking at the age of nine. He
recovered after surgery and was cancer free until his later
years when he had COPD (chronic obstructive pulmonary
disease).

"He retired from Grote and Weigel in 1979. My
parents remained in Tariffville until 1994. Then they
moved to South Burlington, Vermont to live near me and
my family.

"Dad's life was hard, but he always managed to find
some kind of employment. His favorite job was when he

worked in the CCC, since he felt camaraderie with all those
who served with him. He believed that he learned the most
about life while serving at Burr Pond. His other favorite job
was with Fuller Brush.

"My father died on Sept. 12, 1998."

Stanley "Kit" Kaczmarczyk

Stanley "Kit" Kaczmarczyk at his home on Alder Street,
Bristol, CT in approx. 1939. Carol Carter

On March 8, 2009 I received an email from Carol
Carter of Bristol, Conn. She said her father was in the CCC
camp at Burrville and that she had his discharge papers and
a photo.

After contacting her and telling her I was very
interested, she sent me this information.

"My father, Stanley 'Kit' Kaczmarczyk, was born
on Oct. 14, 1914 in Bristol, Conn. His father was Jan
(John) and his mother was Anna Dabkowska. They had
six children: Anna, Rose, Stanley, Jennie, Pauline, and
William. Dad's mother died in 1918 when he was only four
years old. So life was hard for his father and children.

"As a teenager during the spring and summer he worked
at Zarella Farms in Plainville, CT. Dad graduated from
Goodwin Tech in in New Britain where he was enrolled in
a trade program that qualified him to work as a toolmaker.
Several times Dad said he was encouraged to sign up for the
CCC by friends and family members because this job would
help support his family. At that time he was unemployed
and jobs were scarce. His father was also unemployed, not
in good health, and working only sporadically.

"Later my father moved to Plainville, Conn. where he signed up for the CCC on Oct. 16, 1933. He was 19 years old. His records show that he had experience as a tool and die maker. Perhaps he learned these skills at his technical high school. According to his discharge papers he spent two days at Fort Wright. This is where the boys got their physicals and clothing. He then was transported to Torrington, Conn. and taken by truck to Camp Walcott Co 176 in Burrville.

"Although he never expressed his feelings about leaving home, he sometimes said that he missed his family during that time. He often spoke about how cold that winter was.

"He thought the food was pretty good at camp. During the 1990s, pumpkin soup became the latest food fad. He would get this look on his face when he saw it on the restaurant menu. When questioned, he said that one winter (he never said what year) money was so scarce, that the family lived on pumpkin soup. Until the day he died, pumpkin always brought a frown to his face.

"Dad's nickname was Kit. His last name was frequently mispronounced and the first syllable was pronounced as Kich, but the proper pronunciation was more like Kaz. He was known as Kitchie (later shortened to Kit) and he was the catcher during his school years. When the weather was warm, or when there was no snow on the ground, Dad played a 'pick up' game of baseball at camp.

"On weekends he went home if he could get a ride with someone, or if he had money he went home on a train.

"He sometimes talked about a friend who had a motorcycle. This friend would provide him with a ride home on weekends and then pick him up and they would drive back to camp. From the way he spoke about these weekends, I'm not sure whether they were allowed to do this. I cannot recall the name of the friend with the motorcycle, but I can recall that the motorcycle was what was called an 'Indian.' I understand that today it is a collector's item. Sometimes he said those rides back on the motorcycle were very cold and scary, especially on the icy roads.

"In the evenings or weekends that he didn't go home he said he played cards.

"He worked as a laborer and did reforestation work. His work was rated 'satisfactory.'

"On March 31, 1934 he was discharged because his time of service, six months, was up. The Army provided him with transportation from Torrington to Plainville, Conn.

"When Dad came home he found a job as a tool and die maker at Handee Mfg. Co., in Hartford where they made industrial springs. (Many Connecticut companies make various springs for the automotive, medical, firearms, and aerospace industries). Connecticut still has a very active spring industry.

"My father married Jennie Pietrowski on Sept. 7, 1936 at St. Stanislaus Church in Bristol. They had five children: Carol, David, Paul, Paula, and Janet.

"Dad wasn't in WWII because he was exempted from the draft when the war broke out. His job which was critical to the war production and he had two children. My parents often talked about the long work days and work weeks during the war. He left home early in the morning and many nights did not return until 9 or 10 pm. During the weeks that he worked a 'normal day' 7 to 5, he then worked Saturdays and Sundays.

"In 1958 my parents moved to Cranston, Rhode Island and one evening he told us the story about his motorcycle rides back to the camp. That was when he casually mentioned his participation in the CCCs at Burr Pond. During the winter Dad occasionally did some ice fishing with his brothers-in-law at Burr Pond. Spring and fall his fishing partners were his brother-in-law Walt and Walt's wife Jean. Our family swam and picnicked at Burr Pond State Park many Sundays during the summer. Several times my Mom would suggest going to Black Rock State Park. It was a shorter drive there. Dad always insisted on Burr Pond. I think that indicates his pride about the work he had done there and that he cared about the area around Burr Pond.

"From my perspective one of the benefits dad received from working in the CCC was his ability to select and care for trees and shrubbery for transplant in his yard. Before my parents bought their first home, they bought a cottage on a lake. The cottage was bare minimum housing no electricity or indoor plumbing, but they loved summers there. When they purchased their first home, trees and shrubbery were lacking on the property. Early in the fall, just before they closed the cottage, he would go out in the woods and dig up a tree and a mountain laurel to transplant. The trees still survive and so do the mountain laurels. By the way, mountain laurel is the state flower and it is illegal to uproot them in their natural state. Every time he did this, on the way home us kids were terrified that we would be arrested.

"Dad retired in 1977. He died on Oct. 14, 1997 in Cranston, RI."

Edward J. Baczek

Ed and Ester Baczek in 1944. Ellen Amodeo

On Nov. 21, 2008 I received an email from Ellen Amodeo that stated she had read an article in the New Haven Register about my research on the CCC camps in Conn.

"I am the daughter of Edward J. Baczek of Derby who served in the CCC. I don't know which camp he was assigned to but it was near Windsor according to my mom who is 94 years old. I recall my father talked about hitchhiking a ride to where he was assigned. He and his friend would stop for a pizza which was 25 cents. I think my dad's work involved building stone walls or some kind of masonry, but I'm not sure. I just learned, too, that mom's brother, John Natowich of Ansonia, and Dad's best friend was also in the CCC. I hope to come to the dinner at Grassy Hill Lodge in Derby to hear your talk so that I can learn more about the CCC."

Ellen did come to my talk by on Nov. 24, 2008 sponsored by the Derby Historical Society. I told her how to send away for her dad's discharge papers.

Ellen secured her dad's records and also did family research and this is what she learned about her father's life.

"My dad, Edward Joseph Baczek, was born in Shelton, Conn on Nov. 14, 1915. He was the second of the six children of Alexander and Kamila Baczek, immigrants from Poland who arrived in America in the early 1900s. Ed had an older sister Sophie and younger brothers Frank, Zygmunt, Joseph, and a younger sister Helen. The family lived mostly in the Naugatuck Valley cities of Shelton and

Derby although for a while in Waterbury so my grandfather would be closer to his work at American Brass.

"My grandfather would save his earnings and buy houses so he would have rental income. At one time, I believe my grandfather owned land in Oxford. For many years the family homestead would be a farm of approximately seventeen acres in Derby, not far from the Housatonic River.

"My father was around 16 years old when the family moved to the farm. The farm consisted of a house built in the 1800s, a large barn, and several smaller buildings. There was a small orchard with apple trees and one pear tree. My grandfather had milking cows, chickens, and at least one horse so he could plow the farmland.

"According to a story told by my grandmother to my mom, Dad did well in school, even skipping a grade because of his academic ability. Dad's last school was Shelton Jr. High but he left sometime close to graduating Grade 8 to go to work.

"According to his CCC application memorandum, my dad's usual trade or occupation was farm work. He had worked for four years at a farm in Derby for a Mr. Kotkowski earning $5.00 a week and room and board. He then worked for two years as a printing apprentice with a weekly wage of $5.00.

"Also, listed was Dad's last job before joining the CCC. Dad worked for a few weeks at a riding school in Washington, Conn. where he groomed, exercised, and fed horses. Once again he earned a $5.00 weekly wage. His CCC discharge papers state his additional occupations and hobbies: horses and football. He had been unemployed since August 1933 when he would have been close to his eighteenth birthday. Dad probably heard about the CCC from the local valley newspaper, The Evening Sentinel or perhaps from friends.

"Dad's CCC application was stamped on Oct. 9, 1933 and he was directed to report to the US Army Authorities at 6 Church St., New Haven. His closest relative was listed as his mother, Kamila and she would receive his $25.00 monthly wage.

"Then he was sent to Fort H. G. Wright in New York for conditioning. His height was listed as 65½ inches, his weight was 142 pounds, and his eyesight was listed as 20/20. He received the usual inoculations.

"After satisfactorily completing conditioning, Dad was assigned to Company 176, Paugnut State Forest in

Torrington, Conn. According to the dates, Dad must have been with the first group of enrollees at Camp Walcott.

"Being at Camp Walcott wasn't the first time Dad lived away from home. He worked and boarded at a nearby farm in Derby and then lived at a riding school in Washington, Conn. Camp Walcott was the longest distance away from the family home. I'd imagine Dad experienced a sense of adventure. Dad was quiet but sociable – he especially enjoyed talking about gardening.

"I remember my dad talking about being assigned up-the-line in the 3 Cs, his phrase for northern Conn. But I never knew the actual location until I sent for his paperwork.

"I don't have any information or photos about Dad's actual time in camp, but my mom said that he learned how to cut hair in camp. This was a skill he used throughout his life. He would cut my uncles' hair, his brothers', and his brother-in-law's plus his nephews.'

"At camp Dad said he played the trumpet. I remember he would call it the cornet. Dad must have had music lessons in school.

"After serving his two 6-month periods of enrollment, Dad was honorably discharged from the CCC in December 1934. Like his fellow CCCers, he was gaining weight – in Dad's case, 142 lbs. to 149 lbs.

"Dad later worked as a welder for the American Brass Company in Ansonia. Perhaps he learned the rudiments of welding at camp.

"In 1941, he married my mother Esther Natowich, the daughter of Ukrainian immigrants. They had one daughter – me. I was an only child.

"The Natowich family lived about a mile away from our home in Derby on a small farm in Ansonia. My father was close friends with my mother's brother, John, who was my dad's age. My dad's brothers were also friends and fellow athletes with my mom's brothers. I learned last year that my mother's brother, John, was also a CCC boy serving at Camp White in the Peoples Forest in Barkhamsted. I would hear my dad talking with my uncle about his days in the CCC.

"Dad served in the US Navy in WWII. He was stationed at Kaneohe Bay in Hawaii where he was wounded and received a merit of commendation. He was honorably discharged with a rating of Fireman First Class.

"I remember Dad attending a CCC reunion – I believe it was somewhere near New London. I recall how he was very excited about attending this get-together. I may have the poster he brought home from this reunion.

"Along with being a skilled welder, (he was often referred to as Eddie the Welder), Dad was an excellent plumber, a skill he learned in the Navy. He was also a fine carpenter and mason. He did all the stonework for the foundation of his house in Ansonia. He may have learned masonry in the CCC and later perfected his masonry skills, learning from coworkers at the American Brass.

"Whenever anyone needed help – plumbing, welding, setting up scaffolding to paint a house, etc. Dad never said no. To this day, I don't know how he did everything – holding a full-time job, keeping up the family homestead in Derby along with his own house, and lending a helping hand to family and friends. When my husband and I built a house on the family farmland, my dad and a friend did all the plumbing. Dad also did the tile work in the kitchen and put in the concrete sidewalk. Nothing made him happier than the churn of his cement mixer.

"Dad was an avid gardener and he would always be telling my husband and me to plant fruit trees. He planted several fruit trees in our backyard that he transplanted from the family homestead. Dad was chopping wood, into his late seventies. His favorite saying was, 'A little hard work never hurt anyone.'

"Both my dad and Uncle John passed away due to lung cancer, the result of working in the American Brass. Both passed away months apart. Dad passed away, two days after his 83rd birthday, on Nov. 16, 1998 at the Veterans' Hospital in West Haven. He was accorded full military honors at his funeral service."

CHAPTER 20
TORRINGTON / WEST GOSHEN / MOHAWK STATE FOREST

HISTORY

On May 27, 1933 Camp Toumey S-52 Co. 173 was established when the enrollees arrived and set up tents in Mohawk State Forest (MSF) in West Goshen, Conn.[1]

Camp Toumey's main work was in the 3,400-acre Mohawk State Forest. It is the sixth oldest forest in the state. It is located in the southern Berkshires of Litchfield County covering the towns of Goshen, Cornwall, and Litchfield. The forest began in 1921 when the White Memorial Trust donated 250 acres to the state. It got its name indirectly according to Harriet Lydia Clark's, History of East Cornwall. Although the Mohawk Indians did not live there, a legend said that local Indian tribes lit signal fires on the summit of the mountain to warn tribes to the south that the Mohawks were approaching.[3]

The first camp commander was Capt. Allen. He was followed by Capts. O'Leary and Austin. Under Austin's command Camp Toumey was awarded the Honor Flag in January 1935. On Feb 2, 1935 Capt. Hagstrom assumed command. Lt. Dehm took over command in May 1935. Lt. Killen took over in January 1936. Capt. Columbia and Capt. Earl H. Marsden took command in 1937.[4]

Superintendent Herbert J. Ord supervised a large road project at the end of the summer in 1933. It was a new entrance to the Mohawk SP. The state had to rent a right-of-way into the park but by building their own entrance on state-owned land, it cut the cost out of the park budget. Road work continued till the middle of January. 1934 when

Enrollees of Co. 173 pitched their tents in Mohawk State Forest in West Cornwall in 1933. Conn. CCC Museum

heavy snow curtailed construction. The crew then spent three months cutting a line in the forest for fire protection. Road work continued in April 1934. Gravel for the road was brought from gravel pits at Mt. Tom SP.[5]

During the road construction there was a terrible accident when workers were using dynamite. Joseph Roskosky of Terryville was seriously injured when he did not understand a signal during dynamiting. He was taken to the Walter Reed Hospital in Washington where he was given excellent medical treatments and recovered well but he lost the use of one eye. Joseph returned to his camp and worked as a sub-foreman.[6]

In 1934 Camp Toumey's men almost completed the construction of Toumey Road. It began at the Rt. 4 (Bunker Hill) and continued for 2.5 miles to Mohawk Mountain where the fire tower was. At the summit

Sleeping Giant Park Assn.

James W. Toumey

Camp Toumey S-52 in West Goshen was named in honor of Yale Professor James W. Toumey (1865-1932) who was a strong advocate of developing Connecticut's forests and parks.

The camp was named for Professor James W. Toumey (1865-1932) who was the second dean at the Yale School of Forestry. In 1933 under his leadership of the Sleeping Giant Park Association, the land for the park was purchased.[2]

A Nov. 1933 group photo of Camp Toumey. The new barracks are above the group. Gary Potter

(L–R) 1 In May 1935 Lt. Dehm became the new the new camp commander replacing Capt. Hagstrom. Mancuso Family 2 By the winter of 1933 Camp Toumey enrollees had a warm building to sleep in. This was barracks D which had two wood stoves and housed 40 men. Mancuso Family 3 Camp Toumey used a lot of gravel to build roads. The enrollees are loading a truck with shovels. Conn. CCC Museum

enrollees developed a parking area for visitors. Enrollees constructed 10 fireplaces with tables, and 20 toilet facilities along Toumey Rd. They also placed tables where no fires were allowed.[7]

By June 30, 1934 enrollees had improved the condition of the ranger's house which was an old farmhouse. They constructed a new fireplace and chimney, installed hardwood floors, and removed wall partitions. Then they moved a barn and repaired it, to make a machine shop. The final project was the construction of a 20 x 40' warehouse for the camp equipment and a lumber shed for storing sawed lumber from the forest.[8]

On a high hill above the picnic area on Toumey Rd. stands the stone observation tower. The enrollees built it between 1933-34. It is a small circular stone tower. Stone steps with a wooden handrail lead up to the tower. From the tower hikers could see a wooden tower to the N on Lookout Mt. and the hills of southern Massachusetts, and to the west the Catskill Mts.[9]

After one year of work Camp Toumey had been very productive in its forestry work. By June 30, 1934 they had cut 623 cords of wood for fuel and harvested 332 wood posts, 37 poles, and 31,578 bd. ft. of logs. Their silviculture work was also superb. They cleaned 210 acres of deadwood, thinned 383 acres, did reproductive cutting on 40 acres, and cleaned 82 acres for planting, which totaled 715 acres of treated forest.[10]

One of the first tragedies to occur in the Connecticut CCC camps happened in October 1934. While working at Camp Toumey Michael Babier, 19, of Milldale was hit by a falling tree and died. The Goshen medical examiner, Dr. Bradford Walker stated his death was caused by a fractured School. The story was reported in the Nov. 30, 1934 Camp Cross Chronicle. Some of the CCC boys attended the funeral.

During the 1934 tourist season Mohawk State Park was rated as the second most popular camp in Connecticut. In first place was Peoples State Park.[11]

It was not all work and no play for the enrollees in Camp Toumey. The Army provided recreational activities such as baseball, basketball, track, and football. They played other CCC camps and local town teams.

During the winter of 1934-35 the basketball team played in the Litchfield County Tournament. The team also

(L–R) 1 Stone Observation Tower DEEP 2 Camp Toumey enrollees built a road and parking lot to the Mohawk Mt. fire tower that was built in 1922. www.cornwallhistoricalsociety.org

played other CCC camps. There was also inter-barracks competitions that were held at a town recreation hall. There was a boxing team and wrestling team that competed against local CCC camps such as Camp Cross. [13]

A spring dance was held on March 28, 1935 from 8:30-12:30 at the American Legion in West Goshen to honor the new camp commander, Capt. Hagstrom. Buses brought young women from the Torrington area. [14]

The Education Advisor J. S. Bissell scheduled Amateur Night on Wednesday evenings. There were also Smokers held occasionally that included boxing and singing and instrumental numbers. Bissell had three other instructors. W. J. Flynn from Portland, a UCONN graduate, taught English, Current Events, and Arithmetic, and he also coached basketball. A. Weinstein taught Algebra, Dramatics, French, Dancing, and Writing One-Act Plays. J. Cerasole was another instructor. Some of the foremen, officers, and enrollees taught classes such as Photography, Leather-craft, Radio, Typewriting, Model Airplanes, Forestry, Conservation, etc. [15]

As summer approached the May/June 1935 issue of the Mohawk Lookout reported that Camp Toumey's enrollees got their gloves, bats, and balls and began practicing. The camp team played the other CCC camps such as Roberts,

A collage of camp activities and work at Camp Toumey. [12]

The History of Co. 1106-V

Camp #	Camp Name	Date Began	Town
CE-1	Wilson	7-8-33	Barre, VT
P-61	Jefferson	11-5-34	N. Whitefield, ME
CE-11	Charles M. Smith	7-15-35	Waterbury, VT
S-52	Toumey	10-22-38	Goshen, CT
S-66	Beantown	7-26-41	Stockbridge, MA

Co. 1106 had a long and illustrious history. It originated at Fort Devens, Mass., on June 28, 1933. Maj. Floyd D. Carlock, US Infantry was in command of the Veterans. After ten days of conditioning at Devens, they joined the other Veteran companies who were already working on the East Barre dam. They arrived at CCC Camp Wilson and were greeted with a vicious storm.

They worked in Vermont with nine other CCC companies building a dam to control the Winooski River that had caused much flooding in the past.

The Veterans pitched their tents and worked on the camp site. They were preparing it for ten companies that would total 2,500 men and who would arrive soon.

They were armed with axes, shovels, picks, grub-hoes and bars. The veterans went to work removing trees, brush, rocks, and soil until they reached rock on which the main foundation for the dam could actually be started.

Four other companies of about 200 men each dug a 600-foot trench for the conduit (pipe) that would carry the water through the dam. The work was done mostly by hand. The men used 600 wheelbarrows as well as numerous picks, shovels, sledges, and drills.[30]

By the end of October, 1933 the Veterans were assembling the steel base for the dam's outlet and had started pouring cement. As work progressed, in January 1934, Companies 1106, 1108, and 1111 were transferred to the Websterville quarries where they worked four-hour shifts through the exceptionally cold days of that winter, cutting, breaking, and loading granite for the spillway, interior, and face of the dam. The Veterans rode in open trucks three miles uphill from East Barre to the quarry.[31]

Camp Charles M. Smith was at the Waterbury dam site that contained 2,000 men. It was named in honor of Vermont's governor when construction started. The camp was located on both sides of Little River Road, about a quarter of a mile southwest of the dam. Camp Smith "operated as a self-sufficient village, with its own waste and sewage system, police and fire departments, medical dispensary, three stores, a library that contained over 6,000 books, and a 462-seat theater. The 'village' had about 100 buildings, sixteen U- or

L-shaped barracks that were brought from East Barre and Wrightsville and combined, eight T-shaped mess halls, a theater, library, skating rink, chapel, 'Swiss Chalet, officers' quarters, a large infirmary, a school, and camp garden."[32]

A balmy summer passed into a pleasant autumn, and it was time to pack up. Thus, on Nov. 6, (1934) the members of 1106 found themselves away up north in Camp Jefferson at North Whitefield, Maine. For over eight months, they were employed on forestry work, gypsy and browntail moth extermination, and in the construction of campsites for the state. While in North Whitefield, part of the outfit was used for maintenance of the state park around the capitol of Augusta.[33]

On July 15, 1935 Co. 1106 returned to Camp Smith in Waterbury, Vermont. The next day the members began pitching their tents in the valley near where the district school stands. Before winter all were housed in model U-shaped barracks on the North Plateau.

On the Waterbury Dam 1106 Co. was designated as a transportation company and supplied the majority of the truck drivers, bulldozer operators, and equipment maintenance specialists on the project, but because there was a constant shift of personnel the system was abandoned. However, Co.1106 continued to supply the maintenance specialists.

Since its inception, Co.1106 particularly good at baseball, defeating all comers at Camp Wilson in 1934 and winning a mythical championship. In 1935 the Co. again molded a powerful team, advancing to the semi-finals to be eliminated by 1109 Veterans team. Last summer 1106 won the Veterans' Division of the Sixth Dist. League, and was barely nosed out for the district title by the Junior 119 Co.

At the close of the Seventh CCC enrollment period, Co. 1106 was selected as the Outstanding Co. in the Sixth Dist.

On Oct. 22, 1938, 1106 was ordered to transfer to Torrington, where it has been located in the Mohawk State Forest.[35]

Co. 1106 was composed of Veterans many of whom were in WWI. This group of photos show them at Camps Wilson & Smith where they worked on building dams in Vermont. This company came to Camp Toumey in the fall of 1938.[34]

Enrollees like Guysa with guitar organized bands and singing groups at Camp Toumey and performed at the weekly Amateur Night on Wednesday evenings in the rec hall. Anthony Mancuso is on top of table (right). Mancuso Family 2 Camp Toumey enrollees, Ted & "Mac" Mancuso, went swimming at nearby Lake Tyler after a hard day working in the Mohawk State Forest. Mancuso Family 3 One of the more than 100 waterholes constructed in Mohawk Forest by Camp Toumey. These provided a water source for fighting fires. Podskoch

Hook, Cross, Walcott, Robinson, and White. There was also inter-barracks baseball. (3.) There was also volleyball, softball, swimming, boxing, and wrestling, and there were hopes of building a tennis court. [16] They also built an outside basketball court. [17]

Enrollees completed these projects during the month of July 1935: 5 latrines, 1 well, 4 water holes, 1 dwelling erected , landscaped 1 acre, made 65 signs, 4 fireplaces and 34 picnic tables, built 3 miles of Toumey Rd., cut 30 cords of firewood and 500 bd. ft. of logs, maintained 9 miles of road, destroyed 20,000 Ribes, did 520 acres of blister rust control and 525 acres of White pine Weevil control, treated 150 acres gypsy moths, razed one structure, started 5 new picnic tables, cut and marked a 1-mile boundary with discs and surveyed a 1-mile boundary, cut 2 miles of fire lines and put in 85 rods of guard stones on Toumey Rd. [18]

In October 1935 the enrollees had a wide variety of classes to choose from.

Here is the schedule of evening classes:

Day	6-7 pm	7-8 pm	8-9 pm	9-10 pm
Mon	#Radio #Quartet Handicraft #Typing *Geometry	*Civil Service Electricity #Glee Club Handicraft *Bookkeeping	*Chemistry A Physiology #Orchestra Current Events	#Typing D Physiology
Tue	*Arithmetic Novelty Work *Drafting Handicraft #Typing	*Civil Service History *Social Problems *Mechanics Handicraft	*Chemistry B Physiology Current Events	#Typing E Physiology
Wed	*English *Geometry #Radio Handicraft #Typing	Electricity *Bookkeeping #Typing Handicraft	Forestry C Physiology Current Events Debating #Typing	#Typing F Physiology
Thur	#Radio *Drafting #Typing Handicraft	History *Social Problems *Mechanics Handicraft #Typing	Current Events *Drawing #Typing Electricity	#Typing Astronomy
Fri	*Geometry #Radio #Typing Handicraft	Electricity Handicraft #Typing	History Current Events #Typing	Astronomy #Typing
	Motion Pictures (7-9 pm)			

Table Key:

*   Class is held in the White House

\#   Class is held in the instructor's room

A-F   Barracks in which class is held

Handicraft Class in Sign Room [19]

When the mess hall was being cleaned, the boys brought the tables outside and meals were served Alfresco. Mancuso

Camp Toumey didn't have a football team in the fall but the boys practiced basketball on the outside court. Then in November 1935 the boys tried out for the team at the Litchfield Jr. Republic gym. During the winter the team played the CCC teams of Kent, White, Walcott, Roberts, and Cross. The games were held at the Rialto in Torrington. [20]

During November Camp Toumey provided 1,500 chestnut fence posts to the state for highway guide posts: 225 to Canaan & Salisbury; 700 to Harwington; 400 to Hotchkissville; 175 to Goshen. [21]

By the end of 1935 enrollees had built 111 water holes. The young men's hard work wore out a lot of hand tools. They wore out 3 doz. gravel rakes, 8 doz. shovels, and 2 doz. picks doing road work. The machine shop repaired 700 wooden handles for shovels, axes, etc. [22]

The enrollees were happy to hear in January 1936 that they had full privileges to use the gym, swimming pool, bowling alleys, etc., at the Torrington YMCA. [23]

During the 1936 spring flood of the Connecticut River, Camp Toumey sent approximately 150 enrollees to Hartford from March 22 to April 15. [24]

In June 1936 Camp Toumey completed road work on Toumey and Eli Bunker roads. There were now 4.5 miles of auto roads, 20 wood roads, and 6 mi. of foot trails in Mohawk State Park. [25]

By 1937 approximately 7,400 acres had been surveyed and treated for plant and tree diseases and insects. The men did experimental planting on 170 acres and did improved cutting on 400 acres of forest. They also fought a total of 43 forest fires and constructed 28 miles of fire lines. [26]

In 1937 Camp Superintendent Arthur J. Brooks supervised the following work projects: built roads and bridges, fought tree and plant insects and diseases, did forest fire control work, fought fires, did experimental planting, and silviculture work. They also did recreational work: built foot and ski trails and constructed fireplaces and parking areas. [27]

Enrollees spent 150 man-hours guiding tourists who visited Mohawk State Park in 1937.

In road construction, enrollees built 6 miles of Eli Bunker and Toumey roads that led to the Mohawk fire tower. They also built three bridges, one of which was a King Truss bridge. [28]

Education was an important component in camp life. Classes covered academic, vocational, crafts, and forestry subjects. [29]

During the fall of 1938 Junior Co. 173 was removed from Camp Toumey and replaced with a Veterans Co. 1106. They arrived from Camp Charles Smith in Waterbury, Vermont.

The February 1939 issue of the camp newspaper, the Mohawk Lookout listed the camp staff: Capt. Harold E. Whitten was commander assisted by 2nd Lt. Erple Keeney; Dr. Herman E. Schorr was the contract physician; the Education Dept. was headed by Donald C. Pierce assisted by Herbert Welts and William F. Giglio, who was a Recreation Program Director from the WPA; Work projects was headed by Superintendent Arthur J. Brooks assisted by Harry A. Dillon; the mechanic was Merton L. Burgess, and the blacksmith was Joseph E. Hudon. These men were foremen of the work crews: Gregaire J. LeClerc, silviculture; Edward F. Wilcox, junior civil engineer; Joseph A. Roskosky, Carroll S. Dunham, and Paul C. Zimmerman.

Enrollees are lined up for a hot lunch with their mess kits in hand. They were working in the Mohawk Forest. Mancuso Family

CCC enrollees traveling to work by truck on Tower Rd. Mancuso Family

The senior leader was Francis A. Broderick.

The February of 1939 Mohawk Lookout reported these proposed work projects that would begin on April 1, 1939 and extend to March 31, 1940. Three truck trails were on the agenda. The 3 mi. Wadhams Rd. was to be completed and two miles to be graveled along with constructing a few culvert headers. The 3-mile Tower Rd. was still rough and approximately ½ of the road's rock drilling was to be completed. Road construction of Bear Swamp Rd. was to begin with swamping work. Two bridges were planned with a new cement slab on the 18' long stringer bridge on Eli Bunker Rd. and a 16' cement bridge on Bear Swamp Rd. Bunker Rd. was named after Eli Bunker, a friendly Indian who lived nearby. [36]

The following were the proposed silviculture projects. They were to plant 40,000 red pine, white pine, Scotch pine, Norway spruce, Douglas fir, white spruce, ash, and larch. The enrollees had to clear approximately 1000 acres for this planting. Approximately 700 acres, including the Speckle Pond area, had to be treated by scouting and destroying tree insects and diseases. Another 1200 acres of forest were to be treated five miles north of Torrington to Paugnut State Forest.

Bug crews also had work to do. From May 15 to June 20 they scouted the 200-acre red pine plantation in the Mohawk Forest for the red pine shoot moth. In the town of Cornwall crews went out from May 1 to September 1 to eradicate the gooseberry and currant bushes near the white pine trees.

These were the construction projects. Enrollees were to landscape the Hart farm house and build a two car garage. In the machine and sign shop the masonry crew was to build a brick chimney. The last project was the construction of a septic tank toilet at the Ives picnic area. On a high hill above the picnic area on Toumey Rd. stands the stone observation tower. The enrollees built it between 1933-34. It is a small circular stone tower. Stone steps with a wooden handrail lead up to the tower. From the tower hikers could see a wooden tower to the N on Lookout Mt. and the hills of southern Massachusetts, and to the west the Catskill Mts. [37]

Fire prevention was of prime importance. Veterans were to construct 20 water holes and cut 25 miles of fire lines on private land near the Mohawk State Forest.

The May 1939 issue of the Mohawk Lookout reported an effort to buy two new pool tables and furniture for the Rec Hall because there was a disastrous Christmas fire to the building.

Card playing was one of the ways the Veterans used their free time. In the spring a big pinochle and cribbage tournament was held. The pinochle tournament lasted for nine weeks with ten teams competing. The cribbage tournament had eight teams. After these tournaments the veterans went outside in June to play volleyball.

Veterans were elated in May 1939 with the news that beer became available in their canteen. The profit of 2 cents per bottle went to the camp treasury. Veterans were encouraged to be on their best behavior so that they didn't lose this privilege. They were also encouraged to return the bottles to the canteen because they were worth 2 cents when returned to the beer company. [38]

In 1939 Camp Toumey enrollees turned some of the roads through the forest into ski trails. They built the first downhill trail under the direction of Rolf Holdvedt and the Connecticut Ski Council. [39]

"The trail was 7/10 of a mile long, had several sharp turns and a very deep drop. At the end of the trail was a substantial shelter for 20 or more people and fire places were located nearby for warming one's food. From the beginning this ski run had been very popular and at the end of the season a Connecticut State Ski Meet was held here and the drop from the top to the bottom was made in 48 seconds." [40]

In Jan. 1940 the Mohawk Lookout became a weekly paper. The front page released the news that Camp Toumey was designated as the enrollment and replacement center for the Veterans of Connecticut. Enrollees could sign up in Hartford or Camp Toumey. Then they would get processed at Camp Toumey including physicals, filling out forms, and issuing of clothing. Camp Toumey needed 40 new enrollees to bring the camp up to the 200-man level. Once that was achieved the extra Vets would be sent to Co. 2103 in Westfield, Mass. [41]

On Sat., Jan. 6, 1940 nineteen new recruits reported to Camp Toumey in the evening and were at work on Monday. [42]

Each weekend during 1940 a feature movie was shown in the movie room. Weekly speakers came on Tuesdays and spoke to the Vets who were interested. The first speaker in January was Mr. Case of the Southern Telephone Co. in Torrington. [43]

After Reserve Officers were eliminated in some CCC

camps, Camp Toumey's mess director was E. L. Keeney, a civilian whose title was subaltern. [44]

Junior Forester Gregoire J. Leclare and his five-man crew spent two months covering 3,600 acres of Mohawk Forest and were making type maps showing the age and species of all the stands of timber. [45]

In January 1940 District Forester S. D. Parker visited the site where Veterans were constructing a lean-to at the foot of the ski trail. [46] He approved the project which was completed in February.

Also during January the crew led by Foreman Dunham left the Spectacle Pond block in Kent and started cutting at the south end of Compartment 19 close to Bear Swamp Rd. Foreman Dillon's crew was finishing up work in Kent. They were also melting the snow and ice in the Toumey Rd. culverts. [47]

There were two large snow storms on Feb. 14th and 19th. Camp Toumey Vets went out and helped opening the roads. One stretch of road in West Goshen had drifts up to 12' deep. They helped dig out one farmer who had a two-day supply of milk in 20 milk cans and another woman farmer by opening up a mile of road to her farm so she could get feed for her chickens and livestock. [48]

On Feb. 18, 1940 the Litchfield Hills Winter Sports Association had a ski meet at the downhill ski run built by Camp Toumey. Approximately 500 contestants and spectators parked along East St. [49]

On February 22 approximately 70 people used the ski run on Washington's Birthday. Then on the following weekend over 100 people skied on Sunday. There was 3" of powder over a 12' base. [50]

In March 1940 Camp Toumey had the following

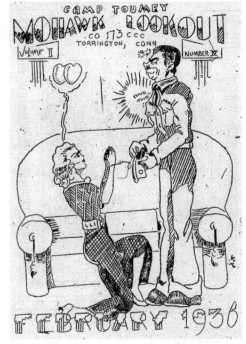

The Education Advisor supervised the Journalism Class that produced a monthly camp newspaper. It gave the boys practice in improving their writing and artistic skills. In 1940 they made a weekly newspaper.[53]

activities for the Vets: Mon. & Thurs. evenings general information movies and film strips; Fri. & Sun. nights feature films shown and funded by Company Fund; religious services every week; weekly recreation trips to town; card & pool games each night; a library containing many books, 24 monthly magazines, and 15 daily newspapers from many parts of New England. [51] The camp also received books in a traveling library that went from camp to camp. [52]

The camp newspaper editorial said that the camp activities were not enough compared with other camps.

The snow storms in 1940 were pretty severe and enrollees were busy clearing the camp and forest roads. They also helped neighboring towns in plowing & shoveling roads. CT CCC Museum

The Camp Toumey garage located a short distance from the camp is still used today by the CT DEEP. Podskoch

CCC enrollees at Camp Toumey operated a bulldozer to build roads in the Mohawk State Forest. DEEP State Parks Archives

Camp Toumey fire crew with their tools: brooms, rakes, and Indian water tanks. Conn. CCC Museum

The Mar. 15, 1940 editorial called for the following: more playing card game, pool and checkers tournaments with adequate prizes; bingo once a week; a bowling alley because there were enough craftsman in camp to build one; a weekly talk by outside speakers; and a company smoker with entertainment once a month with refreshments supplied by the commercial companies who supplied the camp. [54]

During March 1940 Mr. Burger's garage crew was constructing concrete forms to support a 50-hp Hercules motor that would power the camp sawmill. [55]

After the newspaper published the editorial, the administration scheduled tournaments and weekly speakers. One of the speakers was State Forester Austin Hawes.

In March 1940 Foreman Roskosky's crew finished hazard reduction work on Coltsfoot Mt. and moved to Compartment 25 on Milton Rd. where they were working on forest stand improvement. [56]

The ceilings in seven buildings contained a fiberboard called Firetex that had to be removed and placed higher to form a gable peak (cathedral ceilings) like the one in the rec hall. The reason for this was to reduce the fire hazard. [57]

There were a few other camp work projects that began in April, 1940. Dunham's fire crew burned the area below the rec. bldg. in preparation for a bulldozer to level out a future baseball field. The new motor for the saw mill was installed, and plans made to build a new 20' x 30' educational shop building. [58]

The camp newspaper editorials frequently asked for ways to help the Veterans get jobs because most of them were over 40 and who had difficulty getting a job because of their age.

During April 1940, Camp Toumey fire crews were trained and they prepared equipment for the coming spring fire season. Camp Toumey had three trained 20-men line crews with another partial line crew ready if called upon. There were also 2 pump-trained crews consisting of 10-men each. [59]

By June 1940 Camp Toumey completed the construction of Bear Swamp Rd. There were now 9.8 miles of auto roads in Mohawk State Park. [60] The road got its name because the early settlers killed up to 20 bear a year in the Cornwall area. [61]

By the end of 1940 the old Hart place in the Mohawk Forest was renovated by the CCC enrollees and became

When you travel down Toumey road in the Mohawk State Forest you will pass stone chimneys that stand tall like tombstones showing where enrollees ate in the mess hall and played in the rec hall. Podskoch

the home of the forest ranger. Workers also built a lumber storage building. [62]

On July 26, 1941 Supt. S. Niven supervised the closing of Camp Toumey. The US Army retained custody of the camp but the state had to maintain it.

Then on June 21, 1944 The Army turned over Camp Toumey to the State Forestry Department.

LEGACY

Mohawk State Forest is one of the state's largest parks. It offers hikers a 30-mile trail system much of which was constructed by Camp Toumey. Thousands of visitors each year travel on CCC-constructed Toumey Rd. to the top of Mohawk Mt. where they are greeted with spectacular views. Before the fire tower was closed, visitors were able to get an even better view from the observer's cabin. The park is also enjoyed by rock climbers and those who enjoy the diverse ecosystem and natural settings.

Along the park roads are benches and picnic areas developed by the CCC enrollees in the 1930s.

Mohawk SP is also visited by thousands of people in the wintertime, where they enjoy crosscountry skiing, downhill skiing, and snowmobiling.

Directions:

20H-25 Map Torrington West Goshen Camp Toumey

From the Waterbury: take Route 8 north to Exit 42, (Harwinton Exit). Proceed west on Rt. 118 and go 4.9 mi. to the center of Litchfield. Then go north on Rt. 63 and travel 6.1 mi. to the rotary in Goshen Center. Take Rt. 4 west from Goshen approximately 3 miles to the forest entrance for Mohawk State Forest at Toumey Rd. on the left. Then travel on Toumey Rd. (a dirt road) for approximately 2 mi. and the Camp Toumey was on the left. You will find fireplace chimneys and old foundations.

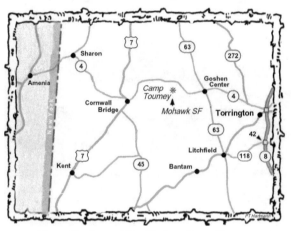

Map – Torrington West Goshen, Camp Toumey

Mohawk State Forest entrance. Podskoch

CCC workers built the first downhill trail in 1939 under the direction of Rolf Holdvedt and the Connecticut Ski Council. In 1946, Walter R. Schoenknecht began leasing the NW of Mohawk Mt. from the state and developed a ski resort. [http://www.cornwallhistoricalsociety.org/exhibits/forests/mohawkski.htm] [http://www.mohawkmtn.com]

301

MEMORIES

Note: Raymond Sanford of Broad St. in Bristol, an enrollee at Camp Toumey, was interviewed by a reporter for the Bristol Press for the June 9th, 1933 issue.

"Young Sanford was one of the group of 11 youths who left with the first contingent from Plainville three weeks ago for Fort Wright. This is the first time he has been home since he joined up. He is in splendid physical condition and says that the life at camp is ideal.

"From Plainville the boys went first to Fort Wright where they remained for a week, during which time they were given a preliminary course in camp and Army life. All the boys were inoculated for the various contagious diseases such as small pox, typhoid fever, scarlet fever, diphtheria, and measles.

Camp Toumey tent camp was established in the summer of 1933 in the Mohawk State Forest. CT CCC Museum

On Thursday, May 18 most of the boys at Fort Wright were sent to their respective forestry destinations. The group in which Raymond found himself, of whom there were 200, took a special train from New London direct for Torrington by way of New Haven and Devon.

"On arrival at Torrington, the boys were taken by bus to the camp site at the foot of Mt. Mohawk in West Goshen. The first afternoon was taken up with pitching tents and building a kitchen. Twenty-four men occupy one tent.

"During the first week in West Goshen most of the time was taken up in camp work and organization, in other words breaking the men in. During this last week the men have been sent out on odd jobs such as grubbing out stumps, cleaning up along the side of the road, and so on. The actual forestry work will come later.

"Ray had some experience in forestry work, and has done a great deal of camping and lived out of doors during the summer months. Consequently he was picked as one of the sub-section foreman, whose duty it is to have charge of 20 men.

"The regular daily routine is as follows: reveille, 6 o'clock; roll call, 6:15; mess, 7 o'clock; policing, 7:30 and out on the job at 8 o'clock. The boys work for 8 hours straight with a few minutes for lunch. The day's work is over at 4 o'clock. After that the time is the boy's except for supper at 5 o'clock. The long evenings make it nice for ball games, swimming and other sports. The boys must be back in camp at 11 o'clock.

"Ray says the biggest sport at night is tipping bunks. You may be sound asleep one minute and the next find yourself on the floor. It's all in the spirit of fun. Yesterday was payday, and the boys were in exceptional form.

"The boys are given arduous work at first, in order that they may be hardened to the job. Most of the boys have stood up well.

"Next week the camp site will be changed, moving from the present location to Tyler Pond. The reason for this is lack of water near Mt. Mohawk. The new camp will be wonderful in one way because it will be right next to the water.

"A little forestry work has been done so far, on killing the blister rust and the European shoot moth. The blister rust originates on currant and gooseberry bushes. This work has been mostly done by the foremen.

"The food, according to Ray, is very good. In the morning pancakes or egg and bacon, at noon meat and potato and at supper cold meats and specialties. Anyone who wants can go back for seconds.

"The fellows can go home every weekend if they so desire. Their attire in camp is blue dungarees and jumper, work shoes, and Army stockings. Outside of camp the boys wear olive drab pants, khaki shirt and regular Army hat. A complete set of toilet articles is given to each man.

"It costs the government 27 cents a day to feed each man which is certainly not excessive.

"Raymond says that he is enjoying the life immensely and that the gang of fellows at Camp Mohawk is one of the best groups in any of the state camps."

"Play the Game"
by James Joyce

The Game of life like any game
Should at first begin,
With an honest and worthy part
And a real desire to win.

But like most games there is a time
When things just don't go right,
We show right then the stuff within
For we either quit or fight.

It's at such a time a man needs most
A background of good training,
So that he may not lose the day
Doing naught but just complaining.

In every game including life
No matter what the outcome,
Just do your best then be at rest
For though you lose you've won.
- Mohawk Lookout, June 1939

"Yellow Holes in the Snow"

Just a little hole in snow
Where you go you see
It tells a story strange but true
That someone had to –

These little holes in snow
Are scattered here and yon,
They multiply mysteriously
Between the night and morn.

Now in our camp we have a dog
A little fellow, too,
He makes his share of yellow holes
But all – he couldn't do.

The yellow holes denote the urge
To ease a heavy load,
That men can't carry further
Than the middle of the road.

The corner of a barrack

Or a can beneath their bed,
And the odor that arises
Makes you think of something dead.

Why you be so lazy
When it's easy to do right
Though no one's there to catch you
In the middle of the night.

Just dress yourselves up warmly
Then hit the old Rose Bowl
Then when the light of day rolls 'round
They'll be one less yellow hole.
- Mohawk Lookout, March 8, 1940

"Tobacco"
by Frank Nibert

Give a man a pipe he can smoke,
Give a man a book he can read,
And he is bright with calm delight
Though the room be poor indeed.

Tobacco is a dirty weed.
I like it.
It satisfies no normal need.
I like it.
It makes you thin, it makes you lean,
It takes the hair right off your bean.
It's the worst darn stuff I ever seen.
I like it.
- Mohawk Lookout, Oct., 1935

Mancuso Family album

303

Alexander Klimak

Alexander Klimak with his wife Grace in 1943. During the Depression he worked at Camp Toumey in West Goshen. Terry Klimak

On May 5, 2008 I traveled to the quaint farm community of Bethlehem, Conn. near Waterbury. I interviewed Alexander W. Klimak who I met at a talk I was giving on the history of the CCC camps in Connecticut.

"My father was Samuel John and during the Depression he worked in the Chase Brass shop as a buffer. My mother Mary worked in the clock shop on watches. They had four children: Edward me, Wanda, and Virginia. I was born in 1921 in Waterbury.

"After my third year in high school I quit, when I was 17 years old. I could not find a job so I joined the CCC with Nicholas Cicchitto who lived on my street. We signed up in the fall of 1938. I wasn't nervous about leaving home. I thought it was an adventure.

"We were sent to Camp Toumey. It was OK. The barracks were clean and the food was good. There were four barracks with three wood stoves in each. The stoves burned 3' long pieces.

"The bathroom was to the right of the camp. It had a coal boiler to heat water for washing clothes. We all did our own laundry.

"They brought logs to camp and cut the wood for the stoves. I worked cutting long logs using a big circular buck saw (also called buzz or cordwood saw) powered by a water-cooled gasoline engine.

"I also worked on the wood pile. I took logs to the saw and carried the cut wood to a pile. That old water-cooled engine went putt, putt, putt, and worked constantly and perfectly.

"On weekends I went to the steel fire tower and was a guide. I described to the tourists what the scenery was. I met a lot of interesting people. I saw some smokes but there weren't any forest fires. There was no observer when I worked there and the next week I did not have to work on the wood pile.

"Then I worked on a gypsy moth control crew. We went into the woods and looked for the gypsy moths.

"In my free time I hung around camp. A truck took guys to Torrington on the weekend but I never went there.

"I went home a couple times on the weekend. I went with my friend, Nicholas Cicchitto. The trucks took us to the Torrington railroad station.

"One time Nick and I got on old Rt. 8 and started hitchhiking. You won't believe it but nobody picked us up. There weren't many cars. We walked all the way to Thomaston. We walked almost all night. Nick called his father and his brother came and picked us up.

"There were no sports teams. The only recreation was playing cards. Sometimes I just hung around and went to the recreation hall. They didn't have a pool table like some camps had.

"After working for six months, I quit to come home and get a job. I think my brother was working in an auto-body shop and he got me a job. It was terrible.

"In 1939 I worked in a Princeton Knitting Mill in Watertown with Nick. We only got 43 cents an hour working the 11-7 night shift. We quit and worked in the Waterbury Clock Shop and Chase Brass Co. where we made shells for the war.

The entrance to Camp Toumey from Toumey Rd. in West Goshen. CT CCC Museum

"In July 1942 I married Grace Guarino. We have two daughters, Tody and Terry.

"Then in September I decided to join the Navy. I went to Quonset Point Naval Station, Rhode Island. I was an aviation metalsmith. Then I got sick and was discharged when I became diabetic.

"I went to Tri-State College in Indiana, studied civil engineering, and graduated in four years.

"In 1948 I got hired with the Department of Transportation of Connecticut. I did road work and then bridge construction. I retired at the age of 60 in 1980.

"In the CCC I learned to be independent."

Alexander Klimak passed away at 90 years of age, on June 11, 2012.

Albert Bellucci

Albert Bellucci of Waterbury wore a CCC hat and jacket at a CCC Reunion in Thomaston. He shared his stories about working at Camp Toumey in 1933. Podskoch

On Aug. 18, 2008 Tony Purrone of Trumbull, Conn. wrote to me after he saw a story in the Waterbury American newspaper about my search for information on the CCC.

"I figure that I should write to you about my 93 year old father-in-law, Albert Bellucci. He joined the CCC under his brother's name, Cesare or Charles, because he, (Albert) was not yet 18 in 1933. Cesare was 19. Believe it or not, Cesare and his father kept all the money that was earned by Albert in the CCC.

"So, Albert, born in 1915, is generally in good health, except for his hearing and he would be surprised to receive

Camp Toumey rec hall. Mancuso Family album

correspondence from you. He's so feisty; he beat me shooting pool today! He remembers stuff from the 1930s like it was yesterday! I love him very much and would like to see him get some recognition for his CCC experiences. He talks about them a lot. I believe he spent time in Goshen, Cornwall, and Fishers Island, NY, off the Connecticut coast. I'd like to meet you and some of the other CCC guys as well."

It was not until July 31, 2010 that I finally got to meet both Albert and Tony at a CCC reunion at the Black Rock State Park in Thomaston. Both enjoyed meeting the other CCC boys and all shared their CCC stories.

Unfortunately, I didn't write the stories down because I thought I'd interview them by phone or at their homes.

My attempts to interview Albert failed because he didn't want to tell others how he joined the CCC under his brother's name. Tony told me:

"Marty, he's afraid that the 'G' Men will come after him and ask for the money back."

So as I was writing my book in 2014, I desperately needed Albert's story. Luckily his daughter, Cheryl Purrone sat down and interviewed him and Tony helped with the wording.

"My father Umberto, later nicknamed "Albert" was born on July 16, 1915 in Rutland, Vermont.

"My dad said, 'My parents were old-fashioned immigrants from Italy. My father, Francisco, was stern and had me get a job at the age of 7. Mother's name was Gesumina and she was quiet and humble. I had two brothers. Cesare was born in 1913 and my younger brother Vincenzo was born in 1923.'"

"I only went to grades 1-8 'cuz Pop told me to get yet another job. I wanted to further my education and play sports but I had to listen to Pop and help my family.

"Then I read about the CCC in the newspaper. I signed up in the spring 1933. I couldn't wait to get out of the house!

"They sent us first to Fishers Island and then on to Camp Toumey in West Goshen, Conn.

"The camp was very good. I had good buddies. There was a nice atmosphere and it was a change of scenery for me. The air was fresh and I was working and making more money than U.S. servicemen during the Depression. They were only getting $21 a month but I got paid a dollar a day. This was $30 a month.

"I made lots of friends but can't remember their names 'cuz many were from different towns and we didn't stay in touch after we left the CCC.

"There were a couple of jobs I had. First I hauled sand in trucks for building roads. Then I did tree work and sprayed trees for insect control. I also cooked part time. The food was excellent.

"In the evening I went to the common [rec] room for music and conversation. I also played baseball with the guys. On the weekends I hit the city of Torrington

"When they wanted me to be a full-time cook I decided not to sign up again. I was discharged in the summer of 1934.

"When I got home I got a job as a truck driver. Then I started working at Waterbury Corrugated as a printer.

"In 1942 I married Estelle Deptula and had a daughter and two sons.

"After 20 years at Waterbury Corrugated, I went to work in 1961 at Boise Cascade as a printer/foreman. In 1981 I retired.

"In 2010 I lost my wife Estelle and I miss her terribly."

Cheryl then asked her father how he benefited from being in the CCC. "I made money and I enjoyed the outdoors. I also learned the value of hard work and appreciated FDR's program to help us guys out."

On March 27, 2014 Albert Belluchi passed away.

Anthony John Mancuso

During the summer of 2005 Elizabeth Rosa of Torrington contacted me by email and asked if I would like to see her father's photo album from his time at Camp Toumey near Mohawk Mt. I certainly did and arranged to meet her at a Starbuck's Coffee House in Colchester.

A few days later I met her and her husband. She showed me her large photo album and shared some of her dad's stories. She also let me borrow the album so that I could scan the photos and use them in my book.

Here is what she told me about her dad's life and time in the CCC.

"My father was born on June 25, 1916. His father was Joseph and his mother was Angelina. My father had a younger sister, Carmela.

"When dad graduated from Hartford High School there were not many jobs for young men and the CCC offered a job and experience. He joined in 1933 and was sent to Camp Toumey in the Mohawk State Forest. I think he didn't mind leaving home and wanted the adventure and learning experience of the CCC.

"He had a very good friend, Red Berman, who may have been in another camp but they went at the same time and kept in touch for many years.

"There are quite a few photos in the album showing Dad and others surveying and using a transit. This was a great learning experience for him. When he left the CCC he went on to get a land surveyor license and did this as a side job over many years.

"On many weekends I know that he often hitchhiked home to see his family. That was quite a trek from Mohawk to Hartford. I think he must have hitchhiked and walked down Rt. 202 to get home. He was fond of his family and

Anthony Mancuso (Middle Row, Right) giving "rabbit ears" to the boy with the pipe and someone giving Anthony "rabbit ears" by the entrance to barracks D. Mancuso Family

306

(Clockwise from Above) 1 In the top left photo Anthony is to the right of the transit. In the lower photo he is marking a 90-degree angle. Mancuso Family 2 The Camp Toumey kitchen in the mess hall. There were three coal cook stoves with chimneys on the left in the area for preparing food. Mancuso Family 3 Camp Toumey survey crew with transit (L–R): Wilson, Anthony Mancuso, Quintas, and Yakso. Mancuso Family

made many trips home.

"I'm not certain when he left the CCC but I thought it was a short term camp I think he was exempt from WWII because he got a job at the Hartford Gas Company where his father worked

"After a short time working for the Gas Co. he worked for the state of Connecticut as a highway engineer. He started work as a transit man, then a junior highway engineer. He then became a senior engineer and finally director. Dad took many engineering courses for his jobs.

My mother was Helen Silvester. My brother Joseph lives in NYC and my brother John lives in Wethersfield.

"Dad's experience in the CCC had a tremendous effect on his life. He learned a skill that carried him through life and he was very successful, retiring as the Executive Director of the State Traffic Commission. I know that the CCC was something he really enjoyed and he talked about it often."

Harold Mattern, Part IV

"I think it was the spring of 1940 that I came to Camp Toumey in the Mohawk State Forest. There were Veterans of WWI. I continued working on measuring the logs and calculating the volume of wood in the downed trees caused by the 1938 Hurricane. I had a veteran as my assistant.

At this time the CCC boys were doing roadwork, gypsy moth eradication, and timber stand improvement. There was a sawmill in camp that produced a lot of lumber for state use.

"I don't think the Veterans went home on the weekends. The state ranger made arrangements for me to leave my car in the state garage.

"The damage in the forest wasn't as bad as the shore. I stayed there till about the fall and then went to Camp Hadley in Haddam."

Company road with barracks on each side is where O'Connell and 200 men lived. The buildings had no insulation but was covered with tar paper to shield the buildings from wind rain and snow. Mancuso Family

Gerald J. O'Connell

Gerald J. O'Connell was always proud of his time
and experience in Camp Toumey in West Goshen.
Gerry O'Connell

On April 4, 2008 I interviewed Gerald J. O'Connell Jr. He told me about his father, Gerald J. O'Connell, who worked at CCC Camp Toumey.

"My dad was the oldest boy in his family. My dad's father, Maurice, had been a bootlegger but with the end of prohibition in 1933 he was unemployed. His mother was Catherine. They had three children: a daughter and two sons. My father was born on June 13, 1918 in Waterbury.

"My dad told me that when he was in high school he heard about the CCC from some guys in the neighborhood who were joining up. He quit school when he was 15. He fibbed about his age and said he was 18. He joined in May of 1933. Dad said he was excited to go. It was an adventure and his folks could use the dough. He got paid $30 a month and $25 went home to his family. He had $5 for spending money. The Army sent him to Fishers Island, NY where he was processed.

"Then he went to the CCC camp in the Mohawk State Forest near Goshen. It was a 'reforestation' camp. They cleared brush, built fire trails called fire breaks, and small ponds to collect water in case of fire. You can still these off Toumey Rd. in Cornwall. They also cut and split wood.

"Dad didn't get injured working but once he tossed a sharpening stone to a buddy. It accidentally slit his buddy's wrist. The kid began to run and the blood was spraying out of his arm. So my dad and his buds had to wrestle the kid to the ground, to calm him down. Then they brought him to the first aid building where he was taken care of.

"One day one of the CCC men asked my dad if he could drive. My dad was 15 but tall for his age. He said, 'Yes.'

"Well, they got in an old WWI truck that you had to double clutch. When they were going down a big hill, the older man told my dad to 'down clutch.' My dad had no clue and the truck picked up speed. Finally, the older man pulled up the emergency break and said, 'Ok kid, move over!' And my dad never drove up at Camp Toumey after that!

"Even though Dad wasn't far from home I don't think he went home like a lot of guys did on the weekends.

"In November 1933 my father was discharged. I guess it was because you could only stay for six months. They later changed it to two years.

"He re-enrolled at high school. Then he worked in a factory.

"In 1940 he was one of the first from Waterbury to be drafted in the Army.

"In 1941 my dad married Dorothy Dickson in August before the war began. Then he was sent to Africa.

"Dad participated in the landings in North Africa. First he was at Casablanca and then traveled across North Africa to Bizerte in Tunisia. Then he was in the invasion of Sicily, Italy in July 1943 at the Gulf of Gela, and the landings in Salerno. Next he was in the Battle of Monte Cassino, and the liberation of Rome in June 4, 1944. He then went on to Florence, and by May 1945 he went to Bolzano in the Italian Alps. It was not too far from the south of Austria.

"He and my mother raised my two sisters Patricia and Mary and me.

"After WWII my dad went to Boston University on the GI Bill and worked at the Post Office back in Waterbury in the summers. He began working in the post office full time by 1950, first as a carrier then as a supervisor. Dad also ran the Postal Credit Union.

"Dad retired in 1980 and passed away in 2004.

"My father learned a lot of things in the CCC. He learned about using a pick, a sledge hammer, axes and things like living in a camp with all types of people. They all served him well later in World War II. He was very proud of his service in the CCC!"

CHAPTER 21
UNION

HISTORY

Camp Graves S-55, Company 174 was established on May 27, 1933 on state land. The camp road was Whipple Lane on the north side of Rt. 190, near I-84 in the town of Union in the NE section of Connecticut.

A group of 204 enrollees and Army supervisors left Fort Wright Army base on Fisher's Island (6 mi. SE of New London) at 9 am on May 27, 1933 and arrived at New London at 10:15 am. The men then traveled by bus to Stafford Springs' freight depot where a group of curious onlookers gathered to greet the men.

The Sunday, May 28, 1933 issue of The Hartford Daily Courant also reported that the camp was located on meadow and forest land that it was to be completed before nightfall and consist entirely of tents. The group was led by Army Captain W. H. Speidel and assisted by Lts. J. K. Mitchell and B. G. Feen.[1]

Three days later a group of five Winsted enrollees went AWOL. They only lasted two nights and were back home on Tuesday. Stanley Kolasinski, one of the five, told a Hartford Courant reporter that they didn't get enough to eat. When asked what he got for breakfast Kolasinski replied, "oatmeal and bacon and eggs." He said that he and the four other Winsted boys weren't the only ones to leave. There were 13 other boys. Kolasinski said that on the trip from New London to Union he received only one potato, two sandwiches, and coffee. At camp that first Saturday night, Kolasinski said he only had bread and coffee. The

A postcard of Camp Graves showing the camp entrance off Rt. 190 in Union. Bob Markovits

Army denied that 18 enrollees left the camp. Winsted town officials were annoyed that these men gave up the opportunity to earn $30 a month. [2]

Company 174 enrollees worked mainly in the Nipmuck State Forest (NSF). State Forester Austin Hawes supervised the state's purchase of the first NSF tract in 1905. It was originally called Union State Forest and was Connecticut's second state forest. Hawes wanted it to be a pine forest because Connecticut had to import most of its softwoods. When the state purchased more land in other towns, the forest was renamed Nipmuck after the native Indians. Nipmuck (also Nipmuc) means "Fresh Water People." Over the years the forest expanded to 9,000 acres that mostly surrounds Bigelow Hollow State Park. Nipmuck State Forest also contains parcels in Ashford and

www.foresthistory.org

Henry S. Graves

The camp was named after Henry S. Graves, the Dean of the Yale School of Forestry. He was born in 1871 in Marietta, Ohio. He graduated from Phillips Academy in 1888. Graves went on to Yale and graduated in 1892 and earned a Masters degree in Engineering in 1900. That year he and Gifford Pinchot founded the Yale School of Forestry, which was the first graduate school dedicated to forestry in the US. Graves joined the US Forest Service and was its chief from 1910-1920. Two years later he returned to Yale. Graves became the Dean of the Yale School of Forestry and served there for 27 years. He died on March 7, 1951.[3]

A group of Camp Graves cooks and servers during the early tent camp days in 1933. Union Historical Society

Camp Graves barracks. The mattresses and bedding are folded on the back of the cots waiting for a new group of enrollees. Union Historical Society

Three Army officers (white arrows) supervising enrollees at Camp Graves. The boys are on trucks ready to work at the nearby Nipmuck and Shenipsit state forests. The truck garage is on the lower left at the entrance to camp on Rt. 190. Gary Potter

The first fire observer tower in Connecticut was located in 1912 above Mrs. Dedi Lawson's cottage on Mt. Ochepetuck in Union. Camp Graves was often called out to help fight fires the observer spotted. Union Historical Society

Stafford. [4]

The 1934 Connecticut State Parks and Forests Report stated that Camp Graves constructed a mile road over Stickney Hill and the entrance road to Morey Pond. They also did work in the Shenipsit State Forest where they improved the road over Soapstone Mountain for two miles.

In the spring of 1934 enrollees did stream improvement projects on Roaring Brook, which flows through the towns of Union, Stafford, and Willington.[5]

Camp Graves also worked on fire prevention. In 1934 they were constructing a 15'-wide firebreak along the

Massachusetts border. They also cleared deadwood from a 100'-wide border area [6]

In 1934 enrollees developed a recreation area on Morey Pond (near the intersection of present-day Rt. 89 and I-84) that included a beach house and a bath house. The men also constructed a trail along the pond, fire places, and tables for picnics. [7]

By June 30, 1934 Camp Graves had accomplished a lot of work in the forest. They cut 633 cords of wood, made 534 posts and 391 poles, and cut 10,310 bd. ft. of logs. Enrollees performed silviculture work in the Nipmuck

Forest. They cleaned 115 acres of deadwood, thinned 112 acres, cleaned 11 acres for planting, and did reproduction cutting (clearcutting) on 14 acres. The total areas treated were 252 acres. [8]

In the fall 1934 the First Annual Inter-Barracks Field Day was held. Some of the featured events were: 50 and 100 yd. dash, running broad jump, and baseball throw. Other competitions were basketball, bowling and boxing. There was also competition with other CCC camps. The camp cross-country team also competed against Norwich Free Academy. [9]

Inter-barracks debating teams were organized and the topic for the Dec. 10 debate was on "Unemployment Insurance." The Education Advisor was John P. Murphy. [10]

During the 1934-35 winter a crew was busy graveling truck trails that had been graded. The crews of Foresters Mason and Hadfield were busy cutting wood and by Jan. 15 had cut approx. 1,000 cords. Also in the woods were two crews using a tractor to haul out cordwood and saw logs. [11]

The education department welcomed new ERA teachers to camp. Edwin T. Tracy of Hartford taught commercial business subjects and was in charge of the Dramatics class. Franklin Learned taught journalism, public speaking, literature, and advanced Algebra. He was also in charge of the Debating Club. Elio Scotta of Stafford Springs taught Elementary subjects and was in charge of the Dramatic Club. [12]

Camp Graves was very fortunate to have teachers who were well educated and talented young men. Lynn Beals graduated from Phillips Exeter Academy and Harvard (1932) with a degree in French. He then completed three years at Harvard Medical School. Elio Scotta graduated from the University of Chicago where he majored in Chemistry and literature. [13]

During January 1935 there were many visiting speakers. The first was Atty. Edward G. McKay the coroner for New London County. His talk was entitled "Carelessness and its Consequences." He was followed by Professor Albert E. Moss, head of the Forestry Dept. at Storrs; Rev. John J. Reilly of Norwich; William McKay, Director of the FERA Transient Bureau of New London; William J. Meagher, J. J. Professor of History, Holy Cross College, who talked about his trip to the Philippines Islands. [14]

The following is a list of Camp Graves Administrators in January 1935: Capt. Walter C. Sage, Company Commander; Stanley Niven, Camp Superintendent; 1st Lieut. Bernard P. Moran (senior officer.), Nathaniel C. Robbey, contract physician; 2nd Lieut. Alexander D. Fraser; and John P. Murphy, Educational Advisor. [15]

The rec hall during the winter was a place that boys gathered after supper and sang, wrote letters, talked about their day, or read a good book. It was also a place to play ping pong or practice for the next minstrel. [16]

On Feb. 6, 1935 Camp Graves' enrollee entertainers traveled to Hartford and performed on radio station WTIC. [17]

On Fri. Feb. 15, 1935, Camp Graves enrollees participated in CCC entertainment at Avery Hall in Hartford. They sang songs, put on skits, and played hillbilly music. [18]

Entertainment continued every Sunday evening at Camp Graves. There was singing, bands and solo

During the 1933-34 winter, manpower and sleds removed cordwood from the Nipmuck SF. Union Historical Society

An Army officer walking up the company road towards the administration building during the winter of 1934. Gary Potter

The rec hall at Camp Graves was a place for the boys to sit and relax in comfortable mission style furniture by the warmth of the large stone fireplace, sing songs by the piano, or play pool. Union Historical Society

Camp Graves had a dynamite cellar built into the earth. DEEP State Archives

instrumentals, and dancing, followed by speeches. [19]

In the Mar. 15, 1935 issue of the Camp Graves News Superintendent Stanley Niven was proud to congratulate his enrollees who came in second place of all Connecticut CCC camps in cutting logs and cordwood. Niven stated that Connecticut State Forester commended Camp Graves for having the best cutting tools in the Eastern District. This showed the excellence of the camp saw filers. He also said that during the summer of 1934 his road crew constructed the truck trail on Soapstone Mt., one of the finest in the state.

During the winter the boys loved the large snowfalls to participate in outdoor sports. The boys enjoyed snowshoeing. Some boys took the "Snow Train" to Brattleboro, Vt. to watch the champion Ski Jumpers. [20]

From September 1934 till May 1935 the gypsy moth crew composed of from 10-20 men covered almost 12,000 acres of woodlands in Union and Stafford Springs. They creosoted 33,605 egg clusters. During the spring the crew began to burlap trees in the most infested areas. The boys use an 8" wide piece of burlap and tied it around at a convenient height. The top part is turned down over the bottom piece of burlap. The caterpillar at its third stage begins going up and down the tree and feeds at night. During the day it seeks shelter under the burlap. The crew comes and picks the caterpillars from the burlap, counts and then destroys them. This has shown to be a successful program. [21]

During the months of February and March there was a tent caterpillar contest. The guy who collected the most egg clusters on their free time and had at least 2,000 clusters would be eligible for the cash prize of $4. Second place prize

was $2. First place went to the boy who collected 4,581 and second place gathered 4,503. There are approx. 300 eggs in each cluster. [22]

On Fri. May 24, 1935 Camp Graves celebrated its second anniversary. Many citizens from the surrounding towns were invited for the festivities. Tours of the camp were given throughout the day. The festivities began at 2 pm with a "Mummers" parade and circus. This was followed by an address by Dean Graves the head of the Yale School of Forestry. State Forester Austin Hawes also spoke congratulating the camp on their accomplishments. At 4 pm various athletic events were held. Then came the

The July 1935 cover of the Nipmuck Sentinel.

A group photo of Camp Graves. CT CCC Museum

banquet held in the mess hall. At 7 pm there were boxing matches. The finale was a dance in the rec hall. Trucks were sent to Stafford Springs to pick up anyone wishing to attend. [23]

The education advisor and Army helped organize dances for the enrollees. The July 1935 issue of the Camp Graves Sentinel reported: "A hot time was had at the camp dance at the town of Stafford Springs. Virtually the entire personnel of Camp Graves moved in mass into town to attend the dance held at the Town Hall. ... Music was furnished by a six-piece band under the direction of Danny Haig. From eight until twelve o'clock the large crowd of dancers thronged the floor of the hall. Many guests were also present from surrounding towns, as well as the usual compliment from Stratford. ... Two policemen and a janitor on duty throughout the evening and expressed themselves as well satisfied by the all-around good behavior of the crowd.

CCC camps throughout the state encouraged religious programs at camp. On June 14, 1935 Rev. Henry Young, a Catholic missionary priest from Boston, held a mission service. He celebrated a mass at 5:30 am in the rec hall and a service in the evening at 7:30. Father Young served as a chaplain in the Army for five years in Panama. After his visit to Camp Graves Father Young visited other Connecticut CCC camps. [24]

In the summer of 1935 Kenneth Holland, Educational Advisor for the 1st Corps Area, gave the Educational Dept. of Camp Graves a "Superior" rating. This reflected the fine work of Ed. Advisor Lynn Beals and his staff. [25]

During the winter of 1935-36 Graves' basketball team started it season at the Southbridge YMCA on Feb. 19. They lost to Camp Fernow by the score of 40-20.

On March 3, 1936 Captain W. F. Conlan was granted a 25-day leave for a rest "in Florida, or some other place where it's damn good and warm," said Conlan. Lieut. Hiland J.

Holt of Camp Stuart was his replacement. [26] Camp Graves was fortunate to have a swim team. They practiced at Connecticut State College indoor pool. Gustave Langner, a former Yale swimming star and Olympic prospect, coached the Graves enrollees who practiced on Wednesday nights. [27]

The 1936 Report of the Connecticut State Parks and Forest stated that the CCC constructed three truck roads in the NSF at Stickney Hill, Morey Pond, and Snow Hill. It also reported that the camp produced these forest products by June 30, 1936: 8,557 bd. ft. of logs; 1,264 cords of fuel wood; 366 poles; and 1,497 posts.

Camp Graves closed on April 22, 1936 and most of the buildings were removed because of insufficient funds to maintain the camp.

In August 1937 The Shenipsit Lookout reported that Camp Graves was to be taken down and the lumber taken to Voluntown's Camp Lonergan to be used for forms in building a new dam.

Later the state traded the 8-acre camp site to George and Lillian Hall for a larger parcel near Mashapaug Pond and Breakneck Pond. In 1955 the Halls sold the land and some CCC buildings to Donna & Rudolph Corsini who presently own the property.

The Corsini's converted the Officer's Building into a home. They planted a tree where the camp flagpole stood. The circle of stones the boys placed around the flag pole are still there today. Podskoch

LEGACY

Camp Graves did a lot of work in the Nipmuck State Forest, such as building roads, silviculture work, and planting thousands of trees. Camp Graves also built many picnic sites and swimming areas at Morey Pond and Bigelow Hollow State Park where thousands of people enjoy fishing, hiking, picnicking, hunting, boating, and snowmobiling.

Directions:

From Hartford travel East on I-84 for approximately 30 mi. to Exit 73. Then go west on Rt. 190 for approximately .04 mile. Camp Graves was located on the right under the large white pine trees at 780 Whipple Lane, Union. The site is now private property owned by Donna Corsini. Please do not trespass.

Bigelow Hollow State Park on Rt. 171 in Union. Camp Graves built a picnic area that included tables, fireplaces, and a boat ramp. Podskoch

Map – Camp Graves, Union

Camp Graves boys built this incinerator at the entrance to Morey Pond SP in the 1930s. For a 25 cents entry fee visitors had a swimming area, picnic tables, and a bathhouse. Podskoch

(L–R) 1 This area was once the entrance to Camp Graves. 2 Donna Corsini purchased the site in 1955. Podskoch

In 1935 CCC boys constructed the road through the Mountain Laurel Sanctuary on Snow Hill Road off Rt. 190 in the Nipmuck SF, Union. They built picnic areas and waterholes for fire protection. CT CCC Museum

MEMORIES

"Only a Truck Driver"
Anonymous

Only a State truck driver am I
You say you think my job is as easy as pie,
First to get out at break of day,
Report to Art Quick, and have him say:
"Warm up your truck for the daily grind"
I often think I'll go out of my mind.
Drive out your bug crew, and do not hurry,
Or you'll get tossed out of camp in a flurry.
This damn truck driving is the bunk
From 9 till 3, I'm a grease ball punk.
Down in the old damp pit I go,
And start dropping wrenches on my toe,
Drop the crankcase, pull the clutch,
If I don't do right, I get in Dutch.
At night I hear some bug man say:
"That crummy truck driver loafs all day."
All those fellers who wisecrack it
Would be the first to quit the "racket."
- Camp Graves News, Mar. 1936

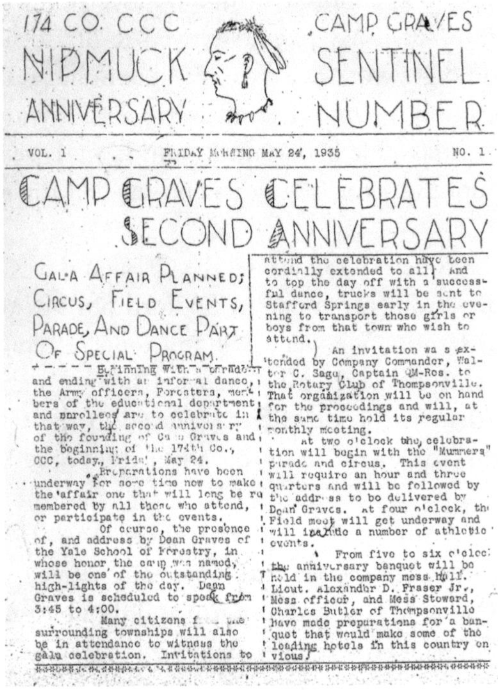

174 CO. CCC — NIPMUCK ANNIVERSARY — CAMP GRAVES SENTINEL NUMBER

VOL. 1 FRIDAY MORNING MAY 24, 1935 NO. 1

CAMP GRAVES CELEBRATES SECOND ANNIVERSARY

GALA AFFAIR PLANNED; CIRCUS, FIELD EVENTS, PARADE, AND DANCE PART OF SPECIAL PROGRAM.

Beginning with a parade and ending with an informal dance, the Army officers, Foresters, members of the educational department and enrollees are to celebrate in that way, the second anniversary of the founding of Camp Graves and the beginning of the 174th Co., CCC, today, Friday, May 24.

Preparations have been underway for some time now to make the affair one that will long be remembered by all those who attend, or participate in the events.

Of course, the presence of, and address by Dean Graves of the Yale School of Forestry, in whose honor the camp was named, will be one of the outstanding high-lights of the day. Dean Graves is scheduled to speak from 3:45 to 4:00.

Many citizens from the surrounding townships will also be in attendance to witness the gala celebration. Invitations to attend the celebration have been cordially extended to all. And to top the day off with a successful dance, trucks will be sent to Stafford Springs early in the evening to transport those girls or boys from that town who wish to attend.

An invitation was extended by Company Commander, Walter C. Sage, Captain QM-Res. to the Rotary Club of Thompsonville. That organization will be on hand for the proceedings and will, at the same time hold its regular monthly meeting.

At two o'clock the celebration will begin with the "Mummers" parade and circus. This event will require an hour and three quarters and will be followed by the address to be delivered by Dean Graves. At four o'clock, the Field meet will get underway and will include a number of athletic events.

From five to six o'clock the anniversary banquet will be held in the company mess hall. Lieut. Alexander D. Fraser Jr., Mess officer, and Mess Steward, Charles Butler of Thompsonville have made preparations for a banquet that would make some of the leading hotels in this country envious.

Camp Graves boys published a monthly newspaper containing camp news, poems, gossip, and cartoons. Here is the May 24, 1935 issue of the Camp Graves Sentinel

A truck driver and his work crew at Camp Toumey. Al Belucchi

Ralph P. Guerra

On Oct. 11, 2009 Ralph P. Guerra of Stafford Springs attended a CCC reunion at the CT CCC Museum. Ralph worked for 18 months at Camp Graves from 1933-35 in Union, Conn. Podskoch

After a CCC presentation at the Woodstock Historical Society in the Palmer Memorial Hall on May 17, 2009, a young man said, "Hi, I'm Pete Tiziani and I'd like you to meet an old CCC boy, Ralph Guerra. I'm not a relative but a good friend and I call him 'Uncle Ralph.'"

Ralph told me he was at Camp Graves in Union in 1933 and he had a lot of stories, but since we didn't have time for an interview I told him that I'd contact him.

A few days later I got this email from Pete. "I just wanted to let you know how much Uncle Ralph and I enjoyed your program in Woodstock on Thursday. It was the second time for me because I previously heard you give

Camp Graves' enrollees moving their mattresses, bedding, and clothing into their barracks. Union Historical Society

A hydraulic jack hammer was used to plant dynamite while building a road through the Shenipsit State Forest. DEEP State Parks Archives

this talk at the Connecticut Forests and Park Association banquet a couple years ago. It was, however, well worth a repeat.

"While returning Ralph to his apartment in Stafford, he provided some additional information about topics that were touched on that evening. One Camp Graves story he told me was how the men went on strike for better food. Whoever was in charge of ordering food for the camp started skimming money to support his 'courting' of a girl in Stafford. The food became terrible, and it smelled like the meat was spoiled. Somehow, the guys gained access to the books and were able to prove the guy was dipping into the till. Ralph said the guy got court martialed.

"The second story concerns Ralph's intimate knowledge of the grease pit. They thought Ralph had something to do with the mysterious disappearance of a

A teamster helped the boys remove cordwood from the forest. Gary Potter

barrel of fish, so they decided to punish him by making him to clean out the grease pit. I got the impression that Ralph didn't take the fish, but knew who did and didn't want to squeal. Apparently, someone didn't want to eat the fish, so the barrel got loaded onto a truck leaving camp, and got dumped in a ravine somewhere.

A few months later I called Ralph Guerra and asked him to tell me about his family and his CCC days.

"I was born on October 21, 1915 in Bridgeport, Conn. There were four children in our family: Arthur, myself, Floyd, and Velma. My parents moved to Stafford Springs so dad could get work as a weaver in the mill. I was 5 years old then. In high school I went to live with my uncle near Worcester, Mass. He had a mushroom farm. I went to the trade school there for four years and studied the electrical trade.

"In October 1933 I joined the CCC and was sent just a few miles from my home in Stafford Springs to Camp Graves in Union. We were living in tents. I remember it snowing and we were still in tents. Later we moved into barracks that had wood stoves. I stayed in the CCCs for 18 months. Living in camp was a fun thing, the best part of my life.

"The Army gave us clothes from WWI. We had hobnail shoes, whose soles had short nails with a thick head sticking out at the bottom for grip and durability. We had woolen shirts and pants, overcoats with big collars, and five woolen blankets to keep us warm.

"When we first got there they gave us a mattress cover

and they told us to go down to a building full of straw. We made our own straw mattresses. It was good sleeping on it. Remember, we were brought up rough on a farm.

"We ate with a mess kit all the time. It had a cup, spoon, knife, and the cover was the dish. For cleaning the mess kit there was a 50-gallon drum on top of stones and a fire underneath. Another barrel had brown GI soap. We dipped the kit into the soapy water and then went to the other drum of hot water to rinse. All year round we did this. At first the mess hall didn't have any heat. We had to drum our feet to keep warm. The following year they put stoves in the mess hall.

"The food was terrible. It was so bad that we went on strike. We found out the Army lieutenant in charge of the mess hall was buying cheap cuts of meat. He was going out with a girl from Stafford and spending food money on her.

"The Army officers ran our camp. We had one Navy officer who was a doctor. He was an alcoholic. We also had a lieutenant and two sergeants.

"In the evening we had a rec hall for activities where we played cards or read. We never had movies. We had rangers who gave us classes on trees, etc.

"On weekends we went up to South Bridge (near Sturbridge) 12 miles north in Mass. We roller-skated there. We could go a long way on our five dollar monthly pay.

"I didn't mind leaving home because it was close by. A lot of guys hitchhiked home but I stayed at the camp because there was more fun there. We hitchhiked on Rt. 20 (now Rt. 190). This was the main road to Boston. There were five restaurants in Stafford Springs that stayed open all night. The boys liked to go there on weekends.

Ralph helped build fireplaces in the picnic areas at Morey Pond. Many of them are in use today. Podskoch

"For recreation we had a baseball team that played the neighboring towns like Rockville in their parks. I played some games at 2nd base. We also had volley ball games. I wasn't very good because I was short, only 5' and weighed 118 lbs.

"One time I almost got in trouble. The first year we had a gravity water tank. I still remember the 2" line that froze up. We started digging up the line. I threw a snowball at the only black guy but no one told him. If he ever found out it was me, he would have killed me.

"There was a camp superintendent, Holstrom, who planned our work projects. He lived down the road.

"During my stay at Camp Graves I had a few jobs. My first job was building a road in Shenipsit State Forest. It was a few miles west of Stafford Springs. We had Chevrolet dump trucks that were only about one-ton in size. They had benches on each side to carry the workers to the site. Every morning we got in and went to Soapstone Mountain. We were building a road to the top of the mountain where the fire tower was. At first there was just a steep walking path to the tower and there was a man tower observer. We improved the fire tower trail. The same trucks were then used to bring up the gravel. One job I had was loading the truck with 6-10 guys other guys. We took turns shoveling.

"While building the road we used a lot of dynamite to blast out the stumps and stones that were in the way. Some places they had horse-drawn scoop to dig out the road.

"In the afternoon a special truck brought us food. They had a large thermal bottle to hold the soup. They also gave us peanut butter sandwiches. The peanut butter had no oil and when you ate it, you couldn't open your mouth. Sometimes they gave us pork chop sandwiches. They baked their own bread and, boy, it was great! We also toasted the bread over the fire. It was so good!

"My second job was chopping cord wood. Everything was by hand. We also cut wood for the homeless. We also brought four-foot length wood to a place called The Hearth Stone near the Colt Fire Arms factory in Hartford.

"We also cut down trees for the guardrails. We took the bark off the logs and dried them. Then we brought them to the highway dept.

"One time I got hurt and went to the infirmary. I cut my big toe with an ax and took off the edge of the toe and you could see the bone. The doctor sewed me up. I stayed overnight. The place had three beds. There was supposed to be somebody there but the doctor left and I was alone.

"I also worked down on Roaring Brook in Ashford where we made a pile of stones in the water that made a pool for the native trout.

"We also worked on fish habitat on the Hop River near Willington and making hiking trails in Bigelow Hollow Park.

"Another project was at Morey Pond. When they built Rt. 84 it split the pond in half. We made a bathhouse, boat dock, and fireplaces. The guy who invented a particular style of fireplace, Mike Julian, was our company clerk who was about 23 and from Stafford Springs. His son later became a selectman. We also cleared the area for a parking.

"After being in the CCC for 18 months, I left in April of 1935 because they said there was a time limit. The first thing I did was get a job working for the WPA. I climbed the really bad Dutch elm trees that were dying. We had a half-inch rope with a large knot at the end. We'd throw the rope over a limb and then climb up the rope. If it was a really bad tree, we cut the whole thing down and trimmed the branches. Then we burned them. I did this for a year.

"Then I worked as an arborist for a company in Thompsonville. I planted trees and put guy wires on them and did landscaping.

"After three years I was drafted in 1942 so I joined the Navy. I was on the carrier Enterprise. We got hit three times by torpedoes. My job was a hydraulic specialist working on planes (Hellcats & Corsairs.) I also did welding. In 1946 I was discharged.

"Then I worked for a private company called the Davey Tree Expert Co. from Minnesota. If a tree was splitting, we put in bolts to tie them together. It was for the wealthy people and they were tough to work for. I also worked in Westchester County New York after an ice storm (during the 1939 World's Fair). We cleaned up the trees.

"I married my neighbor, Mary Scott. We had two children: Sandra and Richard.

"I really liked the CCC and learned a lot. I went all winter long to classes on silviculture and bark reading. I learned all about trees. Later I became an arborist.

"I also learned how not to play poker. I lost all my money. It happened once and I learned my lesson."

On March 22, 2015 Ralph Guerra passed away at the age of 99.

Adolph E. O'Bright

Adolph E. O'Bright worked at Camp Graves and served in the Army in the Pacific theater. Linda Czaplicki

Adolph "Ed" O'Bright was born Dec. 19, 1911 in Manchester, the sixth of 11 children. His parents were Charles and Mary (Patrick) O'Bright.

He was at Camp Graves in 1934 in Union. He started out on KP and learned to cook. Ed said, "The CCC changed my life by teaching me about the environment."

During WWII Ed served in the Army in Guam, the Philippines, Okinawa, and the occupation of Japan. He received the Bronze Star for valor.

Ed married Simone (Guay) and they had a daughter Linda (Czaplicki). Ed also had two step-sons, Ronald Cote and Norman Cote from Simone's first marriage.

After the war Adolph was employed with Pratt & Whitney Aircraft for over 25 years. He retired in 1976 and then worked with Ward Manufacturing in Manchester.

On Oct. 22, 2004 Ed passed away at his home in Manchester.

A Camp Graves baker displaying a fresh tray of muffins. This is where "Ed" O'Bright learned how to cook. Gary Potter

Arthur A. Avedisian

Arthur told of difficulties of growing up during the Depression. He was forced to quit school after 8th grade to help his family. Podskoch

As we sat at a restaurant in Windsor on Aug. 26, 2008, Arthur Avedisian of Windsor, told me about his fascinating life and experiences in the CCC at Camp Graves in Union.

"Marty, I invited you to dinner because I want to tell you about my life. My son John told me about your research on the CCC and he contacted you and helped set up this meeting.

"I was born on Jan. 13, 1914 in Springfield, Mass. My parents were John and Anna. My father owned a small market in Springfield. After my mother died when I was six years old Dad asked a farmer named Pease to take care of me and my older sisters, Rose and Nancy, for three years. Then Dad took us to Hartford to live.

"I grew up at the corner of Franklin Ave. and Brown St. where my father worked at my godfather's grocery store. He gave Dad an apartment on the third floor of his building. When Dad got there he opened a meat department in the store because Dad was a butcher. He could run upstairs to check on us. We literally grew up on the street and I became a con artist.

"This was when prohibition was the law. I watched for the police to warn the people who were making booze in their bath tubs. I whistled a warning if I saw the police.

"Then my godfather sold the grocery store and my father got a job at Pratt & Whitney. He was working about two days a week. There was nobody watching us. We matured quickly. I had to learn how to take care of myself.

"I only went to 8th grade. I quit school then. We had to move and Dad couldn't take care of us all so I went to Wethersfield and worked at Griswold's farm.

"On weekends I'd go caddying at the Wethersfield Country Club. I gave half the money I earned to Dad. I loved my father. Every Sunday he took us to a park and we went swimming and on rides. My sisters and I had only one pair of roller skates. We shared with each other.

"Then I went to Schultz United 5 & 10 Cent Store. I told the owner, 'Give me a counter and I'll sell all the fudge in the store.' The fudge was in the cellar. I proposed putting the fudge in a double boiler downstairs so that the smell would permeate the store. My speech worked and the owner hired me and I sold all the fudge. I was a good con artist. The owners were impressed.

"Another idea I had was filling a balloon with some rice and hitting it like a boxing bag. I gave the customers a speech on how to use the balloon to practice and be able to protect themselves. I sold a lot of balloons.

"Then they put me in the hardware department to sell Walker Turner tools. I taught the customers how to use the lathe and how to build furniture.

"I left that job and bought 'Stuminite' shellac. I went to every store on Main Street and told them, 'This stuff is wonderful. If you buy it, I will put it on for you.' I lied. Once they bought it I never came back.

"News about the CCC was widely advertised. I was 18 when I joined in the fall of 1933. I went with an older friend, Bernard Shaw. He had a car that was helpful in camp. There were other guys from Windsor who also joined and

Marty interviewing former CCC member Arthur Avedisian at a restaurant in Windsor. Podskoch

went to Camp Graves in Union. I got paid $30 a month and $25 went home to my dad. I had $5 for myself and made extra money running crap games. Remember, I grew up on the streets of Hartford and I learned a lot. I learned to fight from Tommy Tucker who was my best friend.

"On my first day at camp they put me on top of the water tower for half the night till they let me down. This was part of the hazing of new recruits. This was just for fun. All the guys were good at camp.

"On my first job I started working in the kitchen. I didn't like the job. Then I worked in the woods with a forester. We became good friends. He taught me two tree diseases: strumella and nectria. For strumella canker he took a hatchet and girdled the tree. A tree infected with nectria canker he said to chop it down. These diseases reduced the quality of the tree. I worked on this for months.

"My next job I worked building a road up on Soapstone Mt. in Stafford Springs. I cut trees and learned how to blow up stumps with dynamite. I had fun driving a grader. It wasn't hard work but pleasant, fun work. It kept me healthy.

"The food we had in camp was good. Any food was good because I was used to eating what my sisters cooked.

"On some weekends we'd go home and my friend, Shaw, got paid for taking other guys home except for me. The car was full and I was strapped to the fender so I didn't have to pay for the ride. The cars didn't go fast in those days. Some cars had to go up the hill backwards in Stafford.

"I dated a girl named Jenny from Stafford Springs Hotel. I met her at a Saturday night dance. I also went to barn dances. I was the most popular guy because I was the best dancer.

"In the evening and on weekends the guys had boxing

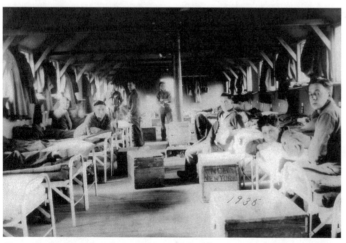

Camp Graves barracks where Arthur said, "In the evening we debated with each other and played craps. I also taught the guys how to dance." Gary Potter

and wrestling matches.

"After working at Camp Graves for a year I came home. My father's friend worked at Taylor and Fenn Company in Hartford where they did metal casting. I asked the superintendent for a job. He said, 'You're not big enough to work.' Just because I was short he didn't think could do the job. I said, 'If I'm no good you have power to fire me.' And I was hired.

"My first job was working in a pattern shop shellacking patterns. It was too boring. Then they put me in a core room. I worked with a machine making cores. I said to myself, 'This is fascinating.' I was moved to a bench and made cores. I was really interested. I wanted to know how to make them better and faster. My advancement was to piece work. I made the cores fast and made money.

"It was war time and I suggested to my boss that he should hire women. I recommended the women do piece work. He agreed and I taught the women how to work. The president of the company recognized my work.

"In 1940 I got married to Betty Carson of Manchester. She was very poor. We met in a night club dancing. We had three children: Margo, Arthur, and John.

"When WWII began I wasn't drafted because I was making parts for submarines using ductile iron."

I asked Arthur what he learned from being in the CCC. He replied, "I didn't learn anything. I grew up on the street. I was self-sufficient. But without the CCC there would have been a revolution in the cities. The CCC kept a lot of young boys off the streets.

"I'll never forget my dad's advice: 'Don't bring shame to the family name.' I never forgot that."

Arthur then showed me papers that told of his accomplishments in the field of metallurgy. He was a member of the Ductile Iron Society and helped found "Ductile Iron News" magazine.

I asked Arthur to explain what ductile iron was. "It is a type of cast iron invented by Keith Millis during the early 1940s. Most types of cast iron are brittle but ductile iron is much more elastic and flexible because it is infused with graphite. Working with ductile iron became my passion and even though I retired, I continue to teach classes about it."

After our meal, I thanked him for his stories and dinner. That fall I invited him to a reunion at the CCC Museum in Stafford Springs and he enjoyed sharing his CCC stories. The following year his son John called me and told me of his father's passing on June 8, 2009.

Harold E. Mattern Part I

Harold E. Mattern in college. Lee Salina

Many CCC alumni and family members told me that I should talk to Harold Mattern because he had the longest duration in the CCC in Connecticut and then worked for the Conn. Park & Forest Commission. They said he had a wealth of information on most of the camps in Connecticut because he worked in many of them.

I finally got to meet him on Sept. 5, 2007 when I visited Harold at his daughter Lee Salina's home in Mansfield, Conn. This is what I learned.

Harold was born on May 10, 1915 in Chaplin, Conn. His father, August, was a farmer who worked at the UConn poultry farm. His mother, Mable (Spooner), had four other children: Florence, Kenneth, Alice, and Wilfred.

Mattern spent most of his childhood in Mansfield, where he attended grammar school and was a Life Scout and Assistant Scout Master in the Boy Scouts of America, Troop 32. He was a member of the 4H Sheep Club and the Forestry Club. He attended Willimantic Trade School and in 1932 he graduated as a plumber. Mattern, however, couldn't get a permanent job. In the meantime he did odd jobs to help his family since he was the oldest boy.

"It was the Great Depression, and my father had lost his job as a tenant farmer. My three brothers and sisters were too young to work. My Boy Scout leader encouraged me to join the CCC. I was eligible because my father was out of work and I was single, out of school, and unemployed. I was just 18 when I joined the corps in Oct. 1934. It was the first time I left home to live elsewhere.

"The Army sent me to Camp Graves in Union. Our work was primarily in Nipmuck Forest. There were 50 guys in each of the four barracks. There were about eight other buildings. The Army lived in the headquarters building. The recreation building included a canteen. The washroom had a shower where we shaved but there were no flush toilets. Next was the mess hall that included a kitchen and a dining room for the officers and tech personnel. Then the infirmary was for the sick. Near the highway was the garage that had a pit that serviced two vehicles. There was also a blacksmith shop near the garage.

"I first worked in the woods cutting cord wood that was later sold. The foreman hired teamsters to haul out wood to the side of the road and to camp. This wood was used to heat the camp buildings. Some grade A wood was given to local towns for the poor for their cooking and heating.

"Then I worked with a surveyor on the state forest boundaries. Francis Bidwell was my foreman. I had this job for about six months. I enjoyed this job. We took lunches with us and toasted the sandwiches over a campfire in the winter. We had mostly peanut butter and baloney sandwiches.

"Next I worked with a gang building truck trails. We had a cleat-track bulldozer. We worked with a mattock shaping the banks of the road. They brought in truckloads of gravel and they used galvanized pipes under the roads. Some guys had the job of building culvert headers.

"Another job I had was fighting fires. We all received fire training and used Indian tanks. A few times we stayed

Camp Graves' young men having fun at nearby Morey Pond. Union Historical Society

the whole night in the woods. One of the chief causes of fires was fires at the town dumps and careless people burning brush and using trash barrels.

"The camp closed in April 1936 and most of the buildings were sold for lumber. There were a lot of poor people and some bought the empty CCC buildings and used the materials to build a home.

"In April 1936 I was 21 years old and I left the Union camp because it was closing. They asked me what camp I'd like to go to. Since Camp Fernow in Eastford was the closest camp about 14 miles from my home I asked for Eastford.

Harold Mattern's story is continued in Chapter 9, Camp Fernow.

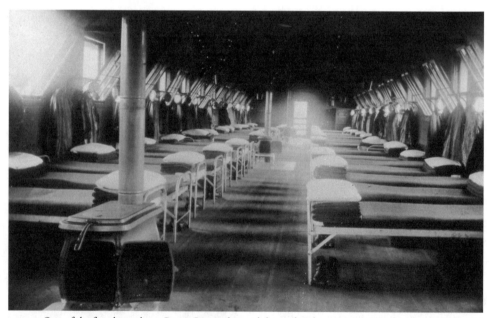

One of the four barracks at Camp Graves that each housed 50 boys. Union Historical Society

CHAPTER 22
VOLUNTOWN

(L–R) 1 During the summer of 1933 the Camp Lonergan enrollees lived in tents while the wooden barracks were being built. Gerry Dembiczak 2 CCC boys Joe Lalla (left) and friend on a bridge leading to a picnic area over Misery Brook with Camp Lonergan buildings in the back. Linda Lalla Lamothe 3 One of the many water holes built by the CCC in the PSF that are still used today. DEEP State Parks Archives

HISTORY

Camp Lonergan S-58 Co. 179 was founded on June 6, 1933 in the Pachaug State Forest (PSF) in Voluntown in eastern Connecticut near the Rhode Island border. Enrollees set up their tents on a brush-covered field next to Mt. Misery Brook. It became the home for 250 enrollees. The camp commander was Captain Leslie Cartwright and C. H. Tracy was the superintendent. The enrollees lived in tents until mid-September when they moved into new wooden barracks.[1]

Enrollees did most of their work in PSF. Here are some of their projects: constructed telephone lines to help prevent forest fires, built fire breaks along the CT/RI border, constructed water holes, removed dead trees, cleared brush 10' along both sides along roads, built roads for cars, constructed 33 recreation areas, did stream improvement projects, planted trees, worked to stop blister rust, surveyed state forest borders, and constructed buildings.[4]

On Feb. 1, 1934 the camp experienced the first enrollee fatality. Robert E. Ringland of Norwichtown was working behind a truck in the gravel pit when he was accidentally pinned between the truck and the gravel.[5]

Maj. Gen. Fox Conner came to Camp Lonergan on April 9, 1934 and awarded Camp Lonergan the prize of being the best camp in New England for the second enrollment period. In fact it was the second time in a year that they won the same prize.[6]

Camp Lonergan was honored again on June 2, 1934 when the Connecticut Forest and Park Association presented a plaque for winning the award for first place of all the CCC camps in New England.

By July 1, 1934 the Connecticut State Parks and Forest Commission reported the following completed work projects of Camp Lonergan: an entrance road into camp, the No. 1 trail through the forest running in a north

Augustine Lonergan

The Voluntown camp was named to honor Augustine Lonergan (1874-1947) who was born in Thompson, Conn. He graduated from Yale University Law School in 1902 and practiced law in Hartford. He was a US Representative for 11 years and a US Senator from 1933-39.[2]

wikipedia.org

Quinebaug Trail travels through PSF and at the junction of Hell Hollow Road passes by Phillips Pond. Co. 179 worked here and developed a recreation area that is still used today. Thurlow Coats

Camp Lonergan boys loading gravel used in building roads in PSF. At times it was a dangerous location with slides and truck accidents. Thurlow Coats

(L–R) 1 A home-made cement roller used for making roads by Camp Lonergan. It was left in the Pachaug SF. Mike Wilk 2 The entrance road into Camp Lonergan was improved in 1934 with a beautiful cedar fence and camp sign. Note the 8-mile speed limit. CT CCC Museum 3 Three CCC boys using a buzz saw to cut up cord wood at Camp Lonergan. Gary Potter

to south direction, a cut-off road traveling northwest from the camp, and five miles of road. Enrollees also began the construction of a fire line on the nearby Rhode Island border. They developed several picnic areas in the PSF. Enrollees also built a lumber shed and repaired the ranger's house.[7]

During this same time enrollees were very active in the production of wood products. They cut 593 cords of wood, 198 posts, 336 poles, and a total of 19,036 bd. ft. of logs.

The PSF contained a large amount of white cedar that enrollees harvested. Then the state purchased a second-hand No. 1 Lane shingle mill to use in the production of cedar shingles. To power the mill the state used a Fordson tractor. The mill was able to produce up to a thousand shingles an hour. These shingles were then used for state construction projects.[8]

During the winter of 1934-35 Mr. "Pop" Williams, the physical instructor, kept the boys busy with activities such as ping pong and pool tournaments, an inter-barracks bowling league, boxing matches, and basketball. The

basketball team played these nearby camps and town teams: Oneco, Plainfield, Camp Fernow, and the sailors at the Groton Submarine Base.[9]

In April 1935 Camp Lonergan again won the title of the best camp out of 104 CCC camps in New England. There were a total of 104 camps competing for the distinction.[10]

As spring approached in 1935 Coach "Pop" Williams started practice for the baseball season. There was inter-barracks competition as well as with other CCC camp teams. The boxers traveled to the Majestic Social Club in Westerly for boxing matches. Lonergan was one of the few camps that had a tennis court and tournaments were held. The boys also began developing a mini golf course.[11]

Camp Lonergan was called out many times to help towns in need. One instance was on a July morning in 1935. At 2:30 am the camp got a call to help the town of Voluntown because a fire was threatening the business section. There was no firefighting equipment in Voluntown. The enrollees, however, were familiar with fighting forest

Pachaug is the Indian word meaning bend or turn in the river. The Pachaug River runs from Beach Pond through the middle of the state forest to the Quinebaug River. This area had been inhabited by the Pequot, Narragansett, and Mohegan Indians.

During the late 1600s colonists and Mohegan Indians joined together and defeated the Pequot and Narragansett Indians. The Indian war veterans were granted a 6-mile tract of land that was called "Volunteers' Town." In 1721 it was incorporated into Voluntown.

The land was farmed and pastured. As early as 1711 mills had formed along the many streams. During the early 1900s farms and mills closed due to advanced technology. The only remaining evidence are the cellar holes, stone walls, stone foundations and parts of dams.

The Pachaug State Forest began when the state purchased land in 1928 in Voluntown. Today the PSF covers 24,000 acres in New London County and is located on the border with Rhode Island. It is the largest state forest in Connecticut.[3]

fires and quickly formed a bucket brigade. The enrollees also climbed on neighboring roofs to prevent the spread of fire. It worked and the town was saved.[12]

In the fall of 1935 the football team won the Eastern Semi-Pro Championship. They played the following teams: Franklyn, Mass., Stafford Springs, State College Freshmen "B" team, Danielson Townies, Norwich Ramblers, and Jewett City.[13]

When the enrollment of the camp was lowered to 200 men, it created space in Barracks No. 6. In December 1935 the barracks was converted into a schoolhouse/social center and turned over to the education dept. The building was divided into four classrooms with sliding walls that provided for classes or large group activities such as movies, amateur shows, lectures, and social gatherings.[14]

By the end of the year Capt. Jules L. Paridaens was camp commander and John P. Roche was the superintendent. Franklin Learned was the education advisor and Richard J. Caines was the camp surgeon.[15]

At the beginning of 1936 Camp Lonergan was fortunate in procuring 25 interchangeable memberships for the Shyma Club in Taftville (approximately 10-miles west of Voluntown). The camp used the basketball court on Monday and Thursday evenings. They also had use of the bowling alleys, reading rooms, pool tables, and other equipment.[16]

Dances were very popular amongst the enrollees. The camp was able to secure the Pachaug Grange Hall for these events. A dance was held in January and Joe Jackson's band of Norwich provided music.[17]

The basketball team had a successful 1935-36. They hammered the CCC Supply Depot of New London 29-13; beat the Battery "E" team in Westerly, RI 49-36; and crushed the Shyma Flashes of Taftville 49-25. The number of games was small due to the severe weather conditions that cancelled many games.[18]

The camp newspaper's February 1936 issue of the Lonergan Log reported the gypsy moth crew was handicapped in traveling through the woods in search of gypsy moth egg masses due to the deep snow.

Another forestry crew was cutting trees in the cedar swamp under foreman Clifford Congden. The purpose was to thin the forest to encourage growth. The cedars were then used to make shingles.[19]

A third project was taking place on Mt. Misery. The men were removing scrub oaks so that in the spring the area could be planted with pine trees.[20]

Work was continuing on the construction of the Green Falls Rd. A crew laid the first surface of gravel and then followed with a finishing layer.[21]

On March 23, 1936, 130 enrollees traveled to East Hartford to help the people whose homes and businesses were damaged from the flooding of the Connecticut River. Enrollees worked in the filth and mud to clean up the unhealthy conditions. The men worked until April 16th and returned to camp. They received many gifts and words of praise for their work.[22]

Ninety-five members of Co. 179 traveled to Hartford on April 29, 1936 where they were honored for their hard work doing relief work for the city. A banquet was held for

179th Company at Voluntown, Conn

Some of the activities at Camp Lonergan found in the First Corps Area, Fifth CCC District Yearbook, 1937

Camp Lonergan enrollees cut cedars in the PSF and made shingles that were used on various state buildings. DEEP State Parks Archives

CCC boys shoveling out trucks in the winter at Camp Lonergan. Gary Potter

(L–R) 1 Co. 179 in Voluntown built this wooden observation tower on Mt. Misery and used it to spot fires. Gary Potter 2 Twelve Company 179 workers taking a break while working in the Pachaug State Forest at Camp Lonergan. Gary Potter

the all the CCC camps that helped. A total of 1,268 CCC enrollees were honored and each received an engraved Ingersoll wristwatch.[23]

In April a dance was held at the Pachaug Grange. The dance drew approximately 70 young ladies from Jewett City, Voluntown, Plainfield, and Norwich. During the intermission food was served and enrollees presented song and dance activities.[24]

When spring came in 1936 enrollees turned to inter-barracks softball games and other sports. Mr. Learned began teaching life-saving classes for the approaching swimming season at nearby Beach Pond. Swimming classes were held later in June. The goal of the camp was to have every enrollee a swimmer. Trucks took the boys swimming nightly when it was warm.[25]

The tennis court was prepared for the tennis season. The clay court had to be leveled and rolled. Boys signed out raquettes and balls. A tournament was later held to find the camp champion.[26]

There were two other popular camp sports. There was an inter-barracks volleyball competition and two horseshoe courts.[27]

Another source of entertainment for Camp Lonergan was a WPA vaudeville show on May 18, 1936.[28]

During 1936 the Federal Government's Resettlement Administration began acquiring approximately 10,000 acres of sub-marginal farmland and woodland in Eastern Connecticut. Some of this was near the PSF and provided forestry and recreation projects for Camp Lonergan.[29]

By July 1936 enrollees completed the construction

of these roads: Green Falls Pond Rd. and No. 1 and No. 2 trails. There were now 11.2 miles of auto roads, one bridge, 43.8 miles of wood roads, and .2 mile of foot trails in PSF.[30]

Enrollees were also busy in the forest doing boundary surveys and type mapping. They surveyed and did type maps of 9,710.66 acres of forest.[31]

In the October 1936 issue of the Lonergan Log was a list of the Technical Dept. that guided the enrollees in their projects: Superintendent John P. Roche and staff: Fred Beard Jr, B. Ripley Park, Jay Ricketts, Clifford Congdon, Emmett Lamb, Milton Arnold, William Mack, James Fuller, and Raymond Linnell.[32]

As the new recruits came to camp in October 1936 the Education Dept. began these classes: spelling, shop math, salesmanship, music, woodworking, journalism, photography, dramatics, leathercraft, forest conservation, tree identification, nature study, first aid, auto mechanics, and camp discipline. Approximately 95% of the camp enrollees attended one or more of the classes. Many learned to read, write, and even dance in their home in the forest.[33]

Camp Lonergan's teams excelled in many sports. In 1936 the football team won the State CCC Football Championship. The team was undefeated and unscored upon. The camp teams also performed exceedingly well against leading semi-pro and pro teams in Conn. and RI.[34]

The August 1937 issue of The Shenipsit Lookout reported that the Camp Graves buildings in Union were to be dismantled and the lumber taken to Camp Lonergan to be used for forms in building a new dam.

The January 1938 issue of the Lonergan Log

A woodworking shop where CCC enrollees learned how to use tools. Gary Potter

The 1936 Camp Lonergan football team won the Connecticut CCC Championship. They were undefeated and unscored upon. Walter Sekula

introduced a new company commander, 1st. Lt. Francis G. Lee and a new camp doctor, David P. German. Franklyn E. Learned continued as Education Advisor along with John P. Roche as superintendent.

Between 1938-39 the WPA constructed a brick charcoal kiln in the PSF. CCC enrollees cleared the forest of downed trees caused by the 1938 hurricane and brought the wood to the kiln for processing into charcoal. There was a twofold benefit of the kiln. It helped remove thousands of trees that were destroyed by the hurricane and it helped remove a fire hazard. The state sold the charcoal to companies and made a profit.[35]

During the winter of 1937-38 the work on the Green Falls Dam was curtailed because of the cold weather. One of the dam's foremen, Joseph Consolini, was transferred to Camp Cross for the winter months. The bug crew, however, continued its search for gypsy moth egg masses on the trees. Albert Thiebault supervised the work. The crew was working in January in the town of Sterling.[36]

Dances continued to be very popular at Camp Lonergan. On Feb. 24, 1938 there were 300 people who attended the company dance at the Pachaug Grange Hall. Young ladies from Norwich, Danielson, Jewett City and Voluntown came to dance with the enrollees. Refreshments and party noisemakers made it a festive occasion.[37]

Camp Lonergan sawyers competed at the 1938 Hartford Sportsman Show. The team of John Sionkowski and Richard Mitchell set a record time of 16 seconds and came in first place in the first heat but a week later they beat their record with a time of 11.2 seconds. This, however, was only good for second place. Another Lonergan team of Nick Martino and Stanley Konn came in a respectable third

place. The sawyers were trained by these camp supervisors: Milton Arnold of Colchester, Leo Cahoon, and Donald Falvey.[38]

A new popular winter activity was added at Camp Lonergan, Bingo. Every week Bingo games were held and a limit of 100 men could play. The camp Exchange gave out 10 prizes each week.[39]

On Aug. 2, 1939 a spot fire occurred in pines that had been destroyed by the 1938 hurricane in Canterbury. The enrollees' quick arrival with their Indian tanks prevented a large fire from developing and limited the damage to just 31 acres.[40]

In October 1939 enrollees were anxious to see their new spruce green uniforms. No more wearing of Army hand-me-downs. The men also received matching dark green overseas caps.[41]

There was also a new education advisor listed in the October 1939 Lonergan Log newspaper. M. W. Price was now directing the education classes and organizing

Co. 179 enrollees used wood to form up a concrete wall for the Green Falls Dam. A cement mixer is in the background. CT CCC Museum

In November 1939 Camp Lonergan was presented the pennant recognizing Lonergan as the third best CCC camp in New England. Twice before Lonergan had won the first place pennant for all of New England.[42]

The January issue of the Lonergan Log described the benefits of being in the CCC. The enrollee received clothing, shelter, food, medical care, and salary. The enrollee received an additional perk when he left the CCC. Each discharged man was allowed to keep his new spruce green suit and enough winter clothing if he was discharged in the winter.

The Conn. Forestry Dept. hired local teamsters to remove the logs cut by the CCC boys of Lonergan. Thurlow Coats

In February 1940 Camp Superintendent John P. Roche reported that the Green Falls Dam was completed except for some landscaping in the area below it. It was one of the largest construction projects in the state. Co. 179 enrollees used rubble and masonry for the construction. The dam was 548' long, 6' wide at its top, and 16' wide at its base. The depth was 10' at the ends and 26' in the center. Enrollees quarried the stone near the dam site. The stones weighed between one pound to five tons each. The total masonry volume was 2,930 yds. A total of 5,553 cu. yds. of material were excavated and 2,840 cu. yds. of backfill were used. The men set up a screening plant in a nearby gravel pit and the men washed all the aggregate at the dam site. The young men used 9,313 bags of cement. The dam entailed 15,853 man-days of work. The workers and foremen were proud that there was no loss of time due to accidents. Three foremen supervised the work: Devine, Lamb, and Consolini.[43][44]

Superintendent Roche reported in March 1940 that since the devastating hurricane of 1938 caused such damage to the PSF, most of Camp Lonergan's work was salvaging the wind-torn timber. He stated that 325,354 bd. ft. of soft wood logs had been removed and taken to the state sawmill. A total of 100,420 bd. ft. of hardwood logs were removed. Some crew members did work on fire reduction. All the lumber produced in the state sawmill was used for state projects.[45]

In April 1940 Camp Lonergan won the pennant as the "Outstanding Company" in the inspection area out of a group of 12 camps. It was the second time Lonergan received this award.[46]

Sports continued to be popular in the spring of 1940.

The teamster dragged the logs to a road in the PSF and stacked it for a later transport to the sawmill. Thurlow Coats

Voluntown CCC boys brought logs to the state sawmill in Voluntown and made lumber that was used for state projects. Thurlow Coats

The baseball field was put into shape for the camp team and for inter-barracks softball competition. The other sports of tennis, volley ball, and horseshoes were also beginning as the weather warmed up.

By July 1, 1940 enrollees had completed the construction of Lawrence and Green Falls roads. There was now one mile of road for every 500 acres in PSF.[47]

Another smaller camp project was the construction of a sawmill shed that had a cement foundation.[48]

Camp Lonergan made a significant improvement in PSF with the tremendous amount of trees they planted. From July 1, 1938 to June 30, 1940 a total of over 250,500 trees were planted: 31,950 red pine; 47,700 white pine; 36,600 scotch pine; 45,600 Norway spruce; 36,850 white spruce; 35,400 European larch; 6,050 pitch pine; 500 Douglas fir; 7,950 jack pine; 4,400 mixed spruce, and 4,800 miscellaneous.[49]

In 1942 Camp Lonergan worked on developing Hopeville Pond State Park into a picnic area. Enrollees began removing short-lived trees such as poplars, alders, and grey birch so that hardwoods (oak, maple, ash, and beech) would take over the area. Their next project was to extend the bathing area by bringing in gravel and sand.[50]

After almost nine years of service, Camp Lonergan closed on May 28, 1942. It was the longest operating CCC camp in Connecticut.[51]

On Aug. 20, 1943 the camp was turned over to the State Forestry Dept.[52]

Eventually all the CCC buildings were removed and lumber was used on state projects. One building was burned by the state. Thurlow Coats

LEGACY

After nine years of work in the Pachaug State Forest, Camp Lonergan has left the citizens of Connecticut with a productive forest that continues to provide thousands of bd. ft. of lumber that is used by the state and also sold to the public for profit. The CCC developed miles of roads and trails for people to escape from the bustling cities and commune with nature. The forest is enjoyed by hikers, hunters, bikers, equestrians, and campers. The ponds and streams provide fishing and swimming.

At Hopeville Pond State Park Camp Lonergan developed picnic areas and expanded the swimming area so that today thousands of people come to the park for swimming, fishing and camping.

Directions:

From Norwich take Rt. 2 south to Rt. 165 on the left. Drive 12.6 mi. and Rt. 165 merges with Rt. 49. Go 0.5 mi. and then turn left onto Rt. 49. Travel north on Ekonk Hill

The January 1940 cover of the Lonergan Log camp newspaper.

Rd. for 0.5 mi. and turn left at Headquarters Rd. (Trail 2) at sign to DEEP Office (approximately 219 Ekonk Hill Rd. for GPS). Travel on this road for 0.8 mi to a Y. The road on the left goes over Mt. Mercy Brook but go to the right. You will see stone pillars on each side. This was the entrance to Camp Lonergan. The camp was on both sides of the road but all the buildings were removed.

Hopeville Pond is located in Griswold along the Pachaug River. DEEP

Map – Camp Lonergan

Green Falls Dam constructed by Camp Lonergan created beautiful Green Falls Pond that is great for hiking, swimming, fishing, and picnicking. DEEP

MEMORIES

"Football"
Bill Smith

Football is here in its colorful splendor,
Leaving thrills you long will remember.
Teams ready to fight – Crowds that cheer.
Coaches anxious as the battle draws near,
Banners are waving – bands start to play,
The whistle blows for the start of the fray,
There goes the kickoff – the crowd comes to their feet,
To cheer on their team in win or defeat.
The play around the end – an off-tackle smash,
A fullback plunge – a forward pass
A man gets away – he's now in the clear,
He sidesteps and twists as the goal line draws near.
A daring tackle, grunt, and fall,
But grimly determined he holds on to the ball.
Last down and seven – a drop kick is tried,
Toe meets the leather – the ball gets a ride.
The kicks away – it's good for a score,
The game is ended – hear the mob roar.
The crowd still cheers though the battle is won,
The band plays on as they never have done.
Excitement, color, thrills, and more
Can be found in just a football score.
There is no game you will longer remember
The football in all its colorful splendor.
- The Lonergan Log, Oct. 1936

331

Connecticut Civilian Conservation Corps Camps

"The Camp Song"
by Bill Smith

We are the boys of Voluntown you hear so much about,
The people stop and stare at us whenever we go out.
We're noted for our talent and the clever things we do,
Most everybody likes us and we hope you like us too.
HEY!
As we go marching and the band begins to P-L-A-Y.
You can hear them shouting,
The Boys from Voluntown are on their way. Hey! Hey!
- The Lonergan Log, Oct. 1936

"The School"
by Kenneth Fleming

The school in camp is to increase our knowledge'
If you learn enough, you are prepared for college

The subjects that are taught are for the benefit of us all
So come on boys, let's answer the call.

From six until ten there is time to spare
For some of us dumbbells who ought to care.

It should be our chief delight
To learn all we can with might.

The instructions are free to all
So all us boys should answer the school call.
The lessons that are taught are grand
And instructors are always willing to give a helping hand.

After you have gone to school
You'll be nobody's fool.

We all need schooling – don't forget!
So straighten up and be yourself yet.

Don't forget that we should grasp it
even if we're not going to college.

Our life is short and our old age near
So do your stuff at school, boys, and you'll have no fear.

Your chances for a job will be fine
And it will be easier for you to have spare time.

Learn while you can and be a well-known man
As knowledge gained is knowledge earned.
The Boys from Voluntown are on their way. Hey! Hey!
- The Lonergan Log, Jan. 1938

Camp Lonergan Mess Hall CT CCC Museum

"The Meal"
by Kenneth Fleming

When we sit down to eat
At first we all grab for the meat
To all of us it's a great big treat.

Next we grab our desert to make sure
In case there isn't any more it's secure

We gobble that down with one bite which is so pure.

We then get other kinds of food
Such as spinach and onions which are good
To furnish us with energy for chopping and sawing wood.

Soon our meal is ended to our dismay –
We are full to the crop and all so gay
All the chow hounds go and hide away.

We leave chow for another day
And then go and hit the hay.
- The Lonergan Log, Jan. 1938

A Camp Lonergan road crew clowning around. Gary Potter

"Safety"
by Kenneth Fleming

At work or at play
Us C.C.C. fellows should be safe and gay.

It doesn't pay to wear a frown
As our aim is to wear a crown.

Men working in the gravel pit
Should be apart so's not to get hit.

A pick or shovel will do much harm
So take precaution and watch your swinging arm.

Men working on the bug crew that wander all day
Should play safe as it will always pay.

Climbing trees and going over hill and dale
Is the bug crew's idea of a fairy tale.

The men that are wood choppers and sawers, too,
Careful of your tools, they are sharp through and through.
The men on the saw should be careful, too
For a mishap would mean an arm or two.
Safety in all walks of life
Should be our main strife.

If we play safe at our work
No one of us will have to grumble or shirk.
- The Lonergan Log, Jan. 1938

"Pay Day"
by Alex Rogulski

When pay day comes I always smile,
And yet I think 'tain't worth the while,
Cause, when in my hand they lay my dough,
I can just imagine where it will go.

And there in line, with itchy palms,
I find my "friends" with outstretched arms.
Tis true, I've saved a little dough,
But that is just a dime or so.

You'll find that too, the dime I mean,
With other coins in the old canteen.
And though I never buy a smoke,
Still, you'll always find me broke.

I ALWAYS find five bucks NOT MUCH
When I have my debs and such.
You see, my friends, 'taint worth the while
When getting paid, to give a smile.
- The Lonergan Log, Mar. 1938

"The Barber"
by Kenneth Fleming

A chatter here and a chatter there –
That's what goes on when in the barber chair.
Every night from six to ten
You will find the barber ready to tend.

He will cut your hair short or long
And gossip gaily with the throng.

He will put tonic on your bean
And make the hair on your dome gleam.

He shaves your face spic and span
And is dangerous with that left hand.
As the razor goes over your face
His hand moves at a speedy pace.

He plucks your eyebrows with a thong
Sometimes short and-sometimes long.
He cleans your ears and shines your nose
And after he's finished you smell like a rose.

Do you know of a barber ever so queer?
Who's so dumb but brings us cheer?

The boys of Co. 179 begin their day with the raising of the flag
as the bugler blows reveille. Gary Potter

He knows his stuff about the old hair
So C.C.C. fellows take the barber chair.

"The C.C.C."
by Raymond Rolfe

The United States has set aside
A place that should be a boy's big pride.
It's a place known as the C.C.C.
A place where boys should like to be.

Go to the city nearest thee
And a man will choose you the boy to be.
Next fill out your application true,
Then sit back and listen and do.

Now is the day that you are to go,
Thou it be in rain or snow...
You're in the camp that will be dear –

Maybe in the woods way back in the rear.

Next to be examined by the Doc, the man
Who always does for you whatever he can;
He puts you in bed when you have a cold
And when you come out you're sturdy and bold.

Marching along to the supply room we go,
Maybe some new or old clothes to sew –
Hats, coat, gloves, and all
Then we're ready for the old work call.

Now we're in the barrack and on detail,
Maybe to put some water in the pails,
Make the bunk nice and neat,
Then pull tight all the sheets.

I wonder what crew I'm going on
Says the young lad with a frown –
Maybe wood chopping or gravel pit
Or with the other men digging a ditch.

Working day is almost done
And we're working far from the setting sun.
Next to get ready for retreat,
Then after that something to eat.

Next, to the mess hall door
Just to eat some chow once more
A slice of bread, butter, and some meat.
After that eight hours of sleep.

Time for the lights to go out
And the boys cut down on their shout,
The life of the C.C.C. has been dear –
Both long weary and drear.
- The Lonergan Log, Mar. 1938

"The Rookies"
by "Foo" Pettibone

"Here's the rookies!" comes the cry
To the "rec" hall we all fly.
To get a glimpse of strange, new faces,
Guys like us from different places.

A SORRY LOOKING SIGHT WERE THEY
Ne're will we forget the day,
Short and tall, fat and lean,
A sadder bunch we'd never seen.

And when at night, they went to mess,
Just what to do they could not guess,
They didn't have the nerve to crab,
When they saw the others grab.

After chow they got their beds
And had a place to rest their heads,
But oh, the barracks roar and noise
Disturbed the peace of our boys.

But soon new pals and friends were found.
Friendship and good will abound.
And when things were serene at ten,
Contentment reigned in Lonergan.
- The Lonergan Log, Oct. 1939

me a large group photo of his camp in 1933. I arranged a telephone interview with her Feb. 22, 2008.

"My father's parents John Baptist and Josephine Paquette were married in 1898. They had 13 children: Grace, Josephine, Delia, John Baptist, Marie, Agnes, Selmar, Effie (Alice), Mary Blanche, Joseph and three children who died. My father was the youngest. His family lived in Sprague (near Lisbon). Dad was born in Versailles, Conn. on June 2, 1912.

"He only went to 7th grade at the Occum Grammar School then quit school to help his family. Dad worked in the forest with his father. His CCC records state he was unemployed since January 1933. He heard about the CCC and went to Norwich and joined on May 29, 1933. He was almost 21 years old. They sent him to Fort Wright on Fishers Island for a physical and conditioning. He was 5' 6" tall. He was there for almost a month and on June 28th he was sent to Camp Lonergan #2172 in Voluntown. Dad was a truck driver and laborer.

"My father liked working at the Pachaug State Forest in Voluntown while in the CCC.

"When he found a job he asked to be discharged. He was honorably discharged on Aug. 30, 1933. Dad got jobs working in mills. He worked in a box factory, Federal

Joseph Graveline

Anita and Joe Graveline of Voluntown. Irene Schott

Anita and Joe Graveline met after Joe was in the CCC camp in Voluntown. Irene Schott

Irene Schott of Voluntown told me when I was speaking at the Voluntown Library that her father, Joseph Graveline, was in the local CCC camp. She also showed

Paper Board Co., in Versailles. Then he worked as a grinder chipper at Electric Boat Co.

"On Jan. 21, 1939 he got married to Anita Gauvin of Taftville. They had three children: Florida, me, and Dolores.

"He retired in approximately 1978 from Norwich Public Works Dep. My father passed away on Aug. 2, 2002 in Voluntown."

Joe Lalla

On May 14, 2009 I met Linda Lamothe at my CCC talk at the Rose City Senior Center in Norwich. She told me her father, Joe Lalla, worked at the Voluntown CCC camp and she showed me some of his camp photos. She wasn't sure when he joined but on the back of one of the photos it said '1934.' A few months later I asked her to tell me what she knew about his life.

"My father's parents were Alexander and Julia. They had six children: John, Victoria, Joseph, Henry, Florence, and Violet. My father was born on Feb. 13, 1915 in Southington, Conn. He started 9th grade and then quit to help his family during the Depression.

"During this time he became a barber. In April 1934 he was unemployed and he heard about the CCC. On July 20, 1934 he joined the CCC. The Army sent him to Fort Wright on Fishers Island for a physical and training. He was 5' 7" and underweight at 133 pounds. The doctor wrote in Dad's records that he had severe varicose veins in both legs and was missing eight of his 32 teeth.

"On July 25th he was sent to the Voluntown camp. He was classified a laborer. I'm not sure what jobs he did but Dad got the nickname 'the Count' at the camp. He was a charismatic person and had a 'valet' who waited on him.

The nickname 'Count' continued for his CCC friends his whole life. Some of his CCC friends were members of the Szablewski family from Jewett City.

"For entertainment Dad liked going to the camp dances. He also played on the football team. I also remember him telling me the story about him and how he and his friends drank too much and fell into a ditch.

"My father was a colorful, strong-minded person, which might explain why he received an administrative discharge after being in Camp Lonergan for 15 months. His work habits were classified as 'unsatisfactory' and he was AWOL on July 3, 1935 and Sept. 22, 1935.

"While Dad might not have been the best candidate for the structure of the CCC, I feel that the CCC experience had a kind of delayed reaction for him. While he may have been a wild and crazy nineteen-year old balking at some of the camp rules, he managed to pull his life together and by the early 1940s, he had established his own business, the Paramount Barber Shop, in downtown Norwich. I guess this might be called 'growing up'!

"My dad and my mother, Elizabeth 'Libby' Jankowski, were married in 1940. They met at a dance held by the CCC in Voluntown. They had me and my brother.

"Dad's barber shop was a center for politicians, factory workers, philosophers, and artists. Often his shop was packed with people; however not all were there for haircuts. Drinking his coffee and shooting the breeze kept customers and visitors coming back.

"Throughout his life, my father was committed to doing for others, including customers and friends who needed a little something. He was a very active member of the Norwich Lions Club for three decades and was awarded 'Most Valuable Member 1960-61.' We still have the plaque.

Joe Lalla (left) and buddy at the entrance to Camp Lonergan. Linda Lamothe

Joe Lalla (left) sitting on the picnic table with pal by the footbridge near the entrance to camp. Linda Lamothe

Through the Lions, Joe became fervently committed to helping the blind and visually impaired. This is the primary focus of the Lions Club, but Joe went above and beyond in helping those in need. I recall him driving an elderly blind woman to visit relatives in western Connecticut several times a year.

"Dad was an avid worker in creating the Tercentenary Celebration of Norwich in 1954. The Lions Club float took him and his fellow Lions countless hours to create.

"Although my dad only had an eighth-grade education, I feel that the CCC helped to educate him in many ways. The self-discipline kicked in a couple years later, and along with that, this young fellow became self-educated. He worked hard to provide excellent educations for his two daughters, who earned Master's degrees in the fields of teaching and library science. I'm very proud of my dad for working so hard, building a successful business, giving back to the community, and creating a wonderful life for my family.

"My father passed away in 1980."

Theodore "Ted" Potocki

Ted Potocki at the Connecticut CCC Museum in Stafford Springs where he did volunteer work. He also donated some tools that he had used in the CCC. Bonnie Potocki

Note: This story contains excerpts from Sharon Kay Smith's interview for her 1996 Master's thesis: "The Legacy of the Civilian Conservation Corps in Connecticut," and information from his daughter, Bonniemay Potocki.

Theodore "Ted" Potocki came from a family of six children. He was the fourth, the only boy. His father was a weaver and loom fixer at Eldridge Mills and at American Woolen Mills but he had limited employment at both companies because of the Depression.

Ted served in the CCC from 1937-1940. He joined in Moosup, Conn. at age 17. He re-enlisted four times. His first assignment was at Camp Lonergan in Voluntown.

Then he was sent to Durango, Col. While there his foreman, George Walters, told him all about Butch Cassidy who used to live in the valley because he liked it there. Later they moved the whole camp to Paradise Valley in Moab, Utah.

Ted returned to Connecticut for his last stint at Camp Robinson in East Hartland.

"The C's changed me for the better," said Ted. "I worked on road building, gypsy moth control, and fire trails. In the evening I took education courses in forestry.

"The Eastern camps offered more education than those out West. I enjoyed the Saturday night dances.

"My most memorable experience in the CCC was, well, everything,"

From 1940-1944 Ted was in the Marines. After WWII, Ted married Annamay (Jolie). They had two children: Harold and Bonniemay.

Bonniemay said, "Mom and Dad lived in Chula Vista, Calif. and Tucson, Ariz. after they were married in 1950 because Dad liked the weather after being out West with the CCC. Dad worked for Rohr Aircraft in California. I'm not sure where Dad worked in Arizona.

"They returned to Connecticut in 1961 and purchased a home in Manchester. Dad worked in carpentry and masonry. Then he went to a sheet metal school. He worked in shops and moved up to Pratt & Whitney. In 1985 Dad retired after working there for 25 years.

"After retirement in 1985, Mom and Dad volunteered as host and hostess at the CCC Museum in Stafford Springs. He loved his work in the CCC and in retirement he joined the National Association of Civilian Conservation Corps. They had monthly meetings where the guys enjoyed sharing their CCC stories.

"Dad was an avid outdoorsman and was active in helping develop the Hockanum River Hiking Trail, a 15-mile trail along the Hockanum River in Manchester.

"In 2001 my father passed away in Manchester."

Bronislaw "Bruno" Dembiczak

Army photo of Bronislaw "Bruno" Dembiczak. Bernice Riha

Walter, Bronislaw, Josephine, and Aniela (Nellie).

"In 1928 my father left Franklin School in Bridgeport after 8th grade. He then attended Congress High School taking their commercial classes at the night school for about four months.

'I don't know what Dad did for a job when he left school but it was probably something to help his family.

"On May 29, 1933 he joined the CCC and went to Fort Wright on Fishers Island for a physical and training. On June 5, 1933 he left Fishers Island and went to the Voluntown camp #2172. He was a laborer and his work was graded as 'satisfactory.'

"After 10 months in the CCC, Dad was discharged on March 31, 1934 and the Army furnished him transportation to his home in Bridgeport.

"After the CCC Dad worked as a stock clerk at Bryant Electric Co in Bridgeport, Conn.

Bernice Riha came to my CCC talk at the Wallingford library on Oct. 23, 2008 and showed me pictures of her father, Bronislaw "Bruno" Dembiczak at the Voluntown CCC camp in 1933-34. She later copied the photos and gave them to her brother Jerry who passed them to me at one of my monthly land trust walks in Colchester.

I finally contacted Bernice in Jan. 2014 when I was writing the chapter on the Voluntown camp. She said that she didn't know that much about her father's activities in the camp but she did find his CCC and Army discharge papers and shared this info with me.

"My father was born on Aug. 18, 1910 in Wallingford. His father, Joseph, was from Rogie, Austria where he worked as a provision dealer. His mother, Annie Bucior, was born in Brzyckwala, Austria. They had four children:

Bruno's friends by their tent in 1933 with their camp dog. Bernice Riha

Bruno (center top row) and his uniformed buddies are waiting for the truck to take them to town for a date, movie, or dance. Bernice Riha

(L–R) 1 In June 1933 Camp Lonergan was in in its early stages. Bernice Riha 2 Bruno is in his CCC uniform with a sporty hat at the entrance to Camp Lonergan. The tents had been replaced with wooden buildings. Bernice Riha 3 Bruno (2nd row right with a hat) was part of the camp's fire-fighting crew with their Indian tanks. Bernice Riha

"Then on Feb. 17, 1942 he was drafted into the Army and had three months of basic training at Fort Devens, Mass. Then he spent 12 months attending Radio Operator School. He then spent 24 months as a radio operator. 'He operated portable radar equipment by manipulating tuning and operating controls while observing readings on oscilloscopes. He plotted and read both polar coordinates and assisted in keeping equipment in good operating condition with the 583rd Signal Aircraft Warning Battalion in the Pacific Theater of Operations.'

"On Nov. 28, 1945 Dad was honorably discharged from the 33rd Fighter Control Squadron at Ft. Devens Army Base as a Private 1st Class.

"He received a good conduct medal in the Pacific Theater, a campaign ribbon with a bronze service arrowhead, an American Theater Campaign ribbon, a Philippines Liberation ribbon with 2 bronze service stars, and a Victory medal.

"After WWII Dad returned to Bryant Electric Co.

"On July 26, 1947 Dad married Margaret Hetesh. I have a brother, Gerald.

"Dad passed away on June 26, 1981."

Carmine Vietri

Camp Lonergan friends Carmine Vietri (left) & Bill Mentillo (front) together with another friend (right). Carmine Vietri Jr.

In the summer 2008, I had a telephone interview with Carmine Vietri at his home in Guilford, Conn.

"On April 7, 1915 I was born in Bridgeport. My father Joseph worked at Remington Arms where he mixed powder. My mom, Assunta, had 10 children: Anna, Amedeo 'Danny,' Rose, Vicki, Theresa, Grace, Marie, Amato, and me. I was the second oldest. My mother's first child, a girl, died on my parents' way to the US from Italy.

"While I was in high school I sold newspapers and shined shoes to earn money to help my family.

"I graduated from high school but couldn't find a job. Then I saw in the newspaper about the CCC and signed up in Bridgeport. I wasn't nervous; I was excited. There were three others guys from Bridgeport who joined.

"We went to New Haven and got a physical exam. Then we went by train to New London where we got on a boat and went to Fishers Island. I had a stye over my right eye and they thought I needed it operated on. The doctor lanced it. I stayed for one week and then went to Camp Lonergan.

"When I got to camp it was in the woods near Voluntown. I liked it. It was exciting. I loved being outdoors. There were a lot of guys that became my friends. One of my best friends, Bill Mentillo, just passed away at 93.

"My first job was in the gravel pit. We loaded trucks with shovels and they took the gravel for roads. Then I was put on the woodchopping crew. We worked in pairs. My partner and I cut down trees that were marked by a state forester, who blazed them with an ax. When our saw or ax got dull, the state foresters came around and sharpened them. Sometimes an axe glanced off a tree and cut a guy's knee. You had to be careful.

"The third job I had was on the dynamite crew. My state forester made me the lead man with the battery. It had to go with me wherever I went. When I gave the order 'fire' the guy on the other side would yell back, 'fire.' That meant it was all clear. Then I hooked up the battery to the wire and

The gravel pit crews often had races loading trucks. Thurlow Coats

A view of Camp Lonergan from a tree. The garage is on the left and the water tower is in the rear. Gary Potter

pushed the plunger down. We were dynamiting rocks for road building. No one was ever injured. We had to keep the dynamite separated from the caps. No one was ever injured.

"My next job was as an amateur photographer. I climbed trees to get a picture of the five barracks, officers' quarters, and mess hall. I had postcards made for the recreation hall. I did it for enjoyment.

"During winter the snow was 1' deep. They said we had to shovel our way to the mess hall or we wouldn't eat.

"I was also a forest fire fighter. I went with a group of guys and carried a water pack on my back. We also carried shovels and pick axes and went onto trucks to fight fires in the woods. Luckily I never got hurt.

"On weekends I used to go to Jewett City to see a movie or have a couple drinks. The last truck back to camp was at 11 pm. I missed the truck a couple times and had to hitchhike 11 miles back.

"About once a month I hitchhiked to Bridgeport on Friday night because I wanted to get home to my family. It took me a couple hours to get home.

"The food was very good. We had good chefs and you could get seconds if you wanted.

"In the evenings we went to the rec hall to play pool or cards. We had other recreation activities. There were football and baseball teams. We brought our instruments and formed a country band. I played the violin. We played at grange halls and square dances. Women brought us food to eat. We had a lot of fun.

"There was an education advisor who scheduled classes. I learned clerical work, typing, and filing reports. I had a part-time job working in the office. At a night class, I got a report card that said I passed an exam.

"I was discharged in December 1934 because I could only stay for one year and three months. When I came home I went to employment offices at many factories searching for a job. I finally got a job working at Manning, Maxwell, and Moore. Then I worked in a machine shop in Bridgeport.

"In 1943 I was drafted into the Army. I went to the SW Pacific islands, Guadalcanal and New Caledonia. I was a radio operator.

"In January 1946 I came home and the next year I married Shirley Jane MacNeil. We had a son, Carmine, Jr.

"I went to work for the Post Office as a letter carrier. After 27 years I retired.

"Once I went back to my old CCC camp with my good friend. It had changed a lot. Nobody was living there. The barracks were empty. I wished I could have stayed longer in the CCC. It was a good healthy life."

Carmine passed away on Oct. 6, 2008

Charles J. Dougela

Charles J. Dougela was born on Nov. 15, 1915 in Waterbury. He had two siblings. His father worked at the Cheney Cloth Mill in Manchester, Conn.

In 1933 Charles went to Hartford and enrolled in the CCC and was assigned to Camp Lonergan in Voluntown.

He was put in charge of the tool shop where he learned how to do repair work. Charles said, "It was an exhilarating experience."

In the evening he attended education classes where he learned basic math and science.

Since the camp wasn't close to a town the boys had to create their own entertainment. One of Charles' hobbies was playing violin. He even got to play on radio station

Charles worked in a tool shop like this one in Eastford where they repaired tools and worked with the blacksmith. CT CCC Museum

parameters

WTIC hosted by Norman Cloutier who had a program that visited CCC camps.

"I enjoyed the music in camp but it was mostly a lot of work. The fun part was when we got to rest," said Charles.

After he left the CCC he married Valeria (Stankevich) and they had four children: Tom, Claire, Marge, and Ray. He and his family lived in East Hartford for over 60 years.

Charles said, "I learned how to respect the outdoors in the CCC just like many of the other enrollees. My experience working in the tool shop helped me get a job at Colt's Firearms Company as a tool and die maker.

On Dec. 10, 2000 Charles J. Dougela passed away.

Drayton Holcomb

Drayton Holcomb (center) with two friends by their barracks. Holly Condon

After searching through a list of CCC alumni interviewed by Sharon Kay Smith who wrote a thesis on Connecticut CCC camps, I tracked down Drayton Holcomb. I was lucky to find his daughter, Holly Condon, in West Suffield, Mass. She said her father lived at the Meadow Brook Nursing Home in Granby. I called him on May 10, 2012 and he told me about his life and his days in the CCC.

"I was born on March 2, 1916 and had two brothers and two sisters: Edith, Carlton, George, and Catherine. My father, Chester, was a farmer and my mother was Rebecca Phelps. My parents met at the New Gate Prison in East Granby that my mother's uncle owned.

"My father got asthma and my brother and I had to

run the farm. Eventually my father had to sell the farm in 1939.

"After my second year of high school I quit school to get a job to help my family. I think my father heard about the CCC from our selectman. In December 1935 I was 18 years old and signed up for the CCC in Granby. It was a way for me to get money to help my family.

"My dad drove me to the CCC camp in Voluntown. It was all right. I enjoyed it there. I was happy to have a job and be able to help my family.

"My first job was cutting deadwood in the forest. Then I became a truck driver. I drove a dump truck in a gravel pit where 3-4 guys loaded my truck. I also drove a rack truck and carried men out to different jobs. I took guys to dances at the Pachaug Grange Hall and sometimes to Jewett City to the movies. They also went to a little restaurant in town. We had a football team and I drove them to play other teams.

"During the flood of '36 I drove truck in East Hartford where the guys cleaned out basements from flooded homes. My job was taking the junk to the dump. At night we stayed at some CCC camp just south of East Hartford.

"Another job I had was driving the Lieutenant to Norwich where I picked up food for our camp. I made this trip at least once a week.

"One time I was driving an Army truck to Boston in a convoy and was sideswiped. Because of that accident I was not allowed to drive Army trucks. I was disappointed after that because I enjoyed that job.

"In the evenings I went to the rec hall and played ping pong and read. We also had a little store where I bought candy. Captain Peradean's office was at the end of the rec

Drayton drove a CCC truck (left) during the 1936 Flood. Roberta Kosnoff Sciacca

hall. He was a nice guy. I enjoyed the boxing matches at camp and playing jokes on new recruits like short-sheeting their beds.

"Sometimes on the weekends I hitchhiked home. It wasn't too hard getting rides.

"Some men in my camp made extra money by cutting hair while other guys loaned out money. Then on payday they waited at the pay line to collect one extra dollar on each dollar they loaned.

"In April 1936 I left the CCC because I had put in two years and that was the limit. Captain Peradean drove me all the way back to Granby.

"I used to cut my neighbor's lawn and she told me that her husband, who was a construction foreman, needed workers. So I asked him for a job. He got me my first job building bridges. My first bridge was over railroad tracks in South Bridge, Mass. Then my second bridge was in Three Rivers, Mass. They had a lot of flooding and there was a lot of construction work.

"Then I did carpentry work and built houses.

"I met my wife, Lois Petit, at Congamond Lake, in Massachusetts. We dated for a few years before getting married.

"In 1940 I worked in Bermuda building a naval base. I was there for two years. The pay was good, too.

"When I came back I married Lois in 1944. We had two girls, Holly and Judy.

"The Army drafted me right after I got married. I was 30 years old. They sent me to Florida for 17 weeks of training and then to France and all the way to Berlin but I didn't see any action.

"I came back to Hartford and bought a gas station and ran it until 1949. Then I met Charlie Kaman of Kaman Aircraft. In 1950 he hired me and I became a foreman in the helicopter blade department. I worked there for over 20 years. I retired in 1971. My wife and I sold our home and we traveled for twenty years all over the US.

"The CCC changed my life because I was able to meet so many fellows who became good friends and we had many good times together. I learned how to take orders and not to talk back."

Drayton Holcomb passed away on Sept. 26, 2013.

Edward Piontkowski

Sharon Viadella of Griswold met me on Sunday,

Edward Piontkowski, 4th from left in the back row, was on the 1934 Voluntown CCC football team. Sharon Viadella

Sept. 29, 2013 at a CCC Museum in Stafford Springs and showed me a picture of her father, Edward Piontkowski, in a Camp Lonergan football team picture. This was the only information she had so I suggested getting her father's discharge papers.

A few months later she mailed me his discharge papers.

Edward Piontkowski was born in Norwich on Sept. 8, 1915. His father, Edward, Sr., was born in Austria and his mother, Amelia, was born in Norwich. They had two sons and one daughter. Edward, Jr., graduated from Greenville Grammar School in Norwich and then worked on farms.

When Edward was unemployed in December 1933, he went to the city of Norwich and Mayor E. G. Moran helped him sign up for the CCC on Jan. 15, 1934. Three days later he signed an oath of enrollment. He was 6' 2" and weighed 172 pounds.

Edward went to Camp Lonergan on Jan. 18, 1934 and worked as a laborer. He was rated by his supervisor as "excellent."

After working at Lonergan for more than a year he was transferred to the Supply Depot in New London on May 23, 1935. Here he did "warehouse supply" work and received a "satisfactory" evaluation. Edward worked there till Oct. 10, 1935.

Then Edward was sent to Camp Fechner, Co. 2102 in Wooster Mountain State Park in Danbury. When he arrived he requested that he be transferred and was told "that this would not be granted." Edward told the officer that the enrollees in the camp were too young and that "he intended to desert." Company commander Capt. Schwartz informed him about the seriousness of this offence. Edward decided not to stay in this new camp and the Army didn't go searching for him. He was formally discharged on Oct. 18, 1935. There were other boys ready to take his place.

Sharon told me, "After my father left the CCC he worked at Electric Boat Co. as a ship fitter.

"My father was married twice, first to a lady named Beatrice. I don't know what her last name was. They had one daughter, Edna. His second marriage was to my mother Evelyn Bernier. I have a sister, Sandra, and a brother, Edward, III. My father died in New London on April 2, 1977."

Sharon was happy to learn a little more about her father after being separated from him when she was just two years old.

James & Philip "Charlie" Marceline

Philip "Charlie" Marceline and his bride Frances on their wedding day March 30, 1951. Manny Cardoza Jr.

Manuel Cardoza Jr. of Preston, Conn. sent me this information about his two half-brothers, James & Philip Marceline who were in Camp Lonergan in Voluntown.

James and Philip's parents were Moses Marceline and Senhernia Gomes both from the Cape Verde Islands. They had four children: James, Rose, Mildred, and Philip. My mother divorced Moses and married Manuel Cardoza. They had five children: Robert, Leo, me, Amaro, and Mary.

My father worked on the WPA. He was a stone mason and worked on the Uncas on Thames TB Hospital. Dad also worked at Rocky Neck State Park building the big pavilion. James only went to 8th grade while Philip went to a couple grades in high school.

They joined the CCC around 1934-35 and were happy to make some money for their family. There were a lot of local boys from Norwich in camp such as the Rizzuto and Ritacco families from Talman St.

My brothers said they lived in barracks. They planted thousands of trees and built bridges at Hopeville Pond State Park. They also built cabins for the rangers.

I was born in 1929 and my half-brothers came home on weekends as long as the weather was good. We lived in Norwich. I remember they had a football game at Hollyhock Island Park. It was actually a landfill. James was tough and he played on the team. I went to see him. He was built like a fire hydrant. They called him "Butchy." Philip, who we called "Charlie," played on the baseball team.

One time a small black lab mix puppy was born in camp and my brother Jimmy wrapped it in a towel and walked all the way home with it. Then he went back to camp. We kept the pup and nicknamed him "Shadow."

My brothers probably left the CCC because they got jobs. Jimmy worked in Electric Boat Co. as a machinist on the last shift and Charlie worked at the VanTassle Leather Factory.

In 1942 both were drafted. They went for physicals and were in great shape. Charlie & Jimmy both went into the Navy.

After the war Charlie became an engineer at VanTassle Leather Factory and Jimmy went to New Britain and got married to a local girl. My brothers never had any children. Charlie died at age 83 and Jimmy died at 92.

Ray Misluk

Former Voluntown CCC enrollee, Ray Misluk, shared his CCC stories with the audience at the Goshen Public Library. Podskoch

(L–R) 1 Ray drove a truck like this one. He also made the coffee at a campfire and helped the workers in their jobs. John Balavender 2 CCC boy searching for gypsy moth egg masses. He painted them with creosote. Conn. Agricultural Experiment Station 3 Ray played pool in the Camp Lonergan rec hall that was similar to the above rec hall in Camp White. Paul Adykoski

As I walked into the Goshen Library to give a talk on Sat. May 3, 2008 about the CCC camps, I saw an elderly man walking in with a young man.

I asked him if he was in the CCC or knew someone who had been in the CCC.

"Yes, I worked at the Voluntown camp in 1934. I'm Ray Misluk and this is my son-in-law, Lowell Wortman Jr. We live in the nearby town of Harwinton."

I asked Ray if he would share his stories with the large audience that came out that day and he agreed.

"I was born in Forestville on April 7, 1919. We desperately needed money to survive so I quit school and joined the CCC.

"My father, Alex, made sand molds in an iron foundry in Plainville during the Depression but he wasn't working that much.

"My mother's name was Dora Karova who was Polish. The children ranged from the eldest Sam, to Jack, Mary, Catherine, Steve, myself, Ann, Michael, Peter, and John who died in childbirth.

"I wasn't that good of a student. I kept failing school and I was so embarrassed. I was 15 years old and still in 5th grade. I had no shoes and not much clothes. I went to school with newspapers under my shirt to keep me warm. There was no food in the house. So I quit school to help my family.

"I heard about the CCC from the welfare department. They wanted to ship me to Oregon but my mother wouldn't let me go because it was too far away. I had a buddy, Robert Duffy, who went to Oregon along with his friend Roy Extrom. Duffy is still alive in Florida.

"My older brother, Steven, was good in sports and he stayed in school. I volunteered to help the family because the other boys were younger.

"It was the fall of 1934 that I first went to Hartford for my physical exam. Then the Army shipped me to Voluntown near the Rhode Island border.

"At first it was hard to leave my family. I got homesick easily but mother needed food for the family so I stayed.

"I was the youngest guy and I was the camp pet. I had friends like Finn Halessey. He told me, 'Ray, if anybody bothers you, let me know and I will take care of them.' He was a big husky guy. I probably weighed about 90 lbs. soaking wet."

Someone in the audience asked, "Ray, what kind of work did you do in camp?"

"I was a truck driver because I just came off a farm and I knew how to drive mules and horses. They gave me a government issued test. I went to Norwich with an officer and he told them I was a good driver. He even lied about my age.

"When I left the camp I got my Connecticut license for 50 cents, and I didn't have to take a test. I drove trucks all my life and never had an accident.

"At camp I drove a dump truck. We used to put 8-10 guys on boards in the back for them to sit. There was a portable canvas top in case it rained.

"I never sat down on my ass; I worked with the guys.

"We always had a campfire. There was a metal coffee percolator and I made the coffee.

"For lunch the sandwiches were wrapped in butcher paper by the cooks and I brought them in my truck.

"Then I was made trail man or leader. My crew was looking for gypsy moths. I marked the trail in and out. I'd have about 20 men in a line. There were a couple of truckloads of guys going through the forest and farm lands. When we found the brown clusters we painted them with creosote.

344

"In the springtime we planted trees and in the winter we chopped wood for the following year. All the camp stoves used wood.

"Then I worked with a blacksmith in his shop. We made wheels for wagons. We also worked on truck bodies and used scrap metal fastened to tie boards.

"On the weekends the guys went to town and went drinking. I never went drinking because my father was a drinker. I didn't want to be like him."

Then someone asked if he ever got sick in camp?

"I had my tonsils out. They took me in a truck to New London and I got on a tugboat to Fort Wright on Fishers Island. The Army had a hospital. They sat me in a chair and wrapped a sheet around me. Then someone snuck up and put ether gas over my face. Six hours later I woke up. There were male nurses who kept saying, 'Wake up chicken! Wake up!'

"While I was there they had me working. I took coal off a barge and shoveled it onto a wagon with a big coal shovel. Then I drove the mules to the hospital from the barge.

"I was there for 2-3 weeks recuperating and then back to the camp.

"I just remembered the jokes guys played on each other, especially the rookies. There was a new group that came every six months. When I first got to camp, they initiated me. After taps at 10 pm I had to go around the camp and yell, 'All is well!'

"Sometimes they sent guys to the kitchen for a pail of steam. Another was to go to the shop and ask for a left-handed monkey wrench."

Ray worked in a blacksmith shop like his one in Eastford repairing tools and equipment. CT CCC Museum

I asked Ray what he did in the evenings and on weekends?

"We played pool in the rec room or went for hikes in the evening. On the weekends, I think it was on Sundays, we went to Jewett City to the movies. They cost 5 cents if you had a nickel otherwise you just walked around town.

"If a guy had a month without any problems, they gave him a day off. We also got extra down time for fighting fires. This was vacation time. One time I stayed home for a week.

"I hitchhiked home most of the time. One time I had to walk and walk because I didn't get a ride. I got flat feet from walking so much. I went to the infirmary and was laid up for four days. They got me arch supports so I could work again.

A lady then asked how the food was?

"We had a colored cook, named Kelly. He was short and stocky. I think he was from New Haven. We had no problems with colored people. We worked together, slept together, and had no trouble at all."

I asked how long did he stay there?

"I got homesick and left in the spring of 1936. I had been there for 18 months. I got a job working for Arbio Road Construction from Hartford and Farmington. I drove a dump truck.

"I met my wife Evelyn Swanson of Forestville through a friend. We married in 1940 and had two girls, Gail and Karen.

"In 1942 I enlisted in the Army. When I got to Fort Devens they found out that I had TB and I wound up in the state sanitarium, Cedar Crest, in Newington for 18 months. My wife was a wonderful person; she came to visit me every day.

"When I was discharged from the Army I took a machine class and got a job in New Departures Co. where I worked in production. I was a ball race grinder.

"I then worked for a repair shop as foreman for 18 years. Finally, I went into business for myself and started an auto body repair shop in Forestville. I owned that for 21 years. I retired in 1980.

"In retirement I bought a farm in Harwinton and made hay on six acres."

Another man asked, "Did the CCC help you in any way?"

"It was a great experience. It gave me a job and helped my family by sending money home. I learned how to work hard chopping wood, how to drive trucks, and how to work with tools."

I asked Ray if he ever went back to his camp?

"Marty, I never went back to camp because I was too busy."

Robert W. Manchester

At Cromwell's Belden Public Library, I met Bob Manchester at my CCC talk on Wed. Apr. 30, 2008. Bob told me his dad, Robert W. Manchester, was at two CCC camps during the early 1930s: Voluntown and Niantic. A few weeks later I interviewed Bob by phone.

"My father was born on Nov. 3, 1914 in Brooklyn, NY. His parents were Norman and Florence May (Wade). They had four children: Norman, Robert, Arthur, and Ethel. My grandmother remarried after her husband died in 1921 and she had three children: Frank, Everett, and Leona.

"In those years, the family was living on Staten Island, NY. My grandfather and his brother Otis were ship's officers (chief engineers) in the U.S. Merchant Marine, sailing on US flag freighters. Interestingly, my grandfather's last ship, the SS Willimantic, was sunk by a German submarine in 1942 off Cape Hatteras, NC. This was many years after his passing in 1921.

"Sometime after my grandfather's passing, probably in the early 1920s, my grandmother moved to the Middletown, Conn. area, where she had some family. She remarried and had three children from the second marriage: Frank, Everett, and Leona.

"Dad was one of the smartest guys I knew but he only went to about 7th or 8th grade because in those days you had to quit school to help your parents.

"Early on in the CCC program, most likely 1933 or

Bob Manchester worked at Camp Lonergan just like the truck driver (right) at the Eastford Camp. CT CCC Museum

1934, Dad enlisted. He was first stationed in Voluntown, Conn. and to my knowledge he truly enjoyed life there. In addition to manual labor, he learned to operate some equipment and drive dump trucks. This would prove helpful for him later on because he became a Teamster driver. Discipline was good and fair. He enjoyed the food, played baseball and cards, and made many friends. According to family lore one time on leave he brought home a friend, who eventually married his sister Ethel. The couple had a long and happy marriage, and my aunt is well and enjoying life at 97.

"Dad was then transferred to a camp at Stones Ranch in Niantic.

"My father left the CCC, sometime in 1935, because in 1936, he was working at A.N. Pierson in Cromwell, then the largest Rose grower in the world. He worked in their large steam plant, installing and maintaining steam and water lines throughout Pierson's vast array of greenhouses. Later in life he also held a plumber's license.

"From the late 1930s until 1941, my father drove tank trucks for the Red Wing Oil Co. in Portland. Red Wing was CALSO (later CHEVRON) distributor of gasoline and fuel oils.

"In May 1937 he married Rita Kelley of Middletown. I was born in 1939 and my brother Dennis in 1945.

"During WWII Dad worked for Andover-Kent Co. in Middletown casting 37, 75, and 105mm shells for the war. During this time, due to a shortage of qualified drivers, Dad drove part-time with his brother Art at Peter H. Mortensen Co., a large bulk petroleum carrier from Hartford. The work was mostly in Connecticut and Massachusetts, with occasional trips from New Jersey to the Boston area. Summer work included hauling road oils (tar). I know that he spent a lot of time in eastern Connecticut. I hope that he had a chance to visit his old camp at Voluntown.

"After the war he remained with Mortensen until the late 1940s when he went to work for American Oil Co. (later AMOCO-BP) in their Rocky Hill Terminal on the Connecticut River. He stayed with AMOCO until the closing of that plant in 1960. He then ran an AMOCO station until his passing at the early age of 57 on Feb. 9, 1972.

"I know that Dad was happy to have served with the CCC, and we often spoke fondly of his experiences. He learned by those experiences the value of hard work."

Voluntown

There were approx. 265 enrollees, officers, foresters, and foremen in the Voluntown CCC Camp group on Jan. 25, 1934. Henry Turcotte was in the 2nd row of seated boys 5th from the right. Irene A. Schott

Henry Turcotte

Henry Turcotte was one of the first enrollees at Camp Lonergan. He is with his wife Eleanore

Irene Schott of Lisbon came to my CCC presentation at the Voluntown Library on Jan. 29, 2008 and told me her uncle, Henry J. Turcotte, was an early enrollee at the Voluntown CCC camp in 1934. He was born on Jan. 17, 1916. He had three brothers: Joe, Fred, and Paul.

Irene said, "I don't know much about his time in the CCC. I remember him saying he was a laborer."

Then she showed me a group picture of the Voluntown camp.

"He married Eleanore Gauvin on May 30, 1939. They had four children: Richard, Raymond, Eugene, and Paula Mae.

"My Uncle Henry was a Marine in WWII. After the war he owned a general store in Norwich. Later he worked for Gillette Wholesale Distributors of Willimantic and Joseph Connors of Taftville as a salesman.

"He passed away on July 19, 1996."

Arthur & Vivian Roode

At my first CCC talk in Connecticut on Jan. 29, 2008 at the Voluntown Library, Arthur Roode told me, "When I was young I remember the CCC boys gathered around Marion's Grocery Store in Voluntown in the evenings. It was a short walk from their camp. They'd be drinking and talking. I was about 10 years old."

Arthur's wife, Vivian Roode, added, "One of the jobs they did was making 'pug holes.' These were water holes all around the area that they built to supply water in case of a fire."

"They were beautiful," said Arthur. "They were as big as this library room we're standing in. There was one by the elementary school. I used to skate on it in the winter."

Carl Stamm standing near a stone-lined waterhole built by the CCC used in forested areas to fight fires. Podskoch

347

CHAPTER 23
WEST CORNWALL / HOUSATONIC MEADOWS STATE PARK / SHARON

Camp Cross Co. 182 group photo. Podskoch

HISTORY

On June 2, 1933 Company 182 was formed at Fort Wright on Fishers Island, NY. A group of approximately 250 enrollees began a three week conditioning program. After 17 days Lt. John O'Leary took 10 enrollees by boat to New London and traveled to Sharon, Conn. to begin establishing Camp S-51. The camp was approximately 4 miles south of West Cornwall's Covered Bridge on Route 7 at the Housatonic Meadows State Park. The camp was named West Cornwall after the nearest post office. [1]

"Early Days of Camp Cross"
by Thomas C. Hood, Camp Superintendent

At 2:25 on a hot dusty afternoon the 182 CO special train pulled in at Cornwall Bridge and out spilled 253 raw recruits anxious to see the kind of place they had landed into. Then Capt. Kennedy asserted himself and men in squads began to unload tents, cots, blankets, kettles, and food into waiting trucks. Superintendent Hood and Foresters Brooks and Cleveland were waiting to act as guides and help where ever possible.

The cavalcade moved out for the campsite where Lieut. John O' Leary with an advanced squad of 10 men had been getting ready for three days. Camp was pitched with the field stoves set up where the garage shop is now located and into long rows of eight-men tents extending out to the camp baseball field. Tents were set up by willing, though inexperienced hands, cots brought in, and blankets unrolled. The well had already been driven and temporary pump working.

Supper was served to a hungry line with new mess kits and canteen the boys sat on the rocks or ground. When the late June dusk came down everyone was ready to turn in on those narrow canvas cots. In the early night a family of wood chucks crawled out of their hole in the middle of the company street to investigate their new neighbors and slunk away undisturbed for the CCC campers were dead to everything.

Next day all were set to work to make a camp. The eight men in each tent were organized into a squad, each three squads had a leader. Capt. Kennedy was an energetic, decisive Commanding Officer. Lieut. Hinckley, an able executive with picturesque language, and Lieut. O'Leary, Mess Officer. The regular Army sergeants Towne, Silveria,

Wilbur L. Cross

The camp was named for Governor Wilbur L. Cross. He was born in Mansfield, Conn. in 1862. His family was in farming and manufacturing. He earned a BA and a PhD at Yale. In 1894 Cross became a professor of English at Yale where he taught for 36 years. In 1931 he was elected governor and served for eight years. The Wilbur Cross Parkway, a limited access road between Milford and Meriden, is named after him. Cross passed away in 1948. [2]

Connecticut State Library, State Archives

and Decker and Poison, the cook, taught the rookies camp wisdom by example and cuss words. Mr. Meadows of payroll fame, was company clerk. Bangs and Stewart, were bosses of camp work. Munn was an Army driver and general mechanic.

On the second day 10 squads of rookies were turned over to the forestry superintendent to begin building the road up the hill to the present campsite. Foresters Brooks, Nickerson, Smith, Dakill, and Ceder cleared the thick briars and brush from the campsite. Leader Wingertaman, "Scotty" McKelvie , and Axel Johnson soon showed their worth. Dickinson was one of the three Connecticut State 1933 graduates who came in as Local Experienced Man.

When the road was completed the camp tents were moved to the present location and mess hall and washroom constructed. When the last of the tents were folded away and the camp moved into barracks the veterans felt that the rugged pioneer stage was by, but the final stroke of weakness was the substitution of spring cots with mattresses for the canvas cots.

The comfort of the enrollees has always been the first objective in this camp but during the first two months in camp, Foremen Smith, Ceder, and Christen bunked in a small tent where all the forestry axes, shovels, mattocks, and nails were kept, as well as the superintendent's office equipment.

A log cabin shop was built of logs carried down from the hillside and became the tool shop, blacksmith shop, garage shop, and superintendent's office. It was considered quite commodious, too. The trucks were left in a neat row when not in use, and a row was staked out where enrollees' cars could be parked.

The welcome yell, "Come and get it!" caused such a stampede on occasions that a cloud of dust obscured the camp and company, punctured only by the sounds of stamping feet. Eating from a mess kit in a downpour of rain stirred the feelings of Lieut. Hinckley so that he contrived a rigging of posts and poles with a tarpaulin cover and breast high tables benches from which the enrollees could eat standing up. This was a stupendous advance in comfort and table manners. "Hinckley Hall" was a noble idea carried to a successful conclusion.

Lieut. O'Leary was promoted to captain and sent to Camp Toumey. Capt. Kennedy was returned to his regular duty. Lieut. Hinckley took over command with reserve officers to train sergeants. Towne and Silveria went back

to Fort Ethan Allen, leaving Munn as senior leader and the CCC was out of its baby days and running on its own manpower. [3]

Projects

The major projects of Camp Cross were developing Housatonic Meadows State Park and Housatonic Forest. The park and forest began in 1927 when the state acquired over 3,000 acres of land owned by an iron company. Over the years the land had been repeatedly clear cut to make charcoal for the iron industry. [4]

The first forestry project was the fire line, 3 miles long in Housatonic Meadows State Park.

State Park, and a fire line and road on Mt. Ragi, 25 miles away from camp. Thickets of dense brush were cleared away in the park, a park road built, and the baseball field improved by removing stone walls and boulders.

Blister rust eradication was started and the construction of Cream Hill Rd. of 1 mile length began. This was the road where a long section of rock face sank into the mud three successive times before a firm road stood to the satisfaction of engineers and foresters. Old fields were cleared and 50,000 young trees planted that fall. The construction of a 2-mile Yelping Hill Rd. was begun that fall and finished the next year. [5]

CCC enrollees constructed ten dressing rooms near the Hollister Pines where there were places to wade in the Housatonic River. Other development projects included cleaning and improving the woods and fields, making parking areas, rebuilding stone walls, developing camp sites and ball fields, and constructing access roads in the park. [6]

Enrollees traveled to the boundary line with NY and began making a fire line. This was a 100' wide strip in which dead trees were removed and a 15' wide center strip in which all trees were removed. [7]

Trail construction work was conducted at the beautiful Dean's Ravine (4 miles south of Falls Village in the Housatonic Forest. Enrollees also constructed fireplaces there. [8]

During the early summer of 1933, plans were made to build a road at Kent Falls State Park, four miles SW on Rt. 7. The road was "to climb on rising diagonals up the west side of the hill eastward of the highway (Rt. 7) which divides the Kent Falls Park area and to give access by car to the fields at the top of the falls directly through park land. That section

Foreman Arthur Ceder supervised Camp Cross workers building a road to the north of Kent Falls required large retaining walls but the road was never completed to the top of the falls. Sheila Ceder

of the park, which offers good picnic possibilities, has been practically cut off from active use, being accessible from the park center only by a foot trail up to the falls ravine, or by a long detour on the public roadways." [9]

"In November 1933, a crew from Camp Cross began working on constructing the road at Kent Falls. After about a month, work was curtailed because of bitter cold weather. In April 1934 one crew resumed working on the road. Then in August a second crew was added. [10] The young men made some progress up the mountain constructing large stone walls but the road was never completed.

Highlights of Camp Cross, 1933

June 2	182 Co. CCC formed at Fishers Island, NY
June 20	Advance guard of 10 men, including Danny Munn, arrive to prepare camp grounds. Superintendent Hood and Foreman Smith and Cleveland on hand to aid them.
June 23	Capt. Kennedy and entire company arrive at camp.
June 25	First detail, a blister rust crew sent out.
July & Aug.	Mess hall, washroom, and recreation hall built.
Sept. & Oct.	Five barracks constructed.
Oct. 6	First issue of Camp Cross Clarion put out.
Oct. 16	Berton Dickinson, former CCC enrollee becomes Forester.

Nov.	Capt. Hinckley becomes commanding officer.
Nov. 27	First mimeographed issue of Camp Cross Clarion. [11]

1934 Projects

Enrollees endured a harsh winter in 1934. In February the temperature went below zero 20 times. [12] The chopping crew worked in forest-stand-improvement and clear cutting in weather 20° below zero. Day after day these CCC men showed that they could courageously endure continuous extreme cold without complaint. The health of the men was very good with few frost bites or colds and no pneumonia. [13]

Activities

On Feb. 28th, 1934 Camp Cross greeted its first education advisor, Ralph White. whose responsibility was not only establishing educational classes but also cultural, social, and sports activities.

The camp basketball team played other CCC camps and local teams. In March 1934 Camp Cross won the CCC State Basketball Championship. [14]

In the May 14, 1934 issue of the Camp Cross Clarion, Mr. White, Educational Advisor, said that Camp Cross is known far and wide as "the singing camp." White said a glee club was formed and enrollee Elmer Trombley was the director. Capt. J William Johnson offered a two-dollar prize for the enrollee who wrote the best Camp Cross song.

To liven up camp life a company dance was held at the Kent Community Hall on May 17, 1934. The cost for admission was one quarter. [15]

Donald Cameron and Mr. Marston, two former movie actors, visited the camp. Mr. Cameron was the male lead in "Alice in Wonderland." Mr. Marsden was one of the motion picture stars of the old silent movies. [16]

In May 1934 the boys constructed a volleyball court at the foot of the hill. Later a barracks intramural league was formed. [17]

That spring one event brought cheer to Camp Cross when the District Chopping Contest was held at Peoples Forest. Camp Cross representatives, coached by Forester John Vising, competed against seven other camps. They came in first, second, and fourth place. [18]

Almost every evening the dramatic club practiced two plays, "The Other Side" and "Three Friends." Assistant

Education Advisor, Charles Cutler, directed the group. The boys performed the plays on June 29, 1934 at the Hartford Community Players' Studio. [19]

A camp dance was held on June 13, 1934 in Torrington. There were 150 members of Camp Cross who danced with Torrington's best debutantes. The mayor of Torrington and his wife chaperoned along with a half a dozen couples from Torrington's best society and a dozen Army and Navy officers and their wives. The refreshments were ice cream and cookies. The dance was held in the Torrington Armory and the price of admission was $.25. [20]

Also in June 1934 Camp Cross held a Field Day to celebrate the first anniversary of the camp. Various activities were held pitting the Pioneers versus the Rookies. Some of the events held were a baseball game, tug-of-war, and various running races. The Pioneers won with 51 points to the Rookies 49. After the competition refreshments were served. Everyone had a great afternoon. [21]

In June 1934 the education dept. provided a lecture series featuring painters, writers, and international travelers. On June 18 George Baer the head of Baers Art School and Arlington Yutzler, an illustrator and cartoonist, who spoke and gave examples of illustrating and cartooning. Dr. J. M. Gilbert of Sharon spoke on ancient and modern life in Rome and Greece on June 19. Then on June 21 Mark Van Doren gave a talk on the pleasure of reading. Later in August Dr. Charles Beard of New Milford and retired professor at Columbia University. spoke on Fascism. [22]

Projects

A view of Camp Cross looking north with Company Street and barracks on left, birch bark fences along walkways, street and walkways lined with whitewashed stones. On the right is the washroom, mess hall, and water tower. Gary Potter

New improvements were made at camp in the spring 1934. The boys filled potholes, created paths, and planted shrubs and evergreens. A fixed bar was installed for gymnastics, and two horseshoe courts were installed. [23]

Camp Cross enrollees planted fruit bearing shrubs such as honeysuckle, dogwood, and bayberry bushes. They planted them along the edges of the new plantations of trees. These shrubs provided food and shelter for birds and animals. A crew of 10 men from camp under the direction of Forester Harry Christian planted approximately 2,000 shrubs and about 40,000 evergreen seedlings on different parts of Cream Hill, Sharon Mt., and Yelping Hill. More planting would take place in the fall. [24]

In August 1934 lectures and entertainment were given in the new outdoor amphitheater. The first event was on Thursday, Aug. 2. Ralph R. White, Educational Advisor, was the master of ceremonies. He introduced Fred Dawless, Pres. Of Crucible Steel Co. of New Haven who spoke on "Selling Yourself by Developing Your Personality." He was followed by the Lakeville Band that performed many songs. Then various groups and individuals took the stage and played music or sang songs. One group was Elmer Trombley playing the piano along with Albano on trumpet. [25]

The boys at Camp Cross also got a little culture when they were invited to hear the Gordon String Quartet at Music Mountain in Falls Village, Conn. They traveled west about 33 miles to get to Music Mountain that began in 1930. The enrollees' went to the concerts on Sunday afternoons and Saturday evenings. At the end of the summer the Gordon String Quartet came to Camp Cross on a Wednesday evening on Aug. 29, 1934 and performed in the camp mess hall.

The quartet was greeted with enthusiastic applauses throughout the evening. At the end of the concert Mr. Gordon said, "It has been a pleasure for us to travel to your camp. The manner in which you received our music is an indication that the appreciation for classical music is gradually coming to the surface among the working classes of America. The C.C.C. and their educational programs are bound to further the average American's appreciation for what deserves appreciation – be it music, literature, drama, or art. We hope to visit Camp Cross again, possibly next spring."

During the intermission of the concert Pres. James L. McCunaughy of Wesleyan University spoke on the topic "Your Connecticut." He said Camp Cross was doing a fine job in the surrounding forest. He complimented the camp on the work done on Yelping Hill where he had a summer house. [26]

Sports were very popular at Camp Cross in the summer. There was an inter-barracks softball league and a baseball team that competed with the neighboring CCC camps, White, Roberts, and Walcott. There was also an inter-barracks volleyball league. Quoits or horseshoes was also popular. [27]

In the fall Camp Cross was fortunate to get athletic equipment from the Taft School in Watertown and the Canterbury School in New Milford. The donations included football, baseball, and soccer equipment. The new supplies were used in inter-barracks competition. [28]

During the first week of October 1934 Educational Advisor Ralph White announced new classes would begin. Enrollees had a choice of these classes: Tree Identification, Insect Life and Plant Diseases, Automobiles and Mechanics, Dynamite and its uses in Roadbuilding, Current Events, Forest Firefighting, Improvement Cutting, Tree Surgery, and Blister Rust & Gypsy Moths. There was also a 12 week course called "Lives of Great Men" taught by Chaplain Honeywell. Dr. DiRago taught Health and First Aid and Charles Cutler taught Public Speaking. Lieut. Clark gave instructions on Photography Developing and Printing. [29]

The Sept. 26, 1934 issue of the Camp Cross Clarion, gave helpful tips to the boys hitchhiking home on weekends. First, "thumb" rides in places where automobiles are going slow. Second, do not go up to cars and beg for rides. And lastly, conduct yourself when writing in a car so that drivers will pick up future C.C.C. boys.

In the fall of 1934 the Camp Cross Players began practicing three one-act plays that were written by Percival Wilde, a local playwright who summered in the vicinity. The boys also performed a comedy play called "The Idllings of the King." Mr. Wright was their advisor and the plays were performed in Hartford at the Hartford Players Studio.[30]

On Tuesday evening of Oct. 23, 1934, 11 trucks loaded with the entire 250 men of Camp Cross drove to the West Cornwall Masonic Hall where they saw a performance of the play "Tommie." The play was organized by the New England Division of the FERA traveling dramatic company. Many of the actors had performed the same play on Broadway. There were two FERA dramatic groups that traveled throughout the state entertaining other C.C.C. camps. [31]

Surveying state land on the rugged stony terrain of Canaan Mt. was very difficult for the Camp Cross crew in 1934-35. Gary Potter

Fall Projects

When Camp Cross opened in 1933 the state owned approximately 10,000 acres of forest land near the camp. Most of the land had never been surveyed before. Camp Cross crews began surveying these three blocks owned by the state: Sharon Mt., Cream Hill, and Canaan Mt. Once a boundary was surveyed, the boys began cutting a 10-foot strip on the outer edge of the state property. They cleared all the trees, deadwood, and trees under 3" in diameter. Trees that were also over 3" thick were also cut. All the brush was dragged back 20' or more and placed on state property. The boundary lines helped adjoining property owners know their boundary thus preventing an owner from cutting on state property. By the end of 1934 Camp Cross survey crews had almost completed all of the Sharon Mt. and Cream Hill blocks. The Canaan Mt. block was the hardest because of the hilly terrain and its poor accessibility and took more time to complete. Foreman C. H. Nickerson and his crew finally completed the survey in Nov. 1934. [32]

In Oct. 1934 the typemapping crew under the leadership of Forester Harry Christen completed the survey of the 6,000 acres on Sharon Mt SF and the Purchase Area. Another crew led by Forester Burton Dickinson began a survey on the Barracks Mt. section of the Cream Hill block. Mr. Christian was then transferred to do improvement cutting. [33]

Work crews began building the Sharon Mt. Rd. in the middle of July and by October about 3 miles were serviceable except for the gravelly parts of the hillier sections. When the road was completed it will be six-miles long. The new road will be of scenic and recreational value and important for fire protection and forest improvement work. [34]

In Nov. 1934 the Conn. Light and Power Co. and their representatives from the Canaan office and the generating plant at Falls Village notified Camp Cross that they could have over 3,000 free truck-loads of gravel to be used on the Cream Hill and Yelping Hill roads. This gravel was very helpful in completing these roads. [35]

Dr. DiRago reported the following major injuries that were treated by him and his staff at the camp infirmary in the Oct. 31st, 1934 issue of the Camp Cross Clarion: one injury due to lack of care of teeth, one due to a scalp wound received from the careless handling of logs, three injuries due to infections of the feet and hands, two caused by axe cuts, and one injury due to blood poisoning from injuries while handling a pick axe. The doctor said most accidents were due to carelessness. He also said that any injuries should come to the infirmary that is open from 7:30 am to 6 pm. [36]

Highlights of Camp Cross, 1934

Feb.	Thermometer goes below zero 20 out of 25 days.
Feb. 28	Mr. White arrives as educational advisor.
March	Basketball team wins CCC State Championship.
April	Capt. Johnson becomes commanding officer.
April 23	Danny Munn, former senior leader, receives appointment as mechanic for Forestry Service.
June 23	First Field Day held. Pioneers beat Rookies 51 to 49.
June 30	Last of Pioneers leave Camp Cross.
Aug.	Camp Cross team wins District sawing championship.
Aug.	Camp Cross team wins District Sawing Championship.
Oct. 4	Capt. Johnson transferred
Oct. 15	Capt. Greenleaf becomes commanding officer.
Dec. 31	Veterans of second enrollment discharged. [37]

Projects

During the winter 1934-35 Camp Cross enrollees were busy searching for caterpillar egg masses. By Feb. 1935 approximately 10,000 egg masses were collected and destroyed by Camp Cross. At the same time about 15% of each CCC camp in Connecticut was also engaged in destroying gypsy moths. [38]

Other projects included improvement cutting on Barracks Mt., led by Mr. Stone. In March a work on a road at Kent Falls was suspended because of the thick mud. A road project was to start on Sharon Mt. where three more miles needed to be completed. Another project for the spring was the planting of 35,000 mostly red pine trees over 35,000 acres was busy cutting four miles of boundaries on Lake Wangum. [39]

Social Activities

A dance was held on March 21, 1935 at the American Legion Hall in West Goshen to honor Capt. Rose and Lieut. F. G. Comerford. Buses picked up girls at the Torrington High School and arrived at the dance at 8:30pm. The dance ended at 12:30 am. [40]

About 30 Camp Cross enrollees traveled to the Kent

The Infirmary in 1937. The chimney is one of the few remaining structures of the camp. Gary Potter

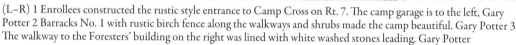

(L–R) 1 Enrollees constructed the rustic style entrance to Camp Cross on Rt. 7. The camp garage is to the left, Gary Potter 2 Barracks No. 1 with rustic birch fence along the walkways and shrubs made the camp beautiful. Gary Potter 3 The walkway to the Foresters' building on the right was lined with white washed stones leading. Gary Potter

Community House on Tuesday night, April 16, 1935 and entertained the local people at a "Smoker." Some of the events that night were: six boxing matches, a comedy boxing bout, wrestling, musical interludes, and a novelty rope skipping act. After the Smoker the boys went to the Pewter Mug for refreshments. [41]

Projects

An effort to beautify the camp was begun in the spring 1935. Grass was planted in 10' wide strips on both sides of the long Company St. Scotch pine trees were planted near the Forester's building and shrubs and flowers were by the barracks. Work was performed on Saturdays and depended on volunteer work from the boys and foremen. [42] Two enrollees, Albano and Glover plus others built a rustic birch fence along the walk between Barracks No. 1 and No. 4, and along Barracks No. 2 and Barracks No. 5. It greatly improved the appearance of the camp. Foreman Mr. White and volunteers built a Chestnut fence along the driveway leading up to the camp. [43]

During the spring 1935 the shoot moth extermination crew supervised by Forester Berton C. Dickinson traveled to many parts of Litchfield County. They first worked at the plantation in Mohawk SF. Then they traveled to the Norfolk water reservoir, Lakeville watershed, and Mt. Riga area. They also worked the plantations at Cornwall, Canaan, Salisbury, and Sharon. [44]

Camp Cross had two fire crews composed of 10 men each and a supervisor. During the spring fire season of 1935, fire crews responded to 16 calls for aid. One fire was in Ellsworth where 20-acres were destroyed. They fought a 40-acre fire in West Torrington and a 25-acre fire on the Norfolk Canaan line. The worst fire was on Bear Mt. that damaged 175 acres. A total of 100 enrollees fought this fire. [45]

Camp Cross was one of the few CT camps that had approximately 250 men. To relieve the overcrowding a sixth barracks was constructed in the spring 1935. It was placed along the back of the other five barracks along the foot of the mountain. [46]

In June 1935 several trucks carried hardwood posts that was mostly maple and cut in the winter of 1934 in the swamps of the Yelping and Cream hills. They were then transported to the creosote to a plant in Portland. The work

(L–R) 1 A CCC enrollee with a stack of logs that his crew had removed from the forest so that more profitable trees could flourish. The logs were then used for firewood at camp. Gary Potter 2 This Adirondack lean-to and fireplace were built by Camp Cross boys at Dean's Ravine. DEEP State Parks Archives 3 A Camp Cross blister rust crew posing with their foreman (right) after searching an area for and destroying Ribes plants that can damage white pine trees. Gary Potter

of the shoot moth crew was completed during this month and they began attacking blister rust. [47]

During the summer 1935 the gypsy moth crew began spraying trees to kill caterpillars. They used a mixture of 300 gallons of water, 15 lbs. of lead arsenate, and two quarts of fish oil. A pump could transport the mixture up to a mile in the woods. Up to 400 lbs. of lead was used in a day by one machine. [48]

There were other forestry projects during the summer. A group of boys and their assistant leader, Dodge, were working on building an Adirondack shelter at the north end of Dean's Ravine. It was constructed of chestnut poles. Enrollees were also building an old fashioned fireplace. Twenty-men under the supervision of forest culture foreman LeClerc did a release cutting in a large area next to the road running from Yelping Hill to Cream Hill. The boys cleared grey birches and other worthless trees so that valuable hardwoods and conifers could flourish. The surveying crew led by Charles Nickerson completed surveying the entire Cream Hill Block. Once the Canaan Mt. Block was finished, all of the Housatonic SF will have been surveyed. [49]

By Sept. of 1935 these were some of the projects that were completed. The blister rust crew supervised by Foresters Dickinson and Griswold cleared over 2,500 acres of Ribes plants. on Sharon Mt. Rd., and Rosata and his crew built stone culverts and bridges. One large bridge culvert was near the Quarry Rd. Camp Cross delivered over 2,000 maple posts to the creosote plant in Portland. The camp was sad that engineer Charles Nickerson who had supervised survey work on Canaan Mt. was leaving to work in Norfolk at the Childs-Walcott Game Preserve. [50]

A foreman (center smoking a pipe) is relaxing with his crew. CT CCC Museum

As winter approached the boys were ready to replace their shovels with an axe. The Nov. 12, 1935 issue of the Camp Cross Clarion described these forest projects for the coming fall and winter. Silva culture foreman LeClerc and his crew continued working on tree release work. So far around 500 acres had been worked in which they were cutting undesirable trees. By the end of the winter they hoped to have covered 1,500 acres of forest on Sharon Mt. Several areas on Sharon Mt. would be clear-cut so that new trees would be planted in the spring. Another project was the cutting of dead chestnut trees on several areas of Sharon Mt. The wood was used for posts, cordwood, and other products. The fall fire season was busy because of the dry weather. The fire crews were called out to fires on Lake Candlewood and the other in East Canaan.

During Dec. 1935 foremen Arthur B. Ceder and Lyle G. Griswold's forestry crews completed approximately 8 miles of boundary cutting on the newly acquired land near Lake Wangum on Canaan Mt. Men working at Kent Falls SP ended their work by Dec. 1st. Foreman Fred B. Smith had a crew begin burning brush on Barracks Mt. in order to control the gypsy moth infestation. [51]

Activities

Two famous Pulitzer Prize writers lived near Camp Cross and enjoyed coming to the camp and talking with the enrollees. During July 1935 Carl Van Doren, a professor at Columbia University, gave an interesting talk about the use of sound effects in making movies. Carl's brother Mark, an English professor at Columbia for almost 40 years, gave a lecture on Shakespeare and the Elizabethan stage. Mark had a tremendous influence on such famous people has Thomas

A large work crew on their one hour lunch break ready for a warm meal brought by truck from the Camp Cross kitchen. Gary Potter

Merton, Allen Ginsberg, and Jack Kerouac. [52]

Weekly "Smokers" began in December and continued throughout the winter. This entertainment included boxing and wrestling matches, skits, singing, dancing, and musical entertainment. There was also smoking! [53]

Highlights of Camp Cross, 1935

March 1	Capt. Greenleaf replaced by Capt. Adolph T. Rose.
March	Enrollees Jasensky & Murphy win first and third prizes in State-Wide Forest Fire Poster Contest.
April	Grass plots laid out along company street.
April & May	Company wins District prize as Honor Company.
May	Company receives new Cletrac Tractor-Trail-Builder.
May 5	CCC Director Fechner visits and inspects camp.
May 16-19	Camp Cross men fight three day fire On Bear Mountain.
June	Barracks No. 6 built and mess hall enlarged.
June 16	A cadre of 23 men leave to form BashBish State Park camp at Copake Falls, NY.
June 23	Second anniversary Field Day held. Barracks No. 1 wins honors. Reynolds awarded Fiengo Cup for doing most for camp.
Aug. 3	Capt. Cohen assumes command of company.
Oct. 1	Leader Albano appointed to Forestry Staff at Camp Toumey.
October	Company strength cut from 252 to 200. Barracks No. 3 made into a schoolhouse. [54]

Camp Cross Staff, Feb. 1936

- Educational Advisor - Ralph R. White
- Camp Surgeon - Dr. L. Arthur Bingaman Munn

Army Personnel

- Capt. Morris G. Cohen
- 1st Lieut. G. W. Youngerman

Forestry Personnel

- Superintendent - Thomas C. Hood
- Asst. Superintendent - Fred B. Smith

Forestry Foremen

- Road Foreman - William K. Brewster
- Road Foreman - Richard Cleveland
- Forest Foreman - Arthur B. Ceder
- Forest Foreman - Lyle G. Griswold
- Blacksmith - John Dellaghelfa
- Mechanic - Damase J. Munn
- Type Map Foreman - Milton C. Arnold
- Type Map Foreman - Richard H. Florian
- Forest Culture - Gregoire J. LeClerc
- Surveyor - Charles H. Nickerson
- Entomologist - Berton C. Dickinson[55]

The 1936 Flood damaged downtown Hartford and other cities along the Connecticut River. Roberta Kosnoff Sciacca

Over 1,000 CCC boys and their supervisors gathered in Hartford ready to enter the Governor's Foot Guard Armory for a dinner in thanks for helping with their flood relief work. DEEP State Parks Archives

KEEP CONNECTICUT GREEN!

(L–R) 1 Ice covered Housatonic River, which destroyed the West Cornwall Covered Bridge and covered the nearby New York, New Haven & Hartford Railroad tracks. Gary Potter 2 The cover of the April 1936 Camp Cross Clarion newspaper was awarded 4 stars by Happy Days for its excellence in writing, layout, and illustrations.

1936 Flood

In March 1936 the Housatonic River rose quickly and washed away the historic West Cornwall Bridge. Camp Cross was called out to help remove large cakes of ice from the nearby New York, New Haven & Hartford Railroad tracks. The camp was called out again on March 23 to do flood relief work at towns along the Connecticut River. One hundred and twelve men were transported to Camp Filley, Company 1195 in Haddam. They worked in that area for over three weeks before returning to Camp Cross on April 10th.[56]

In appreciation for the excellent work done by Connecticut CCC Camps during the recent flood, the City of Hartford invited over 1,200 CCC boys and supervising personnel to a dinner and entertainment at the Governor's Foot Guard Armory in Hartford on April 29, 1936.

The Camp Cross boys arrived at the Armory about 6 pm and had a delicious steak and mushroom banquet topped off with pie à la mode. Each man received a package of cigarettes, toothbrush, toothpaste, and many noisemaking devices. After the dinner the boys were treated to a 21 act vaudeville show. At the end of the evening each boy received an Ingersoll wristwatch as a souvenir for their hard work. [57]

Projects

The Forestry Department was working on two important projects during the summer of 1936. The first was an 8-mile foot trail that would skirt around the top of Canaan Mt. The second project was the construction of The Hatcher Hughes and the Mansfield roads truck trails. The Hatcher Hughes Rd. would be half mile long and connect the Yelping Hill Rd. with the town road going to West Cornwall. The one-mile Mansfield Rd. was going to make the large area east of the Yelping Hill Rd. more accessible.[58]

The September 1936 issue of the Camp Cross Clarion described these work projects of Camp Cross. The first project was the construction of the Clay Beds Rd. in the Sharon block of the Housatonic SF. The 1 mile road would cross from the west side to the east side of the Sharon Forest Rd. that was constructed in 1935. The road got its name from the clay beds that were worked over by four different companies in kilns that processed the clay. Another project was the building of in 8-mile fire break on the top of Mount Riga, the highest mountain range in Connecticut. This area had been the scene of many fires in the past. The blister rust

A blister rust crew from Camp Cross removing Ribes plants (gooseberry and current bushes) from a field. Gary Potter

Boys playing touch football on Company Street with barracks on right. Gary Potter

crew was busy most of the summer destroying the Ribes (gooseberry and current) bushes. The crew covered about 2,000 acres of land in Salisbury and over 90,000 Ribes plants were pulled up and destroyed.[59]

The 182nd Co. at Camp Cross won the contest for honors of best camp in the Army's District. It has won first place two times and has usually been near the top of the list in every competition. The cheerful and respectful attitude of the enrollees has been so marked that a state forestry official once stated that he could usually distinguish a Camp Cross man as soon as he spoke to him by his reply.[60]

23H-20 Photo: Boys playing touch football on Company Street with barracks on right. Gary Potter

During the fall of 1936 the Camp Cross football team was busy getting in shape in competing against other nearby CCC teams. The Hotchkiss School of Salisbury donated properly fitting football equipment for all of the players.[61]

During the winter of 1936-37 there were new classes for the men. In December the State Forestry Service began six conservation classes that were taught by the forestry staff. Then in February the army installed woodworking equipment in two separate rooms in the education building for woodworking classes.[62]

The March 1937 Camp Cross staff contained: Capt. Walter H. Smith and 2nd Lieut. Angelo Iantosca. The forestry department was led by Superintendent Thomas C. Hood, and Asst. Superintendent Richard Cleveland. The forestry foremen were: Joseph E. Bolger, Ernest D. Clark, John Dellaghelfa, Damase J. Munn, William K. Brewster, Berton C. Dickinson, Gregoire J. LeClerc, and Harry A. McKusick. Educational Advisor was Alan O. Lindstrom and Camp Surgeon was William F. Bria.[63]

Throughout the summer of 1937 more than half of the men were engaged in road construction. Work on the Clay Beds Rd. reached the mile and a half point on Sharon Mt. and work was almost completed. Recently a small crew began the construction of a 600' road near Dean's Ravine Recreation Area. The small piece of road is in the town of Cornwall.[64]

The Nov. 1938 issue of the camp newspaper had a new name, Cross Cut. The paper announced that Capt. Johnson was replaced by 1st Lieut. Clifford Perham who was transferred from Brunswick, Vermont.

By Dec. 1938 work on the new Mt. Titus truck trail was completed. The 1¼ mile road lies within the Cream Hill Block of the Housatonic SF. Now crews were able to

do improvement cutting and fire protection work there. Engineer William K. Brewster of Shelton and foreman Edgar Hawks of Winsted supervised the work.[65]

1938 Hurricane

Since Sept. 22, 1938 when Connecticut was hit by a terrible hurricane, Camp Cross crews cut out fallen trees and opened 47.8 miles of fire lines that were mostly on private lands near the Housatonic SF. The camp also had forest fire crews ready for prompt response to calls from the local fire wardens.[66]

During 1939-40 the CCC constructed two more roads: Gold Road and Titus Mountain Road (5 miles NE of West Cornwall).[67]

Forest Products Made and Used in Connection with CCC Work in Housatonic Forest

Biennial Report Ending	Fuel Wood Cords	Posts	Poles	Logs (bd. ft.)
June 30, 1934	643	55	251	2,946
June 30, 1936	1,682 (incl. wood to Kent Camp)	719	69	7,349
June 30, 1938	2,280	6,066	40	13,303
June 30, 1940	2,375	1,379	1,842	20,162

Summary of Acres Planted in Housatonic Forest

Area Planted Before	Total Area Planted	Trees Planted
June 30, 1934	210	76,000
June 30, 1936	268	64,000
June 30, 1938	303	93,541
June 30, 1940	354	111,100

Recreation Facilities in Housatonic Forest

Biennial Report Ending	Fireplaces	Tables	Open Shelters
June 30, 1936	5	6	1

Number of Miles of Roads and Trails in Housatonic Forest

Biennial Report Ending	Miles of Auto Roads	Miles of Wood Roads Passable for Teams	Miles of Foot Trails	Vehicle Bridges
June 30, 1934	3.1	50.8	0.8	1
June 30, 1936	8.9	58	1	1
June 30, 1938	12	56	5	
June 30, 1940	14			

Housatonic Meadows State Park showed a steady increase in the number of visitors. In 1936 over 100,000 visitors came to the park for picnics and camping.[68] From July 1938 to June 30, 1940, 212,178 visited the park.[69]

Camp Cross closed on April 1, 1941. All of the camp buildings were given to the state park.

The 1942 Report of the Connecticut State Parks and Forest stated that all of the CCC camp buildings except for five were taken down and some of the salvaged lumber was used at the state park and the remainder sent to the Rocky Neck barracks during the past winter. The state said they were retaining the five buildings until after WWII in case they were needed for war purposes.

LEGACY

Camp Cross enrollees helped develop the picnic and camping area in the Housatonic Meadows State Park where thousands of people enjoy swimming, hiking, fishing, picnicking, and camping to this day. By planting thousands

Ella Clark found this stone table on Yelping Hill Rd. built by Camp Cross workers. Ella Clark

There are beautiful campsites at Housatonic Meadows SP that Camp Cross built along the Housatonic River. Campers can enjoy fishing, swimming, and boating. DEEP

(L–R) 1 A work crew spreading gravel on newly constructed road in the Housatonic SF. Gary Potter 2 Only two fire place chimneys remain at the old Camp Cross Camp. Podskoch 3 The entrance to the Housatonic Meadows SP that was built by Camp Cross. Podskoch

of trees and thinning the forest of dead trees the CCC improved the land that was devastated by the iron industry through its practice of clearcutting. Today the Housatonic Forest has grown to nearly 10,000 acres. [70]

The enrollees also did work in two other state parks: Macedonia Brook where they built campsites, roads and stone walls and Kent Falls SP where they constructed an uncompleted road near the top of the falls .

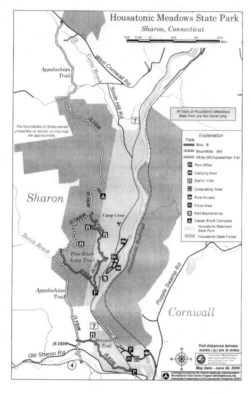

Map – Housatonic Meadows State Park. DEEP

Directions:

From Danbury: Travel north on Rt. 7 into Sharon, CT. The park is located along Route 7 approximately 2 miles north of the intersection with Rt. 4 and approximately 3 miles south of the West Cornwall Covered Bridge.

From Hartford: travel west on I-84 and take Exit 39. Drive west on Rt. 4 to Cornwall Bridge. After crossing the Housatonic River, turn north on Rt. 7 and travel approximately 2 mi. to the park entrance on the right. Continue north on Rt. 7 for approximately 0.3 mi. The entrance to the CCC camp is on the left. There is a field on the right where the garages were. Walk up the road on the left that levels off. You will see the stone chimneys and foundations on the right.

MEMORIES

The boys at Camp Cross had many pet dogs that they loved to have around camp. Here is "Boots" and her pups. Gary Potter

"In Memoriam"
by M. Linsley

Alas a pioneer has gone
To his last resting place
We never again shall hear your bark
Nor glimpse your tawny face.

New Deal, you will be missed by all
Your growls, your yelps, your whines,
Again we would'st see your wagging tail
While resting among the pines.
- Camp Cross Clarion, May 14, 1934

"Hit the Ball"
by Art Pope

(Sung to "Alexander's Ragtime Band")

Come on you 11, come on you all, hit the ball
for old Camp Cross
And if you do, you'll find that you have
the best camp in the land.
Get out of bed first thing in the morn
Never look at work with scorn,

And you'll find out that it's good for you
Oh, do your work, never shurk, and you will finduse 'shirk'
A lot of fun, when work is done and many a good time.
And if you want to be
The Pride of Franklin D.
Come on you all, come on you all,
Hit the ball for old Camp Cross.
- Camp Cross Clarion, May 28, 1934

A Camp Cross barracks ready for inspection. Podskoch

"Our Beds"

You fluff 'em
Puff 'em
Shake 'em
Make 'em
Fuss over 'em
Cuss over 'em
And then fall asleep.
- Camp Cross Clarion, May 14, 1934

After a hard day's work Camp Cross personnel salute the flag
as it is slowly lowered when the duty day is done at reveille.
CT CCC Museum

"Through the Forests"
Anonymous

I am out in the forest where everything is green
I hear some birds whistle and others that sing
But my heart is always yearning for you far away
When you will be with me forever to stay.

And when we are together, God will be our guide
And lead us to happiness that is so far away and wide
That we will leave behind, and with happiness replace
The trouble and the sorrow we both had to face.

As we go through life we will march arm in arm
And we will both keep our chins up
And never say down.
- Camp Cross Clarion, May 28, 1934

Founding of Camp Cross

The main body of men who were to make camp Cross their home arrived on Fishers Island on June 1 and 2nd. After an anxious wait of days and after many false reports and rumors going around the company street that they were going everywhere, but the place where we are today, the true report finally came through. The campsite was called Housatonic Meadows State Park.

Sgt. Towne chose 10 men to go in advance to prepare the company site for occupancy, and help in digging a well.

This advance detail consisted of John Stuart, foreman, Bob Voorhees, truck driver, Jimmy Coles, Tillie Covino, Johnny Russo, Russell Sanford, Danny Munn, R. McLaughlin, John Loch, and John O'Neill. Capt. O'Leary was in charge.

They left Fishers Island early Tuesday morning on June 20 starting out with two army trucks: one of our present trucks, and the other an old army truck. Some of the old timers will still remember what happened to it. Bob Voorhees drove the good truck while an Army mechanic drove the other at least he did his best.

The detail stopped at Capt. O'Leary's home where a hot meal was served. They continued on from there to the camp site. Several miles from it they were met by Mr. Brooks who showed them where the future camp would be.

Arriving at camp about 5 o'clock they set up cook stoves and tents. After a very pleasant meal a group of the fellows took a walk and were introduced to their first glimpse of Cornwall Bridge.

The next day they were introduced to Mr. Hood, Mr. Brooks, and Mr. Bacon. The site for the company street below on the flat was laid out and the brush was cleared. They also aided with the piping of the well and the setting up of the water tank. The following day they had their first taste of axes, brush hooks, and machetes. They had two good work days cutting and burning brush under the direction of Mr. Hood and Mr. Brooks. At the end of the second day they were rudely interrupted by the arrival of the main gang, so more work had to be done before the day's work was finished. This was on Friday, 22 June.

The confusion and enthusiasm of the new arrivals was most exciting. The advance detail was glad to see old friends and to impress on them what they had so recently learned about the forests.

The first details were sent out by the forestry department on the next Monday, 26 June.

After the present site was cleared, the camp was moved up there. Now where there once was only a thick birch cluster stands one of the finest CCC camps in the country. Camp Cross – 82 company C.C.C.

    - Camp Cross Clarion, June 29, 1934

"I Walk Through a Forest"
by Art Verdosci

I walk through the forest,
So calm, so serene,
'Neath wide spreading branches,
Of trees clad in green.

I hear as I listen,
A bird's sweet refrain,
It stops for a moment,
Then goes on again.

The sweet scented flowers,
With fragrance so rare,
Are part of the wonders,
That nature put there.

I come to a hollow,
And pause by a stream,
It's all so entrancing,
It seems like a dream.

But now day is ended,
And I must go home,
To dream of that walk through
A forest – Alone.
    - Camp Cross Clarion, Oct. 31, 1934

"Burp's Whistle"
by Vazuka

I hate to hear Burps whistle blow,
So early in the morn.
It drives me from a bed,
That is so nice and warm.

I like to hear Burps whistle blow,
Right on the dot of noon,
It makes me run like mad,
For my cup and plate and spoon.

I like to hear Burp's whistle blow,
Just when it's supper time,
But best of all, I like to crawl,
In that good old bed of mine.
    - Camp Cross Clarion, Nov. 30, 1934

Camp Cross went to help flood victims in Hartford (above) and other towns along he Connecticut River. Roberta Kosnoff Sciacca

"Bilge Water from the Flood"
by Teop Roop

Departure
While radios and papers flashed,
The stories how the dams had smashed, our caravan of trucks rolled out,
To see what it was all about.

Great Expectations
Adventure pounded in our blood,
When we first left to fight the flood,
But seen soon we found Camp Filley business,
Was just a lot of silly business.

Artificial respiration
There were no uses to be found,
For skill in rescuing the drowned,
The only victim who was smitten,
Was just all water-logged good young kitten.

First Job
We paste along the rivers border
To help maintain the law and order,
The river and our feet were swollen,
But not a postage stamp was stolen.

Second job
With poisoned gases in our smellers,
We cleaned the sewage from the cellars,
We washed the walls and floors with lime,
And waited in the slosh and slime.

Return
Then when our little job was through,
And we returned to 182,
We looked ahead for brighter days,
Camp Cross had Filley beat 10 ways.

Object Lesson
Don't build too near the river's brink,
If you object to stench and stink,
And never let a keg of wine,
Be stored below the sewage line.

Good time
Grapefruit, hot soup, coffee, and peas!
Pass the mashed potatoes, please.
Mushrooms on a juicy steak,
Pie and ice cream – what a break!

Right Time
We're thankful for the cheery call,
To come and get your Ingersoll (watch),
And for the only time we ate,
And found a toothbrush at each plate.
- Camp Cross Clarion, April 1936

Funny

The blister Rust crew left their lunches in a pasture in East Hartland where they were working. When they returned for lunch they saw a Jersey cow eating their lunch. They shooed the cow away and got some of the remaining food. The lunch consisted of 39 oranges, 78 sandwiches, bananas, apples, and prunes. The farmer said when he milked the cow it gave 26 quarts of milk.
- Camp Cross Clarion, Oct. 6, 1936

A Camp Cross enrollee at the entrance to camp on Rt. 7.
CT CCC Museum

**"CCC, That's the Place to Be"
by Ralph Grillo**

Yes, I've joined the CCC
And what has it done for me?
It's given me home, a little cash,
And meat instead of bone.

Many were the nights
When my heart longed for a home,
A place I could call my own,
Where I could work and play,
Get up and say,
This is the place, my home.

Out in the woods,
The birds around,
Trees lying chopped, along the ground,

363

Boys telling jokes, laughing, and singing,
They stop, the child bell's ringing.

No more streets, walking and begging,
Prancing, hiking, and gallivanting.
Yes, I've joined the CCC
That's the place to be.
- Camp Cross Clarion, Aug. 1936

A CCC boy at the rear of Barracks 3 at Camp Cross.
Gary Potter

The Leader's Lamentation

"The time has come," the leader said,
"To make you guys start working,
With dirty bunks, and dirty floors,
Filth in every corner lurking."

"If you guys want a weekend pass,
You'll have to change your ways,
For when next Friday night rolls round,
Every man in the barracks stays."

Up rose and unwise rookie,
And said, "I've worked enough,
I think this cleaning up affair,
Is no nothing but plain guff."

The leader angrily turned on him,
And said, "You better learn the score
For if you don't show production,
You guys will go home no more."

The rookie went to work again,
But grumbling neath his breath,
He said, "If I ever run a crew,

I won't work my men to death."

Today that rookie wears three stripes,
He runs a crew of men,
He pushes, snorts, yells, and grunts,
And is called tough by them.

"The time has come," that rookie now says,
"To make you guys start working,
With dirty bunks, and dirty floors,
Filth in every corner lurking."

And so CCC goes round and round,
You rookies kick, but the time will come,
When you, too, will run a crew,
And be called tough by the others too.
- Camp Cross Clarion, Aug. 1936

CCC Songs

When our camping days are over,
And we camp in dreams,
We can hear the gang ear bending,
Under the barrack beams.

Camp Cross – Camp Cross – CCC
We sing our praise of the
The camp that is in the valley,
We loved our stay with thee.

We dream of days and nights with you,
Filled with work and fun,
Memories of the passing seasons,
And of the friends we've won.

Camp Cross – Camp Cross – CCC
We sing our praise of thee,
The camp that is in the valley,
We loved our stay with thee.

Cheer, Cheer for dear old Camp Cross,
Cheer for the men who put her across,
Send her praises far and wide,
All of her boys are filled with pride.

What though the odds be great or small,
Camp Cross will help us win over all,
If we are loyal, faithful, and true,
We'll get there in all we do.
- Camp Cross Clarion, Aug. 1936

Camp Cross enrollees entertaining friends with country music in the rec hall. Connecticut First Corps 1937 Yearbook

"We're the Happy C.C.C. Boys"
by Marsten Linsley

(Sung to "Marching Through Georgia")

We're that happy C.C.C. Boys
We come from the West Cornwall
We chop the trees, we saw the wood
For Superintendent Hood.
We haul the logs In Dean's Ravine,
Then a lick our mess kits clean
Onward we march through the forests.

Chorus
Hurrah, Hurrah, we are 300-strong,
Hurrah, Hurrah, we tried to meet all tests.
And so with them and vigor, boys, let's harmonize this
song.

We're happy C.C.C. Boys
We come from West Cornwall,
We swing the axes, we grub the hooks,
We sweat for Mr. Brooks.
With Cleveland we've climbed the hills,
They gave us plenty of thrills.
Onward we march through the forests.

We're the Happy C.C.C. Boys
We come from West Cornwall,
We make good roads, we clear the brush
For Mr. Ceder we do rush.
On work on parks, no time is lost
When we by Smith are bossed.
Onward we march through the forests.

We're the Happy C.C.C. Boys
We come from West Cornwall,
The post we peel, the trees we plant
Oh, Christian makes us pant
We survey land for Nickerson,
He keeps us on the run.
Onward we march through the forests

We're the Happy C.C.C. Boys
We come from West Cornwall,
The stones we crush, the rocks we bust.
Visini works us fast.
For Dickinson the bugs we hunt.
It sure does make us grunt.
Onward we march through the forests.

We're the Happy C.C.C. Boys
We come from West Cornwall,
We run the chain, we hold the rod
We toil at Brewster's nod.
With Pickert we kill blister rust,
On this we work hard, we must
Onward we march through the forests.

We're the Happy C.C.C. Boys
We come from West Cornwall,
We're all for you, Lieut. Clark,
You make us toe the mark.
And, Capt. Johnson at your behest
We'll always do our best.
Onward we march through the forests.
- Camp Cross Clarion, May 28, 1934

John C. McKay

John McKay, who worked at the West Cornwall camp in 1933, came to the Chatfield Hollow State Park to celebrate the 75th anniversary of the CCC.

While talking with Harmon Poole of Simsbury, Conn. he suggested I contact John C. McKay, also from Simsbury who had served in the CCC in Cornwall, Conn. I contacted his daughter, Linda Driggs of Collinsville, Conn. and asked her to interview her father.

Q: Dad, tell me about your family:

A: "I was born on June 23, 1914 in Fairmont, W. Va. My father, Dr. Hosmere Clare McKay, was a dentist in our town of Fairmont, W. Va. My mother was Lelia Hess McKay. I was the youngest of five children (Dorothy, Winfield Scott, Hosmere, Bob and John).

"I was 20 days old when my father died. It was on the afternoon of July 12, 1914, when my father, a prominent young Fairmont dentist, decided to try out his new Mitchell Six Touring car. He took with him his chauffeur, his father (Winfield Scott McKay), his young son (Winfield Scott McKay, Jr., age 9) his daughter Dorothy, age 11, and two friends. The car spooked an oncoming horse and the car failed to make a curve and went off the road.

"The elder McKay and Winfield were thrown from the car and instantly killed. Dr. McKay was still alive when assistance arrived and an effort was made to remove him to the hospital in Uniontown, W. Va. But in those days 18 miles was too much for a badly injured man. He was removed from the car and laid in the shade until it was decided to take him to a farm home where he died a few hours later.

"The chauffeur and one friend were also killed. The other friend suffered broken bones and Dorothy had a badly fractured leg.

"In relating the story of the tragedy the New York Times reported: 'For the first time the owners of machines were brought face to face with the awful power of death which they have. In the 53 years since the first accident,' Fairmont has often been faced with the awful losses they can bring."

Q: How did your mother cope raising four children without a father?

A: "My mother was a very strong and determined woman. She had a sister, a brother and several cousins and relatives in the Ohio, West Virginia area who helped in raising the children. Also, the older children helped care for the younger ones. After a while my mother moved to Hartford, Conn. to be near my brother Hosmere, but would later on return to the house in Fairmont to live out her life."

Q: Tell me why you joined the CCC and describe your camp.

A: "After graduating from Hartford High School in about 1933, I read about the Civilian Conservation Corps in the local newspaper. I called them up and they said to come down and I'd be admitted. I signed up in Hartford.

"I didn't mind leaving home. I was glad for the freedom, the outdoor experience and friendships gained from meeting a lot of nice guys. I would learn later that many of the men went on to serve their country and some of them paid the ultimate price.

"They took me to Camp Cross, Company No. 182, in West Cornwall, Conn. about 30 miles Northwest of Hartford. When I got there I started out living in a tent. Later they built wooden buildings. When I arrived there were 4 wooden barracks and 8 tents for the 250 men. There was never more than 250 men at one time. The count was always changing due to being men being homesick or able to get a job.

"At first Capt. Hinkley was in charge of the camp. Mr. Hood, from New Haven was in charge of all the work outside the camp. He was assisted by six young state foresters. Later, Capt. Kennedy took over the camp.

"My older brother Bob, a pre-med student, was also at Camp Cross and worked in the infirmary. Bob did the things the doctor didn't want to do like applying bandages and giving needles.

"I was paid $30.00 per month and $25.00 went for my mother. That equaled $50.00 per month because my brother also sent money to mother. We were very fortunate to be able to send money home."

Q: Who were your good friends at camp? Did you stay in touch with any of them?

A: "While in camp, I made a good friend with a forester, Arroll Lamson, from Simsbury. Although Arroll died in 2007, we maintained a close relationship over the years and attended the same church. Arroll eventually became head of Wildlife for the state of CT."

Q: What kind of job did you have?

A: "Well, we all had our own jobs to do daily which consisted of making our beds, cleaning our foot lockers and getting ready for inspection, but I started out working on a gypsy moth detail. Then I worked on clear-cutting in the forest and building roads on the east side of the Housatonic River along the railroad.

"Later I did surveying with a Yale graduate. There were quite a few guys from Yale. The Depression was a tough time to get a job. We went to the town hall for property records. Much of the land was left by farmers who went West. There were only minimal boundary marks, but we established the boundary lines of the old farms."

"Then I was made Supply Clerk. I passed out pants, socks, shirts, coats and blankets to the new recruits when they arrived at Camp Cross.

"When I was a supply clerk I remember seeing a deer walking down the camp road. Then one guy took an ax and tried to kill it, but he just nicked the deer and he got away."

John McKay (left) and his brother Bob (right) both worked at Camp Cross in West Cornwall. Linda Driggs

Q: What did you and the guys do in the evenings and on the weekends?

A: "We had a group of guys who went out on the weekends to capture rattlesnakes for a bounty and brought them back to camp in burlap bags. Others brought wildlife back to camp, such as a young fox or birds to rehabilitate them.

"Some week nights we had a Sport Night. On one occasion I entered the wrestling competition. I defeated my opponents over three nights and won the championship for my weight class - 145 lbs.

"I would travel about 15 miles to take classes every Friday night at the Torrington Vocational School where I studied Mechanical Drawing. This would later help me get a job at Pratt & Whitney Small Tool Company in West Hartford, CT.

"On Saturday nights we went to Torrington. The town put together a "social" with lots of girls to dance with and have refreshments. On Sunday a truck took us to Torrington for church services.

"I went home to Hartford about every second week traveling about 30 miles one way. I bummed a ride with a teacher who went to Hartford to see his wife who was sick in the hospital.

"One weekend my brother and I decided to go home in uniform. My mother was living with my older brother Hosmere in Hartford. We left camp around 6 P.M. While we were walking and hitchhiking a terrific snow storm began. We made it to Torrington and continued on to Hartford in the storm. My brother wanted to stop but I said, "We have to keep going or we'll both die." We walked and walked and finally got a few rides and got home about 1 pm. It was a hell of a storm.

"Well, the food at camp was 60 percent good and the rest bad. While we worked they brought lunch to us in a special truck. We had WWI mess kits and in the winter, some of the food was frozen by the time it got to us. How does frozen Jello sound?"

Q: How long did you stay in the CCC and what did you do after you left?

A: "I stayed in the CCCs for 6-8 months. One of the guys I lived with in camp knew the Port Engineer of City Fleet in Boston. I wrote him a letter and got a job. I was able to leave the CCCs and join the Merchant Marines. I was about 19 years old. I worked in the engine room. It was a dirty and hot job loading the boilers. I stayed in for nine months. While on board I took some illegal pictures of German and Italian boats that were taking oil out of Corpus Christi, Texas. When I saw that the war was coming, I got the hell out.

"When I left the Merchant Marines, I worked for a paper products company was paid $16.00 a week. A friend from CCC and I went to businesses and supplied them with our products.

"I got married to Muriel Ashford (from Worcester, Massachusetts) in 1936 and moved to Wethersfield, Conn. and then to Simsbury. We had three children: Robert Bruce, Linda Jane, and David Ashford. I would then work at Pratt & Whitney Small Tool Company in West Hartford where they built airplane engines that became very successful. I worked there for 42 years and retired in about 1967."

Q: How did you benefit from the CCC and have you ever gone back to Camp Cross?

A: "When I look back at my time in the CCCs, I learned to be self-sufficient, to get along with people, and to love nature. It built character. In many ways, the CCCs acted as my father; they were strict, fair and set an example for me to follow.

"Yes, a few years ago I went back to see my old CCC camp (Camp Cross), but it was all overgrown, but I did find some of the trails that we built."

John C. McKay died on August 10, 2015.

Joseph Henry Choiniere

Joseph Henry Choiniere (1997) worked as a boxing instructor at Camp Cross in West Cornwall. Joanne Woodworth

Boys practicing boxing at a CCC camp. Theresa Phelps

Joanne Woodworth of Pittsfield, Mass. called me on Feb. 13, 2008 and said her father, Joseph Henry Choiniere, worked at Camp Cross at the Housatonic State Park.

"My father had three siblings Armond, Anne, and Madge.

"His mom died in Bristol, Conn. when he was about four. His dad had diabetes and was in poor health and unable to care for four children. I believe Armond stayed with his father and went in the military while my father, Anne, and Madge were sent to an orphanage in New Britain.

"Dad told us stories about how poor parents who couldn't care for their children. They would drive up to the big buildings on the hill (the home or orphanage) and leave their children.

"My mom was orphaned when she was also very young. Her mom died from pneumonia and her dad was a mason and carpenter in Poughkeepsie and couldn't care for her. He was going to put her on an orphan train but her grandfather agreed to take care of her because he had just lost his wife and daughter at the same time. Mom never saw children (or anyone else for that matter) until she was old enough to go to school in West Cornwall.

"She and Daddy met one Christmas Eve in West Cornwall at the railroad station when they were having a carol sing. Dad was in his CCC uniform and Mom was with her grandfather (Smith). She said he was the most handsome man she had ever seen.

"My dad graduated New Britain High School."

Q: How did your father learn about the CCC?

A: "Dad learned about the CCC from the people who worked at The Klingberg Children's Home where he lived from age five with his two sisters until high school graduation. He was very young when he left the Klingberg

Children's Home. He loved living there. When he was quite old, we took him back to see the barn where his job was to work on the farm."

Q: What did he do at the CCC camp?

A: "He told us he was a boxing instructor. While boxing his nose was broken. Dad used to tell us about his cauliflower ears from boxing."

Q: When he left the CCC camp what did he do?

A: "In 1939 he married my mom, Eleanor Mathews. They had three daughters: Joanne, Lorraine, and Kathy.

"Dad worked on a chicken farm in West Cornwall where he lived with his family.

"He never was in WWII because he had an exemption because he was providing the country with eggs (or that's what he used to tell me).

"When he left the farm, he worked on the Cornwall Highway Dept. until his retirement at age 60.

"An article entitled, 'Highway Crew,' was published in the March 2015 Cornwall Chronicle describing my dad's work for the Connecticut State Highway Department where he worked for approximately 50 years. In 1990 my father and sister Lorraine were interviewed. Dad said, 'During the winter that he worked, the sand was spread on the highways by shovel. There would be two men standing in the corner of each truck, and the truck would go along and the men would take turns in swinging so that they didn't get in each other's way and they would spread the sand so that it covered the entire road.'"

Lorraine added, "My mother was left with two girls and a farm. It was a lot of responsibility for her when he was gone, and he could be gone for 24 hours at a pop. A lot of uncertainty was raised when there was a storm coming in and it was very dangerous for him and my mother was frightened by that."

In the newspaper article Joe described how snow meant overtime for the highway crew.

"The fact that the men then were able to get enough money to pay their bills lent itself to the saying that when it began to snow, for the guys on the highway crew, it was 'pennies from heaven.' And while it was literally pennies, because the pay was so low in those days for those old timers, it did help. The men went along with it. They were glad to get the pennies, although doubted they came from heaven, and they certainly had to work for it."

Joe's daughter Lorraine, a musician and song writer, wrote the following song about his experiences:

"Highway Crew"

Pennies from heaven, when the snow started falling
The jokers at the general store teased the highway crew.
Like my father you might find it hard to join the laughter
After you had done battle with a blizzard or two.

Pennies from heaven, don't you smell the snow coming?
Did you look up last night; see a haze on the moon?
Pennies from heaven, a blizzard by morning.
Mount the plows, load the Sanders, it'll be snowing soon.

Country people are used to hard work and low wages,
For the crew every storm brings the chance for yet more pay,
But the true cost of pennies from heaven is frozen
In lines on their faces that will not melt away.

Q: Did our father ever go back to his CCC camp?

A: "I remember when I was very young, parking the car and walking back to see where the camp had been."

William "Bill" Jahoda

Bill Jahoda beside one of his gardens at his home In Lebanon, Conn.

On April 19, 2010 I visited Bill Jahoda at his home in Lebanon, Conn. I met Bill's wife Margery and he showed me his gardens and the forest that he managed. We then went inside his beautiful home and sat in his living room while he told me about his life.

"I was born on Sept. 21, 1917 in New York City. Later my family moved to Fairfield. My parents were Emil and Mary. I have an older brother Emil.

"My father worked at Handy Harmon in Fairfield as a machinist. The company did silver fabrication and refining. I grew up loving trees. I loved to hold onto a huge chestnut tree and run in the woods with my bare feet.

"I graduated from Fairfield High School where I took commercial courses. I got a job on the night shift at the General Electric factory in Bridgeport. I would eat my lunch at midnight on the grassy mid-area of a road near the plant.

"After three months I had enough of this and decided I would join the CCC. Having always lived in the country and outdoor life was what I hoped for, the CCC looked real good to me. I had a really hard time with my town board that made the enrollment decisions because we were not on welfare. My mother refused to be dependent on aid to survive so I wrote to the State Forester, telling him of my hopes. His answering letter influenced the Board to allow me into the CCC.

"So in early 1936 I was enrolled and assigned to Camp Cross, 182nd Company, Camp #2182 at the Housatonic Meadows State Park along the Housatonic River in Sharon, Conn.

"The CCC camp was an Army-run operation. We lived in Army barracks, with an Army officer and his staff in charge. The outside work in the woods was under a state forestry department staff. I earned $30 per month of which $25 went to my parents and I received five dollars for incidental needs. Of course we also received our clothing, food, and lodging so for those times it wasn't so bad.

"One of the most important decisions of my life was to join the CCC and re-enlist every six months when my enlistment ran out. This decision was responsible for what became a life-long environmental ethic. I spent three years in the CCC and loved every moment of it.

Q: What did you do in camp in the evenings?

A: "Many times I went off by myself and hiked up Sharon Mt. to get more familiar with the woods. Sometimes I went fishing in the Housatonic River. We had two camp dogs and I used to take them with me. One day I was on the side of the river with one dog and the other dog on the other side. Then an adult doe was trapped in the river afraid of the dog's barking. I chased the dogs back to camp. That

allowed the deer to reach shore on my side where she fell down beside me. I patted her until she recovered. I helped her up and she went into the woods.

"Several weeks later while walking slowly near some rhododendrons I heard some rustling. Then I saw a deer feeding on vegetation. I walked slowly up to it and talked in a low voice. She stopped and let me walk up to her. I began patting and stroking her. I'll never forget that wonderful time. Later, I wrote about the experience in the Christian Science Monitor entitled 'A Matter of Trust.'

Q: Who did you work with?

A: "My interest was forestry and I worked mostly with the four foresters who were all young forestry school graduates. They took me out on their personal studies, something from which I benefited greatly. At the camp we did white pine blister rust control, red pine shoot moth control, forest fire control, and wintertime silviculture operations; just what I needed to make me realize that I wanted to have a career in forestry. During my second six-month hitch I was made an assistant leader, which jacked my monthly pay up to $36 a month.

"Two of the forester's, Greg LeClerc, a recent University of New Hampshire (UNH) Forestry School graduate, and Harry McKusick, a recent University of Maine Forestry School graduate, took me under their wings and encouraged me to consider going to forestry school. Mr. McKusick was later to become the Connecticut State Forester.

"Not having a college preparatory background, I decided to try for the two-year Syracuse University Forest Ranger School in Wanakena, NY but the program was phased out and closed the year I was applying. They suggested I at least try to get into a four-year program, and Greg LeClerc's wife even took me up to the UNH for an interview with the Dean. I don't know what he had been

(L–R) 1 Bill Jahoda working in the Housatonic State Forest. Gary Potter 2 Bill Jahoda was a pilot in the Army Air Corps flying cargo planes in SE Asia. Jahoda Family

told but he agreed to admit me into the university if I passed entrance exams in American history, algebra, and geometry, subjects I never had in high school because of my commercial course background.

"Aware of the hurdles in front of me, I went to a second-hand bookstore in Bridgeport and bought history, algebra, and geometry books for less than a dollar. For six months I studied for my exams in camp and out in the woods during lunch breaks. They must have been very kind to me at the university for after the exams they allowed me to enter on probation for six months. If my grades were okay, they would let me stay, otherwise I would have to leave school. Boy! Did I study! All dormitory rooms had been long assigned, but I was able to rent a room in the home of the married daughter of the head of the entomology department who lived closest to the University. Frankly, it gave me a nice quiet, convenient place to study.

"Since I was financially broke, I worked year-round on the University Forest for the Forestry Department under the National Works Progress Authority (WPA), earning $.35 an hour. I also worked for Dr. Woodward, head of the forestry department, on his woodlot cutting trees and also selling some of his Christmas trees during the Christmas season. Another job was working for the wife of the head of the entomology department where I mowed lawns. I also was awarded a few educational scholarships. In addition, I was a proctor in a dorm one year so I didn't have to pay room fees and I also did various income-producing things all the time.

"On Sept. 21, 1938, the day the big hurricane hit New England, I had my 21st birthday. While standing outside in the early evening I could hear the big pine trees crashing down in the college woods. But the most momentous thing that happened to me as an undergraduate was that on Old Home Day of my junior year a classmate, Bill Johnson, from Pittsburgh, NH introduced me to his sister Marjorie, a sophomore student that prior to that time I had not known.

"I studied hard, got excellent grades, and ended up after four years with honors. Since I had taken extra courses I had earned 188 credits instead of only the 144 needed for graduation. I even won the class of 1941 Forestry Cup which is on display at the University with my name engraved on it. It is very interesting to point out that Greg LeClerc, the young forester from the University who had encouraged and helped me to go to the University had won the cup as the outstanding forestry student for the year 1935.

Q: What did you do after the CCC?

A: "In 1939 I left the CCC to go to UNH to get my forestry degree. However, my mother thought I was way out in the woods, and once, when she came up to visit with friends who had a car, I was later told that she cried on the way home. She was so upset that I was far from home and civilization.

"In 1941 during my senior year, I and two friends took exams and passed for induction in the Army Air Corps. I graduated from the university in May and waited for orders.

"I was sent to the Midwest and trained as a fighter pilot on Skymaster planes. Before my company was to join the war effort in Europe, every sixth man in my squadron was ordered to step forward. I was selected as a B-17 Bomber pilot trainer for the war effort.

"It was during that time that I married Margery Johnson in Tucson, Arizona in 1942. We had met at the university through her brother William who was in my class. We had four children: John, Judy, Janet, and Jim.

"Then I was sent to Asia and flew cargo planes from India over the Himalayas (the 'Hump') to Burma and China. We carried supplies for the war against Japan. This was an interesting job since we were flying over mountains that were 20,000' in elevation.

"After the war in 1946 I went back to the UNH for my master's degree. Then I went to Ohio State for my PhD.

"In 1951 I taught Biology at New Paltz State Teachers College in NY and was still in the Air Force Reserve.

On Aug. 21, 2013 CCC alumni (L–R) Hugo DeSarro (Meeker, CO), Bill McKinney (Winsted), Mike Caruso (Madison), Bill Jahoda (West Cornwall), and author Marty Podskoch attended the 80th Anniversary of the founding of the CCC at a reunion at Chatfield Hollow SP in Killingworth. Kira & Lydia Roloff

"At the beginning of the Korean War, I was recalled to active duty as a professor of air sciences with the UCONN Air ROTC Training Program.

"In 1955 I became the state Information & Education Chief of the Board of Fisheries. I had a weekly TV program called, 'This is Your Connecticut Wildlife.'

"Then I took a teaching position at Eastern Connecticut College in Willimantic in 1958. I retired in 1972.

"I also guided many trips for the Audubon Society and Sierra Club."

USAF Lt. Colonel Dr. William John Jahoda, 97, died in his home on Sunday, Jan. 25, 2015. His obituary lists some of his many accomplishments at http://www. potterfuneralhome.com/notices/william-jahoda.

Elmer R. Trombly

In the spring of 2008 Elmer Trombly visited Macedonia Brook SP and told members of the Kent Historical Society and the author about his work spreading gravel on the road that was supported by a large stone wall. The road was approximately two miles long and was built along the eastern base of Cobble Mountain. Podskoch

On April 15, 2008 I interviewed Elmer Trombly at his apartment on Swift Lane in Kent, Conn. He told me that he had been in the CCC for two years at the West Cornwall Camp. The camp was really in Sharon and not far from the Housatonic River. It's in present day Housatonic Meadows State Park.

Elmer said, "I was born on April 23, 1914. My father, Elmer J., was a carpenter but he died young. My mother Edna remarried a man who she met in Broad Brook. I had two older sisters. The eldest died young and my other sister Barbara lives in Broad Brook.

"My family lived in Manchester and I graduated from high school in 1931. In town there was a big cloth factory called Cheney Manufacturing. I tried to get a job but couldn't get one. Then I read in the newspaper that they were looking for young boys to join the CCC. So I went down town and signed up. I was like all young guys happy to get out of town.

"They sent me to West Cornwall camp. It was all right. I wanted to get out and away from home. It wasn't too bad I liked it. I built the road that went through Macedonia Brook State Park. We did all of the work with wheelbarrows, picks, and shovels. Some of the other guys in camp worked at Kent Falls building a road to the top.

"The food wasn't too bad. Once in a while I helped out in the kitchen. During the week we played games like baseball when it was warm. We also went to Cornwall and played the town team.

"I stayed at camp on the weekends. I didn't go home because there was nothing to do there. I went with my buddies to dances in Cornwall Bridge. That's where I met my wife, Beatrice Thompson. She lived on a farm with her grandparents. They were looking for someone to help them milk cows. This gave me a chance to get out of camp. Her grandparents offered to let me stay there and work. I had my own room. I learned how to milk cows. After a while her grandparents decided to give up the farm. I didn't want to buy the farm so I got into carpentry.

"I got married to Beatrice and later was drafted into the Army during WWII. I wound up out West almost in California. Then I heard they were looking for paratroopers. They gave me an extra $50 a month to go to Fort Benning, Ga. I was in the 105th Airborne and sent to England. From there we got into a plane bound for Germany. We flew over an island near Holland. Our plane went around and around searching for a place to land. Then we saw an island and landed. We didn't know it was controlled by the Germans. All of us were sent to Germany and placed in a POW camp for eight months. The soldiers forced us to walk most of the way because most of trains were out. When we got to a camp they made us work in Munich cleaning up the damage from bombing. They didn't give us much to eat. Then the allies were coming closer and closer. They captured our camp and we were liberated. We went back to England and then back to the US.

"After WWII my wife and I went to Kent and bought a four room cape on Rt. 7. My wife lost our first baby and she couldn't have any more. I worked for Joe Gowel doing carpentry work. We built houses.

"I had a friend in the postal service and he helped me get a job as a clerk. Then I became a mail carrier. My route was from Cornwall Bridge to Sharon. Later I retired. My wife passed away and I moved to this retirement apartments.

"Times were really tough during the Depression. I was very lucky to get a job in the CCC. It was good for me."

Elmer R. Trombly died on April 25, 2009 in Kent, after a brief illness. His wife Beatrice died on Feb. 23, 2010.

Joseph Padersky

Joseph Padersky skiing in the Housatonic State Forest where Camp Cross is located. Chris Stratoudakis

Joseph Padersky at the entrance to the Camp Cross Infirmary where he worked. Chris Stratoudakis

"My grandfather, Joseph Padersky was stationed at Camp Cross in West Cornwall where he was a male nurse. I believe he was there from 1935-37.

"He was a lifelong Stamford resident. He was born on June 14, 1914. His parents were Louis and Frances. They had three children: Louis Jr., Betty, and Joseph.

"I don't have many details on his life but I'm sure he was like many of the boys during the Depression who had a hard time getting a job. I have two photos of him at the camp.

"When he was 21 he joined the CCC and was sent to Camp Cross n West Cornwall. His job at the camp was supervising the camp infirmary.

"After working for approximately two years, my

grandfather was discharged from camp. He worked at Yale & Towne Manufacturing Company in Stamford. He worked there for 40 years and retired.

"He married Helen Lenz and they had a daughter Linda and a son Bruce.

"My grandfather died on June 30, 2001. He always spoke fondly of his time in the CCC."

Blanche Marcou McWilliams & Family

In 2008 Father Bill McCarthy introduced me to Blanche Marcou McWilliams at My Father's House, a retreat house in Moodus. Blanche said that she was familiar with the CCC camps near Cornwall Bridge.

"I was born in 1931 and lived in Cornwall Bridge. When the CCC camp was going I remember the CCC boys came to our house to visit my brother Reynold.

"My dad died in 1938 from cancer at the age of 37. There were eight children in our family. A couple of my brothers lived with my aunts and uncles. One brother worked in the area on a farm.

"We moved from Cream Hill near West Cornwall to Cornwall Bridge in 1940. My mom did housework to help support the family.

"I remember going to the Goshen CCC camp for Christmas parties and remember

"When we got there we went to the mess hall where we had a Christmas dinner. There were other families there, too. I was about nine years old and got presents, one of which was a doll.

"I think we went at least two times. Captain Duffy was the leader of the camp."

Then I interviewed Blanche's sister, Pearl DeBarge and their mother Florence who was 100 years old.

Pearl said, "I remember visiting the CCC camp in the [Housatonic] meadows in Cornwall Bridge. I just went a couple times.

"In the Goshen CCC camp my family went a couple times with a Captain Duffy. I only remember going at Christmas. The captain picked us up in an Army truck with other kids.

"There was a lot of food. We ate in what looked like a cafeteria. After dinner we got Christmas gifts. My brother Francis got several metal airplanes that went on the floor. He pulled it back and then it moved forward. I think I got a doll and a dress. I was about 5 or 6 years old.

"Mom worked at the church, St. Bridgette's church in Cornwall Bridge."

Then Pearl's mother, Florence, said, "We went to church and so did Capt. Duffy. I didn't go with them. It was over in Goshen."

"The CCC boys built picnic areas in the state parks."

John Paul Marsan

John Paul Marsan on his wife's family front porch steps in South Norwalk in 1947. Paul Marsan

In 2009 Paul Marsan of Plainville, Conn. contacted me by email to find out about the CCC since his father had been in it. After a few attempts to get together I finally

met Paul at two CCC reunions in 2014. I told him how to secure his dad's records from the National Personnel Record Center in St. Louis and I also asked him to answer a few questions about his dad's life.

After a year he sent me this information.

"My father, John Paul Marsan, was born on July 10, 1919. Both of his parents were born in Canada. His father was Ovila Louis and his mother was Louisa Belec. They lived in St. Theodore Action, Quebec and later moved to Norwalk, Conn. The family was large with 12 children: Bertha, Ernest, Germaine, Armand, Gerald, Lucien, Ovila, Cecile Marie, Gabrielle Marie, Antoinette Marie, Jean Paul (John Paul), Lorenzo (Larry), and Lauette Marie. You can just imagine how hard it was to feed a large family during the Depression. My father, like many of his family, only went to 8th grade and then went out to work to help the family. He did odd jobs for people. In 1936 he got a job working at the Norwalk Pipe Co. He also worked at Durable Metal Co. but from 1938-40 he was unemployed.

"When my father was 20 years old he heard about the CCC from the Welfare Department. He signed up on July 1, 1940 and the Army sent him to Camp Cross, Co. 182 in West Cornwall. His main job was doing silviculture work in the forest.

"In the evenings my father took classes and earned certificates in: Orientation, Elementary Forestry, Tree Identification, Auto Mechanics, and First Aid.

"On weekends Dad went home since it wasn't that far away. Most of the guys in those days hitchhiked.

"On March 3, 1941 Dad was transferred to Co. 180 in East Hartland. Soon after he was honorably discharged on 5/12/41 from 180th Company CCC Camp Tunxis State Forest #S-53 Ct., VII District, because of Employment.' Jules L. Paridaens, the Camp Commander, signed his discharge.

"My Dad was a very hard worker despite the fact he was born with a deformed hand which kept him from being accepted in the service during WWII. His disability did not keep him from being an asset to the CCC and finding work during the war to support his family and then later becoming a longtime chrome plater at Yankee Metal in Norwalk.

"On Oct. 5, 1947 my father married Frances Robinson and they had three children: Barbara, Jean, and me.

"A lot of weekends during the spring, summer, and fall my mother drove my dad and the kids from Norwalk up

Rt. 7 to see the CCC camp. We went to Camp Cross (now the Housatonic Youth Group Camping Area). As a family, we did get out of the car to look around and we realized that this was where he spent time in the CCC until my mother told us on one of our later drives. My father rarely spoke about his experiences during the CCC. He was a very humble and private gentleman. My mother would start telling us about it when she would get closer to the camp's area. She always used the two big Pine trees on the left that were just before the camp as a guide.

"I remember my father said that being in the CCC taught him how to be more independent and how to enjoy the outdoors.

"On July 4, 1978 my father passed away in the Norwalk Hospital. His ashes were scattered at Camp Cross near West Cornwall where he had learned so much."

Art Ceder

Art Ceder worked at these three CCC camps as a foreman and caretaker: West Cornwall, Wooster Mt., and Squantz Pond. Sheila Ceder

Arthur "Art" Bronx Ceder had a life-long interest in conservation. He was born on Feb. 11, 1906 on a barge in the Bronx, NY. His parents, John and Mabel Mercer moved to Burlington, Conn. in 1912. Art had many careers in his life: world traveler, CCC camp foreman, land surveyor in California, and Superintendent of White Memorial Foundation (WMF) in Litchfield. One forestry professor at Yale described him as the best self-taught forester that he ever met. [http://articles.courant.com/2007-08-05/

While working at the West Cornwall camp, Art Ceder, left, is supervising a surveying crew building a road near Kent Falls. Sheila Ceder

news/0708040890_1_litchfield-powerful-influence-uncle-art]

Ceder worked as a foreman at three CCC camps: Camp Cross at Housatonic Meadows in Sharon; Fechner at Wooster Mt., in Danbury; Camp Hook at Squantz Pond in New Fairfield. The following is an excerpt from Ceder's unpublished autobiography, "Working, Wandering, and Wondering." He describes his experiences working at three CCC camps.

At Housatonic Meadows is where I first started with my (CCC) crew of men. There were old stone walls that had tumbled down over the years and we rebuilt some of them. Also, there was a large part of the area in the woods much of which was dead chestnut trees, killed by the chestnut blight about the time of World War I. These were cut and mostly hauled to the camp for fires to keep warm in the winter, which could be exceedingly cold. We also patched up the dirt roads to make them more passable.

Once my crew was sent to Kent Falls State Park where we started to build a new road that would come out at the top of the falls. This was a very rough terrain at the upper end and it needed high retaining walls for a road to reach the top. We did an incredible amount of work and we did build a retaining wall close to thirty feet high but the road was never finished. It needed power equipment and that was not to be had, although we did get two trucks to haul rocks and dirt. The big rocks were loaded by hand which was very wasteful of manpower.

I recall the winter of 1934 which was bitter cold and some days if it was over fifteen degrees below zero we did not go to work until it warmed up to fifteen degrees. On a day like that you could hear the axes chopping away with

375

much vigor as the boys tried to keep warm. We kept weather records and if I recall correctly there were only a few days in the month of February that didn't register zero or below. It did go down to 34 degrees below zero for a day or two. The big dead chestnut woodpile rapidly disappeared. The barracks were built of one inch boards and there was no insulation and they were cold. The stove was kept loaded with wood, but one stove with that bitter weather was hardly enough.

To illustrate how cold it was, there was a crew that worked up on Sharon Mountain cutting big dead chestnuts. One of these was hollow and a frozen rattle snake was found in it. It was brought to camp and Mr. Hood stood inside the door and when one came in he poked that stiff as a cane rattlesnake right close to his face. This usually caused some comments which thankfully there was not room for here. There was some discussion that when it thawed out would it be alive? No one knew, so the snake was placed in front of our fireplace to thaw out. It was carefully watched to see if it was alive. It gradually thawed out and was limp but very dead. So we learned firsthand that if a snake freezes solid, they don't recover.

There was a new camp built south of Danbury called Camp Fechner and I was transferred there. The buildings were completed in 1935, the camp was operational and needed a few foresters so I was detailed there.

The main work there was to see if the Dutch elm disease could be controlled. This was killing all the elm trees about everywhere in the state and it was a very serious problem. The disease was carried by the Dutch elm beetle and it was a fungus I believe. These beetles, when they hatched flew to the tops of the elm trees and if they carried the fungus the leaves turned brown and in a year or two or maybe sooner the tree would die. The beetles laid their eggs in the bark. The dying tree could produce swarms of beetles who spread the disease by flying fairly long distances and landing on an elm tree and it soon was infected.

The method of control was to cut, pile, and burn the entire tree. This was a lot of hard work. The stumps were painted with an oily fluid filled with disinfectant to kill the beetles that might be in the bark.

Much work was done in the surrounding towns but the big swamp near the Danbury Fair Grounds took a tremendous amount of work because the large swampy area supported an almost solid stand of elm trees. We had sometimes huge piles of very heavy logs, tops, and brush.

Sometimes they were fifty feet long and twenty feet high. These were burned when snow was upon the ground. Generally they would burn for several days.

We did other work also. I was assigned to control 'Shoot Moth.' We traveled over a large area looking for this bug which is a pest of ornamental pines. Its egg is laid in the terminal bud and the following spring the moth hatches and eats the new growth, causing the tree to be deformed. Sometimes nearly every bud will be deformed. Control consists of cutting each deformed bud and putting it into a bag to be taken to a place and burned in order to kill the moth inside. When a moth gets to be an adult it leaves the shoot and flies to an area depositing an egg on every shoot. This was a seasonal job for me.

Then I was given a road to build to a fire tower in the town of Redding. This was an easy job as it mostly consisted in hauling gravel to surface the graded road.

Then as time marched on, spring came bringing with it the forest fire season. We covered the northern part of Fairfield County and in April and May we were very busy putting out small grass and forest fires.

One day we put out seven fires in widely separated areas. As there were no radios we had to come back to camp after each fire and then be sent out again. The citizens in the area were very unconscious about lighting fires, going outdoors and burning some papers or other stuff and not

Art worked as a foreman at Camp Fechner in the forests around Danbury where he supervised CCC enrollees in cutting and burning elm trees that were infected by Dutch elm disease.
Sheila Ceder

watching it at all. With a breeze these fires frequently took off and we were kept busy. However, by the end of May the grass and the woods were green and that duty ended.

One of the biggest as well as the most rugged fires was on the hills near Beacon Falls. This fire called out fire departments to protect several houses, but it burned mostly uphill. It was partially on the Water Companies property and it was slow going as it was very steep in many places. Right across the street was a Mars candy factory. I had to use the telephone and the management was very interested in the smoky forest across the road from them. After I had made my phone call someone asked if the men would like a candy bar or so. I said, 'Yes, sir! They sure would!' So I was given all the boxes I could carry back to the fire, passing out candy bars usually two to each fire fighter, courtesy of Mars Company. They were very welcome and they disappeared like magic.

After the fire season was over, I was given the job of surveying the burned areas that we had put out earlier and also the burned areas that fire wardens had put out elsewhere. I was given the lonesome job as I was a land surveyor. I had a record of the acreage reported burned and the idea was to see how accurate these estimates were. I surveyed over thirty acres by compass and pacing, and invariably all were over estimated as much as three times the actual area.

(Note: turn to Chapter 8 for more history of Camp Hook at Wooster Mt.)

(Note: turn to Chapter 8 for more history of Camp Hook at Wooster Mt.)

❧ ❧

The camp (Hook) was closed and I was sent to Squantz Pond State Park as the caretaker and patrolman. There was a lean-to built by the CCC about 100 feet from Squantz Pond and this became my camp for the summer. This was probably the best summer I ever had. There were hikers and campers every weekend and I was soon well acquainted with many very nice people. Across the pond was Joyceland where there were dances every weekend and the campers loved it.

I made one friend who I still have, over 50 years later. He was fishing but without much luck. My patrolling journey went right by him so I stopped to watch his technique. He cast and cast with no luck and then he said, 'You try your luck.' I noticed that he was covering the same area all the time. There was a big ledge and I got a strike from a pretty good 3-pound bass. John became my friend then and

there and every week he, his wife, and child came camping. Also his sister who was studying to become a nurse came camping. He made a boat and left it with me so I could go out onto the pond if I so desired.

(Note: turn to Chapter 7 for more history of Squantz Pond.)

(Note: turn to Chapter 7 for more history of Squantz Pond.)

❧ ❧

As the camping season ended about the middle of September, I was sent back to camp Fechner which had been closed and now was to be torn down. I was to do the tearing down. Also, just before the election in October, President Roosevelt decided the country needed a work program and the work program America or W.P.A. was born. A crew from Danbury was assigned to Camp Fechner. I had to go and pick them up and also take them back daily. We worked up in the woods cutting fire wood which the welfare folk in Danbury would burn the coming winter.

Early in November the election returned Roosevelt to the White House and what do you think one of his early acts was? He closed the W.P.A. as he was now elected for four years and he had a job. If many thousands of others did not work, well he had the economy to think of. Of course before election he couldn't think of that but he did get many tens of thousands of votes because men had a job. Such is politics.

I lived in the old camp infirmary which was very O. K. for baching it. So I alone started to tear down the camp buildings, one at a time. As the boards and 2 x 4s came down they were piled. When the weather turned cold, I worked in the old cook shack making picnic tables for the state parks. I made the top boards, held together by 2 x 4s near each end which fitted exactly into the end sections. I made forms for the tops and the sides and cut the seats exactly to length. These tables were all in sections so they could be transported easily that way.

I had no electric saw which would have been a great boost of production so I sawed each end of every piece by hand. I was working on the cold concrete floor and my feet were cold no matter how fast I sawed. Slowly some saw dust accumulated and I pushed it underfoot and it got to be a couple inches. The State Park trucks came to pick up the loads of these tables and they were easily assembled with just a few nails or spikes. Lumber was not wasted.

When early spring came the State Park Department

needed help elsewhere so I left my Danbury home and went to Hammonasset State Park where they were building a nice boardwalk along the beach front of the big main building.

This was quite a project and they had all the help they could afford getting it ready for the spring opening. It was mostly made from lumber from the hurricane which had knocked down thousands of trees in the state.

✂ ✄

Arthur Ceder then worked for Alain and his sister Mary White, who, in 1913, had established the White Memorial Foundation (WMH) in Litchfield, a non-profit tax exempt organization to promote education, conservation, research, and recreation. Arthur was hired as superintendent and supervised their 4,000-acre wild-life sanctuary.

As superintendent of WMF, Arthur had many accomplishments. He supervised the building of over 20 structures, the construction of many miles of roads, and the sale of wood products: over 4,400 cords of wood, lumber from the WMF sawmill, charcoal, treated poles, sawdust, and maple syrup. [http://www.whitememorialcc.org/newsletter_archives/fall_2007.pdf]

In 1969, Art retired to Florida at age 63. Three years later he married for the first time, to Marjorie Esham.

On July 14, 2007, Art Ceder passed away at the age of 101.

Walter Richard Bartram Sr.

After meeting me at a CCC Reunion 1n 2008, Sheila Hislop of Danbury sent me this information about her father at Camp Cross.

My father's dad, Robert Edward, was a WWI veteran of the US Army. His mother, Martha Beckerle, was the daughter of the prominent and wealthy hat manufacturer, William Beckerle, of Danbury. On Jan. 15, 1914 Walter was born in the mansion of his grandfather Beckerle's estate on Hilltop Farm on Clapboard Ridge in Danbury. He was their only child.

"My father, Walter R. Bartram, was 20 years old when he joined the CCC. He signed up on Dec. 23, 1933 at the Danbury Unemployment Relief Committee in the Danbury City Hall.

"His discharge papers state he only completed 8th grade. Dad was a truck driver but was unemployed since October 1933.

"On Jan.16, 1934 my dad was sent to Camp Cross in West Cornwall. Dad worked in the woods and his work was rated 'satisfactory.' Of his $30/mo. pay $25 was sent to his mother, Martha Ulrich Bartram, at Tower Place in Danbury. He had $5 each month for spending money.

"My dad was 'honorably discharged' on the 31st of March 1934 which was his expiration time. Captain J. W. Johnson was his commanding officer.

On June 13, 1935 Dad married Eleanor Loretta McCauley in Patterson, NY. They had five children; Walter Richard Jr., Joseph Anthony, Wayne Thomas, Sheila Marlene, and Kathleen Annette.

"After the war my father worked as a trucker, mechanic and in maintenance work.

"On April 7, 1975 my father passed away."

During WWII Walter served in the US Army, and was stationed in Ft. Knox, Kentucky. Sheila Hislop

CHAPTER 24
WINDSOR / POQUONOCK

Camp Britton, Company 1193, P-66 was established on June 4, 1935 on Connecticut Agricultural Station Land in the Poquonock section of Windsor. DEEP State Parks Archives

HISTORY

Camp Britton, P-66, Company 1193 began in Windsor on June 4, 1935. 1st Lt. R. S. Pride led a cadre of 23 men from Company 175 (Thomaston) in a five-truck convoy to establish the new camp. They drove north on Rt. 75 to Poquonock, a northern area of Windsor. They turned east on River Road and arrived at state land near the Windsor Agricultural Station. They pitched their tents and began clearing the land for permanent buildings.[1]

On June 5th Dr. J. B. Filip, the contract surgeon, arrived to care for the health of the enrollees.

First Lt. Pride was relieved of his duties on June 24th and Capt. J. G. Farren became the commanding officer. Lt. Windsor became the adjutant and Leroy Johnson became the Education Advisor.

In August, A. W. Jack was assigned as the Camp Superintendent. By September the buildings and the camp were completed and the foremen, along with the rest of enrollees had arrived. The camp formally opened on Sept. 12, 1935. Its principal projects were gypsy moth control, forest improvement, and road construction.[3]

Massacoe State Forest

In 1908 the Eno family sold the state an approximately 120-acre tract in Simsbury to use for experiments in fire prevention and reforestation along a railroad right-of-way which ran through the forest. Mrs. Antoinette Eno Wood, a devoted naturalist, donated funds for the experiments, which sought to reduce destructive fires started by railroad. Trains fueled by coal spewed sparks that started forest fires. Later, diesel engines reduced the amount of fires.

Although the Massacoe Forest experiments did not find a solution to the problem, it did prove that the forest with burned-out areas could be successfully reforested and productive. Much of the reforestation work was done by CCC labor provided by Camp Britton.

State administration and Simsbury residents donated money for materials to develop a recreational area in the forest. In 1933 the CCC built a small dam across Stratton Brook to create Massacoe Pond, which was used as a swimming area until the new, larger pond was built in the park in 1965.[4]

Massacoe State Forest consists of two separate blocks of woodland in Simsbury that combine to total 370 acres. The largest block, Great Pond, is home to the town's biggest

Wilton Everet Britton

Camp Britton was named for Wilton Everet Britton who was the State Entomologist and Director of the Connecticut Agricultural Station. He was born in Marlborough, Mass. in 1868 and received his PhD from Yale University in 1903. He wrote a "Guide to Insects of Connecticut: A State Bulletin." Britton was noted for his research on many insects, particularly mosquitos from the nearby tidal marsh ditches. He died in August 1939.[2]

www.faculty.ucr.edu

This large building contained the Repair Shop, Tool Room, and Blacksmith Shop important in storing and repairing equipment used in forestry projects. This building is still in use by the Thrall Tobacco Farm. Ed Kelly

In 1935 Camp Britton enrollees built the beautiful Stratton Brook Park Pavilion in Simsbury. DEEP State Parks Archives

standing water body, while the 73-acre Massacoe block adjoins Stratton Brook State Park and provides diverse recreational opportunities.

In 1949 Stratton Brook SF was created from Massacoe SF. Architect, forester, and conservationist James L. Goodwin (1881-1967) worked to preserve forest space here and throughout the state. He graduated from Yale in 1910 with a Masters degree in Forestry. He became a private forestry consultant, as well as a landscape architect. From 1913-1914, Goodwin was field secretary of the Connecticut State Park and Forest Commission. He also served as president of the CFPA from 1958-1961. He worked to promote the reforestation of Massacoe Forest and the development of Stratton Brook State Park.

The following is a description of Simsbury State Forest in the August 1938 issue of the Camp Britton Bug.

The Simsbury State Forest has of late attracted much attention from all parts of the state as a result of the many and varied improvements made under the guidance of the state.

The improvements consist of the building of roads, fireplaces, and trails throughout the forest at the most conventional spots. The building of a dam at the Massacoe Pond is still another project conducted under the Simsbury State Forest Improvement Plan.

Camp Britton has been chiefly responsible for the work done at the park and the men are still hard at work making the Simsbury State Forest another of the many beauty sojourns in Connecticut. [5]

Camp Britton also helped the local community. One instance was finding a Mr. Fontaine who was lost in a

nearby swamp for two days. The Windsor Locks Chamber of Commerce commended the men for their service. [6]

1936

In 1936 Camp Britton's staff consisted of the following:

Army: Capt. J. G. Farren, Commander; 1st Lieu. H. R. Isenberg, Adjutant; Dr. J. B. Filip, Camp Surgeon.

Forestry: A. W. Jack, Superintendent; Foremen: H. D. McCracken, A. Barry, F. N. Foisey, A. P. Batayte, James Hull, and Paul Tierney. John Rostock, Mechanic. [7]

During the March 1936 flood, Camp Britton was called out again to help. They rescued victims when the Connecticut River overflowed its banks in Windsor Locks, Wilson, and Windsor. When the river subsided, enrollees spent the next two months cleaning up the same three towns and Hartford. The enrollees cleaned out buildings and sprayed the buildings with chloride of lime. They also buried many farm animals, cats, and dogs. Camp Britton also quartered enrollees from Company 173, who also helped during the flood, at Camp Toumey in the Mohawk State Forest. [8]

To show Hartford's thanks for the work of the CCC, Mayor Spellacy invited the CCC volunteers to the Hartford Foot Guard Armory on Wed., April 29 for a dinner. Governor Cross and the mayor gave speeches of praise for the boys' work. Then the enrollees received a wrist watch as an appreciation for their work. [9]

Camp Britton was known as a bug camp and there were many crews working to eliminate insects that damaged trees. Mr. Foisey's crew was busy searching for egg masses and painting them with creosote. They also were banding the trees with burlap.[10] In September 1936 Mr. Dubiel's bug crew was working on the gypsy moths in the Town of Canton.

From May 1 to June 30, 1936 approximately 111,000 trees were burlapped in West Hartford, East Granby, Suffield, Canton, Farmington, Simsbury, and Granby. During this time 132,344 caterpillars were destroyed. During the month of July 80,193 caterpillars were destroyed. From August 888 acres of forest were scouted in Simsbury and 16,093 egg masses were treated. Five work crews were supervised by these foremen: McCracken, Barry, Colvin, Foisey, and Dubiel.

Additional crews of from 15 to 20 men each were doing silviculture work at Simsbury State Forest in conjunction with gypsy moth control.[11]

A new diesel tractor was delivered to Camp Britton. It had a scraper and other attachments. The 14-15-ton tractor cost about $7,000. It was used to build roads in camp.[12]

Camp Britton did work at the 110-acre Connecticut Agricultural Experiment Station Rainbow Forest near Windsor. In 1902 the first experimental forestry plots had been laid out there. Another experimental forest was at Mundy Hollow near Poquonock. During 1936 a crew from Camp Britton constructed fire lines and cleared along the boundaries at the Mundy Hollow tract. Some of the lines were made into truck trails that helped in fire protection. The enrollees also constructed several fire holes for fighting fires and laid out experimental hardwood plots that would later provide information regarding trees growing in sandy valley soil. At the Rainbow Forest the crews thinned and pruned the trees and cleared and extended fire lines.[13]

Most of the wood removed from these forests was used to heat Camp Britton. Some of the timbers were used to construct bridges while others were used for experiments in treating posts.[14]

Camp Activities

Camp Britton also provided sports and entertainment for the enrollees. In May 1936 an outdoor arena was built. It was used for WPA Band concerts, boxing, and other forms of entertainment. These activities were also open to the public. Captain Farren sponsored Sunday afternoon tea dances. The camp orchestra provided the music.[15]

The August 1936 issue of the Camp Britton Bug had the following description of the July dance:

"Capt. J. G. Farren, highly esteemed commanding officer of the 1193rd company rewarded the enrollees with the dance given at the Poquonock Town Hall, Thursday evening, July 23. About 120 enrollees attended. Trucks were sent out to nearby towns and returned laden with happy young women. The town of Poquonock has as usual its regular quota of lovers of the light fantastic. The WPA dance orchestra of Hartford furnished the music.

"Shortly before intermission a grand March was led by Lieut. Isenberg and a beautiful blonde partner. Refreshments consisting of cookies, ice cream, and lemonade were served."

Camp Britton dances were scheduled for the last Thursday of each month.

On Aug 19, 1936 Camp Britton was awarded the banner, "Honor Company 5th CCC District."[16]

Camp Britton had a few sports in the summer to keep the boys busy. There was a baseball team that played the nearby CCC camps and local teams. There was also a boxing team and matches were held in an open air arena. There were also wrestling matches. Another favorite sport

(L–R) 1 The Army staff that supervised Camp Britton with Capt. J. G. Farren, Commander (center); flanked by two assistants. DEEP State Parks Archives 2 Camp Britton boys helping rescue people and animals in the 1936 Flood in the Town of Wilson along the Connecticut River. Ed Kelly 3 Ed Kelly (2nd row 4th from left wearing glasses) was a member of a bug crew searching for gypsy moth egg masses during the 1935-36 winter with two foremen standing on each side. Ed Kelly

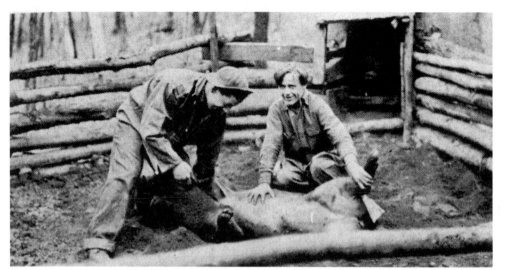

(L–R) 1 Two enrollees with a pig they were raising at Camp Britton. This was an educational project to give the boys experience working with animals.[18] 2 The first page of the Aug. 1936 issue of the Camp Britton Bug.

was horseshoes. There were courts on the east side of the mess hall. Efforts were begun in building a tennis court but work was discontinued until permission was given to purchase tennis equipment such as rackets, balls, and a net.[17]

The camp had its own newspaper called The Bug, since the company's primary work was with insects and tree diseases. In 1936 the name was changed to the Camp Britton Bug.

The educational program at Camp Britton started an agriculture program in which the enrollees began raising pigs. The six KPs. of the camp volunteered to be in charge of the program. They owned eight pigs that were in two pens. Some members thought this might be a good way to make money and they began bidding on the pigs. Eventually ownership of the pigs changed hands four times. The program gave the boys a chance to learn how to raise animals and possibly make money when it was time to sell them. [19]

On Sept. 17, 1936 Capt. Roy J. Honeywell, District Chaplain, came to Camp Britton and showed slides of his visit to Russia. The boys were very interested in learning about the land and people of this Eastern European country. Before he started the program Capt. Honeywell led the boys in songs accompanied on the piano by Carlton Allen. [20]

The Educational Advisor, Mr. Johnson, and Company Commander Capt. Berglund began planning for the fall 1936 educational program. Dramatics was one of the leading programs at the camp. A platform was constructed

in Barracks No. 2 for the stage in practicing plays. [21]

In the fall of 1936 Barracks No. 2 was turned into a recreation hall and was being partitioned into classrooms that helped improve the education program for the camp.[22] The building also had a Reading Room that contained books, magazines, and educational material. By January 1937 the building had folding walls that made three rooms. It also had two stoves, a blackboard, bookshelves, and new lighting. Besides holding classes the walls could be moved for space for dances and plays. [23]

In the fall the Forestry Department led by Mr. Jack, Camp Superintendent, and his foremen taught these classes: Forest Protection; Tree Identification & Wild Life; Roads, Trails, and Structures; Machine Operation & Repair; and General Conservation. At the end of each course the boys who completed the requirements were given a Certificate of Proficiency. [24]

A new program for the Educational Program was classes in the building trades to prepare the enrollees when they left camp to apply for apprenticeships. The classes were Carpentry, Blueprint Reading, Plumbing, Painting, and Masonry. Clerical classes were also offered: typewriting and the operation of adding and mimeograph machines. [25]

The Radio Club was very popular at Camp Britton. Their instructor, Carlton Allen, guided the boys in building and operating a radio transmitter. He also gave classes on international Morse code. [26]

Another popular class was Auto Mechanics taught by Mr. Rostock. There were 20 members who worked with a real motor installed in the rec hall. [27]

In December 1936 the Photography Club was happy to have a new darkroom located next to the lavatory so that they could easily get water necessary in developing photos.[28]

Three enrollees had 30 of their oil paintings from an art class placed on the mess hall wall.

During the winter of 1936-37 the boys turned to indoor sports. The camp basketball team practiced and played games at the Poquonock Town Hall gymnasium. Some of the teams they played were: Spartan AC of Rockville, Windsor Locks, Rockville Falcons, Thompsonville Comets, Glastonbury Ukrainians, and Camp Connors of Stafford Springs. The boys also played ping-pong and pool in the rec hall and tournaments were held for these activities.[29]

1937

There were frequent speakers who gave talks about travel, health, religion, and opportunities in various occupations. On Jan. 25, 1937 F. W. Putnam, representative of the Refrigeration Engineering Institution from Youngstown, Ohio, spoke about the possibilities for employment in the field of refrigeration and air-conditioning. Enrollees were then able to sign up for a correspondence course.[30]

The boys organized a camp orchestra that was called "Camp Britton Gypsies." On, Jan. 7, 1937 the orchestra played at a Christmas party held by the Hayden Station Community Club. The orchestra also played at dances and after the camp basketball games that were held In the Poquonock Town Hall.[31]

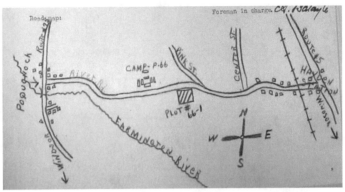

Map – Camp Britton worked with private landowners to show them how to clear the land and plant seedlings. One plot was near Camp Britton in Poquonock (section of Windsor). CFPA Library

Besides taking care of injured and ill enrollees at camp, Dr. Filip, the company doctor, also gave first-aid classes to all the truck drivers. This became mandatory for drivers in case there were accidents on the job or with a vehicle. Classes were also open to every member of Camp Britton.[32]

In February 1937 Superintendent A. W. Jack announced the good news that the ECW drivers of Camp Britton operated their trucks over approximately 150,000 miles without a single accident to either men or equipment. The mileage was calculated from September 1935 to February 1937. He congratulated all of the drivers for their excellent work.[33]

During the spring of 1937 Educational Advisor LeRoy Johnson began organizing an agricultural program for the camp. Enrollees had a plot of land and chose vegetable seeds. At the end of the season the profits would go to the enrollee and the cost of the seeds would be subtracted.[34]

Five gypsy moth control crews searched for egg masses during the winter. Foreman A. Batayte was in charge of the work that was associated with Agricultural Experiment Station Demonstration Plots that were primarily on private land.[35]

On April 4, 1937 Camp Britton celebrated the fourth anniversary of the founding of the CCC. In the morning enrollees cleaned the grounds and barracks because visitors came in the afternoon to look at the buildings, grounds, and enjoy supper with the enrollees. They then went to the Educational Building for programs that included singing and dance. The camp orchestra provided music for a dance that ended at 9:30 pm.[36]

As the spring fire season approached in March 1937 the camp had two trained fire crews each having 10 men and a supervisor. When the camp received a fire call the fire

Two Camp Britton boys won the title of Connecticut State wood sawing champions in 1937. DEEP State Parks Archives

Camp Britton group photo. CT CCC Museum

Camp Britton, closed in 1937, was taken over by Connecticut Experimental Station. The buildings were used for housing migrant laborers from nearby tobacco farms. This post card (c. 1950) had the sign: Windsor Farm Labor Supply Center. Windsor Historical Society

(L–R) 1 Throughout the year people enjoy Stratton Brook SP in Simsbury where they can swim, ice skate, and fish in the Massacoe Pond that was formed when the CCC built a dam in the 1930s. The railroad track going through Massacoe Forest was removed and is now a trail for running, walking, biking, and skiing. Podskoch 2 At Massacoe Forest in Simsbury Camp Britton built the beautiful pavilion, stone fireplace, and chimney used for picnics. DEEP State Parks Archives & Podskoch

crews quickly got into their specially equipped trucks and were off. At one call the crew left the camp in 58 seconds. The fire crews were often the first at the scene before the local fire department.[37]

The Educational Advisor planned to continue classes during the summer. The classes covered a variety of topics such as Pressure Gun Spraying of Cars, Auto Body and Fender Work, Poultry Raising, Flower & Vegetable Gardening, Chemistry, Electricity, and Dancing.[38]

After being in operation for only two years, Camp Britton closed on May 26, 1937. The buildings were turned over to the Connecticut Experimental Station.[39]

The camp was later converted into living quarters for migrant workers on the nearby tobacco farms. Most of the wooden buildings were replaced with concrete and cinderblock buildings. Today the buildings are owned by the Thrall family and house migrant workers from many of the Caribbean nations such as Puerto Rico, Jamaica, etc.

LEGACY

CCCs built a small dam across Stratton Brook to create Massacoe Pond, which was used as a swimming area until the new, larger pond was built in the park in 1965. The handsome rustic picnic shelter located on the eastern bank of the pond was also erected. The pavilion is a well-preserved example of the high-quality structures built by Depression-era relief labor. Of particular significance is the stone chimney, which epitomizes the superb masonry work done by the CCC. [40]

Directions:

From Hartford take I-91 north and travel approximately 7 mi. to Exit 38. Travel north on Rt. 75 approximately 2.2 mi and turn right onto River St. going east to 601 River St., Windsor. Most of Camp Britton was removed and is now the site of CREC River Street School. There is only one CCC garage left on Thrall Tobacco Farm at the rear of the school. The old camp site is now on private property and not open to the public.

The Dec. 1937 cover of the Camp Britton Bug.

MEMORIES

The following are stories and poems written by the boys at Camp Britton in their camp newspaper the Camp Britton Bug.

"A Rookies Song & Story" by Scribblin' Stan

"Oh, we're a bunch of fresh rookies,
Yes, we're a bunch of fresh rookies,
Oh we're a bunch of fresh rookies,
which nobody can deny."

The train wheels seemed to hum this song while it rolled onward to the headquarters at New London. I never heard of any head being divided into quarters so I guess I was a trifle curious about our destination.

Just when I was getting off the train the Porter asked me if I wanted to get brushed off. Humph, naturally I told him I would get off like everybody else, even if I was going to join the Sissy C's. A funny-looking suit one guy had on. He made us march in file. What a fool! Who ever heard of marching inside a file? Gosh, I feel like a Boy Scout on parade.

We were pushed into a room where a whole bunch of male housewives (they wore aprons) jumped on us with a pile of tools which they proceeded to stick into our mouth, ears, eyes, and some places I never knew I had myself. One guy even tried to drive a spike into my arm. Another gawky-looking uniform made me read a sign, then told me that I had poor eyesight. But Holy Cats – I would like to see the fellow who could read and pronounce that word!

Later on another fellow who must have escaped from prison (he wore stripes on his sleeve) gave us a funny-looking suit that he called an 'OD uniform'. He must have forgotten to add the 'OR' because the ODOR made me wish they issued clothespins. The shirt I got was a few sizes too small (about 10) but the pants made up for it because they were at least 10 sizes too large. The suit looked kind of bluish but it turned khaki after I got through taking off about 1 million tags.

After being in camp for almost 3 weeks now, I can say that I am having a grand time and I truly think this is the life. But Gee Whiz, they make us work too hard! After spending the whole day trying to look busy, we are compelled to wash our own knives and forks. Tsk, Tsk.

I've got an errand to do for the big shot in my barracks. But nobody seems to know just where I can find the key to the reservoir.

- Camp Britton Bug, Aug. 1936

"Commandments of the CCC"

1. Members are subject to duty 24 hours per day and seven days per week, if needed. They are required to work for the Forestry Service 40 hours per week. No man has the right to leave Camp at any time without permission of an officer. Weekend leaves are considered privileges and not a right.

2. All members are expected and required do their full duty in assisting to keep the camp site, barracks, and himself neat and in an orderly appearance.

3. Clothing issued by the government is considered the official uniform of the CCC. A mixture of uniform and civilian clothing is strictly prohibited.

4. Absence without leave for one day brings the loss of a day's pay and a trial by Court Martial; absence of seven consecutive days without leave brings about an Administrative Discharge for desertion which is a blot against the member for life.

5. It is the privilege of every member to consult the Commanding Officer at any time about any matter.

6. The ownership and operation of motor vehicles is forbidden to all CCC enrollees.

- Camp Britton Bug, Nov. 1936

"A Rookie's Diary, At the Mess Hall"

First we hear the rattle of a pan, then comes the whistle, and last of all the bugle, and then – we eat. The first few times I was thrown out of the mess hall, but gosh and gee whiz, a fellow can't always remember to wet and comb his hair or wash behind his ears. It's funny I never saw the cooks or KPs wash up. I almost starved the first day at camp. Whenever I said, "Please may I have the potatoes," or "Will someone pass me the hamburger roast?" everybody just looked at me. I didn't eat until I learned to say, "Down with the spuds!" and "Throw over the mashed horse flesh!" Another fellow was asking me to shoot him the cow juice, but I couldn't see any cows around and while I was looking under the table for one I saw him get the milk. The guy was even crazier yet he called for the sneezing powder and he really meant the pepper.

"More dishwater," someone called. A pitcher was thrust into my hands so of course I went to the kitchen sink and brought some. Boy did I get one big surprise of my life when I saw them go drinking it up. I did not know till a while later that I was supposed to be sent after coffee, but it seems that a mistake like that is often made in the kitchen, and there is no difference.

The sugar bowl happened to be near me so I did not have to ask for it, but just as I finished helping myself the guy at the end called for the sand. I saw him looking at the bowl. I never thought I would drink coffee with gravel as sugar in it but it tasted the same to me so I then drank it with a little hesitation.

For the rest of the meal I was in a bombardment of vocabularies. Everyone called for bread in sheets, for spinach as grass, spoons as shovels, forks are called pitchforks, fried worms is spaghetti, eggs as chicken's fruit, and biscuits are cement walls.

I don't know how I ever digested a meal of such a combination got delicatessen a-a-la. After that meal I made my first acquaintance with the well-known CCC pills.

- Camp Britton Bug, Dec. 1936

The Camp Britton mess hall with the Mess Sgt. (standing right) supervising. The kitchen is at the back. DEEP State Parks Archives

"OUT"

Oh, to be out – when the moon is high;
When the twinkling stars
So softly trip by.
When the air is cool –
Tinting red the cheek.
And the crouching shadows,
Are calm and seem so meek.

The moon would glisten
And spread its golden hue;
Would cover all my sadness,
And chase away the blue.
It would bring to me –
The joys I so much crave.
- Camp Britton Bug, Nov. 1936

The Camp Britton Administration building in the winter of
1935-36. Ed Kelly

"The Editorial Room"

Do you hear the hustle and bustle?
And the whizzing and the boom;
Or the ringing and the banging
In the Editorial Room.

Everything is in a hurry there
Everything's all a rush.
The paper's due in a day or two,
And will, of course, be mush.

There are jokes and cracks and Barrack news,
And poetry and dry cartoons-
Lying around here and there,
With room for more not anywhere.

It must be fun to be in there,
To write and type and tear our hair;
And worry as to if we may-
Put out the paper on THE day.
Signed one of them.
- Camp Britton Bug, Dec. 1936

"We, In The CCC"
by Vic Vizvahy

Connecticut boys long for
The site of the city,
'Cause now they're with nature
Which shows them no pity.

But in building roads up these mountains
That will be used for years to come,
They are building a permanent monument
Of what the Connecticut boys have done.
- Camp Britton Bug, Feb. 1937

Ed Kelly

On July 10, 2010 Ed Kelly of Woodbury came to a CCC
reunion at Black Rock SP and shared his stories of working
at Camp Britton in Windsor and Camp Triangle Lake in
Blachly, Oregon.

Marguerite Cogliati saw an article about my CCC research in The Republican-American and contacted me. She said her father, Ed Kelly, originally from New Britain, CT, had been in the CCC and wanted to tell me of his experiences. I arranged to meet him at her home in Woodbury on March 9, 2009.

It was a sunny day as I drove through the quaint town of Woodbury with its many antique stores. Marguerite Cogliati greeted me and took me to meet her father who lived in a small guest house behind her home. Ed Kelly was a jovial man about 5' 9" with a medium build who welcomed

During the 1936 flood, Camp Britton searched for victims by boat and helped clean the streets and homes of debris and mud. Ed Kelly

After working at the Windsor camp, Ed Kelly (2nd row, 4th fr. rt.) was sent by truck to Fort Devens, Mass. and boarded a train with other enrollees to Oregon. Ed Kelly

me into his living room. He took out a photo album and began sharing his CCC stories.

"When I was 18 years old I joined the CCC in August 1935. I joined because times were hard and I was walking on cardboard in my shoes, which was quite common in those days as we couldn't afford to put new soles on our shoes. I just couldn't find a job. I was the eldest in my family of eight children and wanted to help my parents. We were renting a house in New Britain at the time.

"Before I joined the CCC, my dad had a hard time getting a job. After he did well on a government test he got a job in the New Britain post office. My Dad contacted an influential man in town who interceded for me because I was the oldest of eight children.

"They eventually sent me to Camp Britton in Windsor. I had a couple of friends at camp from New Britain: Stanley Stacheelek, Carl Listo, Joe Michaluskas, and my best friend, Johnny Burke."

Ed opened his photo album and said, "Here is a picture of the flood at Windsor Locks during the 1936 flood. We also worked cleaning up in the town of Wilson for several days and then worked in Hartford for a number of weeks in the Front Street area.

"In Wilson we commandeered boats to search for people. Many people were reluctant to leave their homes. There was one Italian man who asked if we wanted a tomato pie for helping him. We said, 'Yes.' That was my first pizza.

"After cleaning up from the flood, we had to take off our filthy clothes and have them run through a steam machine in the laundry. The leaders wanted us to get them

off fast because they were afraid we'd catch a disease. They also had portable showers for us.

"Our camp was near the tobacco farms in Poquonock, which is close to present-day Bradley Airport. The farmers sent buses to all the nearby towns to pick up girls to work in the tobacco fields. Captain Farren, a retired Army officer from East Granby, was assigned to oversee our camp."

Then he showed me another photo of guys climbing trees. "In the winter we looked for gypsy moth egg masses. We'd scout the woods for infected areas. I was a climber. When I found an egg cluster up a tree, I painted it with creosote. One of the many places we went to was in Granby on Copperhead Mountain. Some crews worked around Rainbow Dam. I'm not sure where that was.

"Gypsy moth scouting was hard work because we had to climb mountains and walk through swamps to find infested areas.

"The food at camp was great. I got KP duty every couple of weeks.

"For entertainment they used to have dances at our camp. They also had boxing matches about once a month.

"On some weekends I hitchhiked home. First we went to Hartford and then on to New Britain. One guy named Butler, who lived near my home, had a Model T. He was a friend of a friend and he'd give me a ride back to camp. It didn't happen often.

"The town of Poquonock was mainly Lithuanian. I remember going to one of their picnics. It was the first time I got drunk. I remember lying on the ground and hanging on to the grass.

"After a year in the Windsor camp, I signed up to go out West. In October 1936 the Army sent me to Fort Devens, and from there we went by troop train to Camp Triangle Lake in Blachly, Oregon. This camp was different from Camp Britton where we originally lived in tents. Then we built the barracks, mess hall, and recreational buildings. We built them in sections. There were about six buildings in camp. Here the camp was completed and we lived in established barracks.

"On my first day at Camp Triangle Lake, we were sent out in a convoy to battle a forest fire with a 20-mile front in Bandon. About 25 of us were riding in the back of a ton and a half rack truck with a canvas cover. The driver had no previous experience with a truck with a double clutch. He was driving because all the other members of the camp, including the experienced drivers, were already out fighting the fire. At a sharp left hand turn on the road, the driver lost control and the truck went down a sharp drop, overturning two or three times until it was finally stopped by a very large Douglas fir tree. Once we were able to get out, I saw that my friend, Joe French from Waterbury, Conn., was badly hurt. He was 17 years old and we had become friends while riding out on the troop train. I tried to carry him up the hill to the road to safety when another friend, Joe Oullette, told me: 'It's no use,' and I could see that Joe French was dead. I had lost some teeth and was bleeding pretty badly, but didn't feel anything. I was just thinking of Joe French. Another guy, Gerry Tangonelli, broke his back. Ernie Zick broke his shoulder, and Novak broke his legs. Some of the young men who had been in the convoy were overcome and they sat on the road crying. I had just lost some of my teeth, which was minimal compared to the other injuries.

"After a 100-mile trip with the wounded to an Army hospital in Vancouver, WA, I had lost so much blood that upon arrival I couldn't rise from my seat and had to be dragged inside for treatment. I remember that I was wearing caulk boots with spikes in them and was reprimanded by an orderly for scratching the floors while entering the hospital. I was a patient there for three weeks while I had dental work done. The dentist there said the work was interesting because it was like treating a combat wound.

"After my release I went directly to work at another forest fire. It was the Thanksgiving season and for our Thanksgiving dinner in the woods we had two apple butter sandwiches and an orange; foods I still enjoy to this day.

"My jobs in Oregon included felling timber, driving a truck, operating a steam rock crusher, and constructing a complete telephone line, including poles and telephone wire.

"We were supposed to be in for six months but I stayed longer. After a year my enlistment expired. Then I came home.

"My friend, Ed Conlon, helped get me a job with Prentis Manufacturing Co. where his father was an engineer. I made zippers at 30 cents an hour which added up to $12.00 per week.

"I married Marjorie O'Brien in April 1942. We had ten children: Marguerite, Michael, Peter, Stephen, Mary Ann, Edward, Frances, Andrew, Julia, and Kathryn.

"During WWII I was a sergeant and worked in Advance Ordnance. I was in England, France, Germany, Belgium, Luxembourg, and Austria.

"When I came home I got a job working at the post office in New Britain. Later I became the superintendent there. In 1973 or 1974 I retired.

"When I look back at my days in the CCC I think

Ed Kelly (right) with friend Vic Vizari at Fort Devens waiting to be sent to Oregon in 1936. Ed Kelly

The Army train stopped at a station in South Dakota to give Ed and the other CCC boys a chance to walk around before continuing on to Oregon. Ed Kelly

about what I learned such as swinging a sledge hammer and an axe, and using a two-man saw, skills I never got to use again! Being a member of the CCC in Oregon was overall one of the happiest times of my life. I had good friends and could tell you some interesting tales! The CCC affected my whole life, my work ethic, and the friends I met. Many of them stayed in Oregon or California."

On Nov. 21, 2012 Edward T. Kelly passed away surrounded by his family at his home in Woodbury.

Raphael "Ralph" Donofrio

Ralph Donofrio at age 16. Donna Ford

On March 15, 2009 Donna Donofrio Ford of Suffield wrote to me about her father, Raphael Donofrio, who worked in the CCC.

"Since his name was spelled in different ways: Ralph, Raphael, Refiele, Donofrio, and D'Onofrio, I have had a difficult time finding his CCC records.

"My father's parents were born in Italy. His father, Vincenzio, was a stone mason. His mother, Francesca Tommasino, came to the US in 1910. They had 12 children: John, Andrew, Domenic, Ralph, George, Mary, Pat, Viola, James, Marguerite, and Carmen. Susan died in early childhood.

"Dad was born on May 18, 1915 in Hartford. My father had to quit school in 6th grade in order to help his large family.

"I don't know how he found out about the CCC but he joined and worked at the Windsor camp. The only job

he told me that he did was planting vegetables.

"I don't know how long he stayed at Camp Britton but when he left he worked at the Fuller Brush Co. in Hartford.

"In December 1942 my father married Florence Griffith. They had six children.

"My dad was in WWII. He was in the Army and worked as a cook. One of the battles he was in was the Battle of the Bulge.

"After the war he continued to work at the Fuller Brush Co. He retired in 1971.

"My father died in 1988."

CHAPTER 25
WINSTED / BARKHAMSTED

(L–R) 1 Situated under a mountain near the Farmington River, Camp White Co. #106 was a small village with a mess hall, infirmary, rec hall, administration building, and five barracks surrounding a park like setting with grass, trees, shrubs, and flowers. Paul Adykoski 2 The boys placed whitewashed stones around the camp roads and paths. 106 was the camps' company number. Howard White 3 Connecticut State Forester Austin F. Hawes (right) speaking to members of the CFPA meeting at Matthies Grove in Peoples SF. (CAES)

HISTORY

On May 24, 1934 Camp White S-63 was established by Army Company 106 in Barkhamsted, 5 miles east of Winsted on the west side of the West Branch of the Farmington River in the American Legion State Forest (SF). In 1927 the American Legion Forest was established when the American Legion donated 213 acres to the state. Its WWI veterans had traveled throughout Europe and saw how Europeans had managed their forests. The veterans wanted to provide the citizens of Connecticut with an example of properly managed forest.

Peoples SF, located in the Pleasant Valley section of Barkhamsted, was established in 1924. It got its name because people throughout the state donated money to purchase the land. The Connecticut Forest and Park Association (CFPA) led the effort in collecting donations.

Some of the organizations that contributed were: Daughters of the American Revolution, the Connecticut Federation of Women's Clubs, and many other groups and individuals. Most of the land cost approximately $8 an acre.[1]

Before coming to Barkhamsted, Co. 106 was organized on April 17, 1933 at Camp Devens in Massachusetts. It then went to Martha's Vineyard where the men cut out scrub oak and planted pine trees. They also built roads, installed telephone lines, and fought to eliminate gypsy moths.

Projects

After a year at Martha's Vineyard Co. 106 came to Barkhamsted. The enrollees worked on many projects at the two adjoining state forests. They built roads, nature trails, and a museum, did stream improvement projects, fought tree insects, and improved the forests by doing silviculture and planting trees.[2]

The White Memorial Conservation Center

Alain & May White

Camp White was named after Alain White and his sister, May, who were philanthropists interested in preserving forests in Connecticut. They established the 4,200-acre White Memorial Foundation near Litchfield and Morris. They also donated a substantial amount of land to the state for its forests and parks in the western part of the state. From 1923 to 1928 Alain White was president of the CFPA.

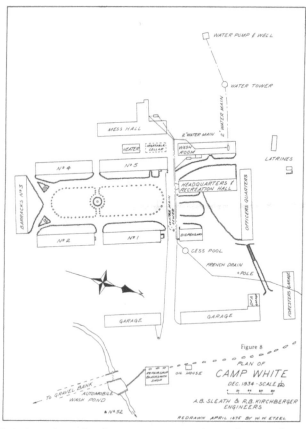

(Clockwise from Above) 1 Map – A Dec. 1934 map of Camp White. Barkhamsted Historical Society 2 The truck garages and blacksmith shop were located below Camp White near West River Rd. The truck drivers are ready to take the enrollees to work. Gary Potter 3 The light coming from the Chaugham cabin near the stagecoach road along the West Branch of the Farmington River was like a lighthouse telling passengers that there were just five miles to go to reach their destination of New Hartford. Barkhamsted Historical Society

Road building was an important project of Camp White. In 1934 the enrollees widened and graveled over 3-miles of Greenwoods Road (formerly Big Spring Rd.), which was the main road through Peoples Forest. They also completed an entrance road to Camp White.[3] By 1936 several other roads had been improved, including the road on the west side of the West Branch of the Farmington River, Beaver Brook, and Pack Grove in the Peoples Forest.[4]

The CCC built many nature trails through both American Legion SF and Peoples SF. In 1934 enrollees built a half-mile instructive nature trail from Matthies Grove through the Ullman Picnic area in the Peoples Forest.[5]

On Aug. 2, 1929 the Matthies family who owned a factory in Seymour, Conn. purchased the 210-acre Ullmann farm, including the house, barns, and outbuildings. In a dedication ceremony, Gov. John H. Trumbull received the deed for the farm from the Matthies family, the largest single donation to Peoples State Forest. The ceremony took place in the beautiful 200-year old white pine grove, which today is called Matthies Grove, located near the entrance to

the park along the West Branch of the Farmington River.

In the American Legion SF the Henry Buck Trail was designed by Henry Buck, a Yale graduate and an outstanding engineer, who designed many state-wide CCC projects. Buck was vice president of the CFPA from 1928-30. The trail begins at River Rd. and travels to the old cheese box (boxes for draining whey) mill and ends at 'Tremendous Cliff' which overlooks the CCC camp. On May 18, 1935 the state dedicated the trail with a large group of friends in attendance.[6]

Barkhamsted Lighthouse Settlement

The CCC boys built the Girard Trail that marks the site of the famous Barkhamsted Lighthouse settlement used to guide the coaches on the stage lines from Hartford. The boys cleaned the Barkhamsted Lighthouse graveyard site and built a wooden stockade fence around it.[7]

After a hike to the settlement, reporter Peter Marteka wrote a story in the Sept. 9, 2011 issue of Hartford Courant:

"The name of a settlement created by James Chaugham, a Native American Indian and his white wife, Molly Barber, in the late 1700s. Soon after they were married, the pair fled Molly's disapproving and angry father up the Farmington River until they reached a terrace in the shadow of Ragged Mountain. The couple had eight children, and soon a community – the Barkhamsted Lighthouse – grew in the woods settled by Native Americans, Europeans and freed and escaped African American slaves.

"The origin of the settlement's name most likely came from stagecoach drivers who traveled along a main road and spotted the smoke or lights coming from the community high on the terrace. Today, only remnants of the community – cellar holes, an old fieldstone cemetery, a quarry, charcoal kilns, and a large stone mortar where corn was ground – remain."

"And there's the Lighthouse," rang the driver's shout,
As down the valley toiled the Hartford stage
Past where the lights were feebly shining out
From cabins high on Ragged Mountain side."
Quote from "The Story of Connecticut" by Lewis Sprague Mills, 1932

During 1934 crews from Camp White fought the spread of gypsy moths. Crews searched for moth egg clusters and destroyed them by covering them with creosote. During the summer they banded trees with burlap to stop the movement of the caterpillars.[8]

In 1934 the young men added a lumber shed to the workshop and built a foundation for the stone administration building.[9]

By June 30, 1934 the enrollees did silviculture work in the forests. In the American Legion SF they cleared 56-acres of dead wood, thinned 148-acres. The camp also made 593 posts, 70 poles, 1,923 bd. ft. of logs, and cut 66 cords of wood for their camp and for park campers. In the Peoples Forest they cleared 205 acres and thinned 466 acres.[10]

Camp White worked on the Whittemore and Matthies campgrounds in Peoples Forest. They cleaned out the pools in the Farmington River and built bath houses. They developed the Ullman and James Stocking picnic groves on Greenwoods Rd. At the Stocking Grove they built an Adirondack lean-to and fireplace for overnight camping. Then they built two other shelters a little farther up Greenwoods Rd. The enrollees protected the big water spring from contamination by stoning it in. They also laid out plans for the Matthies campground and planted shade trees. This area contains 200 year-old white pine trees.[11]

Whittemore campground was named after Harris Whittemore (1864-1927), an impressionist art collector, industrialist, and member of the State Forest and Park Commission. In 1921, Mr. Whittemore began buying parcels of land in the Naugatuck Valley, intending to donate them to the state. He planted 225,000 trees in what is now the Naugatuck State Forest and contributed land and funds to Kettletown and Hammonasset State Parks in addition to other parks in the state and across the country. After his

(Clockwise from Above, Left) 1 Camp White built two bridges across the W. Branch of the Farmington River. The first bridge was the one pictured above that connected the camp to an island in the middle of the river. The stonework was done under the direction of August Casciani. Then from the island they built a lower wooden bridge that extended across the river to the Peoples SF. The bridge was later destroyed in a flood but the stonework remains. DEEP State Parks Archives 2 The wooden bridge that connected the island to the Peoples SF. Doug Roberts. 3 Camp White administrators: Superintendent Edgar Hawks, Capt. Howard Best, and 1st Lt. Hemming. Howard White 4 A gypsy moth crew composed of enrollees Leland and Miranda on the truck and (L–R) are foreman Leblanc and enrollees, Mello, Bowen, Gough and Condon. Howard White

106th Company at Winsted, Conn

Scenes of life at Camp White in the Fifth CCC District First Corps Area Yearbook, 1937.

A September 1935 group and camp photos of Camp White. John Eastlake

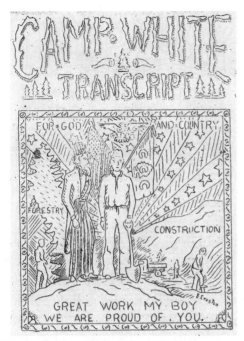

The Nov. 19, 1935 issue of Camp White Transcript was written, illustrated and produced each month by the enrollees under the supervision of the Educational Advisor.

untimely death his family continued to acquire land, and in 1931, almost 2,000 acres were donated in his memory.[12]

The following is a list of Camp White administrators in Feb. 1935: Capt. Howard Best, Commander; 1st Lieut. Robert H. Tiers, Mess Officer; 1st Lieut. Edward P. Bergin, Camp Surgeon; Edgar Hawks, Superintendent; and Richard A. Fear, Educational Advisor.[13]

Camp Activities

Sports were very popular during the winter at Camp White. The camp basketball team played local town and CCC camp teams. Most of the local games were played at the Winsted Y Gym. The ice hockey team won their first five games. Some were played at Granville Pond.[14]

The camp Educational program was limited because it had no permanent instructional classrooms. The program was supervised by Richard A. Fear who was assisted by four FERA instructors: Daniel Connelly, John Midura, Bernard Schulman, and Edward Mularkey. The classes were: Spelling, English, Writing, American History, Arithmetic, Chemistry, Algebra, Civil Service, Psychology, Civics, Journalism, French, Typing, and Dancing. There were also discussion groups on Current Events, Entomology, Blueprinting, and Forestry. Also available were "Amateur Nite" featuring enrollee organized musical programs, a

debating club, a glee club, and a Bookman club.[15]

Enrollees who travelled to the Torrington Trade School during the winter 1934-35 were honored with a banquet on March 16, 1935. The guests included James H. Scully, District Educational Advisor; Fred E. Lukens, Corps Area Educational Advisor; Herbert Jones, Director of the Torrington Trade School; and trade school teachers. Students were presented with certificates many of which were later used to obtain jobs.[16]

A hurricane in September 1934 caused extensive damage to the Wood Creek Dam in Norfolk. Trees were blown down causing the earth above the spillway to flow towards the dam. This caused the water to seep under the trees and under the dam for approximately 20-25'. This was not noticed because the area had been covered with snow and frozen earth. Then when spring came and the earth thawed the dam needed immediate attention. In April 1935 a call was made to Camp White for help. Mr. Mahoney and his road crew were dispatched to Norfolk to help. Enrollees filled 500-600 sand bags and used them to fill the hole. The boys had to walk in 2-3' of frigid water during a snow storm. Then they covered the bags with rocks that forced the water back to the spillway.[17]

In July 1934 a Camp White masonry crew under the supervision of August Casciani began the construction of the Nature Museum on Greenwood Rd. in the Peoples SF. The young men began the difficult task of gathering stone from ledges in the forests within a two-mile area of the park and transporting them to the construction site.

Three months later the camp carpentry crew, consisting of novices many of whom had never used a hammer, was directed by R. Laughlin of the Forestry Dept. The crew used native chestnut and oak lumber. The boys used chestnut for

Nature Museum in People's SF built by Camp White. CT CCC Museum

(L–R) 1 Camp White Army Administrators in 1934: Col. Wilson, Capt. Best, Sanitary Inspector, Lieut. Bergin, and Lieut. Tiers. Howard White 2 The 1936 Flood covered West River Rd. in Barkhamsted. Camp White responded to the blocked road and helped remove the huge ice chunks. Paul Adykoski 3 When New Hartford's homes were destroyed in the 1936 Flood; Camp White went to help residents clean their homes and businesses. http://www.ezoons.com/images/2004/05/flood2.jpg

the beams and paneling while the floor was made of white, red and quarter-sawn oak.

New nature study features were added each month in the summer. The topics were paintings of natural specimens, wild flowers, destructive insects, etc. During their free time enrollees gathered insects, birds, and flower specimens for displays and these were turned over to Mr. Sullivan who was in charge of the displays.[18]

On May 3 Governor Wilbur L. Cross, Director of ECW Robert Fechner, and Col. William L. Wilson came to dedicate the museum. They praised the work of the enrollees and architect Robert Linehard, head mason August Casciani, and carpenter Robert Loughlin. That year the director reported 8,300 visitors to the museum.[19]

The Camp White boys were happy when spring arrived in 1935. Some joined the camp baseball team that played local teams in the Winsted City League. They also played nearby CCC camps like Walcott, Toumey, Cross, and Robinson. A volleyball team played other CCC camps. Some boys played in the inter-barracks softball league, billiards, and horseshoes.[20]

In June 1935 1st Lieut. Robert H. Tiers, who was the Mess Sergeant, assumed command of Camp White replacing Captain Howard Best (since the fall 1934), who was transferred to start a new camp in Agawam, Mass.[21]

The Blister Rust crew led by Mr. Bacon was very busy during the spring and summer. The men traveled through swamps and climbed mountains in search of the Ribes plants that were hosts to the blister rust. By July 1935 the crew had uprooted 10,000 plants. They continued their work on public and private lands until the fall.[22]

A group of 80 New England Society of American Foresters came on Sept. 2, 1935 and camped in tents at Peoples Forest. They inspected the work of the CCC.[23]

In Sept. 1935 the educational advisor was proud to announce the opening of a new Library and Educational Room. It was staffed by an assistant from 10 am to 10 pm. Here enrollees were able to read fiction, non-fiction, and textbooks. There was also a large selection of magazines. It was a place for writing letters home and for instructional classes. The building had two blackboards and two typewriters.[24]

New classes were added to the fall teaching program: Free Hand Drawing, Economics, Handicrafts, and Dramatic Club. E. R. Hawkes was the new Acting Educational Advisor. [25]

In October 1935 Camp White welcomed a new commander, Capt. William F. Moran from Boston. He had served in WWI and also chased after Pancho Villa in Mexico in 1916. Camp White was his first time working in a CCC camp.[26]

On Tues. Nov. 28, 1935 a company dance was held in Barracks No. 6. Approximately 200 enrollees attended. Ladies from Riverton, Winsted, Tarrifville, Simsbury, and New Hartford helped to make the dance a success. Mr. Knott came to the camp two weeks before the dance and had dance classes. These came in handy for the boys with all the pretty young ladies.[27]

In March 1936 issue of The Echo it stated Lieut. John Morrissey assumed command of Camp White replacing Capt. Walter D. Thomas. [The Echo, March 1936, 1.] Howard C. Neal was the camp superintendent. He was assisted by these men: Edward C. Barnes, Robert S. Brown, August Casciani, Howard D. Dick, Paul J. Koistinen, Everett J. Koltz, Philip J. Sullivan, Robert H. Loughlin, Russell Lund, Victor L. Pearson, Allen R. Perry, Raymond E. Shappelle, and Paul Zimmerman.[28]

Dances were very popular for Camp White and

local residents. A dance celebrating President Roosevelt's birthday was held on March 15, 1936 at Red Men's Hall in Winsted. Approximately 400 people danced to the music of the Elliot Bond Orchestra. Lieut. Morrissey and Miss Marian Moxin of Winsted led the "Grand March." [29]

During the winter of 1935-36 there was a large accumulation of snow and when heavy rains came in March the rivers and streams overflowed. At the beginning of the March flood of 1936, Camp White was cut off for two days because of the flooded and ice-covered roads. Enrollees assisted in breaking the biggest ice jam in the history (in the nearby hamlet) of Pleasant Valley.

They followed this by playing a major part in the rehabilitation of New Hartford where on March 18 the almost 100 year-old Greenwoods dam near New Hartford Village broke and flooded the town. Camp Superintendent Homer C. Neal took one hundred enrollees and helped the citizens evacuate the area. Many of the residents were made homeless. The enrollees cleaned up the debris and helped with requests from town officials.[30] "In appreciation for their hard work, they received watches and a royal banquet in Hartford." [31]

After the flood another dance was held on April 1, 1936 at the Red Men's Hall in Winsted. A special award was given to Miss Clara LaRolda of Winsted. Sgt. David J. Larese crowned Clara Miss Camp White and showered her with gifts. This might have been the first time a CCC camp gave such an award. Other prizes were given to Miss Clara

A view of Camp White from the mountain behind camp showing the athletic field (near garage and W. River Rd.) garage, and Amphitheater. CT CCC Museum

LaRolda and Edward Marolda for the best moonlight waltz dancers, and Miss Eleanor Hunt and Henry Laskas won the fox trot contest. Mickey Dill and his orchestra supplied the music. At intermission Camp White enrollees performed vaudeville acts.[32]

Amphitheater

In 1936 Camp White officials selected a natural amphitheater site approximately 100 yards from the camp for a place of weekly entertainment for the camp and the surrounding communities. A weekly series of entertainment events were held on Thursday evenings that began on May 6th and extended for 24 weeks ending on October 15th. The amphitheater held over a thousand spectators. There was no admission charge. A wide-range of entertainment was offered: civic orchestras, symphonies, bands, instrumental soloists, hillbilly bands, dancers, magicians, comedians, minstrels, and tumblers.[33]

Barkhamsted Historical Society

May 6, 1936 at 8 pm was the opening of the Camp White Amphitheater. Capt. William Tasillo and the military band played as the American flag was raised on the newly constructed flagpole over the stage and in the center of the amphitheater. Then Lieut. John Morrisey introduced Miss Camp White, Clara LaRolda. Four girls dressed in white handed bouquets of flowers to Clara, who then introduced Company Commander Capt. Walter D. Thomas, as the band played "Hail to the Chief."

(L–R) 1 Miss Camp White, Clara LaRolda of Winsted, was featured on the cover of the July 1936 issue of The Echo camp newspaper. 2 In 1936 Mr. Lindstrom was the entertainment director at Camp White.

(L–R) 1 Loading the truck with gravel for road construction. The gravel pit was the site of the Amphitheater for Thursday night shows. 2 Barkhamsted resident, Doug Roberts, said, "The Amphitheater was in the gravel pit near the camp. I went to the shows on Thursday evenings. People sat on the gravel bank. They had lights down there at night because power came up River Rd. from Pleasant Valley. The Camp's power came down from Barkhamsted."

(L–R) 1 The Camp White football team played other CCC camps. Paul Adykoski 2 Boys playing touch football on athletic field near garages. Howard White

The band then played several songs followed by several professional vaudeville acts including comedian Miss Frances Odell; yodeler George Carpenter; magician James Brecket; comedy and dancing by Fred Nadeau; a one-arm piano player and a singer, Charles and Lillian Girard; ballad singer Arthur Malloy; and dancers Cosmo and Anita. The master of ceremonies was Stephen Crane. This was followed by community singing, wrestling, and boxing. A special thanks was given to the Hartford Park Dept. which lent the camp bleachers that accommodated 1,500 spectators.[34]

During the summer of 1936 Camp White had new sports: handball, golf, bowling, and tennis. The camp made an agreement with Camp Concord to use their courts. Plans for organizing tennis and golf teams were made for the summer with matches with other camps. The camp also secured uniforms for the baseball, basketball, and football teams. The baseball team played their home games at the Riverton ball field. In May construction began on bowling alleys at Camp White.[35]

When the state took over the nearby old Camp Concord, there were many dilapidated buildings that adjoined the Matthies' House. In 1936 one of the Camp Concord houses was completely renovated and used by the District Forester, S. E. Parker. The house was called the Paige Seaton Cottage in honor of a former commander of the American Legion who pieced together the parcels of land and donated it to make the American Legion Forest.

In 1937 the Matthies House was remodeled into a two-family home. One part was occupied by Foreman R. S. Brown and the other was to be used by the Youth Hostel Movement. Today it is used as the Senior Center.

The enrollees next job was to remodel the Bensen House. All of the renovation work was done by boys from Camp White and supervised by foreman R. H. Loughlin.

5th COMPANY   BARKHAMSTED

First Lt. John Morrissey, *CA.-Res.*, Commanding and Exchange Officer

First Lt. John A. Horton, *Cav.-Res.*, Adjutant

Roster

First Lt. Francis Gallo, *Med-Res.*, Surgeon

William Kent, *CEA*

TECHNICAL PERSONNEL   Homer C. Neal, Supt.; Edward C. Barnes, Robert S. Brown, Asst. Supt.; August Casciani, Howard D. Dick, Paul J. Koistinen, Everett J. Koltz, Philip J. Sullivan, Robert H. Loughlin, Russell Lund, Victor A. Nicola, Everett L. Pearson, Allen R. Perry, Raymond E. Shappell, Paul C. Zimmerman.

LEADERS   Henry Butkiewicz, Norwich, Connecticut; Douglas E. Dodge, Winsted, Connecticut; John H. Fitzgerald, Boston, Massachusetts; Francis G. Lyons, Cambridge, Massachusettes; Harry L. McKinley, Revere, Massachusetts; Howard C. Nelson, Willimantic, Connecticut, Senior Leader; Albert Russo, Thompsonville, Connecticut; Bryant I. Stiles, Hartford, Connecticut.

ASSISTANT LEADERS   A. M. Allemao, Acushnet, Mass.; C. Bacron, New London, Conn.; W. Chambers, Manchester, Conn.; C. Dambrouski, Waterbury, Conn.; T. Danilowicz, Norwich, Conn.; F. Donovan, Brighton, Mass.; A. Giovacchino, Ansonia, Conn.; T. Layden, New Britain, Conn.; F. O'Day, Worcester, Mass.; A. W. Welch, West Haven, Conn.; J. Berry, Waterbury, Conn.; W. Ryznic, Hartford, Conn.

MEMBERS

Eiguier, E., South Boston, Mass.
Alexander, F., Roxbury, Mass.
Angelovich, A., Bridgep., Conn.
Austin, J., Hartford, Conn.
Beaudoin, A., Waltham, Mass.
Beaulieu, R., Hartford, Conn.
Belaski, C., Hartford, Conn.
Bennett, L., Mamaroneck, N. Y.
Black, E., Waterbury, Conn.
Bloomer, G., Watertown, Mass.
Bohmer, F., N. Britain, Conn.
Bolles, W. H., Ken'gton, Conn.
Boslick, J., N. Britain, Conn.
Bowen, R. V., Conway, Mass.

Burdick, H. F., Fitchville, Conn.
Buturle, F. C., Norwich, Conn.
Caisse, J., Waterbury, Conn.
Carter, R., Hartford, Conn.
Chappell, R. H., Man. C., Conn.
Collins, J., Meriden, Conn.
Consic, L., Moodus, Conn.
Cosby, H., Bridgeport, Conn.
Curgio, T., Bridgeport, Conn.
Coutu, N. I., W. War., R. I.
Danila, V. S., Collinsv'le, Conn.
D'Archangelo, D., Brid., Conn.
Delisle, R., Hazardv'le, Conn.
Dinan, J. J., New Haven, Conn.
Dudzik, B., Chicopee, Mass.

Dugoleski, L. C., Ansonia, Conn.
Fahey, M., Hartford, Conn.
Fedor, M., Sandy Hook, Conn.
Ferris, C., Bridgeport, Conn.
Gabrey, F. L., Wareham, Mass.
Gyome, M., Colchester, Conn.
Hathaway, G. S., Hartf'd, Conn.
Hilley, A. R., Watertown, Mass.
Izbicki, N., Norwich, Conn.
Juliano, J., Hartford, Conn.
Kaczka, T. L., Meriden, Conn.
Kelly, T., Worcester, Mass.
King, R., Kensington, Conn.
Labarge, A. J., Ware, Mass.
Lamirand, F., Jewett City, Conn.

Lariviere, E. G., N. B., Mass.
Lasco, F., N. Haven, Conn.
Lebicz, B. C., Cambridge, Mass.
Ledoux, L. R., Worcester, Mass.
Ledwith, P., Hartford, Conn.
Lowles, M. G., Acushnet, Mass.
Martone, A., New Haven, Conn.
Mele, L., N. Britain, Conn.
McAvoy, F. E., Waltham, Mass.
Miller, H. F., Worcester, Mass.
Moore, W., Hartford, Conn.
Morocco, D. J., Bridgep., Conn.
Morrill, H., Hazardv'le, Conn.
Mysz, W., Thompsonville, Conn.
Neary, J. F., Hartford, Conn.

Newell, H. R., Hartford, Conn.
Olsen, J., Dorchester, Mass.
Orio, A. J., W. Haven, Conn.
Orlando, J., N. Britain, Conn.
Pac, J., N. Britain, Conn.
Paradise, A., Bridgeport, Conn.
Pasinok, A., N. Britain, Conn.
Perro, M. J., Worcester, Mass.
Peszko, W., Hartford, Conn.
Pietrowicz, C. J., N. B., Conn.
Poulin, F., Hartford, Conn.
Rose, J. R., Taunton, Mass.
Ross, J., Torrington, Conn.
Sandquist, R., N. Britain, Conn.
Schultz, B., N. Britain, Conn.
Seymour, L., Hartford, Conn.

Shectman, S., Quincy, Mass.
Sheppard, A., E. Weym'h, Mass.
Skovinski, W., Boston, Mass.
Slaby, P., Ware, Mass.
Smith, R., Putnam, Conn.
Traczyk, C., W. Haven, Conn.
Vasso, P. G., Milford, Conn.
Velucci, J., Waterbury, Conn.
Waitkewicz, J., N. B., Conn.
Walsh, P., Worcester, Mass.
Werner, R. L., Winsted, Conn.
Woodard, R. H., Dnbury, Conn.
Zukowski, J., N. B., Conn.
Burrell, W., Kensington, Conn.
Havassy, A., Groton, Conn.
Foley, J. J., Hartford, Conn.
Brown, H. J., E. Lyme, Conn.
Lupo, F., Hartford, Conn.
Podracky, J., Bridgeport, Conn.

Camp White group photo and roster from Fifth CCC District First Corps Area Yearbook, 1937

This was good carpentry experience for the boys that benefited them when they went to apply for a job. [36]

There was a close bond between Camp White and the surrounding communities. One example was in June when over 1,500 members of the St. Joseph's Church in Winsted attended a picnic at the camp on a Sunday in June 1936. [37]

Another example was in August 1936 when 150 members from the Elks Lodge in Winsted and their guests attended a clambake at Camp White. [38]

In June 1936 Peoples Forest had many visitors inspecting the work of Camp White. On June 1 the National Conference of State Parks inspected the park and expressed their approval of the work. Then on June 13 the CFPA came to inspect the park. [39]

In June 1936 Connecticut State Parks and Forest reported that Camp White constructed and maintained 14.8 miles of automobile roads, 22-miles of forest roads, and 14 miles of foot trails in the American Legion and Peoples forests. [40]

In July 1936 the 13th weekly entertainment show was held at the Amphitheater. It featured 12 vaudeville acts. Camp White was the only camp that held weekly shows. [41]

The Camp White Echo reported that in 1935 over 8,000 people visited Peoples Forest and in 1936 more than 12,000 people came to enjoy the picnic areas, hiking trails, recreation fields, and Nature Museum. Visitors enjoyed the oil paintings of native birds, insects, and animals on the nature trails. The flowers, shrubs, and trees were labeled. The Nature Museum had over 200 nature and forestry exhibits. There were also 34 miles of hiking trails that were mostly constructed by Camp White. Russell Lund of the Forestry Dept. supervised many of the projects. [42]

Camp White Forester Pearson received a letter of thanks from District Forester S. E. Parker praising the fire-fighting crew for their work in the Nepaug SF (near Canton) on April 21, 1937. Pearson complimented the boys for their strength and endurance in having to carry water a great distance to reach the fast burning fire. [43]

The fall 1937 Education Program made an effort to prepare the boys for a job. The Educational Advisor selected 45 enrollees to attend evening classes at the Torrington Trade School. They studied these subjects: Machine & Tool Making, Electricity, Carpentry, Radio, Typing, Bookkeeping, and Shorthand. Camp White's Forestry Dept. offered these courses: Elementary Forestry, Roads and Trails, Forest Protection, Auto Mechanics, Tree Identification, and Forest Improvement. [44]

In December 1937 Superintendent Homer C. Neal left Camp White for a position in mining in California.[45] He was replaced by Colonel Otto H. Schroeter who said his big challenge was the construction of a new school building since it was so important to the camp educational program. He said the process gave the enrollees great experience in developing construction skills. [46]

Col. Schroeter was born in Germany where he was educated and then came to the US. He had many engineering experiences including building the Panama Canal. He served in the Army in WWI and said, "My first assignment with the CCC was in 1933 at Camp Graves, in Union where we built Soapstone Mountain Rd., all the Camp Graves buildings, and other minor projects. Then I spent two years at Camp Chapman in Niantic doing work on Rocky Neck SP, Devils Hopyard, and road construction at the National Guard Reservation (Stones Ranch). At Camp Robinson in East Hartland, I spent a year and a half supervising the construction of Dr. Kienholz's house, and the Pell and Morrison Hill roads. In the Christmas season of 1937, I was transferred to Camp White. Our biggest projects here are the rip rapping of the Farmington River along the Matthies' picnic area, the Matthies and Bronson (in which I have made my home) houses, and the King house which is still incomplete." [47]

In the spring of 1938 Mr. Zimmerman supervised the boys in rebuilding Barracks No. 2, which became the school. The new building had a large study hall that could divide into four rooms. In the four corners of the school were permanent rooms. One room was for the educational advisor, the second was for the Press Club, the third was a music room, and the fourth was a private study room.[48]

In March 1938 these were the administrators and foremen. The Army personnel consisted of Capt. Jesse G. Ferren, Commander; 1st Lieut. Bradley J. Donovan, Adjutant; Dr. Harry Shapiro, contract physician; and Herbert T. Baurer, Educational Advisor.

The Forestry Depts. included: Col. Otto Schroeter, Superintendent; Robert S. Brown, Asst. Superintendent; and foremen: Joseph Bolger, August Casciani, Everett J. Koltz, William J. Mahoney, Allen R. Perry, Phillip J. Sullivan, Robert H. Loughlin, John J. Podracky, and Paul Zimmerman. [49]

Looks like these Camp White enrollees are having fun digging a foundation. Barkhamsted Historical Society

Joe Pack getting a ride from John Anderson at a foundation project. Barkhamsted Historical Society

(L–R) 1 The masonry and carpentry crews from Camp White built the District Forester's Office in 1940. CT CCC Museum 2 Camp White had a large fleet of dump trucks, a tractor, and a pickup truck all housed in a large garage. Nadine Logan 3 The "Two-mile trail" was completed and begins near the Camp White gravel pit and goes to a swamp area near the state forest boundary. CT CCC Museum

1938 Hurricane

In September 1938 a hurricane hit New England and it rained for six days. Near Camp White the Farmington River rose from its normal height of 6' at the beginning of the storm to 27' by 7 pm on the sixth day. It flooded roads on the east and west. In some places the depth was 10'. Members of Camp White could not get to the state road but had to climb the mountain and walk two miles. [50]

After the hurricane the entire 106th Co. restored the two-mile road to Riverton. The road was so undermined and washed out that a car could not travel on it. Col. Otto H. Schroeter supervised the foresters and enrollees who did emergency repairs to the road and within a few hours the road was open to traffic. That night volunteer enrollees went to the town of Riverton and helped people escape from the flooding waters. They also helped move furniture to higher ground thus saving residents hundreds of dollars. The enrollees also helped remove fallen trees that damaged homes and property. The boys also patrolled the streets and warned the residents of the rising river. [51]

Then 50 CCC men went to neighboring New Hartford to help the residents clean up after the hurricane. The boys pumped out cellars, cleaned out the mud and debris and sprayed them with lime. The 106th Co. received great praise from the town for their help. [52]

Then Camp White got a phone call to help the City of Hartford. Seventy-five men built dikes to hold back the raging Connecticut River. They continued to stay another day to help. When the greatest danger had passed they returned to camp late that night. [53]

In the fall of 1938 a few CCC camps were closed in Connecticut and enrollees were transferred to other camps. Some men from nearby Camp Toumey arrived at Camp White and veterans welcomed them along with the new

rookies. [4]

In the December 1938 issue of the The White Eagle, Camp Physician Dr. Harry Shapiro wrote an article describing the dangers of social diseases such as gonorrhea and syphilis. He urged enrollees to come to him if they had any questions or concerns.

Then on December 14th Dr. Shapiro invited Dr. Talbot from the State Dept. of Health to show a sound movie on venereal diseases. It explained the causes and results of syphilis and gonorrhea. He also showed a silent movie showing how the disease spread and how the diseases could be cured. [55]

In March 1939 Camp White began work on a new administration building supervised by Col. Otto H. Schroeter. A masonry crew directed by Mr. Casciani built the cellar walls, fireplace, chimney, and a fire proof vault. A carpentry crew supervised by Mr. Laughlin completed the interior and exterior work. The plumbing, wiring, and landscaping were completed by enrollees supervised by Mr. Zimmerman. The building had three large rooms two of which were used by Mr. Hawes and Mr. Parker, and a reception room for members of the State Forestry Department. The project was completed in August 1940. [56]

On the morning of Aug. 1, 1939 at 7:30 am camp mechanic, Mr. Quick, accompanied by six of his trusted drivers left for Camp Buck in Portland to bring back new dump trucks. The trucks were 1939 Ford V-8 that were described by the boys as "streamlined and attractive." They even had ashtrays on the dashboards. The trucks also had hydraulic brakes and special safety glass.

The truck convoy returned at 3 pm and was greeted by enthusiastic boys who were all hoping to get a ride in one of the new trucks. However, before the trucks could be used for work, seats had to be made and the trucks needed

25H-32 Photo: Camp White enrollees worked at the state tree nursery located along the Farmington River in Peoples State Forest. Tony Gagliardi

a thorough inspection. The governors that controlled the speed of the truck were set at 30 mph.[57]

In the Aug. 24, 1939 issue of the White Eagle there was an announcement of a new truck trail that would run from the W. River Rd. at Camp White for 1.2 miles westerly to a dead end near the Legion Forest boundary. It was going to be a single track truck trail designed to open the American Legion Forest for moving t men and firefighting equipment. Col. Otto H. Schroeter, camp superintendent, and foreman William Mahoney were in charge of the 25 enrollees doing the work.[58]

The hurricane in 1938 caused flooding that washed out the nearby Pleasant Valley Bridge. It was being replaced during the winter and spring of 1939 by the A. I. Savin

Construction Co. at a cost of $194,000. The new 27-ton steel bridge was expected to be completed by May 1st and make it easier for residents and Camp White vehicles to get to the Peoples SF.[59]

In May 1940 major repairs were made to the camp buildings. To help prevent fires the Celotex ceilings were raised to follow the pitch of the roof to the peak. This was done so that if a fire developed in the ceiling it would be noticed more quickly. There were also electrical improvements. The old wiring was replaced with BX cables and wherever needed floors were installed. In some of the Army garages a cement floor was installed.[60]

During the first week of June 1940 the 38-man Gypsy moth crew was assisted by a group of 30 men from Camp Hadley. The two crews supervised by Mr. Roberts began spraying in the Peoples SF while another two crews began spraying in Burlington supervised by Mr. Sullivan. Each crew consisted of 15 to 20 men. Each crew had a pump truck with a solution of lead, arsenic, water, and fish oil. A hose was laid out and two men took turns holding the nozzle. On June 28 most of the enrollees from Camp Hadley returned to their camp in Madison.[61]

In August 1940 the boys cleared roadsides in the state forests to help prevent fires that might start from motorists discarding their cigarettes or cigars. One crew was working on Beaver Brook Rd. in Peoples SF. They dragged brush 50 feet from the edge of the road.[62]

In 1940 Camp White completed more projects

This young man (left) is using a hydraulic drill in the quarry to get rocks to build a 627' retaining wall along the banks of the Farmington River (right) to prevent erosion to the Peoples State Park. Paul Adykoski & DEEP State Parks Archives

Capt. George Snyder leading parade of Camp White enrollees in 1939. Lilo Snyder

The entrance to Camp White in Barkhamsted. DEEP State Parks Archives

including Barnes Road in Peoples Forest and an office building for the Western District using wood from the nearby state forests. They used the following materials: shingles, oak flooring, clapboards, and trim. [63]

At the tree nursery in the Peoples Forest the CCC built a pump house to provide water for the seedlings.

By 1940 there was a total of 16.4 miles of automobile roads in the two state forests. [64]

In October 1940 the staff of Camp White consisted of the following men: Capt. George Snyder, Camp Cmdr.; Franklin Newman, Subaltern; Philip Schultze, Camp Physician; and Frederick Kipp, Educational Advisor. [65]

As the US was getting closer to entering WWII Capt. George Snyder was relieved of his command and transferred on Nov. 5, 1940 to return to active duty in the Army Air Corps. [66]

An Army dentist made frequent trips to all of the CCC camps in Connecticut. The Oct. 30, 1940 issue of the White Eagle reported that over a 10-day period Dr. Burston would treat all who needed attention. [67]

Camp White officially closed on Jan. 6, 1942

On Aug. 20, 1943 Camp White was turned over to the Connecticut State Forestry Department. [68]

LEGACY

Camp White was instrumental in developing two parks on both sides of the West Branch of the Farmington River. In the Peoples SF picnic areas are located in the 200-year-old white pine plantation in the Matthies Grove and Whittemore Recreation Areas. The area is the center of river-based recreational activities including trout fishing,

canoeing, kayaking and tubing. Over 11 miles of hiking trails in the two forests provide an opportunity to be close to nature and appreciate its beauty. There are also cultural and historic sites to explore such as the Barkhamsted Lighthouse.

The Nature Museum draws thousands of visitors each year. After sitting idle for 50 years, the Museum was reopened in 1992 under the direction of Marilyn Aarrestad, the Peoples SF supervisor. It was given a new name, 'The Stone Museum.' The curator for the next 15 years was Walter Landgraf. Upon his passing in 2007, the museum was again called 'The Peoples SF Nature Museum.' The purpose of the museum has always been to educate people about local flora, fauna, and history. The area surrounding the museum is rife with natural treasures and interesting tales of the early settlers. All this and more is reflected in the Nature Museum's displays and through interpretive programs. Today the museum is run by Janet Bumstead. [69]

Each year thousands visit the beautiful Nature Museum built by Camp White in the Peoples SF. Podskoch

The entrance to Camp White leads to the old CCC camp site that is now used for Youth Camping. Podskoch

The American Legion SF provides camping opportunities at the Austin F. Hawes Memorial Campground. It is located midway between Pleasant Valley and Riverton on West River Rd. There are 30 campsites where visitors can enjoy the Farmington River for fishing, canoeing, kayaking, tubing, and relaxation.

Another legacy of the work of Camp White are these state forest trails:

American Legion SF

Henry Buck Trail (Blue blazed): Starts at the old bridge site on West River Rd. 2.5 miles north of Pleasant Valley. The trail leads up through the forest to the ruins of an old cheese box mill, climbs the Tremendous Cliffs which offer a good overlook, and continues down the north slope to about .3 miles north of the starting point.

Turkey Vultures Ledges Trail (Blue): Starts on Legion Rd., off of West River Rd., north of the campground. This relatively easy hike leads to a scenic overlook. Distance - .4 miles.

Peoples SF

Agnes Bowen Trail (Orange): Starts at the Museum and proceeds north to the James Stocking Recreation Area, crossing the Pack Trail near Beaver Brook, to Beaver Swamp; follows Beaver Brook Rd. for several hundred feet, proceeding westerly to a crossing of Greenwoods Rd., and southerly to East River Rd. about a mile north of the starting point. The trail is a traditional 1930's ski trail. Distance - 2.5 miles.

Charles Pack Trail (Yellow): Starts at Greenwoods Rd. north of the James Stocking Area; runs southeasterly crossing the Bowen Trail near Beaver Brook; crosses the brook and leads northerly past an old cellar hole, crossing Pack Grove Rd., and through Pack Grove to cross the road again at Beaver Brook Bridge; then, running northwesterly to the recreation area on Greenwoods Rd. Distance - 1.9 miles.

Elliot Bronson Trail (Red): Starts at Greenwoods Rd. near the Museum, runs through the southern portion of the forest crossing a 60' cliff; offers a rugged climb over Ragged Mountain; terminates on a town road near Rt. 181. Distance - 1.5 miles.

Jessie Gerard Trail (Yellow): Starts at East River Rd. near the old Indian Settlement known as Barkhamsted Lighthouse. The right trail fork goes through the lighthouse site and continues northerly to the Chaugham Lookouts. The left trail fork climbs more directly to the overlooks by 299 stone steps. The views from this area are some of the best in the state. Continuing north, the trail passes between the Veeder Boulders to the picnic area on Greenwoods Rd. Distance - 1.3 miles.

Robert Ross Trail (Blue): Starts at the end of Warner Rd., runs westerly to the Jessie Gerard Trail; and then southerly along the west side of the ridge, to the end of King Rd.; proceeds to the Museum and westerly to East River Rd. Distance - 2 miles.

Walt Landgraf (Red): This trail starts near the east end of the Elliot Bronson Trail and leads to an area of rock ledges known as the Indian Caves. For 1500 years soapstone was quarried here by Native Americans. Distance .2 miles.[70]

Directions:

American Legion State Forest

From Winsted take Rt. 44 east to Rt. 318 east to Pleasant Valley; or Rt. 44 west from New Hartford to Rt. 181 north to Pleasant Valley. Then before the bridge over the Farmington River turn left on West River Rd. and travel 2.5 miles to Legion Rd. on the left. Follow the dirt road uphill to the Camp White remains.

Peoples State Forest

From Hartford take Rt. 44 to New Hartford, then continue for approximately 2.5 miles and turn right onto Rt. 318 in Barkhamsted. Go across the steel bridge over the Farmington River and take an immediate left onto East River Rd. The recreation area is approximately 1 mile up on the left and the road to the Nature Museum is on the right.

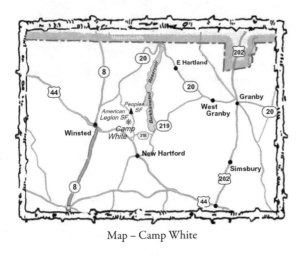

Map – Camp White

MEMORIES

"Extra Duty"
by William Wallace

While reclining on my bunk in a blissful haze of content, after a hard day's work and a good meal, a harsh voice breaks in on my roseate meditations. "Smith, your turn in the kitchen. Grab your mess kit knife." Reluctantly I arise and taking my knife, I depart for another two or three hours work. Thoughts of vengeance and revolt fill my mind. As I near the kitchen door, I notice nine other morose looking men wandering around waiting for orders from the KP Chaser.

For the second time my castles in the air arise as I perceive the others are men with less service than me. With the assurances and confidence of a veteran, I anticipate an easy job, such as working in the tempting confines of the root cellar. For the second time that night my castles in the air go smash, as the bull voice of the KP Chaser bellows, "Smith, the grease trap." With head bent in humiliation and dejection, I depart for the odious and odorous job of cleaning the grease trap.

After two hours of toil at the detestable grease trap, I hear with relief and satisfaction, the new melodious voice of the KP Chaser, "Okay Smitty, scram!"

I return to my bunk with buoyant step content in the knowledge of having completed my turn at the extra duty like a gentleman, and to dream of happy times when all my extra duty days will be over.

- Camp White Static, Sept. 1935

The camp mechanic and a cook join a friend enjoying quiet time with the camp pet near the infirmary. Paul Adikoski

"Perfume of a Different Nature"

To be sure, it's an odor, but not the kind that the young things carry with them to social affairs. No, this odor is a malodorous one. There is nothing like it This Side of Hades.

In order to get the full appreciation of the perfume, one must go up behind the mess hall. There a yawning hole is seen in the earth, and from this cavernous maw there exhales halitosis that defies comparison.

Well – you ask, "Why dig into the decay and cause the air to be filled with bad smells? What's the matter here? Is something wrong?"

Then Teddy Danilowicz gives the questioner near a stony glare and practically yells, "Can't you see the grease trap is broken?"

And so it is. And the cooks and KPs certainly know it's broken, for they have been making love to it for three days now in an endeavor to find what's wrong with it. It seems that the water won't flow down. Now, that's too bad.

But look at poor Vysocka, he is digging in the wrong place. Why he's got a hole dug that is deeper than he is tall. He confers with Lieut. Capasso who gets out the camp map. "Well," says the Lieut., "this map shows the pipeline to run under the ground in that direction. You haven't dug the hole deep enough yet." But Teddy is sick of the whole business. He begins to dig right beside the grease pit. He works long and hard. Finally, he is at the bottom of the affair.

Then it is seen that the pipeline doesn't run as shown on the map. It runs off to one side and under the building itself. Oh, hum, what a life!

Now they are constructing a manhole alongside of the grease trap so if the pipe clogs up again, they will not have to dig any holes in the area again; they can work from the manhole itself. But Teddy is hoping it never occurs again. You know, it was so inconvenient!
- The White Eagle, Oct. 1938

Two enrollees cleaning the grease pit at Camp Toumey.
Elizabeth Germaine

"One Hundred Six"
by Hank Butkiewicz

Down in Pleasant Valley
Nestled back among the trees
Is the one hundred and six
Company of the C.C.C.'s

Our C. O. and his staff
All help in work and play
And they also collect
When there's a fine to pay.

Our Forest Super and his aides,

Are jolly lads what ho',
If they put soft seats in trucks
We'd like them better tho.

Consider now our kitchen staff
Those boys just can't be beat
They now and then fix a dish
No one on earth could eat.

Road building is our specialty
And firefighting, too,
We go to see the Winsted girls
When there's nothing else to do.
- The Echo, March 1936

Camp White boys happy to be with Company 106 in 1935.
Howard White

"Where Am I"

Where am I? Am I in Heaven?
Or am I really with you?
Who are you? Are You an Angel?
Or just a dream too good to be true?
Can moonlight be so enchanting?
Can kisses be so divine?
Where am I? Am I in heaven?
Can it be true that you are mine?
- The Echo, May 1936

"Love Is Like a Cigarette"

Love is like a cigarette
You know you hold my heart
Aglow between my fingertips
And just like a cigarette.
I never knew the thrill of life

Until I touched your lips.

Love so sweet to fade away and
Leave behind ashes of regret
Then with a flip of your fingertip
It was easy for you to forget
Oh! Love is like a cigarette.
- The Echo, May 1936

"Enrollee's Prayer"
by Ralph Bohmer

Here in the C's I sit.
As I think not long ago
When out of C's was I.
My shoes were all worn...
My clothes were torn;
My hair was long, and I was down and out
Now and then I stop to think
And thank the Lord for what He did,
For if he didn't pick the man who's president of our land
I'd still be broke as well as bored.

Now this great man whom Our Lord did pick
Is the one who did the trick.
He gave the call which brought us all
To make this country what it is.
Just think. If you were down and out,
And you couldn't get a job.
And all at once he gave the call
We had waited for, one and all;
To give us homes as well as pay
For which we all do not deserve.

For which I wrote I may be wrong,
But only God gave us three C's.
- The White Eagle, Oct. 1938

A CCC boy on a log fence at Camp White. Paul Adykoski

Camp White mess hall with enrollees lined up for chow and the kitchen serving area in in the rear. CT CCC Museum

"The Big Drink"

No, not of beer. Just water – plain water. And it was everywhere! We know – we're in it. It was no joke to say a fellow was all wet; it was a truth. We were all wet!

The first day, no one minded the little drizzle. But when after a couple of days, it climaxed in a bit of hurricane – well, then we were down and out. The day it rained the hardest the whole overhead was beset with its own problems. The Mess Steward, Teddy Danilowicz, supervised the salvaging of his mess hall and kitchen. The water poured down the mountain in gushing torrents towards the building. It came and then came some more. It looked as though the place would be washed out and Teddy, in white pants and a big raincoat, ran around yelling orders at one and all alike. He would grab a pick to stem the tide, then seeing it ineffective, would drop it in favor of a shovel. He had water on himself, over himself, around him, and in him, too, we guess.

By dint of hustling, his KPs and cooks alike, he managed to get the flood under control so that the stockroom was not flooded, or the fires put out in the ranges. Much credit goes to our Mess Officer, Lieut. Alexander Capasso for his helpful suggestions.

The Supply Steward, Ralph Boehmer, was not omitted from the fury of the waters either. Usually he sits, in the face of community disasters, in the security of his position and just laughs everything off. But the night of the flood, when he saw the waters beginning to invade his sacred supply room which he had thought to be impregnable to anything but fire, dismay was written all over his face. Within an anguished cry of, "River, stay away from my door," he grabbed a broom to sweep the water back over the threshold.

Camp White boys boarding trucks near the garage to work in Peoples SF. Howard White

Finally he accepted the night guard's suggestion to place sandbags in front of the doorway. This accomplished he stood back and viewed the fortunate saving of his precious supply room. He sighed, "Boy, that was too close."

The next day broke in sunshine. It also meant a crew was working in camp on clean-up work and the repairing of damages. Temporary dikes were taken away, fallen leaves raked up, and branches carted away. The road along the riverside was filled in by several crews working busily all day. The day after that, the camp authorities sent 75 men to Hartford to work on the dike, and 50 men went to New Hartford on a clean-up detail.

No matter what or where the inconveniences, the flood gave us a lot of adventure. It did break, at least a little, the routine of camp life – the routine that tends to get monotonous unless something like the hurricane – flood comes along to push us out of it.

- The White Eagle, Oct. 1938

"A Day in the CCC - Building a Waterhole" by Charles Sabatini

We started out in the early morning in trucks. As we got underway, I had the pleasant feeling of starting a new job which was doubly enhanced by our passing of the gravel pit, our job of the previous week, which I had not liked because we never seemed to be accomplishing anything.

When we arrived at our destination, we found that there was a waterhole already made. Our job was to enlarge it to 30 feet in diameter, sloping the sides down to a 5-foot depth. Mr. Brown, who was in charge, first drove in a stake where he wanted the center of the hole. Then by putting his tape measure on the top of the stake at the 15 foot-mark and by driving in stakes at intervals of about 5 feet, 15 feet from the center stake the outside circumference was found. The next thing we did was to remove all the stones and stumps that were inside the circumference. Since the size of some of

the stumps and rocks would necessitate blasting, we had to leave them for the next day. Then began the task of digging out the center and sloping down the sides which was made difficult by the dense undergrowth of roots and ferns, the presence of water already in the hole, and the hard clay we encountered about a foot from the surface.

The purpose of these waterholes is to have enough water ready for the pumps to fight forest fires. When the CCC first built those waterholes, they dug them straight down like a well. Later, however, it was found that animals might fall into them in an effort to get a drink and be unable to climb out and would consequently drown. That is why the waterholes are now built with sloping sides to enable the animals to crawl out.

The best time of the day is at 4 o'clock when with the satisfaction of having done a good day's work you face the cooling breeze on the way home to a much needed shower and a much more pressing need, supper.

- White Eagle, July 26, 1940

A stone-lined waterhole. Al Brown

"Impressions"

When we came to 106
We knew not what to do,
We had to start all over
For everything was new.

Lieutenant Hart came up to us
And said, "Don't be absurd.
You'll find you're part of Camp White now –
No more 173rd.

"Some of the things you may have done back there –
Will be allowed no more;
And don't come in with the excuses
'We did those things before.'"

Surely we thought, "Now we will be tied
With rules and regulations –
And get fined, too." But worst of all,
We KNEW we'd get half rations.

Then we went to the mess hall –
And how those Vets did stuff!
But there must have been aplenty
'Cause we all got enough.

The next AM we made our bunks;
Not one of those beds sagged,
We dusted, shined, and swept – and lo;
Not one of us were bagged!!!

And so the days have turned to weeks,
New things we've seen and heard;
Soon we can say, "We know this place
Like we knew 173rd."

And when we came, we must admit,
No one felt like sticking.
But since we've come to know this place
You don't see us boys kicking.
The Toumey Boys
- The White Eagle, Nov. 1938

CCC man – clean looking, masterful, and direct. He told us what we could expect of Camp White, and what would be expected of us.

After a few days of insipid ease we were sent out to work with the rest of the men. I was assigned to a forestry crew. Our job was to clear away trees that were impeding the growth of more valuable trees.

All of the men worked in pairs. I was placed in the custody of an old timer who was to teach me the ups and downs. He accomplished this capably and was a most pleasant companion. He was intelligent and humorous. Often he kept me laughing for hours.

I soon found out there were excellent educational opportunities in camp. I have undertaken aeronautics and also a high school course.

For recreation we have a hall equipped with pool tables and a ping-pong table. We have quiz programs. These are merely get-togethers in which interesting questions are asked and answered. For a correct answer one is awarded a prize of cigarettes, or a bar of candy. After the quiz we sang popular songs and ballads to the music of guitars and a piano. Time fairly flies, a sure sign that I am having a wonderful time. Hurrah for Camp White. I think it is the best camp in the country.

- The White Eagle, Jan. 1939

The rec hall afforded enrollees a place to relax and have fun playing ping-pong, pool, or card games. Gary Potter

"Impressions"
by D. Majewski

Upon arriving at Camp White my first comment was, "What a drab looking place." I was disheartened almost immediately. However, the aspect soon changed.

As soon as we (I and some other men) were introduced to the commanding officer, I brightened up. Here was a fine

Boys from cities, towns, and farms came to Camp White and learned to work and play together. They developed close friendships that lasted for many years. Paul Adykoski

Doug Dodge

Helen McKee Dodge contacted me after reading an article by Dick Case of the Syracuse Post Standard about my search for CCC alumni and families.

"My husband, Doug Dodge, was at Camp White in Barkhamsted, Conn. I was born in 1928 and grew up in nearby Winsted. I was just a little girl when the camp was going. When I was a young girl, my family went to the American Legion Forest in Barkhamsted for a church picnic. I walked up to the CCC camp and I peeked up the hill. The barracks doors were open and I saw the guys lying in their bunks. I might have seen my husband that day because he was 15 years older than me.

"I also saw the CCC boys walking around Winsted in their uniforms. They were dating all the girls.

"I met my husband when I was about 20 years old. He was working for the CT Gas and Light and Power Co. He was hanging around the bowling alley watching me bowl. One night he offered to give me a ride home. After that we started to date.

"Doug had a friend, Dominic Mitchell, and the three of us used to drive around Peoples Forest where Dominic and Doug saw projects they had worked on. Doug also told me about a culvert he built on Rt. 44 while in the CCC."

Then Helen told me about Doug's early life.

"Doug was born on June 17, 1913 in Stoneham, Mass. (north of Boston). His parents were Ralph and Daisy (Fox) Dodge. He was an only child. His dad worked for the Boston & Maine Railroad. Daisy left her husband when she heard that he had a wife in Maine and another in Massachusetts. Doug's grandmother took him and raised him. He loved his grandmother very much.

"When he got older he couldn't get work. He heard about the CCC and signed up. The Army shipped Doug and a group of guys on a train. They didn't know where they were going. Finally, they wound up in Winsted.

"I'm not sure of exactly what he did or when he was there. He was a big husky guy and seemed invincible. I do know that he went to town and dated the Winsted girls.

"Doug and I got married on April 30, 1955. We had one daughter, Darlene Caley.

"Doug did a lot of good things for the people of Winsted. Doug built baseball dugouts and helped maintain the baseball field. The town even named the field after him. In the winter he cleared the skating pond for the kids."

Helen McKee Dodge passed away on Feb. 10, 2016.

Arroll Lamson

Arroll Lamson's UConn graduation photo. Bob Lamson

Arroll Lamson was born in Bridgeport, on Feb. 4, 1911, the son of George Herbert and Kate (Ballingall) Lamson. Arroll grew up in Storrs, where his father was a dean and professor of zoology. He graduated from Windham High School in 1929. He earned a Bachelor's degree in Forestry from the UConn in 1933.

In the fall he went to work in CCC camps for the State Department of Forestry. His first assignment was as a wildlife foreman in the Pachaug State Forest in Voluntown. Here he was to do stream improvement for fish but since the stream was too sandy he was transferred to Winsted.

At Camp White in Barkhamsted his assignment was doing stream improvement work and building trout ponds. These consisted of logs jammed at the water's edge to divert the flow into pools for the trout to hide. Arroll didn't think much of his efforts because in the spring the Farmington River flowed so fast it washed out what the CCC had done.

He said his workers were a good bunch of boys and he didn't have any problems with them. There were some older men in his group of foremen. One guy, Robert Lund, was forty years old. Arroll called him "Mother Lund." Lund was the motivator in building the Stone Museum in Peoples State Park.

Arroll worked with the boys five days a week. At the end of the work day he returned them to camp and the Army took over supervision. Arroll lived in a separate tent with other foremen and the Army officers who were at the other end his tent. He said the food was decent.

Arroll had a picture of a log bridge the enrollees built to an island in the Farmington River. The enrollees constructed the footings by building log boxes and filling them with stone. This was no match for the spring run of the river that washed out the footings destroying the bridge.

When it was too cold to work in the streams, he supervised the cutting of chestnut trees that were made into fence posts for the highway department.

Arroll's salary was $112.00 a month. His weekends were free so he often drove his car home to Storrs to see his mother or girlfriend.

After working for a year and a half for the CCC he spent a year doing graduate studies in forestry and wildlife at the University of Michigan. Then he worked for two years as Assistant Regional Wildlife Biologist in the Land Utilization Division of the U.S. Resettlement Administration. He completed his graduate studies at the University of Maine, writing a thesis on moose diseases, and received his Master's degree in Wildlife Conservation in 1938. That same year he was appointed Chief of the Game Division, Connecticut Fish and Game Department.

After 35 years of work for the Conservation Department and Department of Environmental Protection, Arroll retired in 1972 as Chief Wildlife Biologist.

On Jan. 27, 2008 Arroll L. Lamson of West Simsbury passed away.

In 1933 Lamson (right) and his CCC stream improvement crew took a lunch break while working on the Farmington River in the Peoples SP. Bob Lamson

Doug Roberts

Doug Roberts speaking at the Barkhamsted Historical Society. Paul Hart

After my talk at the Barkhamsted Historical Society in Pleasant Valley on July 19, 2008, Doug Roberts met me in the parking lot. He showed me a picture of a bridge across the West Branch of the Housatonic River. He said, "I was lucky to save a few things when my house burned and this is one of them.

"We were young kids then and enjoyed hanging around the CCC camp. We knew a lot of the guys. Some people said the CCC stood for Championship Cigarette Chiselers. Those guys were always trying to bum a cigarette.

"There were a few deadly accidents at the CCC camp. One day the Camp White boys were being trucked from Winsted and as they traveled down Hart's Hill Road, the present day Rt. 20, the driver lost control of the truck. At the foot of the hill there were two houses below the road level. The truck ran off the road to the left side. It went between the two houses and hit a tree and a barn. There were four people killed. The accident occurred around 1934.

"Another time a group of CCC boys from Camp Robinson (in nearby East Hartland) was coming home from work. They might have quit early to avoid the approaching thunderstorm. As they were driving it began to rain like the devil so the driver pulled off to the side by a ditch. The guys who were riding in the back of the platform truck didn't have a canvas cover. They hopped off the truck and crawled under the truck body to get out of the rain. Lightning struck up the road and an electric charge went

411

down the stream hitting the boys under the truck. I think there were four boys that were killed.

"On Thursday nights in the summer, Camp White had entertainment down in the gravel pit below the camp. It was like an amphitheater. The entertainment was on a four-foot raised wooden stage covered with canvas. It also had lights. They had musicians, acrobats, boxing, and wrestling. Musicians from the CCC camp and bands from Winsted entertained. People walked or drove from Pleasant Valley and Riverton to be entertained. I went with my folks. The shows started about 7 pm.

"On Saturdays the Army took the CCC boys to movies in Winsted.

"They had dances in Pleasant Valley. There was a barn owned by the state. Now there is just a foundation where it stood.

"The camp also had education classes. I went to a biology class run by Professor Fanclar, from the University of the Philippines. He had a summer home in West Hartland. When he found out that my brother Laurence and I were too young, he kicked us out of class. His class was held in the infirmary.

"I remember seeing the boys working with older men. They had a small crawler bulldozer and dump truck. The guys were building the Greenwood Road (the forestry road just south of Squires Tavern). It joined West Center Hill Road. Most of these projects were Civil Works Program project. The vehicles were from the CCC camp. Boys were operating the equipment and had a new driver about every other day. They surveyed the location of the road, cut the trees, and removed the stumps. Mostly everything was done with a crowbar, rake, and shovel.

"I knew several CCC boys. Doug Dodge married a girl from Winsted. He later became involved in the town recreation program. Harold Kelly married a girl from Riverton. They had about 13 kids. Some live in Winsted.

"My father, Lawrence H., worked for the Forestry Department. He was a member of the committee that worked to acquire the land. He was in charge of the elm sanitation crew for the whole state which cut and destroyed trees infected by Dutch elm disease. He had a 1936 Plymouth state car. In a year and a half he drove over 80,000 miles. Dad had three offices to cover in the state."

I asked him to describe the CCC camp.

"There was a wooden water tower up the hill. The truck garage was near the camp entrance. Trucks had to drive through the stream to the truck garage because there wasn't a bridge. The CCC boys also washed the trucks in that stream.

"A metal shed was near the repair garage where they stored oil and gas. They also had a garage to do repairs. They changed the truck's oil outside. Trucks drove up on wooden planks supported by cement pillars. This enabled the mechanics to work under the vehicles.

"A carpenters' shop was with the blacksmith shop. Ed Barnes was the blacksmith. He was a big muscular guy who lived in Riverton. That's where he also had a blacksmith shop on School Street (now Elm Street) in Riverton. His father had a lumber mill inside the Hitchcock Mill, which made bobbins and spindles for woolen mills. The factory began in 1818.

"Everett Pearson was a forester from Littleton, VT. He rented a house on the east side of the Farmington River. Then he bought land and built a small cabin. Later he built a house in front of the cabin. He got a job as a NYS forester.

"A man from Winsted named Sullivan was a foreman at the camp along with Wendell Roberts. Bobby Brown from Poquonock had a tobacco farm by Rainbow Road. Bobby was also a foreman.

"Allen Perry was in charge of Peoples State Forest. He lived in Squire's Tavern, which also served as the Ranger Headquarters.

"Otto Schroeter was the camp superintendent. I think he was afraid of his enrollees. He always wore a .45 pistol. During the first winter there was a heavy ice storm. The road was a solid piece of ice. He sent guys out with axes to chop out the ice and they wound up destroying all the axes."

"Camp White was a busy place during the 1930s. Those young guys did a lot of work in our forests. There are a lot of people who enjoy coming to Peoples State Forest and probably don't know how the park was established."

Ellwood "Bill" McKinney

On Sept. 30, 2008 a large group attended my CCC talk sponsored by the Portland Historical Society in the Portland Library. We were surprised when William "Bill" McKinney stood up and said that he had been in the CCC and shared some of his stories.

A year and a half later I called Bill and he shared these stories.

"I was born on Sept. 12, 1920 in East Hampton, Conn.

In October 2008 Bill McKinney attended a reunion at the Connecticut CCC Museum and shared his stories about working at Camp White in Winsted. Podskoch

Harry and Bud were my older brothers and we had a sister, Emily. My father, Charles, died when I was 9 years old. My mother, Lillian, supported us by working at Summit Thread Mill in East Hampton.

"After 7th grade I had to help my mother because my brothers and my sister got older and left home. I quit school and worked at the N. N. Hills Co. in East Hampton where I assembled and buffed church and ship bells.

"I can't seem to remember how I heard about the CCC but I did join around 1936. The first selectman took me and a few other guys up to Camp White in Barkhamsted. There were a few buildings including barracks and a mess hall.

"An army captain ran our camp. My forester was Mr. Perry who lived down by the Riverton Inn. He was a very nice man.

"I remember a few of my jobs, including cutting trees in the state forest. We removed dead trees and took some good ones to the sawmill to make boards. I also fought forest fires. One fire started when a farmer was burning on his property and the fire got out of hand. We used Indian water tanks to put out the fire.

"We also built water holes in the forest so that fire fighters could get water when needed. First we looked for a spring. Then we dug a hole and cleaned around it. Next we lined the banks with stones.

"Another job was building roads near Peoples Forest. My job was loading trucks with a shovel. We didn't have front end loaders like today. When it was time for lunch they brought food for us.

"I remember the 'Flood of 1936.' We went into Hartford and filled sandbags near Colt Park.

"A few times I had KP duty. I helped the cook check to see if the meat was done. There were other jobs like peeling potatoes and washing dishes. The food was pretty good and we got plenty to eat.

"After work in the evenings I played pool and cards in the rec hall.

"Sometimes they did tricks on guys. One fellow named Francis didn't like to get up in the morning. So one day while he was still sound asleep they carried him and his bed outside and put him in the stream. Another joke was nailing a guy's foot locker shut. If a guy went home for the weekend, they'd nail his shoes to the floor. He wasn't too happy when this happened.

"On weekends I went home when I could unless we were on fire duty. The Army gave us rides to the train station in Hartford and I'd bum a ride home.

"When I left camp I got a job back at Hills Mfg. Co. I worked there for quite a while.

"In 1941 I married Gertrude Jones of Hebron. She worked in Hills factory with me. I worked for her cousin, Walter, who was a foreman. Then I heard that Pearl Harbor was invaded by the Japanese. It was about a month or so later when my two brothers and I were drafted. I went to Fort Devens and was placed in the infantry. I went to Europe and fought in Germany, France, and Czechoslovakia.

"When I came home from the war, I got a job doing construction work, such as building roads and digging cellar holes.

"Then I went to Standard Nap in Portland and learned machine shop work. When I came home I worked in a machine shop in Newington for Fenn Mfg. We made parts for helicopters. I retired from there at 65 in 1985.

"My wife, Gertrude (Jones), and I had four children: Shirley, Elwood, Kathy, and Michael.

"Once about 1994 I went to see Camp White. Only one building was left.

"When I look back at my time in the CCC I learned to appreciate what I had. I was thankful for the chance to get a job and help support my mother."

Bill passed away at his home in Marlborough on Sept. 19th, 2015.

Matthew Cote

Matt Cote speaking at the CCC Museum Reunion
Stafford Springs in 2012. Podskoch

At the annual CCC reunion at the Connecticut CCC Museum in Stafford Springs on Sept. 23, 2012, I met Matthew Cote of Somers. He told the gathering that he worked at Camp White in Winsted. On Aug. 12, 2013 I talked to him by phone and he recounted his life story and his experiences in the CCC.

"I was born in Enfield on March 13, 1921. My parents were Arthur and Ethel Dunne. They had five children: Harold, Irene, myself, Arthur, and Mildred. My father was a foreman at Bigelow Sanford Carpet Co. in Enfield.

"Dad was laid off and didn't have a job so I didn't go to my senior year of high school. I had to help my family and I searched for jobs. I knew about the CCC because my older brother, Harold, was in the CCC in Arizona, and there were also camps nearby in Windsor and Stafford Springs. So on Jan. 17, 1939 I went to Windsor Locks and enlisted. I was excited about going to camp. An Army doctor gave me a physical and also a pneumonia inoculation.

"The Army sent me and a bunch of guys to Hartford. Then we got in an Army truck that had a canvas top. It was a cold ride to our camp.

"We drove along the Farmington River in Barkhamsted and we reached Camp White on the left side of the road. The truck drove past the garages and up a small hill. The infirmary was on the right with a large stone chimney and then to the barracks on the left. They assigned us our barracks and I got my assigned cot. I was a little nervous at first but I settled down and made friends

"During my two years at camp I had the same job. I worked on gypsy moth control. We scouted the woods for egg clusters on trees. When someone spotted some, we'd climb up. Then we painted the clusters with creosote. If it was too high to climb, someone would throw a rope over a branch and pull a guy up into the tree. I did a lot of the climbing. When we found a lot of egg clusters, we sprayed them with some poison. A truck was brought as close as possible. It had a tank of poison. Someone took a hose that was connected to the tank and walked to the infected trees. Then a pump was started and we sprayed everything. I think we had a mask to cover our faces.

"The food was very good. I loved breakfast. They served eggs, bacon, and cream sauce on toast. For lunch we had a sandwich when we were working in the woods. Someone was designated to start a fire and make coffee. I remember the pork sandwiches that were good.

"They had a rec hall with ping pong tables. I got to be pretty good and the winner kept playing. We played for fun. Our $5 a month pay was not in cash but in ration books. We used the coupons in the PX to buy candy, soda and cigarettes.

"On weekends I went home most of the time. My father would come and pick me up and bring me back home. Sometimes he brought me to Hartford. If I hitchhiked there was no problem getting a ride if you had your uniform on.

"We went to Winsted and drank beer at Johnny's Bar. We also went to Highland Lake. It was a large lake less than a mile from downtown Winsted. We went to a roller skating rink there.

The Camp White quadrangle with the Infirmary (stone chimney) in the right corner. The five barracks surrounded the square with the Administration and Officers' Quarters to the left of the Infirmary. DEEP State Parks Archives

The infirmary chimney is one of the few remaining structures at Camp White. Podskoch

"I played on the camp basketball team. We played at a church in Winsted that had a basketball court in the basement. Maybe it was a Congregational Church. I was a forward and a good shot. I was one of the few who used a one-hand shot which was unusual because they all shot with two hands. We had uniforms and I donated mine to the CCC Museum. I wonder if they still have it?

"I saved up my money and bought an old 1934 Chevrolet for $300. I hid it up along the river just a little way from camp. You weren't allowed to bring a car to camp. Now I could go home on weekends without having to get rides from my dad or by hitchhiking.

"Every morning the Army had us doing short order drills and marches. Then someone complained and the Army stopped doing it.

"I loved camp because I got along with the guys and I became an assistant leader on Feb. 8, 1940 and a leader on Oct. 10, 1940.

"I never got sick in the CCC but guys did get hurt and one guy died. They used to take us to a swimming hole down on the river. There was a big rock right on the edge. Somehow a guy got stuck under the rock and drowned. I was there but no one knew he was missing till we got back to camp. They went down to the river and began searching and they found his body.

"There was another tragedy in our camp when I was there. A truck was coming back from Winsted and it turned over on a really steep road. One boy was tossed out. They found him in the woods dead. He was from Milford

and I knew him.

"On Dec. 21, 1941 I left the CCC because my two years were up.

"I got a job with the Entomology Dept. of the State of Connecticut. They came to my house looking for me because I had two-year's experience in the CCC working on gypsy moth control. I received an excelled evaluation for my work and that helped me get the job. My job was type mapping the state. We'd find a road and count the type of trees in a certain area. They were afraid the gypsy moth would take over all the forest.

"Then on Oct. 12, 1942 the Army drafted me. I went to Fort Devens and then I was sent to the medical corps in Fort Bragg, North Carolina. We went to Utah Beach for the D-Day invasion. I can still remember it was cold and raining. We had a hard time getting into the landing craft. One ship was blown off course and blew up when it hit a mine. I'll never forget it.

"I was in the ambulance corps. In our company we carried out over 30,000 injured and killed soldiers. I was an ambulance driver. We didn't medically treat the injured but just drove the ambulance. We later traveled through Europe and were in the Battle of the Bulge.

"When I got back to the US, I married Helen Firton in 1945. We had two children: Patricia and Dorethea.

"I went to work for Bridge Manufacturing in Hazard where we made wooden cable reels. I was on the go traveling throughout New England. I helped customers with problems. After 52 years I retired.

"Whenever I'm near Winsted I stop by my old Camp White. I only recognize the site of the infirmary. The only thing still standing is the stone chimney. There was a bridge going across the river but it is gone now.

"The CCC had a good effect on me because my experience doing insect control of the gypsy moths helped me get a good state job doing similar work."

Matt Cote passed away on March 20, 2016 the day before his 95th birthday.

Paul R. Adykoski

In 2008 Paul Adykoski attended my presentation at the Cragin Library in Colchester. He showed the audience his wonderful photo album of his time at Camp White. He then trusted me to borrow it so that I could copy it for my book.

Paul Adykoski at his home in Bloomfield where he shared his stories of working at four CCC camps.
Podskoch

On Feb. 17, 2008 I went to Bloomfield to return the album. Paul's wife, Estelle, welcomed me to their home. I sat in their living room and Paul recounted his life and his CCC days.

"I was born in Hartford on June 20, 1918. My parents were Peter and Anna (Sisak) who had two sons and two daughters: Peter, Paul, Helen, and Mary. I was the youngest. When I was just two years old my mother died. It was hard for my dad to raise five children so he remarried. My father, Peter was a tailor but lost his business during the Depression. He then worked at a few stores to feed us.

"After graduating from eighth grade, I quit school to help my dad. I was 16 years old. I picked up jobs here and there. I worked as a hawker for a chow mein company. In the winter I delivered advertisements going house to house for Advo District papers.

"Then I heard about the CCC. In July 1935 I went to an office in Hartford to sign up. The lady asked me how old I was and I said I was 17. She said no, you are 18. So I said OK. I joined the CCC because I wanted to get away from home and my stepmother.

"The Army drove me from Hartford to New London. I went to Camp Chapman in Niantic. For two weeks I stayed there. We took firewood out of the woods and we slept in big Army tents.

"Then I was transferred to Camp Filly in Haddam. My job was as a tree climber looking for gypsy moth egg clusters. I had a can in my back pocket filled with creosote. My job was to paint the clusters with creosote. I wore spurs

to climb but didn't have a belt to hold me on the tree. I had a long rope that we threw over the top notch of the tree. I was attached to a 200' rope with a rope harness around my waist and groin. I twisted my leg around the rope to help climb up. Then I crossed over from one side to the other searching and painting.

"My second job was working at the gravel pit loading trucks by hand. There were four guys loading and it took us about 5-10 minutes. Then the truck took off and we waited for another.

"In 1936 they asked for volunteers to go out west and I signed up. We went by a troop train. It took us a good week. It was summer time so we opened the windows because it was so damn hot in Kansas. The smoke from the locomotive came into our car. It wasn't too nice. I asked, 'When does it rain out here?' All I saw were thousands of jack rabbits and miles of wheat. Then we got to Triangle Lake, Oregon near Eugene.

"My first job was dragging brush to make fire trails. Here is where I learned how to drop trees. Then we used dynamite to remove stumps.

"I stayed there for a little while and transferred to Timber, Oregon. It was a fire camp. I got caught once in between two fires. We had to run like hell, single file to get out. You had to watch out so branches didn't fall on you. We'd work one day and then off the next to rest. They woke us up at 3 in the morning and sometimes we'd have to

Paul Adykoski and friend at Camp White in Barkhamsted.
Estel Adykoski

Paul took this photo of his new CCC Camp White in the winter. Paul Adykoski

On Feb. 2, 2009 (L–R) Paul Adykoski, Anthony Gagliardi, and Joe Prucha reminisced about their experiences in the CCC at the Connecticut CCC Museum.

travel 50-100 miles to get to a fire. We had no chain saws. I dropped trees like crazy.

"In the fall my buddy, Mahoney, got tired of fighting fires and persuaded me to go home. I stayed out of the CCC for the year 1937.

"In the winter I joined again in 1938. They took me by truck to Camp Filly. Then I went to Camp White. I stayed there for two years. I worked doing riprap work on the West Branch of the Farmington River. We worked in a quarry breaking rocks with a jackhammer. We drilled holes and put 'feathers (half-round files) and wedges' into the holes. Then we hit the holes in rotation one after another till it split. Guys then rolled the rocks onto trucks to be used along the river. This helped to prevent erosion.

"When we didn't have enough rock on the ground, we went up and drilled holes in the rock. We used dynamite to cut the cliff down. Then we started again breaking the big rocks.

"In the winter we cut cordwood and piled it up. I studied for a truck driving license and got it.

"In the spring I went back to work in the quarry.

"Someone asked me to work in the canteen so I did. I sold candy, cigarettes, soda, and gum.

"A foreman came along and asked me to work with him drilling rocks for building roads. His name was, Mahoney. He was a nice guy and he gave me rides home on the weekends.

"Then they came out with a new green uniform. It had a wool jacket and pants with a CCC patch. I didn't like it because it was too heavy.

"That year was the year of the terrible hurricane. They sent Col. Schroeter from New London. He took us to the Hartford airport. For a day or two we loaded sandbags for the dikes. We found out we were doing more work than the WPA. The Salvation Army wasn't giving us any coffee but they were to the WPA. The colonel said to us, 'We're getting out of here!' and we went back to camp.

"On the day of the flood four to five guys went to the Farmington River but couldn't walk on the road. So they walked through the woods. It got dark. We took the road from New Hartford to Winsted and followed it. We heard guys hollering to us. They were searching for us.

"On some nights a truck took us to Winsted to get beer or go to a show. One truck on its way home was going down a hill and lost its gears. It coasted and hit a curve. It flipped over. Guys flew out the back and one Negro boy was killed.

"I quit the CCC in December 1939. I went home and lived with my sister, Mary, in Hartford. I took a job driving a truck. I moved furniture from upstate New York to New Jersey and Long Island. My partner was Dominic Crespin.

"After six months I worked at Wire Molding in West Hartford.

"Then in February 1941 I joined the National Guard. After a year the Army drafted me and I went to Ft. Blanding, Florida.

"In 1947 I got married to Estelle and we had one daughter, Laura Ann.

"I went to other US Army camps in the US. In October 1945 I was discharged. I got a job with Northeast Utilities and retired in 1983 after 38 years of service.

Paul R. Adykoski, 97, of Bloomfield, passed away on Sept. 17, 2015.

Walter Landgraf

Walter Landgraf was well known for his work in reopening the Stone Museum at the Peoples State Forest. The museum was built in the 1930s by members of Camp White. It was a very popular nature museum but was closed for many years. Through Walter's hard work the building was restored and reopened in 1993.

For more than 30 years Landgraf was a popular teacher of biology and environmental technology at Northwest Regional District 7 High School in Winsted. In his retirement he gave many lectures at the Stone Museum, and he led nature walks in Peoples State Forest, where a trail is named for him. He passed away on July 23, 2007.

John V. Churney

John Churney of Colchester served in the Army and then joined the CCC where he worked at Camp White in Barkhamsted. Bob Churney

One day while my car was being repaired at Tom Churney's Broadway Auto Service in Colchester, I asked him if he knew anyone who had worked in the CCC. He replied, "Yes, my father worked at Camp White in Barkhamsted." He also told me how to get in contact with his father's good friend in Bloomfield, Paul Adykoski, who also worked at the same camp. Tom then had his brother Bob send me information about their father.

"My father, John Churney, was born on Feb. 20, 1913 to immigrants from Czechoslovakia. They settled in a small town near Canonsburg, Pa. It was a big union town and coal mining area in the southwest part of the state. John's father

was a big union man. He said when they had big mining strikes in the 1920s a lot of the workers were camped out around their house.

"Dad died in the mines in 1929. He was electrocuted and only 42 years old. This had a profound effect on my father and he only worked in the mines for one day.

"In the mid-1930s my father had no work. So he joined the Army and was paid $20 a month. He was a guard at the tomb of the Unknown Soldier. I think he was only in for 1½ years.

"He was not the only one to leave Pennsylvania. His sister Helen left the homestead at the age of 13 when she went to New York City to work. When she was 16 she and her sister Peggy came to Colchester, Conn. to work at Jewish resorts, which were called the Catskills of Connecticut at the time.

"John bought his way out of the Army when he learned he could make more money in the CCC camps.

"In 1937 he came to Colchester by bus. He had no money so his sisters sent him $10 for the bus fare. He joined the CCC and was sent to the Peoples State Forest in Barkhamsted. Each month $25 was sent home to help pay for the rent and food for his family. He just had five dollars each month for spending money.

"Dad told us he was doing carpentry work at camp and also worked down by the Farmington River.

"During his time at Camp White he played ball. He was quite a good football player.

"While at camp he became good friends with Paul Adykoski from Hartford. One weekend Paul and a few others walked down to Canton to the tavern where they could get a pitcher of beer for five cents. On the walk back to camp Paul noticed one of the guys was drunk and couldn't walk. Since it was cold out they couldn't leave him. So they carried him back to camp.

"Another story Dad told us was about a guy named Kozak who was also from Colchester. My father and Paul used to ask Kozak, 'How do you know if your socks are still clean?' John told him to throw them up against the wall and if they stick they are too dirty to wear. If they fall to the floor they're still good to wear. So Kozak was always throwing his socks against the wall.

"While in camp John was planning to sign up for a camp in Colorado but he got a job at International Silver in Meriden, Conn. My father was only in the CCC for about six months. His friend Paul went to Oregon and worked at a CCC camp there.

"In 1939 my father married Theresa Dzagan of Colchester and they had four boys: John, Ronald, Robert, and Tom. He remained in Colchester the rest of his life. Most of his brothers and sisters also settled in the Colchester area.

"After working for a while at the silver company he then worked at Pratt & Whitney for 17 years. While working full time he also raised chickens for the Willow Weaver Hatchery and also grew strawberries, pumpkins, and Christmas trees until he was 85 years old.

"During the 1980s I went to the camp site with my father and Paul. There was only a chimney left where the barracks were in a small opening in the forest. The building he did some work on, I believe, was the main headquarters that is still there and was still in pretty good condition.

"My dad and Paul remained friends until Dad died on Nov. 12, 2000 at the age of 87.

"The CCC camp instilled a good work ethic in my dad and he knew the value of a dollar. These values he passed on to his four sons. His small farm still remains in the family."

Howard White

Howard (left) talking with friend Larry Fitton in the camp courtyard. Rick White

In 2011 Paul Hart from the Barkhamsted Historical Society interviewed Richard "Rick" White whose father, Howard C. White, worked at Camp White in 1934 and 1935.

"My father lived in Brighton, Mass. and was 21 years old when he entered the CCC program. His first camp was the 106th Company in Vineyard Haven (Martha's Vineyard, Mass.) from April 18 until May 24, 1934.

"Then he was transferred to Camp White in Barkhamsted, Conn. from May 25, 1934 until June 30, 1935

"My father said that many of the CCC boys at Camp White could not read or write. Our dad taught classes in reading and writing to his fellow CCCs at Camp White. The classes were probably in the evening.

"Dad was able to come home for Christmas in 1934 but he told his father not to come and pick him up because for just $2 he could take the train from Winsted. Instead he chipped in 25 cents toward gas for the truck that gave him a ride from Camp White to get to the train station in Winsted.

"I'm not sure why my father got the special pass to visit home. It may just have been for a routine visit because it was for the Christmas holiday.

"My father was drafted into the Army and served in North Africa and Italy. He was in Company C, 752nd Tank Battalion when he was discharged at the end of the war.

"Then my father was an electrician in Local 103 IBEW until 1967 when he had a stroke and had to retire. In WWII he was in training running telephone lines before being transferred into the 752nd Tank Battalion.

"In 1951 he got married to Mary Pesaturo. They had two boys and one girl.

"Dad enjoyed being at Camp White but did not talk much about his experiences with his family. He was also very tightlipped about his experiences in WWII and would

A Camp White work crew posing with a cattle skull they found while digging. Rick White

Rick White and members of his family camped in the right corner of this Camp White photo near the remaining Infirmary chimney. Rick White

August Casciani

Gus Casciani supervised the stonework construction of dams, churches, bridges, and a museum in the surrounding towns near Barkhamsted. Doug Roberts

quickly change the subject if asked about the war. I'm sure he had seen some gruesome scenes and hated the sight of blood ever after.

"I was only thirteen years old in 1965 when my father and I visited the location of his camp. I have a picture of us in front of the original woodshed proving it was built by the CCC in 1934-35. It was the only remaining structure of the camp.

"My father would have been among the early boys at Camp White, if not the first. I speculate about whether or not he helped build the structures at the camp. I think my father did cement work among other duties at the camp. When we visited the site that day, the cement bridge was one of the structures that Dad wanted to find and inspect, so this might indicate that he had a hand in its construction.

"My father died in 2000.

"In August 2011 my brother Kevin, his son Christopher, his daughter Nicole, and I visited Camp White now part of Legion State Forest and camped on the site of the Infirmary. We brought our father's photo album with numerous pictures of Camp White and the surrounding area and researched where the buildings and features were located. We unearthed all of the infirmary footings to measure and document its size and location. With dad's photos we were also able to find where his barracks was along with many other landmarks and foundations including what we thought was the septic system in a ravine at the far left end of the camp. It was 6 feet deep by 15 feet wide by 40 feet long.

"My family and I are proud of my father's work at Camp White and his participation in WWII."

On Feb. 14, 2016 I received a call from Anthony Casciani of Barkhamsted who said, "I was told that you were looking for information on August "Augie" Casciani who worked at Camp White in Barkhamsted. He was my grandfather. He came from Italy with my grandmother and lived in New Hartford. My grandparents had four children: Anthony, Mario, Catherine, and Anne. I have a photo of him when he came to our house for Thanksgiving dinner.

"My grandfather did a lot of stonework projects in the area. He worked on both of the large dams in Barkhamsted. He also did the stonework on the Catholic Church in Collinsville. My grandfather also helped build two churches in Winsted that were at both ends of town.

"Another CCC project was the masonry work on the Administration Building on River Rd. The CCC boys built the cellar walls, fireplace, chimney, and a fireproof vault. The building is still used by the DEEP.

"There are still remains of the two stone abutments for the bridge across the Farmington River that my grandfather helped build. The bridge was used to help people cross to the island in the middle of the river.

"One of the stories I heard about my grandfather was one day he was up on a ladder and he wanted a particular stone. He took his axe and threw it near the stone he wanted because he didn't want to come down and get it.

"He died in the late 1950s while I was in the Air Force."

CHAPTER 26
NEW LONDON / SUPPLY DEPOT

HISTORY

In 1900 the Army established Fort H. J. Wright on the western end of Fishers Island. The island is about eight miles long with an average width of 1 mile. Since Fort Wright was seven miles southeast of New London, it was a convenient location to ship supplies to Connecticut CCC camps.

In May 1933 Fort Wright became the supply depot for all the Connecticut CCC camps. Two companies were associated with the CCC program. One was a supply company of 45 men, under the command of Lt. Sawyer, that worked in the Quartermaster warehouse. Another company under Lt. Seward, known as the Headquarters Co., consisted of specialists such as clerks, bookkeepers, carpenters, bakers, typists, and draftsmen.[1]

On June 23, 1933 the two companies were combined forming the 190th Co. with 75 men led by Lt. Seward. Its main task was to supply and maintain all Connecticut CCC camps. The company's daily tasks were typing, accounting, bookkeeping, warehousing, truck driving, baking, supplying food and equipment, and maintenance work.[2]

During 1933 the CCC bakers worked in two shifts to provide the bread for all the camps. In the spring of 1934 this work was discontinued.[3]

Co. 190 men led an isolated life on Fishers Island but did partake in some of the activities of the enlisted Army men at Fort Wright. They went to movies at the camp theater and played sports with some Army teams.[4]

In April 1935, Co. 190 was transferred from Fort Wright to New London and housed in the warehouse. Captain Berglund supervised the maintenance crew that made suitable living quarters for the enrollees.[6]

This was done to avoid the transportation of new enrollees and supplies to and from Fort Wright, the Army moved Co. 190 and all of its CCC quartermaster supplies from Fishers Island to a warehouse at the Government Pier in New London in September 1934. This became the District Supply Base. The company had the gigantic task of loading all the supplies on large barges and transporting them to the warehouse. The project was supervised by Sgts. Baker and Mills. Enrollees also moved the Quartermaster's Office to New London. The men resided at Fort Wright but traveled back and forth each day to work in the New London warehouse.[7]

During this time several qualified CCC clerks were elevated from enrollee to citizen in the District Supply Base. Frank Olszewski became the chief clerk along with these enrollees: Clyde Carrow, Joseph Mason, Joseph Griffin, and Charles Backofen.[9]

Map – Fishers Island, NY approx. 6 miles from New London, CT. http://www.wikiwand.com/en/Fishers_Island,_New_York

26H-2 Photo: Fort Wright Barracks that housed 120 men. http://www.fortwiki.com/File:Fort_H.G._Wright_1902_Barracks.jpg

421

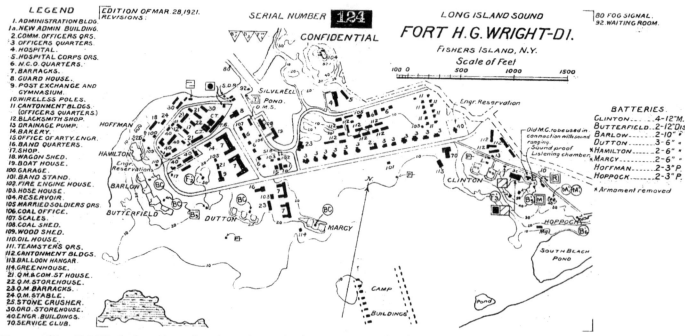

The map of Fort H. J. Wright. http://www.fortwiki.com/images/c/c6/Fort_H.G._Wright_Plan.jpg

One Headquarters' clerk, Clifford Davenport, left the CCC in September 1934 and received a scholarship to Wesleyan University in Middletown when he was selected as the outstanding CCC member in Connecticut. After two years at Wesleyan he was elected president of his junior class. [10]

In the beginning of 1935 Capt. B. R. Whitthorne was in command of the Supply Base and H. G. Bentley was the commanding officer of Co. 190.

The 190th Supply Co. was described in the Nov. 20, 1935 camp newspaper, the Thames Tattler, comparing it to an industrial company. "We have our President who is our Quartermaster. The Vice Presidents are commissioned Army officers who comprise the executive staff. Their secretaries, managers, and foremen are CCC enrollees. These men are known as rated men, leaders and asst. leaders. They are responsible to the officer in charge of their department and come under his supervision and direction."

In Nov. 1935 there were many departments and the key men in the 190th Supply Co were:

1. Administration
Senior Leader, N. T Marshall
Mess Steward, A. Jeronimo
Company Clerk, J. Anderson

2. Supply Dept.

Chief Clerk, T. T. Weekes
Stock Record Clerk, D. Coates
Typist & Stenog, Ben Cholewa
Asst. Leader Clerk, J. Paczkowski

3. Construction Dept.
Plumbing, Ed Breen, Leader
Carpentry, F. Collucci, Leader
Clerk, W. Tucker, Asst. Leader

4. Subsistence Dept.
Shipping Clerk, Joe Genicola, Leader
1st Clerk, Joe Elia, Asst. Leader

5. Purchasing & Contracting Dept.
1st Typist & Clerk, Joe Filo
Typist & Clerk, Joe Perro

6. Transportation Dept.
1st Typist & Clerk, F. Reynolds

7. Headquarters
Mailing Center, Powchak, Leader
Printer, J. Tamerman, Leader
Typists, Stenographers, & Statisticians
Thomas Donnee, Asst. Leader
F. Lajoe, Asst. Leader

E. Olszewski, Asst. Leader
E. Pilewsli, Asst. Leader

8. Fiscal & Finance Section
Finance Clerk & Bkg., L. Zotter
Bookeeping & Clerk, J. Stella
Mail Clerk, H. Lockwood
Typist, J. Makoski

9. Medical Center
Distribution & Clerk, R. Bosco [11]

In August 1935 the 190th Co. received a temporary education advisor, Harry Knott. He organized classes and athletic activities. Some of the classes were: Psychology, English, French, First Aid, Dancing, and Current Events. Knott also arranged for a daily supply of newspapers.[12]

Before there was an education advisor, the enrollees stationed at Fishers Island had few opportunities for activities. Their most popular activities were card playing, checkers, and chess. A writer for the camp newspaper stated: "Reading or studying was almost impossible because of the disturbances caused by younger fellows who found such pleasure in chasing one another all over the squad room and playfully participating in a rough and tumble combat... Some of the fellows just lay or slept in bed continually

(L–R) 1 The Supply Depot was moved from Fishers Island to the New London Government Pier, which is the two-story building behind the trucks near the large tank. The building housed the supplies and approx. 70 CCC boys.[5] J. Wright. http://www.fortwiki.com/images/c/c6/Fort_H.G._Wright_Plan.jpg 2 The Army officers and clerks at the Supply Depot in New London.[8]

and the rest all spent some of those early hours there, or for activity restlessly paced the squad room stopping occasionally to longingly gaze through the windows, or watch the progress in the different games being played."[13]

The Aug. 15, 1935 issue of the Thames Tattler reported the190th Supply Co. organized its first baseball team and played their first game on July 10, 1935. They lost to Niantic's Co. 177 by the score of 1-0. In their next game they came back and defeated Niantic 10-7. (Thames Tattler, Aug. 15, 1935.) On Aug. 13 the baseball team had a close game against Output Clothing winning 4-3 at the Caulkins' ballfield. Then the 190th lost three games to the Groton Transient Camp, 5-3, 5-1, and 15-4.[14]

The 190th Co. also had a Joint Outing with the Groton Transients Camp on Sun., Sept. 8th, 1935. The following events were held: 100-yd. dash, running high jump, running broad jump, obstacle race, three-legged race, sack race, and baseball throw. The final event was a volleyball game.[15]

E. R. A. (Emergency Relief Administration) instructor William Casey organized a swimming team. They practiced for a CCC tourney in Hartford.[16]

Another athletic activity that Knott established was a ping pong tournament. Nineteen members signed up and battled for the first prize, a carton of cigarettes. The runner-up received a pack of cigarettes. The prizes were donated by the PX.[17]

The Thames Tattler reported on Aug.15, 1935 that a Glee Club was organized by music instructor, Mr. Feltcom, who "has made the walls of our mighty mansion echo with the joyful and hilarious singing of the members." It also reported that Mr. Feltcom was going to organize a band "that a few weeks hence, will find the mansion filled with the low throbbing notes of a saxophone, the strumming

The April 1936 cover of the Thames Tattler.

423

Co. 190 held dances at the Odd Fellows Hall in New London.

of guitars and ukuleles, and the tinkling notes of a piano." Feltcorn also provided music instruction every Friday for those interested.

Another organization, the Social Club, was formed in August to improve the social and economic standing of the company. The officers were Pres. Edwin Ratson, Sec. Thomas Weeks, and Treas. Frank Colucci. They organized dances and outings. [18]

Mr. Knott also helped organize a company newspaper called the "Thames Tattler." The newspaper staff was: Salvador Genzano, Albert Beger (Bristol), Thomas Weeks (W. Hartford), Adolf Wrubel (Manchester), Ben Cholewa (Jewett City), Stephen Gulio, and Lawrence Tillinghast. They produced the first issue on Aug. 15, 1935. When the advisor was released from his job, the newspaper staff continued on their own to publish their newspaper and organize activities such as dances. [19]

On Aug. 31, 1935, which was the 5th enrollment period, over 3,000 men enrolled at the District Supply Base in New London. This was the largest in the district's history. In the past, enrollees had been sent to Fort Wright and this wasted a lot of time. Now that the enrollees were processed at the New London Supply Depot, the young men were examined, clothed, and sent to their designated camp in Connecticut. [20]

On September 5th Co. 190 held their first dance. It was at the Starland Dance Hall. Al Rudd's Orchestra provided music and during the intermission cookies and ice cream were served. The dance ended at 10 pm and was followed by a Beauty Contest. The winner was Mary Whittaker of Norwich. Her prize was two pair of lady's hose that were donated by the Bee Hive Dept. Store of New London. [21]

In September 1935 Capt. H. G. Bentley was relieved as commander of Co. 190 and replaced by Capt. W. C. Sage, the former commander of Co.174 of Stafford Springs. A banquet was held on September 9th at Moss Hall in Bentley's honor. [22]

The 190th Co. Supply Depot also provided religious programs. In September Father O'Callahan had a Catholic Mission the week of Sept. 24th 1935. He also visited other CCC camps in Connecticut.

Education classes continued in October. Classes began at 7 pm. Enrollees could take college correspondence courses including: Civil Service, Conservation, Salesmanship, and Etiquette. There were also basic classes: Letter Writing and Grammar. [23]

There were also group sessions for those not taking formal classes and hobby classes such as leather crafts. Enrollees made moccasins, belts, and billfolds. [24]

Other extra-curricular activities such as movies, hobbies, field trips, sports, clubs, and dances were organized by the education advisor. [25] A "Harvest Dance" was held on Nov. 21, 1935 at the Odd Fellows Hall and Harry Feltcorn and his boys provided music. Cookies and sweet cider were provided at the intermission. The enrollees loved their dances and had a "Christmas Dance" on Dec. 19, 1935. [26] The dance was held at the Crocker House and Joseph Tasca and his Cardinals furnished the music. At intermission two door prizes were passed out: a clock and a flashlight. [27]

The sport activities in the fall were: football and basketball. In September 1935 Edward "Bucky" Butkiewicz from Connecticut State College, was appointed the football coach. Twenty men came out for the first practice at the Jennings School playground. There was also a horseshoe tourney. [28]

During the fall enrollment of October 1935 the 190th Supply Co. had to provide clothing and equipment for 1,600 new enrollees. [29] Some of these men stayed in Connecticut but some traveled to other states. The Supply Depot outfitted 380 enrollees who went to the West Coast. There were 164 men who went to Massachusetts. [30]

In November 1935 Co. 190 was saddened when their Education Advisor, Harry J. Knott, was transferred from

(L–R) 1 The 1936 Company 190 New London basketball team.[37] 2 Three Company 190 enrollees in the shipping dept.[44] 3 Two clerks working in the supply room in New London.[47]

the New London Camp.[31] E.R.A. Instructor William Casey became the new Education Advisor. [32]

The 190th Co. football team played its last game on Thanksgiving morning at Camp Wright Field. Although Battery C team crushed Co. 190, 26-0 the team put up a gallant fight.[33] Then the basketball team began practicing for the season at the New London Armory.

At 5 pm on Christmas Eve 1935, a fire broke out in the garage. Luckily the men aboard the boat the "Mine Plantor M. P. Baird" helped alert the CCC enrollees who put out the fire. The damage to the supplies and garage was estimated at $800. A group of enrollees stayed up all night watching for flareups. [34]

The 190th Co. had a good relationship with the city of New London. On Jan. 29, 1936 the Capitol Movie Theater provided 75 free seats for the enrollees to see the movie, "It's a Great Life." [35]

The 190th Co. had their first dance of the year on Jan. 23, 1936 at the Crocker House Ballroom. Edward Chamberlain's Orchestra provided the music. Enrollee Edward Pilewski was praised by his company for inviting a bevy of young ladies to the dance. [36]

In January 1936 the 190th Co. began practicing basketball with a new coach, Edward (Olson) Olszewski from New Haven. In their first game on January 7th the Thames Tattlers lost a close game to the New London Mob 31-27 at the small Methodist Gym with 100 people in attendance. [38]

The Thames Tattlers next game was against a strong team from the 179th Co. from Voluntown. The score was 28-13. [39]

During the month of February and March the 190th Co. basketball team lost to these teams: WPA 28-19, Deep River Falcons 27-22, and New London Mob 51-33. Then the team improved and won their next three games: 27-23 over the Lafayettes, 26-15 over WPA, and 34-33 over the Madison CCC Camp Co. 2101. The team then started practicing for the CCC Basketball Tournament to be held on March 21 at the Willimantic Armory. [40]

The February 1936 issue of the Thames Tattler reported that Co.190 lacked Education and Assistant Education Advisors but the company commander, Capt. Sage, continued to support the existing programs.

During March of 1936 torrential rains and snow melt caused the Connecticut, Farmington, Thames, and Housatonic rivers to flood many towns in Connecticut. The CCC camps responded to the numerous communities who called for help. Camp Fernow in Eastford sent out approximately 50 men and Camp Filley in Haddam sent 150 men to aid many communities along the Connecticut River. [41]

After the CCC enrollees helped in the cleanup of Hartford Mayor Spellacy invited 600 enrollees to a dinner at the Foot Guard Armory on April 29.[42] He also presented each man with a wristwatch.

During March 1936 Co. 190 was busy preparing the new enrollees with transportation, equipment, and food for the new enlistment period. They anticipated 300 new enlistees. [43]

On March 14, 1936 Co. 190 had a spelling bee. Capt. Hensley and Mr. Clyde Carrow were the judges. Around 20 men entered the contest and Burton Margo won. His prize

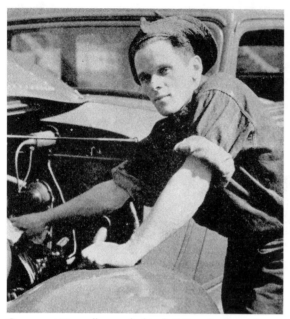

Company 190 enrollees worked in the Motor Pool servicing the cars and trucks.[48]

The Supply Depot had a fleet of cars used by enrollees and Army officials for servicing and inspecting CCC camps.[49]

was five packages of cigarettes. The second place man got three packs and the third place received two packs.[45]

During the April 1936 enrollment period the Quartermaster Office was moved downstairs in the warehouse and the issue bins were moved across the street to Warehouse B.[46] Capt. Walter C. Sage was still the commander of the 190th Supply Co.

The April 1936 issue of the *Thames Tattler* reported that during the month's enrollment, "...some thousand odd men had been going to New London with all Connecticut men coming through the Registration and Transportation Centers located in Hartford, New Haven, and New London. The daily quota fell behind in several instances but on the whole it was fixed at approximately 75 to 100 men per day for six days a week. The processing included a physical examination, the taking of the oath of enrollment, and the compilation of individual records. This occurred daily in the Medical Supply Warehouse.

"In the expansive District Supply warehouse with a clothing issue table extending on two sides, one could find a long line of new enrollees signing for a complete G.I.C.C.C. outfit complete from socks to cap.

"As soon as possible, the men were given a company assignment and transportation to their respective destinations in Connecticut. In special cases, some men were reserved for a few days and then sent to Massachusetts or to distant Oregon on a trans-continental rail movement.

"Approximately 80 per cent of the total enrolled were situated in one of our camps on the very same day that they came through the Registration and Transportation Centers. They went from civil life to camp life in one day.

"When not assisting in the care of the new men, it was necessary for our Supply Company to assist with another great task. With a work crew under his direct supervision, 1st Lt. Phillip Haas, Infantry Reserve, supervised the moving of the District Supply equipment and prepared for the moving of the District Quartermaster office. All men turned out in fatigues to move the racks, tables, supplies, and equipment from the old warehouse space in the dock building to the new site across the railroad tracks. Truckload after truckload of property was transported. Large storage bins too long to carry at one time were cut in half so that 40 men could pick them up, put one end on a truck, and with 2 x 4s underneath for supports, walk behind the truck and move it 1,500.' The enrollees then raised it to the level of the Medical Supply on the second floor of the Quartermaster building. The bins were moved into position and filled. Thus the work in the District Supply was completed."

Thomas Weekes wrote an article in the Sept. 15, 1935 issue of the *Thames Tattler* about the work of the Supply Co. He said that many people didn't even know about the Company and those that did said they were goldbrickers and had an easy job. He countered by stating that the Company often works long hours and sometimes 7 days a week. The 190th Co. was divided into a few crews. The Maintenance Crew was under the direction of the District Construction Officer. It was available at all times to do emergency work throughout the state. The Quartermaster Office had the most enrollees who worked as bookkeepers, mail clerks, typists, and file clerks. Enrollees in the Issue and Commissary Warehouses worked as shipping clerks, warehouse men, and storeroom clerks. In the Motor Pool there were mechanics and chauffeurs. The last department was the District Headquarters where there were clerk typists.

During each enrollment period the departments had extra work. The CCC Clerks in Headquarters Dept. processed the enrollees. The maintenance men helped in the Quartermaster. The Supply Depot provided a hot meal for the recruits at noon. The Supply Dept. furnished clothing for the men and the Transportation Dept. made train and truck connections.

The enrollees had a successful athletic season in 1936. The baseball team was the runner-up in the District Baseball League. The 190th Co. football team was fairly successful, too. In November the Company held a dance on Armistice Day and earned enough money to purchase uniforms for the basketball team. [52]

In approximately 1936 Co. 190 Supply Depot closed when the Portland CCC Camp became the Supply Depot.

John Chase

In the summer of 2008 I met Sharon Niemann Testa of Bristol at a reunion at the Connecticut CCC Museum.

Sharon said her father, John Chase from Bristol, was a member of Co. 190 at the Supply Depot at Fort Wright on Fishers Island. He was a carpenter, an electrician, and a plumber's helper.

Sharon shared his CCC discharge papers and information about his CCC years:

John Chase was born on Sept. 16, 1907 in South Hadley Falls, Mass. On May 2, 1933 he joined the CCC when he was 24 years old. He began working during the infancy of the CCC. Chase was assigned to Co. 172, Co.188 and 190 that were based at Fort Wright on Fishers Island, NY.

On Aug. 15, 1933 he was assigned to work on the 190th Co. utility crew. He traveled to many of the CCC camps in Connecticut and Massachusetts doing plumbing, which was his trade before entering the CCC, and electrical work

On Oct. 11, 1933 he was assigned to the 175th Co. in Thomaston, Conn. and worked as a laborer. He also worked at Co. 176 in Torrington/Burrville, Conn. and at these camps in Massachusetts: Co. 107 Savoy/North Adams, Co. 115 Windsor/Savoy, Co. 196 South New Marlboro/Sandisfield State Forest, and Co. 112 South Lee/Beartown State Forest.

On many of the weekends he hitchhiked to his hometown of Bristol to see his girlfriend, Lorene Maynard. There were some weeks that he didn't come home and he wrote letters to Lorene. His daughter Sharon said she had approximately 75 of her dad's letters. They describe his work and experiences working in Co. 190 and other camps. The

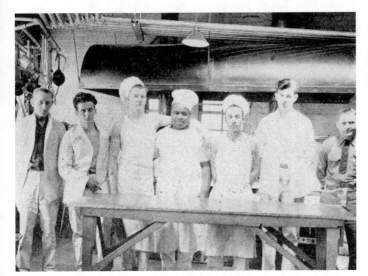

The Supply Depot cooks provided three meals a day for the 70-plus enrollees and a lunch for the recruits who came to register for camps.[50]

Duck pin bowling challenged the boys in the Supply Depot.[51]

letters also show his deep love for Lorene. Here are some of the letters that she shared with me.

May 17, 1933
Fishers Island, NY

Dear Lorene,

Gee Honey but I am lonesome for you. Ever since I have been home I wished I could have seen you last night. Gee I did not know what to do with myself last night. Gee, I guess I miss you pretty badly Dear.

Well, I did electrical work today and it seemed good. I am glad there are only a few of us and there is not much work. Some of the boys are going out next week and I guess it won't be long for us. The sergeant was telling us today that there will be one electrician and a helper to a camp and they will have to maintain it. I hope it will be so because there won't be much work to that. A couple hundred guys (recruits) are expected in tomorrow which means some of us will surely have to leave. Maybe I can come home more often if I get in a camp. I am having an awful time getting used to the eats. Gee but we had a punk dinner but the supper was OK.

How I love you Dear. All I do is think how wonderful you are. I don't know what I would do if I lost you. Gee Honey, but it was awfully hard to leave you Sunday night. I certainly felt lonesome after you left.

I am praying for payday. We expected it sometime this week but we may have to wait until the last of the month. Gee, they took away one of our blankets today. I hope I don't freeze tonight but I guess I will be OK. Gee Honey, I can't think of anything else to say except that I love you. So I guess I will say so long.

Yours forever,
John

❦ ❧

May 19, 1933
Fishers Island, NY

Dear Lorene,

Well Sweetheart, I received your package last night.

Gee it was great. It certainly came in handy as I was awful hungry. I did not eat much for supper so you can see it certainly tasted good. Tell Edith her candy was great. I assume she made it. Gee Honey, everything was good. It certainly did not last long.

Well Dear, I have been shifted again. I am in the 188th Company so when I write, leave off the training Co. and put on 188th Company and I like it better. There are only sixty-one in the company and the eats are great.

Gee Dear, I did not get a letter from you yet today. I suppose it is waiting up at the other company for me.

Honest Honey, I love you more every day and miss you a whole lot. Gee Honey, I don't know where we are going to be sent. No one has gone out yet and no one seems to know where we are going. I wish they would do something with us.

Gee, I was mad this morning. I was an electrician yesterday and today they made me a carpenter's helper but I am OK. Now they sent me back on electrical work this afternoon. So I guess I am all set now.

I am in with a new bunch of fellows and they are all OK. One of them got a package and we all shared it. I did the same with mine. It only lasted about five minutes.

Gee Honey, I have got to find your letter so I will call it quits for now. I love you.

Yours forever,
John

❦ ❧

May 30, 1933
Fishers Island, NY

Dear Lorene,

Well Honey, I have lots to tell you tonight. But first of all I want to thank you for that wonderful package your mother sent. Gee Honey, but you shouldn't have gone to all that trouble and expense. But gee Dear, it was great as I could not have any breakfast when I got back. It certainly came in handy. Gee

Honey, the candy was the best I ever tasted and the cupcakes were great. They were nice and fresh, too, but honest Dear I think it was too much of you to do all that. But I certainly appreciated it. Gee, but it certainly tasted good. It made me wish I was back home again with you.

Talk about rides. I certainly had one coming back. We made the milk truck all right but what a ride. It was a big closed in Mack (truck) and we had to ride the inside with milk bottles and ice. Gee, it was some ride. We were locked in and we had to sit on a case of milk. We had a blanket to sit on so it was not so bad. But Honey, we were cooped up like wild animals for about six hours. Never again for me.

Gee Honey, I was a porter, too. We got a quarter for carrying a lady's bags from the railroad station to the New Britain trolley. Gee, I got quite a laugh about it. We found a nice place near the railroad station to drink beer. I would like to bring you in that restaurant just to try that beer. It was only ten cents a stein.

Well Dear, I got my hair cut tonight. Do you think it will grow out by the time I will be able to come home again?

I fell asleep standing up in the boat this morning but later on we went to work in a tent. I found myself a bunk and dozed off all morning so I feel a lot better. I don't know what I would do if I didn't have your package.

Gee Honey, I guess I have told you all the news and I haven't told you I love you yet. I do worship you. Gee Sweetheart, I don't know what I would do without you. I wish I was home with you Dear.

Yours forever,
John XXXXXXXXXXXXXXXXX

❦ ❧

June 1, 1933
Fishers Island, NY

Dear Lorene,

What a day! Gee Honey. It poured all day long and I had to work out in it. I am pretty well disgusted with this place anyway. We got paid today. I received four

dollars and eighty-three cents. A month's pay!

One of the companies that went out today had a dirty trick played on them. They had to come back again. It was kind of a tough break. I don't know when they go out again. I won't tell you until I really know. Gee Honey, things are not going so good with me. You see I am really on the books as a carpenter's helper and I may have to work as one if I go out to a camp. I think an electrician will get more money. It is a tough break. I didn't get it at first. Ability doesn't seem to count here. Gee Honey, I would give anything to be able to tell them all to go to hell.

We are feeding ninety men in our mess and none of us get enough to eat. Tonight they fed one hundred and fifty. Gee, I guess I will have to go up and get a sandwich. I wish I had some of your candy left. My mother must have got the check by now. Let me know. Will you please?

Gee Honey, I wrote all this letter and I haven't told you I love you yet. Well, Sweetheart, I am telling you now. I guess I feel kind of blue tonight. I wish I was home. Gee sometimes I can't believe I am really here. Gee, I certainly get disgusted sometimes. About the only things I am getting used to are the fog horns. They have been blowing since I came back. Well, Honey. I guess this will be all for now. See you later Dear.

Yours forever and ever. I love you,
John

❦ ❧

June 21, 1933
Fishers Island, NY

Dear Lorene,

Gee Honey, I got a letter from you today that was mailed on Monday. I did not expect to hear from you so soon. Could you get heads and tails to that letter I sent yesterday? I was pretty tired when I wrote that letter so please excuse it. I wondered if you would notice my not watching you until you were out of sight but I already told you in my other letter. I thought I was going to get picked up, but I am glad you noticed it.

Gee honey but I love you. I don't know what I would

do if I could not see you every week. Gee Dear, by the looks of things I guess we will be here for another week. At least we haven't had any orders to move and as far as I know only one has been transferred.

Dear, have you seen anything in the papers about a truck load of C.C.C. turned over? We heard that they had a pretty bad accident but if you see anything about it in the papers, send it. Will you dear?

Gee honey but I love you and certainly miss you. Do you still love me and do you miss me a bit? It seems kind of tough to find anything else to tell you dear and I guess I will get cleaned. You don't mind if I cut this letter a little short? Well honey, I hope I will see you Saturday.

Yours forever,
John   XXXXXXXXXXXXXXXX

❦ ❧

July 6, 1933
Fishers Island, NY

Dear Lorene,

Well Honey, I have just been fighting, that is, I put on a pair of boxing gloves with another fellow. Gee whiz, but I'm tired. It is an effort for me to raise my arms. It is a good thing I had an excuse to write to you or else I would still be boxing.

Well, it seems as though they are rubbing it in kind of hard here. I am in charge of the barracks tomorrow and I guess Saturday besides my own work I have to keep the fire going here. Oh well, I don't care because I can't come home anyway this weekend.

I asked for a transfer but the sergeant said we are going out next week and he asked me to wait. I guess I will have to if he says so. From what I hear there are two groups going out: one to Thomaston and another to Massachusetts. I suppose I will draw the Massachusetts bunch.

Gee Honey, I guess I must be pretty good. I was just asked again to box again. Gee but I would look good with a couple of cauliflower ears. How about it? Do you think you will still love me?

Gee, we had a punk supper. They call it chicken con

carne. I did not eat any of it because I knew from a past experience.

Has George left yet? I won't suppose he has though. I wonder if they are going to enforce the rules about no passes for the month. I don't think I will have to worry because we will be out of here.

Gee Honey, I had better hurry up and tell you I love you. Gee dear it's going to be a lonesome weekend. I hope you won't be lonesome though. Well Honey, don't forget the key. Well Dear, I guess I will close now. I am sending you all my love and kisses. I love you.

Yours forever,
John

❦ ❧

July 12, 1933
Fishers Island, NY

Dear Lorene,

Well. I'm still here and no news about when we are leaving. Gee but it makes me sick. I wish they would tell us something. It doesn't look as though we are ever going out. Oh well, what's the use of worrying about it.

Gee Honey, they shot off one of the big guns today. What a bang! The concussion would almost knock you down. Gee, I certainly got a thrill out of the first one. It broke windows, knocked things off the walls, and blew hats off. It was quite an experience. It was a whole lot different being near it than when we saw it last year from the beach. Well Dear, I am a carpenter now, at least I am making bins for stock.

Gee Honey, I don't know about the passes. I don't think I can get one. I'm going to try hard though. I had hoped I would be out of here this week but as usual I will be disappointed.

Seems funny my mother has not gotten her check yet. I don't know what the delay is. No one else has received one either.

Let me know about the Muscle Shoals (Alabama TVA Project) Dear. Gee, I would certainly like to get a job somewhere, but I hate to leave you. Honest

Dear, I'm crazy about you. I love you. Honest Dear, I am crazy about you. I love you and worship you. Maybe if I can't get a pass I will come home any way. I love you.

Yours forever,
John

      ❧ ❧

August 3, 1933
Torrington, Conn.

Dear Lorene,

Well, I guess I'm in Burrville. It is half way between Torrington and Winsted. I will meet you in Burrville. It is just a wide spot in the road. The other side of that new bridge coming from Torrington. I will be there at the main road around a quarter of four. I like the camp better because the eats are better.

Gee Dear, I haven't time to write since I have to go right back to work. I love you dear and hope you will get this letter on time.

Yours forever, I love you,
John

      ❧ ❧

August 8, 1933
Torrington, Conn.

Dear Lorene,

Well Dear, we got paid yesterday so I am sending home ten bucks. You can take it and buy yourself some stockings with it. I got my raise in the first of July so I received twenty bucks. We all went to Torrington last night and celebrated. Gee Honey, we went to every beer joint in town. One of the boys has not got back yet. We had some fun at the carnival, too.

We are going to East Hartland tomorrow. We finished up today. I expect to be in Thomaston tomorrow as they have had trouble with the generator there and I'm going to try and fix it.

Say honey, I am mad. Gee, I wrote to you but you can't write to me. Well, I couldn't very well since I am moving every week. I am not sure about next Friday night. Dear I am way out in the sticks and unless someone comes after me I will be out of luck. I am going to be thirteen miles from Winsted on a little traveled road.

Gee Sweetheart, I love you and I don't know how I'm going to stand not seeing you this weekend. I hope I can find some way of getting home to you. Well Dear, I guess I will sign off for now. I love you.

Yours forever,
John XXXXXXXXXXX

Chase was discharged from the Thomaston camp on Feb. 31, 1934.

Sharon Niemann Testa said, "My father joined the CCC program so that he would have a steady job. By learning the electrical, plumbing, and carpentry trades he received a higher pay. This allowed more money per month to be sent home to his widowed mother.

After he was discharged from the CCC he worked at New Departure (a division of General Motors) in Bristol for almost 40 years as an electrician. He became a Master Electrician and in his spare time he worked for New England Spring in Unionville as an electrician. He also wired many newly built homes in Bristol."

On March 5, 1993 John Chase passed away and his wife Lorene followed on July 13, 1993.

On Jan. 1, 1935 John Chase and Lorene Maynard were married.
Sharon Niemann Testa

CHAPTER 27
CT BOYS IN OTHER STATES

Joe Iadarola
Buelha, CO

Joe Iadarola of Watertown looking over photos of his
CCC camp in Buelha, Colo. Podskoch

In March of 2009 I visited Joe Iadarola at his apartment in Watertown, Conn. We sat at his kitchen table and he had a few pictures about his time at Camp #2124 in Buelha, Colo. I asked Joe to tell me about his life, family, and time in the CCC.

"My father Pasquale worked one or two days a week at the Scovill Mfg. Co. in Waterbury, as a mold maker. My mother Jenny raised seven children: Paul, me, George, Carmen, Phyllis, and twins Pasquale and Anita. I was born on Nov. 11, 1922 in Waterbury.

"I had a couple years of high school but I quit at 16 to join the CCC. I was the second oldest in my family and I had to help put food on the table.

"They were advertising about the CCC a lot in the newspapers. A couple of my friends were going to sign up with me, but they never showed up because their parents wouldn't sign for them. I went by myself to the Waterbury Town Hall on Jan. 10, 1939, and I signed my parents' names for permission. I and a group of boys were taken to Fort Devens on a regular bus.

"Then the Army sent me and a large group of

Connecticut boys by train to Colorado. The trip was exciting for a while. It was a big adventure for a poor boy like me who had not traveled far. My parents didn't know where I was for a week. I wrote to them from Colorado. They were upset but got over it when they realized what I was doing.

"The CCC camp was near the foot of the Rocky Mountains and SW of the nearest large town of Pueblo. There were ranches all around. I was assigned to a barracks that didn't look too nice but some of the guys were sociable and knew I was young so they took care of me. There were two friendly guys from Connecticut. One was from New Haven and the other was Pat Spino from Waterbury. He is still alive in Waterbury.

"Most of our work was doing projects to help the ranchers. I dug irrigation ditches to help grow grass and diversion ditches to stop erosion. Those ditches were 1' wide and 1' deep.

"We also built basket dams by putting stones in chicken wire. They were placed where the water came down the mountains and caused erosion. These bundles of stones helped hold back the soil. We also planted weeping willow trees along the bundles of stone.

"We also worked making a dam in Rye about ten miles from our camp. It was up in the mountains where a lot of snow accumulated. In the evening the engineers explained what we'd be working on the next day and why we were doing it.

"There were some guys who drove bulldozers building the dam. Then they let everybody get a crack at driving them. Some guys built the forms for the wall for the core of the dam. We had small handfed cement mixers.

"Everybody got assignments. If you were digging ditches you had to sharpen your shovels because there were a lot of rattlesnakes that you had to kill. Those cowboys used to barbeque and eat them.

"The scariest thing was going down this steep mountain every night after work because the road was so steep and there weren't any guard rails.

"Another scary time was when we were fighting a forest fire. It's frightening when the pine trees roar up in flames. It is so scary. We stayed in a side camp and slept in tents. It got very hot and tiring so we took breaks. We went back to the tents at night. We used bulldozers and axes and made firebreaks.

"After work each day we went to the mess hall for dinner. The food was good. We had excellent cooks. One was Lithuanian and the other was Portuguese. If you were on KP for the weekend, one duty was making doughnuts for the whole camp.

"After dinner I took some classes to get my GED in the camp classroom.

"On some weekends we went to Pueblo. It was 60 miles away. We'd go to the drugstore and get a hamburger and a milkshake for 5 cents each. The movies also were only 5 cents. But it was a long ride in and back home in an army truck. We did the trip in one day. It was dark when we got back. They blew taps around 10 o'clock.

"Sometimes I rented a horse from the Three R Ranch in Rye. It cost 25 cents for the whole day. It was about two miles and I walked there. This was a regular ranch. There were a couple of native cowboys in our camp who were leaders and they told me about it. I usually went alone.

"Most of the time it snowed and I couldn't do much because of the frequent storms. Once the sun came out, the snow melted fast. Sometimes when it was nice we played a little volleyball.

"After six months in the CCC I decided to resign and was discharged on July 10, 1939 because my parents wanted me to come back home. I got a job in a grocery store as a clerk and delivered groceries. Benny Ackermann was the owner and a wonderful man. I stayed there for 1½ years.

"In October 1939 I joined the National Guard. I had

At the end of the day the enrollees gathered for the lowering of the flag. Joe Iadarola

to be at the Waterbury Armory one day a week.

"Then in summer of 1940 we went to Camp Drum for two weeks training in the summer. I guess we were getting ready for war.

"I went into the Army in February of 1941. First they sent me to Camp Blanding, Florida. We then went to the Pacific and did coast watches for 10-week periods. I was at Malakula in the New Hebrides Group. My job was watching the water for Japanese.

"Then I went to Bora Bora, an island in the Leeward group of French Polynesia. It was a beautiful island with beautiful people. Here we built a dam. The lessons I learned in the CCC in Colorado benefited me in this job. I was in charge of constructing the dam that would supply water to my camp. There was a pipe that was a half-mile long that carried water to the camp and along the way there were spigots for the natives to use.

"After WWII I got into a training program and went to school for manufacturing engineering.

"In 1946 I married Marie Donato. We had a son Joseph and a daughter Doreen.

"Then I got a job at Mattatuck Manufacturing where I worked for the president. I was in charge of plant operations in Cheshire, and most of the operations in Waterbury. We manufactured cosmetics in Cheshire and automotive parts in Waterbury.

"The CCC was very important to me because of the education classes that I took there in the evening. We had an excellent education teacher who helped me complete my high school education in three months."

Joe Iadarola passed away in 2009.

James Valli
Dolores, CO

James Valli of East Hampton joined the Civilian Conservation Corps in the summer of 1938. He vividly described his trip from Fort Devens, Mass. to the town of Dolores in the SW corner of Colorado. His CCC camp was called Dolores because it was the nearest post office but the camp was approximately 25 miles NW of Dolores in a locale named Lone Dome in the San Juan National Forest. Valli's article was published in the Aug. 19, 1938 issue of the East Hampton News.

Companies 2118 and 2119 boarded Pullman cars, which were to be our homes for the next several days, at

11:30 pm on Wednesday, July 6. We slept overnight on the train, and at 5:15 in the morning, though few were awake to witness it, the train started its grind to Colorado.

On awakening, we found ourselves in western Mass. The only real point of interest at this stage of the journey was the tunnel beneath Jacob's Ladder. Five and three-quarter miles long, it is a sight well worth seeing.

Leaving Mass., we headed north into Vermont as far as Pownal, across the border into New York at Hoosier, and two states were already behind us. Troy, NY was our first stop. We should remember it because we had just finished our first meal on the train. Sausages and spuds, and what a meal! After the first few awkward forkfuls, we managed to get around it.

Albany, the capitol of NY, was the next stop, at 8:15 am. It is a great railroad center. Utica, Schenectady, Syracuse, and Buffalo were the next stops of any importance. These stops occurred in ten hours of the day, before we hit Buffalo at 5:30 pm.

Sighs of relief from both men and joints arose, for here we got out and walked around the platform. The exercise did us a world of good, and though we planned and waited patiently for another workout, this was destined to be the one and only.

Six o'clock found us once again on our way. Every rotation of the wheels, every tick of the clock, and we drew nearer and nearer our destination. We arrived in Erie, Penn., at 7:30 pm, and followed along the Great Lake route, although we were only fortunate enough to see Lake Superior and Erie. Cleveland was next, and we arrived there at approximately 8 o'clock. We saw the home stadium of the Cleveland Indians baseball team, and even though we would have liked to have seen it from inside during a game, no one can say he was sorry he saw it, for few Easterners get the chance.

Most of us were in bed by the time we hit Toledo, and you can hardly blame us. Weary and cramped as we were, the bunks felt better than ever.

It seemed as though we were to get all the tough breaks! First, we had to wait for our trains; then we saw only two of the Great Lakes; and thirdly, we passed through Chicago at 2:05 am on Friday, July 8. Almost all of us were asleep, but the few of us who stood night guard were fortunate enough to catch a fair glimpse of the city. In Chicago we lost the only member of our detachment, one of the men escaping through a window.

At Chicago we caught a glimpse of the stockyards, and quite a sight it was. Reveille found us in Springfield, Illinois, to begin our second day on the rails. The county from that point to Colo. is known as the 'bread basket' of the nation. No name could fit as well this rolling prairie land. Acre upon acre of wheat, corn, potatoes, barley, and many other types of produce stretched before our gaze.

Moline was the next stop. It is the center for the manufacture of farm implements. The John Deere Co. and the International Harvester Co. are both situated here, and many time saving implements are sent from this place to all parts of the US.

Illinois soon passed into the history of the trip, as we reached Rock Island. Here we started to travel on the Rock Island route. From Rock Island to Davenport, Ill. to Iowa, the boundary line was the greatest of all, for the mighty Mississippi River flows there, the barrier between the two states.

Traveling over the river, we saw the famous locks built by the US Army engineers, a great work of mankind, and one of which the engineers may well be proud. It can be seen plainly that they know their business.

The run from Davenport to Des Moines took us through many towns, too small for mention in detail: Wilton, West Liberty, Iowa City, Marengo, Brooklyn, and several others. All are typical Middle Western towns, with few stores and large farms. Des Moines, capitol and the largest city in Iowa, saw us next. The city seems to be like any other in the US. It has noise, pedestrians, motor vehicles, and all the other things related to a city and its daily routine.

Once again upon leaving Des Moines, we travelled through many small towns. Stuart, Anderson, Atlantic, Avoca, and Council Bluffs were among them. Council Bluffs tells us we have seen state No. 7 on our trip. The muddy Missouri River is the boundary line between Iowa and Nebraska. Omaha in that state was the next stop, and Nebraska was State No. 8. It was still a long stone's throw from our destination.

Lincoln, Nebraska was reached about 9 am, Friday. We saw the Platte River on our way, as it rolled onward to add its muddy waters to those of the Missouri, and then to the Mississippi. Night baseball was noted in Lincoln and again we were lucky enough to see the crowds and lights. Memories of another day were all we had left as the lights went out, the night guards were posted, and members of

Company 2118 slept soundly, dreaming of what is to come.

Kansas plains greeted us as we rolled out of bed the next morning. Norton was the first town we passed in Kansas. This land would be a paradise to hunters back East. Jack rabbits were seen in groups of from 10 to 100, large, lively animals running across the prairie, and then lying still, their color blending with the ground. Prairie dogs were another unfamiliar sight which greeted us.

Dry river beds proved to us the real need of trees and irrigation. No one but those who are fortunate enough to see this country can really understand and feel the necessity of our trying to keep these dry river beds flowing with useful water. You will understand that although this land cannot be given away, it is practically useless, and the government has the right idea in spending money to convert it into crop-bearing land.

Goodland was our last stop in Kansas, and at last we reached the state which is to be our home for the next six months or so.

Burlington, Colo. reached at 8:30 am Saturday, was the first stop in this beautiful southwestern state. In rapid succession we passed through Strallon, Flagler, Aniba, Limon, Sinla, Ramoh, Calban, and into Colorado Springs. This city is in a scenic spot, and looming in the background was the mountain of great fame, Pike's Peak, with its summit covered with snow.

Here we changed from the Rock Island railroad to the Denver-Rio Grande route. One hour after leaving Colorado Springs, in the town of Peyton, we saw the foothills of the Rocky Mountains. We have been going skyward for quite some time, and now are up to 3,000 feet. Our trusty engine points its bulky nose southward to Pueblo. We notice that, though the temperature is up it does not seem hot. The air is so dry that the heat does not penetrate as it does in the East.

We arrived in Pueblo at 2:30 pm, exactly 24 hours before we were due at Dolores, our destination. (We were to find that it was still a few hours more to Dolores.).Ever upward we were moving, and as our destination was up to 10,000 feet, we took on a booster engine to help us in the grind.

Minnegua, an Indian village, was next, at 4,808 feet. From here on, we noticed that there was a large Indian population in all of the towns and cities. Greeted with the now famous call of 'Heigh-Ho Silver,' from the train, we saw our first real cowboy riding on his faithful horse, herding cattle. This was at Lime Junction, where the presence of rattlesnakes began to make itself known.

At Walsenburg, we were surprised to find ourselves bleeding at the nose, and we were told they were caused by the altitude. Again we headed west, winding through the mountains. Going through La Veta Pass, we crossed what is known as the Continental Divide. We were still going up when we reached Fir-Summit, Colo., population 12, elevation 10,000 feet, the brakeman checked our brakes, and the booster engine was dropped as we started down the west side of the Rockies.

Again the train twisted and turned over bridges and through tunnels, on our way down. Amid a curious crowd made up of every resident of the town of Alamosa, we climbed singing, and cheering aboard narrow-gauge railroad cars. Narrow was a well-chosen name, the rails being 18 inches closer together than the others. Many who had complained about Pullmans now agreed they were palaces compared to the new cars, with their hard seats and backs reaching only to our shoulder blades, on which we had to sleep. How? No one who did can remember.

Sunday morning, as we traveled through a part of New Mexico, the only towns worth mentioning were Chama and Lumbert. North once again, we travelled into Colo., and after 10 hours of backbreaking seats, cold sandwiches for rations, a continuous jerky motion, and a slow pace, we reached Durango.

Company 2119, which filled half of our train, left from here for its camp nearby, 40 miles from town. Seven hours later we arrived at Dolores, journey's end. With light and happy hearts, we once more had the feel of solid ground beneath our feet. Upon first sight, the town gave us a sickening feeling. Twenty-four miles to this? What could a bunch of fellows do here?

We were to find out, however, that though small, Dolores was by no means without enjoyment for us. Now a month later, there are many who are willing to re-enlist. Conn., Mass., Vt., NY., Penn., Ohio, Ill., Iowa, Neb., Kan., and New Mex., are all behind us, and we have settled down to make our stay in Colo. as enjoyable and as educational as possible.

My personal opinion is that any fellow who is not employed should join the outfit, and travel to this great western world. After all, travel is the best education a person can have.

(Special thanks to East Hampton Librarian Sue

435

Berescik for finding the article)

Frederick T. "Fred" Skripol
Palisades, CO

Fred in 1945 serving in the Merchant Marines.
Dave Skripol

Fred Skripol was born on July 25, 1921 in Hartford. His parents were Paul and Anna. The Skripols were a large family with six children. Fred was the fifth. One of Fred's older brothers was at Camp Fernow in 1936. In June 1938 Fred joined in Hartford. He and a group of boys were sent to Fort Devins for training.

A group of 200 boys from Waterbury, New Britain, and Hartford traveled on an Army train to Camp Mesa near Palisades, Colo. They did a lot of work helping the local farmers and ranchers.

After six months Fred was transferred back to Connecticut and sent to Camp Fernow in Eastford.

Fred told writer Sharon Kay Smith: "My most memorable moment in Colorado was when I drilled, set dynamite, and turned the detonator for the first time by myself. The blast went right. It had great power. I had a tremendous feeling of doing a job right.

"Some boys from camp made extra money playing with a small dance band in camp.

"Our camp had a loan shark who was from Waterbury. If you borrowed from him the interest rate was forty percent. If you didn't pay you got beat up.

"I learned discipline, workmanship, respect for authority, and how to take charge."

During World War II Fred served in the Merchant Marines.

After the war he worked with Fuller Brush Co. for over 30 years. He also worked part time as an officer with the Windsor Locks Police during the 1950s. Then he worked at Hamilton Standard and retired in 1987.

Fred and his wife, Anna M. (Ackerman), had four children: Frederick, Robert, David, and Betty.

Skripol was a charter member of the National Association of Civilian Conservation Corps Alumni. He served as president of Chapter 130 for over ten years and was instrumental in the formation of the CCC Museum in Stafford Springs.

On Jan. 30, 2000 Fred passed away at the age of 78.

Joe Arnold
Grand Junction, CO

Joe Arnold of Guilford worked at CCC camps in
Cornwall and Grand Junction, CO. Podskoch

In the spring of 2008 Nancy Arnold contacted me after reading a newspaper article about my CCC presentation at the New Haven Library on March 26th, 2008. "My husband Joe was in the CCC and he has a lot of stories to tell," she said. I then arranged to visit her and Joe the following week at their home in Guilford.

The Arnolds lived in a beautiful home right next to the water on Whitfield St. There was a exquisite view of brown sea grass blowing in the March wind. Nancy welcomed me and introduced me to Joe and we sat at the dining room table and I asked him about his life.

"I grew up in Larchmont, NY where my father, Augustus, had a very successful roofing business that employed 12 men. Our home was the former Joyce Kilmer home."

Kilmer wrote the poem "Trees" that I had to memorize when I was in my elementary school in Pennsylvania. I still can recite it from beginning to end.

"My mother Marguerite had four children: Marguerite, Eugene, and John. I was the eldest. I was born on March 28, 1918. I had a good life and finished 9th grade when my father lost his roofing business due to the Great Depression. He tried several small businesses and eventually went to work for his brother out of town. My family lost our home and we moved to New Haven, Conn.

"Then my father left my mother with four children. I had to quit school and help my mother. I read about the CCC in an article in Time Magazine. In approximately March 1937 I went to the town hall and signed up. They sent me to Camp Cross in West Cornwall in the northwestern part of the state. The camp was in the Housatonic Meadows State Park. This was a real adventure for me. I didn't mind leaving home because it was peace time so I could come home frequently.

"At Housatonic Meadows I felled trees and it was all done by hand. There were no machines then."

"Then I had a chance to go out West and was transferred to a CCC camp in Grand Junction in western Colorado.

"In 1938 I was in CCC Company 2120, in Grand Junction, Colo. The Palisades Camp BR-59 was about 30

Joe Arnold drove a truck at the CCC camp in Grand Junction, Colo. Stephen Arnold

miles east of the Utah border, a place of high mesas, dry but fertile when irrigated.

"The Colorado River ran through the valley and most of our work involved building and repairing the irrigation canals critical to the peach and melon agriculture of that area. The mild, sunny weather with the flat alluvial valley soil was unbelievably fertile to my New England eyes. This was one of the places where the desperately poor Okie and Arkie families of 'Grapes of Wrath' fame arrayed en masse in their broken down trucks and cars at harvest time. Some even came by foot from the freight yards in Grand Junction, 13 miles to the west.

"The CCC operated under a dual management. The camp area was under the jurisdiction of the Army with a uniformed officer in command and more or less Army procedures in effect with the important exception that one could leave before an enlistment period was completed. Our clothing was standard army issue except that our pea coat-type jacket was dyed green. The work activity was under the jurisdiction of the Department of the Interior, with its rangers supervising the work.

"Most of the enrollees were teenage or early twenties New Englanders reflecting the mix of ethnic Europeans typical of our home states. To the native Anglos of early settler heritage, our faces, names and manner were alien. Still, we got along quite well.

"The work was surprisingly challenging. We operated trucks, bulldozers, cement mixers, and all great for teenage boys. More importantly, a lot of the manual labor was manly, body-building activity dear to the hearts of young men. But most important of all we were doing something worthwhile and getting paid for it at a time of record-breaking unemployment and poverty. The pay was thirty dollars per month, twenty dollars of which was sent home. Time off was the standard Army thirty days per year.

"I can offer you some stories I wrote for the edification of my sons to give them some idea of an era that they were not likely to imagine.

"The CCC enrollee had several favorite pastimes. They were for me softball, movies, and taking trips. If you were from the East and the camp was in the West this was done by hopping freight trains, a venture more or less permitted by the railroad during the Depression. My camp was in the West."

Joe told his son Stephen about his adventures in the CCC and Stephen posted them at this website: http://

"Travels with Jimmy"
Part One

"Jimmy Skowron was a strange sort of buddy for me to hook up with. Quiet, noncommittal and taciturn, like many people of Slavic background and so different from my Irish-Italian world of ebullient noise. He was from the small town of Willimantic with its row houses and nineteenth-century mills enshrouded in the gray depression of the 1930's – grim enough to inspire even a nice Polish-American boy to seek out sweeter climes.

"Initially this odd-couple alliance was based on a shared interest in the adventure of seeing the world. It was only later that I learned of the humorous, music-loving, knowledgeable and steadfast sides of my quiet travelling buddy.

"The Denver and Rio Grande Railroad freight yard in Grand Junction was the beginning and ending terminal of our three major trips. To get to and from there from our camp we needed only hitch a ride, usually from one of the camp rangers.

"Our first trip was to San Francisco. This, the shortest of our three major trips, was one of the most exciting in as much as it was a completely novel experience for Jimmy and myself. Neither of us had even been in a freight car much less ridden in one.

"In a preliminary visit to the freight yards we learned

Joe in downtown San Francisco. Stephen Arnold

that we could select the freight line for our destination. Each rail car had a routing schedule in a bracket on the outside. En route we also learned that one's fellow travelers and even some railroad hands in a freight yard were kind enough to give guidance, including which railroads didn't tolerate riders on their freight lines and which places – cities, yards, or general locations – it was best to steer clear of. To me it was remarkable how tolerant many of the railroads in the west were in letting people, often whole families with all their possessions, hop their freights. Some even added a few boxcars with bench seats at the end of the freight line. A pragmatic gesture in recognition of the dangers of riding in the open. It was also recognition that in those hard days of the Great Depression, desperate people were willing to take desperate risks.

"It was early in May when Jimmy and I left Grand Junction on the first leg of our trip. We were going to Salt Lake City. We were to be gone about a week and we needed to carry both cold and warm weather clothing. I carried my gear in a battered steel suitcase I bought in a secondhand store in Grand Junction. Two teenagers in quasi army clothes carrying suitcases were a real laugher to your standard hobo in tattered clothes with his gear in his big belly bag.

"We arrived early in the morning and by 10 we caught our next ride to Winnemucca, a small town in the central Nevada desert that looked like a movie set for a cowboy western. This leg was our first experience in riding on the top of a boxcar. We had a grand view of the Great Salt Lake and we also learned how cold it was in early May in the desert once the sun went down. By about midnight we got off shivering in the Winnemucca yard, which consisted of a few watering stations and some sidings.

"After a restless night in an empty boxcar on a siding, Jimmy got up and walked around. For all his quiet, taciturn manner he was very much at ease meeting strangers. He dragged me along still shivering and sleepy to meet the boys. There were about 10 of them, some young but most a good deal older but only two with the resigned manner of professional hobos. They seemed amiable enough and invited us to sit around their early morning fire. A couple of blackened coffee cans suspended on wire over the fire were bubbling away. One of the men pulled a small bag from his pocket and carefully metered out a few spoonfuls of something that was to be coffee du jour into the cans of water. After a bit of stirring the same man gingerly removed

Joe's CCC camp near Grand Junction, Colo. Stephen Arnold

one of the cans, took a swallow and passed it to the man next to him. Each in turn exclaimed how good it was. It reminded me of the peace pipe ritual in early westerns with white men making reconciliation gestures with the good red man. One dared not refuse to take a few puffs, or, in this case, a few sips. I took my swig and quickly passed the can to Jimmy. I waited until the attention was far enough away, turned around and as unobtrusively as possible spit out the poison – it was god-awful. Small wonder when I found out the water was from a drain pool alongside the furthest siding.

"Later that morning we caught a ride that would bring us into downtown San Francisco with two short stops en route. By evening we were climbing the gradual east slope of the Sierra Nevada range on the California border and by morning were on top, where we stopped in the midst of evergreen trees glistening with ice crystals. On this leg we had the dumb luck to ride in a boxcar.

"We carried as much food as possible with us, eating out in the most frugal of establishments only when necessary. En route such places were rickety shacks in hobo jungles along freight stops. They were run by enterprising hobos serving the simplest of fare. The cuisine and service would make Dickens wince, but one couldn't expect much considering the prices, which ranged from eleven cents to twenty-four cents for the deluxe menu.

"We started down the west side of the Sierras about noon taking only two hours to reach the valley compared to the five hours it had taken to get into the mountains. It was a startling transformation from thirty-degree icy weather to the mid-seventies warmth of orange groves and palm trees. Just the kind of novelty we were hoping to experience.

"At this last stop before our triumphant entry into San Francisco, we experienced our first exposure to the ever-present hard-nosed side of riding the rails. We were stopped on a siding with a swampy area on one side and orange groves on the other. When a pickup with two men stopped alongside our freight, Jimmy and I guilelessly stood and watched them, not noticing that the more experienced riders on the freight were ducking for cover. Not running was a display of in-your-face arrogance to the two railroad bulls that jumped out of their pickup, billies in hand. We got the message too late. After being cursed out and whacked around, they shoved us into the shallow swamp. They left shortly afterwards. Two of the experienced gentlemen of the road who had hidden in the reefer jumped out and helped us out of the water. We were more chagrined than hurt.

"We learned that even on lines with a tolerant policy towards those hopping their freights there were well-known railroad bulls who got their jollies beating up riders ignorant or arrogant enough not to hide or run away when confronted. It wasn't the last or worse experience of this kind, particularly for me.

"We were on our way again, and reached the Oakland side of San Francisco Bay late at night. We had a particular thrill of accomplishment, realizing that we had reached the Pacific coast. The next day we rode right through the city streets of San Francisco, even daring to wave to people at crossings.

"We checked in at the Y-room rates fifty cents a day. Even though it was mid-morning we went to bed, expecting to get up by late afternoon. We didn't awake until the next morning.

"We had a great time in San Francisco doing the usual tourist things: cable cars, Joe DiMaggio's restaurant on the Embarcedaro, Chinatown, and other free points of interest. We probably went through four or five dollars apiece in our three-day stay.

"The return trip was relatively uneventful; until things went wrong while riding on the top of a boxcar at night in the Nevada desert. Despite our experience in desert nighttime temperatures, we took a chance, since there weren't any empty cars and we were running out of time. We did learn to use our pants belt to strap ourselves to the catwalk.

"In the middle of the night the train stopped at a water tower, and I told Jimmy I had enough of the freezing ride.

We just had to find a sheltered ride to stay where we were and hope to find a better ride the next day. I started to climb down the ladder just as a passing train sped by on the same side about three or four feet away. My hands were numb from cold, and I lost my grip on the top rung of the ladder and fell between the two trains. This was as much of a scare for Jimmy as it was for me. We just had to find a safer ride.

"I waited on the ground while Jimmy ran up and down the line of boxcars until he found an open and empty reefer. In we climbed and snuggled down in the relatively comfortable wire mesh cage, being careful to latch the trap door open. Since we didn't have a flashlight we couldn't tell what, if anything, was in the main compartment of the car. Just before dawn a railroad brakeman, making his rounds, closed the trap door and moved on before we had a chance to holler out. My latent claustrophobia kicked in, spurring me to a panicky and incessant banging on the trap door. It seemed like forever, but in about half an hour, someone unlatched the door and let in the early morning light, enabling us to see the cargo in the main compartments. We were riding with blocks of ice in stacks separated by straw packed to the roof of the car.

"We were about one or two hours west of Salt Lake City. It took about that long sitting on the catwalk to warm up. We got back to camp on time.

Part Two

"Bolstered with the assurance that we were now seasoned Knights of Road, Jimmy and I decided to take advantage of the ten-day Christmas vacation coming up. A trip in the dead of winter posed special challenges. Rides had to be inside, no riding on the top of a boxcar, special attention to proper clothing and the destination must be southern.

"We decided to go to Mexico. Not only was it south but equally important was its aura of daring. Although our destination was technically Mexico, it was just a trolley car ride across the Rio Grande, from El Paso to Ciudad Juarez.

"On Christmas Eve we hopped an empty boxcar on the first leg going east across the continental divide to Pueblo. Joining us was Carl Schmidt; the best athlete in camp, level headed and equally inspired to see the world. Carl's companionship turned out to be fortunate.

"Besides our heavy wool clothing, including long johns, we each carried two wool blankets rolled up. We

needed every bit of this cover going over the 11,500' pass before dipping down to Pueblo. Minus thirty degrees is normal winter temperature for this run in the winter.

"We spent most of Christmas day in the freight yards in Pueblo, the grimiest part of a hardened mining town not partial to hobos of any persuasion. Though undaunted we were not happy to learn that the freight for our next leg to Amarillo would not stop in the Pueblo yards but would slow down enough to catch it on the run. Since empty boxcar doors would be shut our next best bet would be reefer cars with the reasonable expectation that in the winter the ice compartments would be empty. Our freight lumbered into sight in the late afternoon going slowly enough so we could grab a ladder rung with one hand and a foot hold on the bottom rung. It does not take much imagination to realize that this trick was more dangerous than we were willing to risk. We were about to give up when an empty coal gondola was sighted. We went for it, throwing our gear aboard as we ran alongside freeing both hands to grab the boarding ladder. When we clambered aboard, we were surprised to find a passenger, a young man who must have hopped aboard farther up the line. He, like most men riding the rails in those days, was going somewhere, anywhere, in search of a job. This random, unorganized searching was their only hope, more myth than substance, but better than the flat-out hopelessness of where they were.

"The train speeded up almost immediately, eliminating any consideration of getting off. I stayed with our gear while Jimmy and Carl went in opposite directions looking for an available reefer. This was our next hard-learned lesson. In the winter the cargo in the reefer boxcars obviously did not have to be refrigerated but they did need to be protected from the cold. Reefer cars carried perishable goods and they protected them from freezing with coal burning heaters in the ice compartment, which was not vented. Death head placards warning of the dangers of asphyxiation were plastered on these cars.

"There were no empty reefers. With our six blankets, we cowered in one corner of the gondola as much out of the wind as possible. Our fellow passenger did not accept our offer to join us – too proud to take help from a couple of kids. Fifteen hours later when we reached the warmer plains of Amarillo, it was nine degrees. Our fellow traveler was dead.

"By late afternoon we picked up the freight for our next big leg-heading southwest through New Mexico on this wedge shaped route to El Paso. On this third day with very little sleep, I began to come apart. The more rugged Carl and Jimmy coped with the ordeal better than I did. They became very concerned when I began to shiver uncontrollably. There was no question that the next ride had to be an inside berth. Jimmy found an empty reefer. I was carried aboard and immediately collapsed into a sleep so deep that I wasn't aware that my face was resting on the steel grill floor of the reefer. The crosshatched impressions of the grill didn't fade away from the side of my face until later the next day.

"Tucumcari, in northeast New Mexico, was our only stop before El Paso. Another surprise. The yards in this pip-squeak town were shared by another rail line that was less tolerant of free riders than the one we were riding. Apparently one railroad bull kept surveillance over the small yard. When Jimmy and Carl climbed out of the reefer, they were immediately grabbed. I was still too out of it to realize what was going on, but I was shocked into awareness when Mr. Bull picked me up by the hair and stuck his gigantic pistol into my face. We were not welcome was the message.

"Once again we were lucky after being kicked out of the yard to run across some experienced travelers who came to our rescue. The drill was to wait for dark on the outskirts of the yard and catch our slow-moving freight on the run. This time we used our belts to make a sling to carry our gear, thereby freeing our hands to make a relatively safe boarding. Again we got lucky when we found another empty reefer. By morning the temperature was decidedly warmer so we left the cramped reefer for a pleasant outdoor open flat car carrying a load of lumber. We rode this into El Paso.

"We treated ourselves to the upscale seventy-five cent room of the local Y for our two-day stay. Carl insisted we splurge on restaurant meals, going all out for the deluxe fifty-cent menu.

"The main event of our two days was a trolley car ride to Juarez and a walk around town. As depressed as much of existence was at home, we were not prepared for the grimness of Mexico. The one room shacks and open sewers of the slums were a real shock. We were glad to return to El Paso and its clean palm-lined streets and seventy-degree midday weather.

"On the return trip, our big concern was how to get around Mr. Bull at the Tucumcari yards. We decided to jump off before coming to a stop and either duck down right away or scoot to the two-lane road that paralleled the tracks. We did both and set off walking to the northbound side of the rail yard expecting to hunker down near the track and catch the freight on the run. Apparently three frumpy teenagers were types not dear to the heart of the locals since we had no luck hitching a ride and had to walk the approximately two miles to a dirt road that ran between the main highway and the train tracks.

"Shortly before dark our train could be seen leaving the yard. We should have realized that something was amiss when we saw the freight travelling much faster than usual and much too fast to board on the run. We stood in the dirt road watching helplessly as our ride disappeared. When the caboose went by, there on the other side of the tracks was Mr. Bull in his pickup. We quickly turned around and beat it to the highway, where we got lucky and hitched a ride in a mail truck. I was never sure why the driver picked us up when we were turned down cold by others. Perhaps he recognized our CCC uniforms and decided we were not the stereotypical threat to local security.

"Our mail truck ride got us to a crossroad complete with a gas station/bus stop combo, a general store, a few other small nondescript buildings, and a bar with swinging doors. The whole setup was right out of central casting with real cowboys whooping it up in the bar and old codgers with droopy mustaches sitting around a potbelly stove in the gas station/bus stop.

"This was the middle of nowhere. All sagebrush-covered plain with purple-colored mountains in the distance. It was obvious that our only hope was to catch the midnight bus to Amarillo even though the cost would just about wipe out our cash. And wait we did fascinated by the spitting skill of the tobacco-chewing elders who prefaced every sentence with a lob of juice to the spittoon as much as six feet on the fly. When we told them that we were from the east, they were generous with their condolences, having much sympathy for anyone having to live in such crowded proximity. We tried not to look at each other as we graciously acknowledged their comments.

"We were directly across the street from the bar where the ruckus was getting a little high – just typical Saturday night shenanigans. Two of the cowboys spilled out through the swinging doors in a whirl of flying punches. The eventual loser was seen on the ground, having not been too successful in dodging the kicks of his opponent. The good old boys hesitated long enough to acknowledge the fracas before getting back to their chompin' and spittin'.

"'Looks like old Zeke's gettin' stomped on' was the only comment offered. I was sure that some director in puttees and knickers was going to appear shouting into his microphone calling for a break in the action.

"Old Zeke joined us on the bus to Amarillo, needing help to get his seat in front of me. His head was wrapped with gauze but, still quite drunk, he was feeling no pain as he sung for a good hour while he dripped a steady stream of blood over the back of his seat onto my foot rest.

"The ride from Amarillo to Pueblo was uneventful. Our big concern was rationing our meager funds to buy food for the final leg across the divide and home. Our freight stopped for a few hours on the last day in Leadville, near the top of the divide, all-deep snow, tall evergreens and giant coal-burning engines, spouting smoke and spitting steam. I was ravenous, but with only fifteen cents my only hope was a nearby dingy eatery frequented by the railroad men. I ordered a bowl of chili, the only dish I could afford. I had never eaten chili much less the Tex-Mex hot stuff they offered. Three gulps into the bowl of fiery coals and my mouth and gullet were on fire. Three glasses of water didn't do much to quench the flames to the amusement of the hardened customers who were enjoying the predictable outcome. Starving though I was I couldn't finish the chili. I slinked out back to the boxcar; spewing breaths of fire all the way home.

Part Three

"With the experiences of our first two trips in mind, Jimmy and I sat down to plan our biggest, and ultimately, our last trip. We had had enough cold weather derring-do and risky rides on the tops of boxcars or locked in reefers. Also, having a congenial third person with us was a sensible arrangement that added to our security.

"So we recruited Jeep Caratazolia from Providence. Jeep was some sort of a contraction of his first name, or it might have been some reference to a character from Lil' Abner comics. He was tall, broad shouldered with a ready smile and easy disposition. This was to be his first experience hopping freights, and he was quite willing to leave the planning to Jimmy and me.

"Jimmy laid out an itinerary that included Boulder Dam, Los Angeles/Hollywood, and the World's Fair in San Francisco, all in a two-week schedule. We were each to start with five months savings – $25; enough to cover all expenses based on our experience in frugal living on the road.

"In mid-August, we left Grand Junction for Salt Lake City, where we found an empty mail car, complete with seats and running water; an unprecedented luxury all the way to Las Vegas.

"Boulder Dam had only recently been completed and was fast becoming a tourist attraction. We left our luggage, including my new battered steel suitcase, with the stationmaster in the tiny Las Vegas depot and hitched a ride to the dam, where we spent the day.

"Las Vegas looked a little raunchy to our New England sensibilities, so we decided to dip into capital and spend the night in a flophouse rather than risk bunking down in the freight yard. For 25 cents you got a cot with blankets in a large space about the size of a high school gym. The looks of the clientele, mostly older men of desperate resignation, were not particularly reassuring. It was a short stay. I no sooner got myself tucked in when I realized that I was being eaten alive. One look with my handy flashlight at the bedbugs crawling all over me and I was up like a shot. That was enough for Jimmy and Jeep, and we packed up and left, much to the consternation of the grimy proprietor, who felt demeaned by our eastern sensibilities.

"We had learned that unlike San Francisco, one could not ride a freight into or out of the Los Angeles yards. We decided that the San Bernardino/Riverside stop, about 60 miles east of Los Angeles, would be as close as we could get and still be reasonably close enough to try hitchhiking into town.

"Riverside was a particularly beautiful valley of orange orchards and snow-capped mountains. We got off our boxcar next to an orange-packing facility where there were several 20-foot high piles of oranges in various stages of ripeness. After helping ourselves to all the good oranges we could carry, Jeep decided we should play "King of the Hill" in the tallest pile. After enough of this horseplay, I asked one of the packing house workers why the company was letting the oranges rot when there were plenty of people who would be glad to have them. His explanation was that there was an overproduction of oranges that year and, in order to maintain the expected market price, they needed to limit the number of oranges that were to go to market. My first lesson in capitalist marketing.

"I was not very happy with that answer, particularly considering the desperate poverty of so many Americans in a decade-long economic depression. This was a time when many people began to question the logic of a market system with a high capacity for production but with a constrained system of distribution. This was also a time of almost no economic safety net providing for the vagaries of a free enterprise system. Free in this instance to go without in a world of potential plenty. I never forgot this graphic lesson.

"Hitchhiking was not done well by more than two people together. Since Jeep was the inexperienced traveler in our trio, Jimmy and I tossed a coin to decide which of us would hitchhike into LA alone. I won the dubious honor.

"It was early evening when I arrived in LA. We had agreed that we would meet in the railroad station in downtown LA. Surprise! When I asked directions to the station from a cabby, he asked me, 'Which one?' Which one? How could there be more than one?

"'Well, kid,' he said. 'Ordinarily there is only one, but tonight there are two. They are having the inauguration ceremonies for the new one, and at midnight they are closing the old one.

"With only a fifty-percent chance of picking the right one, I gave up and went to the downtown Y. Jimmy guessed that they would find me there.

"Jimmy particularly enjoyed the bus tour around Hollywood and our visit to a studio. We had been gone five days and already had spent nine dollars each. But Jimmy just had to have a Hollywood T-shirt, even if he had to go on limited rations.

"Getting out of LA, we were faced with the same problem of hitchhiking out to a rail terminal far enough out of town. We chose Santa Barbara, and we decided that I would go alone and meet in the Santa Barbara freight yards.

Jimmy (left) and Joe visiting Boulder Dam. Stephen Arnold

"I was happy to get a ride most of the way with a young couple even though I had to stretch out on top of their luggage with about six inches of head room. I arrived in the middle of the night, and very cautiously crept around looking for a safe place to sleep. Again I got lucky. I found an empty day coach on a siding. The seat backs were adjustable and when turned to face one another I could stretch out on one seat and put my feet on the other, keeping care not to forget that there was a twelve-inch gap in the middle.

"After about an hour of restless tossing, I decided that the prudent thing to do would be to check the door at the other end of the car in the event a quick exit was called for. When I was about to try the door I felt a hand on my shoulder. My heart sank.

"'Never mind, kid. It's open,' was the scary admonishment from a disembodied voice in the last seat. I thanked him and scurried back to my double seat bed.

"Early the next morning I got up to find breakfast and my buddies. Intuition suggested that a posh town like Santa Barbara was not the sort of place that entertained hobos with any degree of hospitality and would likely have railroad personnel that shared such sentiments. So with considerable caution, I hustled from row to row of freights working my way out of the yard.

"Almost there I was blocked by a very long freight that had a break in the middle with a separation of about three feet between the two halves. I stopped between the uncoupled cars, looked around cautiously, stepped out and the two cars slammed together.

"I hadn't heard the donkey engine used to shuttle cars around the yard. They would puff along and then shut off the power to coast into a tie-up. That was just the moment I chose to step between the cars.

"A brakeman saw the whole scene. Too far away for me to hear his scream, he must have shut his eyes to the expected tragedy. After bawling me out he calmed down enough to point out the railroad men's hash house with a warning not to come back.

"It is quite apparent that Jimmy and I survived these adventures simply because time after time we were just plain lucky. The luck continued. When I entered the restaurant, there was Jeep, big grin and all. Jimmy was out scouting around for me. He eventually showed up and we set out to plan our escape by freight.

"Jimmy decided that we simply could not take a chance in sneaking around the yard and risk getting caught after being told very directly not to come back. We decided to rely on the favorable view that most people had of the boys in the CCC. I was selected to plead our case with two of the railroad men in the restaurant, explaining that we were on vacation and had to get back to camp in Colorado. They put us in an empty boxcar and wished us good luck. Pretty smart that guy Jimmy.

"The rail line north ran very close to the coast, sometimes riding on cliffs just above the beach. It was a spectacular trip with the constantly changing scene at one time or another duplicating the topography of different parts of our country. Small wonder that the movie industry settled in California.

"Before leaving Santa Barbara, we shopped around for the least expensive food we could buy to take with us on the 20-hour trip to San Francisco. Two items we came to regret were day old Italian bread and three large cans of California sardines packed in brine or something like it. We probably had no more than a pint or so of cheap soda pop to drink. After eating the sardines and bread for lunch and downing the pop, we were in for about six hours of torturous thirst before reaching our first stop at Salinas.

"My twenty-nine year old son is typing this round of teenage adventures. He can't imagine how anyone could be so obtuse to dangerous situations nor so blithe of spirit to launch off into the unknown. A few moments of recollection of his teenage and young adult life were enough to squelch such unthinking arrogance.

"From our YMCA base in downtown San Francisco, we made a three-day foray to Treasure Island, a landfill in the harbor and venue for the 1938 World's Fair. Seven of

In 2008 Joe Arnold (right) and an unidentified CCC alumni celebrated the 75th Anniversary of the CCC at Camp Roosevelt in Killingworth, Podskoch

my precious twenty-five dollars went to the risqué Sally Rand's Nude Ranch, a diorama of a western ranch where cowgirls pranced around in inane imitation of ranch life clad in cowboy boots, beaded shorts, and a Stetson. All those boobs were almost more than three Catholic boys could be expected to withstand.

"On the first leg of the trip home, the only freight available required our riding on the top of a boxcar. Since the weather was warm and we were not making a long leg through the desert at night and because we were running out of time, we hedged in our policy of not riding in the open. We were clipping along through endless acres of wheat, or what I imagine was wheat, when one of us started some horseplay – both dumb and dangerous.

"We CCC men were always treated with kindness by the general public but necessarily so by small town police and by some railroad police (when hitching rides) though these were the exceptions.

"The CCC gave its recruits a chance to see the U.S. It also made it a lot easier to understand how to get along in the Army.

"After about a year and a half in Colorado I came home in 1939. I joined the National Guard and was activated into the U.S. Army at the beginning of World War II. I was stationed for two years on Ascension Island, located halfway between Brazil and Africa.

"After the war I went and sat on a bench on the New Haven green to think over what my talents were and to plan a future. I was 27 years old. The one talent I thought I had was dancing. I got a job teaching dancing at the Arthur Murray dance studio. My aptitude tests from the army indicated other talents, and I was told it would be a shame not to get an education.

"I went to the high school to see if I could take classes for my GED high school diploma. The lady said that I had to first take a test. After the test the lady corrected it. I asked her when I could start classes. She replied, 'You're not going to high school son, you're going to college.' I was so surprised and happy.

"I went to Southern Connecticut State College and studied engineering. The school was at its early stages and my classes were in a garage. After I got my undergraduate and graduate degrees in engineering I began teaching industrial engineering at the University of New Haven in 1958. In 1961 I became the chairman of the department.

"In 1962 I married Nancy Rodriguez and we had three

sons: Stephen, John, and Patrick.

"In the 1980s I visited the town where my CCC camp was and spoke with someone from the local newspaper who told me the old camp site was now a waste disposal site. They did remember the days when the camp was operating in the area but couldn't recall anyone that was still around that I could talk to."

Joe retired from teaching in 1987 after thirty years and became involved in many projects in my town of Guilford. He also got involved in national politics. One summer, Joe worked with young Bill Clinton on a U.S. Senate campaign. Joe and Bill used to sit on Joe's deck overlooking Long Island Sound while eating steamers.

Joseph Arnold passed away on Thurs., March 18, 2010.

Walter Sekula
Meeker, CO

Walter Sekula of Norwich speaking at a CCC reunion at the Connecticut CCC Museum. Nancy Eve Cohen

In 2007 I first met Walter Sekula at a CCC reunion at the Connecticut CCC Museum in Stafford Springs, Conn. He was a short man about 86 years old with a robust voice. He told me that he and a group of other CCC alumni organized the CCC Museum in Stafford Springs, Conn. a few years before. Walter was also an officer of the National Association of the Civilian Conservation Corps Alumni's Northeastern Region Chapter #170. This group had monthly meetings for many years and gathered CCC memorabilia for the Museum. They also donated their time to act as guides for the museum.

Walter was so thankful for his experience in the CCC and he wanted to spread its history to everyone he met. When I told him that I was going to write a book on the history of the CCC camps in Connecticut and needed to do research, he volunteered to accompany me. During 2008 he traveled with me when I gave talks at some 60 libraries and historical societies throughout the state.

He just loved to tell the audiences about his days at the CCC camp in Meeker, Colo. He also helped me locate the many CCC campsites in Connecticut. As we traveled he introduced me to many CCC alumni that I was able to interview for my future book.

On one of our trips I asked him to tell me about his family and early life.

"I was born in Jewett City on Oct. 16, 1921. My parents, Joseph and Sophia, had a large family: Maria, a baby girl (died in childbirth), Kristina (lived only a short while), Mary, Stanley, Peter, John, and me. I was the youngest and wore all the hand-me-downs except Mary's bloomers.

"I only went to two years of high school and quit. I heard about the CCC at my Boy Scout troop. I was the first Eagle Scout in town. In July 1938 I and seven other guys went to the town hall in Jewett City. The eight of us then went to New London on a bus to get processed and signed up. We stayed overnight in a hotel.

"As a youngster I was all excited about going to a new land. They told us we'd probably spend two or three months out West and then be shipped to Alaska.

"The next day we took a train to Fort Devens in Ayer, Mass. We had physicals, shots, and got our uniforms. We were issued old World War I uniforms that smelled of moth balls. Solid wool! Only good thing about that even though it got wet and was awfully heavy it kept you warm, very warm. Matter of fact it was warmer if it got wet in the rain.

"We slept in tents. They were forming groups to be shipped out West. Every day we had calisthenics and policed the area for a few weeks.

"One day they asked what guys had a Connecticut driver's license and to step forward. So I stepped forward. We marched to the barracks and they gave us each a wheelbarrow. They told us to fill it with coal and bring it back to the coal bins. That was the first and last time I volunteered for anything.

"Then the Army filled six trainloads full of enrollees and I was one of them. We boarded the train and it took about a week to get out to Colorado. Many times we were placed on a sidetrack to let the express trains go by.

"The train made three stops in Colorado. The first was Glenwood Springs. My group got off at Rifle, Colo. The train continued to the Palisades camp at Grand Junction.

"When we got off the train, they told us to line up by the Colorado River. We were happy to jump in the river clothes and all because we didn't have a shower in a week. It was hot and stuffy on the train ride so that we kept the windows open and were covered with black soot and cinders from the locomotive.

"The Army had a rack truck that we climbed into and it drove us 43 miles to Meeker. There were no seats. We stood up all the way hanging on to each other. On the way it rained and hailed and it was hot. It was a typical New England weather day.

"It took us what seemed like all day to get to camp because the road was dirt.

"When we got to the campsite there were tents set up for us by a cadre of boys from Oklahoma. They had a meal for us and after we went to the supply tent for two blankets and quilts. We were laughing like crazy because we didn't think we needed all those blankets. But the Okies said, 'You just wait till 11 o'clock and it will be cold!'

"We were on a mesa and stayed in tents. We dug a septic system. There were no wooden buildings like we had in Connecticut camps. We had to wait for a train to bring prefab barracks.

"First we dug holes for piers and built the floor. When the walls came we just bolted them together. We had four barracks for the men, a mess hall, rec hall, and a cooks' quarters because they worked 24 hours on and 24 hours off in two shifts. We also built an officers' quarters, infirmary

Three of the five barracks at the Meeker CCC camp. The boys planted flowers to beautify the camp. Sekula

(4 beds), and the latrine. Inside there was a long seat with holes on both sides. We sat back to back on the john. There was no flush. They threw lime down the hole to keep the flies and odor down. Underneath the latrine's wooden floor was a clay-lined ditch that ran right down the center of the building. The waste flowed down the ditch to a cesspool.

"There was a wash room at the other end of the lavatory with showers and sinks. The shower had a pipe with showerheads on each side of the pipe. They had a coal boiler in the washroom that heated the water for the latrine and the kitchen.

"We also built a rec room that had a PX, a pool table, ping-pong table, cards, dominos, books, and magazines. Outside the rec hall we had a boxing ring.

"We played a few games such as football and softball but no basketball. We didn't play any other CCC camp teams. We just made up teams in camp, like one barracks against another. The closest town was Meeker and that was 13 miles away. It only had a grade school.

"It took almost four months to improve the town's impression of us. They thought we were hoodlums and gangsters from the cities. After several months we got acquainted with town people. They invited us to their ranches for dinner and we rode their horses. They invited us to town dances and we got rides to town in the rack trucks. We also had dances at our camp.

"During the week we had freedom to go anywhere we wanted from 6 pm to 6 am. So some of us walked to town as a group. They had a building called the 'Past Time.' They sold 3.2 beer. They had a radio and pool table. We stayed till the place closed and walked back to camp.

"There were some guys from Connecticut and they heard about the hurricane that hit our state. They were worried about their families so they went AWOL. Some came back to camp after they helped their family. The Army wasn't that strict.

"I wasn't homesick. I had good friends from my hometown plus we met other guys and we became friends.

"The food was terrible at first because we had a Mexican health officer who served beans, beans, and more beans. I never knew there were so many varieties. We had beans for breakfast, in our lunch sandwiches, and for supper.

"I was a 'dog robber.' That was the name they gave me because I was a waiter for the officer's mess. I was chosen by Lt. Gagney because I was clean-cut.

"One morning three men waiters and I were working

Walter Sekula (on right) with two friends in the CCC
in Colorado. Sekula

when the officers were eating supper. Lt. Gagney who was in charge of the kitchen, called me over and said, 'There is something wrong because it is quiet in the mess hall. Go and see what is happening.'

"I looked in and nobody was there. I looked out the front door and all the men were lined up but weren't coming in. I reported back to the lieutenant. He got up to see what the problem was. A spokesman for the enrollees said, "We are fed up with the meals especially the beans. We want some good red meat and some better meals!'

"Lt. Gagney told the captain and he came out and asked them what their problem was. They stated again what their problem was. He said this is what they were sending us for rations and that is what we are using. The enrollees replied: 'We are not going to eat or work until this problem is resolved.'

"The captain said, 'Tomorrow you will have breakfast as usual and you better be ready for work at 8 am or else.

"The next morning the men didn't go into the mess hall and at 8 the trucks were ready, so all the guys got behind their trucks and sat down on the ground.

"Then the captain said, 'I will report this to headquarters in Grand Junction. The men were on strike all day. Then at night the JAG, Judge Advocate General, came to camp and went to the mess hall to listen to the boys' complaints. He listened and walked through the kitchen and saw the rations. He said, 'I promise to get back and resolve the problem tomorrow, but I want you to go back to work. I guarantee your problems will be resolved.'

"We had a medical officer, Campanella, who was of Mexican origin. He said to the JAG: What's wrong with beans? All my life I was brought up eating beans and look at me.'

"In about two or three days a truckload of new rations

came. We even got sides of beef and better rations.

"Just talking about the beans I remember this song we used to sing." Then Walter sang:

"The coffee that they serve you they say is mighty fine. It's good for cuts and bruises and tastes like iodine. I don't want no more of the CCC. Gee but I want to go home.

"We had a group of guys from New Haven, Conn. and veterans from other camps. They came from Connecticut camps in Portland and Madison. There were 50 guys from each camp. So half of the camp was veterans and experienced. There was one guy named Manchetti whose brother was a heavyweight boxer. This guy was a bully and picked on everybody until one day he picked on a guy named 'Red' from Danielson He was a tall lanky guy. He got fed up with him picking on him and other guys.

"One day Manchetti challenged him to a fight in the ring. After supper they got into the ring and the whole camp gathered around cheering for "Red." About halfway through the first round, Red hit Manchetti and he fell down to the canvas. He was knocked out. When he came to, there was a surprised look on his face. He said, 'You did this to me?' 'Yes,' said Red. 'Well, are you happy now?' Manchetti got up and shook his hand and that was the end of Manchetti's bullying. He couldn't do enough for Red after that."

Then I asked Walter what jobs he had at camp.

"The first job I had was digging out the grease pit with a couple guys. We finished it and put a wooden cover over it and covered it with some dirt. I told the guys to stand on the pit and I was going to take a picture of them for a job well done. As I focused them with my box camera. I told them to stand still. I looked into the view finder and I said, 'You guys are moving. Stand still.' The reason the guys were moving was because the weight of all the guys on the cover caused it to fall in. It's a good thing it wasn't filled with grease.

"We had to dig out the pit and used heavier timbers for support.

"The men at my camp were busy building roads, reservoirs, diverting water in the mountains to ponds for sheep and cattle. This was public grazing grounds.

"We built drift fences for the saving of vegetation of the land.

"The guys built branding corrals for the cattlemen and for the sheep we built sheep dips. The sheep went through three different dips to get rid of the dirt, etc. before shearing.

They were shallow runways that were built of concrete. The water came down the mountains and went into the sheep dips that were close to the White River.

"I called the sheep the 'stinking wooleys.' You couldn't see the sheep in the distance but you could smell them before you heard them. The sheep came in like a river. They came in by the thousands. The leaders had bells on them. You could smell them for miles. You'd find 2-3 men who had a chuck wagon. They rode on horses and through whistles and hand signals they guided the dogs who did all the herding.

"Most of these type of sheep came from the Pyrenees Mountains in France.

"I worked on access roads to grazing grounds and water. We used picks, shovels, and wheelbarrows. We had no trees for shade.

"We had a man called 'Horn' who was a forester in charge of the foremen. They were not LEMs but from the Colorado Forestry Dept. They were very good to work for.

"During hunting season in the fall they had 10 days of hunting in our area. So we were restricted to camp during this time. We picked up stones, made sidewalks and beautified the camp ground.

"After the hunting season was over, they organized groups to go out in different directions to see if there were any wounded or dead animals. We picked up a lot of mule deer and elk, brought them back to camp, and dressed them. The rancher had a very large root cellar so we hung the carcasses up in his cellar. Whenever we needed meat we just went over to Iva Schultz's ranch. Our camp was on his property.

"They also had state checkpoints for hunters to bring

One joke the CCC boys did was move a new recruit's bed and place it on the roof of the barracks. The rookie had a hard time finding his bed at night when he came into the barracks to sleep. Sekula

their game for inspection and registration. There was one close-by our camp. We helped weigh them and take samples. They also extracted some teeth for tests.

"In the fall our captain was invited to a hunting lodge that was also a rangers' station on Trappers Lake. The first time the captain took six guys with him to help push out vehicles if we got stuck in mud or snow. I was one of the chosen men. As we came down the mountain I could see a wide brook down the center of the valley. On each side of the brook were ranger cabins. On the mesa there were corrals for mules and horses.

"I always liked the out-of-doors. I learned that we could apply to be a forest ranger. Three of us, Rudy Wojtowicz, Stanley Tracz, and I were like the three Musketeers. So after the first hunting trip we applied to be rangers. Because of our CCC experience Rudy and I were accepted but Stanley was one half inch too short. We tried everything to get him to pass. We put things in his shoes but they said take off you shoes. So it didn't work. We tried having Stanley lay down to make his spine longer. We carried him back into the office to be measured but he was still too short. So we finally gave up. We said if Stanley can't join, we all will stick together and not join. This all happened after we had been there for one year.

"During the winter we used soft coal in the barracks stoves to keep us warm. The guys who slept near the stoves would sweat. There was a night watchman who went from building to building to make sure the stoves were working and he would add coal if needed. He made sure that the stoves in the kitchen were well-heated by 3 am when the cooks got up to start preparing for breakfast."

At one of our CCC gatherings Walter added, "There wasn't anyone in camp who knew how to play the bugle to wake the guys up at 6 in the morning. One guy in camp, however, knew how to hook up a record player to the camp PA system. So every morning he played this same country song that boomed across the camp." Then Walter began singing the song and the audience had a good laugh.

"I forgot to tell you that we were paid five dollars each month. The captain paid us in silver dollars and he had his revolver on the table. This was the day that the loan sharks would be there to collect money that they had loaned out during the month.

"We also used to play jokes on each other especially the new recruits. One joke was putting corn flakes in a guy's bed so that when he crawled in there was a lot of crunching

Walter Sekula by a CCC statue in Maine.

sounds and an angry guy who now had to clean his bed. Sometimes they'd put a dead rattlesnake or a scorpion in someone's bed. That really scared them.

"Then there was the snipe hunt. They'd take the rookies, blindfold them, and lead them into the middle of the woods. Then they took off the blindfold and gave them a burlap bag and said, 'We want you to stay here and we're going to drive snipes to you. They are a small bird. We want you to catch them and bring them back to camp. Of course there was no such thing as a snipe and we just left them in the woods till they realized that they had been fooled.

"In July 1940 I left camp because the project we worked on was going take two more years. I figured two years away from home was enough so I went home.

"When I came home there were only factory jobs so I worked for a local farmer picking Brussels sprouts. Then I worked in a factory weaving shop. I didn't like it, because it was too noisy. My buddies said we don't want to be like our parents so we said let's join the Army.

"We signed up in October 1940. We were shipped from New London to Fort Devens and were back in the same tents we were in two years before. Our drill sergeant Casey was an ex-CCC senior leader. So we had 90 days training and got a furlough. I was assigned to the signal corps. I was called out to be shipped to Camp Falmouth, Cape Cod. They said they were forming a new camp and that we were in the coast artillery. I said that if I had a choice it would not be artillery. He said, 'Shut up and do as you are told. You guys were trained as cooks in the CCC and that is what you three will do together.' We were at Otis Field.

"As soon as I was sworn in the Army I was made a

sergeant in charge of 14 men because they figure the two years I had in the CCC prepared me to be a leader. I had the discipline, the respect for myself, and respect for others. That was the difference."

Then I asked Walter, "When you look back at your time in the CCC what did the CCC accomplish?

"The program was good. It helped the country. It gave us jobs and money to families to recover from the Depression. It also strengthened the youth to fight WWII.

"For myself I learned how to get along with others. I learned about our country. I learned how to play the guitar from Shorty Genest from Taftville, Conn. I learned about life."

Over the years Walter saw that many states were honoring the CCC alumni by erecting a beautiful statue of a CCC worker. Walter urged his CCC alumni to raise money for a Connecticut CCC statue. They had fundraisers but not enough to pay the cost of the statue.

As the years passed many of the CCC alumni passed away and the few men remaining were unable to achieve their dream of seeing a CCC memorial statue in their state. Now it is sad to know that Walter, who passed away in 2012, will never see his dream come true. Now his only chance to see a statue is from above when the CCC children and friends raise the rest of the money to erect a statue to honor these great men.

In 2014 Walter's daughter, Pam Brand, started a campaign to raise funds for her dad's dream of placing a CCC Worker statue in the Chatfield Hollow State Park.

Hugo DeSarro

In Jan. 2009 I stopped at my favorite restaurant, "The Cooking Company" in Tylerville near Haddam Conn. I asked a worker, Annette DeSarro Bellows, if she had any family members in the CCC. She said her dad, Hugo DeSarro, had been in Colorado and that he lived in my town of East Hampton. She gave me his phone number.

I called Hugo and arranged for an interview in February. Here is what he told me about his life and experiences in the CCC.

"My mother, Louise Martino, had 13 children, but one died at a young age. There were six boys and six girls. I am the last surviving child. There were some days when I didn't have a shirt to wear to school because the other kids got to them first. I remember going to school without a shirt and

Hugo DeSarro talking at a CCC Legacy Gathering in Connecticut in Sept. 2015. He told of his experiences at a CCC camp in Meeker, Colo. in 1938.

was sent home.

"When I got older I tried to help my family. During high school I worked after school and weekends at chicken farms. After I graduated I worked in horse stables as a groom, cleaning stables and helping saddle up riders. I worked at Keney Park Riding Stable in Hartford, the Hobbie Horse Stable in Watertown, and the Farmington Polo Stable.

"Then I hitchhiked to Florida with some friends in search of a job. We started with an old automobile, an Overland, and each day we got several flat tires. I only had $6. We didn't have enough money to get a place to sleep so we stopped at the police stations and asked if we could sleep there. We slept in jails all the way down and back. When we got to Florida we only stayed a few days because there were no jobs.

"On our way home our car broke down and we hitchhiked the rest of the way home. It was hard finding rides in Pennsylvania and we walked practically all the way through that state. It was quite an experience.

"In 1937 I graduated from Weaver High School in Hartford and worked at many jobs. I and most people just didn't lay back and wait for a job; we looked hard. I walked from one end of Barber St. to the South end of Hartford and stopped at the many offices and asked if they had any work.

"Everybody knew about the CCC. It was in the newspapers. No one had jobs and it was popular for boys like me who wanted to work and earn money.

"In the spring of 1938 I signed up with other guys

in the Hartford Armory and we got our physicals. I was anxious to get in and help my family.

"We went by train to Fort Devens, Mass. After that we took a slow ride way out West. I didn't know anyone on the train. My brother Alvin also joined the CCC and he went on another train to Grand Junction, Col.

"The trip took about a week. For most of us it was our first time away from home. At first there were no real cooks on the train. They didn't even know how to cook spaghetti. It stuck together like a loaf of bread so we had to cut it with a knife. On the second day they got a better cook.

"Sometimes our train had to pull over on the side and wait for trains to pass. We sat in seats and at night above us there were beds that we pulled down to sleep in. We had to climb up to get in. Some people just slept in their seat.

"The ride was interesting. We passed cities, farms, and forests. To pass the time we played cards.

"After 3 to 4 days we arrived in Grand Junction, Col. in the western section of the state. We went in buses and trucks to Meeker in northwestern Colorado. It was a small place. The only activity in town was the card games in the saloon.

"Our camp was on a ranch about 5 miles from town. The ground sloped to the White River. We often saw ranchers ride by on horses and wagons.

"We lived in barracks. The Army supplied us with old WWI Army clothes. There were no CCC uniforms like at other camps back East.

"In our camp we had some displaced Polish kids (DPs). They were young Polish citizens who escaped from Hitler's invasion into Poland.

"During the spring there were a lot of bugs. We wore jackets over our heads to keep the insects from our faces.

"We had a water barrel fastened on the side of the truck. One day the water didn't taste good but we drank it because we had worked hard and were really thirsty. That night, before going home, a bunch of guys unfastened the barrel from the truck. They emptied the water and a mouse floated out. It was all smooth and shiny. Guys got sick from the sight but no one threw up.

"The second job I had was cutting short cedar trees. We cut off the branches and the ranchers used the posts for fences.

"The next job was killing prairie dogs. We lined up and carried a canvas bag filled with poisoned grain. Ranchers didn't like them because they dug holes and the horses and cows accidentally stepped in them and often broke their legs. We spread out about 50 feet apart and if we saw a hole we put the poison in it.

"Another job was searching for rattlesnakes. The ranchers didn't like them because they sometimes bit the ranchers' horses or cows when the animals got curious and sniffed them. The rattlesnake often bit them on their muzzle and the animal died from the poison. We walked abreast about 30 feet apart and searched for the snakes. When someone saw a rattler in a mesquite bush they'd say: 'Here's one.' Everyone gathered around the bush. They then had to tease or drag the snake out because once you poked them they attacked. They were big snakes compared to our Connecticut domestic snakes.

"The only other thing we did was kill the porcupines because they ate the bark of the trees, which caused the trees to die. Also, farm animals sniffed the porcupines and got the barbs stuck in them. This led to infections and death.

"One time I got sick. They warned us about ticks that carried Rocky Mountain fever. When we worked we often got ticks on us. So in the evening we paired off and examined each other naked. Sometimes they found them under their arms, on eye lids, and in skin creases. I got a fever and started for the infirmary. On the way I passed out. When I came to, several companions helped me to the infirmary. The doctor examined me and said I had a tumor on my chest. He said they wouldn't operate until it got bigger. His diagnosis worried me for several years until I had another physical exam in the Army. The Army doctor examined my chest and said not to worry because it was just my sternum and everyone had one.

"There wasn't much fooling around in camp. We had to work hard. The bed inspections were very strict. You couldn't fight or you'd be punished with KP duty. It was very military. We marched to the mess hall and for the raising and lowering of the flag. It was a great experience for young men. We should have it today.

"I never really suffered because I didn't have enough money because I had food, clothing, and a place to sleep. Money only became a problem when you lost in a card game and had to wait till payday to settle up.

"Payday came at the beginning of the month. We had to line up either outside or inside to get your 5 dollars. There were two lines. One was for the guys being paid and the other line was for the guys waiting to collect money that other boys owed them. The officers sat at a table and paid us in five silver dollars. I often wished that I had saved the silver dollars because they are worth a lot today.

"In the evenings we went into the rec room and played pool, craps, or cards. We played for pennies and nickels. Sometimes we read. I loved to read. We had good times. We told stories and jokes. The canteen was in the rec hall and that is where we bought magazines, candy, soda, popcorn, and cigarettes.

"On the weekends we went to Meeker on Army trucks on Saturday afternoon and stayed till 8 pm. Almost every weekend the ranchers played stud poker at the saloon. Each person knew the other really well and there wasn't any bluffing. We also went fishing in the river near camp and there were a lot of fish in it.

"Sometimes we hitchhiked to Grand Junction where they had a lot going on. It was about 100 miles away. We went to the movies and had a drink or two. We walked around and met some girls but there was no attachment. In those days everybody picked you up when you were hitchhiking. They were generous in giving rides, not like today.

"The food in camp tasted good because we were hungry after a hard day's work. We lined up and marched to the mess hall. We stood at a table until they told us to sit. There were eight guys to a table. When we sat everybody grabbed. The food was good. Sometimes they had fish but it wasn't too popular. One day when I was on KP there were big pots of fish left over and they threw it away.

"After supper I just read a lot. Sometimes I joined other guys and played pickup games of baseball, football, or horseshoes. There were no sports' teams that went to play other CCC camps. We were isolated.

"I remember the mosquitoes were horrible! There were so many it was like a cloud. We put a hood on and used grass to wave in front of our faces to brush them away. That's why I didn't want to join again. So after my six months were up in the fall I was discharged and came home by train.

"When I came home I went to work for a bank and shoveled snow for apartments that belonged to the bank and insurance companies. Then I worked for the Fuller Brush Co.

"Right after WWII began with the bombing of Pearl Harbor, I was waiting to be drafted. My friends who I had worked with at the horse stables and I decided to volunteer so we could choose the service we wanted. We applied to join the cavalry in El Paso, Tex. because we liked working with horses. Then I got a letter saying they weren't enlisting men into the Army cavalry.

"So instead my friends and I chose the coast artillery. We went to Fort Devens, Mass. and then to Fort Eustis in Virginia where we had basic training. I had a good grade on the IQ test and I had three choices: officers' training school, military police, or aviation cadet.

"The last sounded exciting to me. I went to Hemet, Cal. in the San Jacinto Valley. I took college courses and learned about flying, the weather, etc. The training took six months. Then we went to Santa Anna, Calif. where we slept in tents. I flew a single wing plane.

I went to school to be a bombardier, but I didn't like it. I found out that the bombardier was usually the first to die. So, I decided to transfer to be a pilot and went to flight school.

"We used to hitch rides with the more advanced student pilots and I hitched a ride with a student who was flying long distance. The plane had a rough landing and I was knocked unconscious. The Army now considered me a risk because I got a concussion and they moved me to the military police. I was stationed in Hobbs, New Mex.

"Then I was transferred to Utah and on to Florida. I was discharged from the Army in 1945.

"In June of 1946 I married Marietta Randazzo from Hartford. We had three girls: Doreen, Nancy, and Anita.

"I went to the University of Connecticut and majored in English under the GI Bill. In 1950 I graduated, and then got my master's degree in literature from Trinity College in 1951. I worked at nights in the Hartford Post Office.

"I took a civil service examination and went to work for the City of Hartford in the Welfare Dept. as a social worker. In the evenings I worked as an adjunct instructor in English at the University of Hartford. From 1958 to 1965 I was a 'Great Book' discussion leader in the Hartford Public Library neighborhood branches.

"From 1959-1965 I also taught evening classes for the Hartford Board of Education adult classes. In 1965 I was an instructor at the University of Hartford Evening School where I taught grammar and literature until 1973.

"In 1976 I retired from the City of Hartford.

"Over the years, I wrote poetry, three plays, two novels, and published many poems, articles and short stories. I have been writing a weekly Point of View column for the Rivereast weekly newspaper.

"Being in the CCC was a great experience because I

traveled and saw so many wonderful places. I learned to work with others. I enjoyed being with people. We sang going and returning from jobs in the back of army trucks.

"I think the program should be revived. Our kids today need to get out into nature and away from TV. It should be a national program. Many teens could profit from the experience. An increasing number of teens are getting in trouble with drugs, drinking and reckless driving. It would be a big relief for parents to know their children were leading a disciplined life."

Conrad Lussier
Palisades, CO / Voluntown, CT

Paulette Traichel of North Windham called me and said that her father, Conrad Lussier, worked at two CCC camps, one in Colorado and the other in Connecticut. She wanted to know how she could donate his photo albums to the Connecticut CCC Museum where he and my mom used to visit.

"A few weeks later I met her husband Helmut at a restaurant in Willimantic and he let me copy some of the photographs. I then called Paulette to learn more about her father.

"My father was born in 1916 in Willimantic. His father, Eugene, was a watchman at the large American Thread Co. in Willimantic. His mother, Ernestine, had three children: Conrad, Aldege, and Wylda.

"Dad graduated from 8th grade and quit school in

"What a great adventure my father and his friends had traveling to other states and seeing the beauty of the West from the top of a box car." Paulette Traichel

order to help his family since he was the eldest. He heard about the CCC and when he was about 16 years old signed up. The photos in his albums show that he was in Voluntown, Conn. and Palisades, Colo. I'm not sure of the dates when he worked since I don't have his discharge papers.

"After the CCC he was in the Army and during WWII he was in the Hawaiian Islands. One of his jobs was working on a burial detail.

"When my father came home from the war, he worked as a meter reader for the Connecticut Light & Power Co.

"In January 1947 he married Lucy Tirone and they had me and my brother Paul.

"He worked his way up in the power company and became the Collections Manager. My father retired in 1984 when he was 66 years old.

"His time in the CCC had a big effect on him and his family. He was so grateful that the money he earned was able to help his family. My dad loved adventure. He loved traveling out West.

"On Jan. 6, 2001 my father passed away."

Two CCC boys with the camp dog on bags of cement. Paulette Traichel

"During their time off my father (center in boxcar) and his friends liked to hop trains and ride in boxcars." Paulette Traichel

(L–R) 1 "At the Voluntown camp there is a photo of boys clearing trees after the 1938 Hurricane." Paulette Traichel 2 Boys lined up for chow at the tent mess kitchen in Palisades, Colo. Paulette Traichel 3 In 1936 CCC boys worked on irrigation canals in Colorado. They had heated enclosures for the cement to cure during the winter. A cement mixer is on the road above the canal. Paulette Traichel

(L–R) 1 Boy on the tractor used to pull the grader that leveled the walls of the irrigation ditches. Paulette Traichel 2 "He never talked much about his days in the CCC but I think he did construction work in Colorado where the photos show the completed cement wall." Paulette Traichel 3 Conrad and his fellow CCC boys boarding a train to go back home in Connecticut. Paulette Traiche

Raymond Carlson
Meeker, CO

Raymond Carlson sitting on the steps of his CCC barracks in Meeker, Colo. Rosalyn Lachapelle

Rosalyn G. Lachapelle of Voluntown contacted me in the spring of 2011 and said that she saw an article in the Norwich Bulletin about my gathering information on the CCC. She told me her father, Raymond R. Carlson, was in the CCC and stationed in Meeker, Colo.

She said, "I do remember my dad telling me that while at the CCC camp, he and another fellow hopped a freight to California to see a boxing match. They hopped a freight going back to Meeker, too! They were gone a week and no one missed them while they were gone.

"Also, he told me that one time, while walking the tracks, waiting to hop a freight train, he saw a fellow walking towards him. It was dusk. Dad spoke to him, but the fellow never answered and walked right through him. He told me it scared the hell out of him! I bet! Ghosts on the tracks! He could hardly wait for the next train to come through."

A few days later I called Raymond at his home in Ledyard.

I asked him to tell me about his family and why he joined the CCC.

"My father was Cornelius "Raymond" Eskil Carlson and my mother was Agnes Myesky. I was the oldest followed by Harry (Bud) and Joyce. I was born on Oct. 19, 1918. During the Depression my father drove a trolley.

"When I was in 9th grade I quit school because I was an outdoorsman and hated being inside. Things were rough

so I thought I'd help my family out by joining the CCC. I'd also get to see what the West was like. I joined in January 1938 and signed up for six months.

"I went with a group of guys to Ft. Devens and was there for 4-5 days. They gave us shots and clothes. Then we got on an Army train for the long trip to Colorado. Leaving home didn't bother me because I was young and could adjust to anything.

"It was winter and it was pretty cold up there. Our camp was in the Indian Valley. I heard they discovered uranium there and destroyed the area. It was such a beautiful peaceful place.

"I met a few guys from Connecticut. One was Tony and another was 'Copperhead' who had red hair and was from Wallingford."

Q: What work did you do at camp?

A: "I didn't like my first job where I was building roads in Indian Valley. Then they transferred me to the kitchen and I became a second cook. I had to be there about 6 am and get breakfast ready at 7. There were about a dozen guys working in the kitchen. I know we peeled a heck of a lot of potatoes. For lunch I made sandwiches for the guys to take with them to where they worked."

Q: Did anything unusual or funny happen at camp?

A: "The food got so bad at camp because the main cook got too repetitious and boring. The whole camp rebelled and went on strike. I remember the lieutenant sat on the kitchen steps with a revolver and said he'd shoot anyone who advanced towards the cooks.

"Those damn ticks were as big as rabbits. You went to bed at night and woke up in the morning and had 4-5

On weekends Raymond Carlson and other CCC boys visited the town of Meeker, Colo. for entertainment. Ray is leaning against a hitching post where the cowboys tied their horses. Rosalyn Lachapelle

tics imbedded in the back of your legs. Some caused Rocky Mountain fever.

"We had a greenhorn who took all the bedding, sheets and blankets and spread them out in the sagebrush to air out and, boy, did he get chewed out by the captain.

"There were a lot of CCC camps where the boys couldn't stand the Army discipline and being away from home so they left camp. The Army wrote them up as AWOL in their records but they didn't chase after them. I saw a lot of freight trains going by the station in town with ex-CCC boys and hobos sitting right on top of the boxcars.

"A man named Schultz was the owner of the ranchland that our camp was on. He had a daughter named Avis. I met her along the river one day. She was a nice person. We got along well with the local farmers but there were some people who didn't seem to appreciate us being out there.

"Once I got lost mountain hiking and I got pretty scared. Then I followed the sun and the stream till I got back to camp."

Q: What did you do in camp in the evenings and on weekends?

A: "I hung around camp, talked with fellas, read books and magazines, and sometimes walked or hitchhiked to town (6 mi. away).

"Sometimes my friends and I went to the nearest town, Meeker. I remember when the cowboys came into town on horses and tied their horses to a hitching post. The cowboys stayed the whole weekend, played cards, and drank.

"One night I was walking from Meeker back to camp and I met a mountain lion. It was about 6 feet long. I tried to advance near him but he didn't move. He just growled. I knew the sheepherders were coming through soon and I decided to wait it out. We both glared at each other until a truck pulled up and the cat bounded into the bushes.

"I left camp one day and roamed the mountains and they all looked the same. So as I headed back to camp, I found a flat plateau or field. It was loaded with Indian pottery in good shape. I went back to see it again but it was gone or maybe I was confused and couldn't find the right field.

"Other times I fished the nearby White River with worms. I caught rainbow trout.

"One time I went with the captain to Trappers Lake and enjoyed taking pictures. It was beautiful up there.

"There wasn't much sports recreation. The land was pretty rough for sports."

Q: How long did you stay in the CCC and why did you leave?

A: "I stayed in till June 1938. I decided not to sign up for another six months because I thought I had enough and I wanted to go home.

"When I got home I walked right into the '38 Hurricane in September. My first job was working for a veterinarian in Norwich. I just assisted him putting animals to sleep. One time a guy brought in a goat with a chain on its neck and it was all infected.

"I then got a job working as a cook in a restaurant and I got a lot of compliments.

"In 1942 I was drafted into the Army and went to Fort George Wright in Spokane, Washington. I worked in the surgery department in the hospital.

"Then I met my wife, Maxine Stowell, at an ice skating rink. In about eight months we got married on Sept. 25th 1943.

"After I was married they were looking for men to work in the maternity ward and I got the job.

"My wife and I eventually had four children: Roslyn, Naomi, Greg, and Saralee. Then we adopted Paul & Gayle who were Sioux Indians.

"After WWII I worked for the American Thermos Bottle Co. and US Finishing Co. in Norwich. Then I worked at the J. B. Martin Velvet Mill. My last job was at the Norwich Post Office.

"When I retired I did a lot of fishing and photography. I also traveled. Every year my wife and I went out West but I never went back to my campground. I'm glad I didn't see it become a modern town.

"I think that the time I spent in the CCC helped me grow up. It was a good experience."

Raymond Carlson passed away on Nov. 16, 2011.

John "Jack" Scully
Sunbeam, CO

I was searching for stories on the Internet about the CCC in Connecticut and I found a John Scully who in 2008 wrote in the Guilford Forum that he was in a CCC camp in Sunbeam, Col.

On Dec. 10, 2014 I called Jack to see if he was still alive. A man answered and I asked if Jack Scully was home. The man replied, "I'm Jack Scully!" I was overjoyed that I was speaking to a CCC boy who was still alive. I read the

John "Jack" Scully at his home in Newington where he shared his stories and photos of his CCC days in Sunbeam Colorado. Podskoch

notes on him that I found on the internet and he said it was all correct. So I asked him if I could interview him about his life and experiences in the CCC.

"My life began on Feb. 20, 1920 in Hartford. My parents were John W. Scully and my mother was Irene Halloran. Dad worked for Lincoln Dairy in Hartford. There were five children in my family. I was the eldest followed by Dorothy, Evelyn, Louis, and Irene.

"My school buddy in Hartford was Bill Keyes. Every day we both walked from Franklin Ave. to Burr School on Wethersfield Ave. Bill left school early and joined the CCC and went to Delores, Col. He said he liked it so I decided to join with the hopes of being sent to his camp. When I told my mother I wanted to join the CCC she insisted that I finish high school first. So after I graduated from high school I signed up expecting to join Bill in Colorado. I did not realize at that time how big a state Colorado was.

"On July 5, 1939 I signed up in Hartford and the Army sent me to Fort Devens, Mass. Then I was placed on a train with other recruits and sent to a Camp in Sunbeam, Col. It was a terrible trip. It was July and it was really hot. We stopped on a side track in the Chicago Stock Yards and it stunk like hell. We couldn't shut the windows because of the heat. On the trip we went through seven tunnels that were interesting.

"The train finally stopped in Craig and they took us west to our camp in Sunbeam. Our group was called Company 2127. There were farms all around us. We lived in barracks. There were two big potbelly stoves on each

end of the building that burned wood. The officers warned us about fires. They said if there is a fire: 'Take your foot locker, throw it high out the window, and don't let go of the handle.'

"The guys in camp were mostly from Connecticut, Rhode Island, and the Boston area. One of my best friends was a guy named Deacon.

"My first job was working on an earthen dam. We were building a spillway that needed a lot of broken rocks. Our job was breaking the stones using sledge hammers.

"Then I was sent to build a side camp with about 15 men and a foreman. It was 30 miles northwest of our camp in Irish Canyon near the Wyoming border. Our job was to build an earthen dam. We went to a spring and dammed it up to form a small pond. Another group of guys was building a support for a metal water tank. A pump was used to draw the water from the dammed pond into the tank. Then guys laid pipes from the tank to our camp below. Our side camp had three wooden buildings. We built a shower room, and a wood stove heated the water. The cook had a separate building for cooking and he slept there, too. The last building was our barracks.

"One morning we woke up covered with snow because we hadn't finished the roof. After that we made sure the roof was a priority.

"In the fall of 1939 we had a week's vacation and Kelly (from Boston) and I decided to go see the World's Fair on Treasure Island in San Francisco. One of the foremen at Sunbeam gave us the name and address of his brother in San Francisco and asked us to look him up. We Left Sunbeam

Scully was in great shape doing a lot of outside physical work at Camp Sunbeam from 1939-1940. Jack Scully

The Golden Gate International Exposition

The Golden Gate International Exposition, held at San Francisco's Treasure Island, was a World's Fair celebrating, among other things, the city's two newly built bridges. The San Francisco-Oakland Bay Bridge opened in 1936 and the Golden Gate Bridge in 1937. The exposition opened from Feb. 18, 1939, through Oct. 29, 1939, and from May 25, 1940, through Sep. 29, 1940. (http://en.wikipedia.org/wiki/Golden_Gate_International_Exposition)

A 1939 post card of The Golden Gate International Exposition. http://www.treasureislandmuseum.org/wishyouwerehere/

and started hitchhiking west. We went through Meeker and lucked out on a good pick up. The gentleman who picked us up asked if we could drive and we assured him we could. So he explained to us that he had taken a train from California to Chicago to buy a new car. He heard he could pick it up cheaper in Chicago than in California. So he said he had to be back by Monday in order to go back to work so he wanted us to drive at night while he caught up on his sleep. This was a big break for us as he drove all day and we drove all night in his brand new car. We must have left camp on a Saturday morning and got picked up the same day. I do not even remember the make and model of the car but it was brand new and only had a very few miles on it.

"On Sunday morning we arrived at Burbank Cal., his destination, and then we had to hitchhike north to San Francisco. We finally made it and looked up our foreman's brother who showed us all around San Francisco. I remember him taking us up to a very high hill where we had a good view of the San Francisco Bay Bridge.

"We stayed in a hotel and next day we took a trip to Treasure Island and explored the wonders of the World's Fair. We had our picture taken with a Japanese girl to send home to our family.

"The next day we started back to Colorado via the northern route. We got a few good rides along Route 80, but we got stuck in Elko Nevada. We ate there and walked to the outskirts of town to start hitchhiking again. I remember there was a billboard where we were waving our thumb for the few passing cars. On the billboard there were a lot of comments on how many days previous hitchhikers had been in this same spot waiting to be picked up. So we thought we were really stuck there for the rest of our lives.

"When evening came we went back to town and ate and spent the night there and came back out the next day. But luck was with us. We did get a ride all the way across the Great Salt Lake into Ogden, Utah. He dropped us off there and we hitched various rides back to camp. We lucked out.

"In the late fall of 1939 our camp was asked by forest rangers to assist in counting the deer and bears killed by hunters in our area. We had a small trailer packed with food for a couple of weeks and a portable tent for sleeping quarters. They informed me that I was the cook. So I remember I made a very big pot of oatmeal that first day, but nobody cared for oatmeal, and they had very little of it. So I was stuck with finishing up a lot of oatmeal as it seemed a shame to throw it all away.

"We were stationed at the edge of the White Forest and assisted the rangers in their count and checking of deer and bear. The hunters would bring them down out of the mountains draped over their cars or trucks and we would stand by and watch the rangers check the animals for disease while they measured them and took other information, especially about the location where they were shot. I forget how long we spent on this particular assignment, but we all thought it was very interesting to watch these rangers do their job.

"There was one morning when we woke up and looked out our windows. We only saw white. It wasn't snow but thousands of sheep the ranchers were bringing in for sheering.

"My third job was working in the blacksmith shop in the winter. I liked that because it was warm working there. I got up early, walked up to the blacksmith shop and started the potbelly stove. The stove in the blacksmith shop was not as big as the ones in the barracks, but the shop was smaller.

"We repaired a lot of tools. It was mostly picks that

seemed to break off their pointed edge. It was probably due to chopping on frozen ground when the crews were building roads. Deacon Wilczek, the blacksmith, was the one who heated them up in a hot furnace and I was the one who put new handles on them. After Deacon heated up the picks in the forge, he shaped them with a heavy hammer. When he put a new point on them, he would reheat them in the forge and watch the color. He said he was looking for a straw color. He knew what he was looking for and when he saw the right color he would grab the pick by tongs and shove it into a barrel of water to cool it off. It was very interesting to watch him work the forge. I do not remember how long I worked in the blacksmith shop, but we were kept busy with a lot of broken points on tools that winter. Deacon was an easy guy to work with and I enjoyed working with him. He did most of the hard stuff and instructed me on just how to shave down the handles which were reinserted to picks, sledge hammers, shovel handles, and other tools that needed repair.

"In the springtime we built culverts using cedar logs. One day the roads were windy. We heard a roar and our foreman Gil yelled, 'Get out of the culvert fast!' We ran like hell.

"There was a large roar and a gigantic wall of mud from a flash flood came roaring down the mountain. It washed away all our equipment and all of our work went down the stream.

"I never got really sick but I had bad teeth. The Army had a traveling dentist. He pulled six of my teeth. Oh, that night I had a bucket of blood next to my bunk from spitting. It was terrible night.

"Guys used to kill the rattlesnakes to make belts. One guy killed a king snake and the foreman yelled at him because those snakes killed rattlers.

"I remember one incident at camp that was funny as hell. Most of the guys were from Massachusetts, Rhode Island, and Connecticut. We weren't used to anything fancy. We were given old WWI uniforms. In the winter they issued us long johns underwear. We never wore them before. We put them on and danced all around the bunks because it was a novelty.

"They had a lot of ticks in the cedar trees we were cutting down. We cut down the trees and took truckloads over Rabbit Ear Pass to the town of Walden where there was another CCC camp. We met a guy up there named Sandy. He was a tough guy, a real Texan.

"When we came home after handling the cedar trees, we took a shower. A guy in camp was collecting ticks from us and put them in a jar. I have no idea why he did this.

"One day I had a fever and didn't know what it was from. I went to the infirmary and discovered a tick in my crotch and it was all red. The doctor took a bottle of iodine and put it on the tick. It killed it and then they pulled it out. All the sheep we saw also had ticks.

"In our free time while we were at the side camp we hunted for arrowheads. I also learned how to play chess from a guy from Boston.

"At our main camp we had a basketball team. One time we played the local firemen's team. That's where we met Sandy again. We got there early and went to a gin mill. Sandy bought us a bottle of beer and everyone else in the bar. Then the cook walked in and didn't want to be outdone by Sandy so he bought everyone a beer. It went on and on until the table was full of beer.

(L–R) 1 Francis Mann, a CCC enrollee, displayed the head of a big buck that he shot. It had a 46.5" antler spread. Jack Scully 2 "One time we took a rec trip to Rock Springs, Wyo. When we got there we just looked around, had lunch, and then came home. We also saw girls and that was the first time we saw girls in a long time." Jack Scully 3 "Here is a picture I took of one of the fellows in my barracks. They started to give him a haircut but he ended up with a 'baldy.' He looked like a convict. Then about nine other guys in camp got one." Jack Scully

"Then we had to go and play basketball. One guy on our team named King was really good and carried us during the game. It's a good thing because everyone was looped. I didn't know who won the game because I drank too much.

"In the spring and summer we played baseball games in back of camp.

"On the weekends we did our laundry, changed our bunks, and slept. On Saturday morning they inspected our barracks and in the afternoon we went to the movie house. One time when I went to the movies I gave the person a ten dollar bill and he gave me nine silver dollars back. The coins were so heavy I walked sideways into the theater because it weighed me down.

"Sometimes on Sunday a priest came to camp for mass.

"The food at camp was OK but we went on strike once because the food was too repetitive. The top sergeant was mad as hell. He blew his whistle in the morning for us to leave our barracks and begin working but nobody came out. It was finally resolved when they got a new cook. My favorite food was hamburgers.

"I was in Colorado for two 6-month stints but after a year I decided to go home. Well, I had gone out there to meet my buddy but didn't get into his camp. Then I heard from him and he said he had joined the Army. I didn't want to join the Army so I went home. I was discharged from camp on June 23, 1940 and travelled by train for five days and arrived on June 28th at Fort Devens, Mass.

"I loved it out there in Colorado, the country and fresh air. When I got home I couldn't find a job and I wished I was back there working.

(L–R) 1 Gil Redick was a foreman at the Sunbeam CCC camp. 2 Camp Sunbeam enrollees helped the Colorado Game officers in registering and inspecting deer and bear at an inspection station in Hayden, CO. Jack Scully

"In 1941 I got a job with Adley Express as a clerk in West Hartford. My buddy and I heard about a class that was being taught w in Springfield, Mass. So we went there and learned doing inspections for the government. We were taught how to use gauges. After that we got a job at Colts Manufacturing in Hartford.

"Then in June 1942 I joined the Army and was sent to Fort Devens. From there I was transferred to Fort Mead. Next I went for training at Fort Bragg, NC and was in the Ninth Infantry Division. We were shipped to North Africa. Here we stopped Rommel and his German army. Then we went to Sicily. After Italy we went to England to prepare for the invasion into France. Our group went in on the second day of the invasion of Normandy, France. We landed on Utah Beach and fought the Germans through France and all the way to Germany.

"After the war I came home in Oct. 1945. I went to Bentley School of Accounting in Boston. I was there for two years. Then I worked for Downing & Perkins Trucking Co. in Hartford. I worked there for 12 years. My final job was working for Schuster Express in Colchester where I did accounting. I retired in 1982.

"In 1949 I married Margaret Elizabeth Lyman. We had four children: Margaret, John, Kathleen, and Thomas.

"My wife and I took a motor trip out to Colorado as we were going to visit my son who was in Texas at that time. So we crossed the Rocky Mountains at Rabbit Ears Pass and went to Craig and Sunbeam. I had a hard time finding my camp. Then I spotted a small sign saying 'Sunbeam.' I drove to a farmhouse and a bunch of dogs surrounded us. Then a lady came out of the house and quieted the dogs. We asked her where was my old CCC camp? She said, 'The camp was right across the road.' I walked over but there were only cement pilings. The rest of the camp went to seed.

"I also remember visiting 'The Serpent's Trail' in the CCC but could not remember where it was. From Sunbeam we drove down to Grand Junction and spotted the sign for Colorado National Monument. We had a Senior Citizen Pass for National Parks so we took a ride into the park which we thought was a great place. But what was interesting was when they gave us a directory of the trails through the Monument, I saw the Serpents Trail. It was located on the opposite entrance to the one we had used to enter the Park. As it was only a one-way trail we did not get to see it. But while in the CCC our foreman Gill Reddick had taken a truckload of us on a recreational trip there. We had a very good driver. Gill Reddick rode with him in the front seat giving him directions about taking all the twists and turns up this treacherous trail. One curve ran into another curve as we ascended the mountain. A couple of turns were so sharp that the truck had to back up a couple of times to make the turn. The drop on either side of this trail was about 1000 feet. We were all very excited about this ride and a little frightened about the drop on either side. We were in an opentop rack truck and were packed in with about 30 guys. So when we looked out all we could see was the drop on the side of the mountain. It was scary but we were young and just very excited about the whole trip.

"After our visit to Monument Park, my wife and I drove through the town of Grand Junction in the southwest corner of Colorado and that is where I think I saw a mailbox with the name Reddick on it. It made me think that my old foreman lived there.

"When someone asks me what I learned in the CCC my time working in the blacksmith shop stands out the most. There I learned how to fix tools. Building the side camp was also interesting. I think the CCC program should be revived today to give young people a job building our country."

Frank Renzoni
Palisades, CO

Frank Renzoni came to a CCC Reunion at Burr Pond State Park near Torrington in 2010 where he enjoyed sharing his stories about his CCC days in Colorado.
Podskoch

"I was born on Jan. 13, 1921 in Waterbury. My father, Innocenzo, was a shoemaker in Naugatuck, but lost his job during the Depression. He then worked in shoemaker shops to support our family. My mother, Maria (Ciarleglio), had five other children: Lena, Joseph, Vinnie, Tony, and Victor.

"It was in the newspaper that I learned about the CCC. In April 1938 I went by myself and signed up in Waterbury. I was 17. They sent me to Fort Devens, Mass. I didn't mind leaving home at all.

"We were loaded on a train that went out West. It was interesting going through the Royal Divide and Moffit Tunnel. The views and scenery were very pretty.

"I remember when we got out there in the afternoon it was hot. They issued each of us five blankets and a quilt. I said, 'What are these for?' They said, 'You'll need them!' That night it dropped to 35 below zero. We had three potbelly stoves that were white hot.

"Our camp was in a valley. The one thing that I remember was the cleanliness of the barracks. We had to take our blankets and shake out the dust with another guy. When the Captain hit the bunk with his riding crop and dust came up from the blanket, he'd rip the whole thing off our cot and we'd have to do it all over again. If our barracks had too many bad points, the whole barracks had to whitewash the whole building. He also had a white glove that he rubbed over the walls and if there was dirt, he'd motion to the Master Sergeant. All the bunks would be taken out and we had to wash the floor and clean everything. Every Saturday we had to clean the whole barracks and shine our shoes.

"We never had refrigeration. They dug a hole in the ground and hung the meat down there. It got mildew but it was aged and great. I remember going down there for eggs.

"I had a couple of friends in camp that were also from Connecticut. They were Joseph Augistini from Bridgeport and Joseph Amoranti from New Haven.

"Our camp was building the High Line Canal, which was a tributary of the Colorado River. It was used by farmers for irrigation. I was goldbricking a lot of the time. I mostly did pick and shovel and cutting brush work. Then I was startled by a big bull snake that was about 5' long and 8" in diameter. They'd be laying there and I'd get startled and run like hell.

"I had one fellow who was a veteran in camp. He told me what to watch out for when they try to do jokes on me. They had tricks to have rookies water the flagpole to make it grow. They also would make you go to the motor pool to ask the foreman, Walter Moss, for a sky hook. There is no such thing.

"Another joke was to have you go to the motor pool to get a bunk stretcher because some tall guy's feet went over the bunk. Another trick was taking the rookies on a snipe hunt. There is no such animal. They sent rookies into the woods with a burlap bag and told them to yell, 'Over here snipe!' The more gullible you were the more they gave you.

"I was also forewarned by this older guy on how to avoid work. He said to bring along a pile of comic books and to hide in the truck and read. If they found me, I'd say I just came from some hard job and was so tired I was just taking a rest.

"After work we went to eat in the mess hall. We had two shifts for eating. The food was good. Whatever it was, it was good, except for the first three days. There was a stew that wasn't like the kind Mom made and I started to groan. The mess sergeant heard me and said, 'What's wrong?' I told him I didn't care for the stew. He replied: 'I want to see you in the kitchen.' I thought he was going to give me some better food, instead he said, 'Frank, I want to see you in the morning after reveille.

"The next morning I went to the kitchen. He put me on KP duty: I had to wash dishes and peel potatoes. The dishes were endless. This taught me to never complain. I really started eating after that. It didn't taste bad at all.

"After dinner we'd go outside and sing songs with someone who had a guitar or tell stories and jokes. Some guys would walk to town. It wasn't far to Palisades. It was a

The entrance to Camp Mesa BR-50 near Grand Junction in the SW section of Colorado. CCC Legacy

tiny town with one store and dirt streets.

"On the weekends we took a truck to Grand Junction to walk around and see if we could meet some girls. They had a very small movie theater and no bars. One time we went to a rodeo. It was interesting.

"In camp they had a ball team that I think played other companies. But I wasn't into sports and didn't get involved.

"After a while, about five months, camp life wasn't going too well and I decided not to sign up for another six months. So I went home. It took about four days by train. We had something like a Pullman car. The food was not bad. The smoke and dirt came into the car just like when we went West. I do remember the beauty of the West.

"Honestly I learned to get along with everybody. I learned to get along with ignorant guys who didn't even know their own name. I think we gave them a nickname: 'Chucky'.

"When I came home I went to work for Princeton Knitting Mills in Watertown and got 25 cents an hour. It was the only job I ever lost. I took it hard. Then I went to work for Max Weinbach Upholstery. We made sofas and chairs. I was learning to be an upholsterer.

"I joined the National Guard and then after a month we were federalized. I left Waterbury in 1940. I went to Florida and after a year I hated the company commander. I heard they were looking for air cadets. When I went to the commander and asked to take the test he gave me permission. I looked on the board for the names of the guys who passed and my name was there. I asked him for permission to go to the school but he refused to let me go even though I had passed the test.

"Then my company was sent to Georgia. After Pearl Harbor I was shipped to Bora Bora in the Pacific Ocean.

Camp Mesa BR-59 was located along the Colorado River. The camp's main task was rehabilitating the Grand Valley Project that was begun in the late 1800s. It was an irrigation project that converted arid land to fertile farm-land. The camp was established in 1935 and they worked for six years to repair irrigation projects: they lined and reinforced large segments of the main canal; replaced culverts, flumes, and drops; installed drains and did rodent and weed control. CCC Legacy

It was the most beautiful island I had ever seen. We fixed the road so when the General drove on it, he wouldn't drop any cigar ashes on himself. Then they looked for air cadets again. I took the same test but flunked out. Seventeen other guys passed the test to be pilots and they were shipped to Germany where they were shot down. I was lucky that I flunked the test.

"We then went to the Coral Sea and moved onto islands but everything was safe. I was able to make it to the end of the war without any injuries.

"After the war I had many jobs. The one I had the longest was when I worked at Meriden Auction Rooms. It was a furniture and appliance store. I was a salesman and I was there for 17 years. Then I was out of work for a time till I worked for Hallocks Furniture.

"In 1947 I married Mary Calvo of Waterbury. We had two sons: Ted and Richard. We were married for 47 years. She died in 1993. I felt like I was in a shell. I didn't want to be in public. One day after seven months a voice said, 'Till death do us part.' It jelled in me. I had to continue my life.'"

"I feel that everyone about 18 years old should serve either in a CCC camp or in the Army. Then they will learn to take care of themselves. They will meet people from all over the country. Many of the boys at my camp were without education but I learned to get along with them."

On April 11, 2014 Frank passed away at the age of 93.

Pat Spino
Pueblo, CO

In 2010 Pat "Patsy" Spino of Naugatuck enjoyed telling CCC stories at a CCC Reunion in the Goodwin State Forest in Hampton, Conn.

Joe Iadarola of Watertown told me that a friend of his, Pat Spino, grew up with him in Waterbury and was also with him at Camp #2124 in Buelha, Colo. Joe gave me his phone number and I promised to call Pat.

On March 16, 2009 I interviewed Pat "Patsy" Spino by phone at his home in Naugatuck, Conn. He told me about his family and time in the CCC.

"I was born in Waterbury on Nov. 22, 1920. I had an older sister named Adeline. My father Mike died when I was young. My mother, Concetta, remarried a man named Pasquale who worked for the town of Waterbury.

"When I was in school I lost my hearing when I got an eraser stuck in my ear. I had trouble learning and didn't do well in school. Then years later a doctor took it out. It still looked brand new. I also think my hearing problems came from swimming a lot in really dirty water.

"When I went to high school I only stayed for two weeks and then quit. It was hard getting a job so I just had odd jobs.

"In 1939 when I was 19 I heard other guys talking about the CCC so I signed up. I was surprised when they took me.

"I felt good about going away. We went to Colorado by train. The trains were going fast. At night we slept in sleeper cars. It was a long trip, about five days.

"Our camp was just before the Rockies near Pueblo. When we arrived at camp, I looked at the mountains and I said to myself, 'I bet I could walk to the mountains in five minutes.' I found out how wrong I was when we drove by truck towards the mountains to work. We drove about 35 miles but we still weren't there.

"I never got homesick but one guy was so homesick he cried every day so they shipped him back to Massachusetts."

Q: What jobs did you do and what did you do in your free time and on weekends?

A: "My main job was digging irrigation ditches. We saw a lot of snakes. We always brought a shovel with us to go to the bathroom for protection in case we saw any snakes. And each day at noon a truck came down and brought us lunch.

"After work we came back to camp and had supper. The food was great. I gained 24 pounds in three months. I only weighed 120 pounds when I arrived. They called me and my friend Charley Bredice the 'Chow Hounds' because we ate everything.

"Then we had free time in the evening. We just got

together and played games. I played a lot of baseball with the guys. There were times I stole bread and butter from the kitchen and we went behind a mound of dirt, built a fire, and ate. Some camps had a boxing ring but ours didn't. There was one guy who bragged about being a great fighter. Then my friend beat him up.

"On the weekends we stayed at camp. One time, though, a truck took us to Pueblo. It had one big street. We went to a whorehouse. They charged a dollar. I wasn't nervous because I did a little at home. Three girls paraded in front of us and asked, 'Who wants to go first?' One guy named Carbo had never been in a place like this said, 'I'll go first.' He went around the corner and was done before he got in bed. We laughed so hard. I wanted to go twice but I only had one dollar. There were a lot of whorehouses in town and the girls were hanging out the windows calling you in.

"When we came back from town we went straight to the infirmary and the doctor gave us liquid for inside the penis and lotion on the outside. Every Sunday morning the doctor went through camp, checking us out for any diseases.

"They had some education classes in the evening but the only class that I went to was when a guy came to camp and taught us magic tricks. I had a trick I did for the guys. I had a glass that had a hole in the bottom. When I lifted it up flowers came up. Guys wondered how they got in there. I didn't tell them that there was a string attached to my stomach. It happened so fast.

"After six months in the CCC I was going to sign up again but my mother said I should come home because she had a job for me.

"When I came home I had a job in the Shoe Hardware Co. working on machines. I quit after a few months and got a job in the Rubber Shop Co. in Naugatuck. I worked there for 30 years.

"In 1941 I married Emilia and we had four children: Sandra, Donna, Robert, and Chris."

Q: Did you participate in WWII?

A: "No, because of my poor hearing. I went through grammar school without hearing anything.

Q: What effect did your time in the CCC have on you?

A: "It was good for me. It was different. I had a great time in the CCC and I'd do it again."

Pat Spino passed away on July 9, 2013.

Martin O'Brien
Bartlett, NH

Martin O'Brien of Naugatuck worked at the CCC camp in Bartlett, NH. Philip O'Brien

On June 6, 2008 I interviewed Martin O'Brien by phone and he shared his life story and experiences in the CCC.

"My parents Martin and Ellen O'Brien had seven children: Nell, Janet, Mary, Michael, twins Joseph & James, and I was the youngest.

"I was born on July 4, 1917 in Waterbury. My father worked in a rubber shop on Maple St. where he made shoes.

"I graduated from elementary school, but when I was 15, I dropped out of school with my brother, James, who was in 11th grade. My family needed money for food. I worked in a gas station, a glass factory, and then the rubber shop. I serviced a conveyer and made $18 dollars a week.

"My brother Jim joined the CCC two years before me. That's how I learned about the CCC. He came home almost every weekend with his buddy Edmond Lawlor. They hitchhiked down Rt. 8.

"So on my birthday, July 4th, 1935, I signed up to join the CCC. I met two buddies when I was examined; Bill Donavan and I forgot the other guy's name.

"It took about two weeks before we were taken to Bartlett, NH. The town was in the eastern part of the state on Rt. 302. We started off sleeping in a tent for about two weeks. When the barracks were completed we moved in. It rained a lot. It was nice inside and the roof didn't leak like our old tent.

"Our camp was building a road to Saco and another camp was doing the same coming from Saco. We were chopping trees for the new road. One group chopped trees down, one took off the limbs, and another cut the logs into lengths. I was lucky that I never got injured working."

Q: Did anything scary or funny happened at his camp?

A: "We were going into the town of Bartlett to a movie house. There were 22 of us in an Army truck. As we were going down a steep hill, the driver lost brakes, and we went flying down the hill. When we reached the bridge we banged off both sides of the metal bridge going across. Finally, there was a runaway truck trail that he ran up. Then we sent one of the guys who knew someone in the area. He called camp and they sent help. It took from 2 am to 4 am for them to reach us. They took us home and it was almost 6 am so we stayed up and went to eat.

"Then we went on a truck to work. At our 10 am break time, we all fell asleep and it was the best sleep I ever had.

"Another scary thing happened when they called in a LEM to show us how to use an axe. Our lieutenant said we had to go. So we went. The man got up and made one swing. It bounced off the log and hit him in his left foot. Blood was gushing all over. They wrapped his legs in towels and rushed him to Boston.

"There was also some fun and jokes. Sometimes we put shaving cream in a guy's bed that was also short-sheeted. Then they had to hit the shower fast to clean up. One guy used to snore so they picked up his bed and put him in the field to have some quiet in the barracks."

Q: What did you do in your free time?

A: "In the evenings there was a guy who played a guitar while others sang. We also loved to listen to one radio station that had music. It was in one big tent that was our rec hall. One night when lightning hit we all ran outside. The lightning damaged the radio and that was the end of our entertainment. We also threw a football and played catch. There wasn't much open space at our camp for baseball.

"We liked to hike a lot. One time a bunch of guys went for a walk. We got a call from them and they were seven miles away and we had to go and pick them up.

"One time we visited Mount Washington. We had a big gang. One group hiked up and the other rode up. Then they reversed it on the way down. It was nice walking up. It was so beautiful. They told us to wear a jacket. By the time we got three-quarters up it was really cold. At the top it

was really windy and we went inside a huge lodge. It was a weather station."

Q: How was the food at camp?

A: "It was excellent. We had a big breakfast and a light lunch with fruit. Then at night we sometimes had steak. We were buddies with the cook because we helped him the first night when it started to rain. We helped him put up all his pans so that he could reach them. After helping him he told us, 'Whenever you need anything let me know. I will never forget you.'

"That night we lost our raincoats. So we told our cook that we were stuck. He called over to the supply clerk and told him our problem. He told the clerk, 'If you want to eat, you better get three raincoats over here quick.' And we got our raincoats. We never forgot him. He also told us that if we ever get hungry to just come down.

"One day we were moping around. The cook asked us, 'Why are you so sad?' We said we were on KP but we'd rather be out chopping wood. The cook called the guy who made up the lists and told him to take us off the list, and we were never on the KP list again.

"In September 1935 I decided not to sign up for another six months in the CCC because I didn't make enough money to live on. I was smoking like a smoke stack and needed more money. I heard from my oldest brother that jobs were opening up. So I finished up my hitch on Sept. 30th and went home. I think someone in camp gave me a ride to Bartlett and my brother came to pick me up.

"When I got home I went to US Rubber Co. to apply for a job. I sat in a room and waited for the boss to see if there were any jobs. One day I stayed after everyone left. The boss came out. 'Didn't you know there was no work?' he asked. 'How is your math?'

"I said, 'Fine.' He sent me to the doctor for an exam. I came back and the boss said, 'Can you get to work tonight?' I told him I could start right now if he wanted. Since women couldn't work after 11 pm, I got the night job of picking and counting parts of a shoe. After that I moved up in another job in the company.

"I married Mildred Mannion on June 29, 1940, and we had four children: Philip, Paul (died), Sharon, and Olive."

Q: Were you in WWII?

A: "No, I had an abscessed ear."

Q: Did you ever go back to your CCC camp?

A: "My son Philip and I went up there to try and find the site but couldn't find it.

"The government should never have stopped the CCC because it took us off the streets. It helped me and my family."

Martin passed away on March 21, 2013.

Joseph "Joe" Bernard Callinan
Claremont, NH

I was asked to speak about the history of the Connecticut CCC camps at a CCC Statue Fundraising at the Norwich VFW on Sunday, June 1, 2014. Pam Brand, daughter of CCC alumni Walter Sekula, organized the gathering. It was Walter's dream to have a CCC statue for Connecticut. In 2012 Walter passed away but his dream was kept alive by his daughter, who decided to organize a drive for a statue. The first event was in Norwich, the home of her father.

It was at this fundraiser that I met Tom Callinan who said that his father, Joseph Bernard Callinan (JBC), was a CCC boy in Claremont, New Hampshire and he was honored to sing CCC songs to help with the fundraising.

Tom, Connecticut 's first Official State Troubadour, had served in the Marine Corps during the Vietnam era, and then become a teacher. After 1977 Tom devoted his life to traveling throughout the state and beyond singing folk songs and also composing his own songs. He spent that afternoon singing songs and the following original CCC song. He dedicated it to his father.

"The Boys of the C.C.C."
by Tom Callinan

In the grip of the Depression in 1933,
A plan to jump-start our economy
Was developed to help uplift the down and out,
And the C.C.C. helped to bring that change about.
When times were tough, and hope was dim,
With hard work, and discipline,
hand-tools, brawn and dedication
They tamed the wilderness, and transformed our nation.

Refrain:
Clearing land, building dams, on behalf of Uncle Sam
We're the boys of the C.C.C.
Connecting bridges to dreams, over rivers and streams,
And planting billions of trees.
We still walk in their footprints in this land of the free,

From the North to the South, and from sea to shining sea.
Providing access to America's beauty
We're the boys of the C.C.C.

A dollar a day and three hots and a cot
May not seem like an awful lot
But hard work sure beat standing in lines
For soup and bread or turning to crime.
Erecting towers to scan for forest fires,
Planting tons of poles to string electric wires,
Controlling erosion with the sweat of their brow,
Paving miles and miles of roads that still are used now

Refrain

Bridge:
As they stood and worked together,
their pride and skills did grow,
And when our land was threatened by a foreign foe,
Those "soil soldiers" became fighting men,
Who marched away with confidence,
our nation to defend.

Refrain

After Tom's performance I asked him to tell me about his dad's time in the CCC.

"My father, Joseph Bernard Callinan, enlisted in the CCC on Aug. 26, 1935. He reported for duty at Fort H.G. Wright on Fishers Island, NY where he served as a laborer for nine days, during which time he turned 20. He was transferred on Sept. 4 to Camp 1185 in Claremont, NH, where he served as a truck driver.

"Dad's discharge papers state that two-and-a-half

Tom Callinan composed a CCC song to honor his father who worked at a camp in New Hampshire. http://www.crackerbarrel-ents.com/Callinan/news.htm

"The composite of my father shows the young, almost cocky Joe Callinan (c. 1935), contrasted with the maturity he acquired during the war where he served in France (c. 1945)." Tom Callinan

months later, on Nov. 18, he was found to have a car in his possession at camp by Dr. Cohen, FTCP (Field Trains Command Post).

"On Nov. 19, JBC was administratively discharged for maintaining and operating a motor vehicle in violation of CCC regulations. With no prior strikes against his record, he pleaded guilty, and didn't wish to appeal the verdict. That's it.

"My thoughts: as a poor young man at barely 20 years of age, I can't believe there would've been any way he could have had the money to buy a car, so I don't know if he was moonlighting, doing some repair-work on the side, or how he might have come to be in possession of a motor vehicle. I would love to know, but alas, the record doesn't go into further detail. I would think if there had been an allegation that he had stolen it, he would have suffered a much more serious penalty than an administrative discharge. Maybe he was just joy riding in a vehicle he had been working on ... I don't know.

"I was totally surprised by this revelation. Whenever he spoke of his time in the CCC, all he ever said was that he worked on a dam-building project, and that he was proud of his service. I wish he were still around (for countless reasons), but especially to shed light on what actually transpired on Nov. 18, 1935.

"But regardless of whatever this youthful indiscretion might have been, we were all 20 years old and rebellious and/or foolish at one time or another. So, needless to say, my love and respect for my dad are undiminished by this discovery, and I still wholeheartedly support the CCC."

I asked Tom to tell me about his father's early life and family.

"My father was born Sept. 2, 1915. His parents were poor but religious immigrants from Ireland. His father, Michael Callinan, came from County Clare, Ireland. He worked as a laborer and teamster. His mother, Bridget Delia Kearns was from County Wexford, Ireland. She worked as chambermaid in her Aunt Mary's boarding house, and later cleaned railroad cars for the NYNHHRR in New Haven. Michael and Bridget met in Fair Haven, Conn. and were married in 1903.

"Dad was the sixth of seven children. His siblings were Tom, Mame, Ceil, Peg, Ellen, and Francis. My father dropped out of high school in either 1932 or 1933 while his brother Tom, the eldest male in his family, was in Ireland, helping their grandparents. Jobs were hard to find, so my Dad joined the CCC.

"According to family legend and lore, he worked on a dam-building project in the Claremont, NH area.

"Dad was very athletic, so he probably boxed and played other sports.

Q: What did he do after he left the CCC?

A: "He worked for United Illuminating Co., in New Haven. Dad then served with the 83rd Infantry Division in the European Theater during WWII and was honorably discharged after the war.

"When Dad came home he became a sheet metal worker in 1946 at Standard-Knapp Mfg. Co., a division of EMHART. He was later promoted to a set-up man.

"That same year Dad married my mom, Ann M. Coleman, on Feb. 20, 1946. They had four children. I was the eldest followed by Tim, Terry, and Jo-Anne.

"Dad earned a high school diploma in 1956 and was very proud of this accomplishment. He retired in 1978.

"On Sept. 24, 1978, Dad died in Middletown.

"I'm delighted that my father will be part of your book, because even though his time in the C.C.C. was short, I know it made a lasting impression on the man he became."

Larry Lavigne
Alfred, ME

My friend Hugo DeSarro, who had been in the CCC in Colorado, told me that a man at the East Hampton Senior Citizens Center had also been in the CCC. Hugo said that I should stop by to talk to him because the CCC

Larry Lavigne of East Hampton told about his life in Maine and his experiences working at the CCC camp in Gardner, Maine. Podskoch

man was there every day.

On Jan. 2, 2015 I was on my way to the East Hampton Library and as I passed the Senior Center I decided to see if the CCC man was there. I asked a secretary if she knew a man that might have been in the CCC. I also added that Hugo knew him. She replied, "It's probably Larry Lavigne and he is over there playing a card game on the computer."

We walked over to Larry and the secretary asked him if he was in the CCC and he said, "Yes, in Maine. I was in Alfred, Maine for three years and they had us trying to stop the gypsy moths."

I asked Larry if I could stop by the following week to ask him about his time in the CCC. "Sure," he replied, "I'm here every day of the week. A bus picks me up at my house at 10:30 and takes me home at 3:30. I love it here."

On Mon., Jan. 5, 2015 I interviewed Larry at the senior center.

"I was born in Brunswick, Maine on July 20, 1922. My parents, Francis and Marian had eight children: Morris, Annette, Lew, Percy, me, Terry, Francis Jr., and Lorraine was the baby.

"My father was a weaver at Bates Manufacturing Co. in Lewiston, Maine. Then during the Depression it was hard for my father to get a job. It was tough to feed eight kids. He got a job with the WPA working on the streets.

"I went to St. Peter's School. My father made me quit school and get a job after eighth grade. The Depression was awful. I got a few jobs. I worked with a guy who picked potatoes and I sold them to my brother-in-law. Then I

worked for my uncle who worked in a brickyard. I used to put them in an oven and that was hard work.

"In the summer of 1938 I heard about the CCC from my Uncle Lyon. I went to the city hall and told a man that I wanted to join the CCC. That day I signed and they shipped me in an Army truck that picked up kids in our town and others.

"The trip was about an hour and a half to Alfred. The camp was about 15 minutes away. There were guys there just like me who didn't know anyone and someone explained to us what to do. It was like the Army where you made your bed and did KP duty. Some guys were from Lewiston, Sanford, Springfield, and Augusta. They were from all over. I wasn't homesick because I made friends easily.

"In the barracks there were coal stoves. We had to get coal from a pile about five minutes away. There was a fireman whose job it was to stay up all night and fill the stoves. We had to keep the widows open about an inch in case of carbon monoxide. Usually the leader of the barracks had the best spot sleeping by the stove. In the summer he had his own room with his own bed.

"My first job was looking for gypsy moth egg masses and we painted them with creosote. We had a can filled with creosote attached to our belt. We had a small brush like you used to polish your shoes to paint the gypsy moth eggs. We made a saddle out of a rope to sit in and we pulled ourselves up the tree. We started from the top and worked our way down. There was a forester down below telling us what to do.

"Besides that we also fought fires. We carried big water tanks on our backs. That was really hard work.

"There were other crews doing jobs. One built waterholes that provided water in the forest when there was a fire.

"In the winter the town picked us up and we worked with them plowing and sanding the roads. Sometimes we had to shovel sand from the trucks.

"After a day's work we had supper in the mess hall. The food was good. Sometimes I did KP duty. I washed the dishes, frying pans, and sometimes a huge pot about this size he said holding his hands about 24 inches apart.

"We went back to the barracks after eating and played cribbage. Some played poker. They played for cigarettes not money.

"One guy tried to play a trick on me by 'short-sheeting' my bed. But before I went to bed someone told me what had been done and he said, 'When you go to bed just pull the cover up and not the sheet.' So I pulled up only the cover and climbed into bed and nicely said, 'Good night guys.'

"In the summer we went to Sanford and worked at the town beach. We painted and cleaned the bathhouses. If they were too bad we took them down and built new ones. We also did work like this in other towns.

"Some weekends we went to Old Orchard Beach and went swimming, played football, and watched the girls. It was a beautiful beach with about five lifeguards.

"We also went in an Army truck to the movies in Sanford. In the winter it was cold in the back of the truck. They just had a canvas top and our breathing helped to warm us up. We liked to look at the girls."

I asked Larry if he ever got hurt or sick?

"No, I never got hurt or sick but there was an infirmary. It was staffed by a CCC boy who was like a nurse and he gave out medicine.

"We had a colonel who was in charge of our camp. He was a good guy.

"If you got in a fight you had to watch out for the other guys because they got after the guy who started the fight.

"Nobody stole anything from anybody because if anyone found out, your name was mud. You were a crook.

"You had your own locker where you kept your underwear, uniform – everything.

"There was a canteen and if you owed them money you paid on pay day. I'm not sure if they had cigarettes but I didn't smoke. There was one guy who had a machine and he rolled his own cigarettes. He used Bugle tobacco. They sold tobacco, candy, and soda. I bought candy. Butterfingers was my favorite."

I asked if there were any team sports in camp?

"We went to Sanford high school where we played baseball and football. These were all pickup games.

"Sometimes on weekends I hitchhiked home. It was about an hour away and it all depended on how long I had to wait for a ride. Most of the time we were lucky to get a ride because we wore our green CCC uniform.

Q: Why did you leave the CCCs?

A: "I stayed for about three years. After the colonel said that he was leaving (I guess he knew the war was coming) a lot of guys didn't sign up again.

"When I came home I got a job again in the brickyard. When it closed I got a job in the shipyard in South Portland. I cleaned inside the ships where they stored the oil. I worked

there for one year and Uncle Sam called me. I was just 21 when I was drafted.

"The Army sent me to the South Pacific I was at Guadalcanal and Bougainville in the Solomon Islands, New Guinea, and the Philippines. I was in one battle in Guadalcanal. The river was red from blood.

"I was in the Army for about two and a half years. When I came home I worked in a shoe factory. There I met Cecile and we got married in 1947. She died in 1990. We had three boys: Donald (died in childbirth) Gary, and Francis.

"My wife's brother went to Bristol, Conn. for a job in New Departure Co. He told my wife there were jobs in the state. So Cecile said let's go to Connecticut because there wasn't any work in Maine. I got a job in Pratt & Whitney and was gun sprayer. I sprayed parts of engines, etc. My family and I lived in East Hartford. I retired in 1983.

"I learned a lot in the CCC. I learned how to take care of myself and not depend on anybody. I wish they had it again. It would take the kids out of the streets where they are shooting one another."

Emanuel "Manny" Monopoli
Chaco Canyon, NM / Augusta, MT

Emanuel "Manny" Monopoli (right) working with two other CCC enrollees in the woods near their camp in Chaco Canyon, New Mexico. Manny Monopoli

I called Emanuel "Manny" Monopoli in Melbourne, Florida, on May 23, 2012 and his wife, Mary, answered. I was elated to find that he was alive and could tell me about his life and adventures in the CCC. He was born in Scranton, PA just 18 miles from where I grew up near Wilkes Barre. We talked about the great Italian restaurants and the making of wine. He then told me about his family and his CCC adventures.

"My father, Andonia, came from Italy and went to Scranton where he worked in the coal mines. When he had trouble finding work during the Depression he got a job with the WPA. He had a large family to raise. My mother, Anne Maria, had 10 children besides me: Veto, Matthew, Santé (who joined the CCC after me and worked in Glacier National Park), Mary, Salvator, Tony, Danny, Frank, Margaret, and Anne.

"I only went to 9th grade because I had to get a job and help my family. My neighbor, who was in the CCC and played the bugle in a CCC camp, told me to go down to the Armory and sign up. I signed up in January 1939.They put me and a couple of my neighbors, including Joseph Tucker of Minooka, on a train and sent us to Chaco Canyon, the site of Chaco Culture National Historical Park (northwest corner of NM).

"When we got to camp they had wooden barracks not like some other camps where the guys lived in tents. I loved being there because I was doing something for my family. I liked being with the guys and learned how to get along with them.

"The guys found out that I knew how to cut hair so I began cutting hair in my barracks. I made 25 cents a head and sent the money home to my parents. I learned how to cut hair because I had worked as an apprentice in Scranton and also from my brother who was a barber.

"Then one day the leader of my barracks said, 'The Captain wants to see you.' I got a little nervous and wondered what he wanted.

"I went to the Captain's office and he said, 'I heard that you're cutting hair in your barracks and that you do a great job. I want you to be the company barber.'

"The next day the Captain took me to the nearest town of Gallup and bought me a barber's chair and all the things a barber needed. During the day I did my regular job and at night I cut hair. On payday the captain handed me a check for $35 dollars that was extra pay for being the camp barber.

"Each month I had a different job in camp. They did this to give us a variety of jobs. My first job was cutting trees in the woods and making fence posts for the ranchers. Then I worked with a crew building roads. When we finished, we planted grass along the road. My next job I learned how to drive a bulldozer. The next job I had was masonry work. We went to canyons where water poured down and did a lot of erosion. We built little dams using rocks and cement. My last job was truck driving. I drove a 1935 dump truck that didn't have a door. Here is where I learned how to shift without using the clutch. I carried rock, sand, gravel, and cement to jobs.

"The food was good. I can't complain. It wasn't like the Italian food I had at home, but I still remember my first meal: pork chops, creamed corn, mashed potatoes and gravy followed by apple pie and ice cream.

"In my free time I fooled around or played baseball, nothing serious. There were camp teams but I never applied because I was too busy cutting hair.

"In those days we used a straight razor when we shaved the guys. One time I had a cloth around the guy as I was shaving him. Then another guy came into my shop and began arguing with the guy in the chair. The guy in the chair got up and began swinging his two arms while I was shaving him. His arm bumped my arm with the razor and cut my eyebrow. I went to the infirmary and got three staples from the medic. I didn't get any shot or nothing. There was no doctor.

"There was one serious accident at the camp. Two boys went exploring near a high canyon and accidentally fell and died.

"After six months in June 1939 I signed up again, and they sent me six miles south to Farmington, NM because they were closing the Chaco camp. At this camp we worked on roads and cut down trees. Another job we had was at Crownpoint, NM. There was a huge, tall rock that was threatening to fall on Indian ruins. We worked behind it and removed soil to make the rock go backwards. After I got home in 1940 I heard the huge rock fell partly on ruins.

"For fun we used to catch bull snakes and put them around our necks. Then we'd walk around camp showing off. They weren't poisonous like the rattlers we saw. These snakes could kill a rattler.

"In the evening some of the guys listened to the radio or played guitars. One guy from West Virginia, Weaverland, played his guitar. He was good.

"My job was again driving truck. One day the chief mechanic called me into the office and said, 'I have a new Ford truck for you.' I was pretty proud to have it. Then one day I drove a load of gravel where there was a small drop off.

There was a guy who was jealous that I got the new truck. He said to back up further and I got stuck. I said to the guy, 'Why did you tell me to keep going when you knew I'd get stuck?' He didn't say anything.

"When I got back to the camp the chief mechanic said, 'I guess I have to take you off the job because you got stuck with the new truck.' I told him this guy was watching me and told me to keep going. The chief replied, 'You shouldn't have listened to him.' So I lost my truck driving job.

"I used to cut hair pretty nearly every night. Then I'd write letters or listen to the radio.

"On the weekends we went to town on a school bus. One time I got busy and forgot about the time. When I went to get a ride back to camp the bus had gone already. I had to get back so I didn't miss roll call in the morning. I began walking the 18 miles back to camp. It was pitch dark. Coyotes were howling and I was afraid that I might step on a snake. Thank God nothing happened. I made it back to camp at 6 am when everybody else was getting up. I was sure tired that day.

"One time I had an argument with a guy in the mess hall while eating. We started to throw our fists. The sergeant came over and stopped us. He said, 'Tomorrow we are going to build a ring and you two are going to fight three rounds.' The next day we fought and after the fight the guy said to me: 'I'm glad the bell rang because the last punch you threw I really felt it and I pretty near fell down.' After that we became good friends.

"I stayed at Farmington till December 1939 and then they sent me to Augusta, Montana. It was winter up there but not unbearably cold.

"When I got there the guy in charge said, 'You have quite a driving record. You are going to drive a stake body truck.' My job was driving about 30 guys to their job. I also had to gather firewood, build a fire, and make coffee for the guys. I got water from a stream and wrapped the coffee in cheese cloth.

"My brother, Santé, was also in the CCC and stationed at Glacier National Park. One time he travelled about 200 miles to visit me. The next day our camp was going to have an inspection and I had to cut the hair of all the 200 guys. I asked Santé to help and he did. We cut hair all night.

"After my six months were up in June 1940, I went back home.

"I had different jobs. I worked for a car parts company. Next, Shiner's Bakery, then to Cake Bakers of America.

"In 1942 I joined the Navy and was stationed on the 'Essex' aircraft carrier. I was mostly in the Pacific Ocean. In November 1945 I was discharged.

"I went to an upholstery school in Scranton, PA. To help us get back on our feet the state of Pennsylvania gave veterans $20 a week for a year. I then tried being a barber.

"In 1948 I married Mary Desando and we have three sons: Anthony, Michael, and James.

"Since there weren't many good jobs I went back to Connecticut to work. I lived in Milford and worked as a mason. After 10 years I was 40 years old and tired of masonry. It was too tough a job and I went back into the barber business. I worked for JV Hair Design in Stratford and was then living in Shelton. I stayed with JV Hair Design till I was 75 and retired. Then my wife and I moved to Meriden and stayed for 10 years.

"When I was in Meriden a state senator passed a law that granted me and other veterans a high school diploma for our service in WWII.

"I used to have CCC meetings once a month in Milford. We also met in Enfield. It was good to get together with other guys. I did this for about six years. Then when I moved to Meriden I stopped going because of the traveling.

"Working in the CCC was good for me. I learned how to communicate with people. Nobody ever talked bad about the CCC. We all learned something."

Peter Wonsewicz
VA / PA / NM

Peter Wonsewicz proudly shows a photo of the CCC camp in Cuchillo, New Mexico where he worked to help farmers. Podskoch

At the Annual CCC Museum Reunion in Stafford Springs on Oct. 11, 2008, I met Peter and his daughter Julia Wonsewicz from East Hartford. He told me he had worked at CCC camps in three states. I followed up with a telephone interview with Peter on March 12, 2009.

"I was born in Georgetown, Penn. on Oct. 10, 1920. My father, Peter, was laid off when the coal breaker burned down in Georgetown. He had to search for jobs to help his family survive. My mother, Jadwiga, had six children. She lost two before I was born: girl at three years old from the flu and another at child birth when the doctor broke her neck. I was born next followed by Ralph, Valentine, and Geraldine.

"I only went to 9th grade because I had to help my family. It was rough during the '36 flood. Word got around the neighborhood about the CCC. My cousin was going to go with me but he changed his mind but I still joined. I weighed only 113 pounds and was 5' 5" tall.

"When I left home I felt good because I wanted to see what the world looked like. I signed up at the Kingston Armory on April 19, 1936. We left from the railroad station in Wilkes Barre. We traveled to Fort Meade, Md. and stayed there for six days for conditioning.

"Then I traveled by train to Chatham, Va. My first camp was Co. 378. It did soil conservation work. It was near a small town and a lot of farms. We planted a lot of Southern pines. We also built check dams. When there was a gully, we built steps with stones or concrete so the stream wouldn't wash away the soil.

"Then we worked on farms. We put logs on fields that were plowed to prevent soil erosion.

"We also fought one forest fire. We used Indian tanks and stayed there for about 24 hours till we put out the fire.

"I was only 15 years old and so light that the guys picked me up on their shoulders and had a lot of fun with me.

"At our camp we dammed up the brook and made a swimming hole. When a storm came and washed the dam out, we'd go through the nearby farmer's high corn and swim in our birthday suits in deep areas of the stream.

"Another job was when a farmer called us from a field that we were working in and asked us to clean out his mule barn.

"One time there was a swarm of honey bees flying near our camp. This boy in camp who was a farmer went to the kitchen and banged a pan with a metal spoon. The queen bee came down to a limb on a tree and the whole swarm of bees hung onto the queen. The boy called someone nearby who had bee hives and he cut the branch off and took it home.

"On another day we went to help two farmers with a stallion and a mare. The mare was in heat. They put a bar between the mare and the stallion. Then when they figured the stallion was ready they took the tease bar down and the stallion took over.

"In the evenings we played baseball in a field. There was no rec hall like other camps but there was a PX to buy soda, candy, and cigarettes.

"Lights went out at 9 pm and then we all went to sleep because we had to get up at 6 am.

"Guys liked to play jokes. One was to put corn flakes in a bed. When the guy crawled in, he got a crunchy surprise. They also caught some snakes and put them in beds.

"They liked to play jokes on new recruits. They'd send them to the kitchen for a bucket of steam. The recruits believed this and everyone laughed when they tried to get that bucket of steam.

"I was lucky because the guys didn't play jokes on me. The older guys took care of me.

"My mother missed me and she found me a job at a furniture store. She wrote a letter asking that I be discharged. Air Reserve Capt. William H. Thomas who was in charge of the camp discharged me. On Aug. 10, 1936 I was discharged.

"I came home but I wanted to be back at a camp. For about a year I worked at a few jobs. First I worked in a rock quarry and then for the state in Nanticoke. We ripped up trolley rails and loaded them onto cars.

"On Oct. 27, 1937 I reenlisted in the CCC. I went by

Peter went to the Cedar Run campsite near Williamsport, PA where he worked on roads, trimmed trees, and built fire trails. John Eastlake

471

train to Cedar Run, Penn. near Williamsport where I had been at Co. 328. There we did roadwork, built fire trails, and trimmed trees.

"One suppertime we went on a hunger strike because they weren't giving us enough to eat. They had to go somewhere to get us some meat to feed us and after that we never went on strike again.

"One day this guy asked if anyone wanted a ride to Wilkes Barre. He had a car. On the way we passed a lady hitchhiking. There were six of us, three in the front and three in the back. We stopped and she got in and sat in the back on one of the guy's lap. She only had to go about 6-7 miles. Then she got off. When we got to Wilkes Barre we were supposed to go back the following day but we were delayed because the guy said he wasn't leaving till the next day.

"When we got back we were AWOL. For our punishment we had to put on hip boots and go into the grease pit. We cleaned the walls with brushes and rinsed them down. Boy did that stink!

"One day in July they asked for volunteers to go to New Mexico. I and about 15 others volunteered. We left on the 13th of July 1938. We were taken by truck to Tobyhanna, Penn. and got on a train to New Mexico.

"The land was beautiful and flat. We got off the train at Engle. It was a cattle loading area. There were only about ten people and two houses. My daughter, Julia, and granddaughter, Felicia, visited there in 2007. It hadn't changed much.

"A truck took us over Elephant Butte Dam to get to Cuchillo, New Mex. It was in the southwestern part of the state. The camp was a Division of Grazing camp that worked with ranchers to protect the federal grazing lands from over grazing. It was situated on a 250,000-acre ranch.

"We didn't stay long. They asked for 26 volunteers to go to a side camp on another ranch and I volunteered. When we got there, it had small barracks that housed only six men. It had a building with a shower and toilet.

"There was one foreman who supervised our camp. We dug fencepost holes and waterholes, which were like a dam built in a gully. We loaded dirt on flatbed trucks and brought it to form a dam. They were designed to catch water when the rainwater came off the mountains. Then the cattle had enough water for weeks and months.

"In fall we took loco weed and burned it because it caused brain disease to farm animals.

"We didn't have any stoves in camp but it never got below freezing. They just heated water for showers and cooking.

"There were a lot of rattlesnakes but nobody got bit.

"Every weekend we went to Hot Springs. Today it's called Truth or Consequences. The older guys went to beer joints and I and younger guys went to the movies. There were no churches.

"The food at camp was good. We ate a lot of spaghetti. For lunch we had sandwiches with tea and coffee.

"On Dec. 18th, 1938 I was discharged and came back home. I left the CCC because my father had a job for me in the coal mines. You had to be 21 years old to work there. I was only 18 but I told them I was 21. There was also a company rule that family members weren't supposed to work together but my father and I worked together. It was near the East End of Wilkes Barre. It was in a 3' high coal vein.

"The first day they put explosives in a burlap bag and I carried it down the slope. I crawled on my hands and knees. I was working with my dad. We drilled holes with a jackhammer. Then we had to fill the hole with explosives. We had to pack the hole with moist dirt. Dad said you had to piss on the dirt and put it into a tamping bag. Next we pushed the bag into the hole behind the dynamite. Then we went to a safe place, hooked up wires to a plunger, and pushed down on the plunger.

"After working in the mines for two years I went to New Britain, Conn. and got a job in Stanley Works. My job was moving materials.

"I joined the Navy in April 1942. While at the Naval Training Station in the Great Lakes, I met an old CCC friend named Cook. I learned how to cook in the Navy where I was a cook and a butcher. I was in the Navy for 45 months and discharged in January 1946.

"When I got back to Connecticut I went to a culinary school in New Britain, but I never went into that field. I got a job at Pratt & Whitney in the shipping dept. Then I moved on to other jobs in the company.

"In 1947 I got married to Frances Paczkowski. We met in Hartford at the Polish Home. We had one daughter, Julia.

"After working at Pratt & Whitney for 32 years I retired.

"I went back twice to my old CCC camps in Cedar Run and New Mexico.

472

"Today I help my daughter plant, clean, and cook.

"The CCC was a great experience for me. I was a poor boy from Pennsylvania and I got to travel to many places. I got to meet a lot of guys and I learned how to get along with people."

John Koes
Wellsboro, PA

John Koes of Colchester was in a CCC camp in Wellsboro, Penn. where he had a serious injury that caused a lifetime disability. John Koes

Betty Koes of Colchester called me in September 2013 and said that she and her husband had read an article in the local paper about a CCC reunion. They wished that they had known about it because Betty's husband, John, had been in the CCC in Pennsylvania. They were from the Wilkes Barre area where I grew up so we did a lot of reminiscing and I made an appointment to see John.

On September 17 I went to Colchester. Betty greeted me and introduced me to John. We sat down at the kitchen table and John told me about his life and time in the CCC.

"I was born Nov. 2, 1919 in Duryea, Penn. My father, Nicholas, worked in the coal mines and my mother, Mary Matrona, had two boys and two girls: Helen, Harry, Dorothy, and me.

"I only went to eighth grade and quit school to help my family. I was 12 years old and worked on Doreo's farm. I did almost everything, including picking radishes and tomatoes and weeding. They paid me 10 cents an hour and 75 cents a day.

"In the winter there wasn't any farm work so I didn't do much.

"My brother, Harry, was in the CCC in Meshoppen, Penn. so that is how I knew about the CCC. He was a leader. He stayed as long as he could, two years.

"In the spring of 1937 I joined the CCC. I was 17. I signed up in Pittston. A bus picked me up at my home and drove me to Wilkes Barre. Then I walked across the bridge to the Kingston Armory. They examined me and I got on a train. They took us as far as Troy, Penn. and we got on a truck that took us to the Darling Run Camp #1354 near Wellsboro.

"I wasn't nervous even though I didn't know anybody. It was a beautiful place. The camp was in a canyon near the river and the train passed right by our camp. There was a water tank for the trains right by our camp.

"When I got to camp my first job was pulling gooseberry bushes and putting them on piles. We did this whenever the bushes were near white pine trees because they caused blister rust.

"On my next job I worked on the Colton Point State Park. We went in the woods and found a big pile of sandstone rocks. We split them to build fireplaces. Then we loaded stones on the trucks and hauled them to Colton Point State Park.

"On the weekends during the summer they gave me a job of doing a camp survey. I sat at the entrance and looked to see what state the campers were from and how many people were in the car. From this information the state got an idea of how many fireplaces and campsites they should build in the future.

"Our camp was in such a beautiful place. I went

On Saturday John Koes was all dressed up to go to the town of Wellsboro to look for some fun. John Koes

A fireplace built by members of John Koes CCC camp at Colton Point SP. https://commons.wikimedia.org/wiki/File:Colton_Point_State_Park_Fire_Grate.jpg

fishing a lot in the nearby stream. The fishing was excellent. Someone had dammed up the stream in the summer and created a nice pool for swimming.

"We also kept busy playing baseball, pitching horseshoes, and shooting pool in the rec hall. Our camp had baseball and basketball teams that played other CCC camps. We had our own baseball field in camp.

"On Saturday night we either went to Wellsboro or Galton. We walked around and looked in the stores. There was a park in Wellsboro and that is where we looked for girls. Sometimes I took girls to the movies.

"I remember one guy, our cook, who married a local girl whose father owned a restaurant in Wellsboro.

"During the winter we picked up brush and put it on piles that we later burned. We didn't have to go out and work if the temperature was below zero.

"My next job was working in the woods taking the bark from trees. One day I was shaving the bark off a log with a drawknife. As I pulled the knife towards me it hit a knot. So I tried again and pulled the knife harder but the knife hit my knee and cut my kneecap. They took me to the infirmary. I spent a day or two there and it got infected. Then they took me in the camp ambulance to the nearby Blossburg Hospital.

"After a month my knee got worse and they took me to Walter Read Hospital in Washington, D.C. on Dec. 8, 1939.

"The pain was awful. They gave me some medicine to help. I had two surgeries and my leg was completely stiff. They had tubes in my leg to draw out the infection. My left leg was held up in the air. I didn't know if I'd ever be able to walk well again. I laid on my back for almost six months. I still have sores on my back. Today my leg is still stiff and I can't bend it.

"While in the hospital I had a friend who was also a patient. When we were getting better we decided to take a bus down into the city.

"My parents came down once to visit me. My cousin John Koes drove them to Washington.

"I stayed there till October 1940. Then the Army sent me home by train. I got to Wilkes Barre and got a bus to Duryea. I couldn't get a job but got training for radio repair in a rehabilitation program in Wilkes Barre. After that I worked in a silk mill in Duryea. Then I got a job in an iron works in Pittston. It was a defense plant where we made armor plate for tanks during the war. I tried to join the Army but I was 4-F because of my knee.

"I met my wife, Betty Turner, on Dec. 26, 1943."

Betty then added, "My cousin and I were walking to Old Forge to visit another cousin. As we walked, John and his friend, Bob Lackenby, were following us and whistling at us. I had on a cashmere coat and John kept saying, 'I like your coat.' He invited me out for New Year's Eve to go to the movies with Bob and my cousin. They had $2 between them and that was enough for a ticket and refreshments.

"We dated for two years and got married on June 16, 1945 and had three sons: John, William, and Nicholas."

John added, "We moved to Connecticut in 1956 when Betty's brother got me a job at Pratt & Whitney as a machine operator. I retired in 1983.

"I have gone back camping with my family by my old CCC camp," said John. "I also went hunting and fishing in that area. One time while hunting I met my former foreman, Wayne Banks."

Betty said, "John had several lawyers trying to get some kind of compensation for his injury in the CCC but he never got any help."

John passed away on April 11, 2014.

Robert Claffey
Rickers Mills, VT

I met Robert Claffey at a CCC reunion at the Connecticut CCC Museum in May 2008. About two months later I interviewed him by phone on July 20th. He told he worked in a CCC camp in Vermont. I asked him to

Robert Claffey worked as a cook, orderly, baker, laborer, and truck driver at Camp S-59 Co. 1162 in Rickers Mills, VT.

tell me about his family and why he joined the CCC.

"My father William went off his rocker when my mother died. I was two years old. Dad was drinking and remarried. I went to live with my mother's sister Anna Cahill and Uncle Jack. They lived in Hartford and they moved to Bloomfield. Then we moved back to Hartford. My uncle was a photo engraver for the Hartford Times.

"My sister and two brothers were also separated and lived with relatives. Mary went to live with Aunt Mary in New Jersey. Joseph lived with my father's sister Aunt Matilda and Uncle Bill Harding, and William stayed with Aunt Sarah.

"I went to Hartford schools but when I was in Weaver High in Hartford I dropped out after two years. I was 18 years old.

"My aunt and uncle had three children and we got along well. I helped with the cooking and washing floors. I also worked at their grocery store on Saturdays and made $2. I gave the money to my aunt.

"The Child Welfare Department was paying my aunt and uncle to keep me, but I wanted to get out and be on my own. I read about the CCC in the newspaper and it sounded like a good way to earn money and be independent.

"I went to the town hall and signed up on Aug 6, 1935. I went to New London for my physical.

"Then on July 6, 1936 the Army sent me to Camp S-59 Company 1162 in Rickers Mills, a hamlet in the town of Groton, Vt. Our camp was in the Groton State Forest. My first job was an officer's orderly. The officers had cabins with their own rooms. I made their beds and served their meals. At night I helped the baker with pies and cakes.

"I was the officer's orderly until Aug. 6, 1936 because when the baker left, I took his job. I had had a lot of experience cooking and baking with my aunt. I held this job for about five months. "On Sept. 6, 1937 I became the 2nd cook and later the 1st cook.

"On Jan. 11, 1937 I left the kitchen and began working outside. My new job was as a laborer doing a lot of cutting wood. I did this work until April 16th when I had an accident while cutting a tree that was hung up on another tree. When I tried to cut it the top fell. It missed my head but it landed on my hand. It broke my thumb and two fingers. My thumb had a compound fracture. I guess they didn't supervise me well. I shouldn't have been cutting it down. I was sick in the line of duty.

"On March 12th the Army sent me to the Station Hospital at Fort Ethan Allen in Burlington. My thumb was really black and badly infected. The doctors thought they would have to cut it off but one doctor put silver nitrate on it and my thumb was saved. I was in the hospital for about a month. I came back to my camp on April 16th.

"After my injury on Sept. 25, 1937 I became a truck driver for a short time. I drove big Reo Speed Wagon dump trucks. The enrollees were busy building roads, making picnic areas, and doing silviculture work such as thinning trees. They went out to work when it was 30 below zero.

"Then I was moved back to working in the kitchen with the 1st cook. It was a lady from town and she was great. She did a lot of homecooked meals that the guys liked. The food was pretty good. It was better than overseas when I was in the National Guard.

"Sometimes we went to town. It was about 3 miles away. There was a restaurant we'd visit. There wasn't anyone who drank or smoke.

"Sometimes I drove guys in a rack truck to town. We'd go to Wells River and Ricker Mills.

"On Sept. 25, 1937 I was discharged. I had been in the CCC for two years and that was the limit. The Army furnished me transportation from Ricker Mills to Hartford, Conn. I was able to include all these dates because I had my discharge papers."

He showed me them and he was proud of his written performance comments of "Excellent" and "Satisfactory."

"When I came home I bought a car for $50 in New Haven because I wanted to drive out West. My friend

Norman Sullivan, who I met at my CCC camp, wanted to go with me. We first stopped in New Haven to join the Navy but Norman failed the physical so we left for California.

"It took us about two weeks. We had some flat tires in Arizona. I stayed in California for two years. I worked as a waiter in LA and helped a couple in their restaurant. Then I got a job on a farm with room and board. It was a truck garden ranch.

"I came back and stayed with my Aunt Anna. Before the war I joined National Guard and I drove an ambulance. When I went to Camp Edwards they needed a cook and I got the job because I had CCC experience. I was made 2nd cook and a month later 1st cook.

"When I was shipped to Australia I was made a mess sergeant. I stayed there 3½ years but I didn't like it there.

"In 1942 I married Rita Maloney in Hartford. We had seven children: Robert, Gregory (died), Noreen, Kevin (East Granby), Karen, Neal, and Keith.

"My wife and I got an apartment in Hartford. I got a job as milkman. Then I went to trade school and became a carpenter. I got a job at Metropolitan District Water Bureau and I was in charge of maintenance for the whole district. I retired at age 62."

Q: What effect did your years in the CCC have on you?

A: "I learned cooking, baking, truck driving, and a lot of things I would never have learned. I really enjoyed it. I even wanted to join again."

Robert "Bob" Claffey passed away on June 30, 2013.

Manuel "Manny" Almada
Brunswick, VT

On Aug. 28, 2009 Ray Bedard of East Hartford invited me to his home to meet his good friend, Manny Almada, who like Ray was in the CCC. As we sat drinking coffee in Ray's kitchen Manny told me about his early life.

"My parents Frank and Maria came to the US from the Azores, islands 1000 miles off the coast of Portugal. My father worked at the Royal Typewriter Co. in Hartford but was only able to work 2-3 days a week. Then during the Depression he only worked one day a week. My parents had a hard time providing for three growing sons. I was the eldest and my brothers were Alfred and Albert.

"My dad said to me, 'Why don't you go to the Azores and live with your grandparents?' So I went and stayed

To help his parents during the Depression Manny lived with his grandparents in the Azores. He is dressed up for his job in a hotel. Manny Almada

there for two years. They were living on Santa Maria Island.

"My father was desperate for a job and went to the Dominican Republic to work but got malaria.

"Then I went and lived on St. Michael Island for four years. I got a job in a hotel to earn money.

"One day an American freighter stopped at the island and a passenger asked me how did I know how to speak English. I replied, 'I'm from the US.' He said, 'Come with us on my ship and be our mess boy.' I took his advice and travelled to the US.

"When I got to Connecticut I went to my uncle's home in Newington and lived with him. I worked mowing lawns in West Hartford.

"Then I travelled to other towns for jobs. I went to Naugatuck and worked as a pin boy in a bowling alley and got 5 cents a game. In the summer of 1938 I went to Diton, Mass. and worked for truck farmers where I picked beans all summer.

"I only went to about a month in 9th grade and dropped out to find a job. In October I went to the town hall to see if someone could help me find work. A lady said, 'Why don't you join the CCC?' It sounded good so I signed up. The Army took me to a CCC camp in Brunswick, Vermont. It was in the northeast part of the state near the New Hampshire border in what they call the Northeast Kingdom."

Q: What was camp like and what jobs and projects did you do?

A: "There were a few barracks where the guys lived.

Every morning we stood by the flag pole and saluted the flag. The Army officers ran the camp and they were nice to me. They gave us WWI uniforms to wear.

"I was a carpenter's helper for Mr. Young who was a ranger. I was in a group of five guys who went up Stone Mt. in the town of Guildhall where we built an observer's cabin near a fire tower. I did the painting inside and out of the cabin. It was beautiful up there. We also built trails for the tractor to go to the fire tower.

"Another job was building a road. We lived in a side camp for this job.

"We built another large side camp with a big barracks near a fish hatchery that was about 2-3 miles from the Canadian border. We built wooden water troughs down to the fishery. We worked there for a few months."

Q: What did you do in the evenings and the weekends?

A: "We went over to the rec hall and played pool. We didn't have much money to spend. On the weekends we went about 15-20 miles to the town of Groveton, New Hampshire. We went to the movie theater or just hung around town. Sometimes we went to square dances at Island Pond. It was a small railroad town with a pond that had an island. One time we hired a boat to take us around the pond. Sometimes on weekends a priest came to camp and said Mass."

Q: How was the food?

A: "The cooks were very good. The main cook had been there for quite a few years. The officers kept him because he was so good. I had KP duty and had to peel potatoes. I probably got it because my bunk wasn't made the right way. When we ate in the mess hall we sat at tables with eight guys. I loved the flapjack pancakes."

Q: Did you do any sports at camp?

A: "I played volleyball. I didn't make the baseball team because I couldn't see the ball well."

Q: How long did you stay and why did you leave?

A: "After a year I had enough of the cold and heavy snow. I wasn't going to spend another winter in Vermont.

(L–R) 1 The Brunswick, Vermont CCC camp where Manny Almada lived for a year. 2 CCC enrollees used a Cletrac tractor to bring supplies up to the Stone Mt. fire tower where they were building a cabin. 3 A view of the observer's cabin from the fire tower on Stone Mt. All photos courtesy Manny Almada

Manny (standing) and four other CCC boys lived in a tent and a lean-to while building a cabin for a fire tower observer on Stone Mt. in Vermont. Manny Almada

Ray Bedard, left, and Manuel "Manny" Almada shared their stories about working in the CCC. Podskoch

So I was discharged in October 1939. I went back to Newington and got a job in a small factory called Carling Tool. I adjusted electric plugs and operated a milling machine. Then I got a job at Pratt & Whitney where I worked using a file to take out burrs on the parts.

"Then when WWII started I joined the Navy in 1942. I loved being on a ship. I was shipped to Newport, Rhode Island and attended a school for a gunner. I became an armed guard on the SS Aguastar. It was a freighter.

"After the war in 1945 I got married to Rose Frias and we had three children: Richard, Joan, and Pamela. I also went back to work at Pratt & Whitney and retired after 40 years."

Q: What did you learn in the CCC?

A: "I learned how to get along with others. I learned carpentry and painting skills. They helped me later in life and I was able to do things by myself. I had a good time in the CCC."

Manny Almada passed away on April 26, 2016.

Joseph H. Peterson
East Burke, VT

Joseph H. Peterson worked on the toll road to the summit of Burke Mountain while he was enrolled at the CCC camp in East Burke, Vt. Joe Peterson

On May 31, 2008 I met Joe Peterson at the Putnam Library where I was speaking. He said his father, Joseph H. Peterson, was in Camp #232 in East Burke, Vt.

A few weeks later he sent me information that he found on the camp and what projects they were working on.

"I got to looking into the Vermont CCC, and came up with something that gives you the layout of the project where my father (Joseph H. Peterson) was located. East Burke is in the very northeast part of Vermont, above St. Johnsbury and Lyndonville. He worked on the toll road to the summit of Burke Mountain.

"In 1912, East Burke native turned millionaire businessman, Elmer Darling, who owned the mountain at the time, built a picnic area, camp, and a tower atop the mountain."

More changes were to come in 1933, when during the Depression, the Civilian Conservation Corps (CCC) began the painstaking construction of an auto road up the mountain. Campsites and a fire tower were also built. The toll road was completed in 1935 and was named Merrill Highway, in honor of state forester Perry Merrill – a man who worked tirelessly to bring a number of Vermont ski mountains to life. This included Burke Mountain and also Jay Peak Ski Resort, the Northeast Kingdom's only other ski mountain, located about 50 miles to the north. The tower toppled during the Hurricane of 1938, but was replaced with one made of steel.

"My father didn't remember the camp being that high on the mountain, but I guess it was. The notch you see looking across the valley contains Lake Willoughby, the site of another CCC project.

"One memorable story my father told was that while there (in winter) his appendix either ruptured or was in danger of it, and he had to be brought to Plattsburgh, NY to have it removed. The three hour or so trek across the state of Vermont was excruciating in the back of an army truck, but I guess the Army's nearest operating hospital was Plattsburgh. "No doubt there was a hospital in St. Johnsbury or any number of other places where the job

An early photo of Camp #232 in East Burke, Vt. The CCC boys played an important part in developing Burke Mt. for skiing. http://www.northlandjournal.com/stories/stories37.html

could have been done in no time, but it had to be an Army facility.

"After his time in the CCC, my father got work with HH Wright, a watch repair/jewelry company in Worcester, Mass. He met and married my mother in 1937. He attended the watch repair school at the Waltham Watch Co, in Waltham, Mass. For the next while, he worked in watch repair, in Worcester. By 1941, he had two children, and opened his own watch repair business. I came along in 1943.

"After WWII, his brother came home from the service, also attended the Waltham school, and joined my father in the watch, clock, and jewelry business. My father died in 1970."

Fred D'Onofrio
Niantic & Lacomb, OR

Fred D'Onofrio at Camp Chapman in Niantic in 1934.
Frieda Moroniti

Frieda Moroniti of North Branford wrote to me as to how she could get more information about her dad in the CCC. She stated, "I believe my dad was at Camp Chapman in Niantic and maybe later went to Camp Crabtree in Lacomb, Oregon. I also thought I remember him telling me he had gone to Oregon. I do have a banner of a CCC Camp with the Co. #2106 on it."

"My dad was born on Aug. 19, 1917. My father's parents were both born in Italy. His father came to America when he was in his 20's. His parents had 6 boys: Louis, Albert, Michael, Anthony, Edward, and my dad. His

mother passed away when he was 3 years old and his father passed away when he was 13 years old."

I told Frieda how to get her dad's discharge papers. A little while later she wrote:

"I did obtain his CCC discharge papers. He was enrolled on May 2, 1934 when he was 17 Dad was sent to the Niantic Camp. He told me that one of the things he learned in the CCC camps was building roads at Devil's Hop Yard and at Rocky Neck State Park. I think he also worked on the stone pavilion there at Rocky Neck.

"Dad signed up to go out West and was sent to Camp Crabtree in Lacomb, Oregon. I don't know what type of work he did there.

"On March 31, 1936 Dad was discharged from the CCC on his return from Oregon at Fort Devens, Mass.

"He was never in the service because he told me he was hit by a truck while riding a bike and had injured his leg. One was slightly shorter than the other and he couldn't enlist.

"From his experience building roads in the CCC, I gather he became interested in construction. When he was discharged from the CCC camp he went to night school to learn drafting. He worked for a local construction company. Then around 1937 he started his own company, The D'Onofrio Construction Co.

"On April 29, 1940 my dad married Theresa Pellegrino. They had four children: Marianne D'Onofrio, Ph.D., of East Haven; Anita (John) Finta of Branford; Freida (John) Moroniti of North Branford, and the late Fred D'Onofrio, Jr.

"My father passed away in 2007."
Here is a Diary of Fred's trip to Oregon:

"A Cross Country Trip"

Friday Oct. 25, 1935

It was a very cold Friday morning on Oct. 25, 1935, and a long journey lay ahead for some 450 enrollees and officers from all parts of Connecticut who were assembling in New London, Connecticut to leave for Albany, Oregon. The party I was in consisted of 124 enrollees and one officer who didn't mind the cold that morning. We were all the more or less excited as the lights were turned on in the barracks that morning at four am, After a good breakfast at 4:30 am we got aboard the trucks and at 5:15 am we left Camp Chapman, Niantic, Conn. to journey to

New London some 10 miles away at a speed of 20 mph. The excitement had died down and hardly a word was uttered as we journeyed to New London. Let me say at this point that the convoy of six trucks reminded me a great deal of the "Don Patrol" which I saw so much of in the movies. Arrived in New London, at 5:50 am. We waited until 8 o'clock when we got aboard the long train of 13 Pullman cars and two baggage cars converted into kitchens. The meals were going to be served to us in our seats. Each car consisted of 39 men. There were three men to a birth and the leaders and assistant leaders had special compartments. We were all very comfortable. Our train finally pulled out at 9 am. We pulled into New Haven, at 10 am. Here we changed from a steam driven to an electric engine. Passed Bridgeport in 20 minutes which impressed me very much. The captain's wife was at the station to see the train go by. Passed through Stamford at 11 am and passed through Greenwich at 11:15 am. Arrived in New York City at the Penn. Station at 12:10 pm. From the top of Hells Gate Bridge we had a perfect scene of the city; we also saw the Empire and Chrysler buildings looming over all of the other buildings. We had a very good view of the Washington Bridge. Leaving New York via Pennsylvania Railroad we were soon speeding into new Jersey City. At one 10 pm we went through the Hudson Tunnel under the Hudson River. We soon left New Jersey behind and were in Pennsylvania. Past Lancaster Penn. at 3 pm and saw large farmlands with great plains The cattle stockyards were fairly large. Passed by a U.S. Army air base at 3:30 pm. Pulled into Harrisburg, Penn. at 3:45 pm. It was really our first long stop as we took on water here and changed to a steam engine. It is a large city with big mills; we also saw the capital of Pennsylvania. Left Harrisburg at 4:10 pm and into the Allegheny Mts. at 4:25 pm which is very dangerous if you travel fast. Passed Newport Penn. at 4:40 pm. We saw a large race track, and after this we passed through the mining country. The first town we saw was Keystone Penn. at 5:15 pm. Here we saw the rayon manufacturing company that makes ladies hosiery. Stopped at Altoona, Pennsylvania at 6:35 pm. This was the city of 90,000 and an extra engine was put on to climb a mountain 1500 feet above sea level. Stepped on the top of the mountain to disk connect the extra engine. Passed through Bethlehem, Pennsylvania at 9:30 pm here we saw the sky all lit up by the huge blast furnaces, a continual stream of steel mills and plenty of smoke. We arrived in Pittsburgh at 10 pm this was all we saw on our first day out as we all retired.

Saturday, Oct. 26

Saturday morning, Oct. 26 having left Penn. and passed through Ohio during the night, we find ourselves this morning pulling into Richmond, Indiana at 6 am Central Time. Stopped at Richmond for water. After we left Richmond we saw beautiful farmlands and the sunrise a beautiful picture. Passed the town of Greenfield, Indiana at 6:18 am. Here we saw the Libby Biological Laboratories--a very nice building. Passed Indianapolis, Indiana at 6:35 am., the city made famous for its auto racing. Passed by the Indiana big flower mill. We passed, I might say, miles and miles of large cornfields. Just before pulling into the city of Terra Haute, Indiana we saw large stacks of baled hay burning. We also saw the large plant of the American Can Co. We saw a CCC Camp Marshall just after leaving Terre Haute. Passed Effingham Indiana. At 9:30 am, some 10 miles out of Effingham, we were allowed to detrain for a half hour to get some exercise. Passed the Pet Milk Co. at Greensville, Indiana at 11 am. We are now leaving the state of the sycamore trees and into the state of Illinois. We didn't see much of this state to write about. Entered Missouri at 11:45 am and we were all excited about crossing the Mississippi River. Before crossing the river we saw very large slaughter and packing houses, also large cattle pens. Right on the banks were shacks by the hundreds all occupied by colored people. We are now crossing the Mississippi River a dirty and muddy river with its great steamboats you see in the movies. Stopped at St. Louis Missouri at 12:20 pm. It started to rain here while at the station. They have a very large railroad yard here. Left St. Louis at 1:10 pm. At 2:20 we had a little trouble as the cook's car caught on fire, but no damage was done. Since leaving St. Louis we followed the Mississippi River and crossed it again at New Haven, Missouri. At 2:45 pm we saw USS Snag Boat right on the river. At 3:45 pm passed the Missouri State Penitentiary. Just before entering Jefferson City, there were a set of wonderful buildings with bars on the windows to keep the people from getting in and bothering the people inside. Next came the capital in Jefferson City, a beautiful building but the grounds were terrible. We also saw WOS broadcasting station. Passed Kansas City at 6:45 pm. It rained all the afternoon and during the evening so the beds looked inviting. Early as Lowell Thomas would say, "So long until tomorrow."

Sunday, Oct. 27

Sunday morning Oct. 27, we arose at 6:15 am and found out that we were in the state of Kansas. The weather was still foggy. Saw my first ranch house; saw large herds of cattle on the range. Also saw a long train of cattle cars headed for St. Louis. After passing this grazing land, we passed through Scott City, Kansas at 8:50 am. Here we saw one of the oldest trains on a siding. The whole length of Kansas is just plains, very few trees, and hills. We finally cleared out of the fog and mist. Passed the town of Leoti, Kansas and not a tree in sight for acres. No wonder they have tornadoes and dust storms; mile after mile and not a tree or hill insight, just long wide planes. Passed the town of Horace, Kansas at 11:15 am. Stopped just out of the town for exercise. One of the porters scared up a jack rabbit. After leaving here we saw four cowboys riding the range in full outfit. Passed Sheridin, Kansas at 11:50 am. Here we saw cowboys on a round up. Shortly after this we left Kansas and entered Colo. at 12:15 pm. The first town we saw was Eads, Colo., a typical western town with a small race track. Stopped at Ordway, Colo. at 2:35 pm and was welcomed by three girls. It is also called the Sugar City, as there are large sugar refineries here. A very interesting city with rodeo grounds and a small corral. We also saw some of the soil erosion projects. After leaving Ordway at 2:45 pm we saw train loads of sugar beets, then large fields of beets and honeydew melons. This state is noted for its picturesque scenery. On the right of us was nothing but desert and sand dunes with holes from 6 to 12 feet deep and not a sign of water anywhere. On our left there was a beautiful wooded land and in the distance white covered mountain tops for a background. We can now see the Rocky Mountains quite plain with the twin mountains looming over all. Pulled into Pueblo, Colo. at 4:10 pm, a very large nice city with a fairly good size railroad yard. They have quite a few foundaries and one of the biggest stockyards I have seen so far. We ate our supper at the station. While we were waiting to have the brakes put on and to attach an extra engine, we saw steers and they were being shipped to the stockyards. Left Pueblo at 5:05 pm and passed a CCC camp some 10 miles out of Pueblo. Darkness was falling fast as we entered the Rocky Mountains. We followed the course of the Green River that makes it the more exciting. Then the going through the Royal Gorge and under the highest bridge in the world 1,050 feet above the Green River. All the while the raging train is plowing its way up to the highest peak of

the states. After going up to the mountains halfway, we stopped at the city of Solida, Colo. A town you wouldn't dream about way up on the mountains with a beautiful center,. Stopped here to fill up the engine with water to climb 7,000 more feet in elevation. Then the riding up the highest point of the Rockies where the snow was about 2 feet deep and it must have been below zero weather. At 2:30 am we past the snow and started to coast down the Rockies.

Monday morning, Oct. 28

Monday morning Oct. 28, we pulled into Grand Junction, Colo. at 6:15 am Mountain Time to disconnect the extra engine. As long as I live I don't think I shall ever see such a magnificent sight as the rising sun on the mountains. Words just cannot describe it. We entered into Utah at 6:35 am. The first town we passed was Cico, Utah, a typical Mexican town. A short way from here we saw flocks of sheep, I should say numbering into the thousands with pack mules and sheep herders. Passed Green River, Utah at 9:45 am. Here we again entered into the waste lands, nothing but sand dunes, bone dry coules, etc. Stopped on the desert to let a fast freight through, and many of the boys picked up relics and souvenirs. I was glad to leave this God forsaken land. Passed Helper, Utah at 12:40 pm, the center of Utah's mining industries. A short ways from here we saw a shooting spring; the water rising to say about 6 feet into the air. After this we went around the mountains and had to stop at Thistle, Utah at 1:50 pm to repair the brake bands and cool off the hot boxes. One thing that has impressed me very much is the good roads that they have out here in the West. Passed the town of Murray, Utah at 3 pm. Here we saw the Utah Ore Sampling Co. We are now nearing the Mormon city, ordinarily known as Salt Lake City. Stopped at Salt Lake City at 3:45 pm where we changed engines and took on water and bread. Saw the Mormon Tabernacle, also the state capital. Left Salt Lake City at 4:45 pm and we saw the Great Salt Lake. We had the pleasure of seeing the setting sun on the lake. Passed Brigham, Utah at 7 pm and shortly afterwords we passed the largest dam I ever saw, Echo Dam on Bear River. This is about all we saw of Utah and we all retired.

Tuesday, October 29

Tuesday morning October 29, we were in the state of Idaho and looking into the state of Oregon across the Snake River. Crossed the Snake River at 7:15 am Pacific Time. The first town we came to was Huntington at 7:35 am. Started out at Huntington with two engines. Passed Durkee, Oregon at 8:15 am. Quite a site here with the clouds covering the mountain tops and snow is beginning to fall. We are now 3,820 feet above sea level, but gradually going down. Each town we pass has the elevation on the sign at the depot. Stopped at the town of Encina, Oregon at 9:15 am to detach one of the engines. Left and Encina and then into Baker, Oregon at 9:35 am. Here we saw large lumber mills; we also saw a CCC camp. Snow now covers the ground. Stopped at La Grande at 10:50 am to take on coal and water. Passed Meadian, Oregon at 1:15 pm. Still snowing with about 4 inches already fallen; we are still going down the mountains. This snowstorm is turning out to be a young blizzard. The mountains are a beautiful site with clouds on the top and snow on the ground. Passed another CCC camp at Mission, Oregon. We also passed a state game farm and a state fox farm. Passed Pendleton, Oregon at 3:20 pm. The city that is famous for its rodeos. We joined the Columbia River at this point that is famous for its salmon. Passed Wellington, Oregon at 5:20 pm. We are practically down to sea level. Passed Hood River, Oregon at 6:25 pm. We now have 12 inches of snow and it is still coming down. At 7:12 pm we saw a huge dam, the Bonneville Dam being constructed by U. S. Engineers on the Columbia River. It was started Oct. 10, 1934. We arrived in Portland, Oregon at 9 pm. It is a very large city. We had to spend another night on the train as we arrived too late to go on to Albany, Oregon.

Wednesday, Oct. 30

Wednesday morning Oct. 30, left Portland at 3:30 am and we were up at 4 am. Arrived in Albany, Oregon at 6 am. There is a light covering of snow here. This is the end of our trip as far as trains are concerned. Five days and five nights was plenty. We have covered about every kind of land: plains, mountains, forests, swamps, deserts, and what have you. There isn't much we haven't seen with the exception of a few cities we have passed during the night. I must say that a queer coincident is that we crossed 13 states, we had 13 cars in our train, and we had 13 porters. What 13 means to us I don't know but I do know that we are here in Oregon until April 1, 1936. Now to go on with our story. We detrained at Albany, Oregon and got aboard the CCC trucks

that were waiting for us. Left Albany at 7:15 am and finally reached our destination at 8:10 am.

Fred D'Onofrio
2106th C.C.C.
Camp Crabtree
Lacomb, Oregon

Thomas Farrell
MA / OR

Tom Farrell worked as a cook at a CCC camp in Oregon and then made cooking his career. Farrell Family

The Sept. 8, 1986 issue of the Willimantic Chronicle interviewed CCC boys who attended a large gathering of over 1,000 Connecticut CCC alumni at Rocky Neck State Park. Thomas Farrell of Saybrook was one of the interviewed CCC Alumni. He said that he had worked in Oregon.

In December 2011 I contacted Farrell's home. His wife Marjorie said her husband had passed away. I asked if she could tell me about Tom's life and participation in the CCC.

"Yes, I'll try. My husband was born on Nov. 4, 1914 in Brockton, Mass. His parents were Thomas and Mary. His father worked as a welder in Weymouth.

"Tom had five sisters: Geraldine, Florence, twins Dorothy & Virginia, and Kathleen.

"After graduating from high school in Brockton, he joined the CCC because his mother was so poor. His father was a drinker so she left him and raised the kids alone. I think one of his friends joined and he decided to join, too."

Q: What kind of work did Tom do?

A: "At the Oregon camp Tom helped build roads, plant trees, and was introduced to the culinary arts which eventually became his livelihood. It was in the camp kitchen where he did most of his work. It was in the kitchen where his interest in cooking thrived. This would have a great effect on him when he later looked for a job.

"On the weekends and free time he hiked from one place to another. They were in godforsaken country. Tom also loved to play ping-pong. They also played sports like basketball. I have a picture of him playing baseball in camp. He also had a girlfriend. But he didn't drink like the other guys in camp because he saw its effect on his family caused by his father's drinking."

Q: Did he say how the food was at camp?

A: "It was probably horrible but he learned how to cook for over 200 men. Later on he became a good chef.

"He got injured when he fell down a mountainside riding in a truck and injured his left hand. He wasn't treated properly and his hand was deformed till the end of his life."

Q: What did he do when he left the CCC?

A: "Tom went to the shipyard in Weymouth, Mass. and worked as a welder during WWII. Then towards the end of the war he joined the Army and was shipped to Japan as part of the Army's occupation. He was there for at least a year. "During WWII, Tom worked as a welder at the Quincy, Mass. Then towards the end of the war he joined the Army and was shipped to Japan as part of the Army's occupation. He was there for at least a year.

"After the war we got married on Sept. 5, 1945. We had three children: Valerie, Alison, and Glenn.

"Tom spent many years as the head chef at the Wollaston Golf Club in Milton, Mass. In 1962, Tom and I moved our family to Old Saybrook. We loved living here. Tom founded the Colonial Catering Service and ran it until his retirement.

"When he retired here in Saybrook he established the ping-pong, horseshoes, and pool clubs. He had them playing all up and down the coast. He made all the plans for all the tournaments for adults. In fact they are going to name the new pool room after Tom. Tom practiced every day except Sunday. He enjoyed ping-pong and pool very much.

"His experiences as a cook in the CCC had a big effect on his cooking career in Massachusetts and Connecticut."

Tom is wearing the light colored neck tie directly under the center of the Brimfield State Forest sign. Glenn Farrell

Thomas Francis Farrell, 96, passed on Dec. 23, 2010. His wife Marjorie followed on Nov. 20, 2012.

In June 2016 I was fortunate to talk with Tom's son Glen of Old Saybrook and he had this additional information and a photo of his father:

"My father entered the CCC in 1934 at Brimfield State Forest, Brimfield, Mass. which was Company 135. In November 1935 he joined Company 2113 in Heppner, OR. I don't have any information on when he left the CCC.

"He had a tough childhood growing up in the Brockton, Mass. area. He had five sisters and his father left the family destitute because of a drinking problem. So the CCC was one of the few options open to him.

"My dad enjoyed all sports and, while in Heppner was approached by Oregon Normal School in Monmouth, Ore. to play basketball for them for the winter of 1936 and then onto to the State College. At the time my father was known as 'Slim Farrell' in the basketball ranks. Unfortunately, he suffered serious injuries in a logging truck roll over while building roads out of the Heppner camp. That ended his basketball playing days and a shot at college."

William "John" Nenninger
Triangle Lake, OR

In the summer of 2008 I met Gary and Kathy Nenninger at a relative's party. I asked Gary if anyone in his family had been in the CCC. He said, "Yes, my father was in a CCC camp in Oregon. I'll bet he'd enjoy telling you about his experiences but I'll warn you, he's hard of hearing and you have to speak really loud."

John Nenninger was drafted into the Army at the end of WWII. Gary Nenninger

I replied, "It won't be a problem since I've been interviewing old timers for the past ten years and many have a similar problem."

We arranged for a day and time and I visited Gary's parents' apartment in Cromwell on Sept. 14, 2008.

Gary introduced me to his father William who said that he likes to be called John. Gary also introduced me to his mother Constance. I asked John about his early family life and how he got into the CCC.

"I was born on Aug. 15, 1918 in Meriden. My parents were Frank and Dora. My father worked as a steeplejack. My mother had five children: Frank, Doris, me, Marion ('Honey'), and an infant who died. I also had a half-brother, Jim Liverman. My father was in WWI and when he came home they called him 'Kaiser' because he was German.

"I only went to 6th grade and quit because I had no shoes or proper clothes. Those were the days when we had nothing to eat. To help my family I worked in the tobacco fields picking tobacco.

"In the fall of 1935 my mother found out about the CCC at the town hall when she was getting slips of paper for food because we were poor. When she came home she told me that I could get a job with the CCC. I went to Middletown and signed up on Oct. 7, 1935. Then the Army sent me by bus to New London where I got a physical exam.

"I then went to the Cobalt CCC camp for two weeks of conditioning. The Army officer asked if anyone would like to volunteer and go out West. I signed up and I was to go to Oregon. I went to Fort Devens, Mass. and waited for a train to go West.

"On Oct. 23, 1935 I and a large group of guys boarded a train. After almost a week we arrived on Oct. 30th. We were about 20 miles from the Pacific Coast and the weather wasn't that cold. There were a lot of forests with Douglas fir trees. The Army took me and the other enrollees by truck to the Triangle Lake CCC Camp Company #2107."

Q: What jobs did you do there?

A: "My first job was doing trail construction. I worked as a trail blazer. We cut a path through the woods using brush cutters. The next job we did was building bridges on back roads. We built box culverts using cedar wood. At camp we had our own sawmill and cut trees and made lumber out of them. Our boss was forester James W. Kibby.

"We had a bulldozer when we were building a road. There was another CCC camp that was coming towards us and we finally met them. While we were working we stayed at a side camp where we lived in tents. We also helped build a stone crusher to make gravel for the road.

Then John showed me a picture. "I was 17 years old. I lied about my age to get into the CCC. They gave me a skinhead haircut just like they did in the Army.

"One time we went to town to help put out a fire. It burned about 15 miles before we put it out. We also fought a fire at North Bend. A lot of animals like bear and elk came out after the fire. At camp we had a nursery to take care of the injured and young animals.

"After the fire we cut down the dead trees and we planted millions of trees. Then we laid tracks for trains to take the logs out.

"If lightning struck and started a fire deep in the woods, we used pack horses and mules to help fight the fires. One time we stayed 21 days fighting a fire in the town of Notre.

"We also built a wooden tower on a mountain. It took us a long time to just get to the top of the mountain. We pitched tents and cooked our meals there.

"One time we built a bridge to a family's house. Another time we dug a ditch to put pipes in so that people could have running water.

"We also built a telephone line from the town of Triangle Lake to our camp."

Q: How was the food and what did you do in the evening and weekends?

A: "The food was very good. We all had to take turns working in the kitchen.

"Some guys took evening classes. I took a woodworking class. We had a PX where we bought doughnuts and coffee.

We had movies in the rec hall. We didn't have any dances because there were no girls for miles.

"For sports we played games between other barracks. We played basketball, softball and had boxing. I won 12 matches and lost three. There was also swimming at Triangle Lake.

"One time we took a train to Eugene and had a recreation day with other CCC camps.

"Here's a picture of me dressed up going to town. That's what we did for recreation on the weekends. In town we went roller skating or just walked around.

"After two years I left the CCC on Sept. 21, 1937 because they were closing my camp and I wanted to go home. I was discharged on Sept. 30, 1937 at Fort Devens.

"When I came home I wanted to learn a trade. I went to Quoddy Village in Maine. The school was part of the National Youth Administration. I learned plumbing, ground improvements, and garage work. I left there on Dec. 15, 1938. Here is my diploma.

"Then I came home and went to Cromwell and worked in a factory. My next job was driving a delivery truck for Southern New England Ice Co.

"In 1940 I married Constance Russo and we had four children: Gerald, Gary, Debora, and Jon Scott.

"During the war I worked for the Russell Mfg. Co. I got a deferment because we made camouflage webbing for the war effort. Then in 1945 I was drafted and served in the Marines for two years. When I returned home I continued working for the Russell Co. In 1983 I retired after 40 years.

Q: Did you learn anything while in the CCC?

A: "Everything! I learned carpentry, construction, plumbing, mechanics, baking, and timbering. I was also a surveyor's helper. I learned so much in my years in the CCC."

Then John proudly showed me a letter of recommendation from his forestry foreman:

Blachly, Ore.
Sept. 17, 1937

Nenninger has worked for me the past year. He is a good timber faller and bucker, worked on road construction and maintenance, horse trail construction, and maintenance. He is fair at carpentry and good surveyor's helper. He is quick to learn and is a good helper on most any job and shows very good character.

James W. Kibby
Forestry Foreman

(Clockwise from Top, Left) 1 CCC camp Triangle Lake located in the western part of Oregon. Gary Nenninger 2 Triangle Lake boys atop a huge Douglas fir tree they loaded on a trailer. Gary Nenninger 3 John Nenninger, left, and friend are dressed up for a weekend trip to town. Gary Nenninger 4 John said, "At night I went to the rec hall and played pool, checkers, cards or just read." Gary Nenninger 5 John said, "Here's a picture of our barracks where we had to take everything out and scrub the floor." Gary Nenninger

On January 27th, 2015 I emailed John's son, Gary, a draft of his dad's life and CCC experiences for my book. The next morning I got this reply:

"The night Dad passed away he was in the hospital with a broken hip. When I told him his condition, I could tell he took it bad. I tried to encourage him but they were going to take him for more x-rays. It was after midnight so Kathy and I said our good-byes. Then he said to me, 'I'm going to Oregon.' I said to him, 'That's good Pop, when are you going?' 'Tonight,' he answered.

"I did not catch on to what he meant, but at 2:20 am I got a call from the hospital saying he just stopped breathing. They could not revive him. As soon as I heard that, I remembered the last thing he said to us, 'I'm going to Oregon tonight.'

"Dad always wanted to go back to Oregon and visit his old CCC camp. Now I knew he did."

On Monday, May 10, 2010 John passed away at Middlesex Hospital.

John Bowey
Lacomb, OR

On July 31, 2010 John Bowey attended a CCC Reunion at the Black Rock State Park in Thomaston and described what he did at a CCC camp in Lacomb, Oregon during the Depression. Podskoch

After speaking at the Thomaston Library in the winter of 2008, I received this letter from John Bowey of Waterbury:

Marty,

After reading an article about you in the Waterbury newspaper I want to tell you that I also joined the CCC. In Oct. 1936 I went to a camp (Voluntown) near Jewett City. We were asked if we wanted to go to the West Coast. All I knew about the West Coast was sunny California and I wanted that. So I volunteered.

But instead of California, it was Lacomb, Oregon. There we made fire trails in the mountains. It did not snow but it rained almost every day. We each received a canvas suit and we worked in the rain. The trees were as big as the California redwoods. There were no power tools then. Everything was done by hand. Every day at work we received one jelly and one cheese sandwich.

On Saturday night we went to town to the movies. The admission was 10 cents but the CCC paid 5 cents. Haircuts cost 5 cents and a post card with a stamp was one cent. Letters only cost 2-3 cents.

There was a bar in town and we had been told to stay out and we did.

Winter was tough and six months was enough for me and I came home in March 1937.

There were no TVs and only old fashion washers. There were no dryers or radios. It was a good experience.

John Bowey

A few months later on June 19, 2008, I visited John at his home on the hill in Waterbury where there is a large cross that is lit up each evening. John's wife Mae greeted me at the door and welcomed me to the living room where John was. Then John began telling me about his life.

"I was born on March 13, 1919 in Waterbury. My father John worked at the American Brass. My mother Ann had four children: Joseph, Anna, me, and James.

"I only got to 6th grade and quit. I just hung around and took whatever jobs I could get. My friends went into the CCC about a week before me and I got jealous and joined. They went before me and stayed in Connecticut camps, but when I signed up I was first sent to a camp in Voluntown. They lined us up and said who wants to go to the West

Coast. I thought of nothing else but sunny California. So about 2 or 3 from Waterbury signed up with me, and they took us up by truck to Fort Devens, Mass. Leaving home didn't bother me. I thought I was going to California and was excited.

"Then we got on a train to Oregon, We ate on the train and were given mostly sandwiches. Sometimes the train stopped and we got out to stretch.

"When we got there we were all surprised. The town was very small. Our camp was outside in the woods and there was not much around us. The nearest house was about a half a mile away, and the closest town was Macomb. It had only 10 houses and a store."

Q: What kind of jobs did you do and what did you do in the evenings and weekends?

A: "We were making fire trails and cleaning up brush in the woods. Out there it rains all the time.

"In the evenings we didn't do much. We had a rec hall that had a little library and a ping-pong table.

"On Saturday nights they took us into the town of Albany that had a theater and a bar. We were told to stay out of the bar and nobody went in but we went to the movies for a nickel. There wasn't even a restaurant in town."

Q: Why did you leave the CCC and what did you do when you came home?

A: "I didn't sign up again because six months was enough out there in that rainy weather. If I was there in the summer I might have stayed longer.

"When I got home I think I got a job delivering freight for a trucking company. I also worked in a restaurant doing a little bit of everything. Then I got a job in American Brass Co. There I did a lot of different jobs too. After that I was a bartender for a few years and later a house-to-house bread man and then a milkman. After that I owned the Mary Carter Paint Store in Bristol for 18 years. Then I just had a few other jobs."

Q: Did you participate in WWII?

A: "No, I got a deferment because I was working in the brass factory , that produced materials for the war effort.

"During the war I got married on Feb. 16, 1942 to Mae Lally. We didn't have children."

Q: What effect did the CCC experience have on you?

A: "I learned how to take orders and how to take care of myself while I was in the CCC."

John Bowey passed away on Sept. 3, 2014 in Waterbury. His obituary in the Sept. 7th issue of Waterbury Republican

American stated that John swam daily at the YMCA and was a regular walker at the Waterbury mall each morning. He loved watching horse races, and both he and his late wife, Mae, were avid baseball fans. They enjoyed their winters in Florida. It also stated: "Throughout his working years he met and befriended many loyal and frequent customers. He leaves behind a legacy of giving of self to those in need."

Walter Nizgorski
Medicine Bow, WY

Walter Nizgorski of Derby shared his stories of working at the CCC camp in the Medicine Bow National Park near Centennial, Wyoming. Podskoch

After meeting Walter Sekula from Norwich at many CCC reunions, he often told me that I should visit his CCC friend, Walter Nizgorski, who lived in Derby, Conn. He always referred to him as "The Sheriff."

On Nov. 24, 2008 I finally met "The Sheriff" when I was asked to speak at the Derby Historical Society dinner and meeting at the Grassy Hill Lodge in Derby. He told me that he was sent to a camp in Wyoming near Medicine Bow National Park where I had camped in 1967 when I was on a cross-country trip with my good friend John Sadell from New Jersey.

On March 18, 2009 I interviewed "The Sheriff" by phone and he told me about his life.

"My life began in Derby on Sept. 17, 1919. My father Joseph worked at American Brass in Ansonia and my mother was Magdalena. Her first three children died of influenza. Then she had five more children: Henrietta who is a nun in the Holy Family of Nazareth, Helen, Theodore, Minnie, and me, the baby of the family.

"I went three years to trade school and did mostly woodworking. I learned about the CCC from my friend, Johnny Barto.

"One morning Johnny came to my house. I was going to visit my cousin in Union City and Johnny came with me. As we were walking down Main St. we saw a bunch of guys in front of city hall. We asked what they were doing and they said they were joining the CCC. So we liked the idea and we went in and signed up. We lied about our age and we were to go out West. His parents didn't know till they got a post card. We got on a bus and they took us to the National Guard Armory in Hartford. They gave us a box lunch and we got on a train for Fort Devens, Mass.

"The first thing they gave us was post cards. The Army told us to put our family address on them so we could tell our parents that we joined the CCC and that we would write to them when we got to a camp.

"They gave us clothing and put us on a train on a Tuesday and shipped us out to Wyoming. On the fourth day it was Good Friday. They had pork chops but we couldn't eat them because we were Catholics and we couldn't eat meat. It was a fast day. We stopped at a station and a priest was there. We told him our predicament. He told us we got an absolution and could eat meat. We were happy.

"On the fifth day we got to Laramie at 4:30 in the morning. Army trucks were waiting to take us to camp. We asked how far it was to camp and the driver said, 'It is just a few miles.' But he lied because it was 30 miles.

"At 6:30 am we got into camp and got breakfast. It was Easter Sunday. The lieutenant said, 'Does anyone want to go to church in Laramie for Mass?' So a bunch of us went and rode in an Army truck.

"The camp was on a high hill and it took us two weeks to get used to the altitude in order to work.

Q: How did you feel about leaving home?

A: "I'm an adventurer. It was something I've done all my life so it didn't bother me to go away from home. Since our camp had over 100 boys from the Naugatuck Valley, it was easy to make friends and feel at home. Some of them went to school with me.

"I was assigned by the rangers to clean up the road from Centennial, Wy. to Colorado. It was hard work and I didn't believe in it. Since nobody wanted KP duty my friends and I signed up for KP permanently. We also got

$6 extra for doing the job. All the guys in camp chipped in money to pay us. We got up with the cooks at 6 am and got breakfast ready for 7 am.

"The food was good. Our cook was 5' 2" and he was good. We were able to get enough food. We also got meat from government lambs. Any lamb left over after the season we could keep them. The rangers also went out and shot deer for us.

"When I had a day off I went with a crew that was putting up fire towers. I stayed with the ranger. He asked if anyone wanted a trout. We went to the hatchery that had millions of trout. The hatchery men took a net and got some 16" trout. The ranger brought them back and cleaned them. He had a grill and cooked them for us.

"We took it easy in the evenings and played baseball and football. Some guys played football and got injured and they went to the infirmary but I never got hurt or sick. We had three guys from Ansonia High School and they threw the football around a lot.

"The only thing close by was the town called Centennial that was a mile away. It was a 'big' town with a population of four. That's a little exaggerated but it was really small. There was a country store, gas station, and a small inn. Across the street was a big dance hall. On Saturdays it was crowded and we were advised not to go but we did.

"On weekends a couple of trucks went to town and some guys stayed for the weekend. The churches also had dances. We even had people who would take us into their homes.

"Most of us were Catholics and on Sunday a truck took us to church for Mass. We stayed in town till 4 pm when a truck came and picked us up.

"One time we went to Frontier Days in Cheyenne for the big rodeo. A couple guys signed up there for the Army and then went back to camp because they had to get approval to leave camp. Two of the guys were in WWII and died at Corregidor".

Q: Were there any fights in camp?

A: "No. If you got into a disagreement, you both went behind the barracks with boxing gloves and settled it."

Q: Why did you leave the CCC?

A: "I was there for six months. When my term was up I signed up again but I got a letter from American Brass Co. to come to work where my father worked. I took the letter to the lieutenant. The policy was you could leave if you had a job. There were about a dozen of us who decided to go back home.

"When I got home I worked at American Brass in Ansonia.

"In 1941 I married Tessy Kopec and we had one daughter Frances who now is married and lives in North Branford. She has three children.

"In 1943 I joined the Army. I was a combat engineer with the 8th Armored Division and I was in the Battle of the Bulge.

"After the war I went back to work at American Brass and retired in 1966. Then I went to Miles Laboratory in West Haven and worked in security."

Q: Have you ever gone back to your CCC camp?

A: "No but I'd like to go back because one of the Air Force guys I met in WWII told me he went to my CCC camp for R&R during the war and that it was a beautiful place."

Q: How did you benefit from being in the camp?

A: "I was the youngest and spoildest kid in my family because I was the baby of the family. The CCC taught me how to make a man out of myself and how to take care of myself. There were boys there who had a choice of either going to reform school or the CCC. It was good for them, too. They all turned out well and many served in WWII."

Walter passed away on March 24, 2013.

Stanley Hallas
Split Rock, WY

Stanley Hallas at the Greenwich Public Library in May 2008 where he told the audience about working in a CCC camp in Split Rock, Wyo. Podskoch

"On May 30, 2008 I interviewed Stanley Hallas by phone. I had previously met Stanley at my CCC talk on May 30, 2008 at the Greenwich Public Library. He also brought a large photo of his camp in Wyoming that he let me copy. Here is what he shared with me about his youth and experiences in the CCC.

"My father's name was Joseph and he worked for RB & W Bolts and Nut Factory in Port Chester. Dad died in 1930. Some jerk ran up on the sidewalk and killed him. There was no insurance. My mom signed up for relief. They also wanted to take the children away from her and put us in a home. My mother said, 'You can shove it up your duppa. You're not taking my children.'

"My mother, Regina Stempien, was a tough individual. She came by herself to the US from Poland when she was 13. She had a big sign that said: 'I'm Polish and I can't speak English.'

"She had five children. Joseph was the eldest, born in 1910. He was like our father and you did not mess around with him. Next was Harry, me, Helen, and Sophie. I also had a younger brother named George who died at the age of two. I was born on March 18, 1922. My poor mother suffered trying to raise our family during the Depression.

"I graduated from 8th grade and went to trade school to be a tool maker. I stayed there for about a year and then quit.

"My best friend's brother, Butch Hupal, was in the CCC and he said he liked it. Then I saw in the Greenwich Times that they were looking for young men for the CCC. My friend, Frank Muskus, and I went to the welfare department in Greenwich to get information about joining. From there we went to Hartford to sign up.

"About two weeks later they called us up. We went to Hartford Armory and then up to Fort Devens, Mass. It was then that I saw those crazy soldiers in foxholes and it was raining. They were shooting at airplanes with wooden guns. I decided I'd never join the army. Later when I left the CCC I joined the Navy.

"I was homesick. It's a good thing I had Frank. The Army put us on a train and we were told we were going out West to Wyoming.

"The trip took us four days and four nights. We stopped in Chicago and saw the stockyards and we picked up some cattle. They were right behind the engine and boy did it stink. The train had three engines and as it went around a big bend, boy did we get the soot. We had the windows open because it was so hot. I slept with my friend on the chairs that converted to beds. We had a lot of eggs and sandwiches to eat. It tasted so good because my mom didn't have much food.

"Our camp was located in Split Rock, Wyo. Company 2129 (approximately 60 miles N of Laramie, in SE Wyo.). When we got to camp the captain asked for college grads but no one stepped forward. Then he asked for high school grads and a few stepped forward. Then he asked for grade school grads and a few more stepped out.

"Then he said I want all you dropouts to watch the high school grads pick up cigarette butts so that you can get educated.

"My first job was on a surveying crew of four people. My job was to hammer the stakes into the ground. Another guy looked through the transit and gave me the signal to move to either side. Then I placed a stake. One guy held a pole and the 3rd guy sharpened the stakes for me. We had a surveyor from Kentucky, Campbell was his name. He was a leader, a '45er'. He got 45 dollars a month. He also drove the pickup truck.

"One day I went to the infirmary for the rocky mountain spotted tick fever shot. It was so powerful they broke it up into four shots. My friend Frank worked in the infirmary and the guys passed out from the heat and the shot. One day Frank said, 'Come and help me get these guys in bed.' Frank got $36 a month because he worked in the infirmary and was classified as an assistant leader."

I asked him if any strange or funny things happened at camp.

"We had a fight with the Rhode Island guys. We said our state was better than theirs, and we had a water bucket fight.

"On Thanksgiving we had a big meal and they invited the local ranchers for dinner. Someone put GI soap into the coffee for a trick. That night I had to take a crap. I quietly opened the barracks door and there were guys all over outside with the runs. Oh jeez, I wonder what the ranchers thought of us.

"Across from the camp was the MacIntosh Ranch. They had a daughter and the 2nd Lt. was dating her.

"Most of the time I liked the food. We didn't have much of anything at home. We had the Army guys come and teach our boys how to cook.

"I only went to the nearby towns two times, once to Rawlings and once to Casper. When I went to Casper with

Frank he said, 'Let's not go back tonight (Sat).' So we rented a room. Naturally there were no trucks back on Sunday. We walked and walked. You would only see one or two cars a day. We walked to Devils Gate, a total of 42 miles. Then we got a ride on an oil truck. We stopped at a restaurant in Muddy Gap for a coffee. We heard some people say they were going to our camp to watch the movies. We asked them for a ride, but they said they didn't have any room. So the two of us rode on the fenders. It was summertime. The car had a radiator with a thermometer on it. What a ride! We were happy to get back to camp."

Q: Did they have any recreation at your camp?

A: "There were no sports. I decided to take up taxidermy. I bought a .22 rifle and went looking for coyote or something, but I didn't shoot anything.

"I stayed in the CCC for a year and left in the summer of 1940.

"When I came home a friend of mine, Mike, said, 'Do you know how to drive a dump truck?' I said, 'Yes.' I didn't know but I wanted a job. So he showed me how to drive. I began working with him for the Nichols Estate. They sold topsoil. Chester Arnold drove that same truck before me. Then he went into the bakery business with his brother Paul. I used to get their leftover bread for free. It later became the large Arnold Bread Co.

"Then when WWII broke out I didn't want to be in the Army so I joined the Navy. My experience in the CCC helped me because I knew how to get along with people.

"After the war I married Ethel Burns in 1946. We have a daughter Ruth and a son, Joseph. I also have three great grandchildren, Arthur, Evelyn, and Edward.

"I worked at Electrolux in Greenwich as a floater repairman. We had a conveyor belt adding parts to the motor. My job was that I could fill in any position. I was very fast. I worked there for 43 years. They moved in 1985 and I retired at age 62.

"I took my wife, daughter, and son three times to Wyoming to see my old CCC camp in 1969, 1970, and 1982. Then in 1988 I took just my wife. There is nothing left just the stone paths and the water tower.

"We stopped to see Jim Falow who had been the superintendent of our camp and he was Indian. We visited Jim in the town of Lander and he took us all around the town. He was so proud of me. Lander was near an Indian Reservation and we had liberty to go there but I never went there.

"One time one of our guys, 'Big Stoop,' got hit over the head with a whiskey bottle. Many years later I saw him in the Electrolux factory where I worked. I said to my friend, 'Boy he looks familiar.'

"The next year I saw him again and went up to him and said, 'I know you from somewhere.' He replied, 'I was in a CCC camp in Wyoming.' I replied, 'Oh, you're Big Stoop.' And he said, 'Yes.' That was unreal.

"The greatest thing that I learned from being in the CCC was getting along with all the different types of people."

Stanley Hallas passed away on Oct. 28, 2014 in Greenwich.

"Serving in the CCCs Put Me In Touch With the Nation: The CCC Experience of Edward Glannon" Presented by Patricia (Glannon) Wiley

Edward John Glannon at the time he was in the CCC.
Pat Wiley

The following interview is from an audiotape Edward Glannon made with Jan Dunbar, on June 30, 1979, for a local radio station, when Glannon was visiting West Yellowstone.

I came into Yellowstone the first time in 1933. I was a scholarship kid at the Art Students League in New York City. I was twenty-one. After my fellowship dried up, I had no money. One day I was offered a chance to go into the CCCs and I jumped at it. I traveled West on a train with other members of my CCC group.

We came into Yellowstone on a June morning. It was so beautiful coming up the valley toward Yellowstone with snow on the ground and on the pine trees. The town was romantic, like a movie set. It was small with a few stores along Main Street. The air was so clean. It was so promising. It made me feel that my luck had changed. I didn't feel so pessimistic.

The train went right into the station at Yellowstone. There were trucks to pick us up, 245 men and 30 from Bozeman. Some were supervisors and some were workers. The group wasn't exactly welcome. The CCC men had a bad reputation. Many had drifted around; some were criminals who joined to suspend sentences. The people of Yellowstone were afraid of the camp men.

We were setting up a camp on the western side of Hebgen Lake. The ranger there was Mr. White. We put up tents. Those were tough times. It rained a lot. We were divided into crews, and given a variety of jobs to do. We creosoted telephone poles, built fire lines, put telephone lines up to lookout posts, and fought forest fires. I was on a very big fire near Livingston.

My first assignment was a carpenter's detail. We built the mess hall. Mr. Sam Cox, a manual training teacher from Bozeman, was in charge of the mess hall job. The government sent Mr. Bill Cowan for a biological detail. We dug larkspur out where it was poisoning the animals. People had plowed up the land. The buffalo grass was ripped up. We needed to get it back into some kind of proportion. We poisoned a lot of animals. Those were drought years. Gophers multiplied and ate the new grass before it could get established. Their predators were gone. It took 30 years for the land to come back. It was a heartbreaking place, but it came back. When I look at that valley now, I can't believe it. The grass is back, the cattle are visible.

Mr. Henderson, a blacksmith, sharpened tools. He taught us about snakes. The three Frieze brothers from Bozeman worked with the CCC men. There was a detail working on roads around the lake, but I wasn't in that group.

Mrs. Kvosanmacher, who lived on a ranch in the area, baked a cake for our crew every day. She was so grateful for the work being done.

Some people in Yellowstone thought the men were a bunch of atheists. Sam Eagle came on a number of Sundays and brought ministers. The captain gave orders that the men had to attend. Sunday was the only day off to wash clothes. Each man had one outfit, an old WWI uniform. They wore half of the clothes while washing the other half. The fellows were resentful about the ministers. The men would sing part of a hymn and then go right into "Sidewalks of New York."

We didn't get to town much. We were only allowed to come in limited numbers – around 20. There wasn't much to do in town. The Frieze boys told me all summer there was a girl in town they wanted me to meet. I went into town to arrange a railroad ticket back to New York. I met Helen Eagle, Sam's daughter, who later came to NY City to go to library school at Columbia, and we later married.

I went back to NY in the fall after serving for four months. I got word my scholarship had been renewed, and I was released early.

Being in the CCCs was precious and affected me all my life and my attitude toward America. Performing service for the nation was so important. I've heard (in 1979) that people were trying to organize alumni of the CCCs with the hope the government would repeat such programs. I'd like to see every American put in a year's service for the nation. There was so much suffering in 1933. Getting these kids out into the clean and open country was a good idea.

Being in the CCCs gave me a chance to see the nation and a chance to meet people from other parts of the country. I learned a lot about relating to men, to fellow workers. This helped me later when I worked in a boy's club and later became a teacher. It helped me to understand the problems of the country. The CCCs contributed to the nation's understanding of the importance of ecology. It was then that I made the most important decision I would ever make: It became my dream as a landscape painter to express the feeling of the land.

Glannon later wrote in his journal: "That first trip west had a profound effect on me and anything I would ever do because of the expanse, the grandeur, the largeness of what I saw. It put me in touch with the nation."

Edward Glannon was born in 1911 in Pittsburgh,

Penn. He began teaching at the Gramercy Boys Club in New York City under a Public Works of Art Project. He then taught for many years at the Fieldston Ethical Culture School in Riverdale, NY. He taught art and ethics. The last 12 years of his career he taught art at Roslyn High School. This is kind of amazing for a man who never finished high school. He was forced to go to work to help support his large family. He was self-educated. For many years he led Great Books Groups at the Bryant Library as a volunteer.

Edward Glannon taught art for many years and painted the American land all his life. To see images of Edward Glannon and his paintings (including a painting of Hebgen Valley), visit www.edwardglannon.com. To view his lithographs, visit www.oldprintshop.com.

Peter Miezejeski
OR / VT

Peter Miezejeski worked at four camps over 2 ½ years: East Hartland, Conn; Sublimity, Ore; Waterbury, Vt., and Haddam, Conn. Delcie McGrath

On April 6, 2015 I received an email from Delcie McGrath of Essex, Conn.

"My sister, Sandy Olson, told me about the Connecticut CCC book you are writing. Our father and I believe some other people from Deep River, Conn., were in several of the camps in Conn. My father saved his original Certificate of Discharge from the Civilian Conservation Corps. I made copies for you."

The records showed that Delcie's father, Peter was 18 years old when he enrolled on July 12, 1934 at Fort H. G.

A Glannon painting of Wyoming where he worked in the CCC. Patricia (Glannon) Wiley

Wright. He was 5' 5" tall with blue eyes, brown hair, and a ruddy complexion. He was sent on July 12, 1934 to be a laborer to East Hartland, Conn. He did reforestation work and received "Satisfactory" ratings for the three employment periods. After working for 14 months Peter was "Honorably Discharged" on Sept. 30, 1935 by Capt. W. B. Smith. He was sent to Winsted where he was given transportation to his home in Deep River.

The next year Peter needed a job and rejoined the CCC and was sent again to East Hartland's Camp Robinson on Oct. 30, 1936 where he continued to do reforestation work. He worked for five months and his work period ended on March 31, 1937. He received an "Excellent" rating from his foreman.

Then Peter volunteered to go out West and on April 11, 1937 the Army sent him by train to Sublimity in the central part of Oregon near Mill City. His CCC Co. 2106 worked constructing buildings, trails, bridges, retaining walls, and other park infrastructure.

After his six-month period on Oct. 8, 1937 he received a "Satisfactory" rating. He decided to sign up again and was sent to Waterbury, Vt. where he worked in Co. 1108 working on flood control and building a dam. This turned out to be a short stay of two months and he was then sent to Haddam, Conn. to Camp Filley Co. 1195. He worked as a laborer in the surrounding Cockaponset State Forest where he was close to his home farm in Deep River.

On Feb. 18th 1938 he became sick and was taken by camp ambulance to New London and then on a ferry to the Army hospital at Fort H. G. Wright on Fishers Island, NY. After 10 days he left the hospital and resumed work at Camp Filley on Feb. 28, 1938. He worked in Haddam to the end of his 6-month period and was "Honorably Discharged" by his Commanding Officer, E. G. Schwartz on March 31 with an "Excellent" work rating. He had served approximately 2 ½ years in the CCC.

I talked to Delcie in June 2016 and she said, "The only pictures from this period are at Sublimity, Ore. He was in Oregon with his brother Paul. Paul met a girl near camp and eventually married her. He found work in logging but later died at a young age in a logging accident.

"I later visited my father's old camp site in Oregon and got to meet some of my Uncle Paul's family. I had never met them before. I also visited my dad's CCC camp that is now Silver Falls State Park. Some of the CCC buildings have been preserved.

Peter (right) with friends in the woods at his camp near Sublimity, Ore. Delcie McGrath

"My father never really talked much about his experiences in all of these camps so that is why there is such a short description. He did, however, take our family to Vermont to see the large dam he worked on.

"My sister sent me the 'Interview Questions' you gave her. Here is information about my father's life.

"Dad was born in Staten Island June 29, 1917. His parents, Vincent and Anna, came from Poland. They met in Staten Island, married, and had 13 children in this order: Charles Michael, Thomas, Paul, Peter, John, Edward, Vincent, Lillian, Genevieve, Joseph, Janina, Stanley, and Mary.

"The family moved to Deep River, Conn. in 1925. My father went to only the 8th grade and worked to help his family. When he was 18 he enlisted in the CCC possibly because his brother, Paul told him about it. His work in the CCC helped his family financially and he learned a lot of skills.

"When he left the CCC he worked for the WPA. Then he got a job at the nearby Essex Machine Works Co.

"In 1942 my father enlisted in the Army. The next year he married Virginia (North) and they had six children: me, Walter, Sandra, Kent, Karen, and Deanna.

"After the war he had many odd jobs until he found a permanent job at Essex Marine Railway where he worked for approximately 30 years.

"My father passed away in Essex on Aug. 9, 2002."

Joseph "Ray" Bedard
Athol & Baldwinsville, MA / Albany, NY

Ray Bedard learned how to drive a bulldozer in the CCC like the one he is standing near at the Connecticut CCC Museum in Stafford Springs in 2010. Podskoch

On Aug. 29, 2008 I visited Joseph "Ray" Bedard at his home in East Hartford. His daughter Joan had read about my search for CCC men and called me and said her father had been in the CCC in Massachusetts.

When I knocked on the door his wife, Irene, graciously welcomed me into their home. I, of course, began singing the old song to her, "Goodnight, Irene." It isn't very often that I get to meet an Irene. She laughed and then introduced me to Ray who was seated at the kitchen table and was happy to meet me.

"My real name is Joseph but everybody calls me Ray. I was stationed at three CCC camps. One was in Athol, Mass., the second was Baldwinsville, Mass., and finally Albany, NY. I loved it and the food was great,' said Ray."

Q: Could you tell me about your early life and family?

A: "My parents were both from the small town of Saint-Agapit just west of Quebec. My father, Arthur, couldn't find work and moved our family to the US. My mother, Alphonsine had lost three children to the influenza outbreak in Canada. My parents crossed the border in June of 1923 and came to Lawrence, Mass. where there were a lot of woolen mills. My mother was pregnant with me. I was born on Dec. 28, 1923. She had a total of ten children. The eldest was Rose followed by Alice, Armand, me, Robert, Philip, and Paul.

"I never finished high school but quit on my 16th birthday, halfway in 9th grade because I had to help my family. It was during the Depression and jobs were scarce.

"I signed up for the CCC in Lawrence, Mass. and was sent to the camp in Athol, Mass. I was a little anxious about leaving home but when I got there I met a lot of nice guys. Two of my best friends were Ricardo Nobrega from New Bedford and Albert Davis from Woburn. We were always together. On the weekends the three of us hung around a skating rink in Gardner, Mass. There were a group of girls we called the 'Moocher Gang' that we hung around with. Almost every night they paid our entry fee.

"I also had a friend Bob Barnett. He was from my hometown. I got to see him only once after we were discharged.

"My job at camp was driving trucks and operating heavy machinery. They taught me how to drive a grader, bulldozer, and a crane. After the Hurricane of 1938 there were a lot of downed trees. I operated a crane and picked up logs and guys cut the wood into cordwood. Then they placed it along the tote roads.

"Besides cleaning up the dead trees we built roads and fought forest fires."

Q: Did you ever go home on the weekends?

A: "Never! The only time I went home was when I was discharged.

"I was too busy having fun. During the week after work we played baseball. They weren't organized games, just pick-up games.

"My buddies and I were then transferred to the Baldwinsville, Mass. CCC camp. We did a lot of the same

Ray Bedard proudly served in the Army during WWII and participated in the invasion of Normandy.
Joan Bedard Rogers

494

work that we did at the Athol camp. We worked together.

"Then we were transferred to a camp near Albany, NY. We didn't stay long. My three friends didn't like it. We were more isolated than Athol and the camp was coming to a close along with other camps in the US. Since our six-month term expired we asked to go back to our camp in Baldwinsville and I was discharged.

"My two friends and I went to the Simplex Clock Co. in Gardner, but we never got hired. Then we got a job as attendants at a mental institution where we got room and board.

"Then in May 1943 I was notified by the draft board that I was going into the Army. I was shipped to Devens Army Base and then to a camp in Mississippi. I then went to Europe and participated in the Normandy Invasion. I met a CB (Construction Battalion) and asked him if he knew my brother Armand who was also a CB. He said, 'Do you mean 'Frenchie'?' and I said, 'Yes.' And I got to meet my brother. Amazing!

"After three years in the Army I came home and got a job in the post office in Lawrence, Mass. I married Irene Gagne and we had six children: Richard, Tommy, Elaine, Joan, David, and Gloria.

"On Sept. 19, 1985 I retired from the post office.

"The CCC was good to me. I learned to drive a truck and run machinery. I enjoyed my CCC life!"

Frank Evans
Holyoke, MA

Frank Evans at a CCC Reunion at Upton State Park in Massachusetts. Podskoch

Diane Dungey of Woodstock, Conn. contacted me in the summer of 2015 and said her father, Frank Evans, had worked in the CCC. I asked her if I could interview him as soon as possible. Diane arranged for a telephone interview on Aug. 31, 2015.

Before the interview, however, I was fortunate to meet Frank Evans at a CCC Reunion at Upton State Park in Upton, Mass. on Aug. 29, 2015. Two days later I interviewed Frank and he told me about his life and experiences in the CCC.

"I was born on Nov. 4, 1921 in Westborough, Mass. Both my mother and father worked during the day and left us at our neighbor's farm. I was just three years old when my parents broke up and I continued to live with the Stamford family. Mr. Stamford was Polish and his wife was Swedish. She was a very good cook. They were very nice and kind to me. As I got older I worked doing chores on the farm."

Q: How did you learn about the CCC?

A: "I lived near the Upton CCC Camp 1205 in Westborough. The camp was just about two miles from the Stamford farm. There were about 100 pigs on our farm. Mr. Stamford and I collected garbage at the CCC camp and brought it back to the farm for the pigs. They had good garbage that the pigs loved.

"Then the Stamfords pulled me out of my first year of high school to work on the farm. I lost out on education, but I got a lot of experience, which I am really happy about.

"When I was 17, I joined the CCC in April 1939. I felt good about going away from home. I was sent to the Mt. Tom Camp, Holyoke, Mass.

"The camp was very nice. I liked being there. The food was great and I had good friends. One of my good friends at camp was Oliver Charrette who came from Pittsfield. He was transferred from his first camp to Mt. Tom to be near his mother."

Q: What kind of work did you do there?

A: "My camp built a lot of roads. I ran many types of equipment: a stone crusher, tractor, bulldozer, and trucks. Our camp had Reo rack trucks and Dodge dump trucks

"The 1938 hurricane hit Mt. Tom pretty hard and we removed downed trees.

"During my two years in camp I never got injured or sick. Some guys did get injured but it was mostly from swinging an axe and getting cut."

Q: Did anything funny, scary, or sad happen to you while at camp?

A: "The guys liked to give hot feet. If you laid down in the afternoon with your shoes on, they put a match between the sole of your shoe and then lit it. Your foot would start to get really hot and wake you up. Then you'd start dancing around the barracks. I learned to always take my shoes off if I laid down."

Q: What did you do on weeknights and weekends?

A: "I usually read in the barracks and just hung around camp. I didn't do any drinking like some of the other guys.

"There were three stoves in each barracks. I hated that stinky soft coal. It really smelled bad.

"On the weekends I chauffeured our company captain. On Saturdays I drove him to his home in Stafford Springs. I always kept his car polished. Then on Sundays I picked him up about 3 pm and brought him back to camp. He was a nice guy."

Q: How was the food?

A: "The food was excellent. They made cakes that were great. Since I was a truck driver and worked at the garage I never got KP. I was the head truck driver. I liked bulldozer work the best of all the machines I operated."

Q: Why did you leave the CCC?

A: "After two years I got a job. The camp superintendent saw that I did a good job over the two years I was in camp and said that I should get out and get a job. He took me to Quonset Point, R. I. where there was a lot of construction work going on. I joined the union and I did work all over the state in construction for 42 years.

"Shortly before my 21st birthday in 1942 I was drafted into the Army. The CCC was the same as in the Army, only you learned to shoot. I learned discipline there. You got up at 6 am and you hollered out your name when they called it.

"During WWII I was sent to Europe. I was in the infantry for two years. I was mostly driving trucks. Then they finally switched me to doing construction work which I had a lot of experience doing.

"While in the CCC I met my wife Alice through a friend. She came from East Hampton, Mass. We got married on June 27, 1942. We have a son Frank and daughter, Diane."

Q: When you look back at your time in the CCC what did you accomplish?

A: "The CCC had a good influence on me. It was there that I learned how to operate heavy machinery and eventually got a union job where I worked for 42 years. I retired from Perini Construction Co. in 1983 after working

for them for 20 years.

"I have gone back to my old camp about 30 times where I took a lot of people hiking over on Mt. Tom.

"My wife and I have traveled a lot around the US and what impressed me was seeing the different national parks. Much of the work the CCC did is still intact.

"I gave the Connecticut CCC Museum a few of my CCC items like my trunk. It was there that I met Walter Sekula. Walter was also in the CCC and worked hard to develop the CCC museum. Over the years, we became good friends and traveled together to CCC functions. Do you want to make their relationship clearer?

"My experience with the CCC traveled with me throughout my life. It enabled me to have a successful career and through a friend I met in the work program, I met my wife, Alice."

Carl Frank Leiner
Chicopee Falls, MA

Carl Leiner at the entrance to CCC Co. 1156 in
Chicopee Falls, Mass.

At my talk on March 9, 2009 at the New Town Library I met Audrey Leiner DeBlasio. She told me her father, Carl Frank Leiner, was in the CCC and she promised to send me information about him.

On May 24, 2009 she sent me this information: "Here is what I can tell you about my daddy and the wonderful man he was.

"Carl Frank Leiner (pronounced 'Liner') was born Oct. 12, 1916 in New Britain, Conn. His parents, Anton

(L–R) 1 CCC boys standing by the US flag during retreat at the end of the day. 2 A few of the camp buildings at Chicopee Falls in 1936. 3 The Infirmary is immaculate, well-provisioned, and ready for the coldest day. All photos courtesy Audrey Leiner DeBlasio

Leiner and Johanna Binder Leiner, were immigrants of Rax in Jennersdorf and Burgenland, Austria. Anton arrived through Ellis Island on March 27, 1909 and Johanna Binder arrived Sept. 4, 1907. Anton and Johanna met, married, and settled in New Britain, Conn.

"My grandparents had seven children who survived to adulthood. My dad, Carl, was the 3rd oldest of six boys and one girl. The children were in this order: Anthony, New Britain; Joseph, Higganum; Carl F., Bolton; and John, Frank, Sylvia Fredericks, and Edward all of New Britain. I never knew my grandparents. They also had a daughter, Anna, between Joseph and my dad who only lived six months.

"My dad went to grammar school and Jr. High until age 16. Then he went to trade school at night. During the 1920s he was also a delivery boy for The Hartford Courant in New Britain.

"My dad joined the CCC on Nov. 14, 1935 just after turning 19. Daddy's two older brothers, Tony and Joe, had married and moved away from home. His youngest brother, Eddie, was 7 years old. My dad was now the oldest at home, and his parents had separated leaving his mother alone with the four younger ones. My grandfather was apparently an abusive alcoholic. Dad joined the CCC to help his mother financially to raise the younger ones and keep the family together. My Uncle Eddie will tell you that my dad was the one who kept the family together. He was the glue. Uncle Eddie said my dad made it his duty to make sure the family was stable before getting married. When the kids were younger, the family had to be separated into foster homes or with relatives while their mother was hospitalized. It was Dad who made sure they all got back with his mom as a family when she recovered. My Uncle John, who was two

years younger than my dad, took over daddy's job at the Pongrantz Grocery in New Britain when my dad went into the CCC.

"Although Daddy was a Connecticut boy, he was sent to Chicopee Falls, Mass. I understood it was because the Connecticut camps were full and the extra boys were sent to other states.

"From Nov. 1935 to June 1937, my dad was a hospital orderly at the infirmary.

"After my dad died, I found this May 17, 1936 Springfield Republican article that described dad's camp and what he did there:"

"CCC Boys at Chicopee Achieve Unique Record for Work and Health"

Anybody who thinks youths in their 'teens and early twenties can't be happy under rigid disciplinary measures should take a few minutes off someday and ride out to Sheridan Street, Chicopee Falls, to the Civilian Conservation camp – the camp that has made a name for itself among hundreds of others throughout the country for actual conservation accomplishments and high standards of health among the personnel. Partly because the camp is situated in a remote district adjacent to the watershed of the Chicopee water supply system and partly because the citizens are not aware of the spirit of hospitality that pervades the entire encampment, this spot is seldom visited by the ordinary Sunday driver.

The camp occupies a sizeable plot of land about a quarter-mile from the end of the immense tobacco plantation of the American Sumatra Wrapper company. It is set back about 100 feet from the road and is partly sheltered by a growth of trees. The buildings include separate shelters for the officers and foresters, a mess hall for the officers and boys, the administration building and recreation hall, a huge garage to house the camp's trucks and the barracks. The hospital building is the first to greet the eye on entering the enclosure.

Washing dishes is one of the more important items in the camp's problems and to this end an outdoor dishwashing shed has been erected. Dirty dishes are put in three barrels filled with water and placed over a big furnace. The plates are tempered to fresh water during the cleaning process and by the time they reach the boiling water in the third barrel they are spic and span. A rectangular plot of ground gives the visitor a feeling of entering a parkway once he gets inside. During their spare time the boys have planted numerous flowering bushes to beautify the place.

Living here is a group of almost 200 eager, ambitious youths taken out of the ranks of the unemployed in their respective cities and put to gainful employment in a healthy atmosphere. Hailing mainly from the state of Connecticut, they represent practically every nationality on the face of the globe. They have been transferred from a state of harmful inertia to a scene of intense activity where the food is good and lodging excellent.

There is a fixed routine for every day in the year with instructors on daily duty, teaching English, history, photography, geography and even ballroom dancing.

"Complete Hospital Unit"

Chief among the camp's attractions is the cozy little hospital with a six-bed ward, an operating room and all the appurtenances of a well-equipped medical institution. Splendid work on the part of the camp physician and surgeon, Dr. Paul H. Davis, a native of Boston, has placed the Sheridan Street camp on a standing second to none in the country, as far as health is concerned.

Dr. Davis has been gratified with the results of his talks to the boys on hygiene and has kept them in fine condition by compulsory periodic examinations. He has handled something like 400 cases since he was assigned to the camp from the Fort Devens hospital last fall and has supervised extensive improvements on the infirmary. The young physician recently took visitors on an inspection trip through his building and proudly showed his anteroom where he personally mixes medicine used at camp.

Asked what were the chief causes of trouble, physically, Dr. Davis stated that hernias were by far the most common. There have been innumerable cases of cuts and other afflictions and injuries brought to his first-aid room but none ever proved serious after treatment. During the winter just passed, the camp emerged practically unscathed, with serious illnesses reduced to a minimum.

Due to inoculations of Faelten's anti-pneumonia coccic serum during the early part of the winter, there were comparatively few cases of the dreaded pneumonia. There was one case of lobar pneumonia but the patient recovered completely. Inspection of every boy before he takes up his duties at camp has reduced the danger of spread of venereal diseases to nothing. Any youth found carrying a social disease is promptly stricken from the lists. All the boys are advised as to the proper procedure for any contingency.

Besides keeping the campers in good health Dr. Davis trains orderlies. He has two camp members on duty at the hospital 24 hours a day. These two boys, Kimball and Carl Leiner, both of New Britain, Conn., are experts in ministration to the sick. They have been taught every phase of nursing and could stack up well with any R.N., Dr. Davis stated.

The doctor himself must be ready to handle any emergency that may occur when the public is concerned.

(L–R) 1, 2 The Infirmary is immaculate, well-provisioned, and ready for the coldest day. Audrey Leiner DeBlasio 3 Carl Leiner (left) with a friend on the camp ambulance that was used to transport serious cases to the Army hospital at Fort Devens, Mass. Audrey Leiner DeBlasio

The cooks stored perishable foods in the root cellar. Audrey Leiner DeBlasio

During the flood the medical department of the camp functioned 24 hours a day to aid flood sufferers. One day a two-year-old lad was rushed into the infirmary in a cyanotic state. He had been playing with a bean in his mouth, which became lodged in the trachea. Quick action, including the delicate operation of removing the bean, brought the youngster back from almost positive death.

Besides his medical duties, Dr. Davis inspects the meats and vegetables. All food handlers are examined weekly and every last man in the encampment has received inoculations against typhoid and small pox. For his good work, Dr. Davis recently received a letter of commendation from the general of the area.

Lieut. Philip N. Gallagher of Cambridge is in charge of the camp. In talking with Lieut. Gallagher, one learns that the daily routine consists of rising at 6 am, breakfast at 6:30, doing general housecleaning from 6:50 to 7:50 and starting work in the field at the watershed at 8. Their jobs consist of riprapping, roadwork, transplanting, and brush cleaning. The day's work is ended at 4.

As a matter of interest, it was learned that the camp spends about $3000 a month for food, uses 125 pounds of potatoes in a meal and one-quarter of a beef. At breakfast the camp consumes 40 quarts of milk and 40 dozen eggs. To the man primarily responsible for their well-being, they seem to forever swear allegiance. President Roosevelt is their god.

❈ ❈

"While in the CCC as a hospital orderly, my dad of course became friendly with Dr. Paul Davis and the other orderly, Louis Kimball. Based on my dad's photos I would conclude that he had friendships with Lt. Harry Jenkins, Red Aldrich, and Ralph "Dinny" Goudreault. My dad visited with the Goudreault family in Haverhill, Mass. in

June 1937 a few months before he was discharged from the CCC. My dad was a very friendly and likeable guy with great morals and principles, so I imagine he got along pretty well with everyone.

"As hospital orderly, Dad was transferred from Chicopee Falls Co. #1156 on June 25, 1937 with 'manner of performance' as 'excellent.' He was transferred to the 1174th Company in Westfield, Mass. on June 25, 1937 to work in forestry getting rid of the gypsy moths. He was in with the 1174th Co. for a little over a month until he was honorably discharged from the CCC on Aug. 4, 1937 to accept employment.

"For his work at the CCC, daddy's mother, Mrs. Johanna Leiner of Cherry St., New Britain, received $25 per month. Daddy received an allotment of $4.80 each month. He wasn't a smoker and didn't gamble, so I'm not sure what he did with his money. My guess would be he saved it or sent it home, too.

"After Daddy was honorably discharged, his first job was as a zipper machinist. He made 36 cents an hour on a three-month trial basis, and then made minimum wage of 40 cents an hour. He worked in factories in New Britain and tried completing his high school equivalency but there were transportation problems. He had to turn in his registration on his car so that his mother could qualify for welfare benefits. From Sept. 1942 to Sept. 1943 Daddy worked as a machine setup man for New Britain Machine Co.

"From Sept. 24, 1943 until he was honorably discharged on Nov. 14, 1945, Daddy served in the U.S.

Lt. Harry Jenkins was one of the Army junior officers in May 1937. Audrey Leiner DeBlasio

(L–R) 1 When their service was done, the boys were taken home by the Army. 2 The Mess hall and an altar up front where religious services were held. 3 Jeep, Moon, Johnnie, and Roger were some of the cooks at the camp. All photos courtesy Audrey Leiner DeBlasio

Navy. He served as a Water Tender Third Class on the USS LST 906 and LST 526 in the European-African-Middle Eastern area. LSTs were cargo ships which carried tanks, bulldozers, ammunition, and occasionally troops to Italy, France, and Africa.

"The following information about my father is from an interview with his granddaughter, Rebecca Schraffenberger, about his Navy experiences:"

❦ ❧

'Grandpa Carl can only remember one instance in which the LST 906 encountered real danger. He told me: 'It was March 17, 1944. The ship was delivering a load of cargo to Marseilles, France, from Palermo, Sicily, when it encountered three German torpedo boats. We turned back, and sailed around the islands of Corsica and Sardinia. It was about 550 miles and the ship could only go six miles an hour, so it was a big delay. The engine room was ordered to go flank speed, which was about 11 miles per hour. I thought the ship was going to shake apart. It's like pressing the gas pedal to the floor of your car.'

'Five months later, on Aug. 15, 1944 Grandpa Carl saw something he would never forget. Carl and his friend, Freddy Fisher, were on the bow of the ship. There were ships everywhere as far as you could see. They saw aboard another ship none other than Winston Churchill. "Churchill gave us the V-sign for victory." Carl remembers Freddy asking, "Who's the fat guy with the derby and the cigar in his mouth?" Carl replied, "That's Winston Churchill!"

'The crew of the LST 906 also saw other famous people. In fact, they came aboard. The ship went to Northern Italy and picked up the survivors of the heroic 442nd Army unit, which was comprised of Japanese Americans. These men would go on to rescue a Texan battalion from the Nazis in the French Vosges, and become the most decorated unit of

the U.S. Army in all its history. Carl recalled that most of the members of the 442nd were awarded Purple Hearts, for the bravery and determination they exhibited despite their wounds.

'Most of the sailors on the LSTs came home without a scratch. Grandpa Carl was not one of those sailors. One day, he missed the last rung of a ladder and fell three decks down onto the steel floor below. Back up the ladder he climbed, but at the top he passed out. He stayed aboard the ship for three days and three nights under the ship doctor's care. Then he was sent to an Army hospital, where he stayed for six weeks so his cracked ribs could heal. There he saw great suffering. He recalls seeing an Air Force captain named Tom Maloney being brought in. Maloney had been shot down over France, and had parachuted onto a beach. He was walking on the beach and stepped on a land mine. A Frenchman found him and brought him to the hospital.

'Grandpa Carl said, "His legs were just so bandaged up. They were like that (and he motioned with his hands to show the remnants of the captain's legs). There were many cases like that, so I couldn't feel sorry for myself."

'While Carl was in the hospital (I recall he was in the hospital in Italy), the LST 906 was shipwrecked on the rocks at Cartagena, Spain. So, after Carl got out of the hospital, he was assigned to a different ship, the LST 526. Aboard that, he traveled back and forth from Sicily to Africa along the Italian coast for a while.'

❦ ❧

"Two years after the war, Daddy met my mother, Catherine Kurys, on a blind date. She was at New Britain Teachers College. They married and had seven children: Carol Schraffenberger, (Stafford Springs); Michael (Bolton), John (Palmer, Ark.), Andrew (Bolton), Diane Leiner (Cape May Courthouse, NJ), Audrey DeBlasio

(Newtown), and Kathleen A. Leiner (deceased).

"Dad worked for the Ward Maier and Co. as sheet-metal worker for over 40 years before his retirement in 1979. He worked a long day to support his wife and seven children. I remember him up at 4 am and out the door by 5 am and not home until 7 pm.

"During his retirement my dad liked to travel a lot with family and friends. My daddy knew how to enjoy retirement life. He made you smile! I miss the sparkle in his eyes when he'd laugh.

"My dad died peacefully at home July 29, 1998 in Bolton.

"After my father died, I showed my dad's surviving siblings the Springfield newspaper article that generated these memories. Here are a couple of CCC stories from my uncles and aunts:

"Aunt Rita Leiner (Uncle John's wife) said, 'Your father liked the CCC. He told me that there were 200+ guys up at the CCC camp and he couldn't get a date. He asked me to fix him up with one of her (Rita's) friends. So when he came home to New Britain one night, I had four of my friends go out to the movies and then for ice cream in John's car. Your daddy was in the back seat with my friend, Ann. I overheard your dad say to Ann, 'You can just call me Doc.'

"Dad's brother Joe said, 'The article about the CCC camp brought back memories of the time Carl, home from leave, needed a ride back to the camp. It was raining when we left New Britain, but the weather was changing. We dropped Carl off at the camp and then the weather started sleeting. The roads were not sanded in those days, and the road changed into a skating rink. We slid off the road many times. We crept along the side of the road for a mile at 5 to 10 mph until we got near Connecticut, where the going got better. Years have passed but I have never had such slippery conditions since.'

"Joe continued, 'I don't know if your father ever told you about an incident that happened at the camp. We were riding to work one day when he told it to me. His version was funny. It seems the cook had a cat to keep the mice away. This cat had the run of the kitchen, sometimes sleeping on the high shelves where it was warmer. It was breakfast time and the boys were coming into the mess hall. Cocoa was served every day and there was a huge pot boiling on the range. The cat woke up and started to make his way along the shelves. Somehow he slipped and fell right into the boiling hot cocoa. The cook yelled for Carl to help him and between them they got the cat out of the pot. Since there wasn't enough time to make another pot of cocoa, Carl and the cook frantically, with sieves, went through the cocoa to get the cat hairs out and then they wheeled the cocoa out to be served. Carl said somebody made a remark that the cocoa tasted different and asked if they had changed their brand.'

"I cried reading this letter from my uncle imagining Daddy telling Uncle Joe this story on the long ride to work probably with tears of laughter in his eyes. My dad loved funny stories."

Harold Oehler
South Lee, MA

Harold Oehler attended the CCC Reunion at the CT CCC Museum in Sept. 2012 and shared his memories working at the Beartown State Forest in South Lee, Mass. Podskoch

At the Connecticut CCC Museum Reunion on Sept. 28, 2012, Harold Oehler told the gathering about his life and time in the CCC.

"When I finished high school in summer of 1934, there was no work to be found. I wasn't quite old enough, but I went to sign up for the CCC anyway. I was just 16. When I went to sign up the 1st Lt. called me in and asked me what year I was born. I told him Oct. 16, 1917 which made me 16 years old. He said, 'Well, that makes you ineligible by one year, but we'll forget about it because you are almost 17.'

"They sent me to Beartown State Forest in Massachusetts. Camp No. 112. It was in South Lee in the southwestern part of the state. I wasn't nervous about leaving home because I was able to come home frequently on the weekends. My first crew foreman, Bill Hogan, was from my hometown of Holyoke, and he'd give me a ride.

"My camp was an interesting place. In my barracks we had three stoves down the middle of the floor. Guys had to carry wood to our barracks from a huge woodpile in camp.

"My first job was building a road around Benedict Pond. We came in after they cleaned up the tree stumps. I was a laborer cracking boulders to make gravel. I believe that road is still there.

"In the winter of 1934 we worked in a wildlife refuge. They used a bulldozer to clear areas to plant bushes that produced food for wildlife.

"I enjoyed hunting and fishing so the CCC helped develop my love of the woods. We did a lot of walking on the weekends. We liked to walk in the wildlife refuge.

"In December we patrolled the roads in the wildlife refuge to prevent hunting.

"The hard work and great food in the CCC had a big effect on me. I grew about 3-4 inches taller and gained about 30-40 lbs. It was all due to my daily swinging of a sledgehammer building the road.

"We also enjoyed visiting a fire tower on Mount Wilcox in the wildlife refuge.

"When we got back to camp after a hard day working, we had what they called retreat and the saluting of the flag. After supper I didn't do too much because I was so tired from swinging the sledgehammer that I went to bed early.

"Our camp was run by Army reserve officers. The training we got really paid off during World War II. We knew what to do and we were in great shape.

"In the spring, Camp No. 112 closed and they shipped me to Cuttingsville, Vt. about 10 miles southeast of Rutland.

"The first thing we did was set up a side camp on Mendham Mt. in Aitken State Forest. It was an abandoned CCC camp. There were three tarpaper covered barracks and a kitchen/mess hall. I worked on a forestry work crew. We cut trees that were marked by the forester. We had about 15 men on our crew. Any tree he marked under 4" in diameter, we had to remove. Anything that was over 4" we girdled the tree. This meant that we cut a circular chip around the tree using an ax. This caused the tree to die. We just cut a few of the limbs off the fallen trees. The snow was so deep we often lost our axes in the snow and had to dig down to find them. The ax was the only tool we carried and in the evening we

had to sharpen it.

"The food was excellent. I still remember running back up for seconds and thirds. I worked hard and ate a lot. I can still remember the large stacks of pancakes in the morning.

"There were heavy snowfalls during the winter of 1935-36. We wore bear paw (oval shaped) snowshoes that helped us be able to walk. If it was below zero we stayed in camp till it got above zero.

"In the spring there was the big flood of 1936. It got quite warm and the deep snow melted very fast. We went a few times where there were road washouts and we cleared them. After the cleanup we continued to remove unwanted trees in the woods.

"On the weekends we went to town. Every Sunday they had a band concert in Rutland. I met a couple girls and went out with them. I went with one or two girls but I still had a girlfriend in Holyoke who was my best buddy's sister who I later married.

"The forester I worked with, Bill Hogan, encouraged me to go to school and study forestry. After two years in the CCC, I was discharged in the summer of 1936. I applied at Massachusetts State College and was accepted in their Stockbridge School of Agriculture where I took wildlife management and forestry classes.

When Harold was in Aitken State Forest, NH. his family left Holyoke and visited him at his CCC camp. From left to right are his father William, sister Mildred, younger brother William, his mother Flora, and Harold with his CCC uniform under his sweater. The photo was right on the road in his side camp. Harold Oehler

"After my first year of college I worked during the summer for the state doing wildlife management work. I even got credit in school for it.

"After two years I graduated in 1938 with honors. In the fall my school got me a job working at a state wildlife refuge in Wrentham, Mass. We were assigned to different wildlife refuges throughout the state. I worked as a surveying group leader.

"For one job we lived in an abandoned CCC camp in Goshen. We mapped and surveyed the refuge. During the summer I had some of the Massachusetts State College students working on my crew.

"In 1940 I got a low Selective Service number. You could avoid being drafted by volunteering so I volunteered and only had to stay in for a year. I went in January 1941. I was stationed in Fort Banks, Mass. Then I was sent to Fort Strong in Boston Harbor and assigned to the anti-aircraft company.

"In 1939 my girlfriend Gladys Laduzenski and I decided to get married because my one year was almost over so we got married. But six weeks later Japan bombed Pearl Harbor and I was in for five more years.

"After we were married there were no passes issued to go home till 1942.

"I stayed with Battery B until the end of 1942. Then I applied for officers' candidate school. In 1943 I earned the rank of 2nd Lt. and was assigned to Georgia. We were officers with black troops and went on maneuvers at Camp Polk in Louisiana. Then they shipped us to San Francisco and sent us to the South Pacific. We landed on Espiritu Santo to relieve a battery for 4-5 months. Then we went to New Britain Island. I was a battery commander in charge of black soldiers in Finschhafen, New Guinea. It was here that black officers replaced the white officers. Then I flew up to Biak Island and was promoted to captain. Later I went to Luzon in the Philippines. We were there till 1945 and we were preparing to go to Japan in the fall. We didn't have to invade Japan because the war was over when Japan surrendered.

"After the war, I worked at Stanley Products. Then I took a job with a retail lumber company in Granby, Mass. I stayed till 1964. I heard from a contractor about a lumberyard for sale in Stafford Springs, Conn. My life changed and I bought the lumberyard. I moved my family and built a home there. My wife Gladys and I had four children: William, Susan, Laurelae, and Harold ('Mike').

For 28 years I ran the lumberyard and retired in 1992.

"I went to my Vermont CCC camp on my honeymoon. Now my daughter lives in White River Junction and I did hunting and fishing in that area.

"The CCC had a positive effect on me. First, it helped me learn how to cope with military discipline and rules. This was of great importance to me during WWII. The Army ran our CCC camp and we lived by the military way. My job in the CCC of working in the forests resulted in me going to college and studying forestry. My first job out of college was working for the state in their wildlife management program. I got into surveying and making maps. I did well in the Army due to my training in the CCC."

John Bauer
Priest River, ID / Red Lodge, MT

While working in the CCC, John Bauer developed his muscles cutting trees, digging ditches, and moving boulders.
John Bauer

In October 2009 I met John Bauer of Glastonbury at a CCC Reunion at the Conn. CCC Museum in Stafford Springs. I asked him if I could interview him about his CCC experiences. He agreed and on Oct. 27, 2009 I visited him at his home in Glastonbury.

His wife Elsie greeted me and invited me to sit with John at the dining room table. I asked him to tell me about his life before he joined the CCC.

"I was born in Brooklyn, NY on April 20, 1922. My father was John S. and my mother was Elfrieda Weisenberger. Before the Depression my father was a carpenter. He made bakery fixtures, displays, and tables in our basement. Then Dad lost his business and was struggling to take care of our family. I was the eldest and I had a brother name Arthur and a sister Arleen. My father got a job with the WPA when he couldn't get work."

Q: Why did you join the CCC?

A: "I was one of the fortunate boys who graduated from high school in December 1939. A lot of the boys in the CCC quit after 8th grade. After I graduated from school I couldn't find a job. Then while looking through the newspaper there was an ad for the CCC. I was looking for adventure but it was difficult since I'd never been away from home. I had to help my family and joined in April 1940.

"They sent me to Fort Dix and when I got there it was raining and muddy. Then I was sent out West by train to Idaho. It was the worst experience. We rode on a train for five days. We were issued one small towel and there were no showers. It was hot so we opened the windows but the smoke from the engine came in and we were black and dirty. They issued us a mess kit that included our eating utensils and we had to somehow clean them.

"Another hard part of the trip was the sleeping arrangement. Three of us were assigned to a seating area. The seats folded down for two to sleep and on an upper berth for one. One of our guys was a big Italian. I slept on the lower bunk with him. I thought he was a member of the Mafia and he'd rob me but he didn't.

"As night came we passed through Pittsburgh, Penn. and we could see the red light of the steel blast furnaces.

"Along the way we stopped in St. Louis, and got out to walk around. We bought postcards to send home.

"On the fifth day we landed in northern Idaho and a truck took us to our camp, F-127 Co. No. 1235 in Priest River. Our camp was in a valley. There was a single board bridge across a really scary turbulent river that led to the forest.

"It was at camp that I learned how to use an axe, a crosscut saw, and how to cut a tree down. It was a good experience. Later on when I got married to Elsie we bought land and I cut down 153 trees.

"There was this lumberjack foreman in camp who could throw an axe into a tree. He did this to get our attention. One time he threw the axe and it stuck about 10' high into a tree. Then he told a guy to get a branch and knock it down. He had to be careful that he didn't get hit by the falling axe. The lumbermen we had were tough, even

John Bauer exploring the mountains near his CCC camp near Red Lodge, Mont. John Bauer

tougher than the cowboys.

"We were issued boots with thin screws called calks at the bottom of the boots. We didn't know why they had them. Then we learned that when you're working in the evergreen forest, the duff on the ground is slippery and the calks helped you get a grip.

"After Priest River our company moved to Camp F-11 Company 1223 in Red Lodge, Mont. and we worked in Custer National Forest in southeastern Montana. We lived in tents with five guys in each. It had a cone-shaped wood stove that went through the tent roof. The stove was in dirt with 2 x 4s around it. We slept around the stove for warmth.

"In our tent we had an unusual man named Marty Gitiman. His father was a barber. He was a spoiled kid. He asked us to shave him and we refused so he got mad at us and left our tent.

"For breakfast we were given 2-3 eggs and a frying pan. Marty asked us how to break an egg. I said, 'Watch me.' Then he asked me to help make his bed, too. He was a pain.

"The best fella we had was an orphan named Charley. He had to do a lot on his own and we became good friends.

"There was an incident with a dog in camp. He was a stray and we fed him. The next day he came back whimpering with quills in his mouth. We got some chloroform from the infirmary to put it to sleep and we pulled out the quills. The quills were like arrows with barbs. There were some even in his mouth. We got most of them out and he left our camp groggy. He found a spring and laid down in it. Four days later he returned and he was so skinny. We fed him and he got better.

"Two Army lieutenants made sure we kept our beds orderly and the tent clean. We stayed at this camp for five months. Our job was mainly constructing the camp. We cleaned out the trees, found a spring on the hill, captured the water, and piped it down to our camp.

"We also worked in mud, cut trees, and moved boulders. I was working with guy named Escobar who was from the Philippines. He was short, extremely stalky, and muscular. We were a team. We developed a reputation for hard work. The foreman sent us to move boulders that others couldn't budge. Another job I had was working on a ditch.

"We had trouble with ticks where we were working. Every night we had to check ourselves. We smoked cigarettes and when we found a tick we put the cigarette on it to back it out.

"In high school I majored in architectural drawing. Because of this training I got the job of drafting the office building that was going to be built. "In the town of Red Lodge there were 10 saloons and 10 stores. On the weekend cowboys and CCC boys came into town. The saloon walls were lined with buffalo and elk heads.

"One day when we were getting back from town on leave in the Army truck, one guy we called the 'Nose' began to irritate Escobar. We called him the 'Nose' because he was always asking questions. Escobar who had been drinking got really angry and he was yelling that he was going to throw the 'Nose' off the truck. I was afraid that he would really throw him off so I had to distract hm. I began singing,

'I am a rancho grande,

I love to roam out yonder,

Out where the Buff'lo wander,

Free as the Eagle flying,

I'm a-roping and a-tying...'

"Everyone, even Escobar, began singing that Mexican cowboy song. It distracted Escobar and 'Nose' made it back to camp alive.

"Another thing we did on Saturdays and Sundays was a lot of walking and exploring the area around our camp."

Then John brought out his CCC photo album.

"This is a photo of Charley who was an orphan. We liked to climb trees and mountains. We saw a lot of deer. This land was absolutely wondrous. Just imagine me coming from the city and climbing these huge mountains.

"As we were climbing a mountain we found a cave and then an old mine. Nearby here was an old abandoned truck and cart used in the mining. We also found an old cabin. We were tough and young and had so much fun exploring.

"I took pictures and sent them away to be developed. I had some colored to what they thought it should be.

"There was a farm close by and we were accepted by the farmers. We were able to ride their horses.

"In Red Lodge they had a rodeo. There were real Indians who set up their teepees. I got to ride on a horse there.

"One weekend we went to Billings, Mont. The Army took a group of guys who had good behavior. From there we went to Yellowstone Park. There were a lot of turns and switchbacks on the road. It was quite a ride going on the mountains.

"When we got to Old Faithful Lodge they threw out garbage for the bears to feed on. Our group had to go in a cage with stadium seats. Then they locked us in the cage. The ranger told us what was going on. Then about 20-30 bear came and started eating in front of us. There were even coyotes nearby."

Q: How long were you in the CCC and why did you leave?

A: "I only signed up for six months. I understood that I was going to be drafted. I had technical skills and the companies were looking for machinists back home.

"When I came home at the beginning of summer in 1940, they were looking for a foreman at Sperry Gyroscope

John Bauer showing photos of his days in CCC camps in Idaho and Montana. Podskoch

505

Co. in Bradley Field. I got a job and then moved to Lake Success, in Long Island.

In the fall I returned home and women were now working in the plant because of the war.

"In December of 1943 I was drafted. Since I had flat feet and bad eyes I was placed in the Navy instead of the Army. We trained men in Cape Cod for work on aircraft carriers. A whole crew came to our base for training and then we trained another crew.

"On a summer vacation in 1943 I met my future wife, Elsie. My parents invited Elsie to come to dinner. When we met we were immediately attracted to each other. She also loved to travel just like me."

Then Elsie, who was working nearby in the kitchen, added, "I was born a gypsy and loved to travel. We were married the following year and we had two daughters: Janet and Lynne."

John continued, "When I came home from the war I worked again at Sperry Co. which had moved back to Connecticut.

"In my 40s we built this house we are living in. The land was all woods. We bought the first lot from the Williams Soap Co. family.

"When our girls began college, I decided to go to school, too. At 50 years old I got my teaching degree from Central Connecticut. I got a job teaching industrial arts in Glastonbury School. I enjoyed teaching drafting, woodworking, graphic arts, and carpentry.

"After 15 years of teaching I retired and Elsie and I enjoyed camping, traveling, and spending winters in Florida.

"I learned a lot in the CCC. One of the important ones was how to be independent. I also got to see the beautiful Rocky Mountains. There I learned to love the outdoors and its land. I had the desire to see and experience a lot of things. My wife and I made many trips out West. We enjoyed camping for 50 years."

On Monday July 27, 2015 John Bauer passed away.

Sal Maggio
NV / ID / OR

Caroline Dobbins of Danbury, Conn. contacted me in August 2008 and invited me to her home to interview her father, Salvatore "Sal" Maggio, who had been in the CCC in Idaho, Nevada, and Oregon.

Sal Maggio at his home in Danbury telling about his western travels in the CCC. Podskoch

Caroline sent for her father's discharge papers, which helped us piece together Sal's CCC life at the various camps he worked.

On Aug. 28, 2008 I visited Sal. We sat in his apartment kitchen and had an afternoon glass of wine which he enjoys every day.

"You can probably tell that I'm not from Connecticut. I was born in Manhattan on Sept. 26, 1922. During the Depression my father, Valentino, was out of work but eventually got a job knocking down buildings and working as a bricklayer's helper. Our family was on welfare and my mother, Maria, got free milk, butter, and cheese. It was hard for my parents to provide for their five children. I was the second eldest in my family so the older children had to help by working. I had three sisters, Betty, Grace and Tina and one brother, Paul.

"When I was 17 I heard about the CCC. My good friend Fred and I signed up in Manhattan on July 2, 1940. We had just finished our junior year at Murray Hill High School."

"On July 2, 1940 the Army sent me by train to Fort Dix, NJ for conditioning and training. Then on July 9th I went by train to Co. 1212 Camp F-1 in Lamoille, Nevada. We lived in tents that had wooden floors and we fought sage brushfires.

"After a week the army sent me on July 18th to Co. 291, Camp F-412 in Ketchum, Idaho. We did road construction work using picks and shovels. We also built wooden bridges.

"On October 14th our company moved to camp F-66 in Grimes Pass, Idaho. Here again we did road construction work. This was another short stay for me.

"The army transferred me to Co. 1231 in Canyon City, Oregon on Oct. 23. I stayed there for eight months and worked as a mechanic and also telephone line maintenance. We also cut trees. Our foreman painted or marked the dead trees that needed cutting. Then we cut the trees down and cut the wood in pieces using a two-man saw. Then we split the wood and removed it.

"The food at camp was very good. At dinnertime they gave us two salt tablets because we sweated a lot.

"Each month the army sent my mother $22 and I got $8 for myself. I went to the camp canteen to buy treats.

"At this camp they had education classes. I took first aid and mechanics classes. I enjoyed doing mechanics and I attended classes for two and a half months. In my free time I liked reading non-fiction books and magazines.

"After dinner we sat around and threw the bull. Sometimes we went to the rec room and played ping-pong. Once a week we went into town. We walked around and talked with people. Some of us went to a farm and rode horses bareback. The people were very friendly.

"I made a lot of friends in camp but I never kept in touch with them."

Sal handed me his camp yearbook and talked about some of his friends and camp pictures.

"After six months in the CCC I re-enrolled on Jan. 1, 1941.

"At the end of my second six months I decided to go back to NYC and get a job. I received an honorable discharge and left Oregon on June 25, 1941. When I got home I applied for a civil service job with the VA Administration. I got a job and worked in Manhattan doing clerical work.

"In 1943 I was drafted. After basic training in Fort Dix I went by boat to Naples, Italy, then to Casablanca, Morocco, and back to Naples. While there I lost a toe due to frostbite.

"After the war I worked as a clerk for the VA and then with the post office.

"I met Vienna Grimaldi at a Horn and Hardart Restaurant in 1947. We got married on June 13, 1948. We had 4 children: Richard, Robert, Lorraine, and Caroline.

"Then I worked for the Social Security Administration and retired in 1979.

"I think the CCC was good for me and the other guys. The working never killed anybody. It got us in good physical condition. I was also able to earn money to help my family.

It was a good thing.

"When I was in the CCC I learned a great deal, like how to take care of myself and to be a responsible person. I made a great many friends and I have all of their names and old addresses in my book. For a while we kept in touch, then gradually it stopped. My stay there still brings back great memories. On the train ride going from state to state to the west coast, I not only got to see a bit of the country, but we had so much fun. We sang and laughed and had lots to talk about. We continued to do this at the bonfires at camp. While I was at camp we met many friendly farmers, who would let us ride their horses bareback. One of those farmers gave me deer horns which were beautifully mounted. When it was time to leave I didn't have room in my trunk to take it home, so I gave it to a friend to take home and send it to me (he never did). Cutting down those massive trees, enjoying a totally different part of the country, and meeting people from other parts of the country are experiences that I have kept with me for a lifetime and I am so thankful for!"

Sal showed me a plaque with his Army picture and medals earned in WWII. Caroline Dobbins

CHAPTER 28
CCC REUNIONS

Connecticut CCC Reunions

During the 1980s and 1990s many Connecticut CCC alumni and their families joined the National Association of CCC Alumni (NACCCA), which was organized in 1977. There were five Chapters in Connecticut: #92 Milford, #130 Windsor Locks, #138 Ansonia (Derby), #147 Norwich (Willimantic), and #170 Stafford Springs (Eastford). Chapter 130 was founded by Peter J. Arsenault in 1983. The chapters met regularly and alumni shared stories and worked to promote the history and achievements of the CCC. Some members attended national gatherings of NACCCA while some Connecticut members became national officers.

In 2007, the Civilian Conservation Corps (CCC) Legacy was established through a merger between the Camp Roosevelt CCC Legacy Foundation and the National Association of CCC Alumni (NACCCA). The purpose of CCC Legacy is to continue the promotion of the CCC in America. CCC Legacy has an annual Gathering in different parts of the state. In September 2015 The CCC Legacy held a "Gathering" in East Windsor, and many CCC alumni, family, and friends attended.

50th CCC Reunion at Rocky Neck State Park

Approximately 1,000 former members of the Civilian Conservation Corps gathered at Rocky Neck State Park on Saturday Sept. 6th, 1986 for a 50th reunion of Connecticut's corps.

About 2,500 guests joined the CCC alumni who spent the day viewing special exhibitions, eating a free picnic lunch, and sharing stories of their experiences in the corps.

The Connecticut Department of Environmental Protection organized the reunion. Reunion organizer, Pam Adams said, "We wanted to honor these people and this seemed like a good time to do it."

Adams stated that the reunion was originally planned to be held at a state forest in northern Connecticut, but there was such a large response of alumni to come that the event was moved to the large Ellie Mitchell Pavilion at Rocky Neck. In the 1930s the CCC cleared the site and the Works Progress Administration (WPA) built the pavilion.

Other CCC Reunions

Other CCC reunions were held at the Connecticut CCC Museum in Stafford Springs and other state parks.

Former CCC enrollees and family members stand in the chow line at the 50th CCC Reunion at Rocky Neck State Park. DEEP

John McKay (right), a former member of Camp Roosevelt, at a 75th CCC Reunion in Chatfield Hollow State Park on Aug. 17, 2008. Podskoch

On Feb. 12, 2009 a reunion was held at the CT CCC Museum: Joe Prucha, Tony Gagliardi, Paul Adykoski, Gov. Jodi Rell, Walter Sekula, and Ray Bedard. Podskoch

On Sept. 20, 2009 a CCC Reunion was held at Salmon River SP in East Hampton: (R–L) Walter Sekula, Harold Mattern, John Bauer, Bill Vance, Angelo Alderuccio, and Hugo DeSarro. Podskoch

On Oct. 11, 2009 Peter Wonsewicz showed his New Mexico camp photo at the CT CCC Museum. Podskoch

CCC Reunion at Burr Pond SP on Oct. 18, 2009: Walter Sekula, Frank Renzoni, Roger Aubrey, and Ray Misluk in front of the stone officers' building built by CCC. Podskoch

On Aug. 21, 2010 at the reunion at Hampton SF. (Front Row, L–R) Frank Renzoni, Bob Fitzgerald, Pat Spino, Marty O'Brien. (Back Row, L–R) Marty Podskoch, Ted Renzoni, Henry Zapatka , Phil O'Brien, and Carl Stamm. Podskoch

CCC alumni (L–R) Martin O'Brien (NH), Frank Renzoni (CO), Gene Belluci (East Hartland), John Bauer (Idaho & Mont.), Joe Prucha and Sam Harrison (Stafford Springs), and Dick Carner (NH) by the CT CCC Museum on Sept. 18, 2010. Podskoch

At an 85th CCC Anniversary Reunion at Chatfield Hollow SP on Aug. 21, 2013: (L–R) Hugo DeSarro (CO), Bill McKinney (Winsted), Mike Caruso (Madison), Bill Jahoda (West Cornwall), Marty Podskoch & granddaughters Kira & Lydia Roloff. Podskoch

On Oct. 11, 2014 Connecticut 's first Official State Troubadour, Tom Callinan, singing CCC songs at CT CCC Museum with alumni (L–R) John Bauer, Peter Wonsewicz, and Roger Aubrey. Podskoch

On July 31, 2013 at Black Rock SP in Thomaston: (L–R) Ed Kelly, Walter Sekula, Al Bellucci, and John Bowey. Podskoch

On Sept. 18, 2010 Frank Renzoni at the CT CCC Museum where he is looking at a photo of his camp at Palisades, CO. Podskoch

On Sept. 23, 2012 nine CCC alumni (L–R) John Bauer, Peter Wonsewicz, Hugo DeSarro, unidentified, Frank Renzoni, Martin O'Brien, Matt Cote, and Charlie Bigelow spoke at the CT CCC Museum. Podskoch

Marty Podskoch speaks at the CT CCC Museum on Sept. 29, 2013 with alumni at the table (L–R) Mike Popovich, Pete Wonsewicz, Bill McKinney, John Bauer, John Koes, Hugo DeSarro, and Charlie Bigelow.

"CCC Legacy Gathering in East Windsor, CT" by Ellen Baczek Amodeo

Thursday, September 24 could not come quickly enough for me. The Civilian Conservation Corps Gathering was meeting in my quaint state of Connecticut and hosted by Marty Podskoch. I had heard Marty speak at a Derby Historical Society meeting years ago. I was fascinated by all the CCC information Marty shared because I am the proud daughter of a CCC boy, Edward Baczek. My dad served from October 1933 to December 1934 in Camp Walcott, Paugnut State Forest in Torrington. Just this spring, I found out that I am the niece of another CCC boy. My mom's brother, John Natowich, served at Camp White in Winsted, according to their youngest brother, Mike. So this gathering from September 24-27 would be a way to learn about my family's CCC history and visit the camps of my dad and uncle.

Our home base for the four days was at the Rodeway in East Windsor. A shuttle was provided from Bradley Airport to the hotel for those attendees who had flown in. We had approximately thirty-four people join the gathering. Quite a few states were represented with attendees from California, Arkansas, Missouri, Virginia, Vermont, South Carolina, New York, Delaware and Texas. Connecticut thankfully displayed its best weather for the four days – sunny with temperatures in the 70s with gentle breezes.

After registering in the ballroom with the beautiful chandeliers, we met fellow attendees, including our honored guests, several CCC boys. They were truly our rock stars! It was so nice to meet the people whose names I had seen in the CCC Legacy newspaper and on the website, including our CCC president, Joan Sharpe. We viewed the displays of CCC memorabilia, books about the 3C's, including Marty's books about the Adirondack area, photos of Connecticut and Vermont camps and much more. This evening we enjoyed wine, several kinds of cheese and various dips and vegetables. The food we were served for the four days was delicious and plentiful.

Marty gave a Power Point presentation of Connecticut CCC camp history and I was excited to see photos of Camp Walcott and Camp White. Next, Kathleen Duxbury spoke about CCC artists. President Franklin Roosevelt had been interested in having a visual history of the CCC camps. Artists had been commissioned to participate in this project, including Marshall Davis, the subject of Kathleen Duxbury's book. I envied Kathleen as she related stories of traveling around the country with her husband in their RV, visiting state and national parks of former CCC camps. Unfortunately, some art work had already been lost over the years but Kathleen's efforts have saved some of the visual history of the 3C's. We adjourned around 8:30 because we were definitely going to need a good night's rest. Marty had a packed schedule of activities for us on Friday.

After breakfast the next day, we met in the ballroom and were welcomed by Connecticut DEEP Deputy Commissioner, Susan Whalen. Susan gave a very heartfelt speech and after Joan Sharpe's comments, I felt ready and fired up for the busy day ahead. We boarded our school bus and off we drove to our first stop, Uncle John's camp, Camp White. Mike Pixler drove two of the CCC boys comfortably in his van. I had not been in a school bus since taking my own classes of first graders on field trips, but our driver was great. The school bus was comfortable enough for me with its high leather seats. We were greeted by a Connecticut parks employee in the picturesque setting of the former Camp White. The Nature Museum was beautiful, a proud symbol of the CCC. There was so much to see in the museum with its exhibits and photographs of various animals, including my favorite, the bear. I wandered outside just to enjoy the tranquillity. Several photos were taken of our entire group and a very poignant one of the five CCC boys. Then, we had to board the bus for our next stop, my dad's camp in the Burrville section of Torrington, one of Connecticut's larger cities. Marty remembered my father was at this camp, so he passed the microphone to me. I spoke briefly about my dad and his enjoyment of his CCC days. Marty gave all family members a chance to share stories while we were traveling on the bus.

Needless to say, I was very excited visiting Burr Pond State Park. Once again, there was a beautiful stone building used as an officer's quarters. There was a plaque in front of this building commemorating the work of the CCC boys. The setting was exquisite with a lovely lake and beach. We ate a hearty box lunch (enough for a lumberjack!) in the picnic area amidst the towering trees. Then we hiked down to the dam built by the CCCers. I truly felt my dad's spirit here – I thought of the stone foundation he had built for his own home, using masonry skills he probably learned at Camp Walcott. My father used to enjoy going to the nearby Goshen Fair. I now wonder if Dad went back and visited his camp area on one of his trips to the fair. I did not want to leave Burr Pond. I could have happily spent my whole day here.

Our next stop was the Eric Sloan Museum in Kent. This museum featured art work by Eric Sloan, a reconstruction of his study, and a collection of early American tools. Once again, we were warmly greeted and given a great tour of the museum. We hopped back on the bus to visit the Macedonian Brook CCC Camp at Kent where we saw the stone walls and the road to nowhere built by the boys. Our bus driver did a super job maneuvering the bus on some very narrow roads. Finally, our last stop was Kent Falls to see the majestic park and trails also built by the Macedonia CCC boys. I was under strict orders by my college roommate Joan to take photos here. Joan had fond memories of visiting this park with her boyfriend (now husband of forty-three years) as members of the SCSU Biology Club.

We arrived back at the Rodeway, tired but happy. I could not believe all that we had seen and done. I had a new-found appreciation for my tiny home state and of course, the work of the CCC boys. We had a delicious buffet dinner of chicken, sausage and peppers, potatoes that melted in your mouth, ziti, salad, green beans with almonds and a scrumptious lemon dessert (we wanted the recipe!). The guests were all given raffle tickets and throughout the evening, Mike Pixler, who is definitely not shy, enjoyed calling out numbers and giving CCC related prizes. Everyone left with a prize – mine was a revised copy of the CCC handbook. I was glad to have this handbook because all I have from my dad's CCC days is a reunion poster. Author Judy Edwards gave an informative talk about the CCC camps in Vermont and then a CCC meeting was held to conclude the day's events.

On our second travel day, we boarded our school bus with a new driver. We were off on a short ride to Stafford Springs, the home of Connecticut's CCC Museum. We toured the museum where one of my favorite exhibits was a CCC uniform. I also took a photo of a poster of a two-

CCC Alumni, family, and friends gathered in front of the Nature Museum built by Camp White in the Peoples SP.

Gathering CCC Alumni enjoyed visiting Burr Pond SP and its beautiful stone building built by the CCC.

man saw team. According to my youngest maternal uncle, this was his brother's job at Camp White. There was also a large notebook with copies of discharge papers of CCC boys. It was quite interesting to read this material since I do not have my dad's discharge papers. The tour had been split into two groups, so it was time to go outdoors and visualize how the CCC camp in Stafford Springs had looked. The Connecticut DEEP employee, Al, was terrific, blending his talk with information and humor. Areas had been roped off so we could picture where all the buildings had been located. We walked on the grounds and saw where the CCC boys had a baseball field, now a wooded area. But you could close your eyes and almost picture the boys running the bases.

Once again, we had to leave too soon for our final stop, Camp Roosevelt, the first CCC camp in Connecticut. We had a long ride, 58 miles from Stafford Springs to Killingworth. But our ride was worth it – Chatfield Hollow State Park was gorgeous. I was discovering another beautiful site in my home state. We ate our luncheon in the picnic area overlooking the lake. The CCC family and friends toured another impressive building, probably used as a canteen/recreation area which featured the CCC's signature stonework – a massive chimney. Everyone was amazed at the dam built by the boys. We walked along the paths and boardwalk for about a quarter of a mile. It was good exercise for us after another hearty lunch. Quite a few people were enjoying the park, including several fishermen and a family celebrating a child's birthday in a pavilion decorated with balloons. It was evident here and at the other parks that the CCC boys' work had lasted through the years. This state park will also be the site of the CCC statue after funds are raised. Our travels drew to a close and we boarded the bus with our great driver for the last time. Evening festivities awaited us. We returned back just in time for our youngest attendee, Daniel to catch the shuttle for the airport and then a flight home to South Carolina. Daniel, our youngest attendee, had been involved in AmeriCorps, the modern day's successor to the CCC.

On our final evening together, we had another delicious dinner featuring a steamship round of roast beef. There were eleven CCC boys in attendance, escorted by their children or grandchildren. It was very moving to hear the boys speak about their experiences in the CCC and their military service. I think we all had a tear or two in our eyes. For me, it was as if I had my dad back for a while. These

On Sept. 26, 2015 the National CCC Legacy Gathering was held in East Windsor. These 11 alumni attended: (Front Row, L–R) Richard Chrisinger, Charlie Bigelow, Hank Sulima, Jack Scully, & Harold Oehler; (Back Row, L–R) Samuel Williams, Larry Lavigne, Hugo Desarro, Walter Atwood, and Roger Aubrey.

CCCers had all served in WWII, like my dad a wounded Navy veteran. Their courage and resilience amazed me. The CCC boys were presented with several gifts including CCC tee shirts and the beautiful calendars compiled and donated by Naomi Shaw and her father, Richard Chrisinger, one of the proud CCC boys. Mike Pixel was busy again with his raffle prizes, including books written by and donated by Marty and the other authors. Tom Callinan, the CT State Troubadour and a "CCC kid" sang his songs, including some great original compositions honoring the CCC. Later, the Dukes of Hazardville entertained us with their music. It was a perfect evening, the finale to a great gathering in Connecticut of CCC family, friends and historians.

Thank you to Marty Podskoch for organizing this gathering – I enjoyed myself immensely and I have a new-found appreciation for the beauty of my state. Kudos to Joan Sharpe and all the CCC Legacy officers for their diligent work in keeping the CCC boys and their work in the public's attention. Finally, thank you Dad and Uncle John for your service in the CCC. My dad would have turned 100 in November – I know he would be so happy that I attended this Gathering!

NOTES

Chapter 1 History
1 Diane Galusha, "Another Day Another Dollar: The Civilian Conservation Corps in the Catskills, Black Dome Press Corp., Hensonville, NY, 2009, 7.
2 Ibid.
3 Ibid., 7.
4 Ibid., 8-9.
5 http://www.nps.gov/archive/elro/glossary/roosevelt-franklin.htm.
6 Edgar Nixon, "Franklin D. Roosevelt and Conservation, 1911-1945," Hyde Parke, NY: Franklin D. Roosevelt Library; 1957, 3-4.
7 Galusha, 15.
8 http://www.nps.gov/archive/elro/glossary/great-depression.htm.
9 Arthur M. Schlesinger, Jr., The Age of Roosevelt, III: The Politics of Upheaval, Boston: Houghton Mifflin Company, 1960, 251.
10 George P. Rawick, "The New Deal and Youth: The Civilian Conservation Corps, the National Youth Administration, the American Youth Congress," unpublished Ph.D. dissertation, University of Wisconsin, 1957, 18-29.
11 "Message to Congress on Unemployment Relief, March 21,"The Presidential Papers of Franklin D. Roosevelt, 1933.
12 John Salmond, The Civilian Conservation Corps, 1933-1942, A New Deal Case Study, Durham, NC: Duke University Press, 1967, 14.
13 Stan Cohen, The Tree Army, A Pictorial History of the Civilian Conservation Corps 1933-1942, Missoula, MT: Pictorial Histories Publishing Co., 1980, 6-7.
14 Ibid., 2.
15 NYS Conservation Department Annual Report, 1934, 141.
16 Mark Neuzil, "Roosevelt's Tree Army," The History Channel Magazine, November/Dec. 2010, 57.
17 Salmond, 90-91.
18 Ibid., 33.
19 NYS Conservation Department Annual Report, 1934, 141.
20 Salmond, 34.
21 Franklin Folsom, Impatient Armies of the Poor, Niwot, Colorado: University Press of Colo., 1991, 310-322.
22 Galusha, 41.
23 Harper, 104, Salmond, 111.
24 NYS Conservation Department Annual Report, 1935, 170-171.
25 "Youths, 17 May Enter the CCC," Plattsburgh Daily Press, Sept. 27, 1935.
26 Salmond, 58-59.
27 Charles Price Harper, The Administration of the Civilian Conservation Corps, Clarksburg Publishing Co., Clarksburg, W. Va., 1939, 39-41.
28 Salmond, 59-61.
29 NYS Conservation Department Annual Report, 1937, 19, 134.
31 Ibid., 133.
32 Salmond, 137-138.
33 Ibid., 176.
34 http://www.ccclegacy.org/CCC_Brief_History.html.
35 Salmond, 200.
36 Ibid., 200.
37 NYS Conservation Department Annual Report, 1941, 113.
38 Salmond, 208-210.
39 Ibid., 211-212.
40 Franklin D. Roosevelt, letter to James McEntee, March 25, 1942.
41 NYS Conservation Department Annual Report, 1942, 109.
42 http://www.ccclegacy.org/CCC_brief_history.htm.
43 Austin Hawes, History of Forestry in Connecticut, CAES Archives, 189-212.
44 http://www.thesca.org/.
45 Galusha, 181.
46 http://www.americorps.gov/about/ac/index.asp.

Chapter 2 Camp Organization
1 Charles Price Harper, The Administration of the Civilian Conservation Corps, Clarksburg Publishing Co., Clarksburg, WV, 1939, 39-41.
2 http://www.ccclegacy.org/Camp_Roosevelt_68B9.php.
3 Salmond, 135-136.
4 Cohen, 46.

Chapter 3 Enrollee's Life in Camp
1 "The Conservation Corps, What It Is and What It Does," Civilian Conservation Corps Office of Director, Washington, D. C., June, 1939, 10.
2 Cohen, 47.
3 Hawes, 188-189.
4 Ibid., 189.
5 "The Conservation Corps, What It Is. . . , 8.
6 Hawes, 114.
7 Salmond, 51.
8 Ibid., 53.
9 NYS Conservation Department Annual Report, 1935, 170.

Chapter 4 Work Projects
1 Hawes, 182.
2 Ibid., 182.
3 Ibid., 183.
4 Ibid.
5 Ibid., 184.
6 Ibid.
7 Harper, 65.
8 Hawes, 185.
9 Ibid., 212.
10 Ibid.
11 Ibid., 185.
12 Ibid.
13 Ibid., 186.
14 Ibid., 187.
15 Ibid.
16 Ibid., 187-188.
17 Ibid., 184.
18 Ibid., 188-189.
19 Ibid., 189.
20 Ibid.
21 Ibid.
22 Galusha, 102.
23 Hawes, 191-192.
24 Ibid., 192.
25 Ibid., 193.
26 Ibid., 190.
27 Ibid., 193.

28 Ibid., 193-194.
29 Ibid., 194.
30 Ibid.
31 Ibid.
32 Ibid.
33 Ibid.
34 Ibid.
35 Ibid.
36 Ibid.
37 Ibid., 194-195.
38 Ibid., 195-196.
39 Ibid., 196.
40 Ibid.
41 Ibid.
42 Ibid., 198.
43 Ibid.
44 Ibid., 199.
45 Ibid.
46 Ibid., 199-200.
47 Ibid., 200.
48 Ibid.
49 Ibid., 200-201.
50 Ibid., 201-202.
51 Ibid., 202.
52 Ibid., 193.
53 Ibid., 203.
54 Ibid., 204.
55 Ibid.
56 Ibid.
57 Ibid.
58 Ibid., 205-206.
59 Ibid., 206.
60 Ibid., 207.
61 Ibid., 207-208.
62 Fifth CCC District First Corps Area Yearbook, 1937, 43.
63 Hawes, 209-210.
64 Ibid., 206.
65 Ibid.
66 Ibid., 21.

Chapter 5 Clinton

1 http://www.ct.gov/dep/lib/dep/forestry/management_plans/cockaponset_plan.pdf.
2 http://www.ct.gov/dep/cwp/view.asp?a=2716&q=325182&depNav_GID=1650.
3 Ibid.
4 Report of the Connecticut State Parks and Forests, 1934, 77 & 81.
5 Report of the Connecticut State Parks and Forests, 1936, 23.
6 http://familytreemaker.genealogy.com/users/e/l/l/Thomas-A-Ellis-Aberdeen/WEBSITE-0001/UHP-0052.html.
7 http://en.wikipedia.org/wiki/Oak_Lodge.
8 Report of the Connecticut State Parks and Forests, 1934, 85.
9 Report of the Connecticut State Parks and Forests, 1938, 39.
10 Report of the Connecticut State Parks and Forests, 1942, 55.

Chapter 6 Cobalt

1 Report of the Connecticut State Parks and Forests, 1934, 72.
2 http://ct.gov/dep/cwp/view.asp?a=2697&q=322834&depNav_GID=1631
3 http://www.ct.gov/caes/lib/caes/documents/publications/

bulletins/b254.pdf.
4 http://magic.lib.uconn.edu/magic_6/raster/37800/aerial/1934/05994_to_07137/CT1934_06981.pdf.
5 Report of the Connecticut State Parks and Forests, 1934, 76.
6 Report of the Connecticut State Parks and Forests, 1934, 77.
7 Report of the Connecticut State Parks and Forests, 1934, 78.
8 Report of the Connecticut State Parks and Forests, 1934, 81.
9 Report of the Connecticut State Parks and Forests, 1934, 100-101.
10 Fifth CCC District First Corps Area Yearbook, 1937, 71.
11 Report of the Connecticut State Parks and Forests, 1936, 70.
12 Report of the Connecticut State Parks and Forests, 1936, 26.
13 Report of the Connecticut State Parks and Forests, 1938, 16.
14 Report of the Connecticut State Parks and Forests, 1938, 39.
15 Fifth CCC District First Corps Area Yearbook, 1937, 55.

Chapter 7 Danbury / Squantz Pond

1 Report of the Connecticut State Parks and Forests, 1934, 73.
2 http://en.wikipedia.org/wiki/Squantz_Pond_State_Park.
3 http://www.examiner.com/article/squantz-pond-s-council-rock-offers-hikers-a-slice-of-new-england-s-history.
4 Charles W. Brilvitch, A History of Connecticut's Golden Hill Paugussett Tribe, The History Press, 2007, 13–14.
5 http://www.ct.gov/dep/cwp/view.asp?A=2697&Q=322864.
6 Ibid.
7 Report of the Connecticut State Parks and Forests, 1934, 28.
8 Ibid., 76.
9 Ibid., 100.
10 Ibid., 29.
11 Ibid., 101.
12 Ibid., 81.
13 Ibid., 20.
14 Report of the Connecticut State Parks and Forests, 1936, 25.
15 Ibid.
16 Report of the Connecticut State Parks and Forests, 1938, 16.

Chapter 8 Danbury / Wooster Mt.

1 http://web.cortland.edu/woosterk/locher.html.
2 http://www.ccclegacy.org/CCC_Brief_History.html.
3 Fifth CCC District First Corps Area Yearbook, 1937, 77.
4 Report of the Connecticut State Parks and Forests, 1936, 64.
5 Ibid.
6 http://www.elmcare.com/disease/dutchelm/history_of_dutch_elm_disease.htm.
7 Fifth CCC District First Corps Area Yearbook, 1937, 77.
8 Ibid.
9 Camp Fechner News, June, 1936.
10 Fifth CCC District First Corps Area Yearbook, 1937, 77.
11 Camp Fechner News, March, 1937.
12 Fifth CCC District First Corps Area Yearbook, 1937, 77.
13 Camp Fechner News, June, 1936.
14 Camp Fechner News, Jan., 1937.
15 Camp Fechner News, June, 1936.
16 Camp Fechner News, Apr., 1937.
17 Camp Fechner News, March, 1937.
18 Report of the Connecticut State Parks and Forests, 1938, 15.

Chapter 9 Eastford

1 Fernow Forum, June 28, 1935.
2 Ibid.
3 Report of the Connecticut State Parks and Forests, 1934, 20.

4 http://www.ct.gov/dep/cwp/view. asp?a=2697&q=322842&depNav_GID=1631.
5 http://www.ct.gov/dep/cwp/view.asp?A=2697&Q=322842.
6 Fernow Forum, June 28, 1935.
7 http://en.wikipedia.org/wiki/Bernhard_Fernow.
8 Ibid.
9 Fernow Forum, June 28, 1935.
10 http://shs.umsystem.edu/historicmissourians/name/l/lyon/index.html.
11 Fernow Forum, March, 1934.
12 Ibid.
13 Fifth CCC District First Corps Area Yearbook, 1937, 49.
14 Report of the Connecticut State Parks and Forests, 1934, 81-82.
15 Report of the Connecticut State Parks and Forests, 1934, 82.
16 Fernow Forum, June 28, 1935.
17 Fifth CCC District First Corps Area Yearbook, 1937, 49.
18 Fernow Forum, June 28, 1935.
19 Report of the Connecticut State Parks and Forests, 1936, 69.
20 Fernow Forum, June 28, 1935.
21 Ibid.
22 Report of the Connecticut State Parks and Forests, 1934, 100.
23 Report of the Connecticut State Parks and Forests, 1934, 101.
24 Fernow Forum, June 28, 1935.
25 Ibid.
26 Ibid.
27 Fifth CCC District First Corps Area Yearbook, 1937, 27.
28 Fernow Forum, June 28, 1935.
29 Fernow Forum, Feb., 1935.
30 Fernow Forum, Oct., 1935.
31 Fernow Forum, June 28, 1935.
32 Ibid.
33 Ibid.
34 Ibid.
35 Ibid.
36 Fifth CCC District First Corps Area Yearbook, 1937, 78.
37 Fernow Forum, June 28, 1935.
38 Fernow Forum, Aug., 1935.
39 Ibid.
40 Ibid.
41 Fernow Forum, Sept., 1935.
42 Ibid.
43 Fernow Forum, Nov., 1935.
44 Ibid.
45 Fifth CCC District First Corps Area Yearbook, 1937, 49.
46 Ibid.
47 Ibid.
48 Fernow Forum, Feb., 1936.
49 Report of the Connecticut State Parks and Forests, 1936, 170.
50 Fernow Forum, June, 1936.
51 Fernow Forum, Feb., 1936.
52 Fifth CCC District First Corps Area Yearbook, 1937, 49.
53 Ibid.
54 Fernow Forum, July, 1936.
55 Fifth CCC District First Corps Area Yearbook, 1937, 49.
56 Fernow Forum, Nov., 1936.
57 Fernow Forum, Feb., 1937.
58 Fernow Forum, Mar., 1937.
59 Fernow Forum, June 29, 1937.
60 In Fernow, May 27, 1939.
61 In Fernow, Sept. 9, 1939.
62 In Fernow, April, 1939.
63 In Fernow, July 1, 1939.
64 In Fernow, Sept. 2, 1939.
65 In Fernow, June 17, 1939.
66 In Fernow, June 3, 1939.
67 In Fernow, June 17, 1939.
68 In Fernow, July 8, 1939.
69 In Fernow, Aug., 1939.
70 In Fernow, Aug. 26, 1939.
71 Report of the Connecticut State Parks and Forests, 1940, 53.
72 In Fernow, Aug. 26, 1939.
73 Ibid.
74 In Fernow Sept. 9, 1939.
75 In Fernow, Sept. 16, 1939.
76 In Fernow, Sept. 30, 1939.
77 Ibid.
78 In Fernow, Oct. 21, 1939.
79 In Fernow, July 22, 1939.
80 http://www.fosa-ct.org/Reprints/Spring2006_ArthurBasto.htm.
81 "Skill and Equipment of CC Men Is Praised," In Fernow, Oct. 21, 1939.
82 "Camp Orchestra Is Organized," In Fernow, Oct. 21, 1939.
83 "Keen Competition for Movie Passes," In Fernow, Oct. 7, 1939.
84 "Program of Orientation Is Used with Much Success," In Fernow, Oct. 7, 1939.
85 In Fernow, Oct. 28, 1939.
86 In Fernow, Dec. 16, 1939.
87 In Fernow, Nov. 4, 1939.
88 In Fernow, Nov. 11, 1939.
89 In Fernow, Nov. 25, 1939.
90 Ibid.
91 In Fernow, Dec. 2, 1939.
92 In Fernow, Dec. 9, 1939.
93 In Fernow, Dec. 23, 1939.
94 In Fernow, Feb. 3, 1940.
95 In Fernow, Feb. 10, 1940.
96 In Fernow, Feb. 24, 1940.
97 In Fernow, March 10, 1940.
98 In Fernow, March 30, 1940.
99 Report of the Connecticut State Parks and Forests, 1940, 52.
100 Ibid., 53.
101 In Fernow, July 20, 1940.

Chapter 10 East Hampton

1 Fifth CCC District First Corps Area Yearbook, 1937, 65.
2 http://www.fs.fed.us/aboutus/history/chiefs/stuart.shtml.
3 First Corps Area, Fifth CCC District Yearbook, 1937, 65.
4 Ibid.
5 Ibid.
6 Camp Stuart Courier, Nov., 1935.
7 Camp Stuart Courier, Dec., 1935.
8 Camp Stuart Courier, Nov., 1935.
9 Ibid.
10 Camp Stuart Courier, Dec., 1935.
11 Camp Stuart Courier, Feb., 1936.
12 Camp Stuart Courier, Jan., 1936.
13 Camp Stuart Courier, Dec., 1935.
14 Ibid.
15 Camp Stuart Courier, Feb., 1936.
16 Camp Stuart Courier, Dec., 1935.

17 http://www.past-inc.org/historic-bridges/covered-comstock.html.
18 Camp Stuart Courier, Jan., 1936.
19 Ibid.
20 Ibid.
21 Camp Stuart Courier, Feb., 1936.
22 Ibid.
23 Ibid.
24 Ibid.
25 Camp Stuart Courier, April, 1936.
26 Stuart Gusher, May, 1936.
27 Stuart Gusher, Aug., 1936.
28 Stuart Gusher, Nov., 1936.
29 Ibid.
30 Ibid.
31 Ibid.
32 Ibid.
33 Stuart Gusher, Nov., 1936.
34 Ibid.
35 Stuart Gusher, Jan., 1937.
36 Stuart Gusher, Feb., 1937.
37 Fifth CCC District First Corps Area Yearbook, 1937, 65.
38 Camp Stuart Courier, Nov., 1936.
39 Ibid.
40 Fifth CCC District First Corps Area Yearbook, 1937, 65.
41 Camp Stuart Courier, Feb., and Nov., 1936.
42 http://www.ct.gov/dep/cwp/view.
asp?a=2716&q=325184&depNav_GID=1650.
43 Fifth CCC District First Corps Area Yearbook, 1937, 65.
44 Report of the Connecticut State Parks and Forests, 1934, 81-82.
45 Fifth CCC District First Corps Area Yearbook, 1937, 65 & 78.
46 Camp Stuart Courier, April, 1936.
47 Fifth CCC District First Corps Area Yearbook, 1937, 66.
48 Stuart Gusher, March, 1937.
49 Ibid.
50 Ibid.
51 Report of the Connecticut State Parks and Forests, 1934, 39.

Chapter 11 East Hartland
1 Fifth CCC District First Corps Area Yearbook, 1937, 43.
2 http://mssa.library.yale.edu/obituary_record/1925_1952/1940-41.
pdf.
3 Report of the Connecticut State Parks and Forests, 1934, 77.
4 Fifth CCC District First Corps Area Yearbook, 1937, 43.
5 http://pdfhost.focus.nps.gov/docs/NRHP/Text/86001761.pdf.
6 Report of the Connecticut State Parks and Forests, 1936, 69.
7 Report of the Connecticut State Parks and Forests, 1934, 75.
8 Ibid., 80.
9 Ibid., 78.
10 Ibid., 80.
11 http://www.munic.state.ct.us/HARTLAND/
HHSCampRobinsonW.htm.
12 Report of the Connecticut State Parks and Forests, 1934, 78.
13 Ibid., 77.
14 Ibid.
15 Ibid., 96.
16 Robinson Register, Nov., 1935.
17 Report of the Connecticut State Parks and Forests, 1936, 70.
18 Fifth CCC District First Corps Area Yearbook, 1937, 43.
19 Tunxsonian, Nov., 1936.
20 Tunxsonian, Jan. & Feb., 1937.

21 Ibid.
22 Ibid.
23 Ibid.
24 Ibid.
25 Ibid.
26 Tunxsonian, Mar., 1937.
27 Ibid.
28 Ibid.
29 Tunxsonian, Dec., 1937.
30 Ibid.
31 Tunxisonian, Feb., 1938.
32 Spectator, April, 1938.
33 Ibid.
34 Ibid.
35 Ibid.
36 Spectator, April, 1938.
37 Ibid.
38 Spectator, May, 1938.
39 Fifth CCC District First Corps Area Yearbook, 1937, 43.
40 Report of the Connecticut State Parks and Forests, 1940, 52 & 54.
41 Fifth CCC District First Corps Area Yearbook, 1937, 43.
42 Ibid.
43 Ibid.
44 Ibid.
45 Report of the Connecticut State Parks and Forests, 1942, 55.
46 Report of the Connecticut State Parks and Forests, 1944, 75.
47 Ibid.

Chapter 12 Haddam
1 Report of the Connecticut State Parks and Forests, 1936, 54.
2 The Filley Flash, Aug. 1, 1934.
3 Report of the Connecticut State Parks and Forests, 1936, 54.
4 Ibid., 73.
5 http://www.ct.gov/dep/lib/dep/forestry/management_plans/
cockaponset_plan.pdf.
6 Filley Flash, Sept., 1934.
7 Filley Flash, Sept., 1934.
8 Ibid.
9 Fifth CCC District First Corps Area Yearbook, 1937, 67.
10 Report of the Connecticut State Parks and Forests, 1934, 77.
11 Report of the Connecticut State Parks and Forests, 1936, 69.
12 Report of the Connecticut State Parks and Forests, 1940, 52.
13 Ann T. Colson and Cindi D. Pietrzyk, ed., Connecticut Walk
Book East, Rockfall: Connecticut Forest & Park Association, 2005,
93.
14 Ibid., 89-91.
15 Report of the Connecticut State Parks and Forests, 1934, 78.
16 Ibid., 82.
17 Report of the Connecticut State Parks and Forests, 1940, 53.
18 Report of the Connecticut State Parks and Forests, 1934, 84.
19 The Filley Flash, Aug., 1934, 4.
20 Ibid.
21 The Filley Flash, Sept., 1934.
22 Fifth CCC District First Corps Area Yearbook, 1937, 67.
23 The Filley Flash, Aug., 1936, 3.
24 Ibid.
25 The Filley Flash, Oct., 1934.
2 Ibid.
27 The Filley Flash, Nov., 1934.
28 Ibid.

29 https://en.wikipedia.org/wiki/Alexandra_Tolstaya.
30 The Filley Flash, Nov., 1934 and Sept., 1937.
31 The Filley Flash, Sept., 1934.
32 The Filley Flash, June, 1936.
33 Fifth CCC District First Corps Area Yearbook, 1937, 67.
34 Ibid.
35 The Filley Flash, June, 1936.
36 Ibid.
37 The Filley Flash, Jan., 1937.
38 Turkey Hill Observation Tower Site (Connecticut Forest & Park Association, Rockfall, CT. n.d.).
39 The Filley Flash, May, 1939.
40 The Filley Flash, June 24, 1939.
41 The Filley Flash, May, 1939.
42 The Filley Flash, June 24, 1939.
43 The Filley Flash, July 1, 1939.
44 The Filley Flash, June 24, 1939.
45 Report of the Connecticut State Parks and Forests, 1942, 65.
46 Report of the Connecticut State Parks and Forests, 1944, 76.
47 "CCC Camp Designated a State Archaeological Preserve," Connecticut Woodlands, Spring, 2010, 21.
48 Ibid.

Chapter 13 Kent / Macedonia Brook
1 The Connecticut Park and Forest Commission, 1935.
2 CP&FC minutes, May 8, 1935.
3 Fifth CCC District First Corps Area Yearbook, 1937, 55.
4 Ibid.
5 Ibid.
6 Ibid.
7 http://www.ct.gov/dep/cwp/view.asp?a=2716&q=325234.
8 Fifth CCC District First Corps Area Yearbook, 1937, 56.
9 Macedonian, Feb., 1936.
10 Ibid.
11 Ibid.
12 Fifth CCC District First Corps Area Yearbook, 1937, 55.
13 Macedonian, Mar., 1936.
14 Fifth CCC District First Corps Area Yearbook, 1937, 55.
15 Ibid., 56.
16 Macedonian, May, 1936.
17 Macedonian, June, 1936.
18 Fifth CCC District First Corps Area Yearbook, 1937, 55.
19 Ibid.
20 Macedonian, May, 1936.
21 Macedonian, June 10, 1936.
22 Macedonian, Feb., 1937.
23 Ibid.
24 Macedonian, March, 1937.
25 Ibid.
26 Kent Historical Society, Volume 9, Number 3, Kent, Conn., Dec. 2008.

Chapter 14 Madison
1 The Fifth District Annual Report, 1937, 73.
2 https://en.wikipedia.org/wiki/Arthur_Twining_Hadley.
3 The Fifth District Annual Report, 1937, 73.
4 Ibid.
5 Ibid.
6 Pinch Hitter, Sept. 2, 1935, 7.
7 Ibid., 3.

8 Pinch Hitter, Sept. 3, 1935, 7.
9 Ibid., 6.
10 The Fifth District Annual Report, 1937, 73.
11 The Buzz Saw, Sept. 21, 1935, 5.
12 Ibid., 6.
13 Ibid., 7.
14 Ibid., 8.
15 Ibid., 7.
16 The Buzz Saw, May, 1936, 4.
17 "C. C. C. Men Do Good Work in Emergency," The Shoreline Times, Mar. 26, 1936, 1-2.
18 The Buzz Saw, May, 1936, 6.
19 Ibid., 5.
20 Ibid.
21 The Buzz Saw, July, 1936, 4.
22 Ibid.
23 Ibid., 5.
24 The Fifth District Annual Report, 1937, 73.
25 "Camp Hadley in Madison," The Shoreline Times, Mar. 26, 1936, 1-2.
26 The Buzz Saw, Aug., 1936, 4.
27 Ibid., 9.
28 Ibid., 6.
29 Ibid.
30 Ibid.
31 The Buzz Saw, Dec., 1936, 7.
32 The Buzz Saw, Oct., 1936, 12.
33 The Buzz Saw, Dec., 1936, 10.
34 The Fifth District Annual Report, 1937, 73-79.
35 The Buzz Saw, Dec., 1936, 4.
36 The Buzz Saw, April, 1937, 4.
37 Ibid.
38 The Buzz Saw, May, 1937, 5.
39 Ibid.
40 The Buzz Saw, June, 1937, 5.
41 The Buzz Saw, Feb., 1938, 6.
42 Whisperin's, Feb., 1938, 6.
43 Whisperin's, Mar., 1938, 5.
44 The Buzz Saw, May, 1938, 6.
45 The Shoreline Times, Aug. 25, 1938, 10.
46 The Shoreline Times, Sept. 8, 1938, 10.
47 The Shoreline Times, Aug. 25, 1938, 10.
48 The Buzz Saw, Mar., 1938, 5.
49 Whisperin's, June, 1938, 4.
50 The Buzz Saw, June, 1938, 5.
51 Whisperin's, Sept., 1938, 11.
52 The Buzz Saw, Sept., 1938, 11.
53 Whisperin's, Dec., 1938, 4
54 Whisperin's, Nov. 30, 1939.
55 Whisperin's, Feb. 29, 1940.
56 Report of the Connecticut State Parks and Forests, 1942, 55.

Chapter 15 Niantic
1 http://www.ct.ngb.army.mil/armyguard/facilities/history.asp.
2 "A Brief History of Stone Ranch, East Lyme, Connecticut," Ford Hilton, East Lyme Library History Room, 20-22.
3 Camp Chapman News, June, 1934, 8.
4 Report of the Connecticut State Parks and Forests, 1934, 30.
5 Ibid., 31.
6 Ibid., 30.

7 Ibid., 77.
8 http://www.ct.gov/deep/cwp/view.asp?a=2716&q=325064.
9 Report of the Connecticut State Parks and Forests, 1934, 27.
10 Camp Chapman News, Mar. 21, 1934, 1.
11 Ibid., 3.
12 Ibid., 2.
13 Ibid., 1.
14 Camp Chapman News, Mar. 29, 1934, 1.
15 Camp Chapman News, Apr. 26, 1934, 1.
16 Ibid.
17 Ibid.
18 Camp Chapman News, June, 1934, 4.
19 Camp Chapman News, Nov., 1934, 2.
20 http://www.eastlymehistoricalsociety.org/index_files/Page1095.htm.
21 Camp Chapman News, Sept., 1934, 1.
22 Ibid.
23 Camp Chapman News, Oct., 1934, 1.
24 Camp Chapman News, Nov., 1934, 1.
25 Camp Chapman Clarion, June 10, 1935, 7.
26 Ibid.
27 Camp Chapman Clarion, Jan., 1935, 1.
28 Ibid., 2.
29 Camp Chapman Clarion, May 10, 1935, 4.
30 Camp Chapman Clarion, April 10, 1935, 8.
31 Camp Chapman Clarion, May 10, 1935, 4.
32 Camp Chapman Clarion, July, 1935, 2.
33 Ibid.
34 Report of the Connecticut State Parks and Forests, 1936, 30.
35 Camp Chapman Clarion, July, 1935, 2.
36 Camp Chapman Clarion, July 10, 1935, 1.
37 Ibid.
38 Report of the Connecticut State Parks and Forests, 1936, 64.
39 Camp Chapman Clarion, May 10, 1935, 5.
40 Camp Chapman Clarion, Aug. 1935, 3.
41 Ibid., 3 & 7.
42 Ibid., 5.
43 Camp Chapman Clarion, Sept. 1935, 2.
44 Ibid., 2.
45 Ibid., 4.
46 Ibid.
47 Ibid.
48 Report of the Connecticut State Parks andForest, 1938, 39.

Chapter 16 Portland
1 Fifth CCC District First Corps Area Yearbook, 1937, 71.
2 The Buck Eye, Nov., 1935, 8-10.
3 http://docs.unh.edu/CT/mhdm45ne.jpg.
4 Fifth CCC District First Corps Area Yearbook, 1937, 71.
5 http://ct.gov/dep/cwp/view.asp?a=2697&q=322834&depNav_GID=1631.
6 http://www.minrec.org/labels.asp?colid=282.
7 Fifth CCC District First Corps Area Yearbook, 1937, 71.
8 Report of the Connecticut State Parks and Forests, 1934, 58.
9 Report of the Connecticut State Parks and Forests, 1934, 35.
10 The Buck Eye, Nov., 1935, 8.
11 Ibid.
12 Ibid., 1&3.
13 Ibid., 3.
14 Ibid., 7.
15 Ibid., 3.
16 Ibid., 8.
17 The Buck Eye, Nov., 1935, 5.
18 The Buck Eye, Jan., 1936, 2.
19 Fifth CCC District First Corps Area Yearbook, 1937, 71.
20 The Buck Eye, Dec. 8, 1939, 2.
21 Fifth CCC District First Corps Area Yearbook, 1937, 71.
22 Ibid., 69.
23 Ibid., 71.
24 The Buck Eye, Mar. 1937, 1.
25 Fifth CCC District First Corps Area Yearbook, 1937, 71.
26 The Buck Eye, Nov., 1936, 1.
27 Ibid., 2.
28 Ibid.
29 The Buck Eye, Dec., 1936, 2.
30 The Buck Eye, Jan., 1937, 1.
31 The Buck Eye, Jan/Feb., 1937, 1.
32 The Buck Eye, Dec., 1936, 2.
33 The Buck Eye, Jan/Feb., 1937, 11.
34 Fifth CCC District First Corps Area Yearbook, 1937, 71.
35 The Buck Eye, Mar., 1937, 6.
36 The Buck Eye, Apr., 1937, 4.
37 Ibid.
38 Ibid., 1.
39 Report of the Connecticut State Parks and Forests, 1940, 76.
40 The Buck Eye, Feb., 1938, 4 & 6.
41 The Buck Eye, Apr., 1938, 6 & 7.
42 The Buck Eye, Jan., 1939, 6.
43 The Buck Eye, Apr. 5, 1940, 3.
44 Ibid.
45 The Buck Eye, Nov. 3, 1939, 3.
46 The Buck Eye, Sept. 29, 1939, 4.
47 The Buck Eye, Sept. 22, 1939, 1.
48 The Buck Eye, Oct., 6, 1939, 1.
49 The Buck Eye, Oct. 13, 1939, 1.
50 The Buck Eye, Oct. 20, 1939, 3.
51 The Buck Eye, Oct. 13, 1939, 1.
52 Ibid.
53 The Buck Eye, Dec. 2, 1939, 2.
54 The Buck Eye, Dec. 8, 1939, 1-2.
55 The Buck Eye, Dec., 15, 1939, 1.
56 The Buck Eye, Apr. 12, 1940, 3.
57 The Buck Eye, Jan. 26, 1940, 2.
58 The Buck Eye, Feb. 9, 1940, 3.
59 The Buck Eye, Feb. 2, 1940, 1.
60 Ibid., 2.
61 The Buck Eye, Apr. 19, 1940, 2.
62 Ibid., 3.
63 The Buck Eye, Feb. 9, 1940, 1.
64 The Buck Eye, Feb. 16, 1940, 4.
65 The Buck Eye, March 15, 1940, 1.
66 The Buck Eye, Apr. 5, 1940, 2.
67 The Buck Eye, Apr. 18, 1940, 2.
68 The Buck Eye, May 10, 1940, 3.
69 The Buck Eye, May 24, 1940, 2.
70 The Buck Eye, May 17, 1940, 3.
71 Ibid.
72 The Buck Eye, May 24, 1940, 3.
73 Ibid., 3.
74 The Buck Eye, June 21, 1940, 3.

75 The Buck Eye, Aug. 9, 1940, 2.
76 Ibid., 3.
77 The Buck Eye, Sept. 12, 1940, 1.
78 Ibid., 2.
79 Ibid., 1.
80 The Buck Eye, Oct. 25, 1940, 2.
81 The Buck Eye, Nov. 26, 1940, 2.
82 The Buck Eye, Nov. 8, 1940, 3.
83 The Buck Eye, Nov. 22, 1940, 2.
84 Report of the Connecticut State Parks and Forests, 1940, 76.
85 Ibid., 53.
86 Ibid., 59.
87 Report of the Connecticut State Parks and Forests, 1942, 55.

Chapter 17 Stafford Springs
1 Fifth CCC District First Corps Area Yearbook, 1937, 59.
2 Shenipsit Lookout, June, 1936, 2.
3 Fifth CCC District First Corps Area Yearbook, 1937, 7.
4 http://www.arlingtoncemetery.net/fox-conner.htm.
5 Fifth CCC District First Corps Area Yearbook, 1937, 59.
6 Ibid.
7 Shenipsit Lookout, June, 1936, 2.
8 First Corps Area, Fifth CCC District Yearbook, 1937, 59.
9 Shenipsit Lookout, June, 1936, 4.
10 http://www.ct.gov/deep/cwp/view.
asp?a=2716&q=332506&deepNav_GID=1650.
11 Fifth CCC District First Corps Area Yearbook, 1937, 59.
12 Ibid.
13 Ibid.
14 Shenipsit Lookout, June, 1936, 7.
15 Fifth CCC District First Corps Area Yearbook, 1937, 59.
16 Ibid.
17 Shenipsit Lookout, June, 1936, 8.
18 Fifth CCC District First Corps Area Yearbook, 1937, 59.
19 Ibid., 57.
20 Shenipsit Lookout, June, 1936, 46.
21 Ibid., 10-12.
22 Report of the Commission on Forests and Wildlife to the Governor, For Fifteen Years, July 1, 1930 to June 30, 1945, Hartford, 1945, 35.
23 Shenipsit Lookout, Oct., 1936, 4.
24 Shenipsit Lookout, Nov., 1936, 1.
25 Ibid., 2.
26 Shenipsit Lookout, Nov., 1936, 2.
27 Shenipsit Lookout, Jan., 1937, 15.
28 Fifth CCC District First Corps Area Yearbook, 1937, 59.
29 Ibid.
30 Shenipsit Lookout, July, 1937, 1, 6.
31 Shenipsit Lookout, Sept., 1937, 3.
32 Ibid., 6.
33 Ibid., 16.
34 Shenipsit Lookout, Feb., 1939, 9.
35 Shenipsit Lookout, May, 1939, 10.
36 Shenipsit Lookout, June, 1939, 17.
37 Ibid., 17.
38 Shenipsit Lookout, July, 1939, 1.
39 Shenipsit Lookout, Oct., 1939, 14.
40 Shenipsit Lookout, July, 1939, 3.
41 Shenipsit Lookout, Oct., 1939, 13.
42 Shenipsit Lookout, Dec. 2, 1939, 22.

43 Shenipsit Lookout, Dec. 8, 1939, 4.
44 Shenipsit Lookout, Feb. 23, 1940, 4.
45 Ibid., 1.
46 Ibid., 2.
47 Ibid.
48 Report of the Connecticut State Parks and Forests Commission, 1940, 52-54.
49 Report of the Connecticut State Parks and Forests Commission, 1942, 55.
50 Black River Democrat, Apr. 29, 1943.

Chapter 18 Thomaston
1 http://www.ct.gov/dep/cwp/view.asp?a=2716&q=325176.
2 http://www.taftschool.org/125timeline/125timeline.html.
3 Fifth CCC District First Corps Area Yearbook, 1937, 35.
4 Ibid., 33.
5 Ibid.
6 The Black Rocker, Aug. 1936, 2 & 4.
7 Report of the Connecticut State Parks and Forests, 1934, 78.
8 The Bristol Press, Dec. 31, 1934.
9 The Black Rocker, March, 1935, 1.
10 Ibid., 3.
11 Ibid.
12 Ibid.
13 The Black Rocker, March 1935, 4.
14 The Black Rocker, Nov. 1935, 2.
15 The Black Rocker, Feb., 1936, 2.
16 Ibid., 2.
17 The Black Rocker, April 1936, 6 & 9.
18 The Black Rocker, Sept., 1936, 1.
19 Ibid.
20 Ibid., 5.
21 The Black Rocker, Sept., 1936, 2.
22 Report of the Connecticut State Parks and Forests, 1936, 69-70.
23 Ibid.
24 The Black Rocker, March 1936, 1.
25 The Black Rocker, Sept., 1936, 10.
26 The Black Rocker, Nov., 1936, 10.
27 Ibid., 4.
28 The Black Rocker, Dec., 1936, p.7.
29 The Black Rocker, Feb. 1937, 12.
30 Ibid., 6.
31 The Black Rocker, April, 1937, 3.
32 The Black Rocker, March, 1937, 1.
33 Fifth CCC District First Corps Area Yearbook, 1937, 33.
34 Ibid., 35.
35 The Black Rocker, March, 1937, 1.
36 Ibid.
37 Report of the Connecticut State Parks and Forests, 1934, 78.
38 http://www.nae.usace.army.mil/Media/Images.
aspx?igphoto=2000724302

Chapter 19 Torrington-Burr Pond
1 Fifth CCC District First Corps Area Yearbook, 1937, 37.
2 Ibid.
3 Ibid.,78.
4 Report of the Commission on Forests and Wild Life to the Governor, July, 1 1930 to June 30, 1945 (Hartford, 1945), 36.
5 Walcott Windbag, June, 1935, 6.
6 Walcott Windbag, April, 1937, 2.

7 Report of the Connecticut State Parks and Forests Commission, 1934, 80.
8 Ibid., 76, 78.
9 Ibid., 82.
10 Ibid., 100, 101.
11 Walcott Windbag, Aug., 1935, 3.
12 Walcott Windbag, May, 1935, 6.
13 Walcott Windbag, May, 1935, 4.
14 Fifth CCC District First Corps Area Yearbook, 1937, 78.
15 Walcott Windbag, June, 1935, 7.
16 Ibid., 1.
17 Ibid.
18 Ibid., 2.
19 Ibid.
20 Walcott Windbag, Aug., 1935, 1.
21 Walcott Windbag, Oct., 1935, 1.
22 Ibid.
23 Ibid.
24 Ibid., 3.
25 Ibid., 1.
26 Walcott Windbag, Nov., 1935, 1.
27 Walcott Windbag, Feb., 1936, 3.
28 Fifth CCC District First Corps Area Yearbook, 1937, 78.
29 Ibid.
30 Ibid.
31 Report of the Connecticut State Parks and Forests Commission, 1936, 70.
32 Walcott Windbag, Sept., 1936, 5.
33 Ibid., 1.
34 Report of the Connecticut State Parks and Forests Commission, 1936, 61.
35 Fifth CCC District First Corps Area Yearbook, 1937, 78.
36 Walcott Warrior, Nov., 1937, 6.
37 Fifth CCC District First Corps Area Yearbook, 1937, 78.
38 Report of the Connecticut State Parks and Forests Commission, 1938, 39.
39 Report of the Connecticut State Parks and Forests Commission, 1944, 68.

Chapter 20 Torrington / West Goshen
1 Fifth CCC District First Corps Area Yearbook, 1937, 31.
2 Report of the Connecticut State Parks and Forests Commission, 1934, 73.
3 http://www.ct.gov/deep/cwp/view.asp?a=2697&q=322836.
4 Fifth CCC District First Corps Area Yearbook, 1937, 31.
5 Report of the Connecticut State Parks and Forests Commission, 1934, 24.
6 Ibid., 85.
7 Ibid., 80.
8 Ibid., 82.
9 Mohawk Lookout, July, 1935, 3.
10 Report of the Connecticut State Parks and Forests Commission, 1934, 100-101.
11 Ibid., 92.
12 Fifth CCC District First Corps Area Yearbook, 1937, 32.
13 Mohawk Lookout, March 25, 1935, 9.
14 Ibid.
15 Mohawk Lookout, May/June, 1935, 3.
16 Ibid., 4.
17 Mohawk Lookout, Nov., 1935, 6.

18 Mohawk Lookout, Aug., 1935, 6.
19 Mohawk Lookout, Oct., 1935, 8.
20 Mohawk Lookout, Nov., 1935, 6.
21 Mohawk Lookout, Dec., 1935, 7.
22 Mohawk Lookout, Jan., 1936, 12.
23 Ibid., 7.
24 Fifth CCC District First Corps Area Yearbook, 1937, 31.
25 Report of the Connecticut State Parks and Forests Commission, 1936, 69-70.
26 Fifth CCC District First Corps Area Yearbook, 1937, 31.
27 Ibid.
28 Ibid.
29 Ibid.
30 http://vermonthistory.org/journal/73/06_Patton.pdf.
31 Ibid.
32 Ibid.
33 Ibid.
34 Fifth CCC District First Corps Area Yearbook, 1937, 20.
35 Mohawk Lookout, April 5, 1940, 1 & 4.
36 Mohawk Lookout, Jan., 1936, 18.
37 Mohawk Lookout, July, 1935, 3.
38 Mohawk Lookout, May, 1939, 18.
39 http://www.cornwallhistoricalsociety.org/exhibits/forests/mohawkski.htm.
40 Mohawk Lookout, May 24, 1940, 1.
41 Mohawk Lookout, Jan. 5, 1940, 1.
42 Mohawk Lookout, Jan. 12, 1940, 1.
43 Ibid., 2.
44 Mohawk Lookout, Jan. 5, 1940, 1.
45 Mohawk Lookout, Jan. 19, 1940, 4.
46 Mohawk Lookout, Jan. 5, 1940, 1.
47 Mohawk Lookout, Jan. 23, 1940, 2.
48 Mohawk Lookout, Mar. 1, 1940, 1.
49 Ibid., 4.
50 Ibid.
51 Mohawk Lookout, Mar. 15, 1940, 1.
52 Mohawk Lookout, May 24, 1940, 1.
53 Mohawk Lookout, Feb., 1936, 1.
54 Mohawk Lookout, Mar. 15, 1940, 1.
55 Ibid.
56 Mohawk Lookout, April 5, 1940, 2.
57 Mohawk Lookout, April 19, 1940, 2.
58 Mohawk Lookout, April 26, 1940, 2.
59 Mohawk Lookout, May 10, 1940, 3.
60 Report of the Connecticut State Parks and Forests Commission, 1940, 52-53.
61 Mohawk Lookout, Jan., 1936, 18.
62 Report of the Connecticut State Parks and Forests Commission, 1940, 53.

Chapter 21 Union
1 "Forest Camp Tents Rise in Union," The Hartford Daily Courant, May 28, 1933.
2 "Five Winsted Boys Leave Forest Camp," The Hartford Daily Courant, May 31, 1933.
3 http://en.wikipedia.org/wiki/Henry_S._Graves.
4 http://www.ct.gov/dep/cwp/view.asp?a=2697&q=322852&depNav_GID=1631.

5 Report of the Connecticut State Parks and Forests, 1934, 81.
6 Ibid., 77.
7 Ibid.
8 Ibid., 100-101.
9 Camp Graves News, Dec. 10, 1934, 2.
10 Ibid., 1.
11 Camp Graves News, Jan. 15, 1935, 1.
12 Ibid.
13 Nipmuck Sentinel, May 24, 1935, 10.
14 Camp Graves News, Jan. 15, 1935, 1
15 Ibid., 2.
16 Ibid., 4.
17 Camp Graves News, Mar. 15, 1935, 1.
18 Ibid.
19 Ibid.
20 Ibid., 3
21 Nipmuck Sentinel, May 24, 1935, 2.
22 Ibid., 8.
23 Camp Graves Sentinel, July, 1935, 2.
24 Ibid., 3.
25 Ibid.
26 Camp Graves News, Mar., 1936, 2.
27 Camp Graves News, Mar., 1936, 1, 3.

Chapter 22 Voluntown
1 Fifth CCC District First Corps Area Yearbook, 1937, 41.
2 Report of the Connecticut State Parks and Forests Commission, 1934, 60.
3 http://www.ct.gov/deep/cwp/view.asp?a=2716&q=325068&deepNav_GID=1650.
4 Fifth CCC District First Corps Area Yearbook, 1937, 41.
5 Report of the Connecticut State Parks and Forests Commission, 1934, 83.
6 Lonergan Log, April, 1935, 1.
7 Report of the Connecticut State Parks and Forests Commission, 1934, 77, 81, 83.
8 Ibid., 83.
9 Lonergan Log, Feb., 1935, 4.
10 Lonergan Log, Apr., 1935, 1.
11 Ibid., 5.
12 Fifth CCC District First Corps Area Yearbook, 1937, 78.
13 Lonergan Log, Dec., 1935, 8.
14 Ibid., 1.
15 Ibid., 2.
16 Lonergan Log, Feb., 1936, 1.
17 Ibid.
18 Ibid., 9.
19 Ibid., 4.
20 Ibid.
21 Ibid.
22 Fifth CCC District First Corps Area Yearbook, 1937, 41.
23 Lonergan Log, Apr., 1936, 1.
24 Ibid.
25 Ibid., 4.
26 Ibid., 6.
27 Ibid.
28 Ibid., 1.
29 Report of the Connecticut State Parks and Forests Commission, 1936, 53.
30 Ibid., 69, 70.

31 Ibid., 1936, 68.
32 Lonergan Log, Oct., 1936, 1.
33 Fifth CCC District First Corps Area Yearbook, 1937, 41.
34 Ibid.
35 Report of the Connecticut State Parks and Forests Commission, 1940, 76.
36 Lonergan Log, Jan., 1938, 5.
37 Lonergan Log, Mar., 1938, 2.
38 Ibid.
39 Ibid.
40 Report of the Connecticut State Parks and Forests Commission, 1940, 69.
41 Lonergan Log, Oct., 1939, 4.
42 Lonergan Log, Nov., 1939, 2.
43 Lonergan Log, Feb., 1940, 6.
44 Report of the Connecticut State Parks and Forests Commission, 1940, 53.
45 Lonergan Log, Mar. 1940, 6.
46 Lonergan Log, April. 1940, 3.
47 Report of the Connecticut State Parks and Forests Commission, 1940, 52.
48 Ibid., 53.
49 Ibid.
50 Report of the Connecticut State Parks and Forests Commission, 1942, 24.
51 Ibid., 55.
52 Report of the Connecticut State Parks and Forests Commission, 1944, 76.

Chapter 23 West Cornwall
1 Fifth CCC District First Corps Area Yearbook, 1937, 47.
2 https://en.wikipedia.org/wiki/Wilbur_Lucius_Cross.
3 Camp Cross Clarion, June, 1936, 7-9.
4 http://www.stateparks.com/housatonic.html.
5 Camp Cross Clarion, June, 1936, 7-9.
6 Fifth CCC District First Corps Area Yearbook, 1937, 47.
7 Report of the Connecticut State Parks and Forests, 1934, 77.
8 Ibid., 80.
9 Ibid., 25-26.
10 Ibid.
11 Camp Cross Clarion, June, 1936, 1.
12 Fifth CCC District First Corps Area Yearbook, 1937, 47.
13 Camp Cross Clarion, June, 1936, 7-9.
14 Fifth CCC District First Corps Area Yearbook, 1937, 47.
15 Camp Cross Clarion, May 14, 1934, 3.
16 Camp Cross Clarion, May 28, 1934, 1.
17 Ibid., 3.
18 Camp Cross Clarion, June, 1936, 7-9.
19 Camp Cross Clarion, June, 29, 1934, 1.
20 Ibid.
21 Ibid.
22 Ibid., 5.
23 Camp Cross Clarion, May 14, 1934, 3.
24 Camp Cross Clarion, June 29, 1934, 4.
25 Camp Cross Clarion, Sept. 26, 1934.
26 Ibid., 6-7.
27 Camp Cross Clarion, Aug. 22, 1934, 3.
28 Camp Cross Clarion, Oct. 31, 1934, 7.

29 Camp Cross Clarion, Sept. 26, 1934, 2.
30 Ibid., 4.
31 Camp Cross Clarion, Oct. 31, 1934, 5.
32 Camp Cross Clarion, Nov. 30, 1934, 5.
33 Camp Cross Clarion, Oct. 31, 1934, 2.
34 Ibid., 4.
35 Camp Cross Clarion, Nov. 30, 1934, 2.
36 Camp Cross Clarion, Oct. 31, 1934, 6.
37 Camp Cross Clarion, June, 1936, 1.
38 Camp Cross Clarion, Feb. 12, 1935, 1-2.
39 Camp Cross Clarion, April 18, 1935, 4.
40 Ibid.
41 Ibid., 1.
42 Ibid., 2.
43 Camp Cross Clarion, June 28, 1935, 2.
44 Camp Cross Clarion, June 4, 1935, 2.
45 Ibid., 4.
46 Camp Cross Clarion, June 28, 1935, 2.
47 Ibid., 4.
48 Ibid.
49 Ibid., 5.
50 Camp Cross Clarion, Sept. 18, 1935, 3.
51 Camp Cross Clarion, Dec. 18, 1935, 3.
52 Camp Cross Clarion, June 28, 1935, 4.
53 Camp Cross Clarion, Dec. 18, 1935, 6.
54 Camp Cross Clarion, June, 1936, 1.
55 Camp Cross Clarion, Feb. 12, 1936, 2.
56 Fifth CCC District First Corps Area Yearbook, 1937, 47.
57 Camp Cross Clarion, April, 1936, 4.
58 Camp Cross Clarion, June, 1936, 14.
59 Camp Cross Clarion, Sept., 1936, 5.
60 Camp Cross Clarion, June, 1936, 7-9.
61 Camp Cross Clarion, Sept., 1936, 12.
62 Fifth CCC District First Corps Area Yearbook, 1937, 47.
63 Camp Cross Clarion, March, 1937, 2.
64 Camp Cross Clarion, Sept. 1937, 6.
65 Cross Cut, Dec., 1938, 2.
66 Cross Cut, Dec., 1938, 2.
67 Report of the Connecticut State Parks and Forests, 1940, 52.
68 Report of the Connecticut State Parks and Forests, 1936, 26.
69 Report of the Connecticut State Parks and Forests, 1940, 32.
70 http://www.stateparks.com/housatonic.htm.

Chapter 24 Windsor
1 Fifth CCC District First Corps Area Yearbook, 1937, 61.
2 http://www.huh.harvard.edu/libraries/NEnats/NEnatsAB.html#A
3 Fifth CCC District First Corps Area Yearbook, 1937, 61.
4 Austin F. Hawes, History of Forestry in Connecticut, CAES Archives, 1957, 124.
5 Camp Britton Bug, Aug. 1936, 6.
6 First Corps Area, Fifth CCC District Yearbook, 1937, 61.
7 Camp Britton Bug, Aug. 1936, 9.
8 Fifth CCC District First Corps Area Yearbook, 1937, 61.
9 Report of the Connecticut State Parks and Forests, 1936, 66.
10 Camp Britton Bug, Aug. 1936, 7.
11 Camp Britton Bug, Nov. 1936, 9.
12 Camp Britton Bug, Aug. 1936, 7.
13 Sixtieth Report of the Connecticut Agricultural Experimental Station, New Haven, 1936, 188.
14 Ibid.

15 Fifth CCC District First Corps Area Yearbook, 1937, 61.
16 Camp Britton Bug, Sept., 1936, 1.
17 Camp Britton Bug, Aug., 1936, 6, 8.
18 Fifth CCC District First Corps Area Yearbook, 1937, 1937, 61.
19 Camp Britton Bug, Nov., 1936, 6.
20 Camp Britton Bug, Sept., 1936, 11.
21 Camp Britton Bug, Aug., 1936, 2.
22 Camp Britton Bug, Nov., 1936, 6.
23 Camp Britton Bug, Jan., 1937, 4.
24 Camp Britton Bug, Dec., 1936, 6.
25 Ibid., 8.
26 Camp Britton Bug, Nov. 1936, 8.
27 Ibid.
28 Camp Britton Bug, Dec., 1936, 2.
29 Ibid., 4.
30 Camp Britton Bug, Jan. 1937, 2.
31 Ibid., 6.
32 Camp Britton Bug, Feb., 1937, 4.
33 Ibid., 6.
34 Ibid.
35 Camp Britton Bug, Feb., 1937, 6.
36 Camp Britton Bug, April 10, 1937, 3.
37 Ibid., 5.
38 Ibid.
39 Report of the Connecticut State Parks and Forests, 1938, 39.
40 http://focus.nps.gov/pdfhost/docs/NRHP/Text/86001731.pdf.

Chapter 25 Winsted
1 http://www.ct.gov/dep/cwp/view.asp?a=2716&q=325054'.
2 Fifth CCC District First Corps Area Yearbook, 1937, 29.
3 Report of the Connecticut State Parks and Forests, 1934, 75-76.
4 Report of the Connecticut State Parks and Forests, 1936, 69.
5 Report of the Connecticut State Parks and Forests, 1934, 76.
6 Report of the Connecticut State Parks and Forests, 1936, 54-55.
7 http://www.iaismuseum.org/research-and-collections/preserve-booklets/preserve-booklet-barkhamsted-lighthouse.pdf#page=16&zoom=auto,-74,60.
8 Report of the Connecticut State Parks and Forests, 1934, 78.
9 Ibid., 82.
10 Ibid., 100-101.
11 Ibid., 80.
12 http://www.mycitizensnews.com/features/2010/01/author-gives-talk-on-whittemore-legacy/.
13 Camp White Static, Feb. 28, 1935, 1.
14 Ibid., 2.
15 Ibid.
16 Camp White Static, April, 1935, 3.
17 Ibid.
18 Camp White Static, Feb. 28, 1935, 1.
19 Report of the Connecticut State Parks and Forests, 1936, 54.
20 Camp White Static, April, 1935, 6.
21 Camp White Static, June, 1935, 2, 8.
22 Camp White Static, July, 1935, 1.
23 Report of the Connecticut State Parks and Forests, 1935, 55.
24 Camp White Static, Sept. 1935, 2.
25 Ibid., 7.
26 Camp White Transcript, Oct., 1935, 1.
27 Camp White Transcript, Nov. 19, 1935, 2.
28 Fifth CCC District First Corps Area Yearbook, 1937, 28-29.
29 The Echo, March, 1936, 2.

30 Report of the Connecticut State Parks and Forests, 1936, 65-66.
31 Fifth CCC District First Corps Area Yearbook, 1937, 29.
32 The Echo, March, 1936, 3.
33 Ibid., 2.
34 The Echo, May 1936, 1.
35 Ibid., 15.
36 The White Eagle, Nov., 1937, 5.
37 The Echo, June, 1936, 2.
38 The Echo, Aug., 1936, 3.
39 Report of the Connecticut State Parks and Forests, 1936, 55.
40 Ibid., 70.
41 The Echo, July, 1936, 1.
42 The Echo, June, 1936, 1.
43 The Echo, May, 1937, 4.
44 The Echo, Oct., 1937, 5.
45 The White Eagle, Dec., 1937, 1.
46 The White Eagle, Feb., 1938, 3.
47 The White Eagle, Feb., 1939, 9.
48 The White Eagle, Mar., 1938, 7.
49 Ibid., 1.
50 The White Eagle, Oct. 1938, 1-2.
51 Ibid., 2.
52 Ibid.
53 Ibid.
54 Ibid., 6.
55 The White Eagle, Dec., 1938, 8.
56 White Eagle, Sept., 12, 1940, 1.
57 The White Eagle, Jan., 1939, 1.
58 The White Eagle, Aug. 24, 1939, 1.
59 The White Eagle, Feb., 1939, 5.
60 The White Eagle, May 30, 1940, 1.
61 The White Eagle, June 14-28, 1940, 2.
62 The White Eagle, Aug. 16, 1940, 1.
63 Report of the Connecticut State Parks and Forests, 1940, 52.
64 Ibid.
65 The White Eagle, Oct. 23, 1940, 2.
66 The White Eagle, Oct. 30, 1940, 1.
67 Ibid., 4.
68 Report of the Connecticut State Parks and Forests, 1942, 61.
69 http://www.ct.gov/dep/cwp/view.asp?a=2716&q=325054.
70 http://www.ct.gov/deep/cwp/view.
asp?a=2716&q=325054&deepNav_GID=1650.

16 Thames Tattler, Sept. 15, 1935.
17 Thames Tattler, Aug. 15, 1935.
18 Ibid.
19 Ibid.
20 Thames Tattler, Sept. 15, 1935.
21 Ibid.
22 Ibid.
23 Thames Tattler, Oct. 15, 1935.
24 Ibid.
25 Ibid.
26 Thames Tattler, Dec. 15, 1935, 12.
27 Thames Tattler, Jan. 17, 1936, 14.
28 Thames Tattler, Oct. 15, 1935.
29 Ibid.
30 Thames Tattler, Nov. 20, 1935, 2.
31 Ibid.
32 Ibid., 5.
33 Thames Tattler, Dec. 15, 1935, 14.
34 Thames Tattler, Jan. 17, 1936, 18.
35 Thames Tattler, Feb., 1936, 14.
36 Ibid.
37 Fifth CCC District First Corps Area Yearbook, 1937, 51.
38 Thames Tattler, Feb., 1936, 20.
39 Ibid., 21.
40 Thames Tattler, Mar., 1936, 21-22.
41 Ibid., 4.
42 Thames Tattler, Apr., 1936, 3.
43 Thames Tattler, Mar., 1936, 2.
44 Fifth CCC District First Corps Area Yearbook, 1937, 51.
45 Thames Tattler, Mar., 1936, 6.
46 Fifth CCC District First Corps Area Yearbook, 1937, 78.
47 Ibid., 51.
48 Ibid.
49 Ibid.
50 Ibid.
51 Ibid., 78.
52 Ibid.

Chapter 26 New London
1 Fifth CCC District First Corps Area Yearbook, 1937, 53.
2 Ibid.
3 Thames Tattler, Aug. 15, 1935.
4 Fifth CCC District First Corps Area Yearbook, 1937, 53.
5 Ibid., 51.
6 Fifth CCC District First Corps Area Yearbook, 1937, 53.
7 The Fifth District Annual Report, 1937, 53.
8 Ibid., 51.
9 Fifth CCC District First Corps Area Yearbook, 1937, 53.
10 Ibid.
11 Thames Tattler, Nov. 20, 1935, 1-2.
12 Thames Tattler, Aug. 15, 1935.
13 Thames Tattler, Sept. 15, 1935.
14 Ibid.
15 Ibid.

BIBLIOGRAPHY

Books

Brilvitch, Charles W. A History of Connecticut's Golden Hill Paugussett Tribe. The History Press, 2007.

Cohen, Stan. The Tree Army, A Pictorial History of the Civilian Conservation Corps 1933-1942. Missoula, MT: Pictorial Histories Co., 1980.

Colson, Ann T. and Cindi D. Pietrzyk, ed. Connecticut Walk Book East, Rockfall, Conn: Connecticut Forest & Park Association, 2005.

Folsom, Franklin. Impatient Armies of the Poor. Niwot, Colorado: University Press of Colorado, 1991.

Galusha, Diane. Another Day Another Dollar: The Civilian Conservation Corps in the Catskills. Hensonville, NY: Black Dome Press Corp., 2009.

Harper, Charles Price. The Administration of the Civilian Conservation Corps, Clarksburg, WV: Clarksburg Publishing Co., 1939.

Hawes, Austin F. The C.C.C. Makes Better Men and Forests in Connecticut. Hartford, Conn: State Forester, 1935.

Milne, George McLean. Connecticut Woodlands: A Century's Story of the Connecticut Forest and Park Association. Rockfall, CT: The Connecticut Forest and Park Association, Inc., 1995.

Nixon, Edgar. Franklin D. Roosevelt and Conservation, 1911-1945. Hyde Park, NY: National Archives and Records Service Franklin D. Roosevelt Library, 1957.

Official Annual Fifth CCC District First Corps Area Yearbook. New London, Conn: Fort H. G. Wright, 1937.

Report of the Commission on Forests and Wildlife to the Governor, For Fifteen Years, July 1, 1930 to June 30, 1945. Hartford, Conn., 1945.

Report of the Connecticut State Parks and Forests. State, Hartford, Conn: 1934-42.

Salmond, John. The Civilian Conservation Corps, 1933-1942: A New Deal Case Study. Durham, NC: Duke University Press, 1967.

Schlesinger, Jr., Arthur M. The Age of Roosevelt, III: The Politics of Upheaval. Boston, Mass: Houghton Mifflin Co., 1960.

Sixtieth Report of the Connecticut Agricultural Experimental Station. New Haven, Conn., 1936.

State of New York, Conservation Department. Annual Reports. Albany, NY, 1933-42.

Newspapers

Black River Democrat
Camp Chapman News
Camp Chapman Clarion
Camp White Static
Camp White Transcript
Hartford Courant
Hartford Daily Courant
Mohawk Lookout
Plattsburgh Daily Press

Shenipsit Lookout
Thames Tattler
The Black Rocker
The Bristol Press
The Buck Eye
The Echo
The Shoreline Times
The White Eagle
Walcott Windbag

Magazines / Newsletters

"CCC Camp Designated a State Archaeological Preserve." Connecticut Woodlands, (Spring, 2010): 21.

Ceder, Arthur B. "The Early Days of the CCC in Connecticut." NACCCA Journal 22 (January, 1999): 6-8.

Kent Historical Society, Volume 9, Number 3, Kent, Conn., Dec. 2008.

Neuzil, Mark. "Roosevelt's Tree Army, " The History Channel Magazine, November/December 2010.

Pamphlets

"The Conservation Corps, What It Is and What It Does." Civilian Conservation Corps Office of Director, Washington, D. C. (June, 1939): 10

Letters

(Franklin D. Roosevelt, letter to James McEntee, March 25, 1942).

Others

Hilton, Ford. "A Brief History of Stone Ranch, East Lyme, Connecticut," unpublished biography in East Lyme Library History Room.

Rawick, George P. The New Deal and Youth: The Civilian Conservation Corps, the National Youth Administration, the American Youth Congress, unpublished Ph.D. dissertation, University of Wisconsin, 1957.

"Message to Congress on Unemployment Relief. March 21," The Presidential Papers of Franklin D. Roosevelt, 1933.

Online Sources

Americorp Corporation for National & Community Service, http://www.americorps.gov/about/ac/index.asp

Civilian Conservation Corps Legacy, CCC Brief History, http://www.ccclegacy.org/CCC_brief_history.htm

Civilian Conservation Corps Legacy, CCC Facts, http://www.ccclegacy.org/ccc_facts.htm

Cockaponset State Forest Management Plan - CT.gov http://www.ct.gov/dep/lib/dep/forestry/management_plans/cockaponset_plan.pdf.

Corrnwall Historical Society, http://www.cornwallhistoricalsociety.org/exhibits/forests/mohawkski.htm

DEEP: Chatfield Hollow State Park - CT.gov http://www.ct.gov/dep/cwp/view.asp?a=2716&q=325182&depNav_GID=1650

Eleanor Roosevelt National Historic Site Hyde Park, NY, http://www.nps.gov/archive/elro/glossary/great-depression.htm

Eleanor Roosevelt National Historic Site Hyde Park, NY, Franklin D. Roosevelt (1882-1945), http://www.nps.gov/archive/elro/glossary/roosevelt-franklin.htm

Family Treemaker Geanealogy, http://familytreemaker.genealogy.com/users/e/l/l/Thomas-A-Ellis-Aberdeen/WEBSITE-0001/UHP-0052.html

Student Conservation Association, http://www.thesca.org/

US Forest Service US Forest Service http://www.fs.fed.us/aboutus/history/chiefs/stuart.shtml

Wikipedia.org http://en.wikipedia.org/wiki/Oak_Lodge

ACKNOWLEDGMENTS

I would like to thank all of the CCC men who shared with me stories of their life and experiences in the CCC. Thanks, also, to the wives and children who remembered the stories of their husbands and fathers and shared these stories, and photos.

To my wife, Lynn for her support and patience over the past eight years of research and writing; to my children, Matthew, Kristy, and Ryan for encouraging and accompanying me on trips and hikes; to my parents, Martin M. and Joan, who instilled in me the importance of hard work and provided me with a college education that enabled me to achieve my goals. To my son-in-law Matthew Roloff who helped me with computer problems and to my granddaughters, Kira and Lydia Roloff, for going on research trips with me and to my new daughter-in-law, Jenna Podskoch for her encouragement.

To the following people I'd like to also give a special thanks:

My dedicated editor, David Hayden, who was always there to correct and guide me through the writing of newspaper articles and this book. I never would have completed this book without his insightful questions and suggestions.

Carl Stamm, a retired Connecticut Conservation and DEP administrator, who traveled with me for eight years searching for CCC camp sites and research materials.

CCC alumni Walter Sekula who visited many libraries and historical societies with me promoting the great work of the CCC both here in Connecticut but also other states.

A special thanks to:

Amanda Beauchemin of Ford Folios who spent many hours and weeks doing an excellent job with the layout and cover design, with the support of her uncle Barry Ford.

My old publisher, Wray Rominger of Purple Mountain Press, who gave me encouragement and support in printing my first book and help in self-publishing.

Retired District NYS Ranger Paul Hartmann who made the maps for this book.

Jordon Ford who helped me with my research at the UCONN Library.

Sandy Anagnostakis of the Connecticut Agricultural Experiment Station for introducing me to the writings of Connecticut State Forester Austin Hawes.

Joan Sharpe, President of the CCC Legacy in Virginia for her research materials and proofreading.

Thanks to the Connecticut DEEP, these administrators and employees for sharing photos and historical information: Deputy Commissioner Susan Whalen; Tom Tyler, State Parks and Public Outreach Division; Diane Joy, State Parks, Education & Outreach; Alan Levere of State Parks & Historic Sites; Elliotte Draegor, CCC CT Museum; and Pam Adams, retired Director of Connecticut State Parks.

I am grateful for the research material and photographs shared by: Jeff Ward of the Connecticut Agricultural Experiment Station in New Haven; Eric Hammerling and the Connecticut Forest and Park Association; Keith Cudworth of White Memorial; The Madison Historical Society; the Thankful Arnold House Museum, Haddam; Sue Berescik, East Hampton Library; Marge McAvoy, Bill Bachrach, and Charlotte & Dick Lindsey of Kent Historical Society; Walt Olsen of the Chatham Historical Society, East Hampton; Paul Hart and Barkhamsted Historical Society; Lisa Malloy of Haddam

Historical Society, and Luane Lange & The Niantic Historical Society.

To these people who helped with the research on and photos of local CCC camps: Ted Schulz, Eastford; Richard Bailey, Alex Sokolow, and Andy Annino Chatfield Hollow; Paul Edman, Jason Engelhardt & Joseph Oslander, Madison; Jim Beschle, Macedonia Brook; Pierce Rafferty, Fishers Island Historical Society; Rick Kelsey & John La Shane, Portland; Marilyn Aristad and Vinnie Messino, Stafford Springs; Ford Hilton and Wilbur Beckwith, Niantic.

Thanks to the following libraries who hosted my CCC talks that resulted in finding many CCC boys and their families: East Hampton Library; Thomaston Library; Voluntown Library; Cragin Memorial Library, Colchester; Babcock Library, Ashford; Cornwall Free Library; Farmington Library; New Haven Public Library; Beardsley Library, Winsted; Woodbury Library; Salem Library; Brookfield Historical Society; Goshen Public Library; Meriden Public Library; Granby Library; Windsor Public Library; Mansfield Public Library; Greenwich Library; Putnam Public Library; East Lyme Public Library; Cheshire Public Library; Middle Haddam Library; Prosser Public Library, Bloomfield; Torrington Library; Groton Public Library; New Britain Library; Public Library of New London; Bethel Library; Seymour Library; Wallingford Public Library; Lucy Robbins Welles Library, Newington; Brainerd Memorial Library, Haddam; Wheeler Library, North Stonington; Milford Public Library; Waterford Library; Killingworth Library; Portland Library; and Sprague Public Library, Baltic.

To these historians and historical societies, thank you for opening your files and pictures to me or hosting my CCC presentations: Danbury Historical Society; Enfield Historical Society; Belden Public Library, Cromwell; Connecticut Historical Society, Hartford; Portland Historical Society, at Portland Library; Pomfret Historical Society; East Lyme Historical Society at Niantic Bay Yacht Club; Kent Historical Society, at Kent Town Hall; Derby Historical Society at Grassy Hill Lodge; Canterbury Historical Society; Newtown Historical Society at Newtown Library; Coventry Historical Society; Plainfield Historical Society; Woodstock Historical Society; East Granby Historical Society; Windsor Historical Society; Bristol Historical Society; Union Historical Society; Franklin Historical Society; Clinton Historical Society at Henry Carter Hull Library, Clinton.

A special thanks to these organizations for hosting my CCC talks: Griswold Senior Center, Jewett City; Seabury Heritage Hall, Bloomfield; Quinebaug Valley Community College, Danielson; Masonicare at Ashlar Village, Wallingford; Meriden YMCA Y's Men Club; Stonington Grange, North Stonington; Shoreline Institute of Lifelong Learning, The Hearth at Tuxis, Madison; Adventures in Lifelong Learning, Rose City Senior Center, Norwich; East Hampton Rotary; Meshomasic Hiking Club, Portland Library; Senior Center New Hartford; Lebanon Historical Society; Sterling Historical Society, Oneco; Jerome Home, New Britain; Ledyard Historical Society; Sloan-Stanley Museum, Kent, and Ellington Boy Scouts.

I thank you each and all for helping me make this historical record possible.

INDEX

CIVILIAN CONSERVATION CORPS MUSEUM
AT SHENIPSIT STATE FOREST

HISTORY

The original name of the CCC Museum in Connecticut was "The Northeast States Civilian Conservation Corps Museum." It was established by NACCCA Chapter 170 members on Jan. 1, 1993 but the official opening was on Memorial Day, 1993. The museum was located in the former headquarters building of Company 1192, Camp Conner, in Stafford Springs, Conn. Within two years the museum expanded from a modest 600 square feet to 3000 square feet.

CCC alumni started the museum because they wanted to preserve the story of their own experiences in the CCC during the Depression. Most of the items displayed such as photos, clothing, scrapbooks, footlockers, tools and other memorabilia were donated by Connecticut CCC and surrounding states' alumni.

One section contains hundreds of photographs of CCC camps, personnel, and projects. CCC alumni donated memorabilia such as CCC awards, uniforms, personal letters, documents, and copies of their discharge papers.

In the second section there are 30 x 40" poster board photos of the 21 Connecticut camps. There is a blacksmith forge and tools used at Camp Conner and displays of hand tools, telephone linemen's equipment, and tools used in ice harvesting, tree planting, forest cleaning, and logging. Another collection has construction equipment used in building bridges, roads, and dams.

Section three is used for meetings, lectures, and watching videotapes of CCC camps and projects.

The fourth section's theme of camp living features replicas of a barracks and mess hall. There was an original cot, bed roll, and foot locker. A mess hall table had various eating and cooking utensils. There was a display of forest fire equipment: Indian water tanks, rakes, and axes.

The fifth section has displays that include states not in the northeast region.

Supervisor of the Shenipsit State Forest, Marilyn Aarrestad, was important in creating and developing the museum. Her interest in the CCC began as a teenager when she worked in the Youth Conservation Corps during the 70s and early 80s at Fort Devens, Mass. She then worked for the Connecticut DEEP. In 1992 Marilyn was instrumental in reopening the idle CCC "Stone Museum" in the Peoples State Forest.

Initially, the museum was operated by volunteers from Chapter 170 and was open daily from 12 noon to 4:00 pm, from Memorial Day to Labor Day. http://www.justinmuseum.com/famjustin/Nestates.html

Over the next few years the number of NACCA volunteers decreased due to poor health and deaths. Then

On Memorial Day 1993 CCC Alumni and friends gathered outside the Northeast States Civilian Conservation Corps Museum for a dedication. *DEEP*

Visitors touring photo displays at the new CCC museum in Stafford Springs in 1993. *DEEP*

The front of the former Camp Conner Administration Building, which has many CCC displays. Podskoch

A replica of a CCC camp office with enrollees doing clerical work. Podskoch

Visitor, Lynn Podskoch, touring construction equipment used by CCC boys. Podskoch

Original CCC cot, trunk, bed roll and uniform display. Podskoch

the Connecticut DEEP began staffing the museum and was open only on weekends from Memorial Day to Labor Day.

The name of the CCC museum was recently changed to the "Civilian Conservation Corps Museum at Shenipsit State Forest." It continues to honor the dedicated men who worked in CCC camps in Connecticut and other states. The size of the museum is the same with its displays, artifacts, and memorabilia of the CCC.

The museum is located at 166 Chestnut Hill Road (Rt. 190) in Stafford Springs, Conn. It is open seasonally Please refer to the Shenipsit State Forest web page for current hours of operation and for the Museum booklet http://www.ct.gov/deep/cwp/view.asp?a=2716&q=332506&deepNav_GID=1650 or call (860) 684-3430.

Directions:

From Hartford take I-84 east for approximately 10 mi. to Exit 67, and go north toward Rockville/Coventry on Rt. 31(Reservoir Rd.). Then after a short distance turn right onto Hyde Ave/Rt. 30. east for approximately 9 mi. to Rt. 190 (Chestnut Hill Rd.). Turn left on Rt. 190 west for approximately 1.5 miles to the museum entrance on the left.

From Enfield take Rt. 190 east for approximately 9 mi. to the museum entrance on right.

CONNECTICUT CCC WORKER STATUE
FUND DRIVE

Statue History

In 1995, the CCC Worker Statue program originated in Michigan through the efforts of the National Association of CCC Alumni Chapter #129. Program coordinator Rev. Bill Frasier had a vision of having a statue in every state. Now the national CCC Legacy organization continues the work of NACCCA to reach Frasier's dream goal.

The CCC Worker Statue is a monument to the builders of modern conservation. Since 1996, the statue has been placed in many locations across the nation as a memorial to the millions of men in America who toiled to improve the management of our nation's natural resources and build the infrastructure of our modern outdoor recreation system.

The presence of these life-size statues in our nation's parks and forests stand as a testament to the pride, hard work, and desire of America's youth of the 1930s.

Sixty-five life-size statues are now placed in parks, forests, and other public venues. Connecticut is one of 11 states (Alaska, Delaware, Hawaii, Mississippi, Nebraska, Nevada, Oklahoma, Rhode Island, Utah, and Vermont) without a CCC Worker Statue. Some states have more than one. Pennsylvania has seven statues.

Connecticut Statue Fund Drive

The goal is to raise $24,000 for a statue to be placed in one of Connecticut's state parks where a CCC camp worked during the Great Depression. It is bronze and 6' tall. As of the summer of 2016 approximately $8,000 has been raised.

If you would like to make a donation, please send a donation to the address below.

Mail your donation to: CCC Legacy, P.O. Box 341, Edinburg, VA 22824. Include your name, address, phone number and email address. Also, please make a copy for your records. Checks payable to "CCC Legacy" and note on your check "for CT Statue". For more information, call 540-984-8735 or email ccc@ccclegacy.org.

Civilian Conservation Corps Legacy, Inc. is a 501(c)3 non-profit headquartered in the Commonwealth of Virginia. All donations are tax deductible. Upon payment of your pledge you will receive an acknowledgement that meets the IRS requirements for charitable donations. Tax ID: 54-2046004

Note: A portion of the proceeds from the sale of this book will be donated to the statue fund.

ABOUT THE AUTHOR

Marty Podskoch with his granddaughters, Lydia and Kira Roloff.
Amanda Beauchemin

Marty Podskoch was a reading teacher for 28 years at Delaware Academy in Delhi, NY. He retired in 2001. Marty and his wife, Lynn, raised their three children, Matt, Kristy, and Ryan, in a renovated 19th c. farmhouse along the West Branch of the Delaware River. He became interested in fire towers after climbing to the fire tower on Hunter Mountain in the fall of 1987. He met the observer, who was in his 60s, chatted with him, and listened to his stories. Marty was hooked. He set out on a quest to find out all he could about the history and lore of the fire towers.

In 1997 Wray Rominger of Purple Mountain Press asked Marty to write about the history of the Catskill fire towers and the restoration project that was occurring in the Catskills.

After interviewing over 100 observers, rangers, and their families, Marty had gathered hundreds of stories and pictures about the 23 fire towers in the Catskill region. In 2000 his book, *Fire Towers of the Catskills: Their History and Lore*, was published by Purple Mountain Press, which also published his second book, *Adirondack Fire Towers: Their History and Lore, the Southern Districts*, in June of 2003 and his third title, *Adirondack Fire Towers: Their History and Lore, the Northern Districts*, in November of 2005.

Marty also wrote a weekly newspaper column, "Adirondack Stories" in five area newspapers. Sam Glanzman, a noted comic book illustrator for the past 50 years, illustrated the stories. After five years of weekly columns Podskoch Press published 251 illustrated stories in two volumes, *Adirondack Stories: Historical Sketches* and *Adirondack Stories II: 101 More Historical Sketches*.

In 2011 Podskoch wrote and published *Adirondack Civilian Conservation Corps Camps: History, Memories & Legacy of the CCC*. Presently he is doing research on the Civilian Conservation Corps camps in Connecticut and Rhode Island.

In the Fall of 2013 Podskoch received the "Arthur E. Newkirk Education Award" from the Adirondack Mountain Club for his work in preserving the history of the fire towers and Civilian Conservation Corps Camps in the Adirondacks and Catskills.

Podskoch's last book in 2014, *The Adirondack 102 Club: Your Passport and Guide to the North Country*, is a comprehensive guide to travelers listing the history and interesting places to visit in all 102 towns and villages in the Adirondacks. It is also a journal and passport, a place to get each town stamped or signed by a store or resident. Your chance to discover the secret and lovely places that the main roads do not reveal. Those that achieve this goal receive a Vagabond patch.

For further information contact:
Marty Podskoch
43 O'Neill Lane
East Hampton, CT 06424
860-267-2442

CCCLEGACY

"Passing the legacy to future generations"

Mission statement:

The Civilian Conservation Corps Legacy is a non-profit organization dedicated to research, preservation, and education to promote a better understanding of the Civilian Conservation Corps and its continuing contributions to American life and culture.

The Civilian Conservation Corps Legacy represents the CCC alumni of America and strives to bring awareness to the heritage of the CCC, CCC alumni, their programs and accomplishments. For many years, alumni across America have elevated their heritage through consistently reminding citizens, historians, and natural resource agencies of its great impact on the American culture.

YOU ARE INVITED

Become a member of CCC Legacy and be an ambassador for conservation heritage.

All enduring facets of American history are nurtured by citizens who care. Membership is open to all and includes "CCC Boys", families, historians, authors, conservation agency personnel and advocates of all walks of life. A membership benefit is a unique newspaper published six times a year and features articles of alumni and camp histories, current reunions and organizational activities.

You are invited to become part of the effort to ensure that the heritage of the CCC is not forgotten. For more information contact:

CIVILIAN CONSERVATION CORPS LEGACY
P.O. BOX 341 — EDINBURG, VA 22824
540-984-8735
ccc@ccclegacy.org - www.ccclegacy.org

More books from Marty Podskoch:

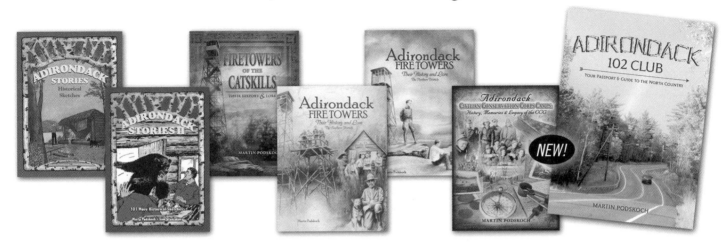

Podskoch Press has a variety of books about the history of the Adirondacks and Catskill regions. *The Adirondack Stories: Historical Sketches I & II* tell interesting stories through the comic sketches of Sam Glanzman, well known *DC Comics* and *Outdoor Life* illustrator. The Fire Tower books tell photo-illustrated stories that Marty researched throughout the region, which led to the development of his Adirondack CCC Camps book detailing the area's growth after the Great Depression. These are wonderful books for those who love the region's history.

Order yours today!

Adirondack Stories, Historical Sketches	$18.95
Adirondack Stories II, 101 More Historical Sketches	$18.95
Two-Volume Set, Adirondack Stories (includes Volumes I & II)	$34.95
Fire Towers of the Catskills: Their History and Lore	$20.00
Adirondack Fire Towers:	
Their History and Lore, the Northern Districts	$20.00
Adirondack Fire Towers:	
Their History and Lore, the Southern Districts	$20.00
Adirondack Civilian Conservation Corps Camps:	
History, Memories, & Legacy of the CCC	$20.00
Adirondack 102 Club: Your Passport & Guide to the North Country	$20.00

Prices do not include shipping and postage. Call or write for total price.

Order these autographed books from:

43 O'Neill Lane, East Hampton, CT 06424
podskoch@comcast.net | 860.267.2442